HISTORY
OF
SANSKRIT LITERATURE

Vol.1

ŚRUTI (VEDIC) PERIOD

By

C.V.VAIDYA M.A., LL.B.

Author of Mahābhārata: a Criticism, Riddle of
the Rāmāyaṇa and Epic India; and
History of Mediaeval Hindu
India, in three Vols. etc. etc.

PARIMAL PUBLICATIONS

DELHI

Published by

Parimal Publications

Office : 27/28, Shakti Nagar, Delhi-110007 (India)
Retail Outlet : 22/3, Shakti Nagar, Delhi-110007 (India)
Ph. : +91-11-23845456, 47015168
e-mail : order@parimalpublication.com
url : http://www.parimalpublication.com

Edition : Year 2011

ISBN : 978-81-7110-047-7 (Set)
978-81-7110-048-4 (Vol. 1)

Price : ₹ 700.00 (Set of 3 Vols.)

Printed by

Vishal Kaushik Printers

Near G.T.B. Hospital, Jagat Puri Vistar,
Shahdara, Delhi-110093

SECTION I–SANHITĀS

History of Sanskrit Literature.

ŚRUTI PERIOD.

SECTION I—SANHITĀS

CONTENTS.

HISTORY OF

SANSKRIT LITERATURE

ŚRUTI PERIOD

SECTION I—SANHITĀS

INTRODUCTION

History of Sanskrit literature is a subject specially of European origin, born of European thought and European research. There is no work in Sanskrit of this kind and modern Indian mind was attracted to the study of the subject, only after European scholars, chiefly German, had written treatises on it. When Sir William Jones, H. T. Colebrooke and other English scholars of the eighteenth century made Europe acquainted with the ancient language of the Hindus and the inestimable literature in it, Schlegel and other German scholars fell to their study with avidity; and later on, when the scholars of Germany became acquainted with the Vedas, the most ancient works of the world, they studied them with a zeal and in a manner entirely their own, indeed as no other people of the west, not even the Hindus themselves, have yet done. They took up the study of the Vedas in the historical spirit and Roth brought out the first book on the Vedas in their historical aspect in 1838 A. D. Weber, however, is the first German Pandit who wrote a history of Sanskrit literature as a whole, which was translated into English in 1852. Max Müller next wrote a history of the ancient literature of India, Vedic and post-Vedic, in 1859. And the latest book on the whole subject, embodying the results of European research down to the end of the nineteenth century, is that of Dr. A. A. Macdonell, Professor of Sanskrit and Fellow of Balliol (Oxford).

The chief difficulty in giving a correct history of Sanskrit literature lies in the fact that most Sanskrit works, especially Vedic and post-Vedic, give no date for their composition, nor also the place of it. Time and place, it is well-known, are the essence of history, the two sides of its body, so to speak; and historians of Sanskrit literature have consequently to find out these from various arguments based on grounds noted further on. The most obvious reason of this non-mention of date in ancient Sanskrit works is that there was no era prevalent in India in pre-Christian-era days. The first era we have in India is the Vikrama era of 57 B. C., originally called the Mālava era; and the next noted era is that of the Śakas commencing with 78 A. D. The Traikūṭaka (249 A. D.) and the Gupta (319 A. D.) eras followed in the 3rd and 4th centuries A. D. It seems probable that the Indo-Aryans got the idea of an era from their contact with the Greeks in the days of Alexander and later, of Menander. The Indo-Aryans, no doubt, lacked the historical sense though they equalled the Greeks, nay even surpassed them, in intellectual vigour. Though they had the word Itihāsa or history already and had works even then of a quasi-historical nature (see Kauṭilya's Arthaśāstra 1–5), they had no idea of true history and chronology. The Greeks, on the other hand, had their Olympic era and wrote good histories even in those ancient days. Thucydides wrote a history of the Peloponnesian war in 430 B. C. which is considered a model even for modern historians. The Indo-Aryans have left no work on history as such written in pre-Christian-era days, though they have left many works on philosophy, grammar and logic written in those days which are masterpieces in these subjects. The Indo-Aryans, it thus seems, took up the idea of an era from the Greeks and first started the Mālava era, an era named after a people, and next the Śaka era also named after the Śakas or Śaka kings generally and not any particular hero. The Buddha and the Mahāvīra eras, though named after these first preachers, probably came into use, not in the 5th century B. C., immediately after their deaths, but some centuries after the dates of their commencement, like the Christian era. Even if we grant that these eras were used from their beginnings, they were unorthodox and were not used by Sanskrit writers who were of the Vedic faith. And further, the whole of the Vedic and most of the post-Vedic literature preceded Buddha and hence there was no era whatever then which could have been used in those works, even if the writers had wished to do so* Later Sanskrit writers never thought of arranging the previous Sanskrit literature chronologically, because the Vedas had already acquired the status of a revelation and it was an item of Indo-Aryan religious belief that the Vedas were revealed at the beginning of creation.

We thus see why the Vedic and the post-Vedic literature contains no date, and why to arrange this literature chronologically is a difficult task. Divergence of opinion on this subject, as will be shown later on, was thus inevitable. It is natural to expect that writers of post-Vikram-era days would mention the dates of their writings and that there would be no difficulty in chronologically arranging them. Unfortunately, however, even here the same difficulty presents itself, though not to the same extent. These writers, probably following the ancient custom of mentioning no dates, give no dates in their works. Thus neither Kālidāsa nor Bhavabhūti, the two most prominent poets of classical Sanskrit, give any clue as to when or where they lived, prospered and wrote; and divergence of opinion consequently prevails among scholars on this subject also. While some place Kāli-

* It is well-known that the theory of Yugas was definitely settled when the Śakas were ruling in Ujjain in the first century A. D. and that the Kaliyuga era though ostensibly counting from 3101 B. C. was never used, indeed was not known, before the 4th or 5th century A. D. or the days of Āryabhatta, the first noted Hindu astronomer.

dāsa in the first century B. C., others place him in the fifth century A. D.; and while Bengal claims Kālidāsa as honouring it by his residence there, Kashmir and Malwa contest the honour with much reason. Bhavabhūti again is placed in the eighth century A. D. while popular tradition looks upon Kālidāsa and Bhavabhūti as contemporaries. There is one advantage, however, in this uncertainty of date and place, viz. that scholars study the works of these authors carefully and write learned papers, marshalling arguments one way or the other, based on references in these works to other works or to noted historical facts and personages, as also on their mention in other authors' works or in dated inscriptions or on social condition etc. depicted in them and so on. Thus research and deep study are strongly stimulated.

But there are other Sanskrit writers of this and even later period who consciously omit to give the dates of their writings in order that they may appear to be more ancient than they really are and even ascribe their authorship to persons of ancient fame. The various Purāṇas pre-eminently come under this description. They are ascribed to Vyāsa, itself a mythical name, and they are always first recited in Naimishāraṇya or the Naimisha forest (Oudh). Some writers again have purposely assumed the name of Kālidāsa or Varāha and a great deal of difficulty is experienced in finding out the true authoriship or the true date of their works.

From the 12th century onward, generally speaking, Sanskrit writers usually mention the date and place of their writings and the difficulty above noticed does not confront the historian of Sanskrit literature in this third period and he has simply to collect the writings and arrange them chronologically from unquestioned dates.

German scholars, as stated above, studied the Vedic literature carefully and deeply and by their historical trend of mind laid the foundations of new sciences with the help of the Vedic language and literature, such as comparative philology and comparative mythology. They thus showed how the Hindus, the Persians, the Greeks, the Romans, the Celts, the Germans, the Scandinavians and the Russians were originally one people, the Aryans, and spoke one language from which the modern and ancient Aryan languages are descended. European scholars again deciphered and studied the epigraphic records of India and from them evolved its history of pre-Mahomedan times, facts from which largely assist the writer of a history of Sanskrit literature. The services of Bühler of Vienna and of Keilhorn of Göttingen in this field of Sanskrit scholarship and the unravelling of pre-Mahomedan Indian history will always be gratefully acknowledged.

But notwithstanding the wonderful acumen and the laborious research of European scholars, there is unfortunately one defect in their way of thinking, namely, their bias in favour of Greek civilization and their consequent inability to concede that the Indo-

Aryan civilization could be so much earlier than the Greek, as it claims to be. When later, Indian scholars began to study the subject, they, having no such bias, naturally doubted the truth of the European view of the antiquity of the Vedas as also of most part of the post-Vedic literature. They declined to believe that the utmost ancient date that could be assigned to the Ṛigveda was 1400 B. C. or that the Mahābhārata could be placed so late as the fifth century A. D. Men like Dr. R. G. Bhandarkar and S. P. Pandit first entered this field of study and these were followed by B. G. Tilak and S. B. Dixit whose labours have established a date for the Ṛigveda which goes so far back as 3000 B. C. at the least. They found out a new method of assigning dates, namely mathematical calculations based on astronomical data found in Vedic literature. It can not be doubted that arguments based on such mathematical calculations are almost unanswerable and it is, therefore, to be regretted that these arguments are not even noticed, much less refuted, by most European scholars and writers on the history of Sanskrit literature. We at least have not come across any substantial refutation of the theories of these authors as propounded in their works. B. G. Tilak wrote his 'Orion or the Antiquity of the Vedas' in 1893 and S. B. Dixit wrote his history of Indian Astronomy in Marathi in 1896. Tilak's work was criticised at the time of its publication and none but

Jacobi, who was independently coming to the same view on astronomical grounds about the same time, accepted his conclusions.

The chronology of the Vedic period, as also of the post-Vedic period, as settled on astronomical basis, thus differs extremely from the chronology given by most western scholars. Hence arises the necessity of presenting to the curious reader a history of Sanskrit literature written from this Indian point of view. The principal landmarks, based on astronomical data in the Indian Vedic and post-Vedic chronology are :–

(1) The date of some Ṛigvedic hymns (4500 B. C., Tilak), evidenced by the position of the vernal equinox in Orion (Mṛigaśīrsha), mentioned therein,

(2) The date of the Śatapatha Brāhmaṇa (3000 B. C., Dixit), evidenced by the mention therein of the rising of the Kṛittikās exactly in the east,

(3) The date of the Maitrāyaṇīya Upanishad (1900 B.C., Tilak), evidenced by the mention of the autumnal equinox in the middle of Śravishṭhā or Delphini and

(4) The date of Vedāṅga Jyotisha (1400 B. C., Tilak and Dixit), evidenced by the mention of its occurrence in the beginning of that Nakshatra.

The arguments for these dates will be noticed in detail in their respective places; but we give here the result as above reached by Tilak and Dixit.*

* There are some Indian scholars who differ from Tilak on the antiquity of the Vedas. While Mr. Pavgi of Poona goes far behind Tilak's date, Mr. Das of Calcutta believes in a still earlier date. These, however, ignore the Śatpatha date.

Western scholars assign to these, dates ranging from 1400 B. C. to 200 B. C. To this extreme divergence in the two views regarding the antiquity of the Vedas may be added the difference of opinion regarding the dates of Pāṇini, of the present Mahābhārata and of Kālidāsa. While Indian opinion would put Pānini about 800 B. C., Mahābhārata about 250 B. C. and Kālidāsa about 50 B. C., Western scholars assign them to roughly 300 B. C., 400 A. D and 500 A. D. respectively. This will show to the reader at a glance how vastly different the Indian view of the history of Sanskrit literature is through almost the first half of its extent and how necessary it is that a history of Sanskrit literature should be written from the Indian view-point.

The determination of the date of Buddha's death about 480 B. C. and of the date of Chandragupta's rule about 300 B. C. assists the determination of post-Vedic and even Vedic chronology to a remarkable extent, as will appear later on. The discovery of the Arthaśāstra of Kauṭilya, alias Chāṇakya, minister of Chandragupta, in recent years has also dispelled the unfavourable views of many European scholars regarding the antiquity of the Indo-Aryan civilization.

THREE PERIODS.

Macdonell divides the history of Sanskrit lilterature into two periods, the Vedic period and the Sanskrit period. But it is more proper to divide the history into three periods, the Śruti period, the Smṛiti period and the Bhāshya period, as we propose to call them. The language of the Vedic literature can be given no other name than Sanskrit. The Indo-Aryans brought with them into the Panjab a branch of the language of the ancient Aryan people which may properly be called, by distinction, Sanskrit. This name no doubt arose later when the Prakrits came into being, by way of opposition, meaning the language of the refined people, as opposed to Prakrit, the language of the common people. But that name has to be carried back to the Vedic times. If Sanskrit is a name which is to be confined to the language of Patanjali's days, Vedic literature cannot come within the range of a history of Sanskrit literature. We may call the Vedic language Vedic Sanskrit, the language of the days of Pāṇini post-Vedic Sanskrit, the language of the days of Patanjali classical Sanskrit and the language of the days of Śankarāchārya and after, modern Sanskrit. The language is the same throughout this length of time, though it has different aspects in these four, rather three, periods, just as English has been divided into old English, Elizabethan English and modern English. It is needless to state that the identity of a language continues so long as its grammar remains practically the same.

The Vedic people actually spoke this Sanskrit language in the form it then had and the Vedic singers did not use an artificial language for their poetry as is sometimes supposed. There was, in the beginning, no Śūdra caste, the Aryans being homogeneous; the cultivators, the warriors and the priests, being of the same Aryan race, were of the same mental and physical capacities. There was then a slight difference between the spoken language of the common people and that of the higher class people, such as exists in every country and at every time. The language of the Vedic common people must, however, still be called Vedic Sanskrit; and it is interesting to find that when the Aryans migrated to the Deccan, they carried words of this Vedic Sanskrit, some of which still survive in the language of the common people of the Deccan. The pronoun 'tyo', used by common people, instead of *to* used by higher classes in Mahārāshṭra, is a survival of the 'tyas' of Vedic times. In short Vedic Sanskrit was a spoken language as well as post-Vedic Sanskrit of the days of Pāṇini. The language had changed visibly by this time; but it was still the same language and Pāṇini gives no separate grammar for Vedic Sanskrit, but simply marks certain peculiarities of the language as used in the hymns. He always makes the simple distinction *bhāshāyām* and *chhandasi* where there are differences. The word *bhāshāyam* used by Pāṇini clearly proves that it was a spoken language of which he wrote the grammar and that the name Sanskrit had not yet arisen, nor of course, Prakrit. Pāṇini belongs to the Panjab and the Aryan people there were still homogeneous though the Śūdra class had long been introduced. The Aryans had, however, spread into the eastern parts of India where the Śūdra population was numerous and had formed certain peculiarities of speech which Pāṇini distinguishes as those of the eastern people (Prāchām). But when, after Pāṇini, the Aryan centre of civilization moved down to the Gangetic valley and further still into the Deccan before the days of Patanjali, the Śūdra class was completely incorporated in the Aryan community and was predominant. Indeed the Aryans, still observing the Panjab rule of marrying into lower castes, married Śūdra wives to a far greater extent here than they had done in the Panjab. The result was that common people and women of even the three higher castes began to speak the Sanskrit language by softening its hard letters and its hard forms. The capacity of the common people and the women had deteriorated owing to the great mixture of blood which manifests itself even now, the people of U. P. and of Mahārāshṭra and Gujarat being distinctly Aryo-Dravidian as found at the census of 1901, while the people of the Panjab are still distinctly Aryan. This led to the rise of what are known as Prakrit languages and the name Sanskrit as opposed to Prakrit. The Prakrits of the different provinces, owing to provincial peculiarities, had distinctive names assigned to them from the names of the provinces where they were spoken. There were thus four principal Prakrits ; 1 Māgadhī (of Magadha and Bengal), 2 Śaurasenī of U. P., Rajaputana, Malwa and Gujarat (from Śūrasena, the middle country of Mathurā), 3 Mahārāshṭri from Mahārāshṭra or Deccan and

4 Paiśāchī, from the country of Piśāchas to the north of the Panjab. It is strange that Macdonell looks upon Mahārāshṭrī as a sub-division of Śaurasenī and as the language of eastern Rajastan (p. 27). Indeed the information given here seems to be incomplete, Apabhranśas being later forms of these Prakrits and Paiśāchī being omitted. Mahārāshṭrī was the most important of these Prakrits and Vararuchi in his grammar of the Prakrit languages (Prākṛita-Prakāśa) gives the grammar of Mahārāshṭrī as the principal Prakrit and notices only the variations of the others.

Thus in this second period, Sanskrit remained as the spoken language of the higher class males only, while all women and the lower classes spoke the Prakrits. Buddha preached to the common people in Pālī, another Prakrit, probably an earlier form of Māgadhī not noticed by Vararuchi who wrote his grammar two or three centuries after Buddha. The Sanskrit spoken by the higher class males was of course understood by the women and the lower class people; for the Prakrits were merely Sanskrit softened and not different languages altogether with different grammars and vocabularies. Sanskrit was, therefore, a spoken language in this period also and, being spoken by the higher class males, it attained a fixed refined form and excellence and it may, therefore, be fitly called classical Sanskrit. This naturally led to a distinctive character in the literature of this period.

The Prakrits were used, Pālī and Māgadhī by the Buddhists and Mahārāshṭrī and Ardha-Māgadhī by the

Jains, for their canonical writings for the first two or three centuries. But the necessity of writing philosophical and scientific treatises as also of controversy with the othodox Hindus who used classical Sanskrit for speech and writing, led the Buddhists and Jains to use later on Sanskrit in their writings. Especially Mahāyāna Buddhism which separated from the old Hīnayāna, under Nāgārjuna in the days of Kanishka in the first or second century A. D., used Sanskrit for its exposition and preaching. We thus have Buddhist and Jain literatures of a high order in this second period, both of them using Nyāya or Logic, the orthodox weapon, in disputations. This second period of classical Sanskrit which commenced from before Buddha i. e. from about 800 B. C. ended in about 800 A. D., when Buddhism was finally destroyed in India by the labours of Kumārila and Śankarāchārya.

For, this same event led to the rise of the modern vernaculars of India at this time. Their relation to Sanskrit is exactly the same as that of the modern Romance languages to Latin which they supplanted. The modern vernaculars have a different grammar from that of Sanskrit and are not inflexional but analytical. Unlike the ancient Prakrits, the modern Prakrits or vernaculars are, therefore, different languages and from their rise we may date the death of Sanskrit as a spoken language. Sanskrit is no doubt used even now for writing by pandits but very few can speak it. It is only the pandits of Tamil, Telugu and Kanarese parts of India that can speak Sanskrit fluently enough. But even these, in speaking, ordinarily use their vernaculars; indeed even in learned disputations they speak in their vernaculars, when they wish to express their thoughts definitely and clearly. From about 800 A. D., thus, Sanskrit may be looked upon as a dead language and all the literature in it that was produced after 800 A. D. is decidedly in a dead language which, therefore, strikes us as artificial. Thus writers of this period do not use the conjugational forms of verbs which do not come to them easily and use instead participles with *asti, karoti* &c. to finish off. Independent thinking also ceased in this period. The Śruti literature being looked upon as revelation and therefore sacred and the Smṛiti literature of the second period as quasi-sacred and the last word, so to speak, in every department of knowledge, the paṇḍits of the third period chiefly wrote commentaries and Bhāshyas on these ancient sacred and quasi-sacred works. This distinctive character is stamped on all the works which were written in this period; whether they be on sacred or profane subjects, whether on religon, philosophy or science. It is hence befitting that this third period commencing with Śankarāchārya (800 A. D.) and coming down to the Veda-Bhāshya of Sāyaṇa in about 1400 A. D. should be called the Bhāshya period. Individual writers like Śankara display high intelligence and vigour of thought and lucidity of expression; but these are directed only towards interpreting old texts or engrafting their own new theories on old texts. Even Vijñāneśvara (c. 1100

A. D.), chief minister of a Chālukya king in the Deccan, could give law in its finished form only by writing his famous commentary, the Mitāksharā, on the Yājnavalkya Smṛiti. The single exception of the Jain Paṇḍit Hemachandra, who wrote in this period an original grammar of Sanskrit defying Pāṇini, only proves the general character of the literature of this period.

The Mahomedans conquered the Panjab about 1000 A. D. and Northern India about 1200 A. D. Under Hindu rule in these provinces, before the Mahomedan conquest, government records were kept in the Sanskrit language, all the kingdoms being ruled by orthodox Hindu kings. Their orders and sanads were issued in Sanskrit, though Sanskrit was a dead language and many treatises on various subjects were written by paṇḍits, chiefly on law for the use of law-courts. Alaṅkāra or poetics is the only subject on which original treatises were written, based on classical epics and dramas. The Mahomedans conquered the Deccan in about 1300 A. D. and the South in 1500 A. D. Vijayanagar, the last Hindu kingdom, produced the well-known Bhāshya of Sāyaṇa on the Vedas. After the Mahomedan conquest in these several provinces, the writing of Sanskrit works practically ceased, though even in Mahomedan times a few treatises, here and there, were written which deserve to be noticed in a history of Sanskrit literature like the Rasa-Gaṅgādhara of Jagannātha. These being of the same nature as the works of the preceding period may be included in it.

For these reasons, therefore, it would be appropriate to divide the history of Sanskrit literature into three periods; viz., the Vedic and post-Vedic period (c. 4500 B. C. to 800 B. C.) to be called the Śruti period, the classical period (c. 800 B. C. to 800 A. D.) to be called the Smṛiti period and the modern period (c. 800 to 1500 A. D.) to be called the Bhāshya period. In the first period, Sanskrit was spoken by all people who were chiefly of the Aryan race; in the second, it was spoken by the high class males while their women and lower classes spoke the ancient Prakrits which were only softened Sanskrit; and in the third period Sanskrit was dead as a spoken language. Naturally the literatures of the three periods differ in language—easy and simple in the first, polished and refined in the second and artificial and pedantic in the third. Then again in the first period, literature is chiefly religious and philosophical and at once became sacred. In the second period literature is highly thoughtful and has become quasi-sacred or authoritative, where not religious, and in the third period literature becomes scholastic though usually full of powerful reasoning and forceful expression.

That this vast literature extending from about 4500 B.C. to 1500 A. D. or over nearly 6000 years is valuable and of unique importance is conceded on all hands. The Vedic hymns, at least three thousand years old if not six, display poetical thought and expression of a high order and they have supplied thinkers with materials for laying the foundation of two sciences viz., Philology and Comparative Mythology. They again supply us with several facts for constructing a history of the common civilization of the great Aryan race. The Upanishad philosophy again rises to the highest point of metaphysical speculation to which human mind can rise. While expounding the most abstruse topics of philosophy, their prose rises to the highest pitch of oratory. Their preaching is so charmingly transcendental that the German pandit Schopenhaur was impelled to exclaim, "O Upanishads ! you will be the solace of my life and the solace of my death." Pāṇini's grammar and Yāska's etymology of the post-Vedic period are the most critical works human minds have produced on these subjects.* In the second period were compiled the Mahābhārata and the Rāmāyaṇa, two epics which surpass in beauty as well as in length every other epic in the whole world. The Indo-Aryans in this period also thought out the problems of logic and metaphysics with an acumen always equal to, if not higher than, that of the Greeks or of modern thinkers of the west. In the third period the Indo-Aryan genius developed these subjects with greater fineness of intellect and particularly Alankārra or poetics was both started and developed in this period

* Dr. MacDonell remarks that in grammar the results attained by the Indians in the systematic analysis of language surpass those arrived at by any other nation (p. 39).

with minute insight into the workings of the human heart and rare appreciation of the beauties of thought and expression.

It is sometimes said that the Indo-Aryans were not able to handle the physical sciences. They undoubtedly cultivated mathematics (arithtmetic, algebra and even geometry); indeed it is the Indo-Aryans who gave the decimal system to the world. They were ahead in the study of astronomy and in the second period, with the help of Greek astronomy, they formulated Siddhāntas which were taken by the Arabs to the west. One great astronomer even propounded the theory of the moving of the earth round the sun seven hundred years before Copernicus discovered the solar system. In medicine again, the Indo-Aryans may be looked upon as the teachers of the ancient medical world. They were already on the path of studying chemistry but their progress was checked by the rise of Alchemy and the idea of Rasāyana or the elixir of life. The one subject on which they have left no works fit to be admired is, as stated before, history.

THE ŚRUTI PERIOD

I GENERAL SURVEY.

The literature of the Śruti or Vedic period naturally divides itself into two portions, the Vedas and the Vedāngas. Vedas again fall under two main heads, the Sanhitās and the Brāhmaṇas. Both these together, according to the orthodox view, form the revelation or Śruti of the Hindu religion. Swami Dayananda, founder of Arya Samaj, who was a great Vedic scholar, denied the Śruti character of the Brāhmaṇas. These Brāhmaṇas are explanatory treatises attached to the Sanhitās, composed by the Ṛishis themselves or their immediate successors. Ṛishis may be defined as the 'composers' or "seers" of Vedic hymns. They are sometimes called Mantrakṛit or composers of Mantras and sometimes, especially in later times, "Mantradrashtṛis" or seers of Vedic hymns, i. e. these hymns are looked upon as seen by the Ṛishis, in other words, as revealed. This sort of sanctity attaches to the original word preached in every religion and we need not wonder that the Vedic Sanhitās attained this sacred character at a very ancient date, indeed even in the days of the Brāhmaṇas themselves. Later literature looked upon the Brāhmaṇas also as revealed and the orthodox dictum now is that Veda is the name applied to both Mantra and Brāhmaṇa i. e. hymns and their explanations (मंत्रब्राह्मणयोर्वेदनामधेयम्). The Brāhmaṇas though unquestionably later than the hymns, as their language indicates, are also very ancient and they may appropriately be treated as belonging to the Veda portion of Sanskrit literature as they contain explanatory notes on the hymns given by ancient sages.

The Vedas are four in number, Ṛigveda, Yajurveda, Sāmaveda, and Atharvaveda. Ṛigveda is unquestionably the oldest of these, that is to say, it contains hymns which are the oldest. Yajurveda contains hymns as well as directions for sacrifices while Sāmaveda contains hymns which are to be sung. The Ṛigvedic hymns are of various nature and not always prayers to gods, nor prayers addressed to the god to whom a sacrifice is being offered. The assignment of Ṛigvedic verses to sacrificial or religious purposes, in other words, their 'viniyoga' is a later affair as we shall see further on. The Ṛigvedic verses are essentially the utterances of the Vedic sages on various topics put in the form of poetry—poetry which is admired even by western scholars. "This lyrical poetry", Prof. MacDonell observes, "far older than the literary monuments of any other branch of the Indo-European family, is already distinguished by refinement and beauty of thought, as well as skill in the handling of language and metre" (p. 29). Ṛik i. e. verse or hymn is distinct from and earlier than Yajus or sacrificial formula, though sacrifice or throwing oblations into fire in propitiation of deities is a form of worship which is common to all ancient people and goes back to pre-historic times. Again singing is natural to man even in primitive ages and devotional singing occurs earlier than singing for love. Certain Ṛiks were, therefore, soon set to singing and they are called the Sāmāni or *good* verses. These Sāmans were sung at sacrifices or at the pressing of the Soma juice, a libation which was peculiar to the Indo-Aryans in their home beyond the Panjab. These three viz. the Ṛik, the Sāman and the Yajus are the oldest divisions of the religious utterances of the Indo-Aryans and they are mentioned in the Purusha-Sūkta, itself a Ṛigvedic hymn, and in this order. The Vedas were thus originally three and they together were called the Trayī Vidyā. Veda itself means branch of knowledge or source of knowledge and is a word at least as old as the Brāhmaṇas. And in one place in the Ṛigveda itself, as shown later on, it is used as meaing sacred word though not the collections of these three forms of utterances, Ṛik, Sāman and Yajus made at some later time and called Sanhitās.

The fourth Veda is the Atharva Veda, recognised as Veda later but before the close of the Brāhmaṇa period. It contains some hymns as old as the Ṛig-vedic hymns, while others are evidently of later date, both from language and matter. The name Atharvan is, however, very old and also belongs to the Iranian people in the form Athravan. The Iranian priests were adepts in magic and used incantations. The Atharva Veda contains mostly verses used for magical purposes as also some verses used for the usual purpose, viz. sacrifice, of the other three Vedas. Its Sanhitā seems to have been put together later as will be shown when we shall speak about it.

Brāhmaṇas or explanatory works grew round each of the three Vedas as also later round the fourth. Each Veda has certain Brāhmaṇas attached to it. These Brāhmaṇas are later works and are in prose, the language of which differs to a considerable extent from that of the Sanhitās. Their latest additions are the Āraṇyakas or theosophical works to be recited in forests and the Upanishads or philosophical compositions made from time to time. Each Veda has thus an Āraṇyaka and serveral Upanishads attached to it. As stated above, this whole Brāhmaṇa literature is considered by the orthodox as sacred and 'Apaurusheya' or not man-made and therefore of equal authority with Mantra and consequently was included in the term Veda. Later still came the Vedāngas or auxiliary works, appendices so to speak, of the Vedas. They are six in number viz., 1 Chhandas or Metre, 2 Jyotisha or astronomy, 3 Kalpa or ritual, 4 Śikshā or rules of pronunciation, 5 Nirukta or etymology and 6 Vyākaraṇa or grammar. There are certain works alone on these subjects which are considered to be sacred works, though not of the same sanctity as Veda, and are learnt by heart by Vaidika Brahmins along with Sanhitā and Brahmaṇa. Their writers are called not Ṛishis but Āchāryas. Most of them fall within the Śruti period as we have defined it, for they were composed at a time when the Vedic language, though out of use, was still understood. But as it had begun to be unintelligible, it was found necessary to write works on the prosody of Vedic hymns and the method of reciting them and soon when the Vedic accents had gone out of use, different schools sprang up which pronounced accents in the hymns and even the Brāhmaṇas differently. These had their different Prātiśākhyas or rules of pronunciation sanctioned by each Śākhā or school. Ceremonial had also begun to differ and hence the necessity for works on ritual also. Sacrifices had again to be performed at particular times and hence astronomy had to be studied and tithis had to be calculated. This branch of study was, therefore, necessary for Vedic sacrificers and required a manual. Lastly the study of grammar and vocabulary of the Vedic language which was going out of use, was a prime necessity and these two subjects were zealously studied for centuries the result of which are two unique works, viz. Panini's grammar and Yāska's Nirukta which have supplanted all works of previous teachers on the subjects and have become the authoritative Vedangas on them. Having taken this general survey of the literature of the Śruti period, we proceed to describe in detail each work commencing with the Ṛigveda Sanhitā.

II THE AGE OF THE ṚIGVEDIC HYMNS AND THE EXTENT OF THE ŚRUTI PERIOD.

The hymns of the Ṛigveda clearly appear to have been composed at different times. There are old and new hymns mentioned even in some of the hymns themselves. Many old hymns are declared to have been lost and Vedic poets often say that they fashion new hymns after the model of the old. The language of old hymns again differs to an appreciable extent from the language of later hymns, especially of the hymns of the tenth Mandala. We have thus to consider the question over what period must these hymns have been composed. Their collection together in the present Saṁhitā text is altogether a different matter; for the date of such collection must be distinct from the date of the composition of the hymns themselves. The date of this collection has, however, also to be determined along with the period of the composition of the hymns, for it will supply the lowest limit of the latter date.

Most European scholars hold that the Ṛigvedic hymns must have been composed from about 1500 to 1000 B. C. Dr. Macdonell thinks that the first collection which was again edited about 600 B. C. after making phonetic changes or Sandhis sanctioned by classical Sanskrit (p. 50) comes from a period which can hardly be less remote than 1000 B. C. (p. 48). Max Müller first assigned these dates from a consideration of the linguistic changes discernible in the language of the oldest hymns and the language of Pāṇini. He thought that there were thus several linguistic layers, so to speak, discernible through the Vedic literature and each layer might be assigned a period of about 200 years. Fixing the date of Pāṇini at 300 B. C. he assigned about 1500 B. C. as the probable date of the oldest Ṛ gvedic hymns. As some of these hymns exactly correspond with some Gāthās of the Iranian Avesta, it is also thought that the Iranian Aryans and the Indo-Aryans separated about this period and the bulk of the Ṛigvedic hymns was composed thereafter in the Panjab. According to most western scholars, thus, the age of the Ṛigvedic hymns extends from about 1500 to 1000 B. C. Of-course these are not exact dates but approximate estimates by centuries.

Many Indian scholars, on the other hand, led by Bal Gangadhar Tilak assign a far different period to the composition of the Ṛigvedic hymns, based on a far more reliable argument than that of language. Mathematical calculations made on the basis of astronomical facts, furnished by some hymns, are more definite and reliable and consequently yield dates which are practically unassailable. What these astronomical facts are and how they can be made the basis of mathematical calculation, we proceed to show in detail.

The rising and setting of the sun give us our lowest measure of time viz., day and night, while the full and new moons give us the dark and bright fortnights, together forming a month, our next measure. Day and night together forming a diurnal day, we have approximately 30 days to the month. The seasons caused by the progress of the sun southwards and northwards have given us the year, our third measure of time and there are approximately 12 lunar months in a solar year. These measures of time must have struck even the primitive man and they are often poetically mentioned in Ṛigvedic hymns such as the year with its 360 days "the wheel with its 360 knobs" The ancients had, however, no measure of time for longer periods; for there is no corresponding astronomical phenomenon so easily marked. It will be remembered that the modern eras have no astronomical basis. The Vedic literature mentions centuries or hundreds of autumns (Śaradām Śatam) and some Brāhmaṇas also mention Yugas, human and divine (mānusha and daiva); but their lengths were not fixed. The Yuga system of later Hindu astronomers is based on a fictitious astronomical phenomenon viz., the starting together of all the planets from the same point in the heavens at the beginning of creation. These facts we mention to explain why there are no chronological data in the Ṛigvedic hymns. (Even if the planets had been known with their revolutions these could only have given periods of 12 and 30 years only.)

The precession of the equinoxes is an astronomical phenomenon discovered about the beginning of the Christian era which can give us a long astronomical cycle of years to measure longer periods than centuries. The Vasanta-sampāta or vernal equinox makes a revolution of the whole ecliptic in about 26000 years and its progress through the Nakshatras or Rāshis will give us smaller measures. The vernal equinox is a point which can be marked by even unintelligent people, though its precession can not be marked so easily, as in the Northern hemisphere it marks the opening of the spring season. In higher latitudes where the sun remains below the horizon for some months, it marks the coming up of the sun above the horizon. Even in the Panjab it could be marked by the ripening of the crops. The Indo-Aryan sages undoubtedly carefully watched the stars and the progress of the moon through them. They also marked the progress of the sun from the southernmost point to the northernmost and exactly fixed the eastern direction by the middle point of this course. We know that the Egyptain pyramids built 3 or 4 thousand years before Christ have corners facing exactly the four directions. It is no wonder then that the Indo-Aryans in ancient days could fix the directions exactly and knew the Viśuvan day. In marking the progress of the sun southwards and northwards, they marked the winter solstice, the vernal equinox, the summer solstice and the autumnal equinox. They also performed sacrifices extending over a year, regulated according to the motion of the sun and by these four days; indeed they looked upon the year as a sacrifice. These facts will show

how the astronomical observations of the ancient Indo-Aryans were accurate and how references to astronomical facts in the Ṛigvedic hymns may be made the basis of mathematical calculation for determining their dates.

It is not necessary for the ordinary reader to have laid out before him the whole theory of B. G. Tilak, propounded in his 'Orion or Antiquity of the Vedas' and it would also not be easy for him to grasp it in all its details. We will, therefore, give the main points of the theory and try to make it as easy for the reader as possible. It is well known that the equinoctial points slowly recede about the circle of the ecliptic, a phenomenon known as the precession of the equinoxes. At present the vernal equinox is behind the Uttarā Bhādrapadā constellation. It has receded to its present position along the Nakshtras one by one and it follows that it was successively in Uttarā Bhādrapadā, Revatī, Aśvinī, Bharaṇī, Krittikā, Rohiṇī, Mrigaśirsha and so on. There are clear references in ancient Sanskrit literature to the positions of the vernal equinox in Aśvinī and Krittikā. The sliding back of the seasons due to this precession becomes marked when the seasons have slided back by about a whole month. Now the ecliptic is divided by the Indo-Aryans into 27 Nakshatras or constellations which means that each Nakshatra consists of an arc of (360 ÷ 27) 13⅓ degrees. It takes nearly 72 years for the equinoctial point to recede one degree, which gives (72×13⅓) 960 years roughly for the precession of the equinoctial point through one Nakshatra are. From this rough rule the reader will understand how from the present position of the vernal equinox in Purvābhādrapadā, calculation can be made as to when it was in Krittikā or Pleiades. This date comes to about 2500 B. C. (960×4½–1920=2400).

Now Tilak has shown that there are several references in the Ṛigveda to the position of the vernal equinox in Mrigaśirsha or Orion also. The Taittirīya Samhitā states that "Phalgunī Pūrnamāsi is the mouth (मुखम्) of the year" a statement repeated in five Brāhmaṇas. Tilak has shown by various arguments that this statement shows that the year must then have commenced with the winter solstice in Phalgunī. If moon was then full in Phalgunī, the sun was then in Mrigaśiras at vernal equinox. That Nakshatra thus had the name Āgrahāyaṇa also, the "first of the year" and the Nakshatra list then must have commenced with it. This name also appears among the Greeks as Orion. There are other passages also in the Rigveda, though not directly yet clearly indicating that the vernal equinox was then in Orion. The story of Prajāpati's head being cut off by Rudra and Indra cutting off the head of his enemy Vṛitra in the form of an antelope, is referred to in R. X 61, 5-7 and in R. I 52, 10 and R. V 34, 2 etc. (Orion, p. 99). Greek mythology also tells us that Apollo hit Orion in its head. These stories are based on the aspect of the stars in the Mrigaśirsha constellation as graphically described by Prof. Whitney. "There is the whole story illustrated in the sky ; the innocent and lovely Rohinī (Aldebarat), the infamous Prajāpati (Orion) in full career after her but laid sprawling by the three jointed arrow (belt of Orion) shot from the hand of the avenger Sirius (Vyādha).* There is again the story of the celestial dog at the gate of heavens, the Canis Major among the Indo-Aryans and the Greeks and the Avesta dog at the bridge. R. I 161, 13 tells us that the dog commenced the year and Devayāna comprised the Vasanta, Grīshma and Varshā seasons (Orion, p. 111). These and various other legends are well explained by holding that the vernal equinox was then in Mrigaśīrsha or Orion. This leads to a date which is (960×2) 1920 years still further back than the Krittikā vernal equinox position and is thus (2500+1920) 4500 B. C. roughly speaking.

Tilak well shows here that the Indo-Aryans and the Iranians must have separated about this time ; for even among the Parsis the Pitṛiyāṇa six monthly period begins with Bhādrapada. The vernal equinox in Mrigaśīrsha beginning the Devayāna period (when the sun is in the northern hemisphere), the autumnal equinox must be in Mūla Nakshatra and the six months of Dakshiṇāyana dedicated to the manes must have begun with Bhādrapada. The feast of the manes of the Parsis falls in this month and that of the Hindus also is observed in the dark half of it.

Tilak further argues that the mention of Chitrā Purṇamāsī also in the Taittirīya Samhitā leads to the

* See also मृगानुसारिणं साक्षात् पश्यामीव पिनाकिनम् in Śakuntalā.

inference that the vernal equinox was once known to be even in Punarvasu, behind Orion and the deity of that Nakshatra being Aditi, it fits in with the Vedic story that Aditi was the mother of gods, the sun from that Nakshtra coming into the northern hemisphere and thus ushering the six months of the gods. "The oldest period in the Aryan civilization may, therefore, be called the Aditi or Pre-Orion period and we may roughly assign 6000–4000 B. C. as its limits." "The finished hymns do not seem to have been then known. Half prose and half poetical *nivids* or sacrificial formulas giving the names, the epithets and the feats of the deity invoked were probably in use. The Parsis and the Greeks have retained no tradition of this period." "We next come to the Orion period commencing from about 4000 B. C. This is the most important period in the history of the Aryan civilization. A good many sūktas of the Ṛigveda, e. g. the Vrishākapi sūkta, were composed in this period and several legends were formed at this time or developed from old ones. The Parsis and the Greeks separated from Indo-Aryans about this time and have preserved these legends about Orion, Agrahāyaṇa among Indo-Aryans and Pauryeni among Parsis" (Orion p. 206–207.)

As stated before, European scholars (except Jacobi) do not believe in this ancient date. "Professor Jacobi of Bonn thinks that the Vedic period goes back to 4000 B. C. a theory based on astronomical calculations connected with a change in the beginning of the seasons which, he thinks, has taken place since the time of the Rigveda period." The argument advanced in refutation of this theory is that "it is based on an improbable assumption of the meaning of a Vedic word which forms the starting point of it." (p. 12). But Macdonell is compelled to concede (one cannot see why) that "meanwhile we must be content with the certainty that Vedic literature in any case is considerably of higher antiquity than that of Greece." But there is no such ambiguity of meaning of a word which can be advanced against the theory of S. B. Dixit by which the Śatapatha Brāhmaṇa is shown to be as old as 3000 B. C. This Brāhmaṇa distinctly describes the Ṛigveda as it is to-day and hence if the date of the Śatapatha is shown to be 3000 B. C. then the Ṛigvedic hymns must certainly be older and their period must lie between 4000 and 3000 B. C.

We will explain this theory of Dixit, as it is almost unanswerable and has not yet, so far as we know, been refuted by anybody, and as it supports almost conclusively the theory of Tilak regarding the age of the Ṛigvedic hymns. In Brāhmaṇa 2 of kānda II Śatapatha says " the Krittikas rise *exactly* in the east" (प्राच्यै दिशो न च्यवन्ते.—The Krittikas do not swerve from the east).* The tense is present and it leaves no doubt that the constellation rose exactly in the east in the days of the Śatapatha writer.

* Winternitz has recently put forward a different interpretation on this sentence. We will answer his arguments later when we speak of the Śatapatha.

We have also shown above that the Vedic Ṛishis carefully marked the heavens and the rising of the stars and that they had marked the eastern direction exactly, like the Egyptian builders of the Pyramids. The statement of the Śatapatha, therefore, is not hap-hazard but must be taken to mean exactly what it purports to mean. The rising of the Krittikās exactly in the east may be made the basis of mathematical calculation, giving the date of this phenomenon. It may be stated that the Krittikas do not now rise exactly in the east but towards the north and from their position to-day we can find the time when they rose exactly in the east. To rise in the east, the Krittikas must be on the equator. They are a few degrees (4° 2′) to the north of the ecliptic. The precession of the equinoxes, we know, continuously changes the position of the equator with respect to the ecliptic and we can see from the diagram given later on, how the equator must once have passed through them, though now it does not. By spherical trigonometry, the latitude of Krittikās being known, we can easily find the position of the vernal equinox at the time when the equator passed through the Krittikās. Shankar Balkrishṇa Dixit has made this calculation and found that the date must have been somewhere about 3000 B. C. He published his views in Indian Antiquary Vol. XXIV in 1895 and so far as we are aware no one has yet refuted this theory. What is sometimes argued against the truth of this theory is that the Śatapatha writer, really of about 600 B. C., merely mentions a fact which was once seen in ancient times, as a present one by reminiscence. But the Krittikās must have swerved from their first position during this long interval of 2400 (3000–600) years and the writer, if he was a Vedic writer, must have marked the rising of stars and seen the new fact and could not have mentioned the old fact as a present one. Moreover, even if we grant this reminiscence theory, it concedes that the fact was once marked by Vedic Ṛishis and was remembered as a formula, which itself takes the Ṛishis back to 3000 B. C. We, however, hold this reminiscence argument to be of no value and if the Śatapatha Brāhmaṇa is itself so old as 3000 B. C. *a fortiori* the Rigvedic hymns must be far older and their period, therefore, may be placed between 4000 and 3000 B. C.

The same conclusion is fortified by two other dates similarly fixed from astronomical data. The date of the Maitrāyaṇīya Upanishad can be fixed to be about 1900 B. C. from the positiou of the vernal equinox mentioned therein as we shall see in detail later on (Tilak's Gītārahasya p 546); and the date of Vedānga Jyotisha can be fixed at about 1400 B. C. from the following statement in it, viz., "The sun and the moon turn towards the north in the beginning of Śravishthā" (प्रपद्येते श्रविष्ठादौ सूर्याचन्द्रमसावुदक् ॥). Now this statement with its present tense occurring in a work on astronomy must be taken to embody an actual fact observed in the days of the Vedānga Jyotisha.

European scholars early saw the importance of this statement and Colebrooke announced that the fact happpened about 1200 B. C. and that, therefore, the date of Vedānga Jyotisha must be taken to be about 1200 B. C. As Vedānga Jyotisha presupposes the whole of the Vedic literature consisting of Samhitās, Brāhmanas and Upanishads of all the four Vedas, it was pointed out to Max-Müller that his assignment of the Rigvedic hymns to the period from 1500 to 1000 B. C. was untenable. S. B. Dixit who has described in detail the method of calculation of this date on the data given by the Vedānga Jyotisha has shown that Colebrooke's calculation was from the beginning of Dhanishthā Nakshatra division, but that if the first star in the Dhanishtha contellation be taken the date goes further back, even taking the star pointed out by Whitney, to about 1400 B. C. It is interesting to note how Max-Müller answered this argument based on mathematical calculation from astronomical data. In his preface to Volume IV of his Rigveda, Max-Müller, admitting first that he had got the mathematical calculation subjected to a scrutiny by Archbishop Pratt, a noted astronomer and that he came to the conclusion that the date of the Vedānga came to about 1181 B. C., remarks curiously enough "This is welcome as confirmatory evidence if we had by internal evidence established the existence of Vedic poetry in the 12th century B. C. By itself this evidence would be of no use for establishing the age of Vedic literature." It is clear from this that

Max Müller was driven into a corner and had to offer some remark in support of his own conclusions. If we had *established* by interval evidence the date of the Vedic literature, then there was no necessity of *any* external evidence. The fact is that the internal evidence of language on which Max Müller proposed his date is so slippery that such date cannot be said to be *established*. For when in a language grammar and vocabulary are studied and fixed, that language changes very slowly and one cannot assign 200 years only for each layer of change. Secondly, the date of Pāṇini taken by Max Müller and other European scholars is itself slippery and, too late as it is, no superstructure can be raised upon it. Thirdly, under such circumstances the unassailable date of the Vedānga Jyotisha arrived at from astronomical data can well be taken as the basis for determining the date of the Vedic literature. The language of the Vedānga and the language of the oldest Rigvedic hymns lie so far apart that the date of the former being fixed even by Archbishop Pratt at 1200 B. C. roughly, the date of the latter cannot be taken to be later than 3000 B. C. We must remember that grammar was begun to be studied even in the days of the Brāhmaṇas. The Śatapatha date again, fixed on astronomical grounds at about 3000 B. C., takes the hymns back to 4000 B.C. And we may safely take the extent of the Śruti period from 4000 B. C. to 1000 B. C. a little after the date of the Vedānga Jyotisha.

The recent finds at Harappa between Multan

and Lahore in lower Panjab and at Mohanjo-daro in Larkhana in Sind cannot, in our view, militate against this date of the Ṛigvedic hymns. That these finds contain no vestige of Vedic civilization may be accounted for in two ways. Either these are more ancient than 4000 B.C. or they evidence the incursion of Semitic culture and settlement during the Vedic period. No date has yet been assigned to these finds; and it is too early to discuss it. But we may mention that the Vedic hymns contain many references to the ocean and also to voyages on the sea. That the Vedic Aryans had sailed down the Indus into the sea and gone as far as Mesopotamia cannot also be doubted. But the chief settlements of the Vedic Aryans were in the Panjab and the U. P. along the Himalayas and had not yet extended into the hot plains of Sind. Sindhu and Sauvīra were long outside the pale of Aryan civilization and it is, therefore, no wonder if Semitic people had founded cities in upper Sind and the lower Panjab. These finds, therefore, can suggest no inferences in connection with the date of the Ṛigvedic hymns or the settlement of the Vedic Aryans in the Panjab. Nay we may point out the fact that Vedic deities are found mentioned in Hittite records recently discovered at Boghazköī in Asia Minor, records which go back to the 14th century before Christ. In the record of a treaty between the king of the Hittites and the king of Mitani, the gods of both kingdoms are invoked as guardians of the treaty, and among the gods of the Mitani appear Mitra,

Varuṇa, Indra and Nāsatya. It thus appears that the Mitani were an Aryan settlement from the Panjab. It can not be supposed that this was an independent Aryan branch which went into Asia Minor from the ancient Aryan home. For Indra is pre-eminently an Indo-Aryan deity and had no existence in that home. That there was intercourse between Mesopotamia and the Panjab in those early centuries is also apparent from certain unintelligible words in one Rigvedic hymn such as 'Turpharū' which appear to be Chaldean. And B. G. Tilak has pointed out that the name 'Yavha' pertaining to God appears as Jehova among the Hebrews. If, then, there was intercourse between Indo-Aryan Panjab and Asia Minor in the 14th century B. C., the coming of the Indo-Aryans into the Panjab and the older Rigvedic hymns may fairly be placed in the fourth millenium B. C.

Argument again in favour of a late date for the Rigvedic hymns is sought to be derived from the extreme similarity of Avestic gāthās and Rigvedic mantras which are sometimes identical. There is no doubt that the Indo-Aryans and the Iranians once formed one people and lived together. They naturally have some mantras in common. But we must remember that Zoroaster did not himself compose these gāthās. He only preserved what had come down from centuries and even if we take 550 B. C. as the date of Zoroaster, that cannot be the date of those gāthās. Indeed, as the Hindus have preserved the Vedic mantras intact for thousands of years, because they have become sacred, so also must the Avestic gāthās have been preserved intact for thousands of years before they were taken up by Zoroaster for his new religion. The date of Zoroaster is, however, much earlier than that taken by European scholars, and Parsi scholars supported by anciant Greck writers place him as early as 2500 to 4000 B. C. We need not discuss Zoraster's date here, as even taking his date to be 550 B. C., the age of the gāthās does and must go far behind him.

Finally, the argument based upon calculations as to how long the Indo-Aryans might have taken to spread from the Panjab to Bengal in the east and the Deccan in the south is as slippery as that based on language. Peoples sometimes spread fast; but sometimes they stand stationary for thousands of years. The Aryans in the north and the Mongolians in the east and the stronger Dravidians in the south might have lived side by side without change for thousands of years and conquest in the east and south may have been by sudden expansion. Indeed, the jungles of the Gondvan country were invaded and cut only under British rule. Burmans and Indians again lived side by side from the most ancient times down to the twentieth centuy A. D.

III RIGVEDA

CONTENTS AND COMPILATION

The Rigveda contains 1017 hymns called Sūktas composed by different Ṛishis or Vedic poets. It exactly resembles "The Golden Treasury of Songs." Some careful compiler has evidently made this collection, with a fixed plan before him, by selecting good hymns from among many then current among the Indo-Aryans, handed down from generation to generation. The plan is evident from the arrangement of the hymns into ten Maṇdalas or books. There is a plan in this division, as the second to the eighth Mandalas contain hymns current in certain Ṛishi families, viz., II Gṛitsamada, III Viśvāmitra, IV Gautama, V Atri, VI Bharadvāja. VII Vasishtha and VIII Kaṇva, respectively. The ninth Mandala contains hymns composed by different Ṛishis in praise of Soma juice, the libation peculiar to the Himalayan regions. The first and the tenth Mandalas contain hymns on miscellaneous subjects and form the van and the rear, so to speak, of the collection. The first hymn is addressed to Agni the most ancient and favourite god of the Aryans and is composed by Madhuchchhanda, who is called

Śatarchin* meaning composer of a hundred verses and the last hymn of the collection is addressed to the unity of hearts of the teacher and the pupil.

The several Mandalas (except of course the ninth) again consist of groups of hymns composed by the same author. There is sometimes a mention of the author of the hymn in one of its verses but usually not and the information about the authorship of hymns must have been separately handed down from generation to generation. As the Ṛigveda soon became the revelation of the Indo-Aryans, it was zealously as well as carefully scrutinised. And Anukramaṇis arose later which gave detailed information about the number of hymns in it, the number of riks in each hymn, the author of each hymn, the deity praised by it and so on. Kātyāyana's Sarvānukramaṇi or table of centents dated about 300 B. C. is available to us and furnishes us with full information about the Ṛigveda. We have simply to note it and present it to the reader in all its principal details.

The Ṛigveda was learnt by heart probably by every Brahmin, Kshatriya and Vaiśya in ancient times. But its length must soon have deterred almost all and to learn it by heart became the occupation of a few Brahmins only. These for their convenience divided it into eight Ashṭakas, each Ashtaka

* Ṛich or Ṛik meaning a verse, Shadguruśisya explains that the poets of the first Mandala are called Śatarchins because the first Ṛishi is a Śatarchin, there being 102 verses of his in this Mandala in the beginning (Sarvānu, by Macd. p. 59.)

consisting of eight Adhyāyas and hence called so. The Ṛigveda was thus divided into 64 Adyāyas or chapters. These chapters are again subdivided into Vargas on what principle cannot be exactly seen. Vargas consist of from one to nine Ṛiks and there is one Varga of one Rik and one of nine Riks. The number of Vargas with 2, 3 etc., to 8 Riks is also counted and the total number of Vargas is 2006.

The reader will thus see, that the eight Ashṭakas and the ten Mandalas cannot be coextensive, the latter being subdivided into Anuvākas which consist of certain numbers of whole sūktas or hymns. These divisions are shown in the following table

Mandala	No of Anuvākas	Sūktas	Ashtaka	No. of Vargas in the printed copies
I	24	191	I	265
II	4	43	II	221
III	5	62	III	225
IV	5	58	IV	250
V	6	87	V	238
VI	6	75	VI	331
VII	6	104	VII	248
VIII	10	92	VIII	246
IX	7	114		
X	12	191		2024*
	85	1017		
				2006

* The difference of 18 is due to inclusion of Vālakhilyas.

That the number of hymns in the first and the tenth Mandalas is the same is an accident and not a conscious arrangement as Dr. Macdonell thinks.

The Ṛigveda has been religiously preserved by the Vaidika Brahmins for these several thousands of years without any variation and there are no various readings in it. Some differences in pronunciation and ritual arose in course of time and these gave rise to what are called *Śākhās* (branches) or *Charaṇas* (feet). The Śākhās of the several Vedas with the parts of India where they are chiefly to be met with, are enumerated in a modern treatise called *Charaṇavyūha* or collection of Charaṇas, the exact date of which we will discuss in a note. This work enumerates five principal Śākhās of the Ṛigveda from among twenty-one said in the Mahābhāshya to be once current and these five are :—1 Śākala, 1 Bāshkala, 3 Māndūkeya, 4 Āśvalāyana, and 5 Sānkhāyana. Each of these had a Sūtra of its own. At the present day only the Sākala Sākhā remains with Āśvalāyana and Sānkhāyana Sūtras. What difference there was in these different Śakhās, so far as the contents of the Ṛigveda are concerned, it is difficult to determine at this date. But the difference must have been insignificant. We are indeed told in the Anuvākānukramaṇī of Śaunaka that there are eight hymns in addition in the Bāshkala Śākhā (Sarva. Macd. p. 51). The modern Vaidikas have preserved one of these viz., तच्छंयोरावृणीमहे etc. which is recited at the Śrāvaṇī but is not found in the Śākala recension. There may have been also some transpositions of hymns or verses in the Bāshkala recension and hence the proverb among Vaidikas which dubs a man as Bāshkala who puts things topsy-turvy. The Śākala Śākhā Saṁhitā was popular from ancient times and has, therefore, now been alone preserved. It has been subjected to careful scrutiny and Śaunaka and Kātyāyana give its contents in minutest details, even the words, nay even the letters in the Samhitā being counted.

There are eleven Vālakhilyas or hymns of Vālakhila Ṛishis (children poets) added as appendix but given in the midst of the Śākala Saṁhitā. These are learnt by heart by Vaidikas, but are not put into the Pada text nor included in the number of words. Thus in the 1017 Suktas, there are 10580 $\frac{1}{4}$ Ṛiks or verses giving 10 verses on an average for each hymn and in these verses there are 153826 words in the Śākala recension of the Ṛigveda and there are altogether 432000 letters which shows that there are about 15 words in each verse on an average and a word on an average consists of three letters.

Long standing tradition recorded in the Mahābhārata (300 B. C.) ascribes the compilation of the Vedas to Krishṇa Dvaipāyana son of Parāśara, called Vedavyāsa for this very reason (वेदान् विव्यास यस्मात्स वेदव्यास इतीरित: and तपसा ब्रह्मचर्येण व्यस्य वेदान्महामति:) (MBh. I. 2) There is no reason why we should not accept this tradition with certain reservations. Krishṇa Dvaipāyana Vyāsa, it must first be pointed out,

*शाकल्यदृष्टे पदलक्षमेकं सार्धं च वेदे त्रिसहस्रयुक्तम्
शतानि चाष्टौ दशकद्वयं च पदानि षट्चेति ह चर्चितानि ॥ ४५
(शौ. अनु Maod. p. 52.)

is a different person from Bādarāyaṇa Vyāsa, author of the Vedānta Sūtras as will be shown in a subsequent chapter. The former again was a contemporary of the heroes of the Bhārata fight which must be placed in 3102 B.C. as Indian tradition, supported by evidence, believes. And since the date of the Śatapatha Brāhmaṇa is fixed by S. B. Dixit, as shown already, at about 3000 B. C. and since the Śatapatha describes the Ṛigveda as we find it to-day, the compilation of the Ṛigveda may fitly be ascribed to Krishṇa Dvaipāyana. There are other indications also. The tenth Mandala which brings together the latest hymns contains a hymn composed by a historical personage connected with the Mahābhārata heroes. viz., Devāpi, uncle of Bhīshma. Another hymn in a previous Mandala mentions Somaka, son of Sahadeva, a Pānchāla king mentioned in the epic. The compilation of the Ṛigvedic hymns, therefore, must have been made a little later than Devāpi and Somaka. This would again make Krishṇa Dvaipāyana a probable compiler of the Ṛigveda. Thirdly, the different Śāknās of the Ṛigveda are, so to speak, editions slightly varying one from another. There are five of them which are now well-known and we may be sure that twent-one were current in the days of Patanjali. When we consider how rigorously Brahmins have preserved the Ṛigveda, a long time must have elapsed after its compilation by Vyāsa down to Patanjali and to Śaunaka, who clearly mentions two versions current in his days viz. the Śākala and the Bāshkala editions. If we, therefore, look upon Krishna Dvaipāyana Vyāsa (c. 3100 B. C.) as the compiler of the Ṛigveda, there is a sufficiently long period of years for various versions of the original Ṛigveda to come into being.

Dr. Macdonell thinks that there were more stages than one in the compilation of the Ṛigveda, that the second to the seventh books of single families must have been first compiled, that the ninth was subsequently added containing hymns addressed to Soma taken from the above family books and that the first book was subsequently added to these, together with the eighth " with which it has much affinity, more than half of its hymns being attributed to the Kaṇva family and the favourite strophic metre of the eighth reappearing in the first." (p. 42) "The tenth book came into existence, when the first nine already existed. Its composers grew up in the knowledge of the older books. The fact that the author of one of its groups (20–26) begins with the opening words " Agnimīḷe " of the first hymn of the Ṛigveda is an indication that the books I–IX already existed in his day *even as a combined collection*." But what ground is there to believe that this author had the nine books before him as a *cumbined collection*? For the words "Agnimīḷe" might have been taken from the hymn of Madhuchhanda alone which, and not the whole first book, might have been before him. Nay more, the occurrence of two identical words at the beginning of two hymns in I and X only may have been a pure chance. Lastly, some of the hymns in the tenth book are old hymns, though many hymns in it are distinctly of late date from their language and contents. In short, the whole Ṛigveda in ten Maṇḍalas may be taken as the work of one compiler, done at one time and need not necessarily be a work successively grown up.

We again differ from the view generally entertained by European scholars that the original work was in a different form from the Saṁhitā form now current. "This phonetically modified form is due to the labours of grammatical editors" (Macd. p. 47) "This text differs in hundreds of places from that of the composers of the hymns, though its actual words are nearly always the same as those used by the original seers. The difference lies almost entirely in the phonetic changes which the words have undergone according to the rules of Sandhi prevailing in the classical language. Thus what was formerly pronounced as "tvam hi agne" now appears as "tvam hyagne" "These phonetic combinations introduced in the Saṁhitā text have interferred with the metre" (Macd. p. 48). The Saṁhitā text embodying such combinations is believed to have been compiled about 600 B. C. (p. 50) as "grammarians like Śākalya and Māṇdūkeya are first mentioned in the Āraṇyakas and Upanishads and hence the Saṁhitā text must have been formulated after the Brāhmaṇas and before the Upanishads."

But this whole argument seems to us to be unsound for various reasons. Is it meant that the Vedic sages did not know the sandhi rules or did not make sandhis in their compositions? For example is it meant that the Vedic seer originally wrote or rather sang 'hi agne' as the metre required, and not 'hyagne'? (hi agne would give three syllables while hyagne would give two). That the old Vedic seers acted upon sandhi rules is certain from many verses in their compositions where such sandhis have been made and where they fit in with the metre *e.g.* पुरुष एवेदं सर्वम्. That their sandhi rules often differed from those of Pāṇini is also certain from several examples such as पशून् तांश्चक्रे and चक्षोः सूर्यो अजायत. Moreover if the Sanhitā text was due to the lectures of grammarians, how were such texts as ऋर्षी॒न्तपस्वतो (x 154) not changed into ऋषींस्तपस्वतो which causes no fault in the metre? How do we then explain such cases as 'hyagne' where the metre falters owing to the shortness of a syllable? The explanation has already been given by Kātyāyana in his Sarvānukramaṇī in the sūtra पादपूरणार्थं तु क्षैप्रसंयोगैकाक्षरीभावं व्यूहेत् (Macd. Sarv. p. 2) which is explained by Shadguruśishya in his commentary in two ways (p. 63) "Kshaiprasaṁyoga means Yakāra-Vakāra-Saṁyoga or Yaṇ-Saṁyoga *i. e.* conjunct consonants with *y*, *v*, *r* and *l*". It seems, therefore, that it was a convention with the Vedic poets that even where Sandhi was made the one conjunct letter or syllable so arrived at should, for purposes of metre, be looked upon as two. Indeed Vaidika reciters even now recite hya as two letters but not as they originally stood viz, as 'hi agne' but as 'hiyagne,' the y being distinctly heard. We may

4

even point out conjunct consonants with y and v being treated as two syllables with i and u added, in reciting, to the previous consonant, even where there are originally not two words joined by sandhi but only one word. Thus in the well-known Gāyatri verse "तत्सवितुर्वरेण्यं &c." the first foot would consist of seven syllables only if ṇya is treated as one syllable. Here there is no sandhi of two words but there is one word only and yet ṇya has to be split up into two letters which Vaidika reciters pronounce as ṇiya. It is, therefore, proper to hold that the ancient Vedic poets had this convention for making up the required number of syllables, viz. splitting one syllable into two especially conjunct consonants with y and v, instead of holding that they did not make any sandhis. Sandhis in sentences are no doubt optional but that is for speaking with facility. No poet would rely upon this in his versification and it is difficult to believe that Vedic poets with such brilliant powers of composition as they exhibit would not make sandhis. The Saṁhitā text is, therefore, the original text of the Ṛigveda; though the word Saṁhitā appears to have arisen after the Pada text was formulated, to distinguish the former from the latter, just as the word Sanskrit arose after the Prakrits were born, though that language is of course older than the latter.

The argument again relied on for fixing the date of the Saṁhitā text is the usual fallacious argument based on non-mention. Because the Brāhmaṇas do not contain any reference to grammatical speculations or terms nor mention any grammarians, it does not, therefore, follow that there were then no speculations or grammarians. Non-mention proves non-existence only when mention is necessary. The Brāhmaṇa-writers might have had no occasion to mention grammatical speculations or they may have not thought the mention necessary even if they had an occasion. Grammatical rules again are enunciated years after the forms are actually used and we may well conceive that the Vedic poets did make sandhis or combinations of vowels at the end of the preceding words with vowels at the beginning of the following ones, long before grammarians arose and formulated the rules of such sandhis. It is only in a dead language that grammatical rules become masters. A living language uses forms or makes sandhis from natural tendencies. It is, therefore, not necessary to hold that the Saṁhitā text arose after grammatical studies had progressed and grammarians had arisen, nor to suppose that the Saṁhitā text arose after the Brāhmaṇas because the latter do not mention grammarians.

The Indian tradition, therefore, namely that Krishna Dvaipāyana Vyāsa made the Vedic compilations before the Śatapatha, the oldest Brāhmaṇa, was composed in about 3000 B. C., may be accepted as reliable. We can not further hold that the Ṛigveda in its compiled form was before the authors of the Yajus's formulæ or Sāman verses. For these two were also collected into Saṁhitās by Vyāsa at the same time from the floating material then existing. These two Vedas, no doubt, contain many verses from the Ṛigveda almost everywhere; but it is not necessary to suppose that they take them from the compiled Ṛigveda. They could do so from hymns as they then separately existed among the Indo-Aryans. There are a few variations in the verses quoted but these are probably due to quotation from memory or to necessity. Ṛigvedic verses are quoted in the Brāhmaṇas and the Sūtras also. But these were quoted after the Ṛigveda was compiled into a fixed form, as the Brāhmaṇas and Sūtras date later than the compilations for reasons mentioned later on ; and the variations in such quotations were often consciously made for purposes of ritual, as held by Dr. Macdonell himself.

While accepting the tradition of the compilation of the Vedas by Vyāsa we may, however, reject that part of it which credits him with compiling the Atharva text also, for we have seen that originally there were three Vedas only, the Atharva Veda being put together later. We may also reject the ideâ suggested later (especially in Vishṇu Purāṇa) that Vyāsa taught the four Vedas to four different pupils, viz. Ṛigveda to Paila, Yajurveda to Vaiśampāyana, Sāmaveda to Jaimini and Atharvaveda to Sumantu. He taught the three Vedas and Bhārata composed by himself to each of his four pupils and to fifth his son Śuka. In ancient times all Brahmins learnt all the three Vedas and division of labour by Brahmins sticking to particular Vedas arose after the Brāhmaṇa period at least. It is hence that we find the Śatapatha Brāhmaṇa of the Śukla Yajurveda mentioning the Ṛigveda with respect and treating the change of even one word in a Ṛigvedic verse as a thing not to be thought of, indeed as blasphemous. The Śukla Yajurveda arose after Vyāsa had compiled the Ṛigveda, the Krishṇa Yajurveda and the Sāmaveda, as its very tradition (which will be given later on) indicates. The Brāhmaṇa literature of the other Vedas grew up later following the example of the Śatapatha Brāhmaṇa, and when the volume of the literature of each Veda thus became vast and when ritual sanctioned by the different Vedas also differed, Brahmins divided themselves into distinct classes which acknowledged allegiance to particular Vedas only, a fact proved by these different classes of Brahmins being descended from the same Ṛishis and having the same gotra and pravara, as also by the fact that the Ṛishis of the different Vedas are also the same.

This division of Brahmins into Ṛigvedins, Yajurvedins and so on was further necessitated by the increased labour of learning by heart the Pada and Krama texts of the Vedas. The Saṁhitā texts were, as we have seen, formulated about 3,100 B. C. and in the course of nearly a thousand years, the Vedic language became generally unintelligible. Learned Brahmins, therefore, had the Saṁhitā text made explicit by separating the padas or words, so that no ambiguity of meaning might arise and to make the Pada text fixed, they further invented the Krama text in which each pada was twice uttered, once with the preceding pada and again with the succeeding one. Ingenuity further invented the Jatā and Ghana Pāthas or methods of reciting, so that Brahmins of exceptional ability could exhibit feats of wonderful memory by reciting the padas thrice and in different permutations, as well explained by Dr. Macdonell in algebraic terms such as ab, ba, abc, cba, abc and so on.

At what date the Pada text of the Ṛigveda, soon followed by the Krama recitation, was formulated, we have certain indications for surmising. This must have been before the Aitareya Āraṇyaka was composed as there is a distinct mention of it therein. Śākalya is considered to be the author of the Pada text and his name is mentioned in the Aitareya Āraṇyaka. The author of Krama was Gālava of the Bābhravya gotra (M.Bh. XIII, Ch. 341). The Pada and Krama recitations being usually more sonorous than the Saṁhitā recitation, they are specially mentioned in the Mahābhārata where Kaṇva's Āshrama or residential university is described in detail in Ādi-Parva. This makes it certain that Pada and Krama recitation was popular before 300 B. C., the certain date of our present Mahābhārata as shown later on. Śākalya, the author of the Pada text must again be placed before Pāṇini who usually quotes Śākalya the grammarian. Śākalya is mentioned in Aitareya Āraṇyaka which mentions the Saṁhitā, Pada and Krama pāthas as Nirbhuja, Pratrina and Ubhayamantareṇa and gives the different fruits of their recitations. Even Keith gives 600 B. C. as the probable date of this Āraṇyaka and hence Pada and Krama pāthas of the Ṛigveda are certainly not later than 600 B.C. Aitareya Āraṇyaka, as will be shown later on, may be placed still earlier and the Pada pātha seems to be nearly as old as 2000, B.C. Mahābhārata XIII. ch. 134 contains a story that Śākalya performed austerities and propitiated Śiva who gave him a boon by which his son became a famous Sūtra-writer. Unfortunately there is no detail here as to who this Śākalya was and what his Sūtra was about. It is permissible, however, to suppose that Śākalya, the father, was the author of the Pada text and Śākalya, the son, was a grammarian and composed a Sūtra on grammar which is always mentioned with respect by Pāṇini and he is also mentioned in Aitareya Āraṇyaka. Śākalya, however, is a patronymic which may be borne by many-nay hundreds.

The Ṛigvedic verses, as also those in the other Vedas and even the prose portions of the Black Yajurveda use words with Vedic accents called Udātta, Anudātta and Svarita. These accents Sanskrit lost in the days of the Brāhmaṇas and thus long before Pāṇini who, however, gives rules for the accents or svaras for the Vedic language. The Śatapatha and the Taittirīya Brāhmanas alone have svaras while all other Brāhmaṇas have none. The Pada texts of the Vedas have accents. The Pada texts might have been, therefore, formulated even before the other Brāhmaṇas arose though it is possible to hold that the Pada text might have been subsequently formulated with accents according to certain rules following the Saṁhitā accents. As shown by Dr. Macdonell, musical accents existed even in old Greek and some other Aryan languages and these have now been replaced by stress accents. But his view that stress accents exist even now in modern Sanskrit cannot be accepted. So far as we know, there is no accent of any kind in modern Sanskrit, all syllables being pronounced in the same tone without any stress on any syllable. Dr. Macdonell has not given the authority for his opinion and there is no mention of this accent in either Pāṇini or Patanjali or later writers.

It must be said to the credit of the Vaidika Brahmins of India that they have preserved the Ṛigveda and the other Veda texts, difficult as they are by reason of Vedic accents which have disappeared these nearly four or five thousand years, without any deviation either of a word, syllable or accent. The knowledge of the Ṛishis and the Devatās of the various Vedic hymns is, however, preserved in Kātyāyana's Sarvānukramaṇi compiled from Anuvākānukramaṇis, Ārshaanukramaṇis and Chhandonukramaṇis etc., which were older. The Prātiśākhya of Śaunaka is another work which relates to the pronunciation of the Śākala Śākhā and there might have been other Prātiśākhyas, as the name indicates, for other Śākhās also.

Ṛigveda Vaidika Brahmins at present are to be chiefly met with in the Deccan and the Konkan and in some parts of Southern India. There are some Ṛigvedins among Kanojia Brahmins in Northern India, but it is doubtful whether they can produce any Vaidika who can recite the whole Ṛigveda with any of its Brāhmaṇas. The Ṛigveda is the most important and the oldest Veda, yet its adherents are so few and found only to the south of the Vindhyas. The reason of this is not apparent, but that this must have been the case from many centuries is apparent from the fact that Ṛigvedic mss. and recitation are always found with the peculiar letter (ḷ) substituted for ḍ as also (ḷh) for ḍh. These letters and pronunciations are peculiar to Southern India and are to be met with in Dravidian languages only. They are not to be found in the Akshara-vaṭikā of Pāṇini nor in the recitation of the Black Yajurveda and probably not in the recitation of other Śākhās of Ṛigveda itself now extinct. This letter and pronunciation is sanctioned by the Śaunaka Prātiśākhya. Probably he belonged to the south and this way of recitation arose after Pānini, when the Indo-Aryans settled south of the Vindhyas about the 8th century B.C., at least before Buddha, as Dr. R. G. Bhandarkar properly held.

Lastly we have to point out a strange mention about the Śākhās of the Ṛigveda in the Mahābhārata. These are, as stated before, said to be five in Charaṇavyūha; and twenty one in Patanjali's Mahābhāshya; but there is an enumeration of Śākhās in MBh. Śānti. P. ch. 343 (Nārāyaṇīya Ākhyāna) wherein the word 21 *thousand* is used in this connection. It is clear that this is a gross exaggeration; the commentator gives no explanation of the word thousand used here. That it refers to Śākhās is clear from the context and it is extremely probable that Sahasra is a misreading of an original Sākhākam, in the Mahābhārata verse here.* The twenty-one Śākhās of the Ṛigveda, however, are mentioned by Patanjali also and thus are as old as the Mahābhārata of 300 B. C. As already stated five of them were well-known and now only the Śākala Śākhā remains. There seem to be some further variations of pronunciation probably even under this Śākhā as one is actually named as Saiśirīya in the Anuvākānukramaṇi of Śaunaka (Macd p. 51). As the word Pārāyaṇa is used here, this may be a school of Pārāyaṇa reciters i.e. reciters of the whole Veda, and not a Śākhā or school of the Ṛigveda Saṁhitā.

Note:—The two-fold division of the Ṛigveda.

The division of the Ṛigveda into Ashṭakas, Adhyāyas aud Vargas in addition to its earlier division into Mandalas, Anuvākas and Sūktas is almost inexplicable. It is, however, old, as old as Śaunaka's Aṇuvākānukramaṇi i. e. 300 B. C. The principle of this division is unsurmisable, especially it is impossible to guess on what principle the Vargas have been made. We made enquiries of many Vaidika Brahmins on this subject but none could enlighten us. The Vargas consist of one, two, three, and so on up to nine Ṛiks without any reference to the ending or beginning of a Sūkta. So also the Adhyāyas are made to end without regard to the ending of a Maṇḍala;

* एकविंशतिसाहस्रमृग्वेदंमांप्रचक्षते was probably एकविंशतिशाखाकं

thus the seventh Ashtaka, Adhyāya 5 and Varga 29 ends with the first Sūkta of the tenth Maṇḍala. Sūkta, Anuvāka, Maṇḍala is on the other hand an understandable division. A Sūkta is a complete hymn, usually composed by one Rishi and an Anuvāka consists generally of the hymns of one Vedic seer, though where there are many Sūktas of the same seer, they are grouped into more Anuvākas than one. Thus, the eleven Sūktas of Madhuchhanda the first Rishi of the first Maṇḍala consisting of 10 Ṛiks each including that of his son are put into three Anuvākas, while the 12 Sūktas of the Rishi Medhātithi Kāṇva with 143 Ṛiks are put into two. The succeeding Rishis Sunaḥs'epa, Hiraṇyastupa, Kaṇva Ghora etc., have one Anuvaka assigned to their Sūktas which are seven, five eight etc., in number. One Anuvāka may contain, however, Sūktas of more than one Rishi if they are few or single. Thus in the tenth Maṇḍala the first Anuvāka contains Sūktas of more than one Rishi, so also the second and third, tho total number of Ṛiks being 148, 146 and 136. No, Anuvāka ends, we believe, in the middle of a Sūkta. The principle of the division of the Ṛigveda into Maṇḍalas and Anuvākas and their arrangement can be seen from the list of the 1017 Sūktas with their Rishis and Devatās given in the Appendix.

ṚIGVEDIC ṚISHIS.

The definition by Kātyāyana of a Ṛishi is again straight and simple. 'यस्य वाक्यं स ऋषिः' "The person whose utterance it is is the Ṛishi of it." The name of the poet is, however, not usually mentioned in his utterance and as stated before, this information must have been handed down from generation to generation. It probably was not given by the compiler of the Ṛigveda; for it could not then have been necessary to compile Ārshānukramaṇīs or Sarvānukramaṇīs like that of Kātyāyana. Probably the compiler of this golden treasury of songs did not give the names of the seers as they must have been then well-known. But after centuries such Anukramaṇīs became necessary, giving the names of the compilers of the hymns as also the metres and the gods in whose praise they were uttered.

The Āśvalāyana Gṛihyasūtra in its Tarpaṇa Adhyāya (III–4) describes these Ṛishis succinctly as follows*:—अथ ऋषयः शतार्चिनो माध्यमा गृत्समदो विश्वामित्रो वामदेवो भरद्वाजो वसिष्ठः प्रगाथाः पावमान्यः क्षुद्रसूक्ता महासूक्ताः ॥ 1 Śatarchins. 2 Mādhyamas. 3 Gritsamada. 4 Vishvāmitra. 5 Vāmadeva. 6 Atri. 7 Bharadvāja. 8 Vasishtha. 9 Pragāthas. 10 Pāvamānis. 11 Kshudrasūktas and 12 Mahāsūktas. The explanation given of the first two names by Shadguruśishya is untenable. He says that the Ṛishis of the first Maṇḍala are all called Śatarchins, because the first viz., Madhuchhanda has 102 Ṛiks, the rest having the same name by comradeship, while the Ṛishis of the intervening Mandalas are called Mādhyamas* and the Ṛishis of the last or tenth Maṇḍala are called Kshudrasūktas and Mahāsūktas But if the Rishis of the middle Mandalas are included in the term Mādhyamas, where was the propriety of again detailing them as Gritsamada &c.? The libation of water would thus be given over again. We think that the Ṛishis of the first Maṇḍala alone are called Śatarchins and Mādhyamas by Āśvalāyana. These Ṛishis with the number of their Sūktas and Ṛiks are as follows :—

	Name	No. of Sūktas	No. of Ṛiks.
1.	Madhucchandas with his son	10 + 1=11	102 + 11=123
2.	Medhātithi Kāṇva	12	143
3.	Sunahśeph Ajīgarti	7	97
4.	Hiraṇyastupa Angirasa	5	71
5.	Ghora Kāṇva	8	96
6.	Praskanva Kāṇva	7	82
7.	Savya Āngirasa	7	72
8.	Nodhā Gautama	7	74
9.	Parāsara Śaktya	10	61
10.	Gautama Rāhugaṇa	20	204
11.	Kutsa Āngirasa	5	42
12.	Kāshyapa Mārīcha	1	1
13.	Rijāśva Āmbarīsha	1	19
14.	Kutsa Āngirasa	4	39
15.	Āptya Trita Kutsa	1	19

* द्वितियादि नवमान्तेषु मध्यमेषु मंडलेषु मध्यमनामानः

	Name	No of Sūktas	No of Ṛiks.
16.	Kutsa Āngirasa	10	107
	Kutsa thus has	15	165
17.	Dairghatamasa	12	160
18.	Parucchepa Daivodāsi	13	100
19.	Dīrgahtamas Autathya	24	231
20.	Agastya	13	103
21.	Lopāmudrā	1	6
22.	Agastya	11	99
23.	Vishaśanki Agastya	1	16
	Total Agastya	26	224

Those in the above list with verses over hundred are, we think, called Śatarchins by Āśvalāyana and those with verses below one hundred are called Mādhyamas. The Ṛishis of the second to the seventh Maṇdalas are of the famillies of Gritsamada etc. and have separate libations under those names. European scholars do not look upon the eighth Maṇdala as a family Maṇdala but it is treated as such by Āśvalāyana who calls the Ṛishis of this Maṇdala by the name Pragāthas. In this Maṇdala there are 92 Sūktas and 11 more Sūktas called Vālakhilyas are inserted in the middle of it (49–59) ; thus the total number may be taken to be 103. Now these 11 Vālakhilyas are all by Kāṇvas and of the other 92 more than half namely 50 are also by Kāṇvas. And thus this Maṇdala may be regarded as a Maṇdala of the Kāṇva family. Āśvalāyana calls the Ṛishis Pragāthas because Pragātha has a Sūkta in the beginning ; but Pragātha also appears to be a Kāṇva (See Sūkta VIII. 48 and Śadgurusishya's commentary. Macd. p. 136). There are hymns no doubt of other Ṛishis also in this Maṇḍala, but the predominance of Kāṇvas gives their name to the Ṛishis properly enough. The fact that "this Maṇḍala contains fewer hymns than the seventh" (104) cannot indicate, as Macdonell thinks, "that it is not a family Maṇḍala." The number of hymns is irrelevent and it is inexplicable how this argument can be advanced (p. 42). Indeed one may also argue that the 11 Vālakhilyas are added to this Mandala for this very reason to make up the round number 103, if this reason is really important. But it is not so as the several family Maṇḍalas (II–VII) have Sūktas of various numbers as already shown.

The Rishis of the 9th maṇḍala are properly called Pāvamānis and though they are often the same as the preceding Ṛishis they have a separate libation as composers of Pāvamāna (Soma flowing) hymns. Lastly the tenth Maṇḍala contains hymns on miscellaneous subjects, some important and others insignificant and Āśvalāyana groups the Ṛshis of these hymns as Kshudrasūktas and Mahāsūktas, "composers of small and great hymns." The commentator Shadgurusishya explains that the hymns down to the famous Nāsadiya (X 129) are great hymns and the remaining (130 to 191) are small ones. This explanation seems supportable as on looking into the tenth Maṇḍala one does find that the hymns down to 129 (which is perhaps the greatest hymn in the Ṛigveda showing to what philosophic height the thought of the

Ṛigvedic Rishis reached) are both long and important hymns and deserve to be called Mahāsūktas ; the succeeding hymns are almost all of them short poems and are on unimportant subjects. They may fitly be called by comparison Kshudrasūktas.

It must, of course, be remembered that the division into family books is not quite rigid. For we find the hymns of Madhuchhandas Vishvāmitra and Medhātithi Kāṇva given in the first book instead of in the third and eighth. (Medhātithi is again quoted in VIII 31 and 32). The seventh Maṇdala again contains 104 hymns all attributed to Vashistha but his grandson Parāśara son of Śakti is also quoted in the first Maṇdala (65to 76). Probably these are given first in the first book because they are simple and musical, the compiler of the Ṛigveda wishing apparently to begin his golden treasury with the simplest hymns, the first being addressed to Agni the first Vedic deity.

Among the authors mentioned in the 10th Maṇdala there are Rājarshi authors such as Kavasha Ailūsha (X 31), Aruṇa Vaitahavya (X 91), Sudāsa Paijavana (X 133) Māndhātṛi Yauvanāśva (X 134). There is a Sūkta by a Vaiśya, Vatsapri Bhalandana. There are some women authors also such as Apālā, daughter of Atri (VIII 91). Indeed a non-Aryan Ṛishi is also met with viz., Ūrdhvagrāvan son of the serpent Arbuda (X 175).

The authorship of certain hymns seems to have been forgotten and such hymns are assigned to imaginary authors, usually some person mentioned in the hymn and even to the deity praised in it. A conspicuous example of this is the Purusha-sūkta (X 90) which is attributed to Nārāyaṇa or Purusha. The hymn X 103 is attributed to Vena who is mentioned in it but who can hardly be its author. The hymns attributed to Manu Vaivasvata (VIII 27–31) are again attributed to him, because the name Manu occurs in some verses; but we cannot believe that their author was the mythical Manu, son of Vivasvat, a name occurring in the Zend Avesta also. The verses attributed to Urvaśī and Purūravas can hardly be theirs, though, being in the form of a dialogue, they come under the rule "The Ṛishi is he whose speech it is." Lastly, sometimes the Ṛishi is mentioned in the hymn itself with great respect and hence the hymn must be taken as that of a descendant of the Ṛishi, though it is attributed to the Ṛishi himself. The heavenly birth of Vasishṭha is itself referred to in one of his hymns and we may believe the revered ancestor Vasishṭha of the singer had already attained sanctity and the hymn belongs plainly to a descendant of his. We have already quoted a verse from the Mahābhārata wherein it is said that originally there were four gotras only, viz., Bhṛigu, Angiras, Vasishṭha, and Kāśyapa. These were probably the four great Aryan family stocks which came to India first and settled in the Panjab.

The commentator quotes various passages from the Purāṇas as also from Bṛihad-Devatā and other ancient works giving interesting stories about several Ṛishis. These apparently had their origin even in Ṛigvedic days; for the birth of Vasishṭha and Agastya from the twin-gods Mitra and Varuṇa (like the birth of Achilles from Apollo) is mentioned even in a Ṛig-vedic hymn. There are certain indications in the hymns themselves from which such stories might have been formulated. The story how Śyāvāśva, son of Archanānas, son of Atri, became a Ṛishi or composer of hymns is interesting, being a love story. He was enamoured of a princess, but was refused as he was not a Ṛishi (Macd. Sarv. p. 118). The story of Śunahśepa purchased by Hariśchandra's son for sacrifice to Varuṇa and his release by Varuṇa on praying to him and his adoption by Viśvāmitra as Devarāta is well-known and is, we think, as explained at length later on, hinted at in his sūkta in the first Maṇḍala. The stories of Gritsamada son of Śunaka, of Viśvāmitra son of Gādhi, son of Kushika, son of Ishīratha, of Vāmadeva's conversation with Indra from the womb of his mother, of the birth of Angiras, Bhṛigu and Atri from Prajāpati, of Dīrghatamas son of Uchathya, son of Angiras and brother of Brihaspati, of Śakti son of Vaśishṭha burnt by the servants of Viśvāmitra, of Pragāthi son of Ghora who became the adopted son of Kaṇva his elder uncle, of Apālā daughter of Atri having skin disease and propitiating Soma by her sūkta and of Urvaśi and Purūravas, as detailed by Shadguruśishya, may have been current in Ṛigvedic days or may have been conceived in the days of the Brāhmaṇas and fitted on to the various sūktas or individual verses.

R. IX 67 is a unique hymn. It consists of 32 verses. The first three are ascribed to Bhāradvāja, the next three to Kāśyapa and so on to Gautama, Atri, Viśvāmitra, Jamadagni and Vasishṭha who form the well known Sapta-Ṛishis identified later with the seven stars of the Great Bear. The last eleven verses are ascribed to Pavitra Vasishtha. And the most remarkable thing is that the last two verses declare that he who recites or learns these Pāvamānī hymns of the Ṛishis will obtain all the blessings on this earth. These two verses are apparently modern in language and are in the nature of Phalaśruti at the end of the Bhagavadgītā. It seems clear that the Saptarshis were already revered before the end of the Ṛigvedic age and that, therefore, this collection of verses by them into one sūkta was made by a descendant of Vasishṭha named Pavitra, probably an assumed name.

V RIGVEDIC METRES

The whole of the Rigveda is, as we have seen, in verse; but like Homer's Iliad or Milton's Paradise Lost it is not in one metre. With multiplicity of authors, there is naturally a multiplicity of metres. These metres are detailed in the work of Pingala which is considered to be a Vedānga. But it is of a very modern date, for it describes metres of both Vedic and classical Sanskrit. The subject is, however, succinctly yet fully dealt with in Kātyāyana's Sarvānukramaṇī and we give below the details therein given with a few explanations and observations of our own.

The Vedic metre depends solely on the number of syllables in it; there is no restriction as to the shortness or length of the several syllables, a restriction which arose in classical Sanskrit. Macdonell thinks that the foot usually ends in an iambic; but this is not the case. Certain restrictions seem to be observed in many Anushṭup verses, and these were subsequently followed invariably in classical Sanskrit, as we shall show later on. The short definition of metre given by Kātyāyana viz. "The measure of the number of syllables is metre" (यदक्षरपरिमाणं तच्छन्दः Macd. Sarvānukramanī p. 1.) is, therefore, the most proper one. There are fourteen metres in all, the first Gāyatri having twenty-four syllables, the second four more and so on in each of the following metres as under :—

1.	Gāyatrī	24	Syllables,	8.	Atijagatī	52	Syllables.
2.	Ushṇik	28	„	9.	Śakvarī	56	„
3.	Anushṭup	32	„	10.	Atiśakvarī	60	„
4.	Bṛihatī	36	„	11.	Ashti	64	„
5.	Pankti	40	„	12.	Atyashti	68	„
6.	Trishṭup	44	„	13.	Dhṛiti	72	„
7.	Jagatī	48	„	14.	Atidhṛiti	76	„

Gāyatrī has three feet of 8 syllables each, while the rest have four feet of 7 or 8 &c. syllables. But Pankti has apparently five feet with 8 syllables and the last Atidhṛiti with 76 syllables has apparently no feet at all. There is one verse only of this metre. The first seven are the important metres, Gāyatrī, Trishṭup and Jagatī being more important and Trishṭup with four feet of 11 syllables each being the most important, nearly two-fifths of the Ṛigvedic verses being in this metre. Like other Vedic matters the Ṛigvedic metre was also scrupulously examined by the ancient Āchāryas and verses in each metre counted. The numbers, given in Chhandonukramaṇī of Śaunaka, of verses in each metre are, as follows, "in the Śākala recension of the Ṛigveda."

1.	Gāyatrī	2467	8.	Atijagatī	17
2.	Ushṇik	341	9.	Śakvarī	19
3.	Anushṭup	855	10.	Atiśakvarī	9
4.	Brihatī	181	11.	Ashti	6
5.	Pankti	312	12.	Atyashti	84
6.	Trishṭup	4253	13.	Dhṛiti	2
7.	Jagatī	1348	14.	Atidhitiṛ	1
		0747			138

Verses with one foot only	6
„ two feet only	17
Prāgātha Bārhata metre	194
Kākubha metre	55
Mahābārhata metrè	257
Grand Total	10414

These totals are given according to the figures given in the Chhandassankhyā; but there are some discrepancies on actual calculation and scrutiny, as noticed by Macdonell. Perhaps this enumeration simply follows what Kātyāyana and others had stated in their detailed Anukramaṇīs as the words used at the end are "as stated by Ṛishis" The total number of verses or Ṛiks in the Rigveda is, as stated in a previous chapter, 10580¼ and the difference in this and the above total is very small and is probably due to the omission of some verses which are of doubtful metre.

The Vedic poets like all other poets were not, however, hide-bound in the matter of metre and they sometimes used one or two syllables less or more. Such cases have been noted and have been given different names. The sūtras of Kātyāyana on this matter are "ऊनाधिकेनैकेन निचृद्भूरिजौ । द्वाभ्यां विराट्स्वराजौ ।" "With one syllable less and more the kinds of metres would be Nichṛit and Bhūrij; with two they would be Virāṭ and Svarāṭ". Thus Gāyatri with 23 letters would be Nichrid-Gāyatrī and with 25 it would be Bhūrij Gāyatrī. Pankti again with 38 letters (40–2) would be Virāt-Pankti and with 42 (40+2) it would be Svarāt-Paṇkti. It would also be in this case (44–2) Nichṛit-

Trishṭup. We have already referred to the rules by which conjunct consonants ending in र and य and some others have to be split into two syllables and in such cases the apparent shortness of a foot by one syllable can be removed.

There are other varieties with different numbers of feet and with different numbers of syllables such as Kakup, Pada-Pankti, Vardhamāna, Pratishthā, etc. Three feet with eight syllables and a fourth with six is an example of this kind and perhaps it is the origin of the simple Ovī metre in Marathi. There are again Prāgāthas such as Bārhata, Kākubha, and Mahabārhata. The word Prāgātha is interpreted by the commentator as meaning 'mixed'; but perhaps the Ṛishi Pragātha gave his name to this mixed metre. These different varieties show that the Vedic poets delighted in varying the metre in the fourth foot or in adding a fourth foot with less number of syllables or in using mixed-metred feet in their versification, thus destroying the monotony of the song. The last verse in a sūkta is usually of a different metre, an artifice adopted to destroy monotony and also to indicate the end —a practice followed by classical Sanskrit epics.

As stated above, the Trisṭup is the most favourite metre with the Vedic Ṛishis, there being 4253 verses in this metre out of the 10500 and odd in the whole Ṛigveda. The Zend Avesta also contains many verses in this metre of four feet with 11 syllables in each. Classical Sanskrit poets also took up this metre with the additional restriction of fixed short and long in the 11 syllables, borrowed from the most musical of the Vedic verses. Thus यज्ञेन यज्ञमयजन्त देवाः of the Purusha-sūkta would be यज्ञेन यज्ञं अयजन्त देवाः of classical epics. Trishṭup, therefore, is the Indravajrā and Upendravajrā metres of classical Sanskrit. The Jagatī metre with 12 syllables in each foot became the Vaṁśastha and the Śakvari, very favourite with Sāma singers, became probably the Vasanta-tilakā of modern Sanskrit.

The Anushṭup, however, became popular with writers of long poems, indeed of extensive works on any subject in later Sanskrit, because the restriction therein on long and short of syllables is very limited. The seventh syllables of the second and the fourth feet are to be short; so also the fifth of the first and the third. Valmīki is said to be the first poet (आद्यकवि) not of Vedic times but of classical times, because he was the first to utter the first verse in classical Anushṭup with these two restrictions viz. 'मा निषाद् प्रतिष्ठां त्वमगमः शाश्वतीः समाः । यत्क्रौंचमिथुनादेकमवधीः काममोहितम् ॥' The Anushṭup metre has no other restrictions no doubt; but for musicalness certain other musical combinations of three syllables, called Vipulā etc., by Pingala are always to be seen in the best verses of Vyāsa and other writers. Vyāsa, however, in the Mahābhārata, often follows the license of Vedic poets in his Trishṭup verses e. g. आपूर्यमाणमचलप्रतिष्ठम् ॥ (भगवद्गीता)

The names of the Vedic metres are, as may naturally be expected, very ancient. The seven most common are mentioned in R. X, 130; (also in X 14–16) and their invention is attributed to gods. Gāyatrī is said to be born from Agni and Ushṇik from the sun; Anushṭup from Soma, Brihatī from Brihaspati, and Virāt from Maitrāvaruṇa. Indra invented Trishṭup, which is consonant with the fact that Indra is most praised in the Ṛigveda and Trishṭup is the metre most used. Finally, the Viśvedevas created Jagatī. Śakvarī is also referred to in another place as popular with singers. "The Vasishthas gave strength to Indra by their loud chants in Śakvarī" (यच्छक्वरीषु बृहता रवेणेन्द्रे शुष्ममादधता वो वसिष्ठाः ।). Sapta Chhandānsi or seven metres are mentioned often in all the four Sanhitās, as also their names. Indeed Chhandas is a word which goes back to the Indo-Iranian period, appearing as Zend among the Iranians.

VI RIGVEDIC GODS

The hymns of the Ṛigveda are mostly in praise of deities which were probably originally conceived as the presiding deities of natural phenomena. These deities are, properly enough, fire, wind, water, rain and lightning, sun, moon and so on. Many of these deities with the addition of Yama, the Lord of death, are common to the Iranian and the Indian Aryans. Yama is thus Yima with the Iranians and Mitra is Mithra the sun, while Agni (Ātash) is zealously worshipped by both. Indra, however, is the peculiar god of the Indo-Aryan people. The Iranian and Indian Aryans, forming originally one family, subsequently became deadly enemies. Probably they quarrelled over some philosophical tenets and separated. Indra hence is a demon with the Iranians ; Āhura (Asura), on the other hand, is the highest god with the Iranians, but Asura is a demon with the Indian Aryans. The word Deva, in Vedic Sanskrit again, means a god but it means a demon in Persian. The word Asura, however, appears in the Ṛigveda in a good sense also namely "the giver of life or adorable." This sense is, no doubt, a survival from those times when the Iranian and Indian Aryans were one people or lived together amicably.

The Ṛigvedic Aryans were thus originally polytheistic ; but their polytheism like that of the Iranians soon changed into monotheism and they soon came to entertain the notion that there is only one God, of whom the many gods are mere different names or descriptions (R. I, 167 and X, 114). Who this one God is, is sometimes differently conceived. He is conceived sometimes as the Sun, sometimes as Indra and sometimes as Varuṇa who is looked upon as the upholder of Ṛita or order and truth; sometimes as Prajāpati the creator of all living beings. He is also called Purusha. The highest God, in later literature, became, however, Vishṇu, and sometimes Śiva, both being Ṛigvedic deities but not much praised in the Ṛigveda. This monotheism of the Ṛigveda subsequently took the form of pantheism, several sūktas identifying the highest God with the whole universe (see X 121). Dr. Macdonell thinks that the tenth or the last verse in this Hirrṇyagarbha sūkta is a later addition. But it cannot be later than the compilation of the Ṛigveda. For the idea contained in this sūkta is the same as that contained in the Purusha sūkta (X 90)* The later philosophy of the Upanishads which identified the highest deity now called Brahman with both man and the universe had thus its foundation in the speculations of the Ṛigvedic Ṛishis.

The attributes of the Ṛigvedic gods are both Indian and Arctic, except Ushas who is solely Arctic. The goddess Ushas or the Dawn can only be properly conceived, if we believe that her attributes are Arctic in their origin. The short-lived dawn of the Panjab cannot have given rise to these attributes.

* स भूमिं विश्वतो वृत्वात्यतिष्ठद्दशाङ्गुलम् ॥ पुरुष एवेदं सर्वम्

These fitly appertain to the dawn as it is seen in Arctic regions as shown by B. G. Tilak*, circling the horizon for days together. The highly poetical hymns in praise of Ushas with their concepts had their origin undoubtedly when the Indo-Aryans were beyond the Himalayās. The twin-gods Aśvins, however, in our view are not well explained either by European or Indian scholars. Pūshan and a few other gods also defy convincing explanation. The Ṛigvedic gods had become an enigma even in the days of the Brāhmaṇas naturally enough, as hundreds of years had elapsed by their time. The mythological stories alluded to in the Ṛigvedic hymns about the several gods also became unintelligible. Even in the days of Yāska there were two schools of explanation viz. the historical and the natural. With the former school thus, Indra was the slayer of Vṛitṛa; and the releaser of cows, a real Aryan hero who conquered Indian Dasyus; with the latter he was nothing more than the deity of clouds, with their thunder and lightning and down-pour of rain. Modern researchers again see the origin of Vedic mythology in the striking aspects of the starry heavens and of the sun and the moon. In our view all these three schools are together correct. The mythology of the Ṛigvedic

* Tilak has in Orion detailed four peculiarities of the goddess Dawn as depicted in Ṛigvedic hymns. 1 Before the sun comes above the horizon, the dawn lasts several days. 2 Ushas is always spoken of in the plural, their number being thirty. 3 These thirty parts are not distinct but continuous. 4 These revolve round the horizon and come to the same point in twenty-four hours.

gods had its origin in all the three viz., history, personification of nature and poetical allegories based on the position of groups of stars and the appearances of the sun and the moon as they move among them. The Vrishākapi sūkta thus can well be understood on the astronomical basis as explained at length by B. G. Tilak and supported by Greek mythology. But after all, these theories must be treated as probable explanations only and not final truths. Indeed we have to realise that finally true explanations are now not possible, as urged even by the ancient sage Kautsa, a predecessor of Yāska, some thousands of years ago (Macd. p. 61). It is indeed difficult to see how correct explanations of mythological stories or of difficult words* uttered about 4500 to 3000 B. C. could be given by thinkers of 2000 B. C. or of 200 B. C., much more by Sāyana or by Roth the modern German Pandit with his historical sense or the knowledge of the Avesta which itself has become difficult to understand even for Parsi scholars. These observations are made only with reference to certain disputed questions such as whether Nāsatya means "not untrue" or "born of the nose" and so

* We may note here that a very laudable effort was being made at Indore under the patronage of His Highness Tukojirao Holker, the retired Maharaja of Indore, to prepare a directory of Vedic words with their different interpretations given by 1 the Brāhmaṇas, 2 Yāska, 3 later writers, 4 Sāyana, 5. Swaami Dayanand and 6 modern scholars so that Vedic students may see at a glance the different meanings assigned in their historical order. This work, however, remains unfinished.

on. On simple and general matters, the Rigveda is not a sealed book and many unquestioned or indisputable facts may be gleaned from it, as we shall presently show.

We will close this chapter with quoting the conceptions of Āśvalāyana, Kātyāyana and Yājnavalkya, successively ancient Indian thinkers and sages on the subject of the Ṛigvedic gods. In his Grihyasūtra, in the chapter on Tarpaṇa or libations of water (III. 4) Āśvalāyana gives the Ṛigvedic gods as follows:—

देवतास्तर्पयति । प्रजापति र्ब्रह्मा वेदा देवा सर्वाणि च्छन्दांसि ओंकारो वषट्कारो व्याहृतयः सावित्री यज्ञा द्यावापृथिवी अन्तरिक्षं अहोरात्राणि सांख्याः सिद्धाः समुद्रा नद्यो गिरयः क्षेत्रौषधिवनस्पतयः गन्धर्वाप्सरसः नागा वयांसि गावः साध्या यक्षा रक्षांसि भूतान्येवमन्तानि ॥

To all these* may be found hymns or verses addressed in the Ṛigveda. Kātyāyana who precedes Āśvalāyana giving a short synopsis on the subject says, "The gods are of three orders from their place, the earth, the sky and the heavens" (पृथ्वी अन्तरिक्षं द्यौः), respectively represented by Agni (fire), Vāyu (wind) and Sūrya (sun). The Vyāhṛitis (Bhūh, Bhuvah, Svah) are also three. Prajāpati is the god of the three (Vyāhṛitis) combined. Omkāra represents all the gods together or the highest God or Brahman or any one god or the divine soul in man. Other gods residing in the three places are different forms of the three Agni, Vāyu and Sūrya. The different praises (hymns) mention different names for different ritu-

* There is however, so far as we have seen, no hymn addressed to Sāṅkhyas. This word and idea is post-Vedic.

als. Or there is only one Deity, viz., the Great Soul. He is called Sūrya as he is the soul of all beings; says a Ṛishi 'He is the soul of the moving and the stationary (सूर्यो आत्मा जगतः तस्थुषश्च). All other deities are his manifestations as stated in the verse "He is called Indra, Mitra, Varuṇa, Agṇi." Lastly, in a very eloquent passage in the Bṛihadāraṇya Upanishad where Yājñavalkya, while finally saying that there is only one God pervading and upholding the whole universe, first enumerates the gods as thirty three viz. 8 Vasus (earthly deities), 11 Rudras (deities of the sky) and 12 Ādityas (deities of heaven) with two more Indra and Prajāpati. In this classification Indra and Prajāpati have a separate position. (Vishṇu is most probably included in the Ādityas and Śiva in the Rudras).

The Ṛishis sometimes invoke these gods in pairs as Indrāgnī, Agnī–shomau, Mitrā–Varuṇau. Soma is both moon and the herb which gave the oft–praised exhilarating drink to the ancient Indian and Iranian Aryans in their common abode beyond the Himalayas. What this herb was, post–Vedic Indians did not know; nor can it be stated now with any certainty. The Soma plant must remain like many other Ṛigvedic things a mystery. The Soma juice so much loved by Indra or more properly by the Indian Aryans flowed from the herb when pounded with a stone and this flowing juice is deified as Pavamāna Soma and praised in several hymns put together in a special Maṇḍala of the Ṛigveda, the ninth, as stated before.

" Indra is the favourite and national god of the

Vedic Indian (Mac. p 84) and more than one-fourth of the Rigveda is devoted to his praise." He is god of thunder and clouds as also of battles; and drinking Soma he delivers attacks on the enemies of the invading Aryans. He is thus pre-eminently the god of the conquering Indo-Aryans. Agni is the next important god who is praised most. He probably came from beyond the Himalayas where extreme cold emphasised the importance of fire. He is a god both of the Iranian and Indian Aryans; so is naturally Sūrya the sun whose other names in the Ṛigveda are Mitra, Savitṛi and Pūshan. Varuṇa comes next in importance, the deity presiding over Ṛita or order and truth, an ancient Aryan god. How he became in Puranic times the god of water and ocean remains to be explained. He is, therefore, the presiding deity of the west. Ushas is an Arctic deity as stated before typifying early dawn; but strangely enough she has no counterpart among the Iranians nor apparently among the Greeks. So also the Aśvins or twin morning deities. They cannot be the evening and morning Venus or Mercury as is sometimes supposed; for they are always spoken of as morning-deities ushering in the Ushas. They must be Arctic in origin though they defy explanation. Possibly they may be Venus and Mercury when both are seen in the morning before the sun comes above the horizon or before even the dawn of the temperate zone. They are looked upon as physicians. They also succour a person in distress. Bhujyu, foundered in the ocean, was rescued by them by sending their own golden boat. X 65 mentions most gods together viz. Agni, Indra, Varuṇa, Mitra, Aryaman, Vāyu, Pūshan, Sarasvatī, Ādityas, Vishṇu, Maruts, Svar, Brihat, Soma, Rudra, Aditi and Brahmaṇaspati. There are some minor gods also such as Bhaga, Brihaspati, Tvashtṛi, Trita Āptya &c. which are not all explainable. So also are Ṛibhus. All the gods are often invoked together as Viśvedevah.

VII VINIYOGA OR APPLICATION OF HYMNS

Allied with the three preceding subjects viz., Ṛishi (author), Chhandas (metre) and Devatā (deity) of a sūkta or ṛik (which it is considered obligatory to recite first when reciting any ṛik or sūkta) is the subject of Viniyoga or use of the particular sūkta or ṛik. The various Anukramaṇīs give the Ṛishis, Metres and Deities of the hymns, but do not give their Viniyōga. But the reciter of a sūkta or ṛik has to pronounce its Viniyoga or use also. This information is given in Śaunaka's Ṛigvidhāna as also in Bṛihad-Devatā. The sūktas are to be recited in particular sacrifices and at particular rituals or ceremonies and every sūkta, nay ṛik, has its Viniyoga so fixed. The god praised or the nature of the praise usually determines the Viniyoga. But this is not always the case. For the sùktas and the ṛiks acquired the status of Mantras in course of time. Mantras, according to Mantra Śāstra, are efficacious by their sounds and not by their meanings. Hence very often, the Viniyoga has no connection with the meaning of the verse or hymn. There are certain indications or signs called Lingas which determine such Viniyoga. The Brāhmaṇas as well as the Śrauta and Grihya Sūtras declare what Mantra is to be recited at any particular sacrifice or ritual in it or any ceremony and these were the first Viniyogas or assignments which thus go back to the period of the Brāhmaṇas. Besides these, there are other uses assigned in the Ṛigvidhāna such as for medical purposes or for incantations or for atonements (prāyaschittas) or for japa or repeating. This will sufficiently indicate what Viniyoga means without our entering into further detail.

NOTE—PURUSHA-SŪKTA

The Purusha Sūkta (x 90) has, it seems to us, been wrongly understood by European scholars. The title is translated by Macdonell as 'the hymn of Man,' ; but it is more properly the hymn of the all-pervading God. Purusha in this hymn is God as stated by Sāyana. When in the first verse he is described as of thousands (not thousand) of heads, thousands of eyes and thousands of feet, the all-pervading nature of God is hinted at, the heads, eyes and feet of all creatures being His, as is clear from the very next verse which says "all this (present) is Purusha and whatever existed before and will exist hereafter (पुरुष एवेदं सर्वम् यद्भूतं यच्च भव्यम् ।). Again in the next verse it is said, "This is His greatness, nay it is greater than this (world). For all created things are only a quarter part of Him ; the remaining three-fourths are immortal and in the heavens". There can be no doubt, therefore, that this hymn is in praise of the all-pervading God. The idea that this being is sacrificed is indeed novel, but it does not show that this being is a giant (Macd. p. 132) and creation is sacrificing by gods of this giant. The thousands of heads, eyes and feet do not constitute Him a giant. For it is further said that from him was born Virāt and from the latter Adhi-Purusha. (who is spoken of as sacrificed). This is the forerunner of the Sānkhya and even Vedānta doctrines which place two stages between the Unmanifest and the Manifest. With the Indo-Aryans every thing was a sacrifice and creation appeared to them as a metaphorical sacrifice. The metaphor's looking upon the Purusha or rather Virāt or Adhi-Purusha as the animal sacrificed indicates that the Manifest is made of the Unmanifest, that God or Brahman is the Upādāna-Kāraṇa of this created world as the Vedāntins maintain. It is not out of a void or Śūnya, as some believe, but as the Upanishads explain, out of Himself that God has created this world as a spider weaves a web out of himself (यथोर्णनाभि: etc.). The spring is the ghee of the sacrifice and the summer is its fuel and the Śarad (autumn) the oblation. The first thing born out of this sacrifice was Rik, Sāman and Yajuh* This verse is wrongly understood as indicating that the three Vedic compilations were already in existence when this hymn was composed. But this verse does not speak of the Vedic collections made subsequently. It refers in our view to the Riks called Sāman or good verses because they were sung, then to Chhandānsi, not metres but metrical utterances generally, and Yajus or the sacrificial formula. It indicates no doubt that the distinction had arisen between verses sung, verses ordinary and the sacrificial formulae. Then were born horses and cows, sheep and goats &c. The Brahmin was (born from) his head and the Kshatriya from his arms ; the Vaiśya from his thighs and the Śūdra from his legs—typifying the respective occupations of the four primeval castes. The words Mukha and Pāda appear twice and hence they must be differently intrepreted, Mukha as head and mouth and Pāda as legs and feet. Strangely enough Sāyaṇa does not see this twofold meaning. Indra and Agni were born from His mouth, the Sun from His eyes, wind from His breath

* ऋचः सामानि जज्ञिरे । छंदांसि जज्ञिरे तस्माद्यजुस्तस्मादजायत ।

(nose) and the four quarters from His ears. The earth was born from His feet and the heavens from the top of His head. All this description clearly shows that this hymn speaks of the universally pervading Purusha or God and not a giant sacrificed by gods. Indeed the gods are spoken as sprung from Him, Indra, Agni, Sūrya and Vāyu. Sādhyas are distinct from gods and the word pūrva refers to the ancestors in the last verse of well-known Devas.

Prof. V. K. Rājawade, a great Indian Vedic scholar, strangely enough interprets this verse as referring in reality to human sacrifice which was practised by the Rigvedic Aryans (Vividha-Dnyāna Vistāra 1927 April). The sacrifice of creation is not real but only metaphorical and there is no allusion to any actual human sacrifice (see further under White Yajurveda). There are other strange statements in this article of Prof. Rājavade such as the idea that Brahmin, Kshatriya and Vaiśya are words which first appear in this sūkta. These words often appear elsewhere also, though one may concede that this sūkta belongs to the later portion of the Rigvedic period.

VIII ṚIGVEDA AS HISTORY.

Although not directly connected with the history of Sanskrit literature, the subject of the history of the settlement of the Indo-Aryans in India and the state of their civilization as disclosed in the Ṛigveda is interesting and it is usual to insert a chapter on this subject in a book of this kind. The Ṛigveda contains many statements of an unambiguous character which can be made to yield such history. And there are some facts which appear to us to have been wrongly or imperfectly understood by European Vedic scholars. We shall, therefore, try in this chapter to place in short our views on this subject before the curious reader.

The Indian Aryans came to India as a conquering people. All the attributes of their favourite god Indra show this. They conquered the aborigines who are called Dasyus or Dāsas. Their leader was named Vṛitra and Indra, the Aryan leader, exhilarated by the Soma drink, attacked the strongholds or rather fortified villages of the aborigines led by their chiefs having different names such as Bala, Śambara &c. Vritra may be taken to typify an aboriginal chief, historically considered. Indeed a fight with the aboriginal enemy is usually styled Vritrahatyā (e. g. VII 19-10) in the Ṛigvedic hymns. VII, 19 alone mentions Śuśnu, Kuyava, Chumuri, Dhuni and Namuchi. The conquerors were of the Aryan race, of white complexion and with prominent noses. The conquered were without noses and black. They were probably of the Dravidian race though the word Dravida does not occur in the Ṛigveda. (The Dravidian people seem from other sources to have spread from the south which was their stronghold to the north-west corner of India. Dravidian words are still found in the language of the Brahuis of Baluchistan.) The word Arya is, on the other hand, distinctly and often mentioned in the Ṛigveda. The following Ṛik (X 38, 3) is important and interesting. "Whoever wishes to fight with us, Oh Indra, whether he be Ārya (of our own race), Dāsa (aborigine), or A-deva (not Rākshasa, but in our view an Iranian Aryan, one who does not believe in Deva)" shows clearly that the Āryans often fought amongst themselves, usually with the Dāsas and sometimes with the Iranians. The Adevas were worshippers of fire but not of Devas or Indra while the Dāsas worshipped neither fire nor devas. The Dāsas most probably worshipped the *phallus* as they are styled 'Śiśnadevah' in the Ṛigveda. This worship gradually became hereafter the most popular worship of the Hindus who may be looked upon as the descendants of Indo-Aryans and Dāsas coalesced into one people. The phallus, however, was later identified with Rudra of the Ṛigveda who also became the ruler of demons and fiends whom the non-Aryans worshipped.

The Nāgas or Sarpas appear to be a warlike leading people among the Dāsas. They were called so, probably because the serpent was their emblem or because they acted like serpents, attacking stealthily with great impetuosity. We know from the Zend-Avesta that the Septa-Sindhu or the abode of the Indo-Aryans was smitten by Aingra Mainyu with heat and serpents, a correct description of the land occupied by the Indo-Aryans compared with the land of Iran finally occupied by the Iranians. But serpents must have troubled the Aryans even when these two sections were together, because serpents are abhorred even by the Zends. Johak, an Iranian king, had two serpents issuing from his shoulders which always gnawed at his brain. Even among the Jews, the Devil appears in the form of a serpent. We may believe that some war-like aborigines, like serpents, often attacked the Aryans surreptitiously yet vigorously and hence they waged a merciless war with them, from Indra who killed Vṛitra in the form of Ahi, down to Janamejaya who went so far as to carry on a war of extermination against them. The Nagas, however, became less hostile and Aryans often married Nāga wives. We thus find that the Nāgas were admitted to the Vedic pantheon. Who the Gandharvas and Apsarasas were, historically speaking, cannot be well conceived. They too became semi-divine even in the days of the Ṛigveda. They are described as fair and hence were probably Himalayan people and not of the plains. They too seem to have coalesced with the invading Aryans to some extent (as Ūrvaśī married Purūravas). They are among the lesser Devatās of the Ṛigveda and have some hymns in their praise.

The Indo-Aryans, as stated before, rose from polytheism to monotheism and from monotheism to pantheism. They early deified mountains and rivers in their polytheism of nature worship. In the hymn (X 75) to the rivers of their land, the poet mentions almost all its rivers. He, of course, begins with the Indus which was the most impressive of them all, the widest and the longest, the Amazon, so to speak, of India. India is the Greek name for the country derived from this very river and Hapta Hindu the seven-river-land is the name given by the Iranians from which Hindustan, the modern name of the country and Hindus, the modern name of the people, are derived. But it is remarkable that the Indo-Aryans never gave this name to their country or to themselves based on this river name, as we shall show further on. These seven rivers may be taken to be the Indus on the west with the five rivers of the Panjab and with Saraswatī in the east in addition and Kubhā on the west. The name Sapta-Sindhu no doubt occurs in the Ṛigveda but the seven rivers are not there specified. Different scholars enumerate these seven rivers differently, some going to the whole of Asia for them. Having praised the Sindhu in the first four verses of the above noted hymn, the poet next mentions the important rivers to the east of the Indus known to the Indo-Aryans till then. It is curious to find in the fifth verse the several rivers to the east mentioned in order from east to west. Thus we have first the Ganges, next the Yamunā, the Sarasvatī, the Śitudri [Sutlej], the Parushnī [Iravati], the Asikni [Chinab], the Marudvṛidhā, the Vitastā [Jhelum] and Ārjīkiyā with Sushomā etc. (names not identifiable).* It may be noted that Marudvridhā should be taken to be Vipāśā a name also mentioned in sūkta 33 of the third Mandala and in other hymns. In the next verse 6 the western rivers are mentioned as tributaries of the Indus viz., Rasā, Śvētyā [Swat], Kubhā, Gomatī and Kramu [now Kabul, Gomaty, and Kurrum] in order from the north to the south.† It may, thus, be rightly supposed that the land of the Ṛigvedic Aryans extended from the Hindukush on the north-west along the Himalayas south-eastwards as far as the Gangetic valley. The most sacred part of it was the Sarasvatī basin, the river Sarasvatī being praised in several Ṛigvedic hymns. It may be noted that this name may be found among the Persians also as Haraivaiti, another river, however, in the western part of modern Afghanistan and thus was popular among the combined Aryans when they were north of the Himalayas. The Indo-Aryans settled in this plain region and even progressed eastward along the Himalayas as far as the Śarayu in Oudh in Ṛigvedic days, as that river is mentioned in one of its hymns, a name also found among the

*It is remarkable that Panjab has forgotton the Vedic names of their rivers while the less advanced people beyond the Indus have still preserved the Vedic names of their rivers.

† Sāyana looks upon these as the seven rivers viz., 1. Ganges, 2. Jumna, 3. Saraswatī, 4. Sutlej, 5. Parushni (Ravi). 6. Marudvṛidhā (Bias) with Asikni and 7. Arjikīyā.

Iranians as Harayu.

In this land, the Indo-Aryans appear to have come in two stocks and by two routes*. The mythology of the Purāṇas has, it is well-known, its roots in the Ṛigveda. The Purāṇas divide the Aryans into two stocks, the Sūryavanśis and the Chandravanśis. Now though these two names are Purānic and find no mention in the Ṛigveda, there are certain indications in the Ṛigveda itself that the Indo-Aryans came into India in two hordes by different routes and at different times. This theory was first propounded by Dr. Hoernle and was accepted by Sir R. Grierson who has carefully studied the languages of India (Imp. Gazetteer. IV p. 358). He divides Hindi into Western Hindi and Eastern Hindi and the speakers also into two distinct peoples (Census report 1911). Sir H. Risley again took the head-measurements of the people of India at the time of the Census of 1901 and these measurements go to show that there are two Aryan races in India, one long-headed and the other broad-headed. This, in our view, corresponds to the two-fold division of the European Aryans namely, the long-headed Teutons and the broad-headed Celts. The people of the Panjab are long-headed Aryans as also of Rajputana while those of U.P. and Gujarat and the Deccan are broad-headed ones. Now the conclusion arrived at from a consideration cf language agrees completely with that from

* We have treated this subject at length in our paper read before B. B. R. A. S. (Vol. XXIV). We give here its purport.

head-measurements ; and Sir H. Risley's and Sir R. Grierson's views put together lead to the theory that while the long-headed or Solar Race Aryans came into the Panjab through the passes of the Hindukush and spread south-eastwards as far as Oudh and the Śarayu, the broad-headed Chandravanśi Aryans came later like a wedge, in this settled Aryan population, by way of Gilgit and the Gangetic Himalayan valley and coming into the plains spread southwards from Ambala along the Yamunā into U. P., Gujarat and Deccan. Western Hindi is thus found spoken in a triangle with its apex at Ambala and base extending from Gujarat to Jubbulpore (Gujarati being allied to it) and Eastern Hindi is spoken in Oudh, the Panjabi and Rajastani being allied to it (See Census R. 1911). This history of the progress of the two peoples as suggested by considerations of language and head-measurements is also borne out by the Purāṇic accounts regarding the Solar and Lunar dynasties called in the Mahābhārata Aikshvāka and Aila also. The Madra-Kekayas of the Panjab and the Raghukulas of Oudh are solar-race dynasties, while Prayāga was the centre of the Lunar dynasties extending from Magadha on the east through Chedi, Śauraseni, Matsya and Kuru-Pānchāla in the north-west.

This theory of two stocks of Aryans coming into India finds a great deal of support in the Ṛigvedic hymns. The lunar race geneology begins with Purūravas, Nahusha and Yayāti. These three are mentioned in Ṛigvedic hymns. It is still more remarkable that the five sons of Yayāti giving their names to five peoples are mentioned together in R. I. 108-8 (यदिंद्राग्नी यदुषु तुर्वशेषु यद्द्रुह्युष्वनुषु पूरुषु स्थः ॥). The clubbing together of Yadu and Turvaśa here and elsewhere and of Anu, Druhyu, and Pūru shows the truth of the Purāṇic legend that the former two were sons of Yayāti by Devayānī and the latter three his sons by Śarmishṭhā. The Yadu-Turvaśas had no kingdom while the Pūrus became prosperous and founded a kingdom in the Ambala region on the banks of the Sarasvatī to which territory their representatives the Kurus eventually gave their name. The Kurus are not mentioned in the Ṛigveda like the Pūrus; but they are mentioned very often in the Brāhmaṇas.

Having settled in this land and thrust a wedge, so to speak, in the centre of the previously settled Aryans (the Sūryavanśis), these second Aryan invaders tried to conquer the former in the west and in the east. The famous Dāśarājna fight in the Ṛigveda referred to in three important hymns of the seventh Maṇḍala (18,19,33), was fought between Sudāsa king of the first Aryans assisted by Tritsus, descendants of Vasishṭha and ten kings, five of the second Aryan peoples and five of their non-Aryan allies. It seems clear that European scholars are under a misconception as to who Bharatas were, who are referred to so frequently in the Ṛigveda here and elesewhere and are hence unable to rightly understand this Dāśarājna battle. The Ṛigvedic Bharatas are not the Bharatas of the Mahābhārata, the descendants of Bharata son of Dushyanta, who were lunar race Aryans. The Śatapatha Brāhmaṇa distinguishes this Bharata as Daushyanti Bharata. Bharata who gave his name to the Ṛigvedic Bharatas was a solar-race king, a grand-son of Manu, described as the king who gave his name to this land viz., Bhāratavarsha.* Another Purāṇa states that Manu himself was called Bharata† from his feeding the people and Yāska states that Bharata is the Sun himself.

The Bharatas led by Viśvāmitra over the Vipāśā and the Śatadru were thus the first Aryan invaders of solar race who first occupied the Panjab and spread further as far as the Śarayu. The people of this country were thus called in Ṛigvedic days Bharatas, as clearly shown by Viśvāmitra's verse (R. III 33–13) "This Vedic prayer by Viśvāmitra protects the Bharata people‡ Bharata became a synonym eventually of an ordinary Kshatriya and even a Brāhmin (Yāska). The priests of these solar race Aryans or Bharatas were Viśvāmitra, Vasishṭha, Bhāradvāja and Gautama, Ṛishis associated with the solar kings of Ayodhyā and Mithilā even in the Rāmāyaṇa. Sudāsa was a solar race king (this name appears even in the Purāṇic genealogy of the solar race), a king of the Bharatas and he with them was about to be defeated by the ten kings opposed to him, when Vasishtha by his prayer to Indra secured

*तेषां च भरतो ज्येष्ठो नारायणपरायणः। विख्यातं वर्ष-मेतत् तन्नाम्ना भारतमुत्तमम्।१७।
Bhāgavata XII

† वर्षोयं भारतो नाम यत्रेयं भारती प्रजा। भरणाच्च प्रजानां वै मनुर्भरत उच्यते॥

‡ विश्वामित्रस्य रक्षति ब्रह्मेदं भारतं जनम्।

victory to Sudāsa [III. 33] " The Bharatas were like cows without herdsmen but Vasishṭha went before them and led them to victory."* It seems Macdonell interprets this hymn wrongly when he says that the Bharatas were defeated by Sudāsa and Tritsus assisted by the invocations of Vasishtha [p. 155] or when he says that Bharatas were among the enemies of Sudāsa (p. 154). Viśvāmitra could not have in ṭhat case said that his prayer protects the Bharata people. The enemies of Sudāsa and his Bharatas in the Dāśarājna battle were the five Aryan lunar peoples Yadu-Turvaśas etc., and their five non-Aryan allies as detailed in VII 18, 7 viz., Pakhtas, Bhalānas, Alinas, Vishāṇinas and Śivas. Of the Aryans are mentioned Turvaśas, Matsyas, Druhyus, Anus and Pūrus (13 and 14). It is not easy to understand this hymn correctly and completely throughout its length; but it seems that Sudāsa safely crossed the Parushṇi, while when Turvaśas tried to follow him they were drowned. In the fight " 6000 Druhyus and 600 Anus lay dead on the battle-field." Indra and Tṛitsus helped Sudāsa Paijavana who made gifts for the victory which are lauded at the end of the hymn. It is this fight which is called Dāśarājna in R. VII 33, wherein Sudāsa with his Bharatas was victorious. In R. IX 61 it is said that "for Divodāsa Indra smote Yadu and Turvaśa." This was probably the first attempt of the Yadu-Turvaśas to conquer the Panjab. The attempt in the days of his

* दण्डा इवेद्गो अजनास आसन् परिच्छिन्ना भरता अर्भकासः
अभवच्च पुर एता वसिष्ठः आदित्त्रित्सूनां विशो अप्रथन्त ॥

son Sudāsa was the next and the greatest attempt by five lunar tribes with the aid of five aboriginal tribes. R. IV 30, 17–18 show that Turvaśa and Yadu combined also attempted to advance eastwards; but they were foiled beyond the Śarayu by Indra who smote Arṇa and Chitraratha. The Turvaśas eventually became extinct (Śatapatha) and Yādavas and Bhojas settled eventually in Śaurasena territory which according to the Rāmāyaṇa was also first under solar kings (being conquered by Śatrughna from Madhu Rākshasa). The Pūrus, however, hereafter settled firmly on both the banks of the Sarasvastī and prospered. They are located there in the hymn to the Sarasvatī (R. VII 96). They indeed so far prospered that the word "Pūru," like Bharata, later became synonymous with an Aryan soldier or priest. These Pauravas, in later time still, conquered the Panjab, probably before, but certainly in the days of, Janamejaya who is said in the Mahābhārata to have conquered Takshaśilā and hence it is that the Pūrus were found there in Alexander's time. These lunar Aryans, it may finally be stated, were of the same Aryan race though of a different stock, spoke the same language and worshipped the same deities. It is hence that the Vedic poet quoted in the beginning beseaches "Indra and Agni to come to him and drink his Soma potation, even though they might have been enjoying a feast among Yadus and Turvaśas, Druhyus, Anus and Pūrus."

Ṛigvedic hymns thus show that the first Aryans who entered the Panjab through the passes of the

Hindu-Kush were called Bharatas and settled there with their Ṛishis viz., Vasishṭha and Viśvāmitra, Bharadvāja and Gautama, the latter being Āngirasas. It is hence that the word Bharata frequently appears in the sūktas of their Maṇḍalas III, VII and VIII. In his Vedic Index, Macdonell properly observes that the Bharatas are spoken of chiefly in Maṇḍalas III and VII ; but he expresses a surprise that they are associated with Divodāsa and with Bharadvāja in R. VI. But Bharadvāja Āngirasa is also a solar race Ṛishi and he properly associates Bharatas with Divodāsa a solar race king. Even fire has got the name Bharata, being kindled by king Bharata (R. VII 8, 4.)* Agni is frequently given in the Ṛigveda the name of the king who first kindled him in India. In this verse the king Bharata must be taken to be the solar race Bharata. Śatapatha remarks on this verse that Pūru here is the name of a demon and not the lunar race king. Dr. Macdonell observes on this in his Vedic Index that in the days of Śatapatha Pūru, the Aryan king, had already been forgotten. But this is clearly a mistaken remark. It is impossible that the writer of the *Śatapatha* could have forgotten Pūru whom the later Purāṇa writers remembered as a son of Yayāti. The fact is that Pūru here cannot be Pūru the lunar race king. If Bharata is taken to be Dushyanta's son, he is a descendant of Pūru after some generations and cannot, therefore, be his contemporary; nor can he be

* प्रप्रायमग्निर्भरतस्य शृण्वे वियत्सूर्यो न रोचते बृहद्भाः ।
अभि यः पूरुं पृतनासु तस्थौ द्युतानो दैव्यो अतिथिः शुशोच ॥

suppposed to have fought with him. If Bharata is taken to be the solar race king, grand-son of Manu, he cannot even then be a contemporary of the lunar race king Pūru. The only alternative is that Bharata, a solar race king, defeated Pūru a demon, that is, an aboriginal chief, when he conquered the Panjab.

To resume, it is clear from several Ṛigvedic hymns that Bharata, a solar race king, first conquered the Panjab and gave his name to the land and the people. These Bharatas are frequently mentioned by Viśvāmitra and Vasishṭha, their Ṛishis, as also by Āngirasas, notably by Bharadvāja. These Bharatas gradually occupied the country as far as the Śarayu in Oudh. The lunar race Aryans came subsequently via Gilgit and the Gangetic valley into the region of the Sarasvatī where the Pūrus settled and prospered. The Yadu-Turvaśas and Anus and Druhyus, lunar race tribes, tried to conquer the Bharatas in the west and the east but failed, being signally defeated. They appear to have thereafter spread along the west coast of the Jumna southwards as the Chedis are also mentioned in the Ṛigveda. In the days of the Brāhmaṇas the Kuru-Pānchālas became famous. The Kaṇva family seems to be the family priests of the lunar race, a connection mentioned even in the Mahābhārata in the story of Dushyanta and Śakuntalā.

These are the few historical facts gleaned from a few stray statements in the Ṛigvedic hymns, chiefly religious as they are and sung in praise of Vedic gods. There is no reference to the Mahābhārata fight in the Ṛigveda nor to Śrikrishna naturally enough, as it was compiled in our view before both of them. There is, however, a hymn to rain in X which is attributed to Devāpi said to be an uncle of Bhīshma, a Mahābhārata hero. There is also a reference to Somaka, son of Sahadeva, who is presumably the Pānchāla king of the Brāhmaṇas. Finally, there is a reference in X (93, 14) to Rāma who is, according to our view, the hero of the Rāmāyaṇa though Macdonell thinks that the name is that of a Ṛishi. But its being mentioned along with the name of Vena makes it certain that it is the name of a king. The Ṛigveda has, it seems to us, still to be studied carefully for history. The significance of the Ṛishi and the thoughts he gives expression to, the legends and kings he mentions, even the words he uses, have importance in this connection. The word Asura, for example, has two senses in the Ṛigveda and it would be interesting to note which Ṛishi uses it in its higher sense. The Dānastutis have also an importance of their own and the kings mentioned must be traced out in Purāṇic stories. It is, however, to be admitted that not much is to be expected even from this study. Indeed the Āryasamājists hold that Ṛigvedic hymns contain no historical information, nay that they must be interpreted on the basic idea that no historical persons are mentioned therein. Bharata, Sudāsa, Divodāsa and Pijavana, Purukutsa and Trasadasyu are not names of historical persons but are words meaning something else. This view, however, goes too far and taking the natural view that even the Ṛishis could not help referring to historical facts and persons of their times, the history of the Aryan advent into India as sketched above is, we think, plainly indicated in the Ṛigvedic hymns.

Proceeding to sketch the social condition etc., of the Ṛigvedic Aryans, we may at once remark that they seem to have come into India with the incubus of caste upon them. Like the Vedas, however, the castes were three only in the beginning, the fourth Śudra caste being added later in the Panjab itself, and before the close of the Ṛigvedic period (the four castes being distinctly mentioned in the Purusha-sūkta). The three castes were, originally, occupational as with the Iranians and were not air-tight compartments. There was no restriction on marriage, the progeny belonging to the caste of the father. The kings fought, the Brahmanas served at sacrifices and the Vaiśyas cultivated the land. The word Viś meant the squatter or settler and he paid taxes to the king. The hymn to be recited at the coronation of kings (X 173,1) is interesting. The word for the nation was Rāshtra and the nation elected its king who it is prayed "may never be displaced from the Rāshtra, being liked by the people".* Of course the Aryan nations were many and small and often fought among themselves. The Aryan warriors fought from cars or Rathas like all ancient warlike people, Greeks and others. The Vedic Aryans seem to

* विशस्त्वा सर्वा वांछंतु मा त्वद्राष्ट्रमधिभ्रशत् ।

be well advanced in arts. They could fashion Rathas or cars which was an interesting process, carpenters felling trees and fashioning cars out of their wood, a process affording a favourite simile even for the creation of the world. One Rishi exclaims "Where is the carpenter of this creation and what trees did he cut". The simile is often taken for the composing of hymns. There must have been iron tools for this work, though Macdonell thinks that bronze ones were used. Ayas is mentioned in the Ṛigveda and the Panjab contained and contains still iron mines. It is inexplicable how Macdonell remarks that "these two metals (silver and iron) are not found in any quantity in the North-west of India" (p. 151). Gold was of course well known, being found in plenty in the Indus and other rivers and on the surface of the Tibetan Himalayan slopes. Gold was used for ornaments as also as medium of exchange. Brahmins got gold and cows and sheep and slaves as Dakshiṇā at sacrifices. There is no mention of coin, however, and when a poet sings that he who gives "a thousand" as Dakshinā goes to heaven, it is probably a thousand gold pieces of a fixed weight.

The Indo-Aryans unquestionably knew the sea viz., the Arabian sea and there are many references to it, such as in X 123-8, 125-7, 142-8, though Macdonell thinks that they did not. Sindhu is, no doubt, a word both for the sea and a river. But Macdonell thinks that the broad Indus was like the sea to the Indo-Aryans. The argument urged for supporting this view is the usual non-mention argument; "No mention is made of the numerous mouths of the Indus as also of fishing. The word which later is the regular name for sea, the Samudra (collection of waters) seems to mean, therefore, the lower course of the Indus which after receiving the waters of the Panjab is so wide that a boat in mid-stream is invisible from the bank" (p. 143). But this view is not supportable. In the well-known Ṛik (R. X 190; 1) ततो रात्र्यजायत ततः समुद्रोऽर्णवः ।, Samudra with the addition of Arṇava must mean the ocean. Then again Bhujyu when rescued on the sea by the Aśvins was for some days in the waters. Moreover, there seems already to be intercourse by sea between the Panjab and Mesopotamia, as stated before, though it seems probable that Sind was not yet settled by the Aryans in the days of the Ṛigveda. The ocean was known to adventurers who went for trade with other countries by the sea, even Aryan kings like Bhujyu going on the sea. It indeed appears that adventurers went even eastwards and saw the eastern sea; as one Ṛik distinctly speaks of the eastern and western seas (X. 136, 5. उभौ समुद्रावा क्षेति यश्च पूर्व उतापरः)

That portion of the Indus which lies in the Panjab, viz. from its emergence from the Himalayas to its entering into Sind, passes through a very fertile country with very many useful products and it has been highly praised, being the home of the Aryans. These things are noted in a happy manner in a verse of the hymn to the Indus (X. 75-6,8)* The

* स्वश्वा सिन्धुः सुरथा सुवासा हिरण्मयी सुकृता वाजिनीवती ।
ऊर्णावती युवतिः सीलमावत्युताधि वस्ते सुभगा मधुवृधम् ।

products were good horses, good cars, good garments, gold, corn, good wool and honey. The Indo-Aryans had plenty of fine cloth, the art of weaving which, it is said, they probably learnt from the Dravidians. Fine clothes are spoken of in hundreds of places in the Ṛigveda. But it remains to be seen whether cotton cloth was known. Herodutus said that in India wool grew on trees. This shows that the Aryans in their abode beyond India knew wool only. Clothes of barks of trees, flexible like cloth, must also have been known.

The Indo-Aryans were a highly civilised society even then; truth and order being prized, adultery abhorred and theft and robbery looked upon as non-Aryan. But they were a conquering people and seized the lands and cattle of the non-Aryans and even made them slaves like the Greeks or the Germans. Like the latter they were fond of dice, one hymn depicting the sad condition of the gambler who had lost all. When Yudhishṭhira in the Mahābhārata is shown as refusing to decline an invitation to a game at dice and staking himself, his brothers and his queen after having lost his kingdom (it being considered dishonourable to retire when there was still something to stake), it is not an imaginary scene depicted by a poet, but a historical fact of the Ṛigvedic times. Parents and elder brothers had absolute power of disposal over children and younger brothers and a wife was equally a chattel as in the west. The story of Śunaḥśepa, a boy sold by his father for some cows to the son of Hariś-chandra for the purpose of being sacrificed to Varuṇa, is supported by a Ṛigvedic hymn.

The marriage customs of the Vedic Aryans may be shortly described as follows. The father gave away the girl in marriage, as daughters were, like his slaves, his property. They were married when fully grown up. It was believed that three gods Soma, Viśvāvasu Gandharva and Agni enjoyed the girl before her marriage with man. The marriage was performed in the presence of fire to which there was offered a marriage sacrifice and the married couple walked seven paces round it. The bride was fit for consummation and the consummation took place with a Vedic prayer (X, 184). Indeed it seems that sexual intercourse was a formal and religious act and this prayer was offered in order that proper progeny might be born. The bride was sent to the bridegroom's house with many presents as dowry and in a great procession with music. All this is woven in the marriage hymn which describes the heavenly marriage of Sūryā, sun's daughter with Soma, celebrated with heavenly music (X 85). The Indo-Aryans were a fighting conquering people and their usual prayer to the gods was for *valiant* sons. They also prayed for cows, horses, plenty of corn and wealth.

The wife was the mistress of the house, though she was her husband's chattel. She had a right to participate in the performance of all religious ceremonies with her husband and the Yajamāna-Patnī was as important as the Yajamāna at the sacrifice. There were very often co-wives and one hymn (X 145) contains a prayer, while using a particular herb, for the discomfiture of co-wives and the securing of the husband's love. The author of this hymn is said to be Śachī, Indra's wife which shows that the evil of co-wives, then as now, existed in the families of kings and chieftains. The custom of sati, in our view, existed in the days of Ṛigveda as one hymn contains a verse requesting the widow to get down from the funeral pyre of her dead husband (X 18, 8).

The Indo-Aryans were not without superstition equally with modern civilized men. They feared the Rākshasas, also called Yātudhānas ; and there are several hymns for protecting sacrifice from them or driving them away (e. g. X 87 and 162 etc.). These were imaginary beings probably, though it may be suggested that they were the worst of the non-Aryans who ate human flesh and were in fact cannibals. Rāvaṇa their king is not mentioned in the Ṛigveda. Again X. 165 is a prayer to ward off the evil effects of having killed a kapota (wild pigeon). It also mentions that the cry of an owl is ominous.

The Indo-Aryans burnt their dead and there is a hymn to be recited at the burning (X 17). This hymn also suggests that dead bodies were buried sometimes. They worshipped the manes of the dead ancestors and these manes included the most ancient forefathers even up to Vasishṭha (X 15–8). The manes were divided into two classes Barhishadas and Agnishvāttas. They were also invoked as Agnidagdhas and Anagnidagdhas (burnt and not burnt i. e. probably buried). The Śrāddha was a peculiar rite of all the Aryans throughout the world. The sūkta for recitation at Śrāddha (X 15) uses the word svadhā, svāhā being used when sacrificing.

The disease commonly feared by the Indo-Aryans of the Ṛigvedic days appears to be consumption. There are two special hymns (X 161 and 163) to drive away this disease from the limbs one by one of the afflicted person ; and when the bride and the bridegroom enter their house gods are praised to keep consumption away from them (X 85, 31).

Their religion chiefly consisted of sacrifice in fire with oblations of ghee ordinarily and occasionally of animal sacrifices. The various parts of a sacrifice are mentioned in a hymn to Yajna or sacrifice itself (X 130) where are mentioned Ājya, Paridhi, Brahman and Pratimā. Elsewhere we have 7 Paridhis and 27 Samidhs (sticks) and Barhis. Whether there was idol worship then in vogue cannot be stated. But the Ṛigvedic Aryans had certain allegorical conceptions about the figures of their gods. Agni thus had two heads with four horns, three feet and seven hands. But it seems probable that stone or wood images of such figures were not fashioned or worshipped along with sacrifice which, with the praise of the deities invoked, was their only religious worship.

NOTE I—MARRIAGE HYMN OF THE RIGVEDA.

The marriage hymn of the Ṛigveda (x 85) is one of the most imaginative poems in the Ṛigvedic collection. It is a hymn for which no author is assigned. It is put in the tenth or last book and it seems to be a combination by the compiler, of Ṛiks which were usually recited at marriage. Its author is thus the compiler himself, the individual Ṛiks being of unnamed authors. It begins with the allegory of the marriage of Sūryā, daughter of the sun, with Soma or moon (to whom the lustre of the sun is transferred). The twin gods Aśvins (who also seem to have depended on the sun for lustre) were suitors along with the Moon. " But the Sun gave Sūryā who desired a husband, to the Moon." This establishes the fact that Vedic Aryan girls were married when they were fit for consummation or, in Ṛigvedic words, " desired to have a husband ". Suitors came to demand and the father gave the daughter to whom he liked. The Vedic marriage ceremony commenced with the bridegroom's coming to the bride's house and ended at his house with taking her hand in presence of Angi who gave blessings and children to the couple. The bride went to her husband's house in a car drawn by bullocks with music, taking with her the dowry consisting of bullocks, horses, etc., given by the father. The whole scene is made the basis of a metaphoric description in which the heavens take part. The bride went into a joint family where she became the Samrājni (queen) of the dreaded mother-in-law and of sisters and brothers in law. The consummation of marriage then took place and the act was considered to be a religious act with certain Ṛiks to be recited at the time. Valiant sons were prayed for and Agni was supplicated for giving *ten* sons to the couple. We thus see that the Hindu marriage customs of to-day are almost the same as they were five thousands years ago; with this difference viz., that the taking of the bride's hand is not done at the bridegroom's house after the bride is taken there. The Saptapadi which is the most essential ceremony in Hindu marriage to-day and gives it finality must have taken place also as part of the hand-taking, though not specially mentioned in this hymn.

We give below Griffith's translation of the last portion of this highly poetical hymn for the curious reader.

42, Be ye not parted, dwell ye here;
Reach the full time of human life;
With sons and grandsons sport and play
Rejoicing in your new abode.

43–44. Not evil-eyed, no slayer of the husband,
Bring weal to cattle, gentle-hearted,
Loving the gods, delightful, bearing heroes
Bring blessing to our quadrupeds and bipeds.

45, Oh bounteous Indra, make this bride
Blest in her sons and fortunate.
Vouchsafe to her ten sons and make
Her husband the eleventh man.

46, Over thy husband's father and thy husband's
Mother, bear full sway.
Over the sisters of thy lord and his
Brothers, rule supreme.
So may the universal gods, so may
The waters join our hearts.
May Mātariśvan, Dhātā and Tvashtṛi
Bind us close together.

NOTE II—THE DĀŚARĀJNA FIGHT.

The 'Dāśarājna' fight or fight with ten kings, as it is called in the Ṛigveda itself, is described in the Vasishṭha

Maṇḍala in three sūktas viz., VII 18,, VII 19 and VII 33. It would be interesting to give in detail what these hymns say. VII 18 is in praise of Indra and states how Indra enabled king Sudāsa Paijavana, to overcome his enemies in this fight though hard pressed by them. It is highly poetical but rather difficult to understand even with the help of Sāyana's commentary. There are certain details, however, which indubitably appear and we give them from each verse understandable. "For Sudāsa, Indra made the difficult waters (of Parushṇi) shallow and easily passable" (v. 5 first half). "Turvaśa desired to sacrifice and give wealth in alms; he as also the strong Matsyas. The Bhṛigus and Druhyus helped them. But Indra between them saved his friend (Sudāsa)" (v. 6). "The Pakhtas, the Bhalānas, the Alīnas, the Viśaṇins and Śivas* made noise but he (Indra) exhilarated (with Soma offered) brought back the cows of the Arya (Sudāsa) to the Tṛitsus and fought with (or killed in fight) their men" (v. 7). "The evil-intentioned senseless (enemy) trying to divert the strong Parushṇi river, dug her bank; but Kavi son of Chayamana felled down by the greatness (of Sudāsa) lay like the sacrificed animal" (v. 8). Indra made up the breach and Parushṇi flowed as before and

* The first half of this verse was difficult for Sayana to crack with its five words Pakhtas, Bhalānas, Alinas, Vishāṇins and Śivas and he rendered them as cooks (in sacrifice), the speakers of Bhalā (well), the men not grown in Tapas, men with horns to scrach their skin, and the benefactors (by sacrifice) cried loudly (praised Indra), But this is clearly untenable. Pakhta is a word, as pointed out by Sir R. Grierson, still surviving in Pakhtu, a frontier dialect. Vishānins appear to be another non-Aryan tribe like some Red Indian tribes who tied horns to their heads. In our view, this half verse contains the names of the non-Aryan five tribes (like the five nations of America) who assisted the Druhyus and other Aryan kings.

the horse (of Sudāsa) went to the desired place. Indra for Sudāsa killed (subdued - Sayana) the bragging enemies (v. 9.) "King Sudāsa, in his desire for fame, killed twenty-one men of the two Vikarṇas (first half of v. 11), while Indra drowned old Śruta Kavasha after Druhyu". "Those who praised him got friendship" (v. 12). Indra at once broke all their strong places and seven towns. He divided the wealth of the son of Anu among the Tṛitsus. We shall conquer the bragging Pūru in battle. (v. 13). Sixty-six thousand and sixty-six Anus and Druhyus desirous of cows slept (on the battle-field) ; all these are Indra's valourous deeds (v. 14). Indra gave much wealth to Sudāsa (v. 15, 17). Oh Indra ! kill Bheda (enemy of Sudāsa) with thy vajra (v. 18), Indra who killed Bheda in that fight was propitiated by the Yamunā and the Tṛitsus and the peoples, Ajas, Sigrus and Yaksus, made him presents of horses' heads (v. 19). Parāśara, Śatayātu and Vaśishṭha do not forget to praise thee and thus enjoy good days (v. 21). Sudāsa son of Pijavana and grandson of Devavāta* gave two hundred cows and two cars with wives to me who will go to the sacrificial fire (v. 22). Four horses given by Paijavana with gold (trappings) draw me (in a car). Sudāsa whose fame fills the two worlds as giver of wealth has distributed wealth among the leading people. Oh men, please and follow king Sudāsa like his father Divodāsa and may the power of the Paijavana be indestructible and unimpaired (v 25)

The above hymn shows how Sudāsa, son of Pijavana also called Divodāsa, fought on the Parushni against five aboriginal peoples and Anu, Druhyu, Pūru, Matsya and Turvaśa and by the aid of Indra praised by Vasishṭha

* This shows that the Hindu practice of mentioning the father and grandfather to particularise a man is as old as the Ṛigveda.

gained the battle. He conquered as far as the Yamunā, the people on whose bank submitted to him.

R. VII 19 is another important hymn. Though it does not directly mention the famous fight, it mentions Sudāsa and other kings with their fights with Vṛitras. It is addressed to Indra by Vasishṭha or his descendants. "Oh Indra! you protected Kutsa and for this son of Arjuna you killed the Dāsa Suśhṇa and Kuyava (v. 2) You protected Sudāsa who had sacrificed to you, with all your powers of protection; you also protected Trasadasyu, son of Purukutsa and Pūru in his Vritrahatyas or fights with the aborigines (v. 3). Oh Indra of green horses! you killed many Vṛitras for god's sacrifice. You with your good weapon laid low, for Dabhīta, the Dasyus Chumuri and Dhuni (v. 4). You destroyed 99 towns and killed Namuchi (v. 5). You gave abounding wealth to do a praiseworthy thing for Atithigva (Sudāsa or his father Divodāsa-Sāyana), killed Yādva and Turvaśa (v. 8). Oh Indra! by this praise be propitious to men in their fight with Vṛitras (Dāsas) and protect them (v. 10).

R. VII 33 is the next important hymn as it mentions the Dāśarājna fight by that name. It is addressed to the Vasishṭhas generally, by some of their descendants. It opens with "O Vasishṭhas of white complexion and with tufts of hair kept on the right side of the head" &c. (v. 1) This shows that the Vasishṭhas were, like the modern Kashmirians, of white complexion and had a peculiar way of keeping the hair on the head. "With these Vasishṭhas, he (Pāśadyumna) crossed the Indus with ease and with them he killed Bheda easily." (This probably shows that with these Vasishṭhas, the Aryans came from beyond the Indus. The four priestly families which first came thus were, as stated in the Mahābhārata verse quoted before, Bhṛigus, Āngirasas, Kāsyapas and Vasisṭhas). "And

Oh Vasishthas ! by your hymn (prayer) Indra verily protected Sudāsa in the Dāśarājna fight with ease" (v. 3). "In the Dāśarājna fight they (Tristus) were surrounded and being thirsty prayed for water; and Indra heard the prayer of Vasishṭha and made the world broad for the Tṛitsus (v. 5). The Bharatas driving their cows were shorn like sticks and were few. But Vasishṭha was their purohita (Tritsus is another uame for Bharatas) and the people of the Tṛitsus prospered" (v. 6). Sāyana seems to be wrong in interpreting Pura &c., as Purohita. We take it to mean, Vasishṭha went in front or took the lead and hence in the fight the people of the Tṛitsus became victorious. Hereafter the hymn relates the birth of Vasishṭha from Mitra and Varuna who, while sacrificing, on seeing Urvaśi, emitted semen which was kept in a jar from which came out Agastya and subsequently Vasishṭha. It is strange to find that this absurd story of the birth of Vasishṭha (related in the Purāṇas also) is as old as this Ṛigvedic hymn.

A fourth hymn of Vasishṭhas gives the clearest proof of this fight. R VII 83 states "Ten leagued together kings not sacrificing* could not fight with Sudāsa, Oh Indra and Varuṇa ! His sacrifices pleased the gods with oblations" (v. 7). Oh Indra and Varuṇa ! you gave strength to Sudāsa when he was surrounded in the Dāśarājna (fight) where the white-complexioned and hair-tufted Tṛitsus (Vasishṭha's pupils – Sāyana) propitiated you with their prayers and oblations". (v. 8). VII 53 contains a stray reference to

* This might suggest that the ten kings were non-Aryans. But as VII 18 distinctly mentions Anus and Druhyus as slain and Matsyas and others, we have to admit that some of the ten kings were Aryans. Probably these did not sacrifice at the time of the fight, while Vasishṭha sacrificed to Indra when Sudāsa was fighting.

Sudāsa in verse 3. These hymns from the Vasishṭha Maṇḍala show that the Vasishṭhas are full of the memory of this battle wherein the Bharatas or Tritsus, Vasiṣṭha's clan-men, with their king Sudāsa obtained a decisive victory on the Parushṇi (Ravi) by the help of the prayers of Vasishṭhas (the priests of Bharatas). Sudāsa and Pijavana or Divodāsa are solar race kings even in the Purāṇic genealogies, while their opponents Anu, Druhyu, Pūru, Matsya and Turvaśa are lunar race people. Yadus and Turvaśas had attacked Divodāsa himself but they were killed by Indra.

Several attempts have been made to fix the approximate date of this Panipat of Vedic times. A researcher of Poona thinks that the fight took place in the sixth millenium B. C., as it may be believed that Manu was saved from the Deluge, an event of about 7009 B. C. and that Sudāsa was a contemporary of Chitraratha, Manu's descendant in the 19th generation. He also thinks that the Vedic Sudāsa and his father Divodāsa were foreigners, not being mentioned in Purāṇic genealogies. These views are, we think, not correct. Purāṇa genealogies, especially in their earlier portions, are unreliable, as will be shown when we come to the Purāṇas. A Sudāsa appears in the Purāṇa genealogies in the solar line; but he is not the Ṛigvedic king as he is not a son of Divodāsa. He is most probably one of his ancestors, how far removed can not now be stated. He is, however, not a foreigner, but an Indo-Aryan king, as Vasishṭha is his purohita; and his date may be taken to be about 5000 B. C. as he is referred to in some of the oldest hymns of the Ṛigveda.

IX SĀMAVEDA.

The second Veda viz., the Sāmaveda, is a natural outcome or accompaniment of the Ṛigveda. Singing is natural to man when praying and some of the Ṛigvedic verses must have been set to singing, even before the Ṛigveda was compiled. Then again, the Soma juice was an exhilarating drink and when it was offered to the Vedic gods, especially to Indra, the god of war, the Vedic Aryans would naturally fall to singing the praises of Soma and Indra. The Sāmaveda, therefore, was a natural and even a necessary accompaniment of the Ṛigveda, as the book of Psalms is of the Bible. At the Vedic sacrifices there was a special singing priest called Udgātṛi; for every priest could not be a singer, singing requiring god-gifted voice and man-attained excellence. The Hotṛi priest recited the Ṛigvedic verses, the Udgātṛi sang the Psalms and the Adhvaryu uttered the sacrificial formulæ and threw the oblations into the fire. The singer priests, therefore, must have already put together the Sāman verses they had to sing and settled the method of singing them also. Thus must have arisen the Daśatis of the Sāmaveda like the family books of the Ṛigveda, before the Sāmaveda, along with the Ṛigveda and the Yajurveda, was finally put together by Veda-Vyāsa alias Krishṇa Dvaipāyana.

The Indo-Aryans were, during the Ṛigvedic period, as we have seen already, well advanced in civilization. They had probably, though not certainly, found out the seven musical notes and also the different arrangements of these which could be made in singing. "Several references in the Ṛigveda show that even in that early age, the Indians were acquainted with different kinds of music. There were three main types of percussion, wind and stringed instruments viz. Dundubhi, Veṇu and Vīṇā. A Ṛishi states that the sound of the flute is heard in the abode of Yama where the blessed dwell" (Macd. p. 169). "That vocal music had already gone beyond the primitive stage may be concluded from the method of chanting the Sāmaveda, which was probably very ancient, as the Soma ritual goes back to the Indo-Iranian age" "Singing is often mentioned in the Ṛigveda". (Ditto p. 170) We may add that the Sāman verses are more than once mentioned in the Ṛigvedic hymns themselves, as distinguished from Ṛiks and the skill of Vasishṭhas in singing loudly the Śakvari-metred sāmans is also noted in the Vasishṭha Maṇḍala (VII 33, 4 quoted already). In the marriage hymn (R. X 85) it is stated that the two bullocks of the bridal car of Sūryā were prompted by Ṛiks and Sāmans. It cannot, therefore, be doubted that Sāmans or good verses were differentiated even in the early part of the Ṛigvedic period. 'The chants of the Sāmavedin,' Burnell holds, 'may go back as far as the hymns of the Ṛigveda; songs are everywhere among the earliest literary productions and Sāmans are in fact mentioned in the Ṛigveda.'

The Charaṇavyūha says that the Sāmaveda had 1,000 branches or Śākhās. The word 'one thousand', here used, may be taken to mean many or innumerable. Indeed we can conceive that the Sāman verses were really sung in innumerable ways. But only seven Śākhās are named by the Charanavyūha and two of them alone viz. the Rāṇāyanīya and the Kauthuma survive. A real singer of the Sāmaveda is now not available and we cannot tell how the Vedic Aryans sang the Sāman verses. In the printed books the seven notes, Shadja and others, are mentioned; but one of these is taken as the note of singing the whole sūkta. The Uttarārchika sūktas give different notes for singing different triads. It is impossible to say how the Vedic Aryans originally sang the Sāmans; indeed whether they knew all the seven notes,* as Sāma-singing has changed from time to time. A noted Brahmin singer of Gwalior used to sing Sāman verses in all the seven notes and in different arrangements of them called Rāgas; but this can never be conceived as the original method of the Vedic Aryans of chanting the Sāman verses. The word 'Om' is the peculiar property of the Sāmaveda, as the humming of this word must have assisted the singer in steadying his voice as he began singing a Sāman. The word 'Om' eventually became denotative of the Highest Deity and its importance is detailed in the well-known Chhāndogya Upanishad of

*We have not yet come across the names of notes in the Sanhitās, whether Krushta, Prathama &c. or Shadja, Rishabha &c.

the Sāmaveda. That word, with Harih added before it, has now been fixed upon as the word which ought to be pronounced when beginning any Vedic recitation.

In the Bhagavadgītā, Śrīkrishṇa identifies himself with Sāmaveda from among the Vedas. This may be explained in three ways. Singing prayers leads to the highest mental elevation. Then again, Śrīkrishṇa was very probably a follower of the Sāmaveda as in the Chhāndogya Upanishad it is said that Ghora Āngirasa taught a particular Vedānta doctrine to Krishṇa, son of Devakī. Thirdly, Śrīkrishṇa himself was a great singer as the Harivanśa relates that he invented the Chhālikya gāna or singing in concert and the Yādavas sang it. In the Brāhmaṇas themselves, this highest place of the Sāmaveda is already attained, as will be seen later on. The Sāmaveda has, therefore, an importance of its own; but to the Vedic student it has not much importance as most of its verses are taken from the Ṛigveda.

The two Śākhās extant of the Sāmaveda are the Ṛāṇāyanīya and the Kauthuma. The adherents of the Rāṇāyanīya sect are chiefly found in Mahārāshtra and those of Kauthuma are found in Gujarat. The recensions of the two, it is surmised, differ but little. We have before us the Rāṇāyanīya text and not the Kauthuma one. This text contains 1549 verses. It is divided into two books. The first book called the Pūrvārchika (the earlier collection of Ṛiks or verses) consists of 6 prapāthakas or lessons, each prapāthaka having ten Daśatis or decades, each of ten verses. The last prapâṭhaka contains, however, 14 decades and these are not exactly decades, as they contain sometimes less and sometimes more than ten verses. The sixth prapāṭhaka really contains 154 verses and the preceding five 500, making the total of the first book thus 654. The second book called the Uttarārchika (later collection* of Ṛiks or verses) has a different arrangement. There are no decades in the nine prapāṭhakas contained therein and the prapāṭhakas are divided, the first five into two halves and the last four into three halves. Each half lesson contains up to 23 stanzas. But these stanzas usually contain more than two ordinary verses of the same metre.

The Daśatis (decades) of the first book or the prapāṭhakārdhas (half lessons) of the second book cannot strictly be called sūktas or hymns, as they are not the compositions of one Ṛishi. The Ṛishis of their verses are many. They are of course mostly identical with the Ṛishis of the Ṛigveda as the Ṛiks or verses in the Sāmaveda are all taken from the Ṛigveda with the exception of seventy-five. There is an Anukramaṇī of the Ṛishis and Devatās of the Kauthuma text, composed by the Naigeya School. We have prepared a list of Ṛishis and Devatās as printed in the Rāṇāyanīya text and we find a few Ṛishis only who are not included in the Ṛigveda Ṛishi list. As the Daśatīs or prapāthakārdhas contain verses com-

* Caland believes the Uttarārchika to be really the earlier one (Datta). So does Burnell.

posed by different Ṛishis, the question arises on what principle these Ṛiks of different Ṛishis are put together. It is a question difficult to answer. One thing is apparent viz. that the verses in each decade refer to the same Vedic deity. These deities in the first book are chiefly Agni, Indra and Pavamāna Soma. Thus the first Prapāṭhaka contains Daśatis the verses of which are mostly addressed to Agni. It is only rarely that other deities come in, as will appear from the list of deities and verses appended hereto. This observation does not apply to the second book.

The first book with its present division is referred to in the Śatapatha (2nd Brāhmaṇa) as pointed out by Dr. Macdonell. We are, therefore, justified in concluding that this book was compiled by Veda Vyāsa as the tradition is, Śatapatha being posterior to Vyāsa. The second book too may be taken to have been also compiled by him. The Daśatis of the first book, like the family books of the Ṛigveda, were probably older even than Vyāsa and he had merely to collect them together. The prapāṭhakārdhas of the second book may be said to have been put together later than Vyāsa, as it is distinctly called Uttarārchika or later collection. But even this might have been put together by Vyāsa himself from the sacrificial practice of his time, giving selections of Ṛiks made for Udgātṛis for singing at different stages of the sacrifice and in praise of different deities, since these ardhas (halves) are usually in praise of more than one deity. There is thus no obvious objection to accept the tradition of the Mahābhārata that Veda-Vyāsa compiled all the three Vedas; and accepting this tradition the date which we can assign to the compilation of the Sāmaveda is the same as that of the compilation of the Ṛigveda viz., about 3100 B. C. The compilation of the Sāmaveda certainly preceded the Śatapatha which in one place states that there is no sacrifice without Sāman (नासाम यज्ञो भवति) and no Sāma-singing without Hinkāra (नवाहिंकृत्य साम गीयते Ś I 3, 1).

There is a Padapāṭha for this Veda, both Pūrvārchika and Uttarārchika. This text is, Burnell states, attributed to a Gārgya (Introd. to Ārsheya Brā. p. 8. The authority given in a footnote is one Durga on Nirukta IV, 4).

A few remarks of Burnell in his introduction to Ārsheya Brāhamṇa on Sāma-singing may be given here. 'The Sāma chants resemble in some respects the Gregorian or Plain Chant. The Sāman, however, being the older and less cultivated, one occasionally meets with passages which are forbidden by the rules of the Plain Chant. The principle of the modern notation of sāmans in the south is more simple than the earlier one of putting in hundreds of letters. The seven notes are marked by the numerals 1, 2, 3, 4, 5, 6, and the last (almost never used) by 7 or ^. Of these the first is equal to F and the rest to E, D, C, B A, G.' (p. XI.).

Note I–SĀMA–SINGING.

At the present day, very few Vaidika Sāma-singers are found. One does come across, now and then, a Sāman reciter, belonging to the Rāṇāyanīya school, but one is not satisfied on hearing him, that his singing is really the old Sāman chanting of the Vedic Ṛishis. Mr. N. K. Patwardhan, a pleader of Poona has studied Sāma-singing from the Sūtras on Sāmagāna and is trying to settle the ancient mode of Sāma-chanting. A few of the points which he has settled may be noted here for the information of the curious reader.

From the Chhāndogya Upanishad, we learn that Sāma-singing consists of five parts viz., 1. Hiṅkāra, 2. Prastāva, 3. Udgītha, 4. Pratihāra and 5. Nidhana. These, at least three of them, remind us of the Astai, Antarā and Ābhoga of modern Indian singing. The ending Nidhana (coda of European music) usually consists of one vocal sound lengthened through three or four notes and may be compared to the ending supplementary Tāna of Indian modern singing. The modern Rāgas or arrangements of different notes may be equated to the different Sāmans named after a typical song (chāla of Indian music); these names are innumerable such as Vāruṇa, Śaubhara, Brāhma, (we find Brāhma Achhāvāka mentioned in Black Yajurveda Sānhitā) and Rathantara, Vinardi, Yajnāyajnīya, Yodhājaya and so on.

The numbers 1, 2, 3 given above letters in most printed books of Sāmaveda are indicative of Udātta, Svarita and Anudātta; but the numbers given in Sāma-Gāna books indicate notes. These notes are usually 1, 2, 3 and 4 and we even have 5, 6 and 7 and they indicate according to Nāradīya sikshā, Madhyama 1, Gāndhāra 2 and so on in the descending order. Then again the vowels in the original Ṛik, according to the Pushpasūtra have, in singing, to be elongated or shortened or changed (e. g. e into ai). This is what is seen in singing in every language. To an Indian, even knowing English, a verse sung in English becomes almost unintelligible by the various changes in pronunciation. Lastly, some unmeaning sounds or words have to be inserted here and there such as, "Au, hau, vā nā, shom" (called stobhas) to be sung in more than one note like modern Tāna; and some parts of the verse or even of words have to be repeated, apparently unnecessarily.

The Uttarārchika has stanzas usually consisting of three or more Ṛiks, the first of which is always taken from the Pūrvārchika. The two or more following Ṛiks are not tacked on to it so much for continuity of meaning as for sameness of mode of singing. The first verse gives, in effect, the sample mode, they being also of the same metre.

The supplementary Mahānāmnī Ārchika (विद्मा मघवन् विद्मा &c.) given in the middle of the Sāma-Sanhitā is called Aindra-puchchha or the tail of the Sāman of Indra. It is chiefly in Śakvarī metre, some portions being added as Upasarga (see the foot-notes in printed texts). There are thus three Śakvarī stanzas and these are to be sung in a loud voice.

NOTE 2–STRANGWAY'S 'MUSIC OF HINDUSTAN' ON THE MODE OF RECITING THE VEDAS.

Mr. Strangway says (p. 246) that the Ṛigveda was recited originally in three musical notes which have become stress notes, since the beginning of our era, viz. Udātta (raised), Anudātta (not raised) and Svarita (falling accent). No authority is quoted for this statement: so far as we have enquired, Ṛigveda is never sung in different notes, though printed editions give different notes Ṛishabha, Gāndhāra &c. for different verses in the sūktas.

He thinks that the Yajurveda is recited on the notes D

E and F i. e. Rishabha, Gāndhāra and Madhyama. There are different notes assigned for different verses in the White Yajurveda also. As actually recited at present, Yajurveda, Black or White, is recited in one note, though the pitch may be sometimes Tāra.

Mr. Strangway gives valuable information about the Sāmaveda. "There are no melodic figures (modern Rāgas) in Sāma-chanting. Sāma is chanted at the pressing of Soma or the moon-plant and at the worship of ancestors who reside in the moon." This connection of Sāma-chanting with funeral rites is mentioned even in the Mahābhārata where the burning of Bhishma's dead body is described (Śāntip. XVI). "Soma sacrifice involved months in preparation and days in performance." "Other creeds have swept over India and buried the Vedic creed except in the south where even, true Sāma-singers are few and impostors many.

'The Stobhas are Jubilations and are borrowed from the Ṛigveda and the places wherefrom the quotations are taken are called yonis. The gāṇas give directions for singing. The scale of Nāradīya-Sikshā in modern notation is F. G. and not G. A. Sāma-singing circles round one note F or E.

The Sāma-song is divided into five parts as follows ; (1) Prastāva or introductory ascription of praise preceded by the syllable Hum (हुम्) sung by Prastotṛi; (2) Udgītha sung by Udgātṛi, chief Sāma-priest, preceded by the sound Om (ओं) ; and (3) Pratihāra or joining in, preceded by hum (हुं) sung by Pratihartṛi who joins in the last syllable,-sometimes divided into two parts viz : (4) Upadrava or recession consisting of the last two syllables of the Pratihāra, sung by Udgātṛi and (5) Nidhana or Coda, consisting of two syllables or Om (ओम्) sung by all the three priests. For example the first verse of the Sāmaveda taken from R. VI, 16, 10 is divided as follows:-हुं ओम्र इ (प्रस्ताव); ओम्

आयाहि वीतये गृणानो हव्यद्दातये (उद्गीथ); नि होता सत्सि बर्हिषि ओम् (प्रतिहार) - to be divided into निहोता सत्सि ब-(उपद्रव) र्हिषि ओम् (निधन).

This is sung three times over to form a stoma (group). The next eight verses of Sāmaveda are also from the Ṛigveda. The last belongs, however, to Sāmaveda exclusively and forms the Doxology. The first, the fourth and the fifth are stomas ; 6, 7, 8 sung thrice and the other four only once, form in all 19 and are called Bhaktis which are usually 15.

The Gāṇas give directions for prolongations and modifications of vowels as also for the insertion of vowel syllables. These insertions or stobhas are the exact counterparts of sybilex. The rythm of the chant ignores the poetical metre. The names of Sāma-notes are Krushta, Prathama, Dvitīya, Tṛitīya Chaturtha, Mandra and Atisvārya. The authorities on the subject are 1. Rik Prātiśākhya, 2. Bṛihad-devatā, 3 Taittirīya Brāhmaṇa, 4. Sāma-Vidhāna Brāhmaṇa, 5. Pushpasūtra, 6. Sāmatantra and 7. Nāradaśikshā which is quite modern. The Pushpasūtra says that the Kauthumas sing in five notes, some in six and fewer still in seven.

The name Gāndhāra is taken from the country, but Ṛishabha, Dhaivata and Nishāda are inexplicable. Shadja is born of six or father of six. Numerals are placed above the syllables of the texts to indicate substantive notes (प्रकृति). Between them are grace-notes (विकृति). The melodic figures are to be sung after patterns handed down from mouth to mouth and their names are many.

X BLACK YAJURVEDA.

The next Veda is the Yajurveda of which there are two forms, the Krishna or Black and the Śukla or White. The terms black and white do not, in our view, involve any disparagement of the former, though this is sometimes urged. They merely mean, we think, the old and the new, a new party among Hindus being usually termed Śukla even now. Śukla may also perhaps mean reformed. That the black Yajurveda is the older form is admitted in the very legend which explains how the White form arose, a legend which we will detail presently. Yajurveda relates principally to sacrifices and gives the various mantras used in them as also prose formulae relating to the method of their performance. The word Yajuh occurring in the Purusha-sūkta probably means, as stated already, the sacrificial prose formula. These formulæ must have been settled in old times though they may have gradually changed according to the change in language as also in ritual. These formulæ, as preserved in the Black Yajurveda finally compiled by Vyāsa, have accents and hence they unquestionably belong to the Mantra period. The rules of accentuation for the two Vedas are nearly the same, as they are chiefly given by Pāṇini and the Prātiśākhyas. The method of pronouncing the accents in this Veda differs, however, from the older method of the Ṛigveda, being more musical and less rough. Hence the recitation of the

Black Yajurveda is more pleasing than that of the Ṛigveda. Even this accentuation disappeared, as we have seen, in the days of the Brāhmaṇas.

The Black Yajurveda thus consists of accentuated prose interpersed with mantras in verse here and there which are directed to the praise of sacrifice, to the manner of its performance and often to the glorification of the gods to whom the sacrifice is offered. The text of the Black Yajurveda may be taken to have been settled by Veda-Vyāsa at the same time that he settled the text of the Ṛigveda and the Sāmaveda. This text has been preserved to us in more than one recension, the Kaṭha, the Kāpishṭhala, the Kālāpa or Maitrāyaṇīya, the Taittirīya and others. But like the Śākala Śākhā of the Ṛigveda, the Taittirīya recension is the most widely known at present. The Maitrāyaṇīya text which has been published by Schroeder, consists of four books (Kāṇḍas) and fifty-four lessons or Prapāṭhakas, and differs to a considerable extent from the Kāṭhaka text which has also been published by the same scholar. The Taittirīya text has been published in many places and at several times. From the copy before us, we find that it consists of seven books and forty-four lessons, each lesson being further subdivided into Anuvākas. This recension might be later than the Maitrāyaṇīya one as the number of Kāṇḍas is greater though that of the Prapāṭhakas is less. The real difference in extent between the Maitrāyaṇīya and the Taittirīya texts cannot be estimated; especially because there is no index book for this Veda like the Sarvānukramaṇī of Kātyāyana for the Ṛigveda which gives its contents in detail. Such Anukramaṇīs were probably not composed for the Black Yajurveda Sanhitā, because it consists of prose gāthās principally, which cannot be counted and for which no Ṛishi or Devatā can be assigned. Even now the Black Yajurveda followers do not give the Ṛishi or Devatā of any mantra they recite, as the followers of the Ṛigveda do. The Taittirīya Sanhitā mantras need not, therefore, have any Anukramaṇīs. The several Anuvākas, however, always end with a mention of the number of padas or words in the Anuvākas. This is peculiar to this Veda alone. For example, it is mentioned at the end of Anuvaka I Prapāṭhaka I Kāṇḍa I that the words beginning with Isha are forty-three (इषेति त्रिचत्वारिंशत्). If these be added for the whole Sanhitā, the number of Padas or words comes to precisely 110, 296. The mantras or sentences are not numbered one, two and so on, and have not been counted, though the number of Anuvākas has been and comes up to 651 (see note).

Dr. Macdonell observes that the Yajurveda introduces us not only to a geographical area different from that of the Ṛigveda, but also to a new epoch of religious and social life in India (p. 174). This is true to some extent only; for we must remember that, even in the Ṛigvedic age, the Indo-Aryans had advanced in the settlement of the country as far as the Śarayu in Oudh and the lower valley of the Jumna.

The Matsyas and the Chedis are clearly mentioned in the Ṛigveda. The Ṛigveda, however, covers the whole period from the entry of the Indo-Aryans into the Indus valley down to their settlement in the lower portion of the valley of the Jumna. Then again, the Chandravanśi Aryans had settled even in the days of the Ṛigvedic hymns in the region of the Sarasvatī under Pūru and had advanced south-eastward into the Chedi and Matsya countries. The centre of the Aryan civilization towards the latter part of the Ṛigvedic period was already in this Sarasvatī region or Kurukshetra and Sarasvatī is already a sacred river in the Ṛigveda, several hymns in praise being addressed to her. It may safely be held, therefore, that the compilation of all the three Vedas, viz. the Ṛigveda, the Sāmaveda and the Black Yajurveda took place in this region under Vyāsa about 3100 B. C. a little before the great fight between the Kurus and the Pānchālas.

It may here be objected that the language of the Yajurveda strikes us as somewhat modern. But that there is not much difference between the language of the later portions of the Ṛigveda and that of the Yajurveda is admitted by all. Secondly, the language of poetry is always more archaic than the language of prose and the Ṛigveda consists entirely of poems. Moreover the prose in the Yajurveda is simple and must have constantly changed and adapted itself to the changing language and hence there are not many archaic forms or archaic words in the Black Yajurveda. Lastly, even as it is, this language is not that of modern Sanskrit and is distinctly old, as old as the language of the Purusha-sūkta and other later hymns of the Ṛigveda and has still accents as already stated.

With regard to the nature of the civilization and social condition of the Indo-Aryans as reflected in the Black Yajurveda, it may be stated that it does not much differ from that disclosed in the Ṛigveda. Caste had already developed upto the four chief castes in Ṛigvedic times. The Vedic gods appear to be nearly the same, though Ushas, the old Arctic home deity, is nearly obsolete, while Rudra has advanced in public favour. There is a special Rudrādhyāya in the Black Yajurveda which is essentially pantheistic in view. Sacrifice, of course, is the chief object of the Yajurveda and therefore still supreme. The various forms of daily, monthly and yearly sacrifices are detailed in this Veda naturally enough. But there is no mention, so far as we see, of human sacrifice which probably came into prominence hereafter (as we shall show when speaking of the White Yajurveda) when the Aryan kingdoms in India developed in extent and power and the Indo-Aryans, from being a newly conquering people, became the settled inhabitants of the land. There is, however, at the end of this Veda the well-known symbolization of the Aśvamedha,* the phenomenon of sunrise being looked upon as a horse

* This favourite sacrifice of the Indo-Aryans is described in detail together with the strange practice of the queen of the sacrificing king being made to lie with the dead horse. Obscene rites obtained, we know, among Western Aryans also.

sacrifice, the early Ushas being the head of the horse sacrificed, the sun its eye and so on.

The Black Yajurveda has its pada text which must have been formulated like the Ṛigveda-pada-pāṭha when the Vedic language became generally un-understandable. This pāṭha must have, therefore, arisen about the same time as the Ṛigveda pada-pāṭha and must have given rise soon to the Krama-pāṭha also. Who the authors of these pāṭhas were, can not be ascertained with certainty ; but it may be surmised that Śākalya and Gālava were also the authors of the Black Yajurveda Pada and Krama texts as in their days the division of Brahmins into Ṛigvedins, Yajurvedins &c. had probably not yet arisen. The Hiraṇyakeśi Sūtra mentions Ātreya as the author of the Pada text.

The contents of this Sanhitā are interesting and deserve careful study. There are stray references to historical facts and kings here and there. There is thus an interesting reference to Vasishṭha and Sudāsa in the seventh Kāṇḍa (4, 7) wherein Vasishṭha whose sons were killed is mentioned as performing a particular sacrifice to obtain sons as also to secure the friendship of Sudāsa. Vasishṭha's patron Sudāsa was perfectly remembered in the days of the Black Sanhitā.

NOTE:—FURTHER PARTICULARS ABOUT THE BLACK YAJURVEDA SANHITĀ.

The Black Yajurveda, following the popular division of the Ṛigveda, divides itself into Ashṭakas and Adhyāyas. But an Ashṭaka does not always contain eight Adhyāyas, and the Kāṇḍa itself is called an Ashṭaka whether it contains eight or less Adhyāyas, the number of Adhyāyas in the seven Kāṇḍas being 44 (8,6,5,7,7,6 and 5). The Adhyāya is, however, divided into Anuvākas and not into Vargas as in the Ṛigveda. There are further no Ṛiks or Mantras as such but particular sentences or words are quoted as mantras in the Brāhmaṇas. The number of such mantras has not been counted but every set of 50 padas is differently numbered as one, two and so on. Numbers less than 50 are further given in words and these sentences are learnt by heart by those who learn the Sanhitā. The details of the contents of this Sanhitā by Anuvākas and padas is as shown in the following table, Prapāthaka being the same as Adhyāya.

No. of Anuvakas

	Anuvākas in Kaṇḍa or Ashṭaka						
No. of Adhy.	I	II	III	IV	V	VI	VII
1	14	11	11	11	11	11	20
2	14	12	11	11	12	11	20
3	14	14	11	13	12	11	20
4	46	14	11	12	12	11	22
5	11	12	11	11	24	11	25
6	12	12	...	9	23	11	...
7	13	...	...	65	26	...	...
8	22	...	...	..	...	...	...
Total	**146**	**75**	**55**	**82**	**120**	**66**	**107**

Grand Total of Anuvākas 651

Padas 19165; 16583; 10622; 14105; 19406; 16902; 13325

Grand Total of Padas 110296.

The Yajurveda mantras have no Ṛishis; but certain Kāṇḍarshis are worshipped. These are variously given as nine, six, five or four and their names are all, those of gods who are supposed to have seen them. For this the seven Kāṇḍas of the Sanhitā and the three of the Brāhmaṇa are re-distributed into nine or six &c. These new Kāṇḍas are called 1 Prājāpatya 2 Saumya 3 Āgneya 4 Vaiśvadeva 5 Svāyambhuva and 6 Āruṇa; of the remaining three the names are 7 Sānhitī Devatā 8 Vāruṇī Devatā and 9 Yājnikī Devatā. The Prājāpatya Kāṇḍa consists of some mantras from Kāṇḍa I with some from Kāṇḍa II, and so on. The details are given in the Satyāśhādha-Sūtra-Bhāshya-Tīkā by Gopināthabhatta (p. 339 Ānadāśrama Edn.) This seems to have been taken up by the followers of the White Yajurveda also, as the first sūkta in it इषेत्वोर्जेत्वा, the same as in the Black Sanhitā, has Prajāpati assigned to it as its Ṛishi. This practice of assigning gods as Ṛishis where none are known is borrowed from the Ṛigveda practice wherein hymns like the Purushasūkta &c. are attribtued to Nārāyaṇa &c.

The prayer at the end of the Aśvamedha ritual with which however, it is usual to finish every sacrificial rite, small or great, is worth quoting. It breathes a high national spirit aud contains also a correct appreciation of the essentials of national prosperity in Indian kingdoms. This mantra is also taken in the Vājasaneyi Sanhitā (XXVI 22)

"May in the Brāhmin community be born Brāhmins possessed of the lustre of sacred knowledge and may in this state be born Kshatriyas proficient in archery, brave and great chariot-warriors. May cows be milk-giving, oxen able to draw, horses swift, women with graceful persons and young men fond of riding chariots, desirous of winning and fit for appearing in assemblies. May this sacrificer obtain a hero son. May rain come at each time we wish for it, may plants give us good crops and may there be sub-sistence and welfare for all of us."

(आब्रह्मन्ब्राह्मणो ब्रह्मवर्चसी जायतामाऽस्मिन्राष्ट्रे राजन्य इषव्यः शूरो महारथो जायतां दोग्ध्री धेनुर्वोढाऽनड्वानाशुः सप्तिः पुरन्धिर्योषा जिष्णू रथेष्ठाः सभेयो युवास्य यजमानस्य वीरो जायतां निकामे निकामे नः पर्जन्यो वर्षतु फलिन्यो न ओषधयः पच्यन्ताम् योगक्षेमो नः कल्पताम्. The word Brahman is differently interpreted by Sāyana in his Taittirīya-Bhāshya and Uvaṭa and Mahidhara in their Vajasaneyi Sanhita Bhāshyas. Sāyana takes it to be in the locative case and mean "in the Brahmin community," probably in opposition to Rāstre Rājanyaḥ which follows and which cannot, therefore, be taken back. The latter take it to be in the vocative; but they do not give its meaning. We prefer Sāyana's rendering as the Taittirīya Brāhmaṇa begins with the words Brahma and Kshatra with the same meaning. Vaiśyas are suggested by Dhenu and Anadvān mentioned in the next sentence. This mantra is commented on in the Taittirīya Brāhmaṇa also in III 8, 13 and the above rendering is olso supported by the running comment there.).

This prayer is fit for being used as a national prayer in any country, specially in any of the Indian states, even at the present day.

WHITE YAJURVEDA.

The Śukla or White Yajurveda, as stated before, is, by the very legend of its origin, a later form of the Yajurveda. The legend as given in the Mahābhārata (Śānti Parva, Chap. 360) shortly runs thus:—"Vaiśampāyana, the teacher of Yājnavalkya once got angry with him for disparaging his co-students and asked him to leave his school, after returning the Veda taught to him. Yājnavalkya immediately vomitted the Veda the mantras of which burned like hot embers. The other pupils of Vaiśampāyana, assuming the form of the Tittiri bird (which is supposed to be able to eat live coals), ate up the Veda which thenceforth became known as the Taittirīya recension. Yājnavalkya being now without any Veda propitiated the Sun who gave him fifteen new Yajush mantras. He then started a new school of his own, formulating the White Yajurveda Sanhitâ and composing a separate Brāhmaṇa called Śatapatha Brāhmaṇa. The new Sanhitā is called the Vājasaneyi recension because Yājnavalkya learnt the new mantras from the Sun, riding the horses of his chariot." This legend is on the face of it imaginary, being a name legend as Dr. Bühler aptly called such legends. It is clearly based on the names Taittirīya and Vājasaneyi. We may, however, believe that Yājnyavalkya, being dissatisfied with the Yajurveda as taught to him by Vaiśampāyana, founded a new school of his own, reforming the Black Yajurveda Sanhitā by separating the prose Brāhmaṇa portion of it and composing a few new mantras of his own, so that his Sanhitā might fitly be called a new one. The new Sanhitā is based on the Ṛigveda model, however, consisting as it does of verses only. It begins with the verse 'Ishe tvorjetvā' the beginning verse of the old Yajurveda; but even in this verse Yājnavalkya has made certain alterations. He composed a separate Brāhmaṇa for his new Veda viz. the Śatapatha, explanatory of the mantras in his Sanhitā and thus set the way to the followers of the other Vedas for composing explanatory Brāhmaṇas for their Vedas. The White Yajurveda Sanhitā is thus the compilation not of Vyāsa, but of his pupil's pupil and is of the same date as its Śatapatha Brāhmaṇa i. e. about 3000 B. C. a hundred years later than the date of the compilation of the other three Vedas. The Mahābhārata story further relates that at a sacrifice performed by Janaka, Yājnavalkya succeeded in establishing the right of the White Yajurveda to one half of the Dakshinā alloted to Yajurveda, after great contention with his maternal uncle Vaisampāyana, the champion of the Black Yajurveda.

Rao Bahadur P. B. Joshi of Bombay who is a follower of the White Yajurveda has collected information from several Purāṇas regarding the personality of Yājnavalkya which may be looked upon as quite historical and we give below its main features. In Mithilā (Behar) lived a Brahmin named Devarāta, called Vājaseni also, as he distributed much food (Vāja) to the poor. His son was Yājnavalkya. (It seems, however, that he was son of Yajnavalka from which word the patronymic Yājnvalkya would arise). He studied the four Vedas with the pupils of Vyāsa, learning the Yajurveda from Vaiśampāyana who was his maternal uncle also. From the Bṛihadāraṇyaka Upanishad, we find that Yājnavalkya studied Vedānta under Uddālaka Āruṇi who once said to him " Even a stump would put forth branches and leaves, if water impregnated with Vedāntic power were thrown on it." A story is concocted on this statement in some Purāṇas in which Yājnavalkya is represented to have worked this miracle. He no doubt became a famous Vedānta teacher and was adored as such by Janaka, the well-known king of Mithilā. Yājnavalkya had two wives Maitreyī and Kātyāyanī, the former being childless. When he departed to the forest, he expounded his Brahmavidyā to the former. Yājnavalkya who is also called Yogīśvara was, according to P. B. Joshi, a social reformer also ; for the well-known Smṛiti named after him may not be his work but is based on his liberal teaching.

The Sanhitā of the White Yajurveda exists in two well-known recensions, namely the Mādhyandina and the Kāṇva. There is not much difference in these except the fact that the Kāṇvas have the letter and use the sound ḷ as in the Ṛigveda Saṇhitā recension. The Kāṇvas mostly belong to the Deccan and hence probably this use of ḷ among them. The difference is more in the Śatapatha Brāhmaṇa than in the Sanhitā. The White Sanhitā is divided into forty chapters or Adhyāyas and the total number of mantras is found, on acutal calculation, to be 1975, while the Charaṇa-Vyūha gives the number as 1800. A few mantras, therefore, some might say, have been added later than the date of Charaṇa-Vyūha. But the number therein given is really 1900, itself a round figure according to our view.* Dr. Macdonell thinks that the first 18 chapters are the original ones, as these alone are commented on in the Śatapatha. But the number of mantras in these comes up to 1026 only. These mantras are not all metrical, some being in prose. It is only generally true that like the Ṛigveda the White Yajurveda contains Ṛiks or verses only.

There are, however, no sūktas; in other words each Adhyāya consists of one sūkta only which is always long. It is divided, no doubt, into Anuvākas on what principle it is not quite clear, as in the other Veda-Sanhitās. The number of these Anuvākas is 303, as given in the Sarvānukramaṇī of this Veda, printed at the end of the edition of this Veda brought out in the Nirṇayasagar press with Uvaṭa's Bhāshya and that of Mahīdhara. A Ś.kshā attributed to Yājnavalkya himself is also printed. The author of the Sarvānukramaṇī is given as Kātyāyana. It is, apparently, a recent one. Uvaṭa, the first Bhāshyakāra, is a Kashmirian of about 1100 A. D.

* द्वे सहस्रे शते न्यूने मन्त्रे वाजसनेयके। (शते न्यूने साति).

The Sarvānukramanī and the Bhāshya give the Ṛishis of the sūktas or rather Adhyāyas as also the metres and deities as usual. The Rishi names are often conjectural or fictitious; for example, the first Adhyāya or sūkta is attributed to Prajāpati. The last Adhyāya, which is the Iśāvāsya Upanishad, Uvaṭa Bhāshya attributes to Dadhyañ Ātharvaṇa while the Sarvānukrama gives Brahman as its Ṛishi. The Ajmer edition gives Dīrghatamas as the Ṛishi of this sūkta. As the original Black Yajurveda has no Ṛishis, it seems probable that this divergence of Ṛishis in the White Yajurveda is due to subsequent different conjectures about them.

There are different Ṛishis assigned to different parts of the same sūkta or Adhyāya which shows that its verses are taken from different sources and where the verses are taken from the Ṛigveda, the Ṛigveda Ṛishi is naturally assigned to it. But this is not always the case, as the well-known Gāyatrī mantra of Brahmins appears as verse 2 of the 30th chapter and Nārāyaṇa is given as its Ṛishi. The Purusha-sūkta appears as chapter 31 and its Ṛishi is Nārāyaṇa as in the Ṛigveda.

We do not find anywhere the padas in this Veda enumerated, as in other Vedas, either in Bhāshyas or Sarvānukramaṇīs, though there is a Pada recitation for this Veda as for others. Taking the average of words as 15 for each mantra as in the Ṛigveda and three letters for each word, we may find out the approximate extent of this Sanhitā. The Pada saṅkhyā comes to about (1975 × 15) 29625 and the Akshara-saṅkhyā to about 88875. This Sanhitā is, therefore, about one-third of the Black Yajurveda Sanhitā and about one-fifth of that of the Ṛigveda.

The Ajmer edition gives the first twenty chapters as Pūrvārdha and the next twenty as Uttarārdha. This is, however, not an old division. The Charaṇa-Vyūha in giving the extent as 1900 verses says that this number includes the Khila and the Śukriya portions. In the Anuvākādyāya printed at the end of the Nirnayasagar edition, we find that the last five or chapters 36 to 40 are called Śukriya, the number of their Anuvākas being given as 11 and the ten preceding chapters viz. 26 to 35 are given as Khila, the number of Anuvākas in them being 35. It may be added that the four chapters 22 to 25 are called Āśva, the number of Anuvākas iu them being given as 49. These four are indeed Aśvamedha chapters. Uvaṭa's and Mahīdhara's Bhāsyas also call the chapters 26 to 35 Khila and the latter calls the last five chapters Śukriya, quoting a Śruti authorly for the name (दध्यङ् आथर्वणः शुक्रमेतं यज्ञं विदांचकार १४-१-१-२०). The later portion of this Sanhitā, therefore, seems to be chapters 26 to 40.

The nineteen to twenty-one chapters are called in the Anuvākānukramaṇī Saura and the preceding eleven to eighteen Chit ; while the first ten are treated together as containing 119 Anuvākas and are given no name. The first twenty-five chapters appear thus to be the old portion according to both contents and the tradition that 26 to 35 are Khila and 36 to 40 are Śukriya.

The Charaṇavyūha speaks of 17 branches of the White Yajurveda, two of which, the Mādhyandina and the Kāṇva, are well-known. The extent above given is of the first Śākhā Sanhitā while the Kāṇva Sanhitā recension is said to have 2086 mantras including Khila and Śukriya. The Brāhmaṇa of this Śākhā is the Śatapatha of seventeen Kāṇḍas while the Mādhyandina Śākhā recognises Śatapatha Brāhmaṇa of only fourteen Kāṇḍas. The Brāhmaṇa is said to be four times the Sanhitā in the first and three times in the second. This is rather inexplicable unless we hold that the latter divides the Śatapatha into a smaller number of sentences. The Pada, Krama and Jaṭā recitations exist in both these Śākhās.

This Sanhitā gives the subjects nearly in the same order as the Black Yajurveda Sanhitā, the first part of which treats of Pārvaṇa (fortnightly) sacrifices and of Soma in the next and the first ten chapters of the White Sanhitā correspond to these. Next come the fire-altar ceremony called Chit contained in 11 to 18 chapters. Next follow the Sautra or Soma-pressing corresponding to the 19 to 21 chapters and finally comes the Aśvamedha corresponding to which are the 22 to 25 chapters of the White Yajurveda.

The arguments advanced by Macdonell to hold that the first 18 chapters form the real old portion and that there were four stages in the development of the White Sanhitā do not seem to be strong enough. He admits the testimony of Kātyāyana that the chapters 26 to 35 are Khila (26 to 29 chapters being supplementary and 30 to 39 entirely new). And yet he looks upon the first 18 chapters only as old. The only argument for this is that these chapters alone are commented on in the first nine chapters of the Śatapatha. But it is conceded that there are a few comments on the following seventeen also. More or less comment is made according to necessity and importance and hence more or less comment can not be made a basis for inferring that the latter seventeen are not old.

The Yajurveda, both Black and White, extol Rudra which deity appears in their time to have advanced in popular favour. Chapter XVI of the White Yajuh Sanhitā is the well-known Rudrādhyāya of the older Sanhitā condensed and altered here and there. Macdonell points out, however, that even here we do not come across the two names of Śiva, Īsāna and Mahādeva, though other names of Śiva occur. It is still more interesting to remark that there is yet no indication of the identification of the Rudra worship of the Aryans with the Liṅga-worship of the non-Aryans which was an established fact in the days of the Mahābhārata of about 250 B. C. This identification was made later probably than even the Atharvaveda which in its sūktas 4 and 5 Kaṇḍa XV mentions both Īśāna and Mahādeva along with Paśupati, Ugra, Bhava, and Śarva &c. but contains no mention of Liṅga-worship In the days of the Atharvaveda the Aryans had advanced into Aṅga i. e. beyond Benares where it may be surmised that the first identification of Linga-worship with Rudra-worship took place and the Śiva god of which consequently became the holiest in the whole of India.

Both the Yajurveda Sanhitās are mainly concerned with sacrifice and we find most sacrifices described therein. The White Sanhitā, however, goes beyond the Black in mentioning, with many details, Purushamedha or human sacrifce. The Indo-Aryans had horse-sacrifice from the most ancient times; but the Purushamedha is not mentioned both in the Ṛigveda and the Black Yajurveda. According to the 30th chapter of the White Sanhitā, Purushamedha consists of the sacrifice of a hundred and eighty-four human beings! The Aśvamedha is an orgie execrable enough, but this holocaust of human beings, if it was an actual sacrifice, strikes us as both terrible and execrable. It seems to have been borrowed from the non-Aryan cannibal races of the south as some striking similarities are discernible. In the last verse 22 of chapter XXX, eight uncouth men are to be slaughtered in sacrifice to Prajāpati, viz. one extraordinarily tall, short, fat, lean, white, black, hairless and hairy man. These enormities of nature were also favourite victims with the Aztecs of Mexico as also the Rākshasas of Ceylon, as described in the Conquest of Mexico by Prescott and the Rāmāyaṇa of Vālmiki. The Indo-Aryans had by the time of the White Yajurveda extended their kingdoms as far as Mithilā and imperialism had set in. In the Mahābhārata, Jarāsandha king of Magadha is shown as comtemplating the performance of a Purushamedha for obtaining the highest power; and Śrī Kṛishṇa is shown as saying that Jarāsandha deserved death for the same. Purushamedha, therefore, may be looked upon as the wildest and most absurd development of the cult of sacrifice and there was naturally a revulsion of feeling leading on the other side to the highest development of the Vedānta philosophy.

In this chapter the next sūkta is the well-known Purusha-sūkta of the Ṛigveda which does not appear in the Black Yajurveda Sanhitā. It is a strange application of this philosophic sūkta to an actual Purushamedha or human sacrifice. It is probably from this application that certain scholars, notably Prof. Rajawade of Poona, look upon this sūkta as describing an actual human sacrifice which is described therein as *an old* sacrifice and they believe that human sacrifice was an old institution with the Aryans (तानि धर्माणि प्रथमान्यासन्). But we have shown already that this hymn in the Ṛigveda is addressed to the highest all-pervading Purusha or God and has nothing to do with human sacrifice. The creation of the world from Virāṭa Purusha or God Manifest is metaphorically looked upon by the Ṛishi as a sacrifice. Sacrifice is an old rite with the Aryans and even the creation of the world seemed to them to be a sacrifice of the Manifest. Its application, therefore, in the White Yajurveda to an actual human sacrifice, illustrates the immortal maxim of Gibbon, "What is once rhetoric becomes subsequently logic."

It may be objected here that the story of Sunaḥśepa belongs to the Ṛigvedic times and proves the existence of Purushamedha even then. But this story appears to have been elaborated in the times of the Brāhmaṇas after the Vājasaneyi Sanhitā was formulated sanctioning and describing Purushmedha. Secondly, the alleged intended sacrifice of his son by Hariśchandra in pursuance of a vow is a different thing altogether from the Purushamedha described by the White Yajurveda. That story resembles the story of Abraham in the Bible, as we will show later when speaking of the Aitareya Brāhmaṇa which gives it; and the Bible story has never been looked upon as showing that human sacrifice obtained among the Jews.

Sacrifice then attained at this time its extremest development. Nay, as Macdonell truly observes, it became all in all and the correct performance of every detail became all important. "Its power is now so great that it not merely influences but compels the the gods to do the will of the sacrificing priest." Even gods, it may further be remarked, obtained god-hood, by performing particular sacrifices. And this power it derived from the correct pronouncing of the prayer and the sacrificial mantras. If any wrong accent was uttered Indra was believed to strike the utterer with his vajra. Mantras again derived their power not from their meanings but from their words, nay, their sounds. For synonymous words can not be substituted, says the Śatapatha, for the words of any Ṛiks. The mantras which word includes the Ṛiks as well as the prose sacrificial formulas are revealed and eternal and the Ṛishis only saw them as they existed from eternity. As Macdonell points out, one is surprised to find unnecessary words and even sounds in Yajurveda mantras. But this is inevitable when once the theory is established that mantras have power not from their meaning but from their sound. This theory seems to have been fully established in the days of the White Yajurveda and its Brāhmaṇa the Śatapatha. It soon led to the compilation of the Atharvaveda, as we shall presently show, the mantras of which used as charms and spells derive their power from their sounds only. We find sometimes strange words used in such Atharva verses as VI 16-3 (तौविलिकेवेलया वायमैलव ऐलयीत्). Hence also arises the necessity of constantly re-reciting whole formulas with only the change of a word or two, though the repetition strikes us in the present age as absurd; for each rite has to be performed separately with the full wording of the mantra, only suitably changed, in order that it should be efficacious and even legal. Indeed, in many modern Council proceedings in India, one hears such formulas uttered again and again when the Finance Minister puts each item of revenue or expenditure before the Council. These Council proceedings in fact strike one as a sacrifice and one can well realize how the Hoṭṛi, the Adhvaryu and the Udgātṛi repeated formulasover and over again as oblations were offered like items of revenue or expenditure, put for sanction.

Macdonell is, however, we think, not right when

he says "Not only do we find the four castes firmly established, but as one of the later books of the Vājasaneyi Sanhitā shows most of the mixed castes known in later times are already found to exist" (p. 184). The book referred to here is the 30th chapter which speaks of Purushamedha. It is a chapter in the Khila section of the Sanhitā. But keeping this point aside, this chapter does not speak of the mixed castes, but of the several professions which were then practised. The four castes are still the only castes existing and the first four caste victims for a human sacrifice are a Brāhmaṇa, a Kshatriya, a Vaiśya and a Śūdra. Next are mentioned a thief, a fighter, a klība, an iron-worker, a harlot, a māgadha, a sūta, a dancer, an actor and so on. Some of these words are difficult to understand, but that these are different professions and not mixed castes is clear from the last verse 22 of the sūkta which states that the māgadha, gambler, harlot and klība are to be neither Śūdra nor Brahmin. This shows that a māgadha is here looked upon as likely to be a Śūdra or a Brahmin which can only mean that māgadha is not here a mixed-caste man but a singer of praises in a king's court. The Bhāshyakāra Mahīdhara here adds the gloss, "Caste being restricted with regard to these four, the others may be of any of the four castes." Sūta would thus be a chariot-driver and not a mixed-caste man and might be a Brahmin, Kshatriya, Vaiśya or Śūdra by caste. It is curious that Uvaṭa, the earlier Bhāshyakāra, gives no commentary on this sūkta. Māgadha, Sūta &c. acquired caste-meanings later. Mahīdhara, in spite of his last gloss, when interpreting Māgadha interprets it as born in Magadha country or born of a Kshatriya woman from a Vaiśya male, and Sūta as born of a Brahmin woman from a Kshatriya. To our mind, the last verse makes such interpretation incorrect and every one of these words in our view indicates a different profession only, the four castes being the only castes recognised in Vedic days. Even the Atharvaveda speaks of the four castes only as will be shown in the chapter on that Veda.

The history of the growth of the mixed castes may be given here succinctly. Formerly, in Vedic times, as even the Manu Smṛiti lays down, the four castes intermarried in the descending order and the progeny belonged always to the caste of the father. Later on, in Smṛiti period this rule was restricted to the first two wives and the progeny of the dvyantarā wife was assigned a lower intermediate position. Later still, progeny of a wife of a different caste was assigned to a mixed caste, later still to the caste of the mother and finally in the Bhāshya period marriage outside one's caste was altogether prohibited (see our History of Medieval Hindu India Vol III p. 395).

[There is a Sarvānukrama Sūtra for the White Yajurveda attributed to Kātyāyana who is probably the same as the author of the Ṛigveda Sarvānukramaṇī. Although for the Black Yajurveda, the reciting of Ṛishi, Chhandas, and Devatā is not necessary for any mantra (for in fact this is nowhere given, nor can it be given now as stated already), the White Yajurveda mantras require such recital and these are given in this Sarvānukramaṇī Sūtra (printed at the end of the Nirṇayasāgar edition). The metres are the same as those detailed for the Ṛigveda; indeed the same sūtras are repeated here. The Ṛishis are also the same as those for the Ṛigveda. In each chapter there are verses of many authors put together and hence there are many Ṛishis for each chapter and these are given in order in the Sūtra, (alphabetical list of these is appended at the end). The Devatās or deities are also nearly the same as those in the Ṛigveda. Both Ṛishis and Devatās are sometimes imaginary like Prajāpati or Savitṛi, or Nārāyaṇa given as Ṛishis. These have no historical importance as in the Ṛigveda. The Devatās of the several metres are given by Kātyāyana, as mentioned even in Ṛigvedic verses viz. Agni of Gāyatri, Savitṛi of Ushṇik, Soma of Anusṭup, Bṛihaspati of Bṛihatī, Varuṇa of Pankti, Indra of Trishṭup, Visvedevaḥ of Jagatī, Mitra of Virāj, Aruṇa of Svarāj, Prajāpati of Chhandas, Vāyu of Vichchhandaṣ, Purusha of Dvipadā and Brahmā of Ekapadā. He adds 'all Ṛiks are devoted to Agni, all Yajuḥs to Vāyu (Rudra) and all Sāmans to Savitṛi.' This is in some respects true. It is difficult to find out which the fifteen mantras are which Yājnavalkya obtained from the Sun].

NOTE:—PERSONS REQUIRED FOR PURUSHAMEDHA.

The details of the persons, 184 in number, required for Purushamedha given in Adhyāya XXX in detail, are interesting as throwing light on the social condition of the time; and we give these details in this note for the curious reader. First are mentioned the four caste victims; any Brahmin, Rājanya, Vaiśya and Śūdra would do. Next come persons following particular professions or of particular descriptions and it is astonishing that women and even boys are mentioned in the list. Some names are unintelligible though Mahīdhara in his commentary tries to explain them. These we give in Sanskrit as they are found. These persons are as follows:—a thief, a fighter, a Klība, an Ayogū (iron-finder), a Punśchalī (whore), a Māgadha, a Sūta, a dancer, a Rebhya, a Strīsakha, a carpenter, a potter's son, a smith, a jeweller, a Vāpa (sower), an arrow-maker, a bow-maker, a maker of bow-strings, a rope-maker, a hunter, a dog-keeper, a Punjishtha boy, a Nishāda, a madman, a Vrātya, an Unmatta, a Pratipada, a gambler, an Akitava, a female bamboo-basket-maker, a Kanṭakakara, a paramour, an Upapati, a Parivitta (elder unmarried brother), a Parivividāna (younger brother marrying before his elder brother), the husband of a younger sister married before her elder sister, a dresser, a Smarakārī, a companion, an Anurādha, a giver of flower presents, a deformed man, a pigmy, a physician, an astronomer, a teller of omens, an assistant of the same, a Praśnavivāka, an elephant-keeper, a horse-keeper, a cowherd, a shepherd, a goat-keeper, a cultivator, a brewer, a house-guard, a treasury-guard, a charioteer's helpmate, a bringer of fuel (from forest), a keeper of fire, an Abhishektā (bath keeper), a food server, a Peshitā (scratcher of idols), a Prakaritā, an Upasektā, an Upamanthitā, a washer of clothes, a dyer, a man with thievish heart, a tale-bearer (Piśuna), a door-keeper, a fellow door-keeper, a servant, a Paridhānaka, a sycophant, a horse-rider, a body-guard, a heater of iron, a Nisara, a Yoktā, an Abhisartā (tracer of thieves), a Viyoktṛi, a Trishiṇa, a Manashrit, an Anjanakārī (a woman who prepares Anjana or black pigment), a woman who makes scabbards, a sterile woman, a mother of twins, a mother of dead children, a Paryāyiṇi, a woman who is not a mother yet, an Atitvarī, an Ātishkadvarī, a Vijarjarā, a Palikni (white-haired), an Ajinasandha (joiner of skins), a worker in skins, a Dhaivara (fisherman's son), a Dāsa, a Vainda, a Śaushkala, a Mārgāra (hunter's son), a Kaivarta, an Ānda, a Maināla, a Parṇaka (Bhil), a Kirāta, a Jambhaka, a Kimpurusha, a Paulkasa, a Hiranyakāra, a Vānija, a Glavin, a Sidhmala, a Jāgaraṇa (constantly awake), a Svapna (sleepy), a Janavādin, an Apragalbha, a Prachchhida, a Kitava (gambler), an Adinavadarsa, a Kalpina, an Adhikalpina, a Sabhāsthāṇu, (these four are connected with gambling), a Govyachha, a Goghāta, a man who begs for cow's flesh, a Charakāchārya, a Sailaga, an Artana, a Bhasha, a Bahuvādin, a dumb man, an Ādambaraghāta, a player on the vīnā, a Tūṇavadhma, a blower of caunch, a Vanapa, a Dāvapa, a Punschalu, a Kāri, a Śabalya, a Grāmaṇya (the leader of a village), a Gaṇaka (village accountant), an Abhikrośaka (village crier), a Vīṇāvāda, a Pānighna, a Tūṇavadhma, a Talava, a Pīvāna, a Pīṭha-sarpi, a Chāṇḍāla, a Vanśanarti, a Khalati, a Khalvāṭa (bald), a green-eyed man, a Kirmīra, a Kilāsa, a man with yellowish white eyes, a black-yellowish-eyed man and then the last eight, namely one extraordinarily fat, lean, tall, short, white, black, hairless and hairy man. The list is long and tiresome. There are only three Sūta, Rathakāra and Māghadha which can be interpreted as meaning mixed castes; but these are plainly chariot-driver, chariot-maker, and panegyrist-profession man. Low class people of several sorts are mentioned such as Dāsa, Kaivarta, Dhīvara and Chāṇḍāla. Four gambling-house office-bearers are mentioned, but what their functions were does not appear, the Sabhāsthāṇu probably being the umpire. It is probable that these victims were not actually slaughtered. They were bound to the slaughter stakes as for slaughter, and after being Upākṛita or formally dedicated to the respective deities they were released. There is a special deity named for each victim, the deities being thus 184. They include the four Yugas, the five Samvatsaras and other imaginary deities.

It is interesting to note that among the victims appears a charakāchārya who is to be offered to sin or Dushkṛita. If charaka is taken to mean a wandering teacher of the Kaṭha and other branches of the Black Yajurveda, this shows either that these itinerant teachers, mentioned even by Patanjali in his Mahābhāshya, were really a sinful set of men or that there was great enmity between them and the followers of the White Yajurveda. It is necessary to point out that the Taittirīya Brāhmaṇa also mentions this victim and to the same deity viz the deity of sin (Kāṇḍa III 16). Now Uvata and Mahīdhara in their Bhāshyas on Vājasaneyi Samhitā merely explain charakāchārya as चरकाणाम् गुरुम् while Sāyana commenting on the same word in the Taittirīya Brāhmaṇa interprets it as वंशाग्रनर्तनस्य शिक्षयितारम्. Nay he interprets दुष्कृत also differently as दुर्घटकार्यकरणाभिमानिने. Sāyana clearly gives another interpretation to prevent a charaka school teacher from incurring disrepute.

XII THE ATHARVAVEDA.

The last and the latest Veda is the Atharvaveda. That it is not included in the Trayīvidyā is the best proof of its late origin. Yet many of the hymns contained in the Atharvaveda are as old as the Ṛigvedic hymns. Indeed, some of them are taken from the Ṛigveda itself with alterations consciously or unconsciously made, such as the well-known Purusha-sūkta or the hymn to the waters "Āpo hi shṭhā" &c., This Veda chiefly contains mantras used in witch-craft or sorcery, in the curing of diseases, for destruction of enemies, giving encouragement to fighting warrriors and so on. These mantras must have been in use from old times, but they were not taken in the three earlier Vedas compiled by Vyāsa, for the obvious reason that their use was for mundane purposes. Indeed Sāyaṇa observes in the introduction to his commentary on the Atharvaveda that the three earlier Vedas are for spiritual ends while the fourth and last Atharvaveda is for both worldly and higher purposes. In the tenth Maṇḍala of the Ṛigveda, there are a few hymns no doubt intended for earthly use such as the humbling of a co-wife. But the Atharvaveda mainly consists of such hymns and only subsidiarily contains hymns intended solely for sacrificial or spiritual purposes. This Veda, therefore, contains, no doubt, many old hymns ; but its compilation was unquestionably made later than that of the other three Vedas. Vyāsa cannot be its compiler though later tradition started after the Mahābhārata, as given in Vishṇu Purāna, ascribes its compilation to Vyāsa and Sumantu is supposed to be that pupil of his to whom this Veda was specially entrusted. If a surmise is to be made as to who its compiler was, it may be suggested that Pippalāda was the first compiler of this Veda.* From a story in the Purāṇas, it appears that Pippalāda was a sister's son to Yājnavalkya who was sister's son to Vaisampāyana. It is probable that Pippalāda, on seeing that Yājnavalkya formulated a new Veda viz., the Vājaseneyī Samhitā, in protest against Vaiśampāyana, was himself emboldened and he formulated the Atharvaveda by bringing together the incantation mantras and by borrowing certain mantras from the Ṛigveda for ritual purposes in the same way as Yājnavalkya had borrowed some mantras from the old Taittirīya Samhitā. That these incantation mantras were used by Āngirasa sages and by Ātharvaṇas was well known. The name 'Atharvāṅgirasaḥ' or simply Ātharvaṇas or Āṅgirasas denoted usually, in Vedic days even, sorcerers or magicians, a meaning which recieves great support from the evil reputation of Magi priests in Persia. Āṅgirasas are said to be dreadful in

* MBh V. 19 (5-8) mentions that Aṅgiras composed the whole Veda and propitiated Indra who declared that the Veda would be known as Atharvāṅgirasaḥ and that Aṅgiras would have an oblation in sacrifices.

a Ṛigvedic hymn (X 108,10) even. The name which this fourth Veda was given was thus first Atharvāṅgirasah or Āṅgirasa and later Atharva only.

The Atharvaveda gives its own name as Atharvāṅgirasah along with the names of the other Vedas in X 7, 20. (यस्मादृचो अपातक्षन् यजुर्यस्मादपाकशन् । सामानि यस्य लोमान्यथर्वाङ्गिरसो मुखम्). Here and in one or two other places we have a mention of the fourth Veda as Atharvāṅgirasah and XIX 54,5 mentions Atharva and Aṅgiras separately (कालेऽयमंगिरादेवो अथर्वा चाधितिष्ठतः) thus showing that Atharvan and Aṅgiras were distinct personalities connected with the magical mantras. Bloomfield makes a distinction between the two sets, holding that Ātharvaṇa mantras were for good purposes while the Āṅgirasa mantras were for evil. And the evil reputation of the Āṅgirasa priests or mantras is attested to even by the Ṛigvedic verse noted above. But gradually the name of Āṅgirasa dropped out and thenceforth this Veda is generally known, even from the times of the Brāhmaṇas, as Atharva-veda. Thus the Chhāndogya Upnishad speaks of it along with Ṛigveda, Yajurveda and Sāmaveda as Atharva-Veda. The reason seems to be that Āṅgirasas are the composers of many good hymns also in the Ṛigveda. Indeed there is a whole book of the Āṅgirasas, Bhāradvāja and others, in the Ṛigveda. Their composing mantras or incantations for evil purposes was by and by forgotten. Brihaspati became the priest of the gods and he too must have composed mantras for doing evil to the Asuras. It is a remarkable thing that in the whole of the Ṛigveda there is no hymn by Atharvan. He seems to have composed mantras solely for secular purposes even though they might have been for doing good, such as antidotes against snake-poison and so on. His name, therefore, was restricted to this Veda gradually though in Ṛigvedic days Atharvaṇ and Aṅgiras were both known as composers of magic spells. A third Ṛishi appears also in the Atharva-veda as the composer of magic spells viz., Bhṛigu and the Bhṛigus must also have associated themselves with the Āṅgirasas in these practices. But their name also dropped out like that of the Āṅgirasas and for the same reason; and the name Ātharvaṇa finally remained as the name of this Veda. It is interesting to note that the Mahābhārata in a remarkable śloka mentions the four original stocks of Brahmin families as Bhṛigu, Angiras, Kaśhyapa and Vasishṭha. The Ātharvaṇas thus never seem to have come into India, for their name is not included in this list of four, nor is it included in the list of the seven great Ṛishis. Nor is it to be found in the gotra-pravara chapters of the Śrauta Sūtras. There are no Brahmins, so far as we know, who have Atharvan for their gotra or pravara Ṛishi, though many have Bhṛigu and Aṅgiras. The Ātharvaṇas, therefore, it seems, remained outside India and the fact that the word Athravan means a priest in Zend-Avesta strengthens the view that they remained in Persia. This may also account for the fact that no hymn by Atharvan appears in the Ṛigveda, Yajurveda or Sāmaveda.* After the promulgation of the Vājasaneyi Samhitā, Pippalāda probably put together the magic spells which were still current in India, though not considered religious and gave status to them by adding some philosophical, ceremonial and sacrificial sūktas. According to this view, the date of such compilation would be from about 3000 to 2500 B. C. i. e., after that of the Śatapatha Brāhmana composed by Yājnavalkya and before that of the Chhāndogya Upanishad which distinctly shows that the Ātharvaṇa Veda was already enunciated.

This compilation in course of time split into different recensions said to be nine, but two of these

* There are two hymns in Ṛigveda Maṇḍala X ascribed to Bhishak Ātharvaṇa and Bṛihaddiva Ātharvaṇa viz. 97 and 120. The first hymn is addressed to Oshadhis (plants) generally and the name Bhishak appears in one verse of it. It probably means a physician only. The hymn is not of the nature of a spell and medicine, as we know, subsequently became an adjunct of the Ṛigveda. The second hymn (120) is by Bṛihaddiva Ātharvaṇa and is addressed to Indra. The name Bṛihaddiva with Ātharvaṇa added is also mentioned in the last verse of it. The word Ātharvaṇa Sāyana explains as a son of Atharvan. We have, however, no hymn by Atharvan himself in the Ṛigveda and this hymn by one of his sons is the only hymn by an Ātharvaṇa found in the Ṛigveda.

But the sage Atharvan is mentioned in the Vedas as a very ancient sage, as one who first kindled fire. He, therefore, is a real being and belongs to the time when the Indo-Aryans and the Iranians were together in their ancient common home. The Iranians have preserved fire from that time and also the word Athravan meaning a fire-priest. Probably in India other sages kindled fire and even kings and their names were given to these fires which perhaps were, like the Iranian fire, long kept up.

are well known, viz. the Pippalāda or the Kashmirean and the Śaunakīya or the southern, the latter being chiefly current in Gujarat and Mahārāshtra. This latter has been published in several places and has been carefully scrutinized by scholars western and eastern. The Pippalāda recension has not yet been published but a birch-bark manuscript has been found, unfortunately with the first leaf wanting. The Mahābhāshya of Pantanjali mentions "Śam no devi" etc. as the first mantra in the Atharvaveda; but it is not the first mantra in the Śaunakīya recension as it is found and recited in southern India. Now the first page of the Pippalāda recension manuscript being wanting, it cannot definitely be stated if that mantra is at the beginning of the Pippalāda recension, though it is generally believed that it is so. As the Upākarma ceremony among the Ṛigveda as also other Veda Brahmins,when reciting the first mantra of each Veda, does recite this mantra still as the first verse of the Atharvaveda, the Mahābhāshya tradition is indubitably correct and this shows that the Śaunakīya recension was not known to Patanjali. The Pippalāda recension seems really to be the earlier one for other reasons also, as will appear later on. The mantra "Śam no devi" &c. is in the 6th hymn of the first book in the Śaunakīya recension.

European scholars have studied this Veda with their usual thoroughness and Indian scholars from ancient times down to the present have also done the same. For there is a Prātiśākhya of this Veda, as also two Anukramaṇīs, the earlier one being called Panchapaṭalikā. There are two Śūtras attached to this Veda viz. the Kauśika Sūtra and the Vaitāna Sūtra and one Brāhmaṇa viz. the Gopatha. Of these we shall speak later on in detail; but these discuss the Atharvaveda in full detail and help in many ways modern scholars as they helped Sāyana who wrote a Bhāśya on this Veda about 1400 A.D. S. P. Pandit edited this Bhāshya in 1890 in India and Roth, Whitney, Bloomfield and others in the west have also published the Śaunakīya text and even translated it. With the help of these guides it is possible to discuss the various topics concerning this Veda such as its extent, its formation, its Ṛishis, its Devatās and so on. These writers mainly discuss the Atharvaveda in the Śaunakīya recension and not the Pippalāda one, though Whitney has also compared the two recensions carefully and pointed out their differences. We have not the advantage of looking into this recension and we will confine our remarks to the Śaunakīya recension.

The Śaunakīya recension of the Atharvaveda is divided into twenty books called Kāṇḍas divided into Anuvākas and the latter into sūktas in all about 730. We say 'about' explicitly to show that there is a divergence of editions in this respect. Bloomfield gives this number as 730; but Pandit's edition gives the number as 759 while in the Ajmer edition the number is 731 and Whitney gives the number as 598. It seems that the number is increased or reduced according as the editor splits up individual sūktas into two or more according to the ascription or Viniyoga of the parts to different purposes. The matter, however, in all the editions is apparently the same. Similarly the number of Ṛiks (verses) or mantras is given as 6000 by Bloomfield (probably in round figures), while Whitney gives the number as 5038 (p. c. XLVII). Here also probably the number differs owing to the combining or splitting up of verses. It is clear that the Anukramaṇīs have not counted the exact number of sūktas or of verses for this Veda as they did for the Śākala recension of the Ṛigveda, the number of sūktas in which is uniformly given as 1017 and of verses as 10580¼, In Pandit's introduction we find that several Gujarat manuscripts give the number of verses as 6015 while one gives the Granṭha-Saṅkhyā as 6630. As Grantha according to modern Sanskrit writers, means 32 letters this gives the figure for letters as 6680×32=2,13,760 while the number of letters for the Ṛigveda is 4,32,000. The number of hymns and of letters for the Atharvaveda as compared with the Ṛigveda shows that its extent exceeds one-half of the latter by a small quantity. The twenty Kāṇḍas again have been divided into four sets or Prapāṭhakas, the first containing seven, the next eighth to twelfth, the third thirteenth to eighteenth and the fourth the last two. The apparent plan of the compiler of this Veda shows itself in this arrangement. The last two books are practically a *Khila* portion and did not probably form part of the first compilation. Leaving these out of view, we find that the first seven Kāṇḍas contain short hymns on miscellaneous subjects and these again are arranged in this order viz. the first book contains hymns of four verses, the second of five and so on to the fifth which contains hymns consisting of eight verses. The sixth book contains hymns of three verses and the seventh of one verse only. This is the rule, there being exceptions here and there which are looked upon by the Anukramaṇīs as Vikṛiti or abnormal. The second set of books VIII to XII contains long hymns of a miscellaneous character while the third set XIII to XVIII contains long hymns on one subject each. Thus book XIII is called Rohita Kāṇḍa because it has hymns addressed to the red sun; Book XIV is called Vivāha Kāṇḍa, consisting as it does of two hymns on the marriage ceremony. Book XV is called Vrātya Kāṇḍa as it contains hymns addressed to Vrātya; what Vrātya is it is difficult to decide as both Sāyana and Whitney do not explain it; but it is certainly not the Vrātya of the Smṛitis viz. Aryans devoid of the Sanskāra of Upanayana.* Book XVI is on bad dreams and book XVII has one hymn addressed to Vishāsahi or the Trenchant One. Book XVIII is called Yama-Kāṇḍa and it contains many hymns to be recited at funeral ceremonies. This Kāṇḍa is looked upon as inauspicious and is not learnt by heart by Vaidikas. That the first or original compilation was of this extent and in this order is apparent from hymn 23 of the nineteenth Kāṇḍa which is plainly supplementary. This hymn gives in a way the contents of the Atharva-

* Vrātya appears to mean here God himself.

veda and describes its Ṛishis in the manner used by the Āśvalāyana Gṛihya-Sūtra viz. Śatarchins, Mādhyamas, Kshudrasūktas and Mahāsūktas as follows.–

'Svāhā' to the Ṛishis (or sūktas) of 4 verses from among the Ātharvaṇas, of five verses and so on up to Ṛishis of eighteen verses ; then 'Svāhā to the nineteen and the twenty, again Svāhā to the great Kāṇḍa to those of three verses, of one verse, to the insignificant (Kshudra), of less than one verse.' This description is intended to apply to the first twelve Kāṇḍas. For the next five are hereafter described by their names and the number of their hymns as follows:– 'Svāhā to the Rohita hymns (XIII), to the hymns (two) of Sūryā (XIV), to the two Vrātya hymns, (XV) to the two Prajāpati hymns (XVI), to the Vishāsahi hymn (XVII), to the Māngalika hymns (XVIII). The duel number of Vrātya and Prajāpati hymns does not correspond to the existing hymns in these Kāṇḍas. But as the number is significantly correct of the other Kāṇḍas, it is probable that the number of hymns in these two Kāṇḍas has increased after the addition of this nineteenth Kāṇḍa. The hymns of this (XIX) Kāṇḍa, according to Whitney, are distributed over other Kāṇḍas in the Pippalāda recension. Bloomfield has pointed out that with the exception of the Kuntāpa sūktas, the hymns of the twentieth Kāṇḍa are all taken out of the Ṛigveda, being required for recitation at the Soma sacrifice as Śastras and Stotras according to the Vaitāna Sūtra. About 1200 of the Atharva mantras in all are taken from the Ṛigveda chiefly from the tenth, first and eighth books; and of the 143 hymns of Book XX, all but ten are taken bodily without any change (Macd. p. 186).

THE ṚISHIS OF THE ATHARVAVEDA

The above noted hymn XIX, 23 is distinctly a later hymn, describing the Atharva Sanhitā with its hymns as it nearly is to-day. It mentions no names of the Ṛishis of the sūktas but uses the general term "Ātharvana" as it subsequently was assigned to the Ṛishis of this Veda, supplementing the names of Āngirasa and Bhṛigu. Here these Ṛishis are collectively called Ātharvaṇa. The Sāyana-Bhāshya as published by Pandit gives no names of the Rishis or seers of the several hymns; and the Ajmer edition also gives no names of seers. The Gopatha Brāhmaṇa story given in the beginning of the Brāhmaṇa that Brahmā first created Bhṛigu from his sweat and Bhṛigu became Atharvan and the latter became Aṅgiras, that Atharvan performed austerities and twenty Ātharvaṇa Ṛishis were born viz., those of one verse, of two verses and so on and these saw the Āngirasa mantras. "The Ṛishis being twenty the Veda was also divided into twenty Kāṇḍas". This story is no doubt absurd as the twenty Kaṇḍas are not each of a separate Ṛishi and it has been properly rejected by Bloomfield as a later one. But all the same the story belongs to the Gopatha Brāhmaṇa which, though a very late production, cannot be later than the Sarvānukramaṇīs, the older Panchapatalikā and the later bigger one. It seems, therefore, probable that for a long time the Ṛishis of the hymns were called generally Ātharvaṇas or Atharvan and Āngirasa with the addition of Bhṛigu and Brahman here and there. The dates of these two Ankramaṇīs are not known; but apparently they are later than even the Sāyana Bhāshya which could not have ignored them. The Bhāshya does not, therefore, give the Ṛishis of individial sūktas; but Whitney in his translation of the Atharvaveda gives the Ṛishis of the sūktas from the Sarvānukrámaṇīs. These Ṛishi names are very often fancied and fanciful like Uchchhochana, Unmochana &c. The names of the Ṛishis of the sūktas which are taken from the Ṛigveda are taken naturally enough from that Veda, such as Sindhudvīpa the name of the author of the sūkta 'Śam no devī'; but this is not necessarily always the case. Even in the Ṛigveda, the Ṛishi name is sometimes coined from the contents of the hymn; as for example Nārāyaṇa, the name of the Ṛishi of the popular Purushasūkta (X, 90) or Sūryā the name of the Ṛishi of the wedding hymn (X, 85). These names are the same in A. V. This method of coining names is oftener followed by the Sarvānukramaṇīs in assigning authors to the hymns of the Atharvaveda and hymns are assigned to Brahman, Prajāpati, Yama &c. XIX, 13 is assigned to Apratiratha (the matchlesss warrior), a coined name assigned to the author of the same hymn in the Ṛigveda (X 103) also. Hymns against snake poison are naturally enough assigned to Garutman meaning the heavenly eagle. The total number of Ṛishis mentioned in the Anukarmaṇīs is not large and Whitney has given an index of these names which will be found in our general index of Ṛishis given at the end. It is remarkable that for the Vrātya hymns no Ṛishi is assigned and that the Ṛishi assigned to the funeral hymn is Atharvan. There are 175 hymns assigned to Atharvan and 100 hymns assigned to Brahman (Whitney p. 1038) and hence also this Veda may have been called Atharvaveda or Brahmaveda. The hymns assigned to Atharvāngiras are only 17 and to Angiras 15. This will also explain why these names as denoting this Veda subsequently fell out of use. (Atharvāṇgirasa may be explained as a Dvandva compound, meaning Atharvan and Angiras, or more properly perhaps as Ātharvāṇa the same as Āngirasa (Karmadhāraya). Curiously enough, three hymns against worms are ascribed to Kaṇva as also three for winning the love of a woman. Four hymns for success in gambling are ascribed to Bādarāyaṇi. It may, however, be noted that there are very few names of Ṛigvedic fame in the list of these Ṛishis. Vasishṭha, Gṛitsamada and so on are conspicuous by their absence. There are one or two hymns only assigned to Viśvāmitra and Kaśyapa who may have composed some magic spells against evil. The Gāyatrī of Viśvāmitra is strangely enough not to be found in the Atharvaveda. The Ṛigvedic Ṛishis are, however, respectfully remembered among the names or Pitṛis in the funeral Kāṇḍa (XVIII 3 15–16) viz., Kaṇva, Kakshīvān, Purunīdha, Agastya,

Jamadagni, Atri, Kaśyapa and Vāmadeva.* This is natural as the Ṛigvedic Ṛishis and the Ṛigveda as also Yajuh and Sāman were honoured by all Brahmins in Vedic times, no difference based on Veda having till then arisen among Brahmins.

METRES.

The Atharvaveda consists chiefly of verses but there is considerable prose in it also, very often in the Brāhmaṇa style repeating words again and again. The verses are generally in the Anushṭup metre, Gāyatrī and Trishṭup also occurring now and then. It is remarkable that the seven chief metres of Vedic poetry are given by name in XIX and a hymn of the eighth Kāṇḍa (VIII 5-9) gives the number of syllables in them increasing by four successively. That the Vedic poets must have been conversant with the different names and the quantities of the metres they used goes without question; but this reference in the hymn to the several metres and their differing syllables and certain irregularities in them shows that there was already a deal of study in prosody. It seems that the longer metres of more than 48 syllables, Dhṛiti &c. were not yet recognised though stray examples of them do occur in the Ṛigveda. The metrical composition of the Atharva

* कण्वः कक्षीवान् पुरुमीढोऽगस्त्यः श्यावाश्वः सोभर्यर्चनानाः ।
विश्वामित्रोयं जमदग्निरत्रिरवन्तु नः कश्यपो वामदेवः ॥१५॥
विश्वामित्र जमदग्ने वसिष्ठ भरद्वाज गोतम वामदेव ।
शर्दिर्नो अत्रिरग्रभीन्नमोभिः सुशंसासः पितरो मृडता नः ॥१६॥

hymns is, however, irregular and not finished like that of the Ṛigvedic hymns.

DEITY AND ASCRIPTION.

The deities (Devatās) of the several hymns and their ascription (Viniyoga) are also given in the two Anukramaṇīs and they are also given in Sāyana's Bhāshya from the Sūtras and various other sources. The deities are the usual Vedic ones, Indra, Varuṇa, Agni, Sūrya and so on. But there are many hymns in which the deities are quite different being earthly obejects and are not inferable from the contents or their Viniyoga or ascription; they must have been given by the Sūtras and the Anukramaṇīs from actual practice as also from contents though not always suggested by them. As stated already, the hymns to be used solely for sacrifice are very few. Most of the Atharvavedic hymns are used as spells or incantations for various purposes which are grouped under distinct heads by writers as follows:—I Bhaishajyāni or hymns for medical purposes, II Āyushyāṇi for long life, III Abhichārakāṇi for sorcery, IV Krityāpratiharaṇāni for destroying the sorceries of others, V Strīkarmāṇi for securing the love of women, VI Rājakarmāṇi relating to royalty such as for coronation, battles &c, VII Saumannasyāni for securing one-mindedness or influencing assemblies, VIII for prosperity in agriculture, cattle &c. and IX for expiation of sins. There are some highly philosophical and theosophical hymns also, especially in the tenth *Kāṇḍa* which explain why four out of the ten chief Upanishads are attached to this Veda. These varicus purposes are served not only by reciting these hymns as spells but by using certain herbs also and this embodies the earliest attempts at medicine. There is one hymn in XIX reciting the Nakshatras which is an advance on the Nakshatra sūkta of the Taittirīya Sanhitā as it mentions Abhijit. The list, however, begins with the usual Krittikās. XIX 8 the next hymn actually states that the mansions of moon are 28 and also mentions Yogas, while the next (XIX 9) mentions Ulkās or shooting stars and other astronomical phenomena with their astrological evil prognostications.* This Kāṇḍa is a later addition and these facts therein are a further proof of its lateness.

ATHARVAVEDA AS HISTORY.

The hymns of the Atharvaveda are mostly spells and incantations and hence they contain very few facts which can be of historical interest. We rarely come across such a statement as is contained in V 19 भृगुं हिंसित्वा सृंजया वैतहव्या पराभवन् ॥. These hymns extending over a very long period of Indo-Aryan history however, show the social condition of the people during that long period. The Indo-Aryans had advanced as far as Magadha and Anga which are distinctly mentioned in a hymn (V 22) against fever called Takman in this Veda. Takman is called upon

* नक्षत्रमुल्काभिहतं शमस्तु नः शं नोभिचाराः शमु सन्तु कृत्याः ॥
शं नो निखाताबल्या शमुल्काः देशोपसर्गाः शमु नो भवन्तु ॥ 9.

to depart into "Magadha and Anga" on the east and into "Gāndhāra, Mūjavat (Mt) and Bālhika beyond." This shows that the Aryan land extended from Gāndhāra on the west to Anga on the east. Bālhika in this hymn is said to be beyond Mūjavat and thus Gāndhāra was probably included in the Aryan land. The disease prevalent in this Indo-Aryan land was fever as now and it is asked to depart beyond its limits and go to its own habitat viz. Mūjavat, Bālhika and Mahāvṛisha; ओको अस्य मूजवन्तः ओको अस्य महावृषाः। यावज्जातस्तक्मंस्तावानासि बल्हिकेषु न्योचरः ॥५॥ (What this tract महावृष is cannot be determined; but Bālhika is modern Balkh). It is curious to find that in one verse of this hymn (V 22, 7), Takman is asked to go to a Śūdra fat woman and shake her. तक्मन् मूजवतो गच्छ बाल्हिकान् वा परस्तरान। शूद्रामिच्छ प्रफर्व्यां तां तक्मन् वीव धूनुहि ॥ It seems that malarial fevers prevailed more among the Śūdras in the Indo-Aryan land than among the Aryan people.

This and several other hymns chiefly show that the people were divided into four castes. The three higher castes, together called Ārya, being sharply divided from the fourth called Śūdra. The Āryas, however, did not at this time hate or oppress the Śūdras and blessings are invoked on *both* Ārya and Śūdra प्रियं सर्वस्य उत शूद्र उत आर्ये ॥ (XIX 6). The Kshatriya and Vaiśya are mentioned in IV 22 and Indra is asked to make them prosperous. Viś are the settled agriculturist Aryans and form the subjects and the king, a Kshatriya, is their ruler. Brahmins who are mentioned in several hymns had by this time begun to be hated or oppressed by kings and one hymn (V 19) contains several imprecations against such oppressors. Kings and nations where Brahmins are oppressed do not prosper." उग्रो राजा मन्यमानो ब्राह्मणं यो जिघत्सति । परावत्सिच्यते राष्ट्रं ब्राह्मणो यत्र जीयते ॥ (V 9–6). This persecution of the Brahmins was a natural result of their sacred position and it characterised social relations in later days probably, later even than the days of the Brāhmaṇas. The cow was specially prized and revered. A long hymn (XII 4) praises the cow, here called Vaśā; and gifts of cows to Brahmins are also praised. The Indo-Aryans, as stated before, were already divided into three castes and the Śūdra, fourth caste, devoted to the service of the three had already, in Ṛigvedic later days, been included in the state or Rāṣtra. The intermediate castes are, however, not mentioned in the Atharvaveda and they appear to be a still later social development.

The Indo-Aryans were still an argicultural people and the Atharvaveda still prays for prosperity in agriculture, horses and cattle. The people, generally called Viś or subjects, were ruled by kings who were apparently elected and there are hymns for the coronation of kings and for the return of exiled kings. The states, which were always small, were not called kingdoms or Rājyas but Rāshtras (as in XIX 24) which shows that the people were still powerful. The kings were, however, forceful and special ceremonies were performed to make them so, such as the fastening of a maṇi or jewel and of darbha (XIX 27 to

33). The last hymn of XIX mentions Rājasūya. These kings often fought amongst themselves and also with non-Aryan enemies. The cousins or Bhrātṛivyas are often spoken of as enemies and may be identified with the Asuras or Persians. Nīla-lohita is supposed to kill the Bhrātṛivya with his Nīla or blue portion and enemies with the red, नीलेनैवाप्रियं भ्रातृव्यं प्रोर्णोति लोहितेन द्विषन्तम् विध्यति (XV 1–8). These Bhrātrivyas may be their own brother Indo-Aryan kings.

Turning to the social condition of the people, we find the marriage customs still the same as in Ṛigvedic times though the marriage hymns disclose a few changes. Indeed the marriage sūkta of the Ṛigveda (X 85) is taken bodily in the Atharvaveda but with some important changes and is extended into two long sūktas with 64 and 75 verses forming the whole Kāṇḍa XIV. The taking of the hand of the bride by the bridegroom is, as before, the most important ceremony and the gift of the bride rests with her father, the bridegroom going to him to sue for her. But the taking of the bride's hand appears to take place at her house as now and not at the bridegroom's house, as the bridal procession, the most gorgeous function, is mentioned again. Curiously enough, the Atharvaveda sūkta omits the prayer for ten sons appearing in the Ṛigveda sukta. The blemish attaching to the garment worn by the bride at the time of marriage still remains. The consummation mantras are included in the Atharva marriage hymn and it seems that the consummation of marriage took place soon after marriage. Many more mantras are to be repeated and cows and kambals are to be gifted for securing long life and progeny to the couple.

Kāṇḍa XVIII relates to the funeral ceremonies and begins with the praise of the world beyond and Yama, the king of the dead. The ancient forefathers, the Āngirasas, the Navagvas, the Atharvans and good Bhṛigus* are remembered, as also Vivasvān in verses which appear in Ṛigveda also (X 14, 6). The hymns in this Kāṇḍa have many verses common to the Ṛigveda though there are many in addition. Dead bodies were usually burnt; but the Anagnidagdhas are also spoken of. The widow sitting by the side of the dead body of her husband on the funeral pyre in response to the *old custom of Satī*† is also referred to here and is asked to come down. The Kāṇḍa brings together all the mantras to be recited at the funeral ceremony; and the Śrāddhas end with namaskāras to all Pitṛis or forefathers.

The following passages regarding the Atharvaveda from Macdonell attract the attention of the reader. " The spirit which breathes in it is that of a prehistoric age. A few of its actual charms probably date with little modification from the Indo-European period; for, as Adalbert Kuhn has shown, some of its spells for curing bodily ailments agree in purpose and

* आङ्गिरसो नः पितरो नवग्वा अथर्वाणो भृगवः सोम्यासः ।
विवस्वन्तं हुवे यः पिताः तेऽस्मिन् बर्हिष्यानिषद्या ॥ XVIII, 58–59.

† इयं नारी पतिलोकं वृणाना निपद्यत उप त्वा मर्त्य प्रेतम् ।
धर्मं पुराणमनुपालयंती तस्यै प्रजां द्रविणं चेह धेहि ॥ XVIII, 3-1.

content, as well as to some extent in form, with certain old German, Lettic and Russian charms." "It contains more theosophic matter than any of the other Śanhitās. For the history of civilization, it is on the whole more interesting and important than the Ṛigveda itself" (p. 186)

"In Patanjali's Mahābhāshya the Atharvaveda had already attained to such an assured position that it is even cited at the head of the Vedas and occasionally as their only representative" (p. 189).

"Among the cosmogonic and theosophic hymns, the finest is a long one of sixty-three stanzas addressed to the earth (XII 1). The following will give some idea of its contents and style.

"The earth on whom with clamour loud
Those that are mortal sing and dance ;
On whom they fight in battle fierce,
This earth shall drive away from us our foemen
And she shall make us free from all our rivals."

The hymn to Varuṇa (IV 16) exalts divine omniscience in a strain unequalled in any other Vedic poem.

'This earth is all King Varuṇa's dominion
And that broad sky whose bounds are distant;
The loins of Varuṇa are these two oceans,
Yet in this drop of water he is hidden.
He that should flee beyond the heaven
Would not escape King Varuṇa's attention ;
His spies come hither from the sky descending
With all their thousand eyes the earth
surveying" (p. 200–1).

Certain queer statements in the Atharvaveda may finally be noticed. The epithet Nīlalohita is explained by stating that Śava's belly is blue and his back is red (नीलमस्योदरं लोहितं पृष्ठम् XVI 7). This description applies to the rainbow. The Rathantara Sāman is placed in the east, Yajnāyajnīya and Vāmadevya in the south, Vairūpa and Vairāj in the west and Śyeta and Naudhasa in the north. In XV 14 Maruts are placed in the east and Indra in the south. What Jangida (जाङ्गिड) is which is invoked in XX 34 and 35 for protection and for killing of enemies is an enigma. Sāyaṇa explains it as ओषधिविशेष (a kind of herb). It may be noted that Purusha-sūkta appears in this Veda as XIX 6 with a few changes among which is छन्दो ह जज्ञिरे तस्मात्, that the Nakshatras including Abhijit are mentioned in XIX 7 and that Itihāsa, Purāṇa, Gāthā and Nārāśansīs are usually mentioned with Ṛik, Yajuh and Sāman.

NOTE 1—THE KUNTĀPA SŪKTAS.

The Kuntāpa sūktas are given in the Atharvaveda chapter XX (127-136). They are not found in the Ṛigveda Śākala sanhitā as we have it. They must have been taken by the compiler of the twentieth chapter of the Atharvaveda which, as we have said, was added later on for sacrificial purposes, from some other Śākhā of the Ṛigveda or from a khila as supposed by Sāyaṇa. That they are required for sacrificial purposes is certain from Aitareya VI 32, 33 and Kaushītaki XXX 5. The former does not use the word Kuntāpa but the latter does. The former, however, gives the particular names of the parts Nārāśansa, Raibhi, Kāravyā

Parikshitiyā and so on which are assigned to them from actual words used in the verses. The Gopatha Brāhmaṇa follows here the Kaushītaki almost word for word and with certain additions such as an explanation of the name Kuntāpa as will be noted in the section on Brāhmaṇas. Whether the Atharva compilation is referred to here in the Aitareya and Kaushītaki Brāhmaṇas or whether these quote from floating materials or from another Śākhā of the Ṛigveda, it is difficult to decide. It is possible to suggest that the Atharvaveda compilation is earlier than Kaushītaki alias Śāmkhāyana at least, as it gives the name Kuntāpa; and even the Aitareya which, though it does not give the name Kuntāpa, gives the names of the component parts of the hymn, the mentioning of the name Kuntāpa not being absolutely necessary. But we find in Kaushītai (IV 10, 11) a mention of three Vedas only by name and the fourth priest Brahman is shown as knowing and working with the aid of these three Vedas only as in the Śatapatha. The mention of Kuntāpa hymns and the name Kuntāpa, therefore, lead to no conclusion as to priority.

Note 2—THE DATE OF THE COMPILATION OF THE ATHARVAVEDA.

We have taken the date of the compilation of the Atharvaveda to lie between the date of the Śatapatha Brāhmaṇa (c. 3000 B.C.) and the date of the Chhāndogya Upanishad (c. 2500, B.C.). Our dates of these two works are much earlier than the ones assigned to them by European scholars and we will give the detailed arguments for our dates when we come to speak of these works. We will simply show here how the Atharvaveda compilation must be placed after the composition of the Śatapatha and before that of the Chhāndogya Upanishad.

The latter work distinctly mentions, as stated already, Ṛigveda, Yajurveda, Sāmaveda and Atharvaveda and in this order. The Śathapatha in its original extent viz. upto the tenth Kāṇda does not mention the Atharvaveda but mentions the other three Vedas. Bloomfield in his introduction to the translation of Atharvaveda in Max Müllar's Oriental Series has collected together all the references to the Atharvaveda in Vedic literature, thus laying researchers in Vedic literature under great obligation ; and we will draw upon them freely in this note in addition to those we have come across. Most of the suktas of the Atharvaveda which, as we have shown, are generally spells, were undoubtedly in existence long before the compilation of the Atharvaveda was made. It is no wonder, therefore, that the Atharvaveda itself speaks of these spells in some of its hymns as Atharvāṅgirasah along with Ṛik, Yajuḥ and Sāman (A X 7, 20 यस्माद्दचो अपातक्षन् &c. verse already quoted.)

The three-fold division of sacred utterances as Ṛik, Yajuh and Sāman was known even before the Ṛigveda was compiled, from the well-known Rik in Purashasūkta. ऋचः सामानि जज्ञिरे। छन्दांसि जज्ञिरे तस्माद्यजुस्तस्मादजायत ।* It seems there was also

* Swami Dayānand interprets the word Chhandānsi in the above verse differently. He thinks it refers to the Atharvaveda and thus holds that all the four Vedas are indicated in this verse. In support is quoted Gopatha I 1, 29 wherein the chhandas of Atharvaveda is given as 'Sarvāṇi Chhandānsi'. The wording of this verse is no doubt a little ambiguous. But if we believe that the Atharvaveda was not compiled at the time of the Purusha-sūkta, indeed not even the three other Vedas, we must interpret this verse differently. The word chhandānsi can not be taken to mean metres ; being placed along with Ṛik, Sāman and Yajuḥ, it cannot mean metres. We have interpreted the verse as follows—"From that all embracing sacrifice were produced first the Sāman Riks (verses): from it were produced the

then a fourth division viz. of spells and incantations which was known as Ātharvāṇas, Āṅgirasas or both together. The first three, however, are usually mentioned as in A VII 54, 2, XI 6, 14, XII 1, 38, XV 3, 68 ; and it seems clear that their compilation was also already made before that of the fourth ; for the word Veda clearly occurs in A VII 54–2 as applied to these three in the sense of a religious compilation ऋचं साम यद्प्राक्षं हविरोजो यजुर्बलम् । एष मा तस्मान्मा हिंसीः वेदः पृष्टः शचीपते. It is interesting to trace how the word Veda gradually changed its meaning. Here in this verse (A VII 54, 2) it appears to be restricted to the three Vedas. But in the Śatapatha Brāhmaṇa, even in Kāṇḍa XIII, the word means merely a branch of knowledge and is applied to different branches. This passage in Śatapatha XIII 4–3 de-

Chhandānsi and from it was also produced the Yajuḥ or sacrificial formula". Chhandānsi should naturally mean thus the metrical utterances ; being different from verses sung they would refer to the ordinary Ṛiks. This word Chhandas is thus not indicative of any Vedic compilation. It is an old Aryan word, the Zend of the Iranians. It may be translated as a metrical sacred utterance. The meaning metre is a later one naturally arising from this by lakshaṇā. Further the word Chhandas in 'Chhāndogya' cannot mean metre but must mean metrical sacred utterances. The most decisive proof would be the verse in the Bhagavadgītā छन्दांसि यस्य पर्णानि यस्तं वेद स वेदवित्. Here the word cannot mean metres ; for they are seven or fourteen only, while leaves must be innumerable. It cannot mean Atharva verses only. It means here the metrical sacred verses of Ṛigveda or of all the Vedas. The Purush-sūkta verse makes a distinction between the verses sung and those not sung and hence the word there may be taken wholly to mean Ṛigvedic verses. The meaning metre or measure had no doubt already arisen as 'sapta chhandānsi' are also referred to in several Ṛigvedic verses. But it is not its primary meaning. Metrical utterance is in natural evolution earlier than the perception of its measure, the metre.

serves to be quoted in full. After speaking of the sacrificial horse being let loose, the Pāriplava is detailed as follows :—

"First day, Manu Vaivasvata is the king, the subjects (Viśaḥ) are human beings and the Veda of Ṛiks is to be recited to them (तानुपादिशत्युचां वेदः). On the 2nd day, the king is Yama Vaivasvata and the ancestors or manes (Pitṛis) are the subjects ; the Veda of Yajuh is to be recited to them (यजूंषि वेदः). Varuṇa Āditya is the king on the third day and the subjects are Gandharvas, young and well-dressed ; the Atharvaṇa Veda is to be recited to them. On the fourth day, Soma Vaiśravaṇa is the king and the Apsarasas are his subjects ; to them is to be recited Āṅgirasa Veda.* On the fifth day Arbuda Kādraveya is the king and the subjects are serpents and to them is to be recited Sarpa-Vidyā Veda. On the sixth day Kubera Vaiśravaṇa is the king and his subjects are the Rākshasas ; to them is to be recited Devajana Vidyā Veda. On the seventh day Asita Dhānva is the king ; his subjects are the Asuras ; to them is to be recited Māyā Veda. 'Some feat of illusion is to be performed also.' On the 8th day Matsya Sammadas is the king and his subjects are fish and those who kill fish ; to them Itihāsa Veda is to be recited. On the ninth day Tārkshya Vaipaśyati is the king and birds are the subjects as also the killers of birds and Purāna Veda is to be recited to them. And on the tenth day Indra is the king and the subjects are the gods. The Veda to be recited to them is of Sāmans, and a daśata of Sāmans is to be recited (साम्नां दशतं ब्रूयात् ।)."

This long extract we give specially because the passage is of great historical interest in many ways. First

*This mention of two Vedas Ātharvaṇa and Āngirasa in Śatapatha XIII suggests the surmise mentioned earlier that Pippalāda must have put them together after the Śatapatha The material was already there before him.

Sāmaveda is clearly looked upon as the highest branch of knowledge and we thus understand the propriety of the Gītā saying "I am Sāmaveda among the Vedas". The Sarpa-Vidyā and Devajana-Vidyā were again two branches of knowledge which have now disappeared. They are noted in these very words in the Chhāndogya Upanishad along with the four Vedas, but the term Veda is not applied to them. Thirdly, Rākshasas are here said to be the subjects of Kubera Vaiśravaṇa who is, however, later known as the king of Yakshas. This establishes the truth of the story in the Rāmāyaṇa that Yakshas and Rākshasas were one people originally and the word Devajana applied to both Yaksha and Rākshasa. Lastly, the Asuras are a distinct people and their king is Asita Dhānva. Who this person is, neither Vedic nor Puranic legend, so far as we know, tells us.

The connection of Itihāsa with fish and fish-hunters is strange. Perhaps Vyāsa's being the son of Matsyagandhā, a fisherwoman, is here hinted at. The connection of Purāṇas with bird-hunters may similarly be explained by the story of Vālmīki writing the Rāmāyaṇa on seeing a hunter kill a Krauncha bird. These stories, therefore, appear to be very old. The Asuras were well-known for their Māyā and there was some Vidyā then of creating illusions. It is interesting to find that the Gopatha Brāhmaṇa (I 10) gives exactly these Vidyās as the five Upavedas of Atharvaveda viz : 1 Sarpaveda, 2 Piśāchaveda, 3 Āsuraveda, 4 Itihāsa and 5 Purāṇa.

Śatapatha X 5, 2, 20 contains nearly the same idea as is expressed in XIII above given. "The Adhvaryus know it as Yajuḥ, the Chhandogas as Sāman, the Bahvṛichas as Uktha, the knowers of magic (Yātuvidaḥ) as Yātu, the knowers of serpents as poison, gods as Urk, men as Rayī (wealth), Asuras as Māyā or illusion, Pitṛis or manes as Sva-

and Apsarasas as fragrant smell." This shows that magic spells or Yātu were the fourth subject of study in the days of the Śatapatha. These were, thereafter, naturally put together in a fourth compilation which gradually acquired the status of a Veda, having some portions purposely introduced, intended for sacrifice and marriage and funeral ceremonies

Leaving these historical facts unconnected with our present enquiry aside, what is pertinent here to remark is, 1stly, the word Veda has a general sense as a branch of knowledge and has not the restricted sense which later it assumed and is not confined to the four Rik, Yajuḥ, Sāman and Ātharvarṇa. 2ndly, the mention of a daśatī of Sāman shows that the Sāmaveda was most probably already compiled and necessarily, therefore, the Ṛigveda and the Yajurveda as appears from the hymn (A XV 54) already noticed. And lastly, the Atharva-Veda was not yet compiled; for the Ātharvaṇa branch of knowledge and the Āṅgirasa branch are here spoken of separately. The Atharvaveda compilation does not consist of two such distinct parts. The meaning, therefore, seems to be that the Ātharvaṇa or auspicious spells were known as a separate branch of knowledge. The present Atharvaveda itself (A VIII 5, 9) speaks of Āṅgirasī Kṛityās. These two sorts of mantras were, later on, put together not as two distinct portions but as one Veda giving the two sorts indiscriminately. We may, therefore, safely conclude that the present Atharvaveda compilation is later than the Śatapatha Brāhmaṇa even in its later portion. The older portion of the Brāhmaṇa (X 52–20) mentions the inauspicious hymns or spells only as yātu-vidyā; but this does not invalidate the above conclusion, as inauspicious hymns were known long before as a branch of study and are referred to even in the Ṛigvedic hymn of Saramā (X 108, 10).

A more explicit statement is that in Śatapatha XI

Adhyāya 5 section 7 speaking of Svādhyāya or daily sacred recitation. The Śatapatha prescribes Ṛik, Sāma, Yajuḥ, Vākovākya, Itihāsa, Purāna and Nārāśansis here; while in the preceding 6th section, it also mentions Atharvāṅgirasaḥ after Sāmāni and before Vākovākyam. The clearest proof follows in section 8 where the words Ṛigveda, Yajur veda and Sāmaveda are distinctly used and Atharvaveda is not mentioned at all as produced by Prajāpati.* The priests at a sacrifice are spoken of as four viz. Hotṛi, Adhvaryu and Udgātṛi with the fourth called Brahman. It is asked, by what Veda will the Brahman do his duty? (the Hotṛi having the Ṛigveda, the Adhvaryu the Yajurveda and the Udgātṛi the Sāmaveda); and the answer is given that the Brahman should do his duty by the same three vidyas.† In later times, when the Atharvaveda was compiled and had acquired the full status of a Veda, the Brahman was to be a professor of that Veda. We may also point out here a passage in the Taittirīya Brāhmaṇa which will be discussed in full later on, wherein Ṛigveda, Yajurveda and Sāmaveda are distinctly mentioned but not Atharvaveda (T. B. III 12,9). The compilation of Atharvaveda is thus even later than T. B.

The word Veda is found in one verse of the Ṛigveda itself viz: VIII 19, 5. Its meaning there is apparently not so extensive as in the above passage of the Śatapatha and the sentence in the verse viz: "He who pleases Agni with Veda" no doubt contemplates the three Vedas apparently. But as the compilation of the three Vedas cannot be taken to have been made before this hymn was seen, we must interpret the word Veda here as meaning any sacred utterance, though Sāyana interprets it as Vedādhyayana referring to all the four Vedas. The word Veda also occurs in the Atharvaveda

*प्रजापतिस्तपो तप्यत। ...अग्नेर्ऋग्वेदो वायोर्यजुर्वेदः। †यदृचा होत्रं क्रियते यजुषाध्वर्यवं साम्नोद्गीथोऽथ केन ब्रह्मत्वमित्यनया त्रय्या विद्ययेति ब्रूयात्।

hymn already noted (XV 3) and in the seventh verse between the 6th and the 8th noted by Bloomfield and mentioning separately Ṛik and Yajuḥ in the first and Sāman in the second. Here the word must, therefore, mean something else than in the Ṛigveda verse. For in the throne (Āsandi) supposed to be raised for Vrātya, Veda forms the coverlet while Ṛiks form the right strings and Yajuḥs the left strings and Sāman the Asāda. Veda, therefore, here stands for knowledge generally. ऋचः प्राञ्चस्तन्तवो यजूंषि तिर्यञ्चः । ६ । वेद आस्तरणं ब्रह्मोपबर्हणम् । ७ । सामासाद उद्गीथोपश्रयः । ८ । तामासन्दीं व्रात्य आरोहत् । ९ । (Brahmaṇ here stands, to our mind, as distinguished from Veda, for Ātharvaṇa spells. Unfortunately there is no Bhāsya on this hymn). Thus Veda both in the Ṛigveda and the Atharvaveda, as also in the Śatapatha Brāhmaṇa, has not that restricted meaning which attaches to the word in the Chhāndogya Upanishad viz ; the Sanhitās of the four Vedas. The latest meaning of Veda includes the Brāhmaṇas of the four Vedas with their Upanishads (मंत्रब्राह्मणयोर्वेदनामधेयम्) also and is explained in a verse quoted by Sāyana in the beginning of his Bhāshya on the Atharvaveda viz. प्रत्यक्षेणानुमित्या वा यस्तूपायो न बुध्यते । एतं विदन्ति वेदेन तस्माद्वेदस्य वेदता ॥

APPENDIX.

I CHARANA-VYŪHA.

This work is said to be a Pariśishta-Sūtra (or an Appendix from among 18) composed by Kātyāyana. It begins with the sūtra अथातश्चरणव्यूहं व्याख्यास्यामः in the usual form. It first treats of the Ṛigveda and gives its Śākhās or schools as five viz:—Śākala, Bāshkala, Ās'valāyana Śānkhāyana and Māndūkeya. The schools of Yajurveda are given as eighty-six; but these are not enumerated. The Charakas are said to be 12, Kaṭha, Kapishṭhala, Śvetās'vatara and Maitrāyaṇīya being among them, some of these being subdivided into Upaśākhas. The Vājasaneyins are then mentioned with the extent of their Sanhitā and their Śatapatha Brahmaṇa which is said to be four times their Sanhitā. The Vājasaneyins are sub-divided into 17 branches two of which are Mādhyandina and Kāṇva. The Taitirīyakas are of two divisions viz. the Aukheyas and the Khāndikeyas, the latter again being sub-divided into five branches (1) Kāleta (2) Śātyāyanī, (3) Hairaṇyakeshī (4) Bhāradvājī and (5) Āpastambī. The extent of their Veda is 1800 Yajuḥ mantras, twice the same being Padapātha and three times Kramapāṭha. The eighty-six Śākhās mentioned cover both the Black and White Yajurvedas. The Kāṇva Sanhitā is said to contain 2086 Ṛiks including Khila and Śukrīya while their Śatapatha is said to contain 17 Kāṇḍas of 6258 mantras in extent. Sāmaveda is said to have one thousand Śākhās. But Indra killed most because they recited on days prohibited. Two only remain namely Rāṇāyanīyas and Kauthumas subdivided into 10 and 7 branches respectively. Their extent of study is 8000 Āgneya, 400 Pāvamāna and 600

Aindra. The Atharvaveda is divided into ten branches, two of which are Paippalāda and Saunaka and the extent of their Veda is 12000. These are divided into five Kalpas, Nakshatra, Vidhāna, Adhikāravidhi, Abhichāra and Śānti.

In the end the four Vedas are deified and described as four persons with different complexions, features *&c*, a thing which led to the construction of imagss representing the Vedas with different heights The gotra of Ṛigveda is given as Ātreya, of Yajurveda as Kāśyapa, of Sāmaveda as Bhāradvāja and of Atharvaveda as Vaikhānasa. These are undoubtedly imaginary gotras, as no reasons can, we think, be offered for this assignment. There are four Upavedas; Āyurveda attached to Ṛigveda, Dhanurveda to Yajurveda, Gandharva Veda to Sāmaveda and Arthaśastra to Atharvaveda. The six well-known Vedāṇgas are also enumerated ; as also 8 Upāṇgas viz. 1 Pratipada, 2 Anupada, 3 Chhandas, 4 Bhāshā, 5 Dharma, 6 Mīmānsā, 7 Nyāya and 8 Tarka. These clearly indicate that this work was composed after the Mīmansā Śāstra had arisen and, therefore, belongs to about the fifth centry A. D., the age of Śabara Bhāshya or later still, of Kumārila.

The commentator on this Pariśishta, out of the eighteen enumerated, mentions the provinces of India where particular Śākhās prevail. Among the Hirṇyakeśins are mentioned Chīttapolas which shows this commentary to be quite recent, later than the 12th centry A. D. Some of these provinces are imaginary like Śvetadvīpa, but many references are correct.

II REFERENCES TO THE VEDAS & THEIR SĀKHĀS IN THE MAHĀBHĀRATA.

In Śāntiparva chap. 343, the following ślokas occur in the Nārāyaṇīya Ākhyāna. एकविंशतिसाहस्रमृग्वेदं मां प्रचक्षते । सहस्रशाखं यत्साम ये वै वेदविदो जनाः । गायन्त्यारण्यके विप्रा मद्भक्तास्तेऽपि दुर्लभाः ॥९८॥ षट्पञ्चाशतमष्टौ च सप्तत्रिंशतामित्युत ॥ यस्मिन्शाखा यजुर्वेदे सोहमाध्वर्यव ; स्मृतः ।

पंचकल्पमथर्वाणं कृत्याभिः परिबृंहितम् । कल्पयन्ति हि मां विप्रा अथर्वाणविदस्तथा ॥ शाखाभेदाश्च ये केचित् याश्च शाखासु गीतयः । स्वरवर्णसमुच्चाराः सर्वांस्तान् विद्धि मत्कृतान् । यत्तद्धयशिरः पार्थ समुद्रेऽत्र वरप्रदम् । सोहमेवोत्तरे भागे क्रमाक्षरविभागवित् । वामादेशितमार्गेण मत्प्रसादान्महात्मना । पाञ्चालेन क्रमः प्राप्तस्तस्माद्भूतात्सनातनात् । बाभ्रव्यगोत्रः स बभौ प्रथमं क्रमपारगः । क्रमं प्रणीय शिक्षां च प्रणयिता स गालवः ।

We have already said that twenty-one thousand here is a misreading for twenty-one Śākhās of Rīgveda. The thousand Sākhās of Sāmaveda are as old as the Mahābhārata (cir. 250 B. C.), as also the Panchakalpas of Atharvaveda. Of the Yajurveda are mentioned 56 and 8 and 37 Sākhās, the total coming to 101 instead of 86 of the Charanavyuha. Yajurveda was the most prevalent Veda and has even now many Sākhās. It must have been so, in Mahābhārata days, also from the statement of Patañjali that Charakas are found in every village. These and other Śākhās were distinguished by differences of accents and pronunciations. The idea of Vishṇu taking the form of Hayaśiras or horse-headed and reciting the Vedas with their Kramas and diflerent letters is interesting, as showing that the Vaishṇavite Nārāyanīya Akhyāna identifies its god with Vedic lore. Lastly Gālava alias Bābhravya (of that gotra), inhabitant of the Pāñchāla country, is mentioned as enunciating the Kramapāṭha (presumably of all the Vedas), by the method shown by Vāmadeva. How and where Vāmadeva has shown this method has to be found out. If Vāmadeva is a Vedic Ṛishi, he can not be a contemporary of Gālava.

In Śanti. p. chap, 350, it is stated that Apāntartamas, a son of Svyambhū, born from his speech, first divided the Vedas in tha time of Svāyambhuva Manu. In the fourth age viz. Kali, Vyāsa will divide the Vedas-Vyāsa born of Parāśara from the family of Vasishṭha. (अपान्तरतमा नाम सुतः स्वायंभुवः प्रभुः । तेन भिन्नास्ततो वेदा मनोः स्वायंभुवान्तरे । तत्राप्यनेकधा वेदान् भेत्स्यते तपसान्वितः ॥ कृष्णे युगे च सम्प्राप्ते कृष्णवर्णो भविष्यति ॥). We have not come across any reference to Apāntaratamas, a former double of Vyāsa or Krishna Dvaipāyana, in any Vedic literature, This is presumably a new idea and a new name promulgated by Sauti.

There is a mention of a Rahasya Veda composed by Arvāvasu (रहस्यवेदं कृतवान् सूर्यस्य द्विजसत्तमः । वन. 138, 18). The commentator states that the eight lettered mantra of Sūrya (घृणिरिति द्वे अक्षरे सूर्य इति त्रीणि आदित्य इति त्रीणि एतद्वैसावित्रस्याष्टाक्षरपदं श्रियाभिषिक्तामिति काटकब्राह्मणम् ॥) is the Rahasyaveda of the Sun referred to. But the Kāṭhaka Brāhmaṇa is included in the Sanhitā and we are not sure if this mantra is really to be found in the Kāṭhaka Sanhnitā published by Schraeder.

In Anuśāsana p. chap. 314, Śākalya is mentioned as Sūtrakṛit. What Vedic Sūtra this is can not be known. Śākala Sanhitā is well-known and Śākalya's son Sākalya frequently mentioned in Pāṇini's grammar may have composed a Sūtra on grammar.

We have already stated in the note at the foot of page 153 that MBh. V 19 (5-8) mentions that Agniras was the author of the Atharvaveda and that the Veda was, therefore, known by the name of Atharvāngirasah. This does not prove that the name Atharvaveda arose later than MBh.; for we find that name long before in the Chhāndogya. This is simply a reminiscence of the Gopatha story that Aṅgiras was Atharvaṇ himself and composed the Atharvaṅgirasa Veda. It must be ascertained if the Vaitāna Sūtra prescribes an oblation to Aṅgiras and to him alone at sacrifices.

III PURUSHA-SUKTA IN THE FOUR VEDAS.

The Purusha-Sūkta hymn X 90 of the Ṛigveda is taken wholly or in part in all other Vedas. In Sāma-Veda, only the first five verses are taken in P. 6, 13 as verses 3 to 7. There are many changes in these five, the second halves of all except the fourth being transposed ; and there are some changes in words also, such as अशनानशने for साशनानशने. In the Black Yajurveda the whole sükta appears only in T. Āranyaka III as Anuvāka 12. All the sixteen verses are taken and two more in Trishtup are added before the last यज्ञेन यज्ञम् &c. The fifteenth verse सप्तास्यासन् परिधय: &c. is, however, given as seventh. There are no other changes except that तस्माद्विराळ-जायत is recited as तस्माद्विराडजायत, the Yajurvedins not pronouncing d as ḷ. In the White Yajurveda, the sūkta appears as chapter XXXI. All the sixteen verses of the Ṛigveda sūkta are given and six more are added, two of which are the ones given by the Black Yajurveda (T. A.). The Ṛishi of the 16 verses is given as Nārāyaṇa, a name given by all the Vedas; but these added verses are said to be by Uttara Nārāyaṇa which is clearly not a Ṛishi-name but means the later Nārāyaṇa verses. There are some few changes in words, one of which is that instead of मुखादिन्द्रश्चाग्निश्च प्राणाद्वायुरजायत we have श्रोत्राद्वायुश्च प्राणश्च मुखादग्निरजायत. Indra is omitted here altogether. In the Atharvaveda, the sukta appears in Kānda XIX as hymn 6 with 16 verses as in the Ṛigveda, but the 16th verse is entirely different. There are many important transpositions and changes in words, the word in the very beginning being सहस्रबाहु: instead of सहस्रशीर्षा. And we have तं यज्ञं प्रावृषा प्रौक्षन् instead of बर्हिषि प्रौक्षन्. It may finally be added that the verse ब्राह्मणोस्य मुखमासीत् &c. appears in the two Yajurvedas and the Atharvaveda and hence belongs to the original sūkta and is not an interpolation. The Sāmaveda gives only five verses and hence it naturally omits this verse along with eleven others.

IV ALPHABETICAL LISTS OF VEDIC ṚISHIS.

In a history of Sanskrit literature, it is, we think, necessary that lists of Rishis of the several Vedas should be given, Rishis being the authors of complete hymns or individual verses Moreover, as the Pravara system of the Indo-Aryans is based on these Rishis, such lists would be interesting. Lastly it would be worth while seeing which Rishis belong to which particular Veda or to all Vedas. We have, therefore, specially prepared such lists and give them here. It is possible that a few mistakes may have crept in here and there. The names are given according to the English Alphabet.

(1) RIGVEDIC ṚISHIS

The number of the Mandala is given in Roman figures, of sūktas in English figures and of verses in the latter figures in brackets. This list is prepared from the Ajmer edition. It will be seen that most names are of real authors, a few only being imaginary such as gods or Pururavas and so on.

Abhitapas Sauryya X 37
Abhīvarta A 174
Aditi Dākshāyaṇī X 72
Agastya I 165–191
Agastyasya Svasā (sister of Agastya) and mother of Bandhu &c. X 60 (6)
Aghamarshaṇa Mādhuchchhandasa X 190
Agnayo Dhishṇyāh Aiśvarāh IX 109
Agni IX 106 (10–14)
Agni Chākshusha IX 106 1–3
Agni Sauchīka X 51 (2, 4, 6, 8); 52; 53 (4–5)
Agni Sauchīka Vaiśvānara or Sapti Vājambhara X 79-80
Agni Pāvaka X 140
Agni Tāpasa X 141
Agni-Varuṇa-Somānām nihavah X 124
Agniyuta Sthaura or Agniyūpa Sthaura X 116
Aindra (dialogue between Indra and Vasukra) X 28
Ākṛishtā Māshāh IX 86(1–10, 30–40)
Amahīyu IX 53–60
Ambarisha & Ṛijishvan IX 98
Amhomuk Vāmadevya X 126

Dhruva X 173
Dīrghtamas Auchathya I 140–164
Divya or Dakshiṇā Prājāpatyā X 107
Droṇa X 142 (3–4)
Dridhachyuta Āgastya IX 25
Duvasyu Vāndana X 100
Dvita Āptya IX 103
Dvita Mṛiktavāhas Ātreya V 18
Dyumna Viśvacharshaṇi V 23
Ekadyū Naudhasa VIII 80
Evayāmaarut Ātreya V 87
Garga VI 47
Gaurivīti Śāktya V 29
Gaurivīti IX 108 (1–2); X 37 ; 74
Gāthin Kauśika III 19–22
Gātu Ātreya V 32
Gavishṭhira Ātreya V 1
Gaya Ātreya V 9–10
Gaya Plāta X 63–64
Gharma Saurya X 181 (3)
Ghaura Kāṇva VIII 1 (1, 2)
Ghoshā Kākshīvatī X 39–40
Gopavana Ātreya or Saptavadhri VIII 73 ; 74
Goshūkti and Aśvashūkti Kānvas VIII 14–15
Gotama IX 31
Gotama Rāhugaṇa 74–93.
Gṛitsamada IX 86 (46–48)
Gṛitsamada Āngirasa Śaunahotra II 1–3, 8–27, 30–43
Harimanta IX 72
Haryata Prāgātha VIII 72
Havirdhāna Āngi X 11–12
Hiraṇyagarbha Prājāpatya X 121
Hiraṇyastūpa IX 4, 69 Āngirasa I 31–55
Idhmavāha Dārḍhachyuta IX 26
Indra Mushkavān X 38
Indra Vaikuntha X 48–50
Indrapramati Vāsishtha IX 97 (4–6)
Indrāṇī X 145
Indramātarah X 153
Irimbiṭhi Kāṇva VIII 16–18
Isha Ātreya V 7–8
Iṭa Bhārgava X 171
Jamadagni IX 62, 65, X 167
Jamadagni Bhārgava VIII 101
Jamadagni or Rāma X 110
Jaratkarṇa Airāvata Sarpa X 76
Jaritā X 142 (1–2)
Jaya X 180
Jetṛi Mādhuchchhandasa I 11
Juhū Brahmajāyā or Urdhvanābhā Brāhma X 109
Kakshīvat IX 74 I 116–8, 122, 126, (1–5), Dairghtamasa 119, 123–5 Auśija 120–1
Kali Prāgātha VIII 66
Kapota Nairṛita X 165
Kaṇva IX 94 Ghaura I 34–36
Karṇaśrut Vāsiṣṭhas IX 97 (22–24)

Trasadasyu Paurukutsya IV 42, V 27 IX 110
Triśiras Tvāshtra X 8–9 ;
Triśoka Kāṇva VIII 45
Trita IX 33–34; 107; X 1–7;
Trita Āptya VIII 47 ;
Tryaruṇa Traivṛishṇa, Aśvamedha Bhārata or Atri V 72
Tryaruṇa & Trasadasyu IX 110
Tvashṭri Garbhakartṛi or Vishṇu Prājāpatya X 184
Uchathya IX 50–52
Ula Vātayana X 186
Upamanyu Vāsiṣṭha IX 97 (13–15)
Upastuta Vārshṭihavya X 115
Urddhvasadmā IX 108 (8–9)
Ūrdhvanābhā Brāhma X 109
Ūrdhvagrāvā Ārbudi X 195
Uru IX 108 (4–5)
Uruchakri Ātreya V 69–70
Urukshaya Amahīyava X 118
Urvaśī X 95 (2, 4, 5, 7, 11, 13, 15, 16, 18)
Usanas Kāvya VIII 84 ; IX 87–89
Utkīla Kātya III 15–17
Vaikhānasas (hundred) IX 66
Vamro Vaikhānasa X 99
Vāgāmbhṛiṇī X 125
Vāmadeva IV 1–41 ; 45–58
Vasishṭha VII 1–104 ; IX 90 ; 97 (1–3)
Vaśośvya VIII 46
Vasu Bhāradvāja IX 80–82
Vasukra Aindra X 27 28
Vāsukra X 26
Vasukrit Vasukra X 20–26
Vasukarṇa Vāsukra X 65–66
Vasukra Vāsishtha IX 97 (28-30)
Vasumanas Rauhidaśva X 179 (3)
Vasuśruta Ātreya V 3–6
Vasūyus (many) Ātreya V 25–26
Vatsa Āgneya X 187
Vatsa Kāṇdv VIII 6 ; 11
Vatsapri Bhālandana IX 68
Vatsapri X 45–46
Vavri Ātreya V 19
Vena X 123
Vena Bhārgava IX 85
Vihavya X 128
Vibhrāṭ Sūrya X 170
Virūpa VIII 75
Vimada Aindra Prājāpatya or Vasukṛit Vāsukra X 20–26
Vishṇu Prājapatya X 184
Viśvāmitra & Jamadagni X 167
Viśvamitra III 2–12; 24–62
Viśvāmitra Gāthina III 1
Viśvāmitra or Kushika III 31
Vivasvān Āditya X 13
Viśvāvasu Devagano. X 139
Vivṛihā Kāśyapa X 163
Viśvasāman Ātreya V 22
Viśvamanas Vaiyaśva VIII 23–26

Viśvakarman Bhauvana X 81-2
Vṛiśa Jāra V 2
Vṛishagaṇa Vāsi IX 97(7–9)
Vṛishākapi Aindra, Indrāṇī and Indra X 86
Vyāghrapād Vāsishṭha IX 97 (16–18)
Yajat Ātreya X 67–68
Yajna Prājāpatya X 130
Yakshmnāśana Prājā. X 161
Yama X 14
Yama Vaivasvata X 10 (2, 4, 8–10, 12, 14) Yamī X 154
Yamī Vaivasvatī X 10 (1, 3, 5–8, 11, 13)
Yayāti Nāhusha X 101 (4–6)

(2) SĀMAVEDA ṚISHIS

The following list has also been prepared from the Ajmer edition. These Ṛishis are in general real persons like the Ṛishis of the Ṛigveda except some like Agni Tāpasa who is very likely god Agni. Only seven verses are assigned no Ṛishis viz. 8, 1 (14), 8, 2 (19), 9, 1 (2) and 9, 2 (3, 4, 7, 10). These are called Etatsāman or Itisāman. Most of the verses can be traced to the Ṛigveda and their Ṛishis are mostly the same as in the Rigveda. On comparing these two lists, one may say that no name is found here which is not in the Ṛigveda list. The greater number of Sāman verses belong to Vasishtha and next follow Viśvāmitra, Medhātithi, Vāmadeva and Śunaḥśepa as great Sāman chanters.

Abhīpāda Udala P 3, 4 (9)
Agastya U 6, 2 (20)
Agni U 3 (118) Pāvaka U 3, 1 (20)
Agni Chākshuśa 6, 8 (1, 7, 11) Vaiśvānara Pāvaka Bārhaspatya 7, 2 (14), 9, 2 (1) V 1 (20) Tāpasa P 1, 10 (1)
Ākrishta-Bhāshah U 3, 1 (1) 4, 1 (1)
Amahīyu P 5, 9 (1, 4), 5, 10 (4, 8) 6, 1 (1, 8, 9), 6, 2 (14) 6, 10 (48) Āṅgirasa U 1, 1 (8, 10), 1, 2 (17, 18) 2, 1 (2, 5, 15) 3, 1 (2) 4, 1 (13) Dhishnya 4, 2 (12), 5, 1 (17), 5, 2 (19) 6, 1 (8)
Ambarīsha P 6, 6 (6,7) and Rijiśvā U 1, 2 (22, 3) 5, 1 (16), 5, 2 (18), 8, 2 (8)

Irimithi P 3, 9 (3), 5, 1 (7)

Jaya Aindra U 9, 3 (9)

Jamadagni P 3, 3 (7), 3, 7 (3) 3, 9 (4), 5, 9 (7), 6, 2 (12), 6, 3 (17, 2), U 1, 1 (5), 2, 1 (1, 4, 10), 2, 2 (1–2), 3, 2 (6, 16), 3, 2 (11), 4, 1 (6), 4, 2 (4, 13) Bhārgava 9, 1 (9), 9, 1 (17)

Jetā Māshuchhandasa P 4, 6 (2), 4, 7 (4), U 2, 1 (19), 5, 1 (20)

Kali Pragātha P 3, 5 (5) 3, 8 (10), U 1, 1 (14), 8, 2 (13)

Kāmadeva P 1, 3 (10)

Kaṇva P 1, 3 (11), 1, 5 (10), 1, 6 (2, 3, 5), 2,5 (1Ghaura) 2, 10 (6), 6, 5 (7)

Kaśyapa P 1, 9 (10), 5, 9 (6), 5, 10 (6), Mārīcha 6, 2 (8,9) 6, 3 (1–12), 6, 5 (11) U 1, 1 (2), 2, 1 (3), 2, 2 (4), 3, 2(2) 4, 1 (2, 11)

Kavasha Ailūsha P 5, 7 (7)

Kavi Medhāvi P 6, 10 (1), Kāvi 6, 2 (11), Bhārgava 6, 7 (1–3, 5) U 2, 2 (30), 5, 1 (12), 6, 3 (1)

Kautsa Durmitra P 3, 4 (6)

Ketu Āgneya U 7, 1 (15)

Khigana P 6, 7 (6)

Krishna Angirasa P 4, 9 (6)

Kritayaśas Āngirasa P 6, 9 (4). U 3, 2 (17)

Kurusuti Kāṇva U 3, 2 (9)

Kusīda P 2, 7 (8), 2, 8 (3 Kānva), U 1, 2 (6)

Kusīdi Kāṇva P 2, 5 (4)

Kutsa P 1, 7 (4), 4, 9 (11), Āngirasa 6, 5 (9), 6, 14 (3) U 4, 1 (7, 21), 6, 2 (18), 8, 3 (14)

Madhuchhandas P 1, 2 (4) 2, 4 (5, 6), 2, 7 (6, 10), 2, 8(2) 2, 9 (6), 2, 10 (5), 3, 1 (5), 3, 2 (2), 4, 6 (1), 4, 5 (4), 5, 9 (2), Vaiśvamitra 6, 11 (3, 4), 6, 2 (6), 11 (3, 4), 6, 12 (6), U 1, 2 (10), 2, 1 (8), 2, 2 (6, 7), 4, 1 (15), 4, 2 (7), 5, 2 (2, 3), 6, 3 (14), 3, 1 (2)

Māndhātṛi Yauvanāśva U 4, 1 (16)

Manu P 1, 5 (4) Āpsava 6, 8 (6), 5, 2 (17), Sānovarana 6, 6 (4), U 42 (20) Vaivasta P 1, 0 (10)

Madasyu Vāsiṣhṭha P 6, 5 (8) U 3, 2 (20)

Medhātithi Āngirasa P 2, 3(9)

Medhātithi P 1, 1 (3), 1, 2 (6) 1, 3 (12), 1, 5 (8), 2, 5 (5), 2, 6 (2), 2, 7 (3), 2, 8 (7), 3, 3 (4, 9), 3, 4 (1, 7, 8) U 3, 5 (7), 3, 6 (2, 3), 3, 7 (4, 9), 3, 8 (9) with Medhyā P 3, 10 (9, 10), 4, 1 (3, 5), 4, 2 (5), 4, 9 (10), U 2, 1 (6, 7), 2, 2

(2a) SIST OF DEVATĀS OF SĀMAVEDA.

As mentioned on page 118, we give below a list of deities praised in the Sāmaveda prepared from the Ajmer edition. It will be found that Agni, Indra and Pavamān Soma are the three most important deities in this Veda, only a few verses being addressed to others. P indicates Pūrvārchika or the first collection of verses and U the Uttārarchika or later collection. The Roman figure indicates the chapter and the first English figure next given indicates the hymn in it, while the third figure given in brockets shows he particular verse in that hymn.' indicates second half and " third half.

Aditi P II 1 (6)

Āditya P III 7 (3) U IV 8, VI 2

Agni P I 1, 2, 3, 4, 5 (1–7, 9, 10), 6 (7, 4–8), 7, 8, 9, 10 (3–6), III v (1–4, 7–10), 2, V i 1 (1, 2, 7), 5 (8), 7 (112), VI 12 (4, 6, 13), 13 (1), 14 (1)–U I (4, 20, 21) I' 13–16, II 6, II" 5, 17, III 6, 20, III 7, 21, IV 7, 22 IV' 14, V 9, 18, V' 9, VI 1, 10, VI' 1, 2, 7, 10, 13, 14, VI" 12, 16, 17, 18, VII 4, 10–16, VII' 1–14, VII" 5, VIII 1, 3, 7, 12, VIII' 3, 11, 18, VIII" 1, 10, 13, IX 4, 5, 18, IX' 1, 2, 8

Aṅgirah P I 10 (2)

Anna P VI 10 (9)

Āpah U IX' 10

Aśvins P IV 1 (2–3) V3 (10) U I' 15, VIII" 7, 9, 12, 15, 17, IX 6

Brahmaṇaspati P I 6 (2) V II 11

Brihaspati U IX" 2 (1)

Dadhikrāvan P IV 7 (7)

Dyāvā Prithvī P IV 9 (9), VI 13 (8), U VII' 14

Indra P I, 5 (8) II, 3, 4, 5, 6, 7, 8, 9, 10, III 1, 2, 3, 4, 5 (1-8, 10) 6, 7 (1-2, 4-10) 8, 9 (1-3, 5-8, 10) 10 (1-4, 7-10) IV 1, 2 (4-10) 3, 4, 5 (1-6, 9, 10) 6, 7 (1-4, 6, 8) 8 (1–7) 9 (1 8, 10, 11) 10 V 2 (1, 2, 4, 5, 7-10) 3(1-8) 4 (5-6) 6 (1-5, 8-10) 7 (3, 4,

Vājinah P V 5 (9)
Varuṇa P III 10 (5–6), VI 10 (4), U VII′ 6
Vāyu P VI 11 (6) U IX′ 11
Vena U IX′ 13
Vishṇu U VIII 4 VIII′ 5
Viśvakarman U VII″ 9
Viśvedevah P I 10 (1) IV 8 (9) V 3 (9), 4 (8), V 6 (6), 7 (6, 7, 9), 8 (5), VI 10 (6), 11 (5), 12 (9), U 1, 12 IV 23, VII 6, VII″ 13, IX′ 5,6

(3) WHITE YAJURVEDA ṚISHIS.

The Ṛishis of this Veda are given in this list. There are no Ṛishis for the Black Yajurveda which consists mostly of prose sacrificial formulas ; but this Veda consists solely of Ṛiks or verses and their authors or Ṛishis are given from its Anukramaṇi. These are mostly real persons and many of them are the same as those in the Ṛigveda, though the verses may be different. There are several new names such as Yājnavalkya, Śākalya and so on; but as this Veda is later than the Ṛigveda, new names are naturally to be expected. The Roman figures indicate the chapters which always consist of one hymn The English figures indicate the number of Ṛiks or verses in the chapter.

Ābhūti XIX 3–9
Adityas XXXV 1, 3, 5, 8
Adityas or Devas XXXV 3, 4, 6, 9, 12–14, 16, 20, 22
Agastya XXXIII 27, 34, 78, 79 XXXIV 7, 9, 48
Āgastya III 46, 47 V 36–43 VI 1
Agni XIII 20, 21 XXVII 1–7, 10–20
Ajamīdha XXVII 31
Aṅgiras XXVII 34
Āṅgirasa III 1 IV 9 VII 43–48 VIII 1–3 XX 36–46
Apratiratha XVII 33–58, 60
Arṇna & Trasadasyu XXII 18
Asuri III 38–41
Āśvatarāśvi XX 24–26
Aśvinau XX 3 XXVIII 12–23
Ātharvaṇa XXXVII 19–21 XXXVIII 1–4

(4) ATHARVAVEDA ṚISHIS.

This Index was made by Whitney, and was carefully revised by Dr. Ryder, and again by Charles Rockwell Lanman (1905):—We take it here with due acknowledgment.

Agastya VI 133

Angiras II 3, 35 ; IV 39, 1–8 V 12; VI 83–84; VII 50–51, 77, 90; XIX 22, 34–35; see also Atharvāngiras and Pratyangiras and Bhrigvangiras

Angiras Prachetas, with Yama VI 45–47

Atharvan I 1–3, 9–11, 15, 20–21, 23, 27, 30, 34–35; II 4, 7, 13, 19–23, 29, 34; III 1–5, 8, 10, 15–16, 18, 26–27, 30; IV 3–4, 10, 15, 22 (? or Vasistha?) 31, 34; V 5–6, 7–8 (?), 11, 24, 23; VI 1–7, 13, 17–18, 32–33, 36–40, 50, 58–62, 64–69, 73–74, 78–80, 85–90, 92, 97–99, 109–113, 124–126, 138–140; VII 1–7, 13–14, 18, 34–38, 45, 2, 46–49, 52, 56, 61, 70–73, 76, 78–81, 85–87, 91–92, 94, 97–99, 101–106; VIII 7, 9; IX 1–2; X 3, 7, 9; XI 2–3, 7; XII 1; XVII 1–4 (the whole Book) XIX 14–20, 23–24, 26, 37–38 see also Brhaddiva Atharvan; also Sindhudvipa Atharvakriti

AtharvanVītahavya VI 136-7

Atharvāngiras IV 8; VI 72, 94, 101, 123–132 VII 74, 115–118, XIX 3–4, 5 (?) *cf* Angiras

Atharvāchārya VIII 10 ; *cf* XII 5 (Kaśyapa)

Apratiratha XIX 13

Ātharvaṇa *cf* Bhṛigu Ātharuaṇa

Babhrupingala VI 14

Bādarāyaṇi IV 37–38 VII 59, 109

Bṛihasehukan VI 54 *cf* Śakra

Brihaddiva Atharvan V 1–3,

Brihaspati X 6

Brihman V 17, 19, 22, 24, 26, 31–32 II 15–17, 24, 13, III 12, 14, 23, 28, 31 IV 5, 16, 21, 33, 39, 9–10 V 9–10, 20–21, 25-27 VI 26, 41, 54–55, 71, 114–115 VII 19–22, 24, 32, 33, 53 54–1, 60, 66–67, 103, 104 111; VIII 1–2; IX 4, 6–7, 9–10; X 5, 37–41 XI 1, 5 XIII 1–4 i. e, the whole

Śunahśepa VI 25 VII 83
Sāvitri II 26 XIX 31
Savitṛi Suryā XIV (whole)
Śindhudvīpa I 4-5 VII 39 X 5, 7-24 XIX 2
Sindhudvīpa Atharvākṛiti I 6 cf Atharvan
Śintati I 33 IV 13 VI 10, 10 21-24, 51, 56-59, 93, 107 VII 68-69 XI 6
Tvastṛi VI 81
Uparibabhrava VI 30-31
Varuṇa VII 112
Vasishtha I 29 III19-22IV22
Vāmadeva III 9 VII 57
Viśvāmitrā II 17 V 15-16 VI 44 141
Vihavya X 5,42-50 Atharvan
Veṇa II 1 IV 1-2 Śintāti I 33 IV 13 VI 10, 19, 21-24, 51, 56-57, 93, 107 VII 68-69 XI 6
Yama VII 23, 64, 100-1 XII 3 XVI 5-7, 8-9 (?) XIX 56-7 Yama with Angirasa Prācchasa

V. ANOTHER ANCIENT ENUMERATION OF THE ŚĀKHĀS OF THE FOUR VEDAS.

We came across this enumeration recently in the Muktikopanishad and we proceed to give it here in this Appendix. This Upanishad may be dated about 1000 A. D. as it evidently is later than Śankara. ऋग्वेदस्य तु शाखाः स्युरेकविंशतिसंख्यकाः । नवाधिकशतं शाखा यजुषो मारुतात्मजा ॥१२॥ सहस्रसंख्यया शाखा ज्ञाता साम्नां परंतप । अथर्वणस्य शाखाः स्युः पञ्चाशद्भेदतो हरे ॥१३॥

Ṛigveda still has 21 Śākhās and Samaveda the traditional one thousand. But Yajurveda has now 109 and Atharvaveda has 50. Instead of these, Churaṇa-Vyuha gives 86 for Yajurveda and 10 for Atharvaveda. The Mahābhārata of 250 B. C. gives the same number for Ṛigeda and for Śāmaveda ; but it gives (56 + 8 + 37) 10′ for Yajurveda and no Śākās for Athervaveda. The increase in the Śākhās of these two Vedas is not surprizing as these Vedas are not as stereotyped as the other two and as their adherents are more numerous and diffused.

VI SUMERIANS AND INDO-ARYANS.

A Prof. L. A. Waddell in his recent book "Indo-Sumerian Seals Deciphered" holds that the old Sumerians of Mesopotamia (about 4000–3000 B. C.) were Vedic Aryans and that from the seals and signets found at Harappa in Lower Panjab and Mohenjo-Daro in Sind which he has deciphered, there was unquestionably a settlement by sea of these Sumerian or Vedic Aryan people in Sind, at so early a date as 3100 B. C. He further holds that "The same Aryan-Sumerian race eventually came in greater force overland through Persia from Upper Mesopotamia and Asia Minor and making their headquarters in the Gangetic valley, annexed India as the 'so called Aryan invasion of India,' presumably about 700 B. C." (p. 5.) This theory is so extravagant and so directly opposed to the theory of an Aryan Invasion coming into and colonising the Panjab from Central Asia about 4000 B. C. according to Tilak or 1400 B. C. according to most European scholars, and so strongly conflicts with the date which we have assigned to the Rigveda, that it is necessary to examine it critically in this appendix.

One is, at the outset, bewildered by the great number of Sumerian names treated by Prof. Waddell as equivalents of Vedic names. The equation, though ingenious, is a mere fancy prompted by the preconceived notion that the Sumerians were Vedic Aryans. Though similarity of sound may be looked upon as showing identity of persons or things, yet it can only be treated as a suggestion and not a proved fact; and where numerous facts go against such identification it has to be rejected. Thus in the very first chapter, we have Maruts of the Ṛigveda identified with Amorites and Krivis with Syrio-Phoenicians. Two Ṛigveda hymns are quoted in this connection viz. R. V. 53 (9) and R. V.III 20 (24). Now in the first hymn addressed to Maruts, they are plainly looked upon as gods (winds) dwelling in the sky and heaven, (आयात मरुतो दिव आन्तारिक्षादमादुत do 8) and as bringing rain (वि पर्जन्यं सृजन्ति do 6). Moreover verse 9 itself speaks of the upper course of the Indus and not its lower course confronting Sind. We have already stated that the Indo-Aryans lived in the Gāndhāra country on the upper course of the Indus and the Eastern Panjab along the Himalayas and not in the hot western plains about Multan or of Sind. The rivers mentioned in this verse (9) are Rasā, Anitabhā, Kubhā and Kramu, along with the Indus, all western tributaries in its upper course. The poet asks the Maruts not to be stopped by these rivers, nor by the Indus (upper course), but come into the Panjab (Eastern part) and bring showers. The Maruts are no doubt described as human beings, the Vedic poets like poets in other religions, naturally investing their gods with human attributes. The Maruts who succour the Krivis and give them victory, bring balms from the Indus and the Asiknī and the mountains (VIII 20, 24). 'They are clothed in robes of wool' (p. 25), because the Indo-Aryans were themselves clothed in woolen garments, living as they did in the cold climes of Gāudhāra and Eastern Panjab. The Sumerians' also being clad in wool can not, therefore, be made an argument to prove that the Maruts were Amorites or that the Sumerians were Vedic Aryans. These Rigvedic poets speak only of the Kubhā and the Indus and the Asikni and the seas, together with the mountains ; had they come so late as 700 B. C. in the supposed second invasion from Mesopotamia via Persia. they would have spoken of many more places and rivers of those countries.

Prof. Waddell has no doubt brought to the identification of names an extensive knowledge of words in the various Aryan and Semitic languages; but his identifications seem to be very doubtful though ingenious. Thus 'Bhārata' is shown as eventually the origin of 'Britain'. It is not necessary for us to enter into all these identifications. But we must note the following with which we are immediately concerned and which ensue from Prof. Waddell's readings of the script on the seals and signets or amulets.

Harappa and Mohenjo-Daro were, it may be accepted, colonies of Sumerians established so early as 3100 B. C.; but it can scarcely be believed that Sind or Edin was a tributary kingdom of the Sumerian king Uruaś, the same as Uru-Nīna of Lagash and that Uruaś is Haryaśva and A-Madgal is Mudgala of the Indian Purāṇas; or that Pānchāla is Phœnician. Whether the seals found at Harappa are rightly read as Uruaś &c. we need not and cannot discuss. It is a question for Assyriologists who mostly differ from Prof. Waddell, as stated by himself at p. 150. But we may say that when he equates Uruaś with Haryaśva, he makes a far-fetched guess, a guess prompted by his preconceived notion that Sumerian kings were the same as mentioned in the Purāṇa lists. Further does Prof. Waddell hold that these kings mentioned in the Purāṇas never ruled in India, but ruled in Mesopotamia, from whence their names were taken into India by the second invasion of the Sumerians which took place about 700 B. C. !!! It may be pointed out further that Pānchāla is not a Ṛigvedic name, but a name first mentioned in the Brāhmaṇas, nor is Haryaśva, who, in the Ṛigveda, is Indra himself. Puranic geneologies are not as reliable for this period as the names mentioned in the Ṛigveda itself, which is contemporary evidence for kings and peoples of about 3100 B. C.

In equating A-Madgal with Mudgala a Bhārmyaśva, reference is made to Ṛigvedic hymn X 102 from which an interesting story is given at page 38 : "Mudgala owned vast herds of well-pastured kine to the number of a hundred thousand. These cattle were raided by aborigines in his absence and only one bull was left behind. Mudgala harnessed this bull to his chariot and yoked on the other side for balance a stone mace (drughana). His wife acted as charioteer and Mudgala touched the bull with the sacred stone mace of Indra. The bull flew along so swiftly that Mudgala overtook the robbers and single-handed routed them and recovered his cattle". In a seal found at Harappa, the objects figured which Assyriologists could not interpret, show this story according to Prof. Waddell. "Mudgala is figured pointing to the two stone maces and beside them is the chariot—pole from which depend the double harness yokes described in the Vedic hymn with their curved yoking-pins at their loose end" This Vedic hymn is no doubt very interesting and its identification with the scene depicted on the seal is very ingenious. But we have to believe that this Vedic Aryan Mudgala lived in Sind with his one lakh of cows, that when the colony was destroyed, the miracle story went to Messopotamia and remained there for two thousand years and came to India with the second invasion of the Sumerian Aryans via Persia. It is not proved, nor is it even suggested, that the Sumerian settlement advanced into Eastern Panjab. It was killed in Sind about 2700 B. C. and the story of Mudgala and his miracle was related in a Ṛigvedic hymn in Sanskrit about 700 B. C. The Sumerians when they came to India changed their language entirely; for there is no similarity between the Vedic language and the Sumerian. Lastly the figure of the man on the seal need not be that of Mudgala but may be of any cart-driver o old times using stone maces. Indeed, even the name A-Madgala is read by all Assyriologists as Akurgal, as stated by Prof. Waddell himself (at page 32 also). The reading of Bargu as Bhṛigu is also questionable and Mudgala is not of the Bhṛigu gotra according to the Indian genealogies.

It is not necessary to discuss every subsequent identification in detail. Their number is great and includes Kanva (Kaṇva), Barama (Brahmin), 2 Uṣij (slave girl) mother of Asiaś (Auśija) Kakshivan "the far-famed merchant (R. I 112, 11) who, a resident on the Indus, praised the bounty of his patron king Svanaya son of Bhavya (R. I 112, 11 &c.), 3 Taps minister of Saguna of Agda (Indian Daxa of Śaguni of Ayodhya), Sargon I of Agade (Sagara of Ayodhyā), 4 Gudia (Gadhi), 5 Jama-Dagni (Duhgin) 6 Paraśu-Rāma (There is no reference to Paraśu-Rāma in the Rigveda. The hymn ascribed to Bhārgava or Rāma viz. R. X 110 does not mention human sacrifices as supposed by Prof. Waddell p. 60) or Buraśsin, 7 Gal-HA Bargu (Gālava Bhṛigu), 8 Uggu the Kad (Vedic Uchchhai king of Kuru-Pañchālas or Syrio-Phenicians) and 9 Pies or fish (the fish Sun-god) which is the Sumerian origin of Vish in Vishṇu as also of the English fish and the Latin Piscis, *b, p, f, v* being freely interchangable in the Aryan languages" (p. 84). As mentioned before, Puranic stories are not reliable for this period; and we may point out that Sagara is not mentioned in the Ṛigveda nor Ayodhyā (Sagara occurs once only and means the sky in R. X 89, 4) ; nor the legend of Paraśurāma destroying Haryaśva or the Kshatriyas. It is, therefore, improbable that these names are really old and it can not be believed that these names first arose in the Sumerian colony in Sind about 3000 B. C. and thence went into Mesopotamia and came back to India about 700 B. C.

The name Edin of the country of Sind has not, however, been equated to any Sanskrit name (the only name suggested Udyāna being that of a country on the Swat a tributary of the upper Indus. Mohenjo-Daro may be the place where a Sumerian colony was originally established in Edin ; but Daro is not suggestive of any Sanskrit name, though it may be Sumerian—Daru or sea. "As to Mohenjo in view of the prominence given to the buffalo on the seals of Edin, it may be derived from Mahisha, a word derived from the Sumerian Ma-a-su or cattle, still current as Mains" (p. 111). This is perhaps the most curious guess ; but it is true, that the this part of the country is the home of buffaloes, a fact on which we will presently comment.

B Mr. Daji Nagesh Apte of Baroda, in his Marathi pamphlet recently published and entitled "Indian and Sumerian Civilizations," without expressly accepting the readings of the scripts on the seals and signets &c. found at Harappa and Mohenjo-Daro, proposed by Prof. Waddell, properly rejects his theory of two invasions of India by the Sumerians, as also his view that Vedic civilization is derived from the Sumerian. But he suggests that the Sumerians and the Vedic Aryans lived together in the Arctic home of the Aryans and issuing from there and dividing into two branches, went into Mesopotamia and the Panjab respectively. He thus believes that the Sumerians and the Aryans were one people and adduces proof by showing how some Sumerian and Vedic myths are identical. Curiously enough, he does not admit that the finds at Mohenjo-Daro and Harappa are Sumerian in origin, a fact which, we think, one can scarcely deny from the script on the seals &c found there. They clearly are the remains of Sumerian settlements from Mesopotamia. But according to our view the Sumerian civilization is not the same as the Indo-Aryan, nor are the two peoples branches of the same Aryan stock. How the arguments and myths adduced by Mr. Apte are insufficient to prove identity of culture and origin, we proceed to show. The Sumerians may have been Aryan by race as shown by the form of their noses and heads, and they may not be Semitic. Even the Semitic people are treated by most anthropologists as related to the Aryan race and not as Dravidians. But it seems certain that the Sumerians are not a branch of the Indo-European Aryan family and probably did not come from the Arctic home, the exodus from which is described in a passage of the Zend Avesta pointed out by B. G. Tilak.

In the first place, similarity or even identity of myths can not be treated as proving identity of race and culture, unless supported by other arguments. For religious myths are usually based on the different aspects of nature which among all peoples first suggested them their conceptions of gods; and men unconnected often imagine identical or similar stories to explain natural phenomena. Then again myths travel from one community to another in various ways, usually through casual intercourse, often by even hearsay. Hence it is necessary to support arguments derived from myths by those derived from language and from tradition. In the light of these remarks we will examine the myths adduced by Mr. D. N. Apte in his brochure.

Indra is the highest deity with the Ṛigvedic Aryans having displaced Varuṇa who was the highest in oldest times, and Indra's greatest exploit is the killing of Vṛitra. To match with this, Mr. Apte points out that Bel was at first the highest god with the Sumerians, but his place was subsequently taken by Marduk who is the exact counterpart of Indra. The story of Marduk's exploit is given in Sumerian mythology as follows:-He is the son of Ea the goddess of earth. Taimat was a dragon born of primeval waters. Other gods refused to go against her, but Marduk at their prayer attacked Taimat in primeval waters and killed her with his spear and club "He split her up like a flat fish in two halves and bade the waters come forth ; and light was then created, for he overcame the monster as a solar god" (p. 31) "He opened the two gates on both sides of the firmament for Śams (the sun-god), who every day journeys from one end to the other across the worlds. The god then praised Marduk in odes" Mr. Apte hereafters quotes similar poetic descriptions of the feat of Indra killing Vritra from the Ṛigveda. The qutations no doubt show a good deal of diligent diving into the hymns of the Rigveda. But similar poetical ideas are bound to be found in the most distant and unconnected poems and the idea of the strongest god killing a dreadful demon who was in the form of a huge serpent is also likely to occur to any people. The idea of the creation of the world and of light out of some primaeval waters overspread with darkness, is also a natural suggestion and these ideas exist among almost all intelligent peoples. We must mark, however, that Marduk and Taimat are names vastly different from Indra and Vritra. If the Sumerians and the Vedic Aryans had been one people, these names could not have been so dissimilar.

The story of Gilgamesh given hereafter by Mr. Apte seems to be irrelevant, as it has nothing to do with the question of the indentity of Sumerians with the Vedic Aryans and as no counterpart of Gilgamesh is shown among the latter people. The story of the Rāmāyaṇa is not Vedic but is plainly Puranic, though Rāma is a Vedic hero. Further, parallel ideas and descriptions appearing in the

Rāmāyana given by Mr. Apte simply go to prove that poets portray and imagine events in different countries and times in the same manner, because they have the same humanity in them. Such similarities do not prove copyng from one by the other or by both from a common source. The story of Gilgamesh cannot hence be said to have been copiled in the Rāmāyana. The story of the Deluge is next referred to as originally Sumerian and thence borrowed by the Śatapatha. The two stories no doubt are very similar but how do they go to prove that Sumerians and Vedic Aryans were one people? Cannot such legends arise among different peoples by imagining a world defuge from heavy floods which often occur in every country? Even if we grant that the Śatapatha story is a copy of the Sumerian original, as the story is not given in the Ṛigveda, but later, and as communication between Mesopotamia and the Panjab after 3000 B. C. is an undeniable fact, one can believe that the story came from the Sumerians to India and was given by the Śatapatha in its own way, after making suitable changes in it. It is, however. necessary to remark that there is no similarity of names even here and hence borrowing is not as certain as in the case of Taimat, Aligi, Biligi &c borrowed by the Atharvaveda, the date of which we have fixed to be about 2700 B. C. lying between 3000 B.C. and 2350, the estimated period of occupation of Sind by Sumerians. We have even suggested at page 39 that some Indo-Aryan people went into Mesopotamia and Asia Minor and established the kingdom of Mittani.

Mr. Apte next notes the identity of the Indian and Sumerian Yugas. It is mentioned that Yugas and Rāśis were borrowed by the Hindus from the Chaldeans who were great observers of the sky. But this borrowing, Mr. Apte fails to notice, took place far later, indeed after Alexander's invasion, when the Hindus and the Greeks came into close contact about 300 to 100 B.C. In Ṛigvedic times and the days of Vedānga Jyotisha, practically from 3000 to 300 B. C. the Indo-Aryans had their own astronomy based on Nakshatras which are purely Indian. Had the Vedic Aryans come in a second invasion from Mesopotamia via Persia, they would have brought the ideas of Rāśis and Yugas, with them and used them in their Sūtras &c. That there is no trace of Rāśis and Yugas in Vedic literature or indeed in any Indian literature up to 100 B. C. is the surest proof that Indo-Aryans never came from Mesopotamia in Vedic or post-Vedic days. Nay further, as the Sumerians do not show acquaintance with the Vedic Nakshatras which they had settled in Ṛigvedic times, it is nearly certain that the Sumerians and the Indo-Aryans did not live together in the Arctic home of the Aryans.

But besides this dissmilarilty, there are others of an important character between the two peoples. The difference of language is the most striking. We speak open to correction, but we believe that the Sumerian language is not akin to Vedic Sanskrit. Comparative philology, not mythology alone, has established the unity of race of the Indo-Aryans and the Iranians as also of the Germanic peoples and the Greeks and the Romans. The similarity of language between the Vedic Aryans and the Iranians is so complete that whole Vedic mantras are often identical with the gāthās of the Zend Avesta. Similarity of language, mythology and worship leaves no doubt whatever that the Vedic Aryans and the Iranians were cousin peoples, the Devas and the Asuras of Vedic literature. The Asuras are often supposed to be represented by the Assyrians ; but this similarity of name is not backed by similarity of language or of mythology or of worship; and it is a mistake to look upon the Assyrians as the Asuras of the Vedas. The Sumerians similarly can not be looked upon as akin to the Vedic people in consequence of difference of language. Mr. Apte has pointed out the affixes तुम् and अस in Sumerian as identical with तुम् and स्य of Sanskrit. But these few instances can not prove affinity of language, which is established by similar syntax and vocabulary generally.

The names and conceptions of deities are also very dissimilar. We have not Varuṇa, nor Savitṛi, nor Yama among the Sumerians, while Shams is a word unknown to the Vedic language. The word Mitra does occur as pointed out by Mr. Apte, but it is not the usual word for the Sun and it may have been taken from the neighbouring Iranians. Uśas the polar-region-deity is conspicuous by her absence among the Sumerians, while the conception of Istar is not to be found in the whole of Vedic literature. Most conspicuous of all the absences, is that of the deity of fire or god-Agni. Fire and the sun are the most natural gods of people living in the Arctic regions; but fire is not mentioned as a god with the Sumerians or with the Assyrians. It is the highest with the Iranians along with the Sun and they are unquestionably the Asuras of the Vedas. There is no trace of fire-worship, it may be noted further, in the supposed seals of the Kanva and Kakshīvat. It can not be believed that the Sumerians forgot or gave up fire worship when they came to hot lands and took up new gods. Bel, Ishtar and Nini. The Iraniarns and the Hindus have not forgotton or given up fire-worship in the hot plains of the Panjab or of Western India. It is, therefore, difficult to hold that the Sumerians and the Vedic Aryans were two branches of the Aryan people of the Arctic regions.

There are other striking differences in their civilizations and conditions which may also be noted. The Vedic Aryans and the Iranians were worshippers of the cow and cows were plentiful in their lands beyond the Indus as well as in the Panjab. The seals show that the Sumerians worshipped or rather used buffaloes which were plentiful in Sind, their home land. The Rigveda does not mention the buffalo at all. They probably did not know it, as it is stated in the Purāṇas that the buffalo was a new creation by Viśvāmitra. If the Vedic Aryans had come from Mesopotamia, they would certainly not have forgotten the buffalo. Nay more, the Mudgala of the seals of the land of buffaloes can not be the Mudgala of the Ṛigveda who had a lakh of cows ; for there could never have been cows in such plenty in Sind in those days. Then again while the Ṛigveda shows no trace of the buffalo, the Sumerian seals show no trace of the horse which is spoken of constantly in the Ṛigveda and which was so plentiful with the Vedic Aryans. Iron too is not found in the new discoveries but it was plentiful with the Vedic Aryans. It seems, therefore, extremely probable, that the Sumerian finds in Sind and Lower Panjab have nothing to do with the Ṛigvedic civilization, which from astronomical data, is proved to be as old as 5,000 B. C.

It may be stated in conclusion that it is not necessary for our history of Vedic literature to refute the theory of Prof. Waddell or of Mr. Apte that the Sumerians were allied to the Vedic Aryans, or the interesting suggestion of Mr. Apte that they both went from their Arctic home into their respective lands. For all one knows, the Sumerians may be one with the Vedic Aryans from the several points of contact noted by these scholars. But our history requires that the idea of Prof. Waddell that the Rishis of the Rigveda and the Acharyas of the Brāhmaṇas and Sūtras were Sumerians who came in a second invasion to India about 700 B. C. and "not earlier" should be refuted This theory is rejected by Mr. Apte as without any proof and the above facts and arguments, we think, rightly negative it. Mr. Apte's theory about their coming from their Arctic home may be accepted, if it is ascertained that the Sumerian language and Vedic Sanskrit are akin*.

VII KĀTHAKA AND MAITRĀYANĪYA SANHITĀS OF BLACK YAJURVEDA.

These have been published by Shraeder and so far as one can scrutinize them, they are nearly the same, though many minor variations are to be found, made consciously or otherwise for variation as well as for difference of ritual. The Taittirīya Sanhitā seems to be the oldest of all the Black Yajurveda Sanhitās and these later recensions are obviously abridgments though Brāhmaṇa portions still remain. For these recensions, like the White Sanhitā do not separate Mantra and Brāhmaṇa. These Sanhitās, however, are later than the White Yajurveda Sanhitā as will appear from the facts noted further on.

The Maitrāyaṇīya Sanhitā is divided into Prapāthakas or lessons while the Kāthaka is divided into Sthānakas which is a new word in Vedic literature. There are 41 such Sthānakas in the Kāthaka Sanhitā. The last Sthānaka is described as follows :—इति एकोत्तरशतशाखाध्वर्युप्रभेदभिन्ने श्रीमद्यजु-

*Sin (noon) may be the basis of सिनीवाली though the word means food in the Ṛigveda. Yavha, as pointed out by Tilak, appears as Jehova in the Jewish language. But one or two words cannot establish affinity of language.

षैंदकाठके चरकशाखायामिठिमिकायामेकचत्वारिंशं स्थानकं सम्पूर्णम्॥. This is clearly a modern description. What Iṭhimikā is it is not possible to say ; the name is a strange one. Each sthānaka is separately named from its contents. These sthānakas are much smaller than the Prapāthakas of the Maitrāyaṇīya Sanhitā but the contents of subsections which probably are called Anuvākas in both are the same ; and the larger divisions also are on the same subjects such as Agnihotra, Chāturmāsya &c. ending with Aśvamedha, as in the Taittirīya Sanhitā ; and in that last section we have the same mantras relating to the strange rite of the Aśvamedha sacrificer's queen being made to lie with the dead horse. The Kāthaka Sanhitā has accents, throughout both its prose and verse parts ; but some prose in the Maitrāyaṇīya Sanhitā is without accents. The Rudrādhyāya which is so popular a part of the Black Yajurveda is found in both, with many variations and some abridgments, as compared with that of the Taittirīya Sanhitā.

The following interesting statements in the Kāthaka Sanhitā are noteworthy :—

1 The Sanhitā begins with the usual words इषे त्वा and the ending of the first sthānaka is as follows ; इति श्रीयजुषि काठके चरकशाखायामिठिमिकायां पुरोडाशस्थानकं नाम प्रथमं समाप्तम्।

2 मार्डीकं (धेहि जीवसे) and गयस्फानो (2, 14) are reminiscent of Sumerian names.

3 Various Ṛigvedic mantras are quoted now and then e. g. अप्सु मे सोमो अब्रवीत्, जुष्टो दमूना, उप त्वाग्ने दिवे दिवे &c.

4 इष्टो यज्ञो भृगुभिर्यज्ञो दायातभिराशीर्भिर्वा अथर्वभिः ॥ Bhṛigu and Atharvan are Ṛishis of magic spells.

5 The word Veda signifies now the Vedic compilations. घृतवन्तं कुलायिनं रायस्पोषं सहस्रिणम् । वेदो वाजं ददातु मे वेदो वीरं ददातु मे ॥ वृषा वृषण्वतीभ्यो वेदपत्नीभ्यो नमः ॥

6 प्रेयमेधा नाम ब्राह्मणा आसन् some of whom kept Agnihotra and others did not. This refers probably to other Aryan peoples who were, however, treated as Brahmins.

7 प्राचीं दिशमरोचयन् कृत्तिका: The Krittikas' rising in the east is a phenomenon also noted in the Śatapatha. This is the same phenomenon and gives about the same date to this Sanhitā; it is, however, later by a century or two, as will appear further. The Krittikas are seven सप्त वै कृत्तिका:

8 Rohiṇī is also mentioned as also the two heavenly dogs (दिव्यौ श्वानौ). Chitrā is also mentioned as Aindra Nakshatra. The deities presiding over Nakshatras were well fixed.

9 Brahmins, Kshatriyas and Vaiśyas kept Agnihotra.

10 आपो वा अग्र आसीत् प्रजापतिर्वराहो भूत्वा न्यमज्जत् is found here also, the precursor of the Varāha incarnation story.

11 अग्निरश्वो भूत्वा देवानगच्छत् स यत्रातिष्टत्स अश्वत्थः ।।

12 नैमिष्या वै सत्रमासत उत्थाय सप्तविंशतिं कुरुपंचालेषु वत्सतरानन्ववत तान् बको दाल्भिरब्रवीत् यूयं विभजथ अहं धृतराष्ट्रं वैचित्रवीर्यं गमिष्यामि ।। (8, 2) This clear reference to Dhritārāshtra, son of Vichitravīrya, places this Sanhitā a little later than the Śatapatha. Vyāsa cannot be the author of this Sanhitā. Baka, son of Dalbha is a teacher mentioned in Chhāndogya, as also the sacrificers of Nimisha forest.

13 Magic rites are prescribed by this Sanhitā also and it seems that the Atharvaveda had not yet been compiled or had not yet become the Veda of magical rites (अभिचरन् अभिचर्यमाणो वा.)

14 The Vedic metres were yet looked upon as seven only, the subsequent seven were added later (न जगत्या परिदध्यादन्तो वैषः छन्दसाम् 12, 4.)

15 Different animals were offered to different deities (आश्विनमजमालभेत सारस्वतीं मेषीमैन्द्रमृषभं वा वृष्णिं वा). The food oblations were offered in dishes formed of different numbers o: Kapālas, the number strangely being very importan

(अष्टाकपाल द्वादशकपाल &c.)

16 In the Rājasūya ritual, the idea of Rāshtra or state is given expression to (राष्ट्रं दत्त, स्वाहा राष्ट्रदाः &c.)

17 The Mantra तत्पुरुषाय विद्महे महादेवाय धीमहि । तन्नो रुद्रःप्रचोदयात् shows that this Veda is devoted to Rudra-worship. The word Mahādeva is also indicative of a late date. This mantra is used with necessary changes in all subsequent Puranic deity-worships. It is obviously based on the Gāyatri mantra of the Ṛigveda

HISTORY
OF
SANSKRIT LITERATURE

Vol.2

BRĀHMANAS

By

C.V.VAIDYA M.A., LL.B.
Author of Mahābhārata: a Criticism, Riddle of
the Rāmāyaṇa and Epic India; and
History of Mediaeval Hindu
India, in three Vols. etc. etc.

PARIMAL PUBLICATIONS
DELHI

Published by

Parimal Publications

Office : 27/28, Shakti Nagar, Delhi-110007 (India)
Retail Outlet : 22/3, Shakti Nagar, Delhi-110007 (India)
Ph. : +91-11-23845456, 47015168
e-mail : order@parimalpublication.com
url : http://www.parimalpublication.com

Edition : Year 2011

ISBN : 978-81-7110-047-7 (Set)
978-81-7110-049-1 (Vol. 2)

Price : ₹ 700.00 (Set of 3 Vols.)

Printed by

Vishal Kaushik Printers

Near G.T.B. Hospital, Jagat Puri Vistar,
Shahdara, Delhi-110093

SECTION II–BRĀHMANAS

History of Sanskrit Literature

ŚRUTI PERIOD

Section II—BRĀHMANAS

CONTENTS

HISTORY OF

SANSKRIT LITERATURE

S'ṚUTI PERIOD

SECTION II — BRĀHMANAS

I BRĀHMANAS IN GENERAL

Following the example of the S'atapatha Brāhmaṇa, containing explanatory notes on the Vājasaneyi Mantras and exposition of sacrificial procedure generally, a vast Brāhmaṇa literature arose and gathered round the other Vedas in due course. The word Brāhmaṇa (neuter) means a work containing explanation of Brahman or Vedic Mantras. The word has not been explained by Pāṇini, but he uses it in this sense as in the sūtra which refers to Brāhmaṇas declared by the old sages. The word occurs also in Vedic literature including Brāhmaṇas themselves, as meaning Vedic explanation (इति ह ब्राह्मणम्, तस्योक्तं ब्राह्मणम् A. B. VIII, 2 &c). The Brāhmaṇas, besides explanatory notes on Vedic Mantras, contain discussions on the ritual of Vedic sacrifices. Such discussions must have often taken place among Vedic savants, called Brahmavādins even in Black Yajuḥ--Samhitā, and the final or prevailing opinion is usually given. As Winternitz aptly puts it, the Brāhmaṇas are thus "treatises on the science of sacrifice". The Brāhmaṇas also contain legends old and new, i. e. current from the days of Ṛigveda or invented later in explanation of Vidhis (rites) or in praise of them, as also of names. All these are together called Arthavādas by the Mimāṁsakas or professors of the science of sacrifice. Containing explanatory notes and legends, the Brāhmaṇas are naturally in prose, though Gāthās or mnemonic verses occur now and then, embodying traditions or traditional sayings in praise of things or men. Their latest developments are the Āraṇyakas and Upanishads, containing theosophical or philosophical speculations on the nature and meaning of sacrificial rites and the phenomenon of this world and the one pervading essence behind it called eventually Brahman. The word Brahman thus rose gradually from denoting a verse (विश्वामित्रस्य रक्षति ब्रह्मेदं भारतं जनम्) in praise of deities, to Veda generally and finally to the highest thing taught by it. All this literature, the explanatory and theological Brāhmaṇas, the theosophical Āraṇyakas and the philosophical Upanishads goes under the name of Brāhmaṇa and is included in the term Veda or revelation by the orthodox Hindus.

This literature must have been more extensive than what has been preserved, as many authors are mentioned in the extant Brāhmaṇas, as also in the Gṛihya Sūtras, whose works do not now exist. The existing Brāhmaṇas attach themselves naturally to different Vedas and the Sūtras similarly, which arose later. The Gṛihya Sūtra of Āśvalāyana attached to the Ṛigveda thus mentions the following Āchāryas in the Tarpaṇa ceremony. It may be stated here that Āśvalāyaṇa makes a distinction between Ṛishis and Āchāryas. According to him the former are the seers of Ṛigvedic Mantras while Āchāryas are authors of Brāhmaṇas. The Āchāryas of the Ṛigveda are enumerated as follows under the Āchārya Tarpaṇa; Kahoḷa, Kaushītaka, Mahākaushītaka, Paiṅgya, Mahāpaingya, Suyajña, S'āṅkhāyana, Aitareya, Mahaitareya, S'ākala, Bāshkala, Sujātavakra, Audavāhi, Mahaudavāhi, Śaujāṁi, Śaunaka and Āśvalāyana. We cannot tell whether all these had their Brāhmaṇas; but we have the Aitareya and the Śāṅkhāyana Brāhmaṇas extant, the latter being also called Kaushītaki to whom a separate libation of water is offered. The names Paiṅgya and Mahāpaiṅgya &c. suggest that, like Bhārata and Mahābhārata, the Brāhmaṇas of Paiṅgya &c. were extended by other Āchāryas. The extended Brāhmaṇas as also many original Brāhmaṇas, unlike the Mahābhārata, have, however, disappeared.

In the Tarpaṇa ceremony of the Śānkhāyana Gṛihya Sūtra, also attached to the Ṛigveda, we have these Āchāryas and further, Bhāradvāja, Jātūkarṇya, Śākapūṇi and Gautama. In both, after these names, is given a general clause "and others" not mentioned (ये चान्येप्याचार्यास्ते सर्वे तृप्यन्तु). From this and from Pāṇini's sūtra referring to old and new Brāhmaṇas, the conclusion is irresistible that much Brāhmaṇa literature has been lost. Probably the best in it has survived; or it may be that some particular Brāhmaṇas alone have survived by the survival of their Śākhās, as it was impossible to preserve such vast literature by memory, all Vedic works being then taught from mouth to mouth and preserved by memory. It is not easy to find out Brāhmaṇa authors of the other Vedas whose works have been lost. For in their Gṛihyasūtras, there is no Ṛishi Tarpaṇa by separate names, nor of course Āchārya Tarpaṇa. Thus Gobhila Sūtra mentions Ṛishi–Tarpaṇa and Āchārya-Tarpaṇa, but gives no details and includes in one category all the Ṛishis or the Āchāryas (of the Sāmaveda). The Pāraskara Śūtra of the White Yajurveda similarly mentions Ṛishis and Āchāryas generally; so also the Āpastamba Sūtra. The Hiraṇya-keśi Sūtra does the same; but it prescribes a Ṛishi-Pūjā in which besides the well-known seven Ṛishis is placed Agastya in the south and certain Āchāryas are also seated; the names are many and include Kṛishṇa-Dvaipāyana, Jātūkarṇya, Gautama, Vāmadeva and Parāśara; seats in a different place are provided for Vaiśampāyana, Paliñgu, Tittiri, Ukha, Ātreya (said to be the author of the Taittirīya Saṁhitā pada text) and Kauṇḍinya said to be the Bhāshyakāra. Whether these wrote Brāhmaṇas or mere Sūtras cannot now be determined. Indeed they are all now usually called Ṛishis.

We will speak of the Brāhmaṇa literature which survives, in detail presently. This literature is all in prose, as stated already, the language of which strikes us as later than that of the Ṛigveda. It is, however, still not classical Sanskrit nor even the language of Pāṇini. It is still Vedic language. The constant repeating of sentences is a peculiarity of this language derived from the Black Yajurveda Saṁhitā where the first Brāhmaṇa treatment of a subject appears. The repetition, however, as shown before, is necessary; but to us, devoid of all interest in or respect for sacrifice, the reading of the Brāhmāṇas is tiresome and even troublesome, as they contain, in the words of Max Müller, 'theological twaddle.' Probably this led to the composition of Sūtras in the next period. The prose of the historical or philosophical portions of the Brāhmaṇas is, however, vivacious and even graceful. The highest development of Vedic prose may be seen in the prose Upanishads, especially the Bṛihadāraṇyaka which, as we will show later, rivals even the oratory of ancient Greece.

Coming to the deities praised in the Brāhmaṇas, we find generally the old Ṛigvedic deities still praised. But Vishṇu, Rudra and Prajāpati rise to the status of highest gods. Prajāpati, as father of all gods, is constantly referred to in the explanations. We can mark how Indra and other gods declined in power and became simply divine beings who have attained to their godly position by sacrifice.

We next come to the difficult and disputed question regarding the age of this literature. For the development of all this literature, including the Upanishads, that a period of about a thousand years must be assigned is conceded by most scholars. But the *termini*, i. e. the beginning and the end of this period of a thousand years, are in great dispute. We look upon this vast literature as evolved from about 3000 to 2000 B. C., while most European scholars place the Brāhmaṇas from about 1200 to 200 B.C. The chief cause of this extreme divergence of opinion is the difference of dates assigned to the Śatapatha Brāhmaṇa. This Brāhmaṇa is, from the legend of its composition, unquestionably the oldest Brāhmaṇa and its composition, as stated already, must be placed in about 3000 B. C. S. B. Dixit has shown this from the statement in the second Kāṇḍa (accepted by all to be its old part) that the Kṛittikās rise exactly in the east. We have said in our introduction that this theory of Dixit has neither been noticed nor refuted by any European scholar; but in the History of Indian Literature by Winternitz, translated into English and published quite recently, a refutation of this theory of S. B. Dixit is found at p. 298. In a note, Winternitz notices how Dixit, followed by several Indian scholars, has concluded from the above passage in the Śatapatha that it was written in about 3000 B.C. But it is urged in refutation that the sentence 'The Pleiades do not swerve from the east' should probably not be-interpreted as meaning that they rose due east. "The correct interpretation," says Winternitz, "is more likely that they remain visible in the eastern region for a considerable time--during several hours every night-which was the case about 1100 B. C." This interpretation was suggested by a German astronomer, Prof. A Prey (foot-note 2, p. ditto). More recently still, the same argument and interpretation has been put forth by an Indian astronomer, Mr. Daphtari of Nagpur, in the Vividha-Jñāna-Vistāra of Bombay (Jan. 1928), on the basis of the remark of Winternitz or independently. How this interpretation is untenable we shall show in a note, as this subject is rather technical. The ordinary reader can, however, clearly see that the author of the Śatapatha statement could not have meant that the Kṛittikās came on the eastern line two or three hours after their rise. The wording clearly refers to the rising of the Kṛittikās and cannot be distorted to mean something else. But what is a more cogent answer is that this new date for the Śatapatha, viz. 1100 B. C, cannot fit in, unless the date of the Vedāṅga Jyotisha is also shifted onwards. The Vedāṅga Jyotisha must be placed many centuries after the Śatapatha and its date from the astronomical statement in it comes, as already shown, to about 1400 B. C. Even Max Müller could not bring it down to any date later than 1181 B. C. with the help of the astronomer Archbishop Pratt. It, therefore, follows that the date of the Śatapatha must be several centuries earlier than 1180 B. C. Winternitz, therefore, cannot change the meaning of the words of the Śatapatha and assign a new date to it, unless he refutes the date of the Vedāṅga Jyotisha, deduced from astronomical statements in it. This he has not done; for he simply states at page 289 that 'the Vedāṅga Jyotisha being in verse is of a later date'!!!

The S'atapatha is further accented and belongs, therefore, to the Saṁhitā period. It was naturally followed by the Taittirīya Brāhmaṇa which also is accented. The Taittirīyas would be the first to emulate the Vājasaneyins in enunciating a Brāhmaṇa for their Veda. The Brāhmaṇas of the other Vedas followed in due course. These were followed by Āraṇyakas ending in the composition of the Upanishads, ten of which are considered to be the leading ones. Now a subsequent Upanishad, viz. the Maitrāyaṇīya, furnishes us with an astronomical statement on which its date, as already shown, has been calculated to be about 1900 B.C. This supplies us with the second terminus for the age of the Brāhmaṇas, which thus extends from about 3000 B. C. to 2000 B.C. There are many other Upanishads; but they are plainly modern and may be omitted from consideration in settling the period of the Brāhmaṇas as the word is understood by orthodox Hindus.

Prof. Bhagvad Datta of D. A. V College, Lahore in his recent book on the Brāhmaṇas assigns them to the Mahābhārata period; unfortunately he no-where states what this period is. The Mahābhārata, as we have it, is assigned by most European scholars to 500 A.D., whereas we assign it to 250 B.C., a date accepted by Lokamānya Tilak in the Gītārahasya. The Bhārata fight took place in 3102 B. C. according to our view; but most European scholars and Tilak place it from 1400 to 1000 B.C. The Mahābhārata period is thus an indefinite expresssion and leads to no particular date.

Lastly, the Brāhmaṇas developed what is found in embryo in the Samhitās, notably the Black Yajurveda Saṁhitā, in the matter of legends, theological explanations and etymologies. Thus the idea that the gods acquired power by sacrifice is to be found in the last verse of the

Purushasūkta. Again a verse in Ṛigveda VII. 33 states that the Vasishṭhas increased the power of Indra by their loud chants. Vasisṭha's sons being killed is hinted at in a sentence in the Black Yajurveda Saṁhitā as well as in a sūkta of the Ṛigveda. The Śunaḥśepa story is hinted at in R. I. 24 as we shall presently show. The story of the serpents' mother is suggested by R.X. 189. These stories were further developed in the Purāṇas naturally enough.

II THE S'ATAPATHA BRĀHMANA

Speaking now of individual known Brāhmaṇas in detail, we come first to the Śatapatha which we hold to be the oldest of all. Macdonell thinks that it is the latest, except the Gopatha of the Atharva Veda, as it shows an advance in matter, uses the narrative tenses and has a style and language decidedly more developed than the other Brāhmaṇas. But these cannot be said to be decisive factors as they might be due to the higher genius of its writer, viz. Yājñavalkya. As said before, the legend of its composition is acceptable and Yājñavalkya, dissatisfied with the Black Saṁhitā, which, gives both Mantra and Brāhmaṇa together, may be believed to have separated the Mantras and written an extensive separate Brāhmaṇa. This Brāhmaṇa is called Śatapatha, as it has a hundred chapters; but this name must be looked upon as given later on to it. For the Brāhmaṇa has now fourteen Kāṇḍas, the first ten of which, containing 66 chapters, appear to be the old portion of it. In the first five Kāṇḍas, there is a continuous commentary on the first 18 chapters of the Vājasaneyi-Saṁhitā enunciated by Yājñavalkya himself-and Yājñavalkya is mentioned therein by name as the final authority. The next Kāṇḍas, VI to X, do not mention him but mention Śāṇḍilya as the authority. This is, however, no argument to hold that Yājñavalkya did not compose these Kāṇḍas. Yājñavalkya accepts the authority of Śāṇḍilya on their subjects and thus mentions his name. His mentioning his own name in the first five Kāṇḍas cannot also be treated as indicating that these were composed by some other person than Yājñavalkya. For even in some Ṛigvedic hymns, we find the authors mentioning their own names in them. We also find that Jaimini, Bādarāyaṇa and Kauṭalya in their works similarly mention their views under their own names and indicate that they are the final views on the matters. We may well believe, therefore, that these ten Kāṇḍas are by Yājñavalkya and hence are as old as 3000 B. C.

The Mādhyandina recension of the Śatapatha has fourteen Kāṇḍas but the Kāṇva has seventeen. Kāṇḍas XI to XIV or XVII are, however, distinctly later additions. The matters they deal with are later subjects such as Upanayana, Śvādhyāya, Purushamedha and Sarvamedha. We have already seen that the Vājasaneyi Saṁhitā, Adhyāyas 26 to 35, are Khila or supplementary and it is these which contain a description of the Purushmedha. It is, therefore, apparent that when these later Adhyāyas were added to the Saṁhitā, their explanation or exposition was added later in these later Kāṇḍas. Some believe that the tenth Kāṇḍa is also a later Kāṇḍa ; for Kāṇḍa 12 is said to be Madhyamakāṇḍa by some which leads to the same inference, since XII would be the middle of the portion from X to XIV.

The prose of this Brāhmaṇa is accented which, as stated before, proves that it is an old Brāhmaṇa, all other Brāhmaṇas except the Taittirīya being without accents. Macdonell detracts from the value of this argument by observing that "its accentuation differs entirely from the regular Vedic method" (p. 203). But the accentuation of the Vājasaneyi–Saṁhitā also differs from the accentuation of the other Vedas and hence this difference also. This difference was introduced either by Yājñavalkya himself or by the followers of his Veda in later times. The mode, however, of pronouncing the accents is different but not the rules of laying them, so far as we know, which, as given by Pāṇini in his grammar, are applicable to all Vedas alike.

The Śāṇḍilya Kāṇḍas speak of the Gāndhāra, Kekaya, and Śālva peoples while in the other Kāṇḍas are mentioned " hardly any but the eastern peoples or the people of middle Hindusthan", viz. Kuru-Pāñchālas, Kosala-Videhas, Sṛiñjayas and others (p. 213, Macd.) This certainly supports the story noted before that Yājñavalkya was a native of Videha and that King Janaka of Videha was his pupil. But we must remember that there was constant communication even in those days in all the three parts of the Aryan land, viz, (i) Gāndhāra and the Panjab, (ii) Kuru-Pāñchāla and the middle land, (iii) the eastern part, Kosala and Videha. We know that the Brāhmaṇas themselves declare that grammar was zealously studied in the northern part and ritual in the middle. Pāṇini (800 B. C.) was a native of Gāndhāra; and the Kuru-Pāñchāla land was the centre of Aryan civilization. The mention of Gāndhāra and Kekaya alone in the Śāṇḍilya Kāṇḍas does not, therefore, show that they were not composed by Yājñavalkya. It may be that Śāṇḍilya belonged to the north-west and as Yājñavalkya accepts and quotes his authority, he has occasion to mention the northwestern people only. It is not also necessary to suppose that this section is an interpolation in the Śātapatha because it mentions the north-western people only. Even if it is an interpolation, it must be an older section, for the same reason, than the rest of the Śatapatha, older than the first five Kāṇḍas of Yājñavalkya. The conclusion, therefore, is that while Kāṇḍas XI to XIV are, most probably, an addition, the first ten Kāṇḍas of the Śatapatha are a work of Yājñavalkya. The last or fourteenth Kāṇḍa is the well-known Bṛihadāraṇyaka Upanishad, the date of which may be taken to be about 2500 B. C., as we shall show when speaking of the Upanishaḍs and hence the composition of the Śatapatha as a whole belongs to the period from 3000 to 2500 B. C. Thus both by its date and its extreme fulness, this Brāhmaṇa, as Macdonell rightly observes, "next to the Ṛigveda, is the most important production in the whole range of Vedic literature" (Macd. p. 212). It is important for the study of the development of sacrificial ritual, theological speculation and Vedānta philosophy.

It is also important in connection with the history of the Indo-Aryan peoples. It gives several legends in this connection. The legend of Māṭhava is interesting and shows how the Indo-Aryans advanced into Mithilā or Videha, or modern Behar. It is contained in the first Kāṇḍa. From the banks of the Sarasvatī, this king with his Purohita, Gotama Rāhūgaṇa, went eastwards taking their sacrifical fire with them and came to the Sadānīrā, the western boundary of Mithilā. The land beyond was not burnt by Agni Vaiśvānara who stopped on its bank. He, however, said to Māṭhava Videha "To the east of the river be thy abode." The land was then occupied by the king, and the Brāhmaṇas who did not formerly cross the river crossed it. "Even now," says the Brāhmaṇa "this river is the boundary between Kosala and Videha" (I. 4,1). It may be noted that the Aryans had advanced into Kosala in the days of the Ṛigveda which mentions the Śarayu as stated already. The advance into further Mithila mentioned in the first Kāṇḍa of this Brāhmaṇa may, therefore, be put some time before 3000 B. C. The Gotama family even in the Rāmāyaṇa is shown as the family priests of Janaka. Here again Yājñavalkya developed his philosophy. This land in future centuries became also the birth-place of Buddhism and Jainism, which used certain words in special senses such as Arhat, Śramaṇa and Pratibuddha used in this Brāhmaṇa to indicate monks generally. The idea of renunciation took root in this country and grew later into the colossal tree of the renunciation of Mahāvīra and Buddha. Macdonell, however, rightly remarks that these words in the Śatapatha have not yet the sense attached to them by these religions. Arhat, Śramaṇa and Pratibuddha are words which in later literature apply only to Jain and Buddhist monks.

Macdonell also points out that Gautama is the name "which frequently occurs among teachers in the Śatapatha and that name is the family name of the Śākyas of Kapilavastu among whom Buddha was born" (p. 215). It may be added here that the Śākyas were Kshatriyas and their taking the name Gautama is explained in Saundarānanda, a Buddhist poem, on the theory that Kshatriyas take the gotras of their purohitas. The Śākyas, however, are nowhere represented as belonging to the Janaka clan. Āsuri, again, a teacher subsequently mentioned in connection with Sāṅkhya philosophy even in the Mahābhārata is also mentioned in the Śatapatha. Of historical kings, Dushyanta and Bharata are mentioned among sacrificers of As'vamedha(XIII 5,4). Janamejaya is also mentioned who is unquestionably the Janamejaya of the Mahābhārata, the son of Parīkshit, grand-son of Arjuna. The Pāṇḍavas are, however, not mentioned; but this non-mention can be of no historical value as their mention cannot be considered to be necessary. On this and the mention of Janamejaya we shall have to speak in detail when speaking of the Mahābhārata, later on. Lastly, Janaka, mentioned in connection with Yājñavalkya, cannot be identified with the father of Sītā, the heroine of the Rāmāyaṇa, as Macdonell thinks. Janaka is a family name and the Mahābhārata (Śāntiparva) mentions more than one Janaka with different individual names. On this also, we shall have to speak in detail when we come to the Rāmāyaṇa. There are many legends in the Śatapatha, one of which must be mentioned here, viz. the story of the Deluge, so well-known in Jewish history. The man saved in the Śatapatha story is Manu and his boat was tied to a peak of the Himalayas, while in the Jewish story the person saved was Noah and the mountain peak was that of Mt. Sinai. The original story was probably Chaldean as among the Chaldeans, the first man is also named Menon.

2

Note 1 :–Dixit's date of the S'atapatha questioned by Winternitz and Daphtari.

The late S. B. Dixit has fixed the date of the S'atapatha Brāhmaṇa from the statement in it in Kāṇḍa II, "The Kṛittikās do not swerve from the east" (एता वै कृत्तिका प्राच्यै दिशो न च्यवन्ते) to be about 3000 A. D. Winternitz, as stated already, questions this theory of Dixit and proposing another interpretation of the above sentence holds, on a calculation made by Prof. A. Prey, that the date of the S'atapatha is about 1100 B. C. Winternitz admits that if the sentence, quoted above, meant that the Kṛittikās rose due east, the date arrived at by astronomical calculation on this basis by Dixit is correct. We have, therefore, only to see whether Winternitz's interpretation of the sentence is the proper one. He takes it to mean that "the Kṛittikās remain visible in the eastern region for a considerable time – during several hours – every night" (p. 298) and not that they *rise* due east.

Winternitz begins his objection with the observation that "the Indians of the most ancient times were concerned only with the position of the Nakshatras in relation to the moon and not to the sun and that there is not a single trace of any observation of the equinoxes to be found in the most ancient times." This remark is certainly incorrect, as the Indo-Aryans must have observed the position of the sun and the equinoxes in the most ancient times. They regulated their sacrifices both by the moon and the sun; the Pārvaṇa sacrifices (fortnightly sacrifices) by the month and the Sattras by the year. The yearly sacrifice was regulated according to the motion of the sun and the Vishuva day, when the sun is in the vernal or autumnal equinox and when night and day are equal, was the most important day in the yearly sacrifice. The ancient Egyptians and Chaldeans watched the sun, the moon and the planets as they moved through the stars from their flat countries and the Indo-Aryans in the equally flat plains of the Panjab and the Kuru-kshetra must have made correct observations of the progress of the sun as well as of the moon.

But this subject has nothing to do with the rising of the Kṛittikās due east or their being observed in the eastern region. The Kṛittikās were not then in either equinoctial point and their rising in the east is a phenomenon entirely unconnected with the course of the sun and the moon among the Nakshatras. The Kṛittikās are about 4° to the north of the ecliptic and they can never be in either equinoctial point. When it is said that the Vasanta-Sampāta or the vernal equinox was in the Kṛittikās, it is meant that it was in the division of the ecliptic corresponding to the Kṛittikās, or at the utmost, in the point on the ecliptic directly under the Kṛittikā constellation. In order that the Kṛittikās should rise due east, the vernal equinox must be some degrees ahead of this point, as will appear from the following diagram, the

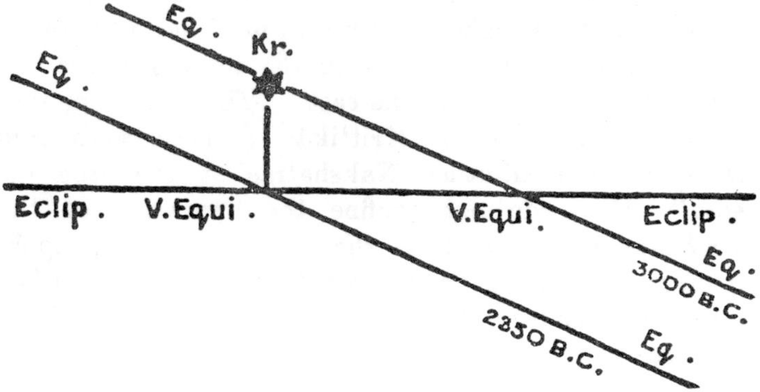

constellations being some to the north of the ecliptic and some to the south.

Now it is well known that the equinoctial points recede constantly through the Nakshatras, its present position being in Purvābhādrapadā. The rising of the Kṛittikās due east means that they were on the equator, which gives the crossing behind the point when the vernal equinox is said to be in the Kṛittikās. This will show to the reader that the rising of the Kṛittikās due east has no connection whatever with the vernal equinox being in the Kṛittikās.

We must, therefore, confine ourself simply to a consideration of what the sentence "the Kṛittikās do not swerve from the east" means. It cannot be twisted to mean that the Kṛittikās come on the east line, some time after their rising, as Prof. Prey takes it to mean. Note 2 at page 298 reads "Prof. Prey informs me that the Pleiades in about 1100 B. C. rose approximately 13 degrees to the north of *the east point*, approaching nearer and nearer the *east line* and crossing it as late as 2 hours 11 minutes after their rise at a height of 29 degrees when seen from a place situated at 25 north latitude." They thus remain, adds Winternitz, long enough to serve as a convenient base for orientation. Now it is not possible to accept this interpretation as the S'atapatha sentence adds to the above sentence "all other stars swerve from the east." The whole sentence is as follows:– "These (Kṛittikās) do not swerve from the east while all other Nakshatras swerve from the east." If we do not confine the appearing of the Kṛittikās in the east to the east point, but apply it merely to coming on the east *line* at some time after rising, the condition laid down in the second part of the above sentence is infringed. For any star that is to the north of the equator within 23° must come on the east line at some time or other after its rising. Moreover, the east point is on the horizon and can be marked easily from an observation circle made on a raised mound; the east line is in the sky and cannot be marked so easily when the Kṛittikās have to come about 29^0 above the horizon, i. e. nearly 1/3 of the heavenly quadrant in a flat treeless country like Kurukshetra. It is questionable if at such an altitude they could serve the purpose of orientation.

Mr. Daphtari takes a different objection to the interpretation which one usually puts on the disputed sentence and urges that the Kṛittikās are not visible as they rise. He states that from observations taken by himself, he finds that the Kṛittikās become visible when they are 13^0 degrees above the horizon. Taking the position of an observer at 30 degrees north latitude he finds by calculation that the time of the Kṛittikās being on the east line when 13 degrees above the horizon, comes to about 1800 B. C. In his desire to find a later date still for the S'atapatha he adds that the Kṛittikās are only faintly visible at 13 degrees altitude. If 2 degrees more are added, then their visibly coming on the east line would lead to a date about 180 years less than the above i. e. about 1600 B. C. This calculation even, as it is given in the Vividha-Jñāna-Vistāra, appears to be incorrect. The figures come to about 2000 B. C. and 1800 B. C.

This is a more ingenious argument than that of Winternitz but it leads to a date earlier by about 7 centuries. Our answer, however, to this argument is the same as above. We must grant that the Indo-Aryans, even so early as 3000 B. C, knew the east point perfectly well. The Egyptions, in the erection of their pyramids built about 4000 B. C. and earlier, had their sides exactly facing the directional points.

Even the east line can again be marked by its position in reference to the east point; and when we say that the ancient Indo-Aryans marked a star on the east line, we must admit that they knew the *east point* exactly. If the coming of the Kṛittikās on the east line at an altitude of 13° was intended, then some other star also at some altitude would come on the east line under this interpretation and the condition 'all other stars swerve from the east' would be infringed.

The observations made by Mr. Daphtari are not convincing. We believe that on dark nights when there is no moon and when the Kṛittikās rise some two or three hours after sunset or before sunrise, as they do at present in the months of Jyeshṭha and Phālguna (June and March), the Kṛittikās must be visible even at 4 or 5 degrees of altitude. But even granting for argument's sake Mr. Daphtari's statement to be correct, we may admit that the ancients could havs inferred from the position of the Kṛittikās a little southwards at an altitude of 13 degrees that they rose exactly in the east point. Such inference would be correct within two or three degrees of the east point which the ancients knew exactly and could not change the date of the S'atapatha by more than a century or two. We, therefore, think that the sentence in question must be interpreted to mean that the Kṛittikās were marked as *rising* due east.

We must lastly consider the supporting argument drawn from Baudhāyana Sūtra by both Winternitz and Daphtari. In the note above mentioned at page 298 Winternitz adds, 'This interpretation of the passage is proved to be the correct one by Baudhāyana Sūtra 27-5, where it is prescribed that the supporting beams of a hut on the place of sacrifice shall face the east and that this direction shall be fixed after the Pleiades appear, as the latter do not dapart from the eastern region. It is true that about 2100 B.C. the Pleiades touched the east line earlier, but they proceeded southwards so rapibly that they were not suitable for orientation'. Mr. Daphtari quotes the same authority and gives further details giving a Baudhāyana statement which in effect means that the builder should mark Kṛittikās or S'ravaṇa for placing his rafters pointed eastwards. He observes. "Here the direction is given for securing the eastward pointing by *seeing* either Kṛittikās or S'ravaṇa, As S'ravaṇa, being always to the north, can never be on the equator in the Brahmrshi country (Kurukshetra), S'ravaṇa can only be seen on the east line when it comes above the horizon above 10 degrees. The word sandars'ana shows that S'ravaṇa is *seen* on the east line after it has risen. If a brilliant star like S'ravaṇa has to come 10 degrees above the horizon, the Kṛittikās have to come even more than 13 degrees, say 15 degrees or 20 degrees, to be seen on the east line." This argument is further supported by Daphtari on the ground that the Kṛittikās are looked upon as a Devanakshatra, which it would not be if their *rising* is intended to be meant in the above passage.

In refuting this supporting argument from Baudhāyana we must first point out that Baudhayana's S'rauta Sūtra cannot be countemporaneous with the S'atapatha Brāhmaṇa and must be placed several centuries after it. Indeed, its very statement giving another Nakshatra for fixing the eastwards of the rafters of the sacrificial hut shows that its date is much later. For while the S'atapatha says 'all other stars swerve from the east,' the Baudhāyana Sūtra gives another star. Hence this method is later and necessarily the meaning is different and even the wording. Baudhāyana uses the word 'diśam na parijahāti' while the S'atapatha uses the expression 'diśo na chyavante'. In the days of the Baudhāyana Sūtra, the Krittikās had ceased to rise due east and and the Sūtra mentions them, only because it was an old custom to use the Krittikās for fixing the eastern direction. That method had become already incorrect and another method and another star had begun to be used. The meaning of the S'atapatha expression cannot, therefore, be settled by the word used by the Baudhāyana Sūtra. As to the Krittikās being looked upon as a Devanakshatra, it has to be remembered that even if we look upon this distinction as based on the sun's being then in the northern course, that would point to the time when the vernal equinox was in the Krittikās and this time has been calculated both by Dixit and others, even Daphtari himself, to be about 2350 B.C. and not 1100 or even 1800 or 1600 B.C. as Winternitz and Daphtari try to assign to the S'atapatha, when even the Bharaṇīs would come into the list of the Devanakshtras.

Note 2 :– Grammarians on the Antiquity of the S'atapatha.

We have already referred to Pāṇini's sūtra पुराणप्रोक्तेषु ब्राह्मणकल्पेषु and shown that he speaks of Brāhmaṇas spoken by old sages and new. In explaining this sūtra Bhaṭṭoji Dīkshita in his Siddhānta-Kaumudī states that the Yājñavalkya Brāhmaṇas are not old and that, therefore, the word Yājñavalkya does not take the pratyaya noted here. This apparently contradicts our view that the S'atapatha is the oldest Brāhmaṇa we possess. It is, therefore, necessary to show how Bhaṭṭoji Dīkshita is wrong in his opinion.

Bhaṭṭoji quotes as an example of an old Brāhmaṇa Bhāllavin, which, being spoken by Bhallu, is called Bhāllavin and those who recite this Brāhmaṇa also go under the same name (भल्लुना प्रोक्तमधीयते भाल्लविन:). Another instance cited by the Kāśikā is S'āṭyāyanin, 'composed by S'āṭyāyana'. This sūtra means thus that a Brāhmaṇa spoken by a purāṇa sage takes the pratyaya *in*. Now, says Bhaṭṭoji, the Brāhmaṇas composed by Yājñavalkya do not go by the name Yājñavalkin but are named Yājñavalka, because Yājñavalkya in not a purāṇa sage. The Tattvabodhinī actually adds the gloss: Yājñavalkya and others are recent sages (याज्ञवल्क्यादयो ह्यचिरकाला: इति भारतादिषु व्यवहार:) as stated in Bhārata and other works.

It is inexplicable how Bhaṭṭoji Dīkshita ignores here the vārtika of Vararuchi on this very sūtra of Pāṇini, viz. याज्ञवल्क्यादिभ्यः प्रतिषेधः। तुल्यकालत्वात्. "This sūtra has an exception in Yājñavalkya and others, as they are of the same time." This means that Vararuchi supplies a defect in Pāṇini's sūtra and states that the pratyaya given by him for the Brāhmaṇas spoken by old sages does not apply to Yājñavalkya and others though these are as old, i.e. as old as Bhallu and S'āṭyāyana, and that Pāṇini should have mentioned this exception. Patañjali gives the vārtika and accepts it without comment. The gloss on Mahābhāshya states that tulyakāla means that Yājñavalkya's Brāhmaṇas are as old as those by S'āṭyāyana and others. It seems thus clear that the oldest grammarians after Pāṇini, Vararuchi and Patañjali, look upon Yājñavalkya's Brāhmaṇas as being as old as those of Bhallu and S'āṭyāyana. This should override the wrong views of Bhaṭṭoji Dīkshita and others. The Tattvabodhinī does not quote the ślokas in the Mahābhārata. The only reference in it to Yājñavalkya is in Anuśāsanaparva where the story of his enunciating the White Yajurveda and the S'atapatha is given and there

Yājñavalkya no doubt appears as a sage later than Vaiśampāyana and others. We must, however, understand that the word purāṇa is relative and he who is purāṇa with reference to some may be new with reference to many others. The real point is whether Yājñavalkya, as a Brāhmaṇa-writer, is a recent writer or an old one and Vararuchi and Patañjali declare that he is as old as Bhallu and S'āṭyāyana. Vararuchi looks upon Pāṇini's not making an exception of Yājñavalkya in enunciating this sūtra as an omission. One may suggest that the use of the word Yājñavalka as denoting a Brāhmaṇa or a reciter of his Brāhmaṇa must have arisen later than Pāṇini and earlier than Vararuchi, who has, therefore, to notice this exception.

But this divergence of opinions among grammarians apart, this sūtra, as interpreted by Bhaṭṭoji even, simply establishes that Yājñavalkya as a Brāhmaṇa-writer is later than Bhallu and S'āṭyāyana whose Brāhmaṇas have not survived. This, however, has nothing to do with the question whether the S'atapatha is older than the Taittirīya or the Aitareya Brāhmaṇa. Now it is clear that the Taittirīya and the Aitareya Brāhmaṇas are not old Brāhmaṇas as contemplated by the above sūtra of Pāṇini. If they had been, the name Taittirīya would have been Taittirīyin and the name Aitareya would have been Aitareyin and the reciters of these would have been called Taittirīyiṇaḥ and Aitareyiṇaḥ. Vāsudevaśāstrī Abhyankar of Poona, who is a good grammarian, contends that the form Taittirīya is established by another sūtra. But he admits that, in that sūtra, old or new sages are not mentioned. And even he could not say that Aitareya is an old Brāhmaṇa-writer; for the name in use for his Brāhmaṇa is Aitareya and not Aitareyin. The extant Brāhmaṇas, therefore, are all out of the province of this disputed sūtra of Pāṇini and we may look upon their authors as not old, compared with Bhallu and S'āṭyāyana. We have to settle their order in time by other considerations and not by this sūtra or any comment on it by Bhaṭṭoji Dīkshita and others, as their comment only means that Yājñavalkya, as a Brāhmaṇa-writer, is later than Bhallu and others and not that he is later than Tittiri or Aitareya.

Prof. Raddi of Deccan College supplies us with an extract from Lagus'abdendus'ekara in which Nagojibhaṭṭa actually finds fault with Bhaṭṭoji Dīkshita for taking no acconnt of the vārtika of Vararuchi ou this sūtra of Pāṇini and looking upon Yajñavalkya and others, through pride, as later than Pāṇini. The extract is as follows:—

याज्ञवल्कानीति। कण्वादिभ्य इत्यण्। ते हि पाणिन्यपेक्षया आधुनिका इत्यभिमानः। भाष्ये तु शाट्यायनादितुल्यकालत्वात् याज्ञवल्क्यादिभ्यः प्रतिषेधस्तद्विषयता च नेति वचनमेवारब्धम्।

III Taittirīya Brāhmana.

Next in point of date and importance to the Śatapatha Br. is the Taittirīya Brāhmaṇa attached to the Black Yajurveda. The rivalry which existed between the followers of the Tittiri school of the Black Yajurveda and the white Yajurveda adherents must soon have led to the enunciation of a Brāhmaṇa, in imitation of the Śatapatha, for the Black Yajurveda. This Brāhmaṇa is accented and, therefore, nearly as old as the Śatapatha. It is indeed accepted by all scholars as an old Brāhmaṇa. Its style is said to appear older than that of the Śatapatha. This is due to its being dominated by the style of the Black Yajurveda Saṁhitā which gives both Mantra and Brāhmaṇa together. The Taittirīya Brāhmaṇa is thus only a continuation of the Brāhmaṇa contained in the Saṁhitā. It has naturally the same style with the same repetition of sentences and gives the same kind of fanciful explanations and etymologies. There are not, however, many legends in it. It cannot be supposed to have been enunciated all at once. As the Purushamedha section was added later to the Vājasaneyi Saṁhitā and certain portions in explanations thereof were added to the Śatapatha Brāhmaṇa, this Purushamedha first appears in the Taittirīya Brāhmaṇa in Kāṇḍa III. It does not, however, give the Purushasūkta yet. The list of persons required as victims at the Purushamedha is nearly the same as in the Vājasaneyi Saṁhitā. But curiously enough, the last two verses are omitted and we will comment on this omission later. Kāṇḍa III appears, therefore, to be a subsequent addition to this Brāhmaṇa, the first two Kāṇḍas being old, their style also resembling the style of the Saṁhitā.

The Āraṇyaka portion of it comes still later. Indeed an Āraṇyaka as such first appears in this Brāhmaṇa: for there is no Āraṇyaka in the Śatapatha. Though the latter has an Upanishad, later named Bṛihadāraṇyaka, it calls itself in reality a Brāhmaṇa. To the Taittirīya Brāhmaṇa are added ten chapters, called Araṇas by the followers of the Taittirīya school. Their names, which have been given to them from the first word in each are: 1 Bhadra, 2 Saha Vai, 3 Chitti, 4 Devā Vai, 5 Yuñjate, 6 Pari Yuvā, 7 Śikshā, 8 Brahmavidā 9 Bhṛigu and 10 Nārāyaṇa. Of these 7, 8 and 9 form what is now known as the Taittirīya Upanishad; and the 10th, Nārāyaṇa, also an Upanishad, is plainly a later addition still, as we shall show when speaking of the Upanishads. There is a Suparṇādhyāya in the last which has become popular with the Vaidikas generally

The Purusha-sūkta of the Ṛigveda, which similarly became popular with all and is taken in the Vājasaneyi-Saṁhitā and also in the Atharvaveda Saṁhitā, is given in the Chitti Araṇa of this Brāhmaṇa. The most popular Gāyatrī, however, appears, it may be added, in the Saṁhitā of the Black Yajurveda itself in two places.

The Taittirīya Brāhmaṇa is divided into books originally called Kāṇḍas, but later, Ashṭakas following the Ṛigveda division; and the first two Kāṇḍas have really eight Adhyāyas, originally called Prapāṭhakas. The third Kāṇḍa, however, has twelve chapters. A chapter is sub-divided into Anuvākas or sections. This name Anuvāka for a section is very old as it appears in this Brāhmaṇa itself in Kāṇḍa III, 10, 10, which is, however, a later addition (एतावन्तुवाकावपरपक्षस्याहोरात्राणां नामधेयानि). These Anuvākas consist of sentences on some particular subject. The number of these sentences is counted and given at the end of the Adhyāya. The number of Padas is, however, not counted as in the Saṁhitā. The number of sentences is counted by tens and each Anuvāka mentions the endings of each set of tens with the number of the remaining sentences given in words. This is in imitation of the Saṁhitā method wherein the padas or words are counted by fifties. One can thus find out the number of sentences in the whole of the Brāhmaṇa. In the 28 chapters or Prapāṭhakas of the three

Kāṇḍas or Ashṭakas, there are said to be about 17480 sentences. The endings of these tens and remainders are given in sentences which are also accented and are learnt by heart by Vaidikas, thus fixing the text almost unalterably.

The contents of the Taittirīya Brāhmaṇa may be given as follows from the printed Sāyaṇa Bhāshya on it, these being mostly, as stated above, in further comment on the Saṁhitā mantras, i. e. in addition to those comments which are given in the Brāhmaṇa portion of the Saṁhitā itself. The first Kāṇḍa contains chapters on Agnyādhāna, Gavāmayana, Vājapeya, Soma, Nakshatreshṭi and Rājasūya. The second Kāṇḍa contains chapters on Agnihotra and Upahomas as also on Sautrāmaṇi wherein Surā or liquor is offered to Agni and drunk instead of Soma and on various Savas such as Brihaspatisava, Vaiśyasava etc. Mantras are given everywhere to be recited by the Hotṛi and the Adhvaryu and these mantras in the form of Ṛiks are taken from the Ṛigveda generally but very often are new. It would be interesting to ascertain which are old and which are new. There are thus mantras to be recited at the time of Rājyābhisheka, of Rathārohaṇa (ascending the chariot) and of Vapana or shaving of the Yajamāna (sacrificing king). The highly philosophical sūkta 129 (नासदासी-न्नो सदासीत्तदानीम्) of the tenth Maṇḍala of the Ṛigveda is strangely enough taken thus in Kāṇḍa 11,

Prapāṭhaka 8, for an Upahoma with water oblations. After this one Ṛik (4) is taken from R. X 81 wherein the philosophical questions are asked,

किंस्विद्वनं क उ स वृक्ष आस यतो द्यावापृथिवी निष्टतक्षुः।
मनीषिणो मनसा पृच्छतेदु तद् यदध्यतिष्ठद्भुवनानि धारयन्

(R. X, 81–4).

What was the wood and what the tree, pray tell us,,
From which they fashioned forth the earth and heaven.
Ye sages ! in your mind, pray, make enquiry,
Whereon he stood, when he the worlds supported.

The Brāhmaṇa-writer answers in a verse probably composed by himself and in the strain of Upanishadic philosophers :—

Brahma the wood and Brahma was the tree,
From which the earth and heaven were chopped out ;
Oh sages ! from my mind I say to you,
Brahma he stood on, when supporting tho worlds.

The Ṛigvedic Ṛishis were speculating. The Brāhmaṇa Āchāryas (this is the word used also by the Sāyaṇa Bhāshya) had developed the Brahman doctrine and had complete answers for all philosophical questions, even while they were engaged in settling the intricate details of sacrifices. In the Brāhmaṇa period, however, the sacrifice was still supreme ; for we find a similar philosophical question put, but answered in the spirit of sacrificers. 'I ask you the farthest end of the earth and the centre of it.' "The altar is the end and its middle, the centre" was the reply.

पृच्छामि त्वा परमन्तं पृथिव्याः पृच्छामि त्वद् भुवनस्य नाभिम्।
वेदिमाहुः परमन्तं पृथिव्याः। &c. (T. S. VII. 4-10).

In the third Kāṇḍa, added later, more detailed information is first given about the Nakshtreshṭi wherein separate Puronuvākyā and Yājyā mantras are given for each Nakshatra. These verses are apparently new Mantras provided for this sacrifice. The 14 Devanakshatras beginning with Kṛittikās are first given and the 14 Yama Nakshatras beginning with Anurādhā are given in Anuvāka 2. Abhijit is now a separate Nakshatra though mentioned in Kāṇḍa I, Prapāṭhaka 5, as an adjunct of Uttarāshādhā only. There are other Ishṭis mentioned in the following two Prapāṭhakas. The 4th Prapāṭhaka gives the Purusha-medha victims. This is a new matter, entirely taken from the Vājasaneyi Saṁhitā. As stated already, this sacrifice did not exist in the time of the Black Yajurveda Saṁhitā. In the following four chapters are treated Yūpasaṁskṛiti, Yajñachchhidra (mistakes in performance) and further particulars about the performance of the Aśvamedha and the various oblations at its Avabhṛitha etc. are given in the 9th chapter. The 10th, 11th and 12th chapters of this Kāṇḍa are called Kāṭhakas by Yajurveda reciters and are very probably still later additions. The Kāṭhaka Saṁhita is different from the Taittirīya and it has no separate Brāhmaṇa. We have looked into the Kāṭhaka Saṁhitā, published by v. Schroeder and we do not find there any matter corresponding to these Kāṭhakas. The pronunciation of some words in them differs, as स्वर्ग is pronounced therein as Svarga instead of Suvarga. So far as we have seen, there is no change in respect of other letters as Macdonell observes (p. 212). Both the Taittirīyas and the Kaṭhas pronounce 'hya' as 'hya' and not 'hiya'. But what is more remarkable in these chapters is that there are fanciful names assigned to each day and night of the first fortnight and also of the second fortnight of months, the names of which are not the usual ones, Madhu and Mādhava etc.; the names here given are Aruṇa and Aruṇarajas and so on, with Mahaśvān for the thirteenth month instead of Aṁhaspati as in the Saṁhitā (III-10); and to fifteen minute divisions of a Muhūrta, itself one fifteenth part of the 12 hours' day. Further astronomical information is given in the fourth Anuvāka of III-10 mentioning the names of the years of the five-year cycle, viz: Saṁvatsara, Parivatsara, Idāvatsara, Iduvatsara and Vatsara. This tenth chapter is devoted to the Sāvitra Chayana or sun-sacrifice.

In the eleventh chapter a story is related how Bharadvāja by 'brahmacharya' obtained only three handfuls of Vedic lore which is ananta "without end" (अनन्ता वै वेदा :) and these three handfuls form the Trayī Vidyā. Here apparently Bharadvāja is credited with knowing or formulating the three Vedas. The fourth, the Atharva-Veda, is yet not known and this shows that the Atharva Saṃhitā was formulated after this whole Bhāhmaṇa, a subject discussed already in a special note. The 11th chapter is next concerned with the construction of the Nāchiketa fire; and in one Anuvāka the story of Nachiketas, sent to Yamaloka by his father, is given. Here final deliverance is said to be obtained by the Nāchiketa fire-sacrifice simply. This story is taken up in the Kaṭhopanishad and developed to teach the Vedānta doctrine of deliverance by knowledge.

In the twelth chapter (Prapāṭhaka) is described in full detail the Chātur-Hotra and then the Vaiśvasṛija sacrifice which is wholly pervaded by the spirit of the Vedānta philosophy, now fully developed. The name means the abandonment of everything and this the philosopher does by a sacrifice. For the Chātur-Hotra are first prescribed seven preliminary Ishṭis to Āśā (hope) Kāma (desire), Brahman (Veda), Yajña, Āpaḥ (waters), Agni and Anurati. Then follow additional oblations to Tapas, Śraddhā, Satya, Manas and Charaṇa. Then coming to the Vaiśvasṛija sacrifice the whole world is brought in for oblations. The whole is symbolical and the several parts of a sacrifice, as mentioned later on and symbolized, are an interesting study for one who wishes to know the several rites in a sacrifice. All animates and inanimates, all males, all females and all sex-less beings, all animals, all stones, all rivers, all plants and trees, all iron, copper, silver and yellow gold are to become the bricks of this sacrifice-altar as also all the directions, all the sky and whatever is in it and all spray and snow, all rays, lightning-flashes, all clouds, all waters in wells, streams and seas, and light, wind, fire, the sun, the moon, Mitra, Varuṇa, Bhaga, Satya and S'raddhā, all the gods, all the stars, all the Ṛiks, Yajuḥs, Samans and Atharvāṅgirasas as also, Itihāsa, Purāṇa and Sarpa-devajanas, all the worlds, days and nights, fortnights and months etc, everything that has been and will be, all this is to be made the bricks. Then the mantras to be recited are given which are probably new. The gods performed the Vaiśvasṛija sacrifice extending over one thousand years. Finally the praise is recorded that one who performs it attains to Sāyujya, Salokatā, Sārshṭitā and Samānalokatā with Brahman. These are the new terms which had arisen describing the final beatitude to be obtained by the Vedānta philosophy, terms, however, used later in a lower sense, as the idea of being Brahman oneself had not probably yet been conceived.

From the above details of the contents of this Brāhmaṇa dealing with sacrifices from the lowest the fortnightly, to the highest the thousand years' one (Sāyana), we can with tolerable accuracy settle the age of it. The Brāhmaṇa consists of three Kāṇḍas, the two first forming the older portion and the last three prapāṭhakas 10, 11 and 12 of the third Kāṇḍa being the latest additions and said to be taken from a Kaṭha Saṁhitā not yet before us. The older portions being later than the old portion of the Śatapatha, the date of which we take to be 3000 B. C., that portion may be taken to be about 2800 B. C. To fix the date of the latest portions we have two data. First the Atharvaveda is not formulated yet as a Saṁhitā. In Kāṇḍa III 12, Atharvāṅgirasaḥ generally are mentioned with Ṛik, Yajuḥ and Sāman and with Itihāsa, Purāṇa and Sarpadevajanavidyā (Anuvāka 8). In Anu. 9 the east is assigned to Ṛik, the south to Yājuḥ, the west to Atharvāṅgirasaḥ and the north to Sāman; but in the next sentence they are omitted. Here the words Ṛigveda, Yājurveda and Sāmaveda are clearly used. We, therefore, can say that this portion is earlier than the Chhāndogya Upanishad wherein the word Atharvaveda appears first, supplanting the compound Atharvāṅgirasaḥ. It is interesting to note that Sāmaveda is always now treated as higher than the other two, as it is next stated that Mūrti (body) is born of Ṛik, all gati (motion) is derived from Yajuḥ and all light (Tejaḥ) is derived from Sāmaveda: again Vaiśyas are born from Ṛigveda, Kshatriyas from Yajurveda and Brāhmaṇas from Sāmaveda. The second data is furnished by the names of months. They are still not Chaitra, Vaiśākha and so on. S. B. Dixit has shown that these month-names arose later, the Vedic names being Madhu, Mādhava and so on and that the conjunctions with the full moon in Chitrā etc. on which they are based indicate that they must have arisen not later than 2000 B.C. This fact we will dilate upon later, but we may take it that the third Kāṇḍa which is so full of all sorts of astronomical names and which cannot but have mentioned the names Chaitra, Vaiś'akha etc., had they existed in its time, must be placed before 2000 B. C. The whole of the Taittirīya Brāhmaṇa may consequently be looked upon as later than the Śatapatha and earlier than the Chhāndogya Upanishad and taking their dates as settled by Dixit, this Brāhmaṇa may be assigned a period ranging from 2800 to 2500 B. C.

Before concluding, we may notice a few interesting social facts which can be gathered from this Brāhmaṇa. One is first bewildered at the number of sacrifices described and the multiplicity of ritual and of mantras to be recited by the Hotṛi and by the Adhvaryu in answer (the puronuvākyā and the yājyā). But it must be remembered that the Vedas were learnt by heart by almost all the Aryans and they all kept the sacrificial fire and performed the ordinary daily and fortnightly sacrifices. The Chhāndogya Upanishad in one place records the boast of

Asvapati that in his kingdom there was no thief and no householder who had not kept the sacrificial fire (न मे स्तेनो जनपदे नानाहिताग्निः). The ritual was therefore, understood by all and was not ordinarily troublesome. Secondly, the ordinary Dakshiṇā of a sacrifice was a cow. She is called Vara (boon) in III 12, 5. In higher sacrifices one hundred cows and even one thousand are prescribed as Dakshiṇā. The country was fit for cow-breeding and the Vaiśyas and even the Kshatriyas maintained large herds of cows and bulls. (See description of Duryodhana's herd in the Mahābhārata). In the jungles of the Panjab and of Kurukśhetra and Rohilkhand, which are many even now, not only are cows plentiful but they give also plentiful milk. Buffaloes are not mentioned anywhere and people drank cows' milk and used it in sacrifice. Indeed in the Vedas cows and sacrifice go together. A four year old cow, especially when pregnant, was the best Dakshiṇā and "secured every blessing": she had a special name Shashṭauhī (III 12, 5). Thirdly, the four-caste system was fully established and was duly respected. The Rājasūya sacrifice was for kings and the highest sacrifice Aśvamedha was for Kshtriyas alone. It is described in full detail in Prapāṭhakas 8 and 9 of Kāṇḍa III of this Brāhmaṇa. It was a Rāshṭra, in other words, national sacrifice and Brāhmaṇas and Kshatriyas joined together for its performance

(8, 4). It proclaimed the independence of the country, the horse being its symbol. When it was let loose, one hundred Rājaputras with the Adhvaryu stood on its east side, one hundred Kshatriyas (not ruling kings) with the Brahman stood on its south side, one hundred Sūtagrāmaṇis with the Hotṛi stood on its west side and one hundred Kshatrasaṁgrihītṛis with the Udgātṛi stood on its north side. The first enabled the king to conquer his enemies, the second made him unassailable, the third made his subjects prosperous (the prosperity being described in detail as plenty of cows, of horses, of sheep and goat, of rice and yava, of Māsha and Tila, of gold, of Hastika, of servants, of wealth and jewels); and the fourth gave the king long life (III 8 & 9).* This shows well how the Aśvamedha was really a national sacrifice and how the three castes stuck to their professions, the Kshatriya warriors, the Brāhmaṇa priests,

* शतेन राजपुत्रैः सहाध्वर्यू राज्यं वा अध्वर्युः क्षत्रं राजपुत्रः। शतेन राजभिरुग्रैः सह ब्रह्मा। बलं वै ब्रह्मा बलमराजोग्रः। शतेन सूतग्रामणीभिः सह होता। अयं राजास्यै विश : बहुग्वै बह्वश्वायै बह्वजाविकायै बहुव्रीहियवायै बहुमाषतिलायै बहुदासपुरुषायै बहुहस्तिकायै रयिमत्यै पुष्टिमत्यै बहुरायस्पोषायै राजास्त्विति। भूमा होता। भूमा सूतग्रामण्यः। ...शतेन क्षत्रसंगृहीतृभिः सहोद्गाता। आयुर्वोद्गाता। आयुः क्षत्रसंगृहीतारः. Compare with this the earlier S'atapatha provision : तस्यैते पुरस्ताद्रक्षितार: उपक्लृप्ता भवन्ति राजपुत्राः कवाचिनः शतꣳ राजन्या निषङ्गिणः शतꣳ सूतग्रामण्यां पुत्रा इषुवर्षिणः शतꣳ क्षत्रसंगृहीतॄणां पुत्रा दण्डिनः शतं XIII 4,1,15. Ugra is not mentioned here. Sāyana explains क्षत्रम् as क्षत्तारः आयव्ययनियुक्ताः तेषां समूहः

and the agriculturist and merchant Vāiśyas. The Śudra was still a servant and impure, not being allowed to milk cows for sacrifice, as the milk was not a fit oblation (अहविरेव तदित्याहुः। यच्छूद्रो दोग्धीति III 2,3,9; Kunte p. 253). From the above description, which is nearly the same as in the Śathapatha, we also find that the warrior caste had begun to be split into two classes, those entitled to rule and called Rājaputras (the word Rajaputra thus is as old as the Brāhmaṇas) and those not entitled to rule and called Ugras. The people of the third caste, the Vais'yas, are named Sūtagrāmaṇīs; the latter word in this compound name plainly means the Patels of villages of modern days. But what does Sūta mean and why are the Sūtas allied with Grāmaṇīs? Similarly the word Kshattra Saṁgṛihītṛi is difficult to explain. Sāyana explains Kshattṛi alone as a mixed caste man born of a Śūdra father and Vais'ya mother; but he interprets Sūta as Sārathi (chariot-driver) and Ugra as S'ura or courageous. It appears that these three words Ugra, Sūta, and Kshattṛi had not yet attained the meanings they later attained as indicating certain mixed castes. We may here draw the attention of the reader to the omission, previously noticed, of the last mantra in the Vājasaneyi Saṁhitā, Adhyāya XXX, which details the victims for Purushmedha, in this Taitirīya Brāhmaṇa Kāṇḍa III, Prapā. 4 where the same Purushamedha is described; this mantra (मागधः पुंश्चली कितवः क्लीबोऽशूद्रा अब्राह्मणास्ते प्राजापत्याः V 30, 22) states that the Māgadha and some others should neither be a S'udra nor a Brāhmaṇa. We have already shown that this condition plainly shows that Māgadha is here not a mixed caste man but merely a panegyrist who might be of any of the four castes. It shows that in the days of the Vājasaneyi Saṁhitā, the mixed castes had not yet come into existence. The omission of the mantra in the Taittiriya Brāhmaṇa might perhaps indicate that mixed castes had come into being by its time. Probably, however, the omission is unintentional, especially as Ugra, Sūta and Kshatṛia used here are still not mixed-caste men. It may, therefore, be inferred that mixed castes had not arisen even in the days of the Taittirīya Brāhmaṇa.

These mixed castes arose later in the same way as the four castes in the beginning, from occupations becoming hereditary. The occupations of charioteers, panygyrists and so on becoming hereditary and the idea of purity of caste gaining stregnth, the children of higher caste men from lower caste wives were first assigned certain occupations and these gradually formed mixed castes which were assigned the old names Ugra and others.

In the above Hastika is not elephant; for elephants can only be maintained by kings and not villagers. It is, however, strange that in the Brāhmaṇas, there is no mention of elephants in the army of kings or in the descriptions of their power and splendour. The Kshatriya is always a car-warrior, like the ancient Trojan or Greek. Probably elephants came in later in the Magadha empire; they were not much found in the Panjab or the Himālayan jungles adjacent to it. The elephant was found in plenty in the jungles of Bengal, the Vindhyas and Aparānta or north Konkan with its dense Sahyādri forests. The Mahābhārata in one place praises the Aparānta elephant as the best.

Finally women were, we find, well-treated and had certain rights. For every sacrifice required the sacrificer's wife to sit along with him. Their presence was not only not prohibited but was necessarily required as that of the king's or governor's consort on ceremonial occasions in modern days. Widowhood was much feared and the blessings invoked on the sacrificer's wife included a wish that she might never be a widow. Ornaments for women were much prized and the priests liked ornaments of women being given them as Dakshiṇā (III 10, 4).

The Brahmins had frequent controversies on questions of ritual and philosophy and particular sacrifices enabled them to conquer their adversaries in disputations. More usually, however, almost every sacrificer wished to destroy "him who hated him or whom he himself hated" योऽस्मान्द्वेष्टि यं च वयं द्विष्मः तं वो जम्भे दधामि. The Indian Aryans were strong in their feelings of enmity. Most often the enemy is called a Bhrātṛivya (cousin). How this word came to be used in the Brāhmaṇas in this sense it is difficult to explain. Perhaps the enmity between the Iranians and Indo-Aryans who were cousins gave rise to this use. But probably this word attained this meaning owing to the enmity which naturally arises in an undivided family between cousins over ancestral property and which is often very deadly as in the Mahābhārata quarrel. The undivided family system certainly existed among the ancient Indo-Aryans as it exists today with its beneficial as well as baneful results. It is hinted at in the marriage sūkta of the Ṛigveda (X 85). But it assumed an evil aspect when the country was settled and there was no room for expansion.

The roots of many Puranic stories lie embedded in the Brāhmaṇas and even in Ṛigvedic hymns. The Kālakañja Asuras are thus mentioned in this Brāhmaṇa (I.). Prajāpati assuming the form of a boar dived below the primeval waters and brought up the earth (I. 2), a story which gave rise to the Boar Incarnation legend of the Purāṇas. In the Rāmāyaṇa we still find Prajāpati and not Vishṇu, assuming the form of a boar. Many similar traces of Puranic stories may be found on a critical examination of this Brāhmaṇa.

Note 1 :– Dakshiṇā or Presents to Priests.

The Ṛigvedic hymns belaud presents to Brahmins or rather sacrificing priests and the Brāhmaṇas do the same to a greater extent. European scholars, not understanding the real nature of these payments, look on Dakshiṇā as a sort of tip or even bribe given to the Brahmins and hence look upon these statements in the hymns or the Brāhmaṇas as proclaiming the selfishness or greed of the priestly class. To understand, however, the real nature of Dakshiṇā as the deserved fee for services rendered with efficiency and great toil, one must translate oneself to the Vedic times when sacrifice was considered as a prime necessity and not a useless or unmeaning, unnecessary or unreal religious ceremony. It was a mistake of Brahmins that they left their services at such sacrifices to be paid for voluntarily. It must be remembered that religious service has to be paid for in every country and in every religion. The method of payment in the western countries under Christianity was and certainly is more practical and straight. The priests are paid fees normally and not as a matter of grace but as a right in the form of fixed salaries out of rates assessed methodically and realised like Government taxes. And these payments of priests and bishops and archbishops are more exhorbitant in reality than Dakshiṇās given to priests even in ancient or Vedic times, not to speak of those paid in modern days. Indeed, one will never come across a Brahmin priest in modern India who lives upon these Dakshiṇās even a tolerably easy life, much less a sumptuous one as is lived by bishops and priests under Christianity or Moulavis and Kajis under Mahomedanism. The Indian priests were and are a poor set of people who eke out a half-starved livelihood from these fees. We never see or read of any Brahmins who have grown rich on Dakshiṇās. Indian history from the most ancient times never furnishes instances of Brahmins, grown lordly by Dakshiṇās or gifts, as Christian history does. There were in Europe bishops owning extensive lands and becoming thus lords and even princes. On the contrary, in India we read of even learned Brahmins as being famine-stricken, as in the Chhāndogya Upanishad.

When a man like Yājñavalkya fought for half the Dakshiṇā payable to the Yajurveda, he was not fighting for a moiety of alms but for half of what was due. The duties of Hotṛi, Adhvaryu, Udgātṛi, and Brahman at a superior sacrifice like the Rājasūya or Aśvamedha were onerous and required a deal of toil and proficiency, acquired by a life-long study. Their duties may well be compared to the duties of Ministers and the Brahman had to perform the duty of the President of a modern Council. He had to watch over and regulate the performance of the sacrifice and to give his ruling on every question of 'in order' or 'out of order' that arose. If Ministers and Presidents of Councils require to be paid high salaries, it is really unthinkable why we should look down upon the large Dakshiṇās paid to these sacrificial priests or wonder that the Brāhmaṇas do not omit to mention what constitutes the priest's payment at every sacrificial act. The pay of the President or Minister must be known before and cannot be left to be decided by the caprice of Government as a sort of Bakshīs or a kind of payment made out of generosity.

The matter will be clearer when we consider how Brahmin teachers taught all Aryan boys at their house and even gave them free boarding. The Guru-Dakshiṇā or teaching fee which they asked for at the end of the whole course was at the lowest fixed at two cows. Compare with this the fee which modern systems of education demand and demand in advance every term or month and which for the total course would amount to the value of several hundreds of cows. It it there-fore necessary to give a caution to the reader not to be misled by remarks about the avariciousness of Brahmin in their demand for Dakshiṇā, made by certain Indian writers even, not to speak of European writers, who have not sufficient knowledge of the real condition of the priestly Brahmins in India, whether in ancient modern times. It cannot be said that Brahmin priests were at any time exorbitant in their demands or that they were more handsomely paid than they deserved, or that Dakshiṇā was Bakshīs paid informally.

Note 2 :- Astronomical Information in T.B

There is a deal of astronomical information in the Saṁhitās and Brāhmaṇas of the different Vedas. But much of it is found in the Taittirīya Brāhmaṇa and we summarise the information given in detail by S B. [illegible] in his unique work on the "History of Hindu Astro-nomy" in its first or Vedic section. Every ancient people must have marked the phenomena of day and night, full moon and new moon, spring and winter The first is the basis of the day, the second of the month and the third of the year (R. I 95-3). But as a fixed number of full days does not constitute the lunar month, nor of lunar months the solar year, owing to the inequality and eccentricity of the motions of the sun and the moon, intelligent nations alone could make progress in astronomical knowledge by carefully watching the motions of the sun and the moon through the stars.

The Ṛigveda hymns frequently speak of 12 months and 360 days in the year or 12 spokes and 360 knobs in the wheel of time (R. I 164-11 and 48). For longer periods than the year we have the word Yuga appearing frequently in the Ṛigveda and divine Yugas and human Yugas are differentiated, (R. VI 8, 5), the latter probably consisting of the usual span of human life. The four Yugas also probably appear to have been known as R. X 97-I speaks of three Yugas, each Yuga being perhaps of hundreds of years. Kṛita, Tretā, Dvāpara and Āskanda or Kali are names found in the Taittirīya Saṁhitā (IV 3-2) first and then in the Vājasaneyi Saṁhitā (XXX-18).

The Yuga of 5 years invented for equating the lunar months with the seasons appears also to be probably as old as the Ṛigveda. The five names of the five-Yuga years, Saṁvatsara, Idāvatsara, Iduvatsara etc., however appear clearly in Vājasaneyi Saṁhitā (XXX–18) and following it in the Taittirīya Brāhmaṇa (III 4), where the victims for Purushamedha are described.

Two months must have been added to sixty lunar months of five years each in order to make five solar years, and it is probable that Adhimāsa is mentioned even in R. I 25–8. The Taittirīya Saṁhitā mentions the names of the 12 months of a year as Madhu and Mādhava, S'ukra and S'uchi, Nabha and Nabhasya, Isha and Ūrja, Sahas and Sahasya and adds two more as Saṁsarpa and Aṁhaspati (Vajasaneyi Saṁhitā XXI-30–34 gives the names Malimlucha and Aṁhaspati for the names in the other Saṁhitā). These month names are based on seasons, the last two being the names of the two months which were added in five years. Sāyana is wrong when he thinks that Aṁhaspati is the name of the

Kshaya Māsa or the month eliminated. This idea of the elimination of a month came in much later than even the Vedānga Jyotisha, in Sidhānta times. Whether two months were originally added at once or at different times as in Vedānga Jyotish is not clear. Whatever the case may be, the two names are still required for the two months.

The Taittirīya Brāhmaṇa (III 8-3) refers to this extra month as the hump of an ox, the year being compared to an ox and the 13th month, an excretion, to its hump. The seasons are usually six as they are experienced in the Indo-Aryan land, viz. the Panjab and the Kurukshetra (IV 4, 11). But sometimes five seasons are also mentioned in the Saṁhitās and in the Brāhmaṇas. This probably is a reminiscence of the seasons in the Arctic regions where the sun remained below the horizon for two months. The year is often compared to a bird, of which the head is Vasanta, the left wing S'arad, the right wing Grīshma, the tail the Varshā and the body Hemanta (III 10-4-1). The sixth season S'iśira is to be included in Hemanta as is expressly stated in many places (e. g. A. B. 1,1) where five seasons only are to be taken for the year. The Romans had ten months only and their year began with March. Similarly among all old Aryan peoples the year was first of 10 months and began with Vasanta.

In the Indo-Aryan land, India, the sun always remained above the horizon; but its course northwards and southwards was markable and the Dakshiṇāyana was considered inauspicious as in Arctic regions. The Vishuvan day was also clearly known and called Divākīrtya (T. B. I 2-4). It is in the midst of the year and certain Sāmans were to de recited. The day joined the northern six months with the southern. The Vedic Uttarāyaṇa was thus different from the modern, as it meant the six months Vasanta, Grishma and Varshā and not Hemanta, Vasanta and Grīshma.

As additional months were to be added to equate the lunar months with solar years, so also some days had to be omitted to equate the lunar month with the rough month of 30 days. A day had to be omitted every two months. There seems to have long raged a controversy over this question, namely, whether a day should be omitted or not as appears clear from the Utsṛijyā Anuvāka (T. S. VII 5 3 उत्सृज्यां नोत्सृज्यामिति मीमांसन्ते ब्रह्मवादिनः). There was a difference of opinion also as to whether a month should begin with new moon or full moon. Some began the month with the full moon, called hence Purṇamāsī (T.S. I 6-7), and some with the new (T. S. VII 5, 11). This difference of opinion still exists in India.

There is, however, no doubt that the phenomenon that the moon was full in certain Nakshatras only was marked. The Chitrā Pūrṇamāsī, the Phālgunī Pūrṇamāsī etc., are mentioned in the Taittirīaya Saṁhitā and Brāhmaṇa. But it is remarkable that the names of months based on these conjunctions, viz., Chaitra, Vaiśākha etc., had still not arisen. Dixit has pointed out that these names first appear in S'atapatha Kāṇḍa XI, which is a later Kāṇḍa (XI 1, 1, 7), in Kaushītaki Brāhmaṇa (XIX 23) and in Panchavimśa Br. (V 9. 9). These names of course do not occur in any of the Saṁhitās but they are also not found in the Taittirīya Brāhmaṇa in which the names Madhu, Mādhava etc. frequently occur. We should expect the names Chaitra and others in this Brāhmaṇa if these names had arisen by its time. According to Dixit, these names must have arisen some time between 2900 B. C. and 1900 B. C. though a more approximate estimate cannot be giver (Dixit p. 132). This is a strong argument to hold that the Taittirīya Brāhmaṇa is older than the XI Kāṇḍa of the S'atapatha, and the Panchavis'a and Kaushītaki Brāhmaṇas.

In the Taittirīya Brāhmaṇa, we find many other astronomical data such as the divisions of day into 3, 4, and 5 parts, the last being Prātaḥ, Saṁgava, Madhyānha, Aparāṇha and Sāyānha (T. B. I, 5-3). See also (S'ata. 2 Br., 9.). The Atharva Saṁhitā. IX 6, 46 states "At sun-rise the Sāma-singer hums (हिङ्कृणोति), at Saṁgava he praises (प्रस्तौति), at mid-day he sings aloud (उद्गायति), in the afternoon he sums up (प्रतिहरति) and at sun-set he finishes his song (निधनम्)". These different parts of singing can only be well understood by a Sama-singer. The division of day into 15 Muhūrtas and of night into other 15 Muhūrtas is not only mentioned in the Taittirīya Brāhmaṇa but different names are also assigned to all these 30 Muhūrtas (III 10,1,2). Nay different names are assigned to the Muhūrtas in the bright fortnight and the dark fortnight (III 10,1,2, and 3). There is a still minuter division of Muhūrtas into secondary or Prati-muhūrtas (III 10,1,4). It is impossible that all these minute divisions and their names should have been in general use. Very probably they are niceties known only to Vaidika astronomers. These names went out of use in later times and are not found in later astronomical works (Dixit page 50).

We now come to the most important astronomical topic, viz. the Nakshatras. Stars generally and then Nakshatras must have been watched in Ṛigvedic days and in Ṛigvedic hymns we have the words Nabhas, Rochana and Stṛī, besides Nakshatra itself, used for stars generally (R.X 68, II 34,2, IV 7,3, X 85, 2). Nakshatra, however, is a word applied usually to those stars near which the moon passes and these were given names in very early times. They were looked upon as 27 in number. Some names appear even in the Ṛigveda such as Maghā, Phalgunī (X 95), or Aghā and Arjunī. But the Taittirīya Saṁhitā in one Anuvāka recites all the 27 Nakshatras with their presiding deities beginning with Kṛittikās (IV. 4, 10). In the Taittirīya Brāhmaṇa (I. 5), the same information is repeated with further unintelligible details as to what precedes and what follows each Nakshatra. The connection of Phalgunī or Arjunī with marriage and the sending of bridal presents mentioned in Ṛigveda X 85 is hinted at here also. In the later Kāṇḍa III, still further particulars are mentioned about these 27 Nakshatras and many etymologies are given of their names, which, often fanciful, are yet more often connected with real astronomical facts upon which these names may have been originally given (VII 1, 1 and 2). The different merits of sacrificing on different Nakshatras are also mentioned. It is important to remark that some Nakshatra names are feminine and some neuter; some are singular in number and some are dual and some plural. There are thus one, two or more stars counted in each Nakshatra.

In the Taittirīya Brāhmaṇa (II 7. I8, 3), the derivation of the word Nakshatra is given as "not Kshatra", which is fanciful. In another place (1, 5, 2) it is stated that stars were called Tārakās, because they floated (अतरत्) over the primeval waters in the sky. The Nakshatras are houses of gods and they are called so because people who sacrifice go (नक्षते) there. The derivations of the names of the several Nakshatras are given diversely in diverse places in the Taittirīya Brāhmaṇa, some of which, as stated above, are fanciful but others are convincing. (Indeed Punarvasu, Chitrā, Maghā and Revatī are names which occur in, the Ṛigveda meaning wealth). In a following sentence, the famous story of Rohinī and Prajāpati is hinted at and the star is said to have ascended into the sky and hence called Rohinī (1 1, 10). In another place it is explained that Rohas or desires (कामाः) are fulfilled by sacrificing on Rohinī and hence that name .(I, 1, 2). In the fifth Anuvāka of the same Kāṇḍa, explanations of the names Jyeshthā, Hasta and Chitrā are given (I 5, 2) and these with Viśākhā and Anurādhā are said to form the Nakshatra-Purusha.

From their singular number the following stars are singular viz., Rohinī, Ārdrā, Tishya, Svātī, Jyeshthā, Mūla, S'ravaṇa, S'atabhishak and Revatī. From their dual number Punarvasu, the two Phalgunis, Vishākhā and Aśvayuj are of two stars each. The rest are plural and their names are used in the plural number. In the third Kāṇḍa, which delights in assigning names to minute things, we have the stars of Pheiades (Kṛittikās) taken as seven and each of these is given a separate name (III 1, 4); S'ravishṭhā (चतस्रो देवीरजराः श्रविष्ठाः) and Proshṭhapadī (Uttarā Bhadrapadā) are stated to consist each of four stars (III 1. 2).

Ṛigveda (I 24, 10) refers to the Saptarishis which appear high up in the heavens (about the North Pole) and it also mentions the two dogs (X 14, 1). These two are also mentioned in the Taittirīya Brāhmaṇa (1. 1, 2). Ṛigveda (V 40) refers to a total eclipse of the sun and how the Atris recovered the sun from the darkness of the Asura Svarbhānu (Rāhu). There is no reference to an eclipse of the sun in the Taittirīya Brāhmaṇa, though there are five in the Tāṇḍya and one in the Gopatha. The S'atapatha also speaks of Rāhu enveloping the sun and of Soma and Rudra securing him (V 3. 2, 2). This can hardly be made a basis for determining the date of the Taittirīya Brāhmaṇa in reference to the other Brāhmaṇas.

Of Tithis, like Pratipadā, Dvitīyā etc., the Brāhmaṇas do not speak. It is likely that the conception of Tithis, irrespective of the Sāvana day, had not arisen nor was the calculation of Tithis, based on the distance of the moon from the sun, easy. The fifteen days and nights of the bright fortnight and of the dark fortnight were, however, given different names which are mentioned in the third added Kāṇḍa of the Taittirīya Brāhmaṇa (III, 10, 1, 1). That these sixty names are mostly imaginary and that they were probably not in much use will appear from the fact that these names have disappeared except Pūrṇamāsī which with Amāvāsyā are names of nights and not of Tithis as at present. Ashṭakā is a name given to the middle night of the dark fortnight which shows that it had a special importance. There were twelve Ashṭakās in the year as well as twelve Purṇamāsīs and twelve Amāvāsyās (T. B. I 5. 12 and III 11, 1, 19). The Ashṭakā is mentioned in the Aitareya and Tāṇḍya Brāhmaṇas also.

Jyotisha and its calculations seem to have incurred popular disfavour as also medicine and medical practitioners, why one fails to see. Among the victims at the Purushamedha we find the watcher of stars and astronomical calculator, Nakshatra-darsha and Gaṇaka, both in the Vājasaneyī Samhitā (XXX 10 and 20) and in the Taittirīya Brāhmaṇa (III 4, 1). Perhaps they are offered, not because they were hated but because they were pleasing offerings to the stars. In Taittirīya Brāhmaṇa, Kāṇḍa III (10, 9) certain astronomers of Vedic times are mentioned, viz , Janaka Ahīna, son of Aśvattha, Devabhāga S'rautarsha and S'usha Vārshṇeya. The science of astronomy progressed as it was a recognised subject of study, Nakshatra–Vidyā being mentioned in the Chhāndogya Upanishad among the subjects studied by Nārada.

IV INTERMEDIATE BRĀHMANAS

The Śatapatha is the oldest Brāhmaṇa though its Veda the White Yajurveda is later than the Black Yajurveda. This Brāhmaṇa was followed by the Taittirīya Brāhmaṇa of the latter Veda. To its two other S'ākhās, viz. the Kaṭha and the Maitrāyaṇīya, we should expect their Brāhmaṇas to be attached. But they never came into being or they have not survived. The Brāhmaṇa of the Maitrāyaṇīya Saṁhitā is said to be mixed up with that Saṁhitā as the Black Yajurveda Saṁhita of the Taittirīyas also contains Brāhmaṇa portions. As to the Kaṭhas, the last three chapters of the Taittirīya Brāhmaṇa, Kaṇda III, viz. chapters 10, 11 and 12 together with the first two chapters of its Āraṇyaka are known as Kāṭhakas and are hence presumably taken from the Kaṭha Saṁhitā or its Brāhmaṇa. The Maitrāyaṇī and Kāṭhaka Saṁhitās have been printed; but we have not scanned their contents. It may however be presumed that these do not much differ from those of the Taittirīya Saṁhitā or Brāhmaṇa. To the Sāmaveda are attached two important and extensive Brāhmaṇas, viz. the Tāṇḍya Mahābrāhmaṇa and the Talavakāra or Jaiminīya Brāhmaṇa. The latter consists of five books, including the Āraṇyaka and Upanishad portions. The first three Kāṇḍas relate to sacrifices, the fourth is called the Upanishad Brāhmaṇa and the fifth, called the Ārsheya Brāhmaṇa, gives a list of the Ṛiśhis of Sāmaveda and is thus, in effect, an Ārshānukramaṇī for this Veda. The Tāṇḍya Brāhmaṇa is also called Panchavims'a from its twenty five chapters and deserves, by its length, the name Mahābrāhmaṇa. Its contents are historically important as it contains a minute description of the sacrifices performed on the banks of the Sarasvatī and the Dṛishadvatī, the rivers which form the two boundaries of Kurukshetra. It also contains the description of a Vrātyastoma or sacrifice for the purification of Vrātyas or Aryans devoid of Vedic rites. The story how Taṇḍi, a Ṛishi, propitiated Śiva by reciting his thousand names is related in Mahābhārata XIII, chapter 14. His son Tāṇḍya is mentioned as a Devarshi sitting in Deva-Sabhā (II,7, 294). He is also mentioned as a Sadasya of King Uparichara and as having praised Vishṇu (XII,337). Whether this Tāṇḍya is the author of the Māhābrāhmaṇa or a descendant of his is a question. The historical and geographical information derivable from this Brāhmaṇa deserves to be collected. There is a Shadvim's'a Brāhmaṇa which by its name forms its supplement. In the last six sections of it, called Adbhuta Brāhmaṇa, sacrifices to obviate the evil effects of extraordinary portents such as the laughing, crying, perspiring, shaking &c. of images of gods are given. This is plainly a very late addition. For image worship most probably did not exist in the Saṁhitā or Brāhmaṇa period. Such evil signs are recorded in the Mahābhārata (XVII) also when the Yādavas were about to destroy one another. Image worship was firmly established at that time, but it existed before Buddha also and is hinted at in Pāṇini's sūtra वासुदेवार्जुनाभ्यां वुन्. Thus this late addition may have been made even before Pāṇini and certainly before Buddha.

There is a Chhāndogya Brāhmaṇa also attached to the Śāmaveda, the last eight lessons of which form the well known Chhāndogya Upanishad. Other Brāhmaṇas of this Veda are Sāmavidhāna, Devatādhyāya and Vaṁśa and are in the nature of Anukramaṇīs giving the Viniyoga, the Devatās and the Ṛishis or teachers of Śāmaveda. We shall speak of these and other minor Brāhmaṇas in detail in a note.

As to the date of the Tāṇḍya Mahābrāhmaṇa it is even in its earlier parts later than the Taittirīya Brāhmaṇa. It is an extensive Brāhmaṇa and gives many details of the sacrificial system now fully developed. It opens thus with the varaṇa or election of priests for Agnishṭoma sacrifice (not given in any Brāhmaṇa) made with great formality and the fee demanded by the Hotri is given as one hundred and twenty cows

(Haug). Fees are indeed prescribed by this Brāhmaṇa as a rule as Vakils' fees are prescribed by rules in British India. Fee was, however, not taken in advance as Vakils' or doctors' fees are taken, which again are more exhorbitant than those demanded by the priests of the Tāṇḍya Brāhmaṇa for performing tedious and onerous sacrificial duties. For, the price of a cow given as Dakshiṇa has been fixed at one rupee and a quarter and one hundred and twenty cows mean in modern currency only one hundred and fifty rupees. Considering the labour and the knowledge and education demanded of the Hotṛi and other priests this remuneration does not seem to be excessive. But this aspect apart, we find from the Taittirīya Brāhmaṇa, as already noticed, that fees were never settled before and that they ranged from one cow to one thousand according to the liberality and ability of the sacrificer. This shows how the latter Brāhmaṇa is older than the Tāṇḍya. Cows, it may be noted by the way, represented the medium of exchange in those days, as corn did in India even down to the British times.

The lateness of the Tāṇḍya or Pañchaviṁśa is also proved by the fact that the names of months like Chaitra, Vais'ākha &c. are found in it, as noted before, and they are not found in the Taittirīya Brāhmaṇa. As pointed out by Dixit, it even mentions Udagayana as falling in the beginning of

Māgha and hence the date of this portion, he thinks, comes down to a little before the date of the Vedānga i.e. 1400 B.C. We will, however, discuss this view in a note along with a similar statement in the Kaushītaki or Śāṅkhāyana Brāhmaṇa.

We next come to the Brāhmaṇas attached to the Ṛigveda. That these were numerous we have already seen from Āśvalāyana's Gṛihya Sūtra Tarpaṇavidhi. But only two of these have survived, viz. the Kaushītaki and the Aitareya. The Kaushītaki Brāhmaṇa is also called Śāṅkhāyana; but from the above Tarpaṇa details, Kauśītaka is a different Āchārya from Śāṅkhāyana; it may, therefore, be inferred that the original Kaushītaki Brāhmaṇa has been lost; there is no Sūtra of that name and we have a Śāṅkāyana Sūtra extant; hence the present Kaushītaki Brāhmaṇa is really that of Śāṅkhāyana. There is another indication, viz. that the Brāhmaṇa of Kaushītaka is called Kaushītaki and it is thus an old Brāhmaṇa, according to the rule of Pāṇini (पुराणप्रोक्तेषु ब्राह्मणकल्पेषु) like Śāṭyāyani and Bhāllavi. The name Śāṅkāyana, however, does not take this suffix and it is a newly enunciated Brāhmaṇa. The present Kaushītaki alias Śāṅkhāyana Brāhmaṇa is a late Brāhmaṇa again from its mentioning the new names of months, Chaitra &c. (see Kaushī. XIX 2, 3). The Brāhmaṇa mentions the names Īśana and Mahādeva of Śiva, and hence it is argued by Weber that "it was composed at about the same time as the latest books of the White Yajurveda and those parts of the Atharvaveda and the Śatapatha in which these appellations of the same god are found" (Macd. p. 206). But this inference is unsound as the occurrence of those names may also and probably does indicate a later date for the former. Macdonell mentions that the Tāṇḍya Brāhmaṇa followers were at feud with the Kaushītakins. Though their Vedas were different, they came into conflict as the Hotṛi and the Udgātṛi came together at sacrifices. This shows that the division of Brahmins according to different Vedic sūtras had not yet arisen.

The Kaushītaki Brāhmaṇa is divided into thirty chapters and the Aitareya into forty, indicating that the latter is later than the former. Both these were known to Pāṇini (see his sūtra त्रिंशच्चत्वारिंशतोर्ब्राह्मणे संज्ञायां डण् V. 1,62). In the list of Āchāryas given by Ās'valāyana, Kaushītaka comes first, then Śāṅkhāyana and then Aitareya. The thirty chapters of the Kaushātaki treat of Agnyādhāna, Agnihotra, Darśapūrṇamāsa and Chāturmāsya, and then the Soma. "The more detailed and methodical treatment of the ritual in the Kaushītaki would indicate that it was composed at a later date than the first five books of the Aitareya. But such a conclusion (it is added) is not altogether borne out by a comparison of the linguistic data of these two works" (Macd. p. 206).

It seems, therefore, that even according to Macdonell, the Kaushītaki may be treated as older than the Aitareya, though some parts of the former (such as XIX), mentioning the later names of months, may be of a date later than that of the Taittirīya Brāhmaṇa.

The priority of the Taittirīya Brāhmaṇa and also of the Śatapatha as compared with these intermeditate Brāhmaṇas is evidenced by an interesting fact. The Ṛishis in the oldest times of the Saṁhitās were looked upon as the authors of their hymns, being usually compared to carpenters fashioning beautiful cars. In the days of the Taittirīya Brāhmaṇa they were probably still looked upon as the authors of mantras (यामृषयेा मंत्रकृतो मनीषिणः। अन्वैच्छन्देवास्तपसा श्रमेण॥ II 88). Later the hymns became divine revelations so completely that the Ṛishis were looked upon as their seers, i. e. as having seen the eternal mantras. The expression अपश्यत् consequently is always used in these intermediate Brāhmaṇas. For example Kaushītaki has एतत्कवषः सूक्त-(RX, 30)मपश्यत् पंचदशर्चम्. Aitareya III 19 has 'Gauravīti, the son of Śakti, *saw* this sūkta' (RX, 73). Tāṇḍya IV, 7, 3 has 'इन्द्रं क्रतुं न आ भर' (RVII, 32, 26), वासिष्ठः पुत्रहतः अपश्यत्. Sāmans also are looked upon as seen; not only the verses but the mode of singing them also.

The question whether Kaushītaki alias Śāṅkhāyana is earlier than Aitareya or Aitareya is earlier is not difficult to decide. Keith looks upon

Aitareya as earlier and treats the mention of Kaushītaki in A. B. VII 11 as an interpolation, a suggestion for which there is no sufficient ground., At least, Aitareya as we have it is later than Kaushītaki. But the Śāṅkhāyana Brāhmaṇa also quotes Kaushītaki very often. It is true that an author often mentions his own name in his own work; especially on disputed points he gives his own opinion as the final opinion. Yet the mention of Kaushītaki may raise doubts. Kaushītaki III 1, on the question of fasting, quotes Paiṅgya for one view and for the other view quotes Kaushītaki. In Aitareya (VII 11) on the same question Paiṅgya and Kaushītaki are similarly quoted. But in a note here Keith in his translation says "this is a mutilated and partially unintelligible version of K.B. VII; cf. Weber". This means that A. B. quotes from K. B. and is thus later.

The methodic and concise treatment of the Kaushītaki is contrasted by Keith with the discursive and extended treatment of the Aitareya, as also the use of perfect as a narrative tense; and these are looked upon as showing the priority of the Aitareya. But these are the peculiarities of individual authors. Some authors are methodical and concise while others of the same time are verbose and diffuse. Some like archaic expressions while others use simple and modern language. These differences cannot, we think, establish priority or posteriority. It may be noted that Ās'valāyana Gṛihya Sūtra mentions three extended Brāhmaṇas, Mahākaushītaka, Mahāpaingya and Mahaitareya. It is possible that S'āṅkhāyana has edited and condensed the first and the present Aitareya *may be* a condensed form of both old Aitareya and Mahaitareya. But there is no doubt that Āṣvalāyana Gṛihyasātra treats Kaushītaka as the older Āchārya.

Note I :- The names Kaushītaki, Aitareya, Tāṇḍya, Taittirīya and others

The names of the two Ṛigveda Brāhmaṇas are usually given as Kaushītaki and Aitareya. The former quotes the authority of Kaushītaki every now and then and this is not strange, as stated already. The name of the Āchārya, therefore, is Kaushītaki without doubt, probably being an Apatya of Kaushītaka. The name of the Brāhmaṇa, written by Kaushītaki, should, therefore, be Kaushītaka according to Paṇini's general rule तेन प्रोक्तम्. This form is actually used in the S'ankhāyana Brāhmaṇa in III, along with Paingya (पैङ्ग्येन प्रोक्तं पैङ्ग्यम्). As to Aitareya the name according to Kāshikā should be Aitareyin as per Paṇini's sūtra पुराणप्रोक्तेषु ब्राह्मणकल्पेषु under which this form is given. The name Tāṇḍya for the Brāhmaṇa may be derived as ताण्ड्येन प्रोक्तं ताण्ड्यम्. For the name Taittirīya, there is a special sūtra of Paṇini तित्तिरिवरतन्तुखाण्डिकोखाच्छण् (IV 3. 102.) &c. The author of the Taittirīya Brāhmaṇa is, therefore, Tittiri.

The name Kaushītaki should be, we hold, Kaushītaka, though as a compound word Kaushītaki Brāhmaṇa would be correct. As to Aitareya, the form Aitareyin is not used in any ancient work and the authority of the

Kāshikā is not decisive ; we need not, therefore, hold that Aitareya is a पुराणप्रोक्त, though the examples given by Bhoṭṭoji, viz. S'ātyāyanin and Bhāllavin are correct, these forms being found actually in Tāṇḍya and Sāmavidhāna Brāhmaṇas.

Note 2 :– Mention of Tāṇḍya in S'atapatha

S'atapatha in its old portion (VI 1, 2, 25) mentions Tāṇḍya 'अथ ह स्माह ताण्ड्यः'. This makes Tāṇḍya earlier than S'atapatha no doubt ; but the Tāṇḍya here mentioned need not be, indeed cannot be, the author of the Tāṇḍya Brāhmaṇa. We know from M. Bh. that Tāṇḍya was a great sage ; and that he gave his name to his descendants who are all Tāṇḍyas. The Āchārya, here referred to, must be earlier than Yājñavalkya, who was sister's son to Vaiśampāyana, pupil of Pārāśarya Vyāsa. From the Vamśa given at the end of the Sāmavidhāna Brāhmaṇa, Tāṇḍya, the probable author of the Tāṇḍya Mahābrāhmaṇa, was pupil of Bādarāyaṇa, pupil of Pārāśaryāyaṇa, pupil of Pauṣhpindya, pupil of Jaimini, pupil of Vyāsa. Yājñavalkya is thus third in descent from Vyāsa and Tāṇḍya is sixth. Yājñavalkya, therefore, cannot refer in his S'atapatha to the Tāṇḍya who was the author of the Tāṇḍya Brāhmaṇa.

V Further Details about the Tāṇḍya Br.

The Tāṇḍya Brāhmaṇa is mainly concerned with laying down the stomas or praise-songs to be sung at the various sacrifices from the lowest Soma to the highest thousand–year Sattra. In mentioning these, stories are related as to who saw these Sāmans and on what occasion and with what result. These stories are usually imaginary ones; but sometimes they contain historical facts. They relate imaginary sacrifices performed by gods or Ṛishis or Prajāpati, usually to obtain Svarga or heaven. Even cows are said to have performed sacrifices and obtained horns. Serpents also, as will be noticed later on, performed a sacrifice, to escape early death. The names of the various Sāmans sung at these sacrifices are often strange; but they are mostly given after the person who saw them. The word "saw" is invariably used throughout this Brāhmaṇa and shows that the Ṛigveda and the Sāmaveda were already divine revelations, the verses now being seen and not composed by their Ṛishis. These names of Sāmans are thus very old and not first given by the Sūtra-writers. Rathantara, Yajñāyajñīya, Vāravantīya etc. are, however, names older still, their derivations being not given even in this Brāhmaṇa; but Abhīvarta, Dyautāna (seen by Dyutana), Gauṅgava, Śārkara etc. are names which are well derived from their seers. The name Jarābodhīya is explained as the Sāman indicated by the initial word Jarā (14,5); see also Rohitakūlīya further on. The Sāyaṇa Bhāshya gives the various mantras denoted by these names; from where this information is given by the Bhāshya, it would be interesting to find out.

Several old Vedic Ṛishis are mentioned such as Bhṛigu, Viśvāmitra, Atri, Śakti (son of Vasishṭha) etc. and the Ṛishi-gotra system appears to be firmly established. The Kāṇvas, Vatsa and Medhātithi, are mentioned in 14,6, 6. In 18, 9, 5 it is in fact stated that the Hotṛi at the particular sacrifice should be of the Bhṛigu gotra. The Śāktyas or Brahmins born in the Śakti-gotra performed a special sacrifice of 36 years (25, 7). The Atri-gotrins are mentioned in 6, 7, 2 where the Ṛigvedic legend is related that the demon of darkness, Svarbhānu, enveloped the sun in darkness and when the gods went to Atri for releasing him, he by his prayers brought out the sun; wherefore, it is added, the Ātreyas are presented with Chandra (which the Bhāshya explains as meaning Hiraṇya or gold and silver). This phenomenon of Svarbhānu Asura attacking the sun is taken advantage of in more than one legend, such as in 8, 6, 13. Two Vālakhilya verses are referred to in 14, 5,4.

Of Brahmavādins (a word often used) or expositors of Vedas, in other words, of Āchāryas or composers of Brāhmaṇas, we find the Bhāllavins (the form used being Bhāllaveyas in 12, 2, 8), mentioned as doing the right thing and Kaushītakas mentioned as doing a wrong thing (17, 4, 3). The Kaushītaki Brāhmaṇa seems thus to be older than the Tāṇḍya. Trikharva-Śākhīyas are mentioned with respect in 2, 8, 3. The word Śākhā is thus at least as old as the Tāṇḍya Brāhmaṇa. But Brahmins do not yet appear to have been split up into Ṛigvedins, Yajurvedins and Sāmavedins who confine themselves to one Veda only for all ritual as at present, since Ṛigveda seems to be drawn upon even in this Brāhmaṇa. The Agastya sūkta 'Kayā Śubha' etc. (R. I. 165) thus is required to be recited in 10. 7. 17 and the Sārparājñī hymn in 9, 8, 7. The simple words तदृग्भ्यनूक्ता introduce a quotation from Ṛigveda in 25.

Indra is the chief god; but he too goes to heaven with the aid of a sacrifice. Prajāpati also creates the world by sacrifice and the help of certain Sāmans. Sacrifice and Sāman are thus supreme. Vishṇu, however, is advancing to the highest position as he is identified with sacrifice; the dictum "Yajña is Vishṇu", constantly referred to in later times, is found in this Brāhmaṇa also in several places (9, 6 etc.); and the Purusha-sūkta verse "यज्ञेन यज्ञमयजन्त देवाः" probably does mean that the gods sacrificed to

Vishṇu. The Sādhya Devas mentioned in this Ṛigvedic verse again are described as ancestors of the Devas or their predecessors who obtained heaven by means of a particular sacrifice (25. 7). Those who do not sacrifice appear to have been persecuted, as Indra is said to have delivered Yatis to jackals (18, 1). The Bhāshya explains the word "Yati" as meaning those who do not perform Jyotishṭoma. It seems, however, that this was a time when the Vedantic philosophy was coming forward but had not yet gained ascendency. Even in the Mahābhārata, Indra is the champion of animal sacrifices.

This Brāhmaṇa almost always prescribes the Dakshiṇā to be given at each sacrifice. It is usually in the form of cows, so many as one thousand cows being prescribed in one place in three instalments of 333 each time. A horse, black in colour, should be given to the Brahman (18, 1) and soma chamasa (spoon) to a sagotra Brahmin. Strangely enough, the Subrahmaṇya gets a he-goat only (18, 8). The Grāvastut gets a she-calf. Pregnant shashṭauhīs (four year old cows) are prized as Dakshiṇā. Gold and silver are also prescribed and apparently nishka was the coin used. Twelve Mānas mean twelve coins or gold-dust packets of a particular weight (18–1) and this is the least, the highest being one thousand Mānas.

The Aryan people were still divided into the three castes, Brahmins, Kshatriyas and Vaiśyas

(2, 8, 2), and the fourth caste Śudra was also included in the community. But the subjects of the king were all Vaiśyas; probably the Brahmins as priests were outside the pale of the king's authority. The Vaiśyas sometimes threw out the king as they formed the Rāshṭra (or state and not kingdom). In 6, 6, 5 a particular sacrifice is mentioned by which the sacrificing Brahmin could help the Vaiśyas (subjects) to destroy the Rāshtra (which Sāyana takes to mean the king). Almost everywhere in this Brahmaṇa 'Viś' means people or subjects who pay taxes. The Vaiśyas were entitled to perform sacrifices (18) and their prosperity in cattle was assured. There was no restriction on marriage, though probably the pratiloma marriage was not practised. But the progeny of Śūdra wives was begun to be looked down upon. There is an interesting story told in 14, 6, 6 which brings this out. Vatsa and Medhātithi were two Kāṇvas; the former was upbraided by Medhātithi as a Śudrā-putra or son of a Śudra woman, whereupon he said "let us throw ourselves into fire and see who is the better Brahmin". Vatsa saw a particular Sāman then and singing it threw himself into fire. "But not a hair of his was singed" (तस्य न लोम च नौषत्). This shows that Vatsa was proved to be a full Brahmin though he was a Śudrā-putra and was taunted as such by Medhātithi. The intermediate castes probably arose hereafter in consequence of this feeling of inferiority.

The Vrātyas mentioned for the first time in this Brāhmaṇa offer a puzzle. Were they Aryans by race who did not observe Vedic customs or were they non-Aryans ? The Vrātyastoma by which they were admitted into the Vedic Aryan fold is described in chapter 17. The Vrâtyas are said in 17, 2, 1, to be 'hīna' as they neither observe a Brahmin's life nor plough nor trade (हीना वा एते हीयन्ते ये व्रत्यं प्रवसन्ति न हि ब्रह्मचर्यं चरन्ति न कृषिं न वाणिज्यम्). ब्रह्मचर्य here means, we think, a Brahmin's life. These were principal Aryan vocations. This sentence is very important. It describes the modes of life of the three castes and kṛishi is here apparently allotted to Kshatriyas, though it properly belonged to Vaiśyas. Or does this sentence simply describe two castes only ? The Vrātyas are further described as putting on red turbans. (According to Sind history, to put on a red turban was the privilege of a Kshatriya and Jāts were punished if they put on red turbans). And they spoke like Dīkshitas or sacrificers though they were not Dīkshitas. These descriptions are not, however, sufficient to determine whether these people were Aryans or non-Aryans. Apparently, the later definition of the Smṛitis that Vrātyas are those Aryans who did not perform the Upanayana ceremony, up to a particular age, correctly describes them. The things to be given at the Vrātyastoma are queer, a turban, a whip, a garment with black border and a black and white deer-skin. There were Vrātyas even among the gods who had to perform a particular sacrifice (24, 18, 1). They performed the sacrifice without consulting Varuṇa. Budha is stated to be the Sthapati at this sacrifice and he is said to be a son of Soma (सोमायनि:).

Who the Sarpas were is also a riddle. They are apparently, like the cows, actual serpents. They performed a sacrifice called Sarpasattra (25, 15,4) in which Jarvara was the sacrificer or Gṛihapati and by means of which they conquered Apamṛityu or untimely death. Among priests is mentioned Takshaka; so also are Dhṛitarāshtra, Airāvata, Arimejaya, Janamejaya and Arbuda. This sattra is the predecessor of the Sarpasattra of the Mahābhārata, which was undertaken, however, by Aryans and for extirpating serpents and not for saving them from untimely death. The names of serpents given here are also to be found among the names of serpent-families in chapter 35 of Mahābhārata, Adiparva; but the names Jarvara and Janamejaya are not found therein. These serpents are described as Abhigara and Apagara and as Shanda and Kushanda, terms which are not well understood. It may be stated finally that in our view these serpents were in reality serpent-worshipping non-Aryan tribes who inhabited the Indian continent before the

Aryans came and who afterwards were so intimate with them that one Ṣarparājñī composed a Vedic hymn and a serpent named Jarvara performed a Vedic sacrifice.

Of historical interest is the story of Viśvāmitra and the Bharatas (who were, as explained elsewhere, the first Aryan invaders of India and not the later Daushyanti Bharatas), led by their king, conquering the Rohita country. This legend is given in 14, 3, 13 and Viśvāmitra is said to have seen the Sāman, called the Rohitakūlīya because by singing it he successfully assailed the Rohita bank. This country is near the Jumna and some people named Saudanti are mentioned here. These people are not mentioned in MBh which, however, mentions the Rohitaka people as conquered by Karṇa and Nakula. The Ṛigvedic kings Trasadasyu, Paurukutsa and Vītahavya are also referred to here.

Of geographical places, the Sarasvatī and the Kurukshetra are mentioned with great respect. Sacrifices were performed at Vinaśana where the Sarasvatī disappears in the sands of Rajastan (25). Plaksha Prasravaṇa is also mentioned as the place where the Sarasvatī rises. Even a Vaideha (Behar) king performed a sacrifice there. The Dṛishadvatī river is also mentioned and Kurukshetra, lying between these two rivers, is extolled as the Vedi or sacrificial altar of Prajāpati. The Jumna is also twice mentioned as the river where the Avabhṛitha bathing should be performed. The twelve years' sacrifice in the Naimisha forest is described in 25, 6, 4. This forest is in Oudh and is frequently referred to in the Upanishads (नैमिषीयानामुद्गाता बभूव- Chhāndogya) and is the place where the Mahābhārata was recited to the Ṛishis by Sauti.

We have interesting references to the subjects of prosody, grammar and arithmetic which were being studied zealously at this time. In 17, 14, 2 are given the numbers above thousand as Ayuta (10 thousand), Prayuta (lakh), Niyuta (10 lakhs), Arbuda (crore), Nyarbuda (10 crores), Nikharva (Abja) and Badva (10 Abjas), a word appearing in Brahmanic gāthās in describing the numbers of cows given as Dakshiṇā by great kings. In 10, 8, 1 are given the Vibhaktis (case-forms) of Indra as Indram (Dvitīyā), Indreṇa (Tritīyā), Indre (Chaturthī), Indrāt (Pañchamī) and Indra (Vocative). In 4, 4, 7 is given the rule that the metres increase by four letters each (a rule thus long recognised before Kātyāyana) and the names of the metres, beginning with Gāyatrī and ending with Jagatī, are given in 9. The several deities presiding over these metres are also constantly referred to.

With regard to astronomy, the information contained in this Brāhmaṇa is not as detailed as in the Taittirīya Brāhmaṇa. The Nakshatras are not mentioned anywhere, either singly or by groups. The five year cycle was known already; but four years only are mentioned by name, Idvatsara being not mentioned (17, 13. 7). This non-mention of Nakshatras or Idvatsara can, however, lead to no inference, as their mention was not imperative.

The names of the different priests at a sacrifice are given in one place (24, 4. 5), as Hotṛi, Adhvaryu, Potṛi, Udgātṛi, Neshtṛi, Achchhāvāka, Maitrāvaruṇa, Brahman, Pratihartṛi, Prastotṛi, Brāhnaṇāchhaṁsi, Grāvastut, Pratiprastotṛi, Agnīt and Unnetṛi with Gṛihapati or sacrificer.

Finally, the humanitarian sentiment was coming forward, as we find that abstention from meat during the four (rainy) months is recommended as pious (न चतुरो मासान् मांसमश्नाति न म्रियमुपैति 17). This is the beginning of that doctrine of Ahiṁsā which was subsequently preached by the Upanishads and the Bhagavadgitā and which later was taken up with vigour by Jainism and Buddhism.

VI The Aitareya Brāhmaṇa

We now come to the Aitareya Brāhmaṇa, attached to the Ṛigveda, which is evidently the last of the Brāhmaṇas composed in the Brāhmaṇa period. The Gopatha Brāhmaṇa attached to the Atharvaveda is, there is no doubt, the latest Brāhmaṇa extant. But the Atharvaveda itself was compiled after the Śatapatha and even the Taittirīya; and hence its Brāhmaṇa, called Gopatha, falls outside the Brāhmaṇa period, as will be shown in detail later on. The Aitareya Brāhmaṇa is, therefore, the latest Brāhmaṇa of the Brāhmaṇa period and, being very detailed, deserves our close attention. It has been carefully studied by European and Indian scholars beginning with Dr. Haug (who has translated it into English) and M. M. Kunte, whose work "The Vicissitudes of Aryan Civilization" is well known; and we will draw upon their views very often in placing the following account of this Brāhmaṇa before the reader.

The author of this great Brāhmaṇa is Mahīdāsa Aitareya, a name mentioned in the Chhāndogya Upanishad. Its date, therefore, must be earlier than that of the latter. The strange legend about Aitareya, given by Dr. Haug from Sāyana, is a name-legend and has no historical value. It states that he was born of Itarā and being not sufficiently clever was disliked by his father. His mother Itarā prayed to mother-earth (Mahī) and by her blessing, Mahīdāsa became a learned man and a Brāhmaṇa-writer. It may be added that Itarā is supposed to be a Śūdra woman and that her son was named Mahīdāsa for that reason. This story is clearly based on the names Itarā, Mahī and Dāsa and may be set aside as unhistorical. Sudāsa, the Ṛigvedic king, may as well be treated as a Śudra on such theories; indeed he has been so treated by some.

The extant Aitareya Brāhmaṇa consists of forty chapters which are put into eight pentads of five chapters and hence called Panchikās. These forty chapters are again divided into Kaṇḍikās the number of which is not fixed: and ranges from 6 to 12. The first pentad has thus 30 Kaṇḍikās, the second 41, the third 50, the fourth 32, the fifth 34, the sixth 36, the seventh 34 and the eighth 28: in all there are thus 285 Kaṇḍikās. The sentences in each Kaṇḍikā are not counted as in the Taittirīya Brāhmaṇa. If they be taken to be about 20 in each Kaṇḍikā, we have about 5700 sentences in this Brāhmaṇa.

"The style of the Brāhmaṇa is on the whole uniform, certain phrases constantly re-occurring. The language is more recent than that of the Saṁhitā; but it is not yet classical Sanskrit. Purely Vedic forms occur such as the infinitive in *tos* e. g. *kartos*, generally dependent on Īśvara,

(Īsvaraḥ Kartoḥ). The bulk of the book appears to have proceeded from a single author though some additions may have been made afterwards of stray Kaṇḍikās. These could be added without disturbance as the number of Kaṇḍikās in a chapter is not fixed" (p. 69. Haug, Intro.). It is probable that a still more amplified work of the name Mahaitareya existed for some time, being mentioned in the Āśvalāyana-Tarpaṇa-Vidhi. But it has now disappeared and this Brāhmaṇa with a few additions has remained, unlike the Mahābhārata which has survived though the Bhārata also, mentioned by Āśvalāyana, has disappeared. The 13th and 14th Kaṇḍikās are thus identical with the 18th and the 19th, as pointed out by Haug: "VII 10 and 11 are looked upon as interpolations having a different language." But it is not necessary to look upon VII 11 as an interpolation from some old astronomical work, because it gives many astronomical details or because it mentions two other Brāhmaṇas. Astronomy was long studied and divergence of opinions among Āchāryas was always noticed with respect.

The Aitareya, being attached to the Ṛigveda naturally principally treats of the duties of the seven Hotṛi priests (who do their work by the help of Ṛigveda Mantras) at the great Soma sacrifices and the royal inauguration ceremony. It naturally does not treat of all the sacrifices, which properly are the province of the Yajurveda, nor of the duties of the Adhvaryu or the Udgātṛi. These it takes for granted as known to the reader. "All minor Ishṭis and sacrifices are excluded, though the Hotṛi priests have to officiate at these, as their duties in connection with these are insignificant. The first two books (Pañchikās) and the first three chapters of the third treat of the duties of the chief Hotṛi at the Agnishṭoma Soma-sacrifice: for this is the model (Prakṛiti) of all Soma-sacrifices which last for one day, and all other sacrifices are its modifications. These duties are mentioned in the exact order in which they are required." It is not possible to go into the details of these duties. "The fifth chapter of the second and the first three chapters of the third book are taken up with the explanations of the Śastras (praise-hymns) of the Hotṛi at the morning, mid-day and evening libations, the morning, breakfast and afternoon teas, so to speak, of modern days). In the last chapter of Book III and the first two of the fourth, the principal modifications of the Agnishṭoma are mentioned and described, viz. Ukthya, Shodaśī and Atīrātra. Then follow Sattras and sacrificial sessions lasting a whole year and the duties of the Hotṛis in these are laid down in the third chapter of the fourth book. The last two chapters of the fourth and the first four chapters of the fifth describe minutely the duties of the Hotṛis at the

Dvādaśāha" (p. 63, 64, Haug).

The whole of the sixth book, after some remarks on the Grāvastut and Subrahmaṇya, treats of the duties of the six minor Hotṛi priests at the great Soma sacrifices which last for one week at least or a series of weeks. (The week with the ancient Vedic people consisted of six days and was called Shaḍaha). The seventh and the eighth books, the most important historically, treat of the peculiar sacrifices of the Kshatriyas. There is here a description of the inauguration ceremony of kings viz., Rājasūya and Mahābhisheka etc. and "the story of Śunaḥśepa, to be recited at the Rājasūya, is related here with great power and imagery (we will notice this story in a note). A Kaṇḍikā mentions here great kings of old so anointed. The last chapter speaks of the appointment of a purohita duly qualified" (page 68).

"The Brāhmaṇa must have been composed from (1) sacred texts and formulæ which were already in use (from Ṛigvedic days, for the sacrifice was a very old institution with the Indo-Aryans); (2) from Nivids and Gāthās including Itihāsa ; (3) Theological expositions; (4) other Brāhmaṇas also." The author has also added many explanations and expositions and remarks of his own. "The Mantras referred to for recital are for the most part to be found in the Ṛigveda we possess. But there are several not to be found. We must, therefore, conclude that Aitareya's Saṁhitā was different from the Śākala Saṁhitā And Āśvalāyana supplies the text of such Mantras (only the Pratīkas being given in the Brāhmaṇa). These are found taken with a variation in the Atharvaveda" (p. 71).

We do not discover in this Brāhmaṇa that Vedantic spirit which became supreme later on in the Upanishads. The work is full of sacrifice and the fruit of knowing its importance is Svarga or prosperity in this world. The words Sāyujyatā and Salokatā do sometimes occur: but the word Brahman is not yet used in the sense of the highest impersonal God. The first sentence, however, of this Brāhmaṇa discovers that the old Vedic spirit is on the wane. Agni is the lowest of the gods and Vishṇu is the highest, neither Prajāpati who is only the creator, nor, Rudra of the Yajurveda, nor Indra, the god of the conquering Aryans. But Vishṇu is not yet the Vishṇu of Upanishads, being not yet identified with Para Brahman as in the line of the Kaṭhopnishad "तद्विष्णोः परमं पदम्."

This again supports the view that the date of this Brāhmaṇa must be taken a little before the date of the Chhāndogya and other Upanishads, i. e. it must be somewhere about 2500 B. C., which, as shown later on, is the commencement of the Upanishad period. The place of its composition must be the middle country or Madhyadeśa referred to with pride in VIII 14 (ध्रुवायां

मध्यमायां प्रतिष्ठायां दिशि). Like the Ṛigveda Saṁhitā, this Brāhmaṇa, however, is now recited in the Deccan only and hence has got the peculiar letter and pronunciation ळ (ḷ) substituted for d. It could not have belonged to the Brāhmaṇa when it was composed by Aitareya in the middle country, but must have crept into it in the Deccan where the Aryans settled about 800 B.C., as already stated.

Many historical and social facts regarding the condition of the country towards the end of the Brāhmaṇa period may be gathered from the Aitareya Brāhmaṇa. The Aryans had spread eastwards into Bengal and Orissa as the Āndhras (pronounced here as Andhras), Pauṇḍras, Pulindas, Śabaras, Mūtivas and other Udantya (?) people are mentioned in VII 18. These are supposed to be sons of Viśvāmitra cursed by him for not admitting Śunaḥśepa to the Viśvāmitra clan. The Aryan invaders in these parts must have been few and must have given up Aryan practices. Vaṅga and Kaliṅga were, we know, long outside the pale of Aryanism and the original Brahmins settled therein (who are cultivators) are still looked down upon as degraded. The centre of Aryan civilization was still the middle country, viz. eastern Panjab and western U.P. in modern language. For here ruled kings called Rājas and the chief people were the Kuru-Pāñchālas and Savaśa-Uśīnaras: तस्मादस्यां ध्रुवायां

मध्यमायां प्रतिष्ठायां ये के च कुरुपञ्चालानां राजानः सवशोशीनराणां राज्यायैव तेऽभिषिच्यन्ते (VIII, 14). Savaśa as a people's name is not found in MBh. The kings in the east were called Samrāṭ, probably because they ruled imperiously a non-Aryan population. The kings in the south were called Bhojas (those who enjoy). They ruled kingdoms on the southern bank of the Jumna. We cannot suppose that the Indo-Aryans had advanced by this time into Deccan or Vidarbha, though kings in Vidarbha also bore this title according to Purāṇas and even Kalidāsa's Malavikāgnimitra. We know that Mathurā was ruled by Bhoja kings and the kings in Dvārakā were also called Bhojas. In the Bṛihadāraṇya Upanishad, Janaka is addressed always as Samrāṭ and Jarāsandha is also Samrāṭ in the Mahābhārata. These two titles Samrāṭ and Bhoja thus continue in Pauraṇic times. Kings in the west were called Svarāṭ (self-ruling or democratic) a term not well understood nor continued in Pauraṇic times. These kings were kings of the Apāchyas and Nīchyas, terms also unintelligible, but showing that these people of the west were looked down upon as base by the middle-land Aryans. The kings of the northern peoples beyond the Himālayas such as "Uttara Kurus or Uttara Madras" were called Virāṭ; probably they were not kings but heads of republics. Imaginary people beyond were named after the real people of the Panjab and this name of the kings and this nature of the people is confirmed by the accounts of them in the Mahābhārata where, in the Digvijaya of Arjuna, it is said that no human being ever went there (Sabhā P.). The Tibetans even in those days also were a sealed people. The kings in the well-known middle country were called merely Rājas. The king who conquered all these kings in the four directions was called Ekarāṭ, the sole king of "the earth upto the seas." The eastern and western oceans were certainly well-known and probably even the southern. He also was called Sārva-bhauma and had all other titles such as Samrāṭ, Virāṭ, Bhoja, Parameshṭhin and Mahārāja etc. This power he obtained by the Mahābhisheka or the grand coronation ceremony (VIII 15).

Higher sacrifices were popular among kings and they raised the power of both Kshatriyas and Brahmins. Indeed, Rāshṭra or nation was constituted by the Kshatriyas and the Vaiśyas while the Brāhmins remained above it. Vaiśyas were agriculturists and payers of taxes to the kings and Śūdras were mere labourers (VII 29). Mixed castes are not mentioned; and we miss the provision made in the other Brāhmaṇas as to how the sacrificial horse in Aśvamedha was to be guarded in its wanderings. The eighth book begins with the praise of Brahman and Kshatra for which Rājanya is another name, as also Ugra, which is also used here in a Vedic verse as an adjective,

(VIII 2). Probably Rājanyas and Sūtas became the headmen of villages. Nishādas, also called Selagas (a word not well understood nor common), lived in forests and led the life of robbers (VIII,11). Janamejaya Pārikshita is mentioned here as a great king who had conquered all kings.

The Mahābhisheka ceremony, which, as in modern days, included Abhisheka with curds, honey, ghee and water (दधि, मधु, घृत and आप्, VIII 20), is extolled by the enumeration of great kings so anointed. The list is first given by the Śatapatha and is thence copied in the Mahābhārata with the traditional gāthās in the Shodaśa-Rājīya-Ākhyāna. The list here begins with Janamejaya Pārīkshita, probably the latest in memory, and mentions 2. Śāryāta Mānava, 3. Śatānīka Sātrājitā, 4. Āmbāshṭhya, 5. Yudhāmśraushti Augrasainya (a new name), 6. Viśvakarman Bhauvana, 7. Sudāsa Paijavana, 8. Marutta Āvikshita (VIII, 21), 9. Anga, 10. Bharata Daushyanti, 11. Durmukha Pānchāla, 12. Atyārāti Jānantapi etc. (VIII, 22). These are mythical kings though Sudāsa Paijavana is well-known from the Ṛigveda and Bharata Daushyanti from the Mahābhārata. It is interesting to compare the three lists and the gāthās quoted therein which seem to form a common folklore. The word badva, meaning a hundred million, appears in all the three in the praise of Bharata. The strange word Mashṇāre is inexplicable.

The social condition depicted in the Aitareya Br. is well described by Kunte in his "Vicissitudes of Aryan Civilization" which properly looks upon the Saṁhitā period as the period of the conquest of India by the Indo-Aryans and the Brāhmaṇa period as the period of their prosperity. "The institution in which Aryan energy was centered at this time was the sacrifice and its performance involved philosophy, trade, military prowess and even cultivation of the soil". Pompous and magnificent sacrifices were evolved which displayed the learning of the Brahmins and the wealth and the power of the Kshatriyas and thus impressed with awe the Vaiśyas and Śūdras. Gilded cloth for elephants and jewels and gold are referred to in VI 27 and IV 6 and chariots drawn by mules and silver carriages in VII 18. The Śūdras unfortunately, like natives in East Africa under European settlements, were not much counted, as they are described as Kāmotthāpya and Yathā-Kāma-Vadhya, i. e. to be ousted and beaten at pleasure. They improved their position in subsequent times as we see from the Sūtras and the Smṛitis. But the Indo-Aryans were a people of a really higher character and more moral than the non-Aryans. For Śunaḥśepa blames his father for being ready to sacrifice him which not even a Śūdra would do (VII,17). We find here an echo of the Anāryajushṭa of the Bhagvadgīta. The Kshatriyas, however.

seem to have been given to drink. In India probably, the invigorating yet not inebriating Soma drink was not to be had and the Sautrāmaṇi sacrifice, it appears, was specially provided to sanctify liquor. A. B. VIII 8 praises Surā as Kshatra or power and the Kshatriyas drank it. Brahmins also drank it at this sacrifice, though not at any other time. The four caste system was firmly established and even the gods had castes. Maruts with Rudras and Vasus were Vaiśyas and Pushan, though alone, was Śūdra (I 9).

The motives for performing big sacrifices were obtaining fame, social position, accomplishment of all desires and success against enemies. But every one could not perform a Soma sacrifice, as the sacrificer was to possess six cows at least before he could perform a Soma sacrifice. A rich man married more than one wife (IV 23). Brahmins learned the Vedas and, when fully equipped, they were called Anūchāna. But sometimes even these did not get any respect and Chāturhotra-mantra recitation in a forest is prescribed for them to earn fame (V. 23). An education system had been evolved. The teacher was called Āchārya. The mode of initiation, the rules of pupilage and the costume of pupils were settled (T.B. III 10, 9, 5); and VII 13 and 23 mention the Krishṇājina of the Brahmacharis. Young men dwelt with their teachers and observed a stern and rigid discipline as Nābhānedishta did (II 15).

"The patriarchical family system prevailed, the father being the master and the judge of the family (vide the Śunaḥs'epa story and that of Viśvāmitra). The mother also consequently had importance and could take her meals before her sisters-in-law" (III 37 तस्मात्समानोदर्या स्वसान्योदर्यायै जायाया अनुजीविनी जीवति). Sons were preferred to daughters, for the prayer constantly is to have Vīras. Marriages were gorgeously celebrated. The marriage gifts (Vahatu) were paraded as the procession went to the home of the bride-groom. Soma mixed with milk was the favourite beverage. The Ṛishis attributed to it their conquests and their knowledge. Next to the members of the family, the cattle attracted the greatest attention. Their pasture grounds were carefully looked after (IV 27) and large sheds were erected for their accommodation (VII 24). The right of possession was the right of property in disputes (VI 28). Brahmins were divided into gotras like Āṅgirasa and Vaiśvāmitra; but adoption into anothor gotra was also in use, as Śunaḥs'epa Ājīgarti, who was originally an Āṅgirasa, became a Vaiśvāmitra (VII 17). The princes often owned only a few villages and extensive forests bordered on every kingdom (III 31).

Note 1 :- The Legend of S unahs'epa and its Meaning.

This well-known legend, told with poetical power in the Aitareya Brāhmaṇa (VII 18), is shortly as follows :– Hariśchandra of the Ikshvāku race had no son. He prayed to Varuṇa, the king (ruler of the world), for a son, vowing to sacrifice him to that deity, and by his favour had a son. On one pretext or another, he postponed sacrificing his son Rohita, until he was grown up enough to bear arms. Rohita fled to a forest, when at last his father could no longer offer any excuse to Varuṇa and proposed to sacrifice him. For six years Rohita roamed in jungles while his father was afflicted with dropsy by the cheated Varuṇa. Once Rohita in his wanderings came across the sage Ajīgarta with his wife and three sons. They were starving and Rohita induced Ajīgarta to sell his middle son S'unaḥśepa for a hundred cows, Ajīgarta being unwilling to part with the eldest and his wife with the youngest son. S'unaḥśepa was offered as a substitute for Rohita and Varuṇa accepted him gladly, saying that "a Brahmin was better than a Kshatriya". S'unaḥśepa, bound to the slaughter-stake, saw no escape from death and, in his despair, prayed to Varuṇa himself and that deity slowly unbound and released him. Viśvāmitra, who was the Hotṛi at the sacrifice, accepted him as his son, as he was loth to return to his father and thus S'unaḥśepa thenceforward became Devarāta Vaiśvāmitra.

Such is the simple story, shorn of the many embellishments added by the Aitareya, which states that it should be related to a king at the time of his Abhisheka by the Hotṛi seated on a golden stool. The Sūtras add that the king should, at the time, be surrounded by his sons and ministers. It is surmised by many from this that in Ṛigvedic times the king's anointment was accompanied by a human sacrifice. But we have already stated that in those times there were no human sacrifices and even the Purusha-sūkta, which is similarly misunderstood does not support such a theory. The S'unaḥs'epa legend is, however, in its origin very old and we do not look upon it as wholly invented by Mahidāsa Aitareya. The idea of sacrificing a son appears even in Jewish ancient tradition, though the Jews had never practised human sacrifice. Sacrifice is a very ancient mode of worship and obtained among the Jews as well as among the Indo-Aryans. And when the Bible relates the story that Abraham was asked by the Deity to sacrifice his son Isaac, we may be assured that the idea of sacrificing a son is natural to man from the desire to offer to the Deity what is dearest to the worshipper. The legend of S'unaḥśepa, therefore, may be taken to be prevalent even before the Ṛigveda compilation. Nay, it is admitted that the S'unaḥśepa account is more natural than the Bible story which mentions God as calling upon Abraham to sacrifice his son Isaac, while the Indian story represents Hariśchandra as himself proposing to sacrifice his son to Varuṇa.

But the legend has been much improved upon by the Aitareya Brāhmaṇa from the hymns of S'unaḥs'epa as they are given in the Ṛigveda (I 24 to 27). In the first place these hymns are supposed to be uttered while S'unaḥs'epa was bound to the sacrificial stake. But if we scan these hymns, it is impossible to look upon them as uttered by the Ṛishi in his helpless condition. Excepting the first (R. I. 24), they do not mention S'unaḥs'epa at all. Thus the words, 'Come to our sacrifice' (इमं नो अध्वरं व्रज I 26, 1) cannot come from S'unaḥśepa, bound to the stake, nor स नो मह्यां, &c, in 27. It seems to us that the hymns 25–27 were composed by the Ṛishi when he was free and independent and a sacrificer himself. The legend of his being purchased for sacrifice and offered at sacrifice is, no doubt, hinted at in I 24. But this hymn plainly belongs not to S'unaḥs'epa but to a descendant of his. It mentions the Ṛishi S'unaḥs'epa and also uses the words 'me' and 'us' (माम्-अस्मान्) which could not both have been uttered by S'unaḥs'epa. S'unaḥs'epa became a famous Ṛishi and his hymns, addressed to various deities, were taken into the golden treasury of songs, prefaced by a hymn by a descendant of his, alluding to the legend which had gathered round the Ṛishi, even before the compilation of the Ṛigveda (see R V 2, 7 also), in the same way as we have hymns of Vasishṭha and his descendents, one of whom alludes to the legend that had gathered round the birth of that great sage.

The order in which the hymns of S'unaḥśepa are arranged in the Ṛigveda is ingeniously but unskilfully taken advantage of in the Aitareya, which represents the Ṛishi bound to the stake as praying first to Prajāpati (क !!!), next by his direction to Agni, then to Sūrya and then to Varuṇa. This is conceivable and these verses are given in the hymn (I 24) composed according to our view by one of S'unaḥśhepa's descendants, though attributed to him, as it alludes to the story. But the Aitareya brings in other hymns 25 to 27, by making Varuṇa direct the sage to pray to Agni; Agni again directs him to pray to the Aśvins, they to some other god and so on the round is again taken. Besides the absurdity of bringing in these other hymns, we have further to dethrone Varuṇa from his kingship and to ignore the fact that he was the deity affronted. It is clear that these other hymns are addressed to different deities at different times by a Ṛishi who is fully at liberty and is prosperous and have no connection whatever with S'unaḥśepa bound to the slaughter-stake. The pāśas referred to in the last verse of I 25 are the usual pāśas of Varuṇa who is supposed to *bind* the sinful; the words uttama, madhyama and adhama qualifying pāśas are figurative ones, though even if interpreted in their ordinary sense they are the usual three ties with which the offender in general is bound and not particularly the victim Ṛishi.

There are other additions which may clearly be detected in the story related in the Aitareya. It does not seem that the adoption by Viśvāmitra was against the wish of Ajīgarta or that Ajīgarta was ready even to take a knife and slaughter his son, because nobody else would consent to do it. This is a hyperbole clearly detectable from the fact that in I 24 S'unaḥśepa prays for respite in order that he may live and see his father and mother (पितरं च दृशेयं मातरं च). We must however, accept the tradition current in the days of the Aitareya that the descendants of Devarāta Vaiśvāmitra, alias S'unaḥśepa Ājīgarti, were the Kāpileya and Bābhrava Brahmins, (Kapila and Babhru being probably his descendants), and the tradition that Viśvāmitra's fifty sons went beyond the Aryan land into Puṇḍra (Eastern Bengal) and further as far as Āndhra and became incorporated with the Dāsas or non-Aryans who inhabited those lands.

What connection this legend has with the anointment ceremony of kings, it is hard to see. But there is no doubt about the fact that this ceremony was never celebrated with human sacrifices.* As said before, human

* Keith has pointed out (p 62 Intro.) that Hillebrandt's view that Rajasūyas were formerly accompained by human sacrifice is not acceptable. "The Purushamedha depicted in S'ānkhāyana S'rauta S. and Vaitana is clearly theoretic and not real.

sacrifice was not an Aryan institution but a non-Aryan one and was borrowed by the White Yajurveda, in its later portion, from Rākshasas. It is possible to suggest that this legend is related to kings at their Abhishekha or crowningceremony to impress upon them the great sanctity of promises made both to God and man. Hariśchandra's name is always connected with truthfulness from this legend.

It is interesting to read the poetical stress laid by the Aitareya on the duty of man to make constant endeavour without despairing, on 'चर वै' or 'move'. Curiously enough the deity which inspires man to make effort is here Indra who is generally supposed to typify the desire to enjoy. Perhaps, as the deity of victory he personifies constant effort.

Two or three interesting facts which appear from the hymns themselves of S'unaḥśepa may finally be noticed. The original of पितेव पुत्रस्य सखेव सख्यु: of the Gītā is found in I 26, 3, viz., सूनवे पितापिर्यजत्यापये । सखा सख्यु: etc. Again the twelve months of the year and the 13th intercalary one are mentioned in I 25, 8. The word chaṇā in I 25, 8 10 probably refers to the grain Chaṇā (gram). In I 27, 6 the river Sindhu (Indus) is mentioned and it is an indication that S'unaḥśepa is an ancient Ṛighi.*

Lastly this legend as related by the Aitareya enables us to fix the date of Aryan advance into Āndhra. Aitareya gives the tradition, probably as subsequently developed but not connected with the original Ṛigveda

* The Aitareya calls this Ākhyāna one of a hundred verses (ऋकशतगाथं शौनःशेपमाख्यानम्) VII 18) though we find the actual number of verses in the hymns of S'unaḥs'epa to be 97. It is not possible to say that we have lost three verses since A. B. S'ata here is not an exact number and we find here the origin of the term S'atarchins applied to most Ṛishis of the first Maṇḍala, as already explained.

legend of S'unaḥśepa, that fifty sons of Viśvāmitra refused to admit S'unaḥśepa to their fold and they were cursed by him to become outcasts and went into the countries of the Pauṇḍras, Pulindas, S'abaras, Mūtibas and Āndhras. We can fix tolerably accurately the dates of Aryan advance into the countrias east of the Panjab. The Ṛigvedic hymns mention the Jumna, the Ganges and the S'arayu. The country of Kīkaṭas is also mentioned in the Ṛigveda as inhabited by non-Aryans. We are thus assured that when the Ṛigveda was compiled by Vyāsa in about 3100 B. C. the Aryans had settled in Oudh. Their advance into Magadha (Kīkata) and Videha (modern Behar) is mentioned in the legend of Agni Vaiśvānara (sacrificial fire) and Videgha Māṭhava, related in S'atapatha, Kāṇḍa 1. The date of this old portion of the S'atapatha is found to be about 3000 B. C., from the astronomical statement therein that "the Krittikās rise exactly in the east". The further advance of the Aryans into the eastern parts of India, Bengal and others, along the sea-coast as far as Āndhra (through Odra or Orissa), is spoken of in this legend of the Aitareya Brāhmaṇa. As the date of this Brāhmaṇa can be fixed at about 2500 B. C. from arguments already set forth, viz., that Aitareya is referred to in the Chhāndogya Upanishad, which again precedes the Maitrāyaṇīya Upanishad, the date of which from the astronomical statement in it has been fixed at about 1900 B. C. by B. G. Tilak, we may be sure that the Aryan advance into Orissa and Āndhra must have taken place before 2500 B. C.

The peoples, Paundra, Āndhra, Pulinda and S'abara are identifiable. But the Mūtibas mentioned among the descendants of the banished sons of Viśvāmitra defy identification. This is a riddle which is worth the attention of antiquarians and sociologists of Orissa.

Note 2 :- Interesting Information from Haug's Introduction to his Aitareya Brāhmaṇa with our remarks where necessary.

1 That part of the Veda which contains the sacred prayers, the invocations of the deities, the chant verses at the sacrifices, the sacrificial formulas, blessings and curses by priests are called Mantras (products of thinking). This word is very old and is found in the Zend Avesta as Manthra. Zoroaster is called Manthran, speaker of Manthras; one of the earliest names for the scriptures of the Parsis is Manthra Spenta.

This shows that the word arose when the ancesters of the Parsis and the Hindus lived together. The Brāhmaṇas arose later when they had divided, as there is no word corresponding to Brāhmaṇa among the Parsis. The idea of the fights of Devas (representing Hindus) and the Asuras (representing the Parsis) mentioned in the Brāhmaṇas arose later (p. 2-3).

2 Sacrifice is a very old institution and one cannot, therefore, make a distinction, made by some, between the Mantra period and the Chhandas period. One cannot assign to the former sacrifical hymns to be treated as late and to the latter, hymns religious and devotional, and therefore early. The horse sacrifice hymn (R I, 162) cannot thus be assigned to the Mantra period as conceived by Max Müller, (viz., 1000-800 B. C.). The names of the deities Indra, Varuṇa, Aryaman etc. found in it are found among all Aryan nations. The sacrificial art had already developed. The fifth verse of the above hymn mentions performing priests, viz. Hotṛi, Adhvaryu, Avayāj, Agnimindha, Grāvagrābha and S'aṁstṛi. In the times of the Brāhmaṇas, no doubt, even a simple Soma sacrifice required sixteen

priests; but the system was well laid already; for among the Parsis we have the Hotṛi as Zota and the Adhvaryu as Rathvi (or Adhyaru).

3 The Pratiprasthātṛi is an assistant of the Adhvaryu as A. B. I 18 calls the two Aśvins the two Adhvaryus. That there was a plurality of Adhvaryus in the time of the Ṛishis, we find from R. II 37, 2 or R. VIII, 2, 4. The fourth priest Agnimindha or Agnīdhra mentioned also in R 11 36, 4 has to repeat "Asto S'raushaṭ" (R 1 139, 1) when the Adhvaryu calls upon him by 'O' S'rāvaya and he takes up a wooden sword called Idhmasannahanī making three knots Trisandhāna." The whole ceremony with the formulas used resembles so closely what is recorded in the Zend-Avesta of the angel Sraosha that we may conclude that the duties of the Agnīdhra were already known before the Iranians separated from the Indians. Vashaṭkāra and Anuvashaṭkāra are mentioned in many Ṛigvedic hymns (e. g. I 120, 4 and VII 15, 6).

4 The fifth priest Grāvagrābha is the Grāvastut of the Brāhmaṇas who recites the Pāvamānya verses when the Soma juice is being extracted by the Adhvaryu. He probably then held the stones for Soma-squeezing. Soma juice (Homa) is known to the Zend-Avesta and the name of the squeezing priest is there Avanan, one who prepares the Havana (Savana-Libation) p. 16.

5 Hotṛi and Adhvaryu are very old and have their counterpart among the Parsis, but not so with Udgātṛi and Brahman. The Hotṛi praises (शंस्) but the Udgātṛi sings (स्तु or गै), see R VIII 1, 1, VI 62, 5 or 69, 2 and the technical terms are Uktha or S'astra and Stoma or Sāma. These names are not found in Zend-Avesta. (It may be noted that chanting is not a part of the Parsi Homa ceremony and we think that Sāma-singing arose in the Panjab the people of which are even now

very fond of singing). Brahman was introduced subsequently but earlier than the Brāhmaṇa period. He is mentioned in R 1, 10, 1. The Brahman's duty is कृणुत as opposed to शंसत and गायत (R VIII 32, 17). In R X 91, 10 Brahman is mentioned with Potṛi, Neshtṛi, Hotṛi and Gṛihapati etc (तवाग्ने होत्रं तव पोत्रमृत्वियं तव नेष्ट्रं त्वमग्निदृतायतः तव प्रशास्त्रं त्वमध्वरीयसि ब्रह्मा चासि गृहपतिश्च नो दमे ॥) The Brahman was looked upon as idle (RVIII 92, 30 and A. B. V, 34). He was the expounder of religious matters (R X 71, 11) and thus "became author of Brāhmaṇas". (This is, however, not necessarily the case as we think that Aitareya was not a Brahman. Probably the authors embodied decisions of the Brahmans given in previous times, like High Court decisions embodied in legal treatises). Bṛihaspati, the teacher of gods, is called Brahman in R X 14, 3.

6 The Agur, the Yājyā mantra, the Vashaṭkāra and the Anuvashaṭkāra are very ancient; for the Agur or introductory formula "ये यजामहे" is found even in the Zend-Avesta, as many Parsi prayers even now commence with "Yajamaide". But the Vashaṭkāra (वौषट्) and Anuvashaṭkāra (श्रौषट्) preceded by अग्ने वीहि ('Oh fire eat') are not found among Zoroastrians as they did not allow anything, flesh or homa or cake, to be thrown into the fire. "Priests have only to show their offerings to that element". It may be added that Zoroaster, probably reformed the old Aryan religion by prohibiting animal sacrifice or the throwing of any oblations into fire as Christ stopped animal sacrifice among the Jews. In both cases, it wrs not the sentiment of Ahiṁsā that was at work, as in India in the Upanishadic days, but the desire to keep God unsullied. This explains why Parsis and Christains, unlike Brahmins, Jains and Vais'yas are flesh-eaters, though they have given up animal sacrifice

7 Haug accepts the date of the Vedānga Jyotisha fixed at 1181 B. C. by Archbishop Pratt and on this date holds that the Brāhmaṇas were composed from about 1400 to 1200 B. C. and the three Vedas were compiled about 2000 to 1500 B. C. "To believe that the observation recorded in the Jyotisha was taken from Babylon or China is absurd." For the Indo-Aryans were required to make such observations for their sacrifices which commenced only on lucky constellations. The yearly sattras, as described in A. B., fourth Pañchikā, were nothing but an imitation of the sun's course. They were divided into two parts consisting of six months each; in the midst of both was the Vishuvan. The Chinese ancient documents, Shu King or book of history, and the sacrificial songs of Shu King go back to 1700 to 2200 B. C. and there is no reason why a similar antiquity should not be assigned to the Vedas (p. 48).

8 That sacrificial speculation had commenced long before the Brāhmaṇas is clear from a reference to it in R. I 95 and the so-called Vāmana sūkta R. I 164. Certain decisions were known as Brahmodya, as mentioned in A. B. 5. 25.

9 The characteristics of the stomas and prishṭhas as given by Haug may finally be given here for the curious reader. Each stoma contains a number of verses chanted according to one and the same tune. The number is often obtained by repetition of the same triplet of verses. The trivṛit (nine-fold) is the symbol of Brahman (theological wisdom) and Agni is its deity. The Panchadaśa (fifteen-fold) is the symbol of power and is appropriate to Indra and Kshatriyas. The Saptadaśa (seventeen-fold) is symbolical of wealth in cattle and belongs to Vaiśyas. The Ekavinśa is to be used for the third libation and is for progeny. Others such as triṇava, trayastriṁśat etc., have similarly

symbolical meanings. Prishṭhas are certain sāmans and their combinations. The two principal ones are the Rathantara and Brihat Sāmans (अभि त्वा सून नोनुम and त्वामिद्धि हवामहे).

Hymns referring to sacrificial facts or names cannot hence be considered as of a late period. The Nābhānedishṭa hymn is also not a late hymn. The story given by the Aitareya Brāhmaṇa is plainly based on the two hymns X, 61-62. He is a son of Manu and the hymns are addressed to the Āngirasas. Nābhānedishṭa represents all births in the universe, the literal meaning of the word being nearest to the navel. He is the guardian of all seeds. Here we have the Zoroastrian idea of the Fravashis, and the word is found in Avesta in the form "nabānazdiśta" an epithet of the Fravashis and signifies the lineal descendants of future generations (p. 5.). The mention of Kakshīvān and of seven Hotris in hymn R. X 61, (16 & 1), is no proof of its late origin. Kakshīvān is many times mentioned, especially in the first book of the Rigveda, as a great chanter and Soma-drinker, a favourite of the Aśvins. He is to the majority of the Rigvedic Rishis a personage of remote antiquity, like Kāvya or Āngirasa. The seven Hotris are, again, mentioned in many places even with their names Potri, Neshtri, Agnīd, Praśāstri and Maitrāvaruṇa (p. 28).

10 The Nigadas and Nivids preserved in the Brāhmaṇas and Sūtras, when compared with the hymns of the Rigveda, are more ancient and served the Rishis as a kind of sacred texts. These are incorporated in hymns e. g. 'Predam brahma', 'Predam sunvatam' etc. The Subramhaṇya formula called a Nigada is found in R. I 51. The word Nivid frequently occurs in hymns, even with the epithet "Pūrva" or ancient (I 89, 3; I 96, 2; II 36, 6). The Marutvatīya Nivid is referred

to by Vāmadeva (IV 18, 7). Aitareya Brāhmaṇa II 33, 34 regards the Nivid addressed to Agni as those words of Prajāpati by means of which he created the whole world. This idea corresponds with the Zoroastrian idea that Ahura Muzda created the world with the Yathā-ahu-vairyo prayer. We actually find that Kutsa, who already, in many Vedic songs, is looked upon as a sage of remote antiquity, says in I 96, 2 that Agni created, by means of the first Nivid, the creatures of Manu (p. 37).

These Nivids cannot thus be regarded as fabrications of priests in Brahmanic times. Their style is that of the hymns. In short sentences, they give the names, epithets and feats of the deity involved. They have no regular metre but a kind of rhythm. They must have been regarded as very efficacious. (See A. B. 2, 33, 3, 10). Viśvāmitra's hymn (III 47) to the Maruts is based on the Marutvatīya Nivids. The many prayer formulas in Yasna which commence with 'nivae ahayemi' (I invite) are of the nature of Nivids (pp. 38, 39).

These remarkable similarities of words and sacrificial procedure in the Zend-Avesta and the Ṛigvedic hymns, pointed out by Haug, show that the sacrifice was an old institution and that the procedure was already developed at the time of the compilation of the Ṛigveda. Haug thinks that the sūktas in the first book are given in that order as they are required in that order for the morning and noon sacrifices (p. 36) and that the hymns of Praskaṇva (R. I, 44 to 51) contain the principal deities and metres of the Āsvinaśastra, the deities even in the order they are praised, viz. Agni, Ushas, Aśvins, Sūrya and Indra (A.B. IV, 7, 11). It may perhaps be argued that the Aitareya Brāhmaṇa gives this order because we find the hymns in that order in the Ṛigveda. Why hymns of particular Ṛishis and in a particular order are given in the first Maṇḍala is an interesting question and Haug's remarks are suggestive. The arrangement of hymns in the tenth book similarly deserves attention.

Note 3 :– Astronomical Statements in K. B. and the age of the Brāhmaṇas they indicate.

We have already noted that the Kaushītaki Brāhmaṇa mentions in many places the new names of months, Chaitra etc. These, as already shown elsewhere, indicate according to S. B. Dikshit, a date from 2900 B. C. to 1850 B. C. (History of Indian Astronomy in Marathi, pp.131-132). This is too wide, though this gives the highest and the lowest possible limits. But we can find a more approximate date from a statement in K. B. I. 3, which is as follows: – " कस्मिन्नृतौ पुनरादधीतेति वर्षास्विति हैक आहुः... मध्यावर्षे पुनर्वसू नक्षत्रमुदीक्ष्य पुनरादधीत... न तस्मिन्काले पूर्वपक्षे पुनर्वसुभ्यां संपद्यते येवैषाषाढ्या उपरिष्टादमावास्या भवति तस्यां पुनरादधीत सा पुनर्वसुभ्यां संपद्यते उपाप्तोऽमावास्यायां कामो भवत्युपाप्तो वर्षासूपाप्तः पुनर्वस्वोः". Keith translates this passage as follows :– "In which season should he re-establish (the fires)? In the rains, some say. In the middle of the rains, with regard to (seeing) the Nakshatra Punarvasus, he should re-establish...In this period (the new moon) does not come into conjunction with Punarvasus in the first (Pūrva) half of the month (पक्ष). On the new moon which follows after (full moon) in Āshāḍhas, he should re-establish (fires). The desire is obtained in the new moon, and in the rains and in the Punarvasus." From this we find that Āshaḍhī or the full moon in Āshāḍha was not in the rainy season. It also appears that the month names were of months ending with Amāvāsyā and not with Pūrṇimā or full moon. On this day we find that the Nakshatra is always (or usually) Punarvasu. And in re-establishing fire on this day, three desired conditions are fulfilled, viz. Amāvāsyā tithi, Punarvasu Nakshatra and the rainy season, if not its middle, its commencement. It must be remembered that in olden times the Varshā months were S'rāvaṇa and Bhādrapada. If you take the middle of the rainy season, we have to fix upon the Amāvāsyā of S'rāvaṇa; but on that day the Nakshatra would be Ās'leshā, two Nakshatras ahead of Punarvasus. (One may look into any Hindu calender and find this; for the Nakshatras and Tithis always remain the same with a little variation). The K. B., therefore, recommends the Amāvāsyā of Āshāḍha as the best day for re-establishing fires.

Now this affords a tolerable basis for calculating the date of this statement. This commencement of the rainy season in the beginning of S'ravaṇa indicates the seasons as they were in those times. At present we have the commencement of rains in the beginning of Jyeshṭha; in Kalidāsa's days they commenced in the beginning of Āshādha (आषाढस्य प्रथमदिवसे मेघमाश्लिष्टसानुम् etc.- मेघदूत). Supposing that the rains are now thrown back about 60 days and taking 72 years roughly for one degree of precession of equinoxes, we find that the rains must have commenced *about (72 × 60) 4320 years ago* in the beginning of S'rāvaṇa. This gives us about (4320 – 1928) 2392 B. C. as the date of this statement; we have already shown that K. B. may be placed in about 2500 B. C.

The note given here by Keith is also very important in connection with this date. Keith points out that the date fixed is a refinement on that of T. S. and S'. B. II. 1, 2, 10 which prescribe merely the Punarvasus and that Bau. S'. S. III 1 fixes the date as the new moon in the Punarvasus *preceding* the full moon in the Āshāḍhas. The first fact makes it clear that Kaushītaki Brāhmaṇa is later than S'atapatha as also Taittirīya Saṁhitā.

The second fact makes it certain that in the days of the Baudhayana S'rauta Sūtra, the rainy season had receded by about a month, so that on the new moon preceding the Āshādhi Pūrṇimā you could never get the Punarvasu Nakshatra.

There is another passage in the Kaushītaki Brāhmaṇa which makes astronomical statements of far greater importance. These are misunderstood both by Dixit and by Keith. We will first give the passage in original in XIX 3 "स वै माघस्यामावास्यायामुपवसत्युदङ्ङावर्त्स्यन्नुपेमे ... तदेनं प्रथममाप्नुवन्ति...स षण्मासानुदङ्ङेति स षण्मासानुदङ्ङित्वा तिष्ठते दक्षिणावर्त्स्यन्नुपेमे वसन्ति वैषुवतीयेनाह्ना ... तदेनं द्वितीयमाप्नुवन्ति स षण्मासान् दाक्षिणेनैति स षण्मासान् दक्षिणेनेत्वा तिष्ठते उदङ्ङावर्तयन् उपेमे वसन्ति तदेनं तृतीयमाप्नुवन्ति ...... तद्वै न तस्मिन्काले दीक्षेरन्नतागतं सस्यं भवति दहरकान्यहानि भवन्ति सवेपमानादवभृथादुदायन्ति तस्मादत्र न दीक्षेरञ्चैत्रस्यामावास्याया एकाह उपरिष्टाद्दीक्षेरन्नागतं सस्यं भवति महान्यहानि भवन्त्यसंवेपमाना अवभृथादुदायन्ति.

On this Keith observes at p. 49 of his Introduction that at that time "the winter solestice was at the new moon of Māgha. This is, however, clearly nothing more or less than the *datum* of Jyotisha and thus yields no date of any assured value for the period in question. If, as is most probable, the Nakshatras were not an Indian invention, but were derived from foreign – probably Semitic–source, it is clear that the date of their fixation would not have the slightest value, save as an upper date for the Brāhmaṇas. At most the Māgha datum tends to render 800 B. C. as a reasonable maximum date of the composition of the Brāhmaṇa literature."

With due humility it may be said that every statement in this opinion is incorrect. In the first place, this passage mentions no Nakshatras (except in the monthname Chaitra). Further, on the question whether the Nakshatras are Indian in origin or borrowed, it may be said that there is no proof that the Nakshatras were borrowed from Semitic or other sources. Their names are Indian; they are mentioned even in the Ṛigveda; their number 27 does not fit in with the Rāśi system which is plainly Semitic. But this Nakshatra question apart, we first have to point out that the Māgha *datum* does not lead to 800 B. C. but to 1400 B. C. as calculated by Dixit, supposing it to be the same as that given in the Vedānga Jyotisha. Even according to Archbishop Pratt, consulted by Max Müller, it establishes a date so far back as 1182 B. C. But this statement is not the same as that of the Vedānga. Considering that Vedānga Jyotisha is not a part of the Vedas and that Brāhmaṇas had been written long before it, the statement could not have been the same as in the Vedānga. Dixit apparently commits the same mistake. Probably he had not seen the original. We have said before that this opinion of Dixit is wrong and we proceed to show here how it is wrong. Dixit does not quote the statement in K. B. on which he bases his opinion. It seems he had not the work before him. The statement in K. B., as understood even by Keith, is that the winter-solstice fell on the Amāvāsyā of Māgha, i. e. the last day of Māgha, while in the Vedānga Jyotisha times it fell on the first day of Māgha. We have already shown that the month names in K. B. are those of Amānta months and not of Pūrnimānta months.

The day recommended had according to K. B. two disadvantages, viz. that at the Avabhṛitha bathing they had to shiver owing to extreme cold and that the crops were not yet in. This clearly shows that the bitterest cold was experienced about Māgha Amāvāsyā, which was natural as it was the winter-solstice day. As at present December 21 or January 1st falls about Mārgashīrsha Amāvāsyā, it follows that the seasons have, since the days of the Kaushītaki, slided back by two months. This is the same conclusion as that afforded by the first Āshāḍhā statment about the rains. As this is an actual observation of the time, it cannot be said that it is taken from some old source. The coming in of crops in Northern India now is about the Amāvāsyā of Māgha, when also the days are longer and there is not much cold. The time for the ripening of crops varies in different provincese and is late in the Panjab and this statement probably belongs to the middle country.

There is one doubtful point here which has to be noted, viz. that the passage speaks of getting the sun thrice, once at starting, again after it has moved northwards for six months and a third time when it has moved southwards for six months. For the second day the word used is वैषुवतीयेन which ordinarily means the day when the sun is in vernal or autumnal equinox. The summer-solstice day may also be taken to be indicated here. It is certain that in the times of the Brāhmaṇas, Uttarāyaṇa had changed its meaning. Previously it meant the time from the vernal equinox to autumnal when the sun was in the northern hemisphere; but as from summar solstice to autumnal equinox, its motion is actually southwards, Uttarayāṇa was taken from winter solstice to summar solstice. It is nearly certain that वैषुवतीय means here the summar solstice; for, if we take it to mean the vernal or autumnal equinox falling on S rāvaṇa Amāvāsyā, six months after Māgha Amāvāsyā, the date of such a phenomenon would be unimaginably ancient.

VII SOME MINOR BRĀHMAṆAS

I The Sāmavidhāna Brāhmaṇa

This Brāhmaṇa has been edited by Burnell with a learned introduction. The Brāhmaṇa clearly belongs to the Sūtra period (2000-1000 B. C.) and not to the Brāhmaṇa period (3000-2000). The language is not verbose and there are no repetitions so characteristic of the Brāhmaṇas. The brevity, often troublesome, of the Sūtras is not, however, found here. Kumārila of the 7th century A. D. mentions eight Brāhmaṇas of the Chhandogas including this Brāhmaṇa, which are, he says, without svaras (Intro. p. 6). There is a commentary on this Brāhmaṇa by Sāyana.

The Brāhmaṇa is divided into three chapters. The first treats of Kṛichchhra, Atikṛichchhra and Kṛichchhrātikṛichchhra which in Smṛitis became the usual penances for sins and offences. It is clear that these provisions were followed by the Dharmasūtras which again became the foundation of the Dharmaśāstras or Smṛitis. Svādhyāya also became a means of purification and even of attainment of desires. The Vedas had long become divine and their learning and their reciting became also sacred. Repeating several times particular mantras or sections secured the desired blessings. A particular procedure for such Japa is prescribed. Bathing thrice a day or standing in water, while reciting, up to the knee, the waist or the neck produced different merits. The ideas of Purāṇic Tapas or religious austerity have thus their root in these provisions.

It seems also that the divisions of Brahmins according to Vedas had already taken place as also the performance of rites by the help of one Veda only. The rites described in this Brāhmaṇa as also the penances are to be observed by the singing alone of particular Sāmans mentioned. Burnell has traced most of the Sāmans mentioned to the Sāmaveda; but there are some which are to be found in the Gānas, viz. Grāmagāna and Araṇyagāna. There are a few which cannot be found and which Burnell thinks must belong to a different Śākhā of Sāmaveda from the one now known.

Curiously enough, although the Atharvaveda was specially compiled for magical purposes, the other three Vedas also began to be used in the same manner in order that each Veda should be independent of others. This Brāhmaṇa prescribes many Sāmans to be sung for such purposes as also for Kāmya rites. The Shaḍviṁśa Brāhmaṇa and the Kaushika Sūtra, as we know, treat of evil omens and the rites for preventing their effects. Burnell points out that the Brāhmaṇa Parimara rite is given in the Aitareya Brāhmaṇa (VIII 28) also, to kill enemies (Intro. p. 23).

Ṛigvedic verses were certainely used similarly and a Ṛigvidhāna must have existed. This is the precursor of Tantric rites. For "there are filthy rites prescribed even in the first part of Aitareya Āraṇyaka" (ibid). In the Sāmavidhāna, we find a rite described wherein fire from a funeral pyre is to be taken to a place where four roads meet and certain Sāmans are te be sung (II, 6, 14) after a sacrifice, while throwing ashes on the bed and in the house of an enemy in order that he may leave the village (See also, III, 6, 12 for killing him). In III 3 a similar rite is prescribed for obtaining a maund of gold by propitiating Maṇibhadra (who is apparently a servant of Kubera) with flesh oblation and the singing of a particular Sāman: अष्टरात्रोपोषितोऽमावास्यायां निश्येकवृक्षे क्षीरिण्यरण्ये मांसं सुसंस्कृतमेकतृप्त्यवराघ्र्यं मणिभद्रायोपहरेदेषस्पते मधुमाँ इन्द्र सोम इत्येतेन हिरण्यद्रोणं लभते (III 3, 3). It even appears that the Purāṇic dread servants of Rudra were already invented. We thus have Vināyaka and Skanda to be propitiated by two Sāmans along with Vishṇu and Rudra by two others in I 4, 6-19.

In Europe, similar magical rites were gone through, such as the making of a wax image of one's enemy and slowly melting it in fire. A counterpart of such rites is found in this Brāhmaṇa wherein an image made of dough of an enemy was to be prepared and cut with a razor and the parts were to be thrown into the fire and the remainder eaten by the sorcerer (II, 5, 4).

The Dhāraṇis of the Tibetan Buddhists are also similar rites.

Charms and amulets are again mentioned; but useful rites for curing diseases are also prescribed. The one for curing Yakshman or consumption (II, 4, 9) is notable, as this was a dread disease with the Vedic Aryans, there being a special sūkta in the Ṛigveda itself prescribed for its cure. There are rites with special chants prescribed for safety of travel etc.

In the third chapter, we have first rites for securing plenty of corn or gold and of cattle and servants, for consecrating a house newly built and for long life. We next have the coronation of kings: if anointed with the Sāman "Ekavṛisha" the king becomes an emperor. The Purohita at this ceremony should be given one good village (in inam), one hundred female slaves and one thousand gold coins (III, 5, 3). For victory in battle, rites with particular Sāmans are prescribed. For killing the elephants, chariot warriors, cavalrymen and infantrymen of an enemy, their images of dough were to be made and then cut with a razor and burnt as oblations in fire with a particular Sāman. For seeing goblins and Gandharvas and Apsarasas, two Sāmans are prescribed for repetition and even gods can be seen by repeating the rite twice (III, 7, 6). A rite is prescribed for finding hidden treasure and another for obtaining whatever is desired. It is interesting to note that there are several rites prescribed for acquiring the power of श्रुतिनिगादिन् i. e. of reciting what is only once heard. The Brahmins had developed memory in reciting Vedas to this high pitch. Finally, there is a rite prescribed for release from re-birth.

From the above description of its contents this Brāhmaṇa clearly belongs to a very late period. It is the immediate precursor of Dharmasūtras. The Vedic sacrifice had receded into the background and Vedānuvachana or recitation of Saṁhitās or Sāmans, Tapas or mortification of the body and fasts were now the popular rites for securing one's desires and the merit of performing sacrifices like the Naimishiya twelve-year Sattra. The state of society is reflected in the fact that the sins for which Prāyaschittas are prescribed are mainly the same as in the Smṛitis. They are :- 1 Teaching the unteachable i. e. the Śudras, 2 Sacrificing for them, 3 Uttering obscene words, 4 Drinking liquor, 5 Killing a Brāhmaṇa, 6 Killing a Kshatriya, a Vaiśya, a Śudra, 7 Taking gifts from a king (for a Brahmin of course), 8 Killing a cow, 9 Marrying before the elder brother's marriage, 10 Sexual intercourse with a Śudra woman, 11 Selling the rasas (milk, honey etc.) and animals (for a Brāhmin probably) etc. The society was then completely divided into four castes and marriage with a Śūdra woman was prohibited. But it is creditable that Brahmins abstained from liquor entirely and that the killing of Śūdras was an offence and a sin.

Finally, we may notice two important statements in the Brāhmaṇa. The seven notes of singing are called Krushṭa, Prathama, Dvitīya, Tṛitīya, Chaturtha, Pañchama and Antya, the last two names being new. We have, however, the old names Mandra and Atisvārya in I 14, the first being Sauma (of Soma) and the second Maitrāvaruṇa. These several notes are used by gods, men, Gandharva-Apsaras, beasts, Pitṛis, Asuras and Rākshasas, and trees respectively. Rākshasas are here, as at present, associated with Asuras and not with Yakshas as in the Śatapatha. The significance of the change will be noticed later. Secondly the Vamśa, i. e. list of teachers given at the end is as follows in the descending order: 1 Prajāpati, 2 Bṛihaspati, 3 Nārada, 4 Viśvaksena, 5 Pārāśarya Vyāsa, 6 Jaimini, 7 Paushpiṇḍya, 8 Pārāśaryāyaṇa, 9 Bādarāyaṇa, 10 Tāṇḍi and Śāṭyāyani and these two taught others. Viśvaksena is probably Shrīkṛishna who was a Sāmavedin. Pārāśarya Vyāsa of Mahābhārata is here given as a different person from Bādarāyaṇi, a fact which we will lay stress on later. Tāṇḍi and Śāṭyāyani were the two Śākhās into which the Sāmaveda has been split and their followers are many. Paushpiṇḍya is an unknown name in Vedic literature.

II Jaiminiya Upanishad Brāhmaṇa.

This Brāhmaṇa, first published in America in Roman characters, has been published in Devanagari by Pandit Ramadeva with a short preface by Bhagvad Datta of D. A. V. College, Lahore. He points out in the preface that the Kena Upanishad, which is a part of this Brāhmaṇa, is said by Śaṁkara to be the ninth chapter of the Talavakāra Brāhmaṇa, while it is in this Brāhmaṇa a part of the fourth chapter. It is clear, therefore, that this is only a portion of a bigger Brāhmaṇa which has not survived. In the portion which has not come to us "there was," says Śaṁkara, "a description in the first eight chapters of various sacrifices; and thereafter was the Gāyatra Sāman described (तदनन्तरं गायत्रसामदर्शनं वंशान्तमुक्तम्)." This Brāhmaṇa begins with the Gāyatra Sāman and ends with a Vaṁśa; then the Kena Upanishad comes, followed by a few more Khaṇḍas.

The Brāhmaṇa is divided into four Adhyāyas which are subdivided into Anuvākas, consisting of two or more Khaṇḍas. The first chapter has 18 Anuvākas divided into 60 Khaṇḍas, the second has 5 Anuvākas and 15 Khaṇḍas, the third has 7 Anuvākas and 42 Khaṇḍas and the fourth has 12 Anuvākas and 28 Khaṇḍas. In all there are 42 Anuvākas divided into 145 Khaṇḍas. If on an average we take 12 sentences to each Khaṇḍa, there are about 1740 sentences in this Brāhmaṇa.

The style of the Brāhmaṇa is the usual verbose style with repetitions and fanciful explanations. The stories told are imaginary as usual. These are, however, philosophical and in the strain of the Upanishads. They copy the stories, given in the Chhandogya, of Kuru-Pāñchāla kings and of learned Udgātṛis. Jaimini is well-known as a Sāmavedin Āchārya and his pupil goes by the name of Talavakāra. The Brāhmaṇa, therefore, naturally treats of Sāmans only and gives philosophical explanations and stories following those given in the Chhāndogya Upanishad. It is even clear that they are borrowed from the latter, as Puranic stories are always borrowed from and modelled after stories given in the Mahābhārata. The borrowing is clear from the additions and extensions made. Thus in I, 17 we find the usual works mentioned, viz. Gāthā Nārāśaṁsīḥ, and Itihāsa-Purāṇa with Kumbya and Raibhī added. What these latter are, we are at a loss to know. There are again the various parts of the Sama--songs allegorically transferred to the seasons Vasanta etc. (वसन्तो हिङ्कारः and so on) in I 12. I 13, 14, 15 again are clearly in the strain of the Chhāndogya. In III 4 we have again लवणेन सुवर्णं सन्दध्यात् सुवर्णेन रजतं &c, with an extension, viz. त्रपुणा लोहायसं लोहायसेन कार्ष्णायसम् and finally चर्म च श्लेष्मणा. In III 5, instead of Yama, Īśāna appears as the lord of the southern direction. It seems almost certain that the Brāhmaṇa was composed after the well-known Chhāndogya: yet it belongs to the Brāhmaṇa period and may thus be placed between 2500 and 2000 B. C.

It is remarkable that Śāṭyāyani is always referred to with respect. Śāṭyāyani is known to be a Sāmaveda-Brāhmaṇa-author who is also very old, from Pāṇini's sūtra already noticed. His name is mentioned in the Vaṁśa (III, 7, 3) in the middle as Śaṅkha Śāṭyāyanī Ātreya which shows that his name was Śaṅkha, his father's name was Śāṭyāyana and his gotra was Atri. Many well-known Āchārya names like Vaiyāghrapadya follow. The Upanishad Brāhmaṇa is also called in one place S'āṭyāyani only (सैषा शाट्यायनि गायत्रोपानिषत्).

Other interesting facts fit to be noted are as follows :-

1. Besides the original unmeaning sounds Hum and Om added to Sāmans, we find such sounds as Ovā, Humbhā etc., and these are variously interpreted in fanciful ways. In III 3 we have even variations of Humbhā (हुम्भा इति ब्रह्मवर्चसकामस्य हुम्बो इति पशुकामस्य हुम्बक् इति श्रीकामस्य).

.2 In III 1, 4 the seven components of Uktha are given as Stotriya, Anurūpa, Dhāyyā, Pragātha, Sūkta, Nivid and Paridhāniyā. These are further explained allegorically.

3 Various Ṛigvedic verses are explained in this Brāhmaṇa in the Brāhmaṇa style, namely, without any real comment but with mere indica-

tions ; and some philosophical riddle questions are answered as in I 14 (इन्द्रद्युक्थमृचद्युद्गीथमाहुः asked by Prithu Vainya to divine Vrātyas) or in I 12 (येमिर्वात इषितः प्रवाति, a question after the Kena Upanishad beginning). To what Veda these belong is not stated nor has its source been traced.

4 We find "Naraka" (hell) mentioned in opposition to Svarga, for the first time probably in Vedic literature, here in IV 4, 25.

5 Here are also found the highest arithmetical numbers, viz., Nikharva, Padma, Kshiti and Vyoma (I 1, 11).

6 Agni is not to be touched with the hand, the foot, or a stick. The sacrificial fire is as respectfully treated by the Hindus as by the Parsis.

7 King Śāryāta Mānava is said in a story to conquer the east. His Udgatṛi was Ayāsya Āṅgirasa, as Bṛihaspati was that of the gods, as Bamba Ajadvipa of the manes and Kāvya Uśanas of the Asuras. The Purāṇic connection of Kāvya with the Asuras is also probably Vedic. Bamba is again a strange name. Ayāsya and Śāryāta are, however, historical and are not connected by the Śatapatha and the Aitareya in the Aśvamedha sacrificers' list.

8 Finally, we find the letter ळ (ḷ) used (अपीळयत्) in this Brāhmaṇa which belongs to the southern recitation. We know that the Jaiminīya Śākhā of the Sāmaveda belongs to Karnatak.

III Ārsheya Brāhmaṇa

This Brāhmaṇa has been published by Sāmaśrami (Calcutta) in Devanagari with the commentary of Sāyana. It has also been published by Burnell (Mangalore) with extracts from Sāyana's commentary, all in Roman characters. The Brāhmaṇa, as its name indicates, gives the Ṛishis of Sāma-songs. But these Ṛishis are different from those given in the printed editions of Sāmaveda. Thus the first verse अग्न आ याहि वीतये &c is attributed to Bhāradvāja in the printed books. In this Brāhmaṇa, in the original and in Sāyana's Bhāshya, it is attributed to Gautama Parka in the first and third Sāmans and to Kāśyapa Barhisha in the second or middle Sāman. It must be remembered that Sāman here is different from the verse itself; for three Sāmans or chants are said to arise from three parts of the verse or portions taken at different times. Whence Sāyana gives this information is not indicated: but he gives the original verse on which the three chants arise. But for this Brāhmaṇa, it would have been impossible for us to know who were the first Ṛishis who chanted the three Sāmans that arise. A great deal of technical study is necessary to understand this subject clearly and it is impossible for us to enter into further details. It may be added that the verse अग्न आ याहि वीतये &c. belongs originally to the Ṛigveda and its Ṛishi there (VI, 16, 10) is Bharadvāja himself as in the printed Sāmaveda.

It is difficult to determine the date of this Brāhmaṇa. The word Smārta which appears in the first or introductory Khaṇḍa "defines its real position" according to Burnell. But it seems that Burnell has misunderstood the word. Its meaning is not the modern derived one. As explained by Sāyaṇa, the word is used in its root sense, viz., "helping the memory" and from the context also this meaning is the only one possible (ऋषीणां नामधेयगोत्रोपधारणं स्वर्ग्यं यशस्यं धन्यं पुण्यं पुत्र्यं पशव्यं ब्रह्मवर्चस्यं स्मार्तमायुष्यं &c). So far as we have looked through this Brāhmaṇa, there is no indication of its date. The order in which the Ṛishis are given follows Grāmagāna and Araṇyagāna of the Pūrvārchika, according to Burnell: but when these Gānas arose, there is no ground to decide. The Sāmans must have been taught orally, for two thousand years at least, before they were written. And it is impossible to say what notation was first adopted to show the notes and the methods. Burnell says in his introduction (p. XXVI) that formerly letters indicating notes were written between the letters of the verse as in the notation of the music of the ancient Greeks, but that later the letters were substituted by numerals in the south. The figures 1, 2, 3, in the printed editions, given above the letters of the verses, indicate not notes but only the stress accents, Udātta, Svarita, and Anudātta as stated already.

It is interesting to note that these accents are not always the same as those in the Ṛigvedic verse. Thus the first yerse in Sāmaveda is written as अ॒ग्न आ या॑हि वी॒तये॑ गृ॒णा॒नो ह॒व्यदा॑तये । नि होता॑ सत्सि ब॒र्हिषि॑ ॥ (VI, 16, 10) in the Ṛigveda. It is written in the Sāmaveda with figures as follows:– अ३ग्न२ आ१ या२हि वी१त२ये२ गृ३णा२नो२ ह३व्य१दा२तये । १नि हो२ता३ सत्सि ब३र्हि१षि२.

In the Sāman way of writing and probably reciting also, the verse thus differs from the Ṛigveda. In Sāma–singing it would be still more different with its divisions into Prastāva, Udgītha etc. When the different gānas arose in Sāma–singing the notes were, in oral teaching, shown by touching the different fingers of the right hand. The first written instructions appear in Nārada-Śikshā and then Gautamī and Māndūkī Śikshās (Burnell Intro. p. XX). The age of these gānas cannot be determined, but they may be taken to be earlier than Pāṇini (*ibid*). Burnell thinks that this Brāhmaṇa is later than Grāmageyagāna in its present form but assigns no date to the latter. There are, however, the following indications to show that it is later than the Tāṇḍya Brāhmaṇa.

Sāma–singing seems to have advanced further by its time and become more complicated than in the Tāṇḍya. Several Sāmans are sung from the same verse which, so far as we can see, was not the case at the time of the Tāṇḍya. Different Ṛishis are mentioned therein as having seen particular Sāmans which were then named after them. This does not signify that there were more than one mode of singing that Sāman The names of the authors of these various Sāmans given in this Ārsheya Brāhmaṇa being different from those given in the Sāṁaveda books lead to the same conclusion. The names strike us often as imaginary. Thus in the very beginning Om is itself treated as a Sāman seen by Parameshṭhin, son of Prajāpati or by Brahman itself and Himkāra is said to have been seen by Vasishṭha or by Prajāpati or by cows. The sound Hum no doubt resembles that of the cow when it calls for the calf; and the Ṛishis, being in constant touch with cows, borrowed that pleasing call. (It is, however, always called Hiṁkāra though it is really Huṁkara). The Brāhmaṇa again quoted in the first Khaṇḍa about the necessity of reciting the Ṛishi, the Devatā and the Chhandas of a mantra is well-known and shows that this Brāhmaṇa is later than the principal Brāhmaṇas, in other words, is later than 2000 B. C.

The first Khaṇḍa states that the person who studies this Brāhmaṇa becomes *Sasthāna* with Ṛishis, a new word used instead of the usual Saloka and it further adds that he is born with the memory of his past lives (स्मरन्नाजायते पुनः ।). These ideas also show that this Brāhmaṇa is later than the other Brāhmaṇas and the principal Upanishads also. But Burnell thinks that this introductory

Khaṇḍa itself is a later addition which is possible. The first Sāman noticed is the well-known Gāyatri and its Ṛishi, i. e. the author of the singing of the verse, is Pushkala and its deity is Agni and not Viśvāmitra and Sūrya as in the original Ṛigveda.

The Brāhmaṇa is divided into three Prapāṭhakas subdivided into 82 Khaṇḍas (28, 25, 29) which consist usually of single but long sentences. The first part is in the Sūtra style: but the second part or index to the Āranyagāna is less artificial (p. VIII Intro., Burnell). Who the author is of this Brāhmaṇa has not been stated and is not known from any source. Sāyana, in beginning his Bhāshya, merely says, "There are eight Brāhmaṇas of the Sāmaveda 1 Prauḍha, 2 Shaḍviṁśa, 3 Sāmavidhi, 4 Ārsheya, 5 Devatādhyāya, 6 Mantra, 7 Saṁhitopanishad and 8 Vaṁśa and that having commented on the first three, he proceeds to comment on the fourth."

VIII GOPATHA BRĀHMAṆA

The Atharvaveda was itself compiled, as we have shown, during the Brāhmaṇa period, presumably sometime about 2,700 B.C. The Gopatha Brāhmaṇa attached to it was composed at a far later period; most probably after the Vaitāna Sūtra, as pointed out by Macdonell, which it clearly follows in its second half. Some passages are taken in it from the Aitareya, the Kaushītaki, the Śatapatha and even the Shaḍviṁśa. Although thus falling outside the Brāhmaṇa period (3000-2000 B. C.), we treat of it here as it claims to be a Brāhmaṇa and is treated as such by later authors, being the only one attached to the Atharvaveda.

This Brāhmaṇa has been edited among others by Rajendralal Mitra in the Bibliotheca India Series and we base our observations on this edition. The Brāhmaṇa is divided into two parts called Pūrva Gopatha and Uttara Gopatha. There are five Prapāṭhakas (chapters) in the former and six in the latter. These contain from 39 to 65 paragraphs or Kaṇḍikās, the Pūrvārdha having 135 and the Uttarārdha 123, in all 258 Kaṇḍikās. These usually consist of five or six sentences which are often very long.

The style of the Brāhmaṇa is that of the other Brāhmanas, involved and desultory. The language is not, however, similar to that of the other Brāhmaṇas, being clearly modern and not Vedic Sanskrit, though Rajendralal thinks that the language is also the same, having the same archaic expressions and grammatical irregularities (p, 11 Intro.) The treatment of the subject is of the same kind as in the other Brāhmaṇas, never detailed and systematic as in the Sūtras, full of imaginary legends and fanciful explanations, always quoting the dictum of the Upanishads, "The gods hate the direct and love the hidden or occult." One is always put in mind of the fact that this queer explanation is first given by the Chhāndogya Upanishad (तस्मादिदंद्रं सन्तमिन्द्रमित्याचक्षते परोक्षेण परोक्षप्रिया इव हि देवाः प्रत्यक्षद्विषः ।). Thus 17 has तं वा एतं वरुणं सन्तं वरुण इत्याचक्षते परोक्षेण परोक्षप्रिया इव हि देवा भवन्ति प्रत्यक्षद्विषः (भवन्ति being added). We have this dictum constantly invoked throughout this Brāhmaṇa. "Myths, legends and parables constitute the staple of the work, but they are short and pointless. They are intended to explain the origin, nature and fruits of particular ceremonies." (Raj. Intro. p. 12).

This Brāhmaṇa was plainly written at a time when the Atharvaveda was not only recognised as a Veda but had even advanced to the highest position among the Vedas. It begins with the legend that Brahman first stood alone, (the wording here is plainly copied from Upanishads "ब्रह्म वा इदमग्र आसीत् ... तदैक्षत ... महद्वै यक्षम्"), that it created first water from its sweat and Bhṛigu from its seed thrown in this water, that Bhṛigu became Atharvan when he looked down (अथ अर्वाक्) and that Atharvan created ten Ātharvaṇa Ṛishis of one Rik, two Riks &c. and from these, the ten Ātharvaṇa Ārsheyas of 11 Riks etc. up to twenty. This refers plainly to the Atharvaveda, as we now have it in two parts, viz. the first half with ten chapters and the second half with chapters eleven to twenty. Indeed it is actually stated that these twenty Ṛishis saw Mantras which form the *Atharvaveda*. From Atharvaveda was created Om, from it, the three worlds, earth, sky and heaven; from them the three gods, Agni, Vāyu and Sun, from them the three Vedas, Ṛik, Yajuḥ and Sāman; from them the sea, from it Varuṇa, from Varuṇa or Mṛityu, Aṅgiras, from him, the twenty Āṅgirasas and from them the ten Āṅgirasa Ārsheyas and from them the Āṅgirasa Veda. (Here Āngirasa Veda is treated as distinct from Atharvaveda). From it was born the word Janat. It stood up and hence the *Aṅgirasas when reciting stand up.* From it, when looking in five directions, sprang five Vedas, Sarpaveda from the east, Piśāchaveda from the south, Āsuraveda from the west and Itihāsaveda from the north, while Purāṇaveda sprang from above, the Dhruvā direction.

The above legend though absurd is very interesting. In the first place, the legend shows that the Gopatha was written at a time when the Atharvaveda had advanced in popular estimation to the first position among the Vedas. Atharvan was Bhṛigu, born from Brahman itself. In previous Vedic literature we find Bhṛigu as a son of Varuṇa, one of the highest Vedic gods, if not the highest. Varuṇa here is born from Samudra, born from the three Vyāhṛitis, born from Ṛigveda, Yajurveda and Sāmaveda, which were born from Oṁkāra, itself born from Atharvaveda. Atharvaveda is thus the first Veda from which the other three Vedas were born through Oṁkāra. "Atharvaveda should, therefore, be studied first by every student before he learns the other Vedas, thus says Vyāsa". Brahman the presiding priest, who before was to do his duty with the help of Ṛigveda, Yajurveda and Sāmaveda was now to be an Atharvavedin.

The directions assigned to the five subsidiary Vedas again are suggestive. Sarpa-Veda was born from the east. Probably the Nāgas were found chiefly in the eastern parts of India. Piśāchas and their allies the Rākshasas were found in the south, there being probably still cannibals to the south of the Vindhyas. The Asuras were in the west and Varuṇa was born of the western sea. They were probably the Iranians or Assyrians or Greeks, with their god Uranus. They were also masters of Māyá or illusion. Mayāsura in the Mahābhārata had such Māyās constructed in the court-hall he built for the Pāṇḍavas. Why Itihāsa is assigned the north and Purāṇa the headward direction is not imaginable. In the Chhāndogya there is a mention of these Vedas as subjects of study; but they are not called Vedas and Itihāsa–Purāṇa is one subject and Sarpa–Devajanavidyā is also one, while Āsuraveda is not mentioned at all.

From the description of the Atharva ten Ṛishis of one, two and so on upto ten Ṛiks and ten Ārsheyas of 11 Ṛiks and so on to twenty, it is, as said above, quite clear that there is here a description of the Atharvaveda as we now have it. What then is the necessity of Viṁśat (20) Āngirasa Ṛishis and ten Ārsheyas and which is their Āṅgirasa Veda is a riddle. The order of these Ṛiks is here reversed. We have first Ṛishis of 16, 15, 12 Ṛiks and then of one, three, four, five, six, and seven Ṛiks. "From it the word Janat was produced and by reciting this word you have all the merit of reciting the Āngirasa Veda." 'This Veda went above' perhaps shows that this is a heavenly Veda not to be found on earth and the word Janat alone survives of it and it is enough for securing the merit of reciting the heavenly Āṅgirasa Veda.

Having discussed this legend of the birth of the Atharvaveda in detail, we may glance over the succeeding contents of the work. We have first the glorification of Om and of Gāyatrī in the remaining of the first chapter. The second treats of the duties of Brahmacharya. A period of twelve years for each Veda is prescribed; but a lesser period according to one's capacity or weakness is also allowed. The third begins with how the Hotṛi should know Ṛigveda, the Adhvaryu Yajurveda and the Udgātri, Sāmaveda, while the fourth, Brahman, should be one versed in Atharvāṅgirasas. Various imaginary legends are then given about priests. In Khaṇḍa 18, we have a detailed description of how the sacrificial animal is to be divided among the priests and others. The fourth chapter relates to the ordination of priests and also to the year as a sacrifice. The fifth treats of the Saṁvatsara Sattra first and subsequently enumerates and describes the various sacrifices, अग्न्याधेयं, पूर्णाहुति; अग्निहोत्रं, दर्शपूर्णमासौ, आग्रयणं, चातुर्मास्यानि, पशुबन्धः, अग्निष्टोमः, राजसूयः, वाजपेयः, अश्वमेधः, पुरुषमेधः and सर्वमेधः. The contents of the Uttarārdha are very desultory. "No subject is taken *ab initio*, but casually with reference to some particular point of doubt. The story of Rudra's fight for a share in sacrificial oblations is given in the first chapter. The second chapter begins with flesh offerings for the various deities. The third chapter relates to the mystic syllables *Vashaṭ* and *Hiṁkāra*. "The last three chapters treat of morning, noon and evening rites in connection, with Ekāha, Uktha, Ekāshṭaka &c." (p. 37)

The author of this Brāhmaṇa is apparently Gopatha. The name Gopatha appears as that of a Ṛishi in the list of Ṛishis of the Atharvaveda, though not in the list of Ṛishis of the other Vedas. The author may, we think, be a real descendant of that Ṛishi. The late Dr. Gune pointed out that the Gopatha Brāhmaṇa was known to Yāska. The latest date for the Brāhmaṇa would accordingly be before 1000 B. C. The earliest date may be fixed at about 1500 B. C., from the fact that the Brāhmaṇa is clearly posterior to the ten principal Upanishads, many expressions and legends being copied from them or invented after their model and from the fact that Kalpa works for each Veda are mentioned in P. V. 25 सन्ति चैवां समाना मन्त्रा कल्पाश्च ब्राह्मणानि च । व्यवस्थानं तु तत्सर्वं पृथग्वेदेषु तत्स्मृतम् ॥

The author probably lived in the middle country, as among the peoples mentioned are Kuru-Pāñchāla, Kāśi-Magadha and other northern ones. From the many details about grammar given in P. I, 24 (ओंकारं पृच्छामः को धातु : किं प्रातिपदिकं किं नामाख्यातं किं लिङ्गं किं वचनं का विभक्तिः कः प्रत्ययः कः स्वरः उपसर्गः निपातः को विकारः को विकारी कति मात्राः कति वर्णाः &c.), the author may have belonged to the north-west. He in one place gives the first Mantras of the three Vedas correctly and for Atharvaveda the first Mantra given is शं नो देवीरभिष्टये &c., the same as given by Patañjali and as recited now by all Brahmins at the time of their Śrāvaṇī, as stated before. The author, therefore, knows the Pippalāda recension only and probably belongs to Kashmir where that recension is found.

The Brāhmaṇa mentions many modern ideas such as ब्रह्म ह वै ब्रह्माणं पुष्करे ससृजे (p. 16) or that a Brahmin should not sing or dance and be called Āglāgṛidha (तस्माद्ब्राह्मणो नैव गायेन्न नृत्येन्माग्लागृधः, P. II 21) or the that gods began a sacrifice which the Asuras and Rākshasas wished to destroy (p. VI, 6) or that 'Om' should be pronounced when reciting any Veda or Vedic verse, or that before beginning any rite, water-sipping or Āchamana should be done thrice. It is interesting to note that this Āchamana or thrice sipping of water is not accompanied by the uttering of names of Shrikṛishṇa, Keshava, Nārāyaṇa and Mādhava as now, but by the sūkta जीवास्थ &c.* What is Pariśumbhana which follows twice, one can not tell (त्रिराचमनं द्विः परिशुम्भनम्).

The last Khaṇḍa of Prapāṭhaka V, Pūrvārdha, consists of verses framed after Vedic mantras in which the greatness of the Atharvaveda is extolled. The sacrifice which is described as सप्ततन्तु and एकविंशतिसंस्थ in the beginning is said to be sevenfold, viz. seven Sutyas (Somas), seven Pākayajñas and seven Haviryajñas, in all twenty-one, and all these are performed by Āṅgirasas. "The followers of the three Vedas go to Trivishṭapa or Tri-

* निरङ्गुष्ठे पाणावमृतमस्यमृतोपस्तरणमस्यमृतायोपस्तृणामीति पाणावुदकमानीय जीवास्थेति सूक्तेन त्रिराचामति (P. I, 39).

diva or Nāka; but those of the Atharvaveda go to the great Brahma-lokas beyond them". These verses are distinctly not Vedic; and there are ślokas also quoted now and then in the book which do not claim to be Vedic. But where Ṛiks are distinctly mentioned as Vedic, being introduced with the words तदेतदृचाभ्युक्तम् &c., the reference is not given and probably can never be traced, though attempts should be made to trace them to the Ṛigveda or the Atharvaveda.

In some cases, however, the Ṛiks can easily be located as many statements in Gopatha are mere copies of those in Aitareya made with a few variations. Thus in U. VI, we have in the beginning तान् वा एतान् सम्पातान् विश्वामित्रः प्रथममपश्यत् which Vāmadeva appropriated (R. IV 19, 22, 23). This is a copy of Aitareya VI. 18. The new Sampāta hymns seen by Viśvamitra and others are then quoted which are the same as those in A. B. with one or two less. Viśvāmitra's new sūktas सद्यो ह जातो वृषभः कनीनः (R. III 48) and अभितष्टेव दीधया मनीषा (R. III 38) which is attributed to Prajāpati in the Ṛigveda are referred to here. Those mentioned as of Vasishṭha are इन्द्रः पूर्भिदातिरद्दासमर्कैः, एक इद्धव्यश्चर्षणीनाम् and यस्तिग्मशृङ्गो वृषभो न भीमः. The first is, however, by Viśvāmitra (R. III 34), the second is by Bharadvāja (R. VI 22), while the third is really that of Vasishṭha (R. VII 19). How these Ṛishis are changed, it is difficult to explain. That some of these sūktas from the Ṛigveda are given in Atharvaveda XIX has already been noted. Thus य एक इद्धव्यश्चर्षणीनां is A. XX 3 and यस्तिग्मशृङ्गो is A. XX, 37. The sūkta सद्यो ह जातः is said to be Pañcharcha (of five verses) in the next Khaṇḍa (U. VI 2); and it is of five verses in the Ṛigveda. Indeed Ṛigveda is the chief basis on which the superstructure of the whole subsequent Vedic literature is raised.

Curiously enough, there are very few statements in this Brāhmaṇa about Dakshiṇās to be given at sacrifices; probably they had become unimportant since the days of the older Brāhmaṇas, as the sacrificial regime was probably over. Indeed in U. VI 14, to take Dakshiṇā is considered to be improper. Further there is no Āraṇyaka or Upanished attached to the Gopatha Brāhmaṇa which makes it certain that it comes after the well-known Atharva-Upanishads.

The last chapter (VI) of the Uttaragopatha mentions many other names of sūktas to be recited by the three priests Maitrāvaruna, Brāhmaṇāchhaṁsi and Achhāvāka, the whole obviously being borrowed from the last chapter (XXX) of the Kaushītaki Brāhmaṇa, such as Āvapana, Kadvanta, Pragātha, Jāgata, Śilpa, Nābhānedishṭa, Vṛishākapi, Vālakhilya, Sukīrti, and Kuntāpa (the derivation of which is given in addition, as burning Kuya or Kutsita; कुयं नाम कुत्सितं भवति तत्तपति तस्मात्कुन्तापः). These Kuntāpas are referred to as 'इदं जना उपश्रुता, the first verse of the first sūkta of fourteen verses'. The Kuntāpa sūktas are given in the twentieth chapter of the Atharvaveda from 127th to 136th and the first sūkta is of 14 ṛiks with इदं जना उपश्रुता as the first. Subsequent three verses are also quoted. These sūktas are from Ṛigveda probably. But they are not found in the Śākala recension. They are quoted in the Āśvalāyana Śrauta Sūtra as already explained and must have belonged to some other Śākhā. A sūkta called Aitasha-pralāpa or the bragging of Aitasha is mentioned in U. VI 13 and the word Pravalhikā is applied to it.

Finally, while Bloomfield considers Gopatha later than the Vaitāna Sūtra, Caland and Keith consider it earlier (Winternitz p. 190). The mention of Kalpa of all Vedas refers, we think, to Vaitāna Sūtra and this should settle the higher limit for this Brāhmaṇa at about 1500 B. C.

ADDITIONAL NOTES ON BRĀHMANAS

I Further Particulars About S'āṅkhāyana alias Kaushitaki Brāhmana

This work quotes the authority of Kaushītaki every now and then, usually in opposition to that of Paingya (as in IV 9–Kaushītaki decides that oblations should be given after darkness is dispelled in the morning;–or in VIII 9) and thus really represents the Kaushītaki school. The name S'āṅkhāyana appears nowhere but he is an Āchārya of Ṛigveda and there is a Sūtra and an Āraṇyaka in his name. He may be taken to be a follower of Kaushītaki and he appears to have reedited the Kaushītaki Brāhmaṇa in a simpler form.

As edited by the Ānandās'rama, the thirty chapters of the work are put into two halves of 15 each. These Adhyāyas contain from 5 to 17 Khaṇḍas, the total for the two halves being 118 and 148, in all 266. The Khaṇḍas are not divided into sentences and are practically long sentences themselves.

This recension almost always uses ळ (ḷ) for ड (ḍ) and thus is a southern one. It is followed in Gujarat which is practically a Dravidian or southern province.

The following interesting facts may be noted: :– (1) In II 2 we have the words Sarpadevajana and Rakshodevajana which show that devajana means higher beings. (2) In 4 we have अप आचम्य (यदप आचम्य व्रतं विसृजते). What was the procedure of Āchamana we are not told. (3) In III we have यजमानस्यार्षेयमाह which shows that the gotra and pravara system was firmly established. (4) In VI we have the generally correct observation that sickness prevails at the junction of seasons (ऋतुसन्धिषु व्याधिर्जायते). (5) In V 5 we have a simile taken from the king's march, in front of which soldiers walk making the road safe (यथा महाराजः पुरस्तात्सेनान्यनीकानि प्रत्युह्याभयं पन्थानमन्वियात्). (6) In V 6 we have a reference to S'rāddha being performed in the afternoon with oblations in the fire called Kavyavāhana (तस्मादपराह्णे पितृयज्ञेन यजते अग्निं कव्यवाहनम्). (7) In VII 8 a S'ikhaṇḍi Yājñasena is mentioned, which name strikes one as that of the brother of Draupadī. (8) In VII 6 the proficiency of northerners in language and grammar is referred to (उदञ्च एव यन्ति वाचं शिक्षितुं यो वै तत आगच्छति तं शुश्रूषन्ते). The fame of Takshiśilā and perhaps of Kashmir was still great as the land of Aryan speech, a fame which they lost long before Mahomedan times, probably in the days of Buddhism. (9) In VI eight names of S'iva are explained but in a strange manner viz. Bhava, S'iva, Paśupati, Ugra, Mahādeva, Rudra, Iśāna and Aśani. These names are assigned to a god born of Agni, Vayu, Āditya, Chandramas, and Ushas, themselves born of Prajāpati. For each name, a separate Vrata or vow is assigned and these vows are:– आर्द्रमेव वासाः परिदधीत, सर्वमेव नाश्नीयात्, ब्राह्मणं न परिवदेत्, स्त्रिया विवरं नेक्षेत, उद्यन्तं नेक्षेतास्तं यन्तम्, विमूर्तमेव नाश्नीयान्मज्जानं च, अन्नमेवेच्छमानं न प्रत्याचक्षीत, सत्यमेव वदेत्, हिरण्यं बिभृयात्. The last is still followed in the Panjab where every Hindu puts golden rings in the lobes of his ears. (10) In VII we are told that Agni is the lowest god and Vishṇu the highest, a sentiment which appears to gain strength at this pericd and is given at the very beginning of the Aitareya Br. (अग्निरवरार्ध्यः विष्णुः परार्ध्यः). (11) In VIII 6 the thirty-three Vedic gods are mentioned and are detailed in XI 6 as in Bṛihadāṇaṇyaka Upanishad. It cannot be said that one copies from the other. Both only describe the prevailing view. (12) What is the Nirukta mentioned in XI, I (उच्चैर्निरुक्तमनुब्रूयात्)? It is not that of Yāska, but its source probably. (13) In XI, 13 it is said that in the other world the animal sacrificed would eat the secrificer. A revulsion of feeling was setting in against flesh-eating and even against animal sacrifice (अमुष्मिन् लोके पशवो मनुष्यानश्नन्ति.) (14) In XIV, 3 we have शोंसावो, शोंसामो and even शोशोंसात्रो and शोशोंसामो to be uttered at Prātaḥsavana etc. In XVII, 7 we have a Sāman named Mārjālīya. (15) In 9 Asurarakshāṁsi are joined as obstructors of sacrifice. (16) In XVII, 8 we have the dictum यज्ञो विष्णुः a favourite sentiment with the Brāhmaṇas commencing with S'atapatha. (17) In XVIII a provision is made for the contingency when the ordained animal dies before it is killed in sacrifice. (18) After Devaloka and Pitṛiloka, Agniloka is described as Jīvaloka, Vayuloka as Amṛitadhāman, Indraloka as Aparājita, Varuṇaloka as Adhideva, Mṛityuloka as Pradiva and Brahmaloka as Rochana. (19) In XXIII 2 an interesting explanation of the name S'akvarī (metre) is given, viz, that Indra was enabled to kill Vṛitra by its help (इन्द्रो वृत्रमशकद्धन्तुमाभिस्तस्माच्छक्वर्यः). The reader will remember that the Mahānāmnī Sāman is specially addressed to Indra and has S'akvarī verses. He will also remember the Ṛik of Vasishṭhas यच्छक्वरीषु बृहता रवेणेन्द्रे शुष्ममादधता वो वासिष्ठाः । (20) In XXV 8 Kaushītaki mentions Baru as the Ṛishi of a Ṛigveda sūkta (X 96) correctly. This is an uncommon name. (21) In XXV 13 Rudra is said to be the oldest and the best of gods (रुद्रो वै ज्येष्ठश्च श्रेष्ठश्च देवानाम्). This is the beginning of the rivalry between Rudra and Visṇu about the highest position among gods. (22) In XXV 15 a Brahmin is asked to reside with a Vaiśya or a Kshatriya or a Brahmin of the same gotra. Brahmins observed the gotra system most tenaciously. (23) In XXVIII, 1 the Praishas and Nigadas are praised (ते ह प्रैषांश्च निगदांश्च ददृशुः यदृग्भिर्यज्ञस्यानाप्तं तदेभिः सर्वमाप्स्याम तानेतान् प्रैषाननुप्रैशान् विश्वामित्रो ददर्श).

II Some interesting facts noted by Mr. Bhagwad Datta in his recent book on "Brāhmaṇas" with our observations where necessary.

1 The word Brāhmaṇas in used in the sense of explanation of sacred verse or ṛik, in S'atapatha XII, 5, 2, 8 (यथर्क्तथा ब्राह्मणम्). The word Bandhu is similarly used for explanation of Yajuḥ (यथा यजुस्तथा बन्धुः S'. VI, 6, 4). The various Brāhmaṇas were the basis on which the Sarvānukramaṇīs were subsequently framed. The authors of many sūktas in the Ṛigveda are thus given in various places in the Brāhmaṇas; e. g. वामदेवः अवैक्षत (Tāṇḍya); एतत्कवषः सूक्तमपश्यत् पंचदशर्चम् (Kau.); गौरिवीति शाक्त्य एतत्सूक्तमपश्यत् (Aita.). We have already noted how S'atapatha (II, 1, 4, 29) refers to the sūkta of Sārparājni आयं गौः etc. (X 189). Tāṇḍya 4, 7, 3 refers to इन्द्रं क्रतुं न आभर etc. (R VII 32, 26) as seen by Vasishṭha. It is, however, we think, not possible that the Brāhmaṇas give all the information required for Sarvānukramaṇis, not even Nirukta, nor the Sūtras. The whole information must have been handed down orally till collected together in Anukramaṇīs.

2 Certain Brāhmaṇas are called Anubrāhmaṇas, a name occuring even in Pāṇini (IV, 2, 62). The small Brāhmaṇas are Anubrāhmaṇas. Even the Taittirīya Brāhmaṇa contains some Anubrāhmaṇas. I, 6 11, 1 says अनुब्राह्मणं च भवति, Mādhava in his Bhāshya on T. B. has अथ राजसूयस्यानुब्राह्मणम्.

3 Of these smaller Brāhmaṇas, Mantra Brāhmaṇa with two Prapāṭhakas and sixteen Khaṇḍas is also called Chhāndogya Brāhmaṇa. It gives Mantras only from the Vedas. (The Upanishad probably belongs to this Brāhmaṇa). From S'ankara's remark on Vedānta Sūtra 3-3-25, it seems that he treats this Upanishad as

forming part of the Tāṇḍya Brāhmaṇa (ताण्डिनां श्रुतिः). There is a Daivata (Sāmaveda) Brāhmaṇa, published by Jīvānanda Vidyāsāgara. There is a Chhando-vichiti Brāhmaṇa, referred to by Pāṇini in Gaṇapātha 4-3-43 wherein descriptions of chhandas are given. There is an Ārsheya Brāhmaṇa containing 3 Prapāṭhakas and 82 Khaṇḍas wherein the Rishis of Sāmaveda are given. The Sāmavidhāna Brāhmaṇa (published by Burnell, London) consisting of 3 Prapāṭhakas and 25 Khaṇḍas gives the Viniyoga or uses of the several Sāmans, some of which are for Abhichāra (magic). There is a Sanhitopanishad published by Burnell (Mangalore) which mentions Araṇyageya and Grāmageya gānas. Finally, there is a Vaṁśa Brāhmaṇa of 3 Khaṇḍas which gives the Vaṁśas of Sāmaveda teachers.

4 Keith in his 'Ṛigveda Brāhmaṇas' argues that Aitareya Brāhmaṇa is old because it has no allusion to S'vetaketu or to Āruṇi (p. 48). But in 6, 30 Bulila Āśvatarāśvi is mentioned who was their contemporary. (We may urge further that non-mention is no test whatever either way, unless mention is necessary). The Aitareya Brāhmaṇa and the Āśvalāyana S'ākhā are found in the whole of the Deccan (तुङ्गा कृष्णा तथा गोदा सह्याद्रिशिखरावधि। आ आन्ध्रादिपर्यन्तं बह्वृचाश्वलायनी ॥ टी. चरण-व्यूह); while in North Gujarāt is found the S'ānkhāyana S'ākhā (उत्तरे गुर्जरे देशे वेदो बह्वृच ईरितः। कौषितकिब्राह्मणं च-ditto).

5 S'añkara quotes Kaushītaki Brāhmaṇa on 1, 2, 28 and III 3, 10 of Vedānta Sūtra.

6 According to Weber, the S'atapatha of 14 Kāṇḍas consists of one hundred chapters containing 438 Brāhmaṇas, having in all 7624 Kaṇḍikās. The Kāshikāvṛitti on Pāṇini IV 2-62 mentions Shashṭhipatha which may be explained as the name of the first nine Kāṇḍas which really contain 60 chapters, thus showing that the

10th to 14th Kāṇḍas are latter additions, a conclusion which we have already accepted, with this difference that the latter portion begins with the XI Kāṇḍa and not the 10th. The Mahābhārata story mentioning how Yājñavalkya composed the S'atapatha states that he composed it including Rahasya, Sangraha and Paris'esha (सरहस्यं ससंग्रहं सपरिशेषम्) The tenth Kāṇḍa is called Agnirahasya, the eleventh contains Sañgraha and 12th and 13th are Paris'esha, the 14th containing the Upanishad. Datta points out that S'ankara on III 3, 19 quotes वाजसनेयिशाखायामग्निरहस्ये शाण्डिल्यविद्यायाम्, thus showing that the 10th Kāṇḍa was known even to S'ankara as Agnirahasya. But he calls it S'āṇḍilyavidyā and thus treats it on the same level as Kāṇḍas VI to IX be longing to S'āṇḍilya.

7 The S'atapatha in XI 5, 1, 10 refers to Ṛigveda Saṁhitā in the sentence तदेतदुक्तप्रत्युक्तं पञ्चदशर्चं बह्वृचः प्राहुः।, describing the dialogue between Urvas'ī and Purūravas; but the sūkta X 95 in the Ṛigveda contains 18 ṛiks and not 15". We may suggest the explanation that this late Kāṇḍa of the S'atapatha refers to a S'ākhā version different from the one we possess

8 The Mādhyandina S'ākhā is found in Anga, Vanga Kalinga and Gujarat. Ujjain Pandits, Harisvāmin and Uvaṭa, wrote Bhāshyas on this version. Further S'atapatha XI 5, 1 gives the whole story of Urvas'ī and Purūravas in a somewhat new form and probably the verses 16-18 in the Ṛigveda sūkta are not required for this story

9 Harisvāmin wrote his Bhāshya on Mādhyandina S'atapatha in the 1st century B. C. (श्रीमतोऽवन्तिनाथस्य विक्रमार्कस्य भूपतेः। धर्माध्यक्षो हरिस्वामी व्याख्यच्छातपथीं श्रुतिम्). This may apply to Gupta Vikrama, but the word Gupta, we think, would not have been kept gupta. This Hari-

svāmin is quoted by Karka in his Bhāshya on the S'rauta Sūtra of Kātyāyana in VIII 19. Vvaṭa wrote his Bhāshya on the Vājasaneyi Saṁhitā in the eleventh century A. D. (मंत्राणां कृतवान् भाष्यं मही भोज प्रशासति). Nīlakaṇṭha, the well-known commentator of Mahābhārata wrote a Bhāshya on the Kāṇva S'atapatha.

10 This Kāṇva S'ākhā version of the S'atapatha according to Caland consists of 17 Kāṇḍas, divided into 104 chapters. The number of Brāhmaṇas is 446 and of Kaṇḍikās 5865, as compared with 7624 of the Mādhyandina version. The difference, however, in reality is very minor.

Datta does not give the province where this S'ākhā prevails; but from Charaṇavyūha and other recent works we find that it prevails in Mahārāshṭra alone. We also find that the letter ळ (ḷ) is used in this S'ākhā as in the Ṛigvedic S'ākala S'ākhā, a peculiarity of Mahārāstra recitation, as stated already, borrowed from the Dravidians of the South.

11 The Taittirīya Brāhmaṇa has in the beginning a Kāṇḍānukramaṇī which mentions the Kāṭhakas added. These thus seem to be old and they include the Purushamedha. It may be said, however, that this Anukramaṇī itself is a late addition.

The Taittirīya S'ākhā is found in Andhra up to the Godāvari and the sea.

Other S'ākhā Brāhmaṇas of the Black Yajurveda are 1 Kāṭhaka, 2 Kālāpaka, 3 S'vetāśvatara, 4 Maitrāyaṇīya, 5 Jābāla, 6 Khāṇḍikeya and 7 Aukheya. The Mahābhāshya has the following sentence (IV 2, 10) ग्रामे ग्रामे काठकं च कालापकं च प्रोच्यते.

12 The Tāṇḍya Brāhmaṇa has 347 Khaṇḍas. It mentions many S'ākhās such as Bhāllavi, Trikharva and Karadvisha and the Bhāllavi Brāhmaṇa appears to have had svaras. In parts of India north of the Narbudda

are found the Mādhyandinī, S'ānkhāyanī, Kauthumī and S'aunakī S'ākhās.

The Shadvimśa has 48 Khaṇḍas; but Sāyaṇa wrote Bhāshya on the last two Khaṇḍas only. I 1, 8 contains comment on the Subrahmaṇya Ṛik mentioned in S'atapatha III 3-4-17. The priests are described as wearing red turbans and having red garments in 3, 8, 28. The morning and evening Sandhyā is mentioned in 4, 5, 8. The four Yugas are mentioned in पुष्ये चानुमतिर्ज्ञेया सिनीवाली तु द्वापरे । खार्वायां तु भवेद्राका कृतपूर्वे कुहूर्भवेत् (4, 6, 5).

13 The Jaiminīya Brāhmaṇa is divided into 3 parts with 360, 437 and 385 Khaṇḍas (total 1182). Its other name is Talavakāra. Kenopanishad is a part of this Brāhmaṇa. The sentences are nearly the same as in Tāṇḍya, but it treats of more subjects than the Tāṇḍya. This is supposed to be composed by Jaimini and his pupil Talavakāra. It is prevalent in Karnatak and many copies are found in Trivandrum (Travancore) also.

14 Other Brāhmaṇas referred to in various works are:– Hāridravika Brāhmaṇa in Sāyana and in Mahābhāshya IV 2, 104, 2 Abhūraka Brāhmaṇa in Taittirīya Prātiśākhya, as also 3 Kankati and 4 Gavaya: 5 Bhāllavin and S'āṭyāyanin in a commentary on Pāṇini. 6 Kālabavi and 7 Rauruki in Gobhila Gṛihyasūtra, 8 Tumburu, 9 Āruṇeya, 10 Saulabhi, 11 Saulavi, 12 Māshaśaravi and 13 Kāpeya mentioned by Vādhula Sūtra. There is a Bashkala and a Māṇḍukeya Brāhmaṇa as already noted. (To what Vedas these were attached we cannot say.)

15 The metals were fully known in this period; gold, silver, tin, iron etc., with some of their properties (लवणेन सुवर्णं सन्दध्यात् &c). Geometry was studied for the construction of altars. Astronomy naturally was studied and geography also. From Vinaśana, the centre of Kurukshetra, the distance of Plaksha Prasravaṇa

is given as 44 Aśvīnas (चतुश्चत्वारिंशदाश्विनानि–A. B.). Svarga is represented as distant by a thousand of the same measure (A. B. 2, 10). 'Thousand' perhaps stands here for thousands, if Svarga was looked upon as not being on the earth. The earth was believed to be surrounded by sea. It was known that the sun really never sets.

16 There are frequent references in the Brāhmaṇas to the four castes and their characteristics. They are thus mentioned in S'ata. V 5, 4, 9. Brahman (Veda) itself is Brāhmaṇa (S'ata. V 1, 5, 2). Brahmins abstained from liquor अशिवं वा एष भक्षो यत्सुरा ब्राह्मणस्य (S'ata. XII, 8, 1, 5). Kshatriyas and Vaiśyas become Brahmins when they are Dīkshita or ordained for sacrificing (A. B. VII 23 and S. B. III, 2, 1, 40). The weapons of a Brahmin are the sacrificial instruments एतानि वै ब्राह्मणायुधानि यद्यज्ञायुधानि (A. B. VII 22). Kshatra was Rāshṭra or nation (A. B. VII 22) and where the Kshatriyas follow the Brahmins that nation prospers (A. B. VIII, 9). The weapons of a Kshatriya are the horse chariot, the coat of mail, the bow and the arrow; एतानि क्षत्रस्यायुधानि यदश्वरथः कवचं इषुधन्वम् (A. B. VII, 9). The nations are the Viśah or Vaiśyas. (A. B. 8, 26). We have already stated that the Brahmin was above the Rāshtra which was formed by the Kshatriya warriors and the Vaiśya agriculturists. The S'ūdras were below the nation, being ordained for service. They prospered by Pādāvanejyā, being created from the feet (Tāṇḍya VI, 1, 11). They had not the right to perform the sacrifices (T. S. VII, I, 1, 6). But Kavasha Ailūsha was originally a S'ūdra who composed a sūkta and became a Ṛishi (A. B. VI, 5).

IX ĀRANYAKAS

Āraṇyakas, with Upanishads usually included in them, are appendices, so to speak, of the various Brāhmaṇas. They are called so, according to orthodox opinion, because they are to be taught in Araṇya or forest or to men who have retired into forest. Thus Sāyaṇa says in the beginning of his Bhāshya on the Aitareya Āraṇyaka अरण्य एव पाठ्यत्वादारण्यकमितीर्यते ।. This word, however, is not explained by Pāṇini who gives a different meaning altogether of this word, viz :– a man who lives in a forest, a forester in fact. Pāṇini does not also use the word anywhere in the sense of a work, as he uses the word Brāhmaṇa, though it is not explained by him ; nor is the word used in any of the Āraṇyakas themselves, as the word Brāhmaṇa is in the Brāhmaṇas. We find that Vararuchi gives a vārtika on this sūtra and adds that the word Āraṇyaka is also used in the sense of study or path or elephant. Thus it seems very probable that this term arose after Pānini and before Vararuchi in the sense of a work to be studied in a forest.

The oldest Āraṇyaka is the Taittirīya Āraṇyaka which probably set the example for the formation of Āraṇyakas or philosophical appendices to the other Brāhmaṇas.

We will speak in this chapter of these Āraṇyakas in order of time reserving the Upanishads which form the most important part of them, for separate treatment in the next chapter. These Āraṇyakas and Upanishads are in fact treated as parts of Brāhmaṇas. Gopatha calls them Rahasya or esoteric treatises.

I Taittirīya Āraṇyaka

This Āraṇyaka consists of ten chapters or Prapāthakas, commonly called Araṇas, which are named as follows from the words with which they begin :- 1 Bhadra, 2 Saha vai, 3 Chitti, 4 Yunjate, 5 Deva vai, 6 Pare, 7 Śikshā, 8 Brahma vidā, 9 Bhṛigu and 10 Narāyaṇīya. 7, 8 and 9 form the Taittirīya Upanishad and 10 is also an Upanishad; but it is of a later date and is indeed treated as Khila. These Prapāthakas or chapters are divided into Anuvākas, the total of which for the nine chapters is 170. The number of sentences in each Anuvāka is given in tens as in the Brāhmaṇa of the Taittirīyas; and the final words of each ten is given at the end of the Anuvāka with the number of sentences remaining over. The chapters contain verses the words in which are accented, as well as the words in prose sentences. These verses are often taken from the Ṛigveda, as we shall show presently. Ṛigveda was still the Veda of all Brahmins.

The first chapter Bhadram relates to the Āruṇaketuka fire and mentions in one place Vyāsa Pārāśarya. The second Saha vai is about Svādhyāya and contains a reference to the land between the Ganges and the Jumna, as a holy land where Munis reside. Strangely enough, we come across the letter ळ (ḷ) in this Araṇa यद्देव देवहेळनम् (II 7) which does not occur anywhere else in the Black Yajurveda. The third chapter Chitti gives mantras for the Chātur-hotra Chitti. One of these happily describes the sun as holding the whole universe; सप्त युञ्जन्ति रथमेकचक्रमेको अश्वो वहति सप्तनामा। त्रिनाभिचक्रमजरमनर्वं येनेमा विश्वा भुवनानि तस्थुः॥. The disc of the sun is the one wheel for his chariot and it has three navels, probably the six seasons in three pairs. The fourth chapter gives mantras for Pravargya. It mentions Kurukshetra and Khāṇḍava, so well-known in the Mahābhārata (कुरुक्षेत्रं वेदिरासीत्। तस्यै खाण्डवो दक्षिणार्ध आसीत्। तूर्णं उत्तरार्धः). This gives the correct position of Khāṇḍava forest as being the southern portion of Kurukshetra, the plain in which Delhi is now situated. This Araṇa gives several mantras of the nature of Abhichāra which perhaps shows that the Atharvaveda had not yet been compiled. Thus IV 27 gives खट् फट् जहि। छिन्दि भिन्दि। &c (इति क्रूरा वाचः) and IV 37 gives a verse ending with खण् फण् भ्रसि. IV 38 indeed says घोरेण त्वा भृगूणां चक्षुषा प्रेक्षे। रौद्रेण त्वा अङ्गिरसां मनसा ध्यायामि। indicating that Bhṛigu and Āṅgirasas were magicians who used spells for doing evil. Mantras for counteracting the effects of evil omens such as the bad cries of eagles, of jackals, of दीर्घमुखी दुहृणू, काकली, गर्दभी वा, of उलूक, of one siezed by an evil spirit (भूतोपसृष्ट) are also given (IV 29, 30). IV 36 gives mantras for destroying vermin (कृमि). The sixth chapter called परे gives mantras required for Pitṛimedha or the burning of the dead, including उदीर्ष्व नार्यभिजीवलोकम्, and other mantras from the Ṛigveda. These contents of the six Araṇas will show that they are not all intended for those retired into forests, some clearly being for ordinary family life. The seventh Araṇa Śīkshā is a grammatical treatise and can certainly not be described as a work fit to be taught in forests, while the 8th and the 9th are philosophical and together are treated as the Taittirīya Upanishad, one of the important ten, as will be noted in the next chapter.

II Aitareya Āraṇyaka

We next come to the Aitareya Āraṇyaka attached to the Ṛigveda which must have followed the Taittirīya Āraṇyaka soon. It consists of five chapters which are treated as separate Āraṇyakas, like the ten Araṇas of the Taittirīyas. Their beginnings are recited separately at the time of the Ṛik-Śrāvaṇī, while the whole Aitareya Brāhmaṇa is disposed of by the single initial sentence of its first chapter viz. अग्निर्वै देवानामवमो विष्णुः

परमः. This shows that the five chapters of the Aitareya Āraṇyaka are looked upon as separate works. Their beginnings are as follows:- 1 अथ महाव्रतम्, 2 एष पन्था एतत्कर्म, 3 अथातः संहिताया उपनिषत्, 4 विदा मघवन् विदा and 5 अथ महाव्रतस्य पंचविंशतिं सामिधेन्यः. These are all in prose which in the fourth only is accented. Verses from the Ṛigveda are frequently quoted with the words तदुक्तमृषिणा. New verses are also to be found introduced with the words तदेते श्लोकाः.

These five Āraṇyakas are divided into 18 chapters subdivided into Khaṇḍas. The first Āraṇyaka describes the Mahāvrata which is a part of Gavāmayana described in A. B. III. The second, in chapters one to three, details the Uktha or Nishkevalya Śastra, the midday Śastra of the Mahāvrata and then treats of Prāṇa and Purusha. The Aitareya Upanishad comes next as chapters 4 to 6. The third Āraṇyaka treats of Saṁhitā, Pada and Krama texts and then of vowels and semivowels &c. This treatment is much earlier than that of Yāska and of the Prātiśākhyas. It quotes Śākalya and Māṇḍūkeya. Keith gives hence 600 B. C. as the date of this Āraṇyaka. But Yāska himself must be placed about 1000 B. C., as will be shown in section III. The fourth Āraṇyaka विदा मघवन् विदा is a very small one and gives the few (9) Mahānāmnī verses to be recited on the fifth day of the Mahāvrata ceremony. And the fifth or the last Āranyaka gives further details about the Nishkevalya Śastra recited at midday in the Mahāvrata. Thus these works by their contents are clearly of the nature of appendices to the Aitareya Brāhmaṇa.

The first three books by tradition are attributed to Aitareya himself, the author of the Aitareya Brāhmaṇa, while the fourth is attributed to Āśvalāyana and the fifth to Śaunaka, teacher of Āśvalāyana. This Āśvalāyana may be the author of the Śrauta Sūtra. The author of the Gṛihya Sūtra is, however, probably his descendant. Keith looks upon Śaunaka (who is also the author of Bṛihaddevatā) as later than Yāska and earlier than Pāṇinī. But Śaunaka, author of the fifth Āraṇyaka, need not be the author of the Bṛihaddevatā. It must be remembered that Śaunaka, Āśvalāyana &c are gotra-names and, therefore, do not always indicate the same person. Keith has pointed out that the first book as also the second mention Mahīdāsa Aitareya and, therefore, are not probably his. The first book does not contain an explicit reference, but the second, in I 8, makes a clear reference to him (एतद्ध स्म तद्विद्वानाह महीदास ऐतरेयः). The word विद्वान् here makes it certain that Mahīdāsa does not mention himself, as authors sometimes do, and the second Āraṇyaka is surely not his.

We have already stated that the Aitareya Āraṇyaka in book III refers to the three modes of reciting the Ṛigveda, viz. the Saṁhitā, Pada, and Krama pāthas, respectively called Nirbhuja,

Pratṛiṇa and Ubhayamantareṇa in it (निर्भुज, प्रतृण, उभयमन्तरेण III 1, 3). The same Āraṇyaka also discusses several grammatical matters such as णकार, and षकार and mentions several grammarians such as Śākalya and Māṇḍūkeya as also Ṛishis named Kāvasheya. It is, therefore, to be questioned whether this third Āraṇyaka really belongs to Aitareya Mahīdāsa who is mentioned in the Chhāndogya Upanishad as an Āchārya who had reached the age of 116 years. Śākalya, the grammarian, however, is a very old author. He may be the same as the Śākalya reputed to be the author of the Pada text of the Ṛigveda and the author of this Āraṇyaka also.

In this Āraṇyaka we have a description of the Veda-Purusha of whom Ṛigveda, Yajurveda and Sāmaveda are shown as limbs (III). The omission of Atharvaveda is puzzling; for if the Atharvaveda is mentioned already in the Chhāndogya Upanishad as a recognised Veda, it ought to have been mentioned in this Āraṇyaka which mentions Śākalya and Māṇḍukeya and which consequently cannot be older than Chhāndogya. The omission may, however, be treated as accidental.

Keith looks upon the Aitareya Āraṇyaka as dated about 600 B. C., as shown above; but its first chapter may be as old as the Aitareya Brāhmaṇa, i. e. about 2500 B. C., and the work of the same author, viz. Mahīdāsa Aitareya.

III Sānkhāyana Araṇyaka

The Sānkhāyana Āraṇyaka is attached to the Sānkhāyana Brāhmaṇa, also called Kaushītaki; but the Āraṇyaka goes under the single name of Sānkhāyana. It follows the Aitareya Āraṇyaka generally. It contains 15 chapters divided into 137 Khaṇḍas. The third to the sixth chapters form the Upanishad, which, however, goes by the name of Kaushītaki. The first two chapters relate to Mahāvrata and are looked upon as actual Brāhmaṇas. There is a reference to Atharvaveda in chapter XIV which is interesting: ऋचां मूर्धानं यजुषामुत्तमाङ्गं साम्नां शिरोऽथर्वणां मुंडमुंडम् ॥ &c has four words meaning the same thing, viz. head; but muṇḍa has a slang appearance and perhaps speaks detractingly of the Atharvaveda. But it is not quite certain if the compiled Vedas are referred to here, though it is nearly certain that the Atharvaveda was already long compiled. Chapter VI mentions Uśīnara, Matsya, Kāsī, Videha and Kuru-Pāñchāla and chapter XIII borrows profusely from the Upanishads, chiefly Bṛhadāraṇyaka. The work, therefore, is very modern, an inference supported by the Vaṁśa which states "We have studied this from Guṇākhya Sānkhyāyana" (गुणाख्यसांखायनादस्माभिरधीतम्). The work is thus admittedly by a pupil of Sānkhāyana or even of his descendant. The Āchāryas then mentioned in the ascending order are:- Kahola Kaushītaki,

Uddālaka Āruṇi, Priyavrata--Somāpi, Somapa, Soma-Prātiveśya, Prativeśa, Bṛihaddiva &c. The combination of Kahoḷa with Kaushītaki is strange as they are distinct Āchāryas.

IV Other Āraṇyakas

The Bṛihadāraṇyaka of the White Yajurveda is an Upanishad and not an Āraṇyaka pure and simple, though it is called so. It has six chapters divided into 44 sections called *Brāhmaṇas* subdivided into Kaṇḍikās. The last two chapters are considered as Khila. The first chapter is taken from Śatapatha Kāṇḍa X, while the other chapters form Kāṇḍa XIV of the Śatapatha. Of this Upanishad, improperly named Āraṇyaka, we will speak in detail in the chapter on Upanishads.

The Maitrāyaṇīya Śākhā of the Black Yajurveda has a Maitrāyaṇīya Āraṇyaka called Bṛihadāraṇyaka also (Datta). It contains the Maitrāyaṇīya Upanishad. Of the Āraṇyaka portion we cannot speak in detail as it is not before us.

There is a Talavakāra Āraṇyaka as there is a Talavakāra Brāhmaṇa attached to the Sāmaveda. It has four chapters divided into Anuvākas subdivided into Khaṇḍas. The tenth Anuvāka of the fourth chapter is the Talavakāra Upanishad. Many mantras are well explained in this work.

There is probably no Āraṇyaka attached to the Atharvaveda, though there are many Upanishads of this Veda; since these are earlier in date than the Gopatha Brāhmaṇa, it may be taken that these Upanishads separately existed and are not parts of any Āraṇyakas.

Finally, with regard to the age of the Āraṇyakas, it may be stated that the several Araṇas or chapters were compiled at different times. Some of them are obviously later than the Chhāndogya and Bṛihadāraṇyaka Upanishads from which they copy copiously statements and even sentiments.

The Upanishads which T. A. and A. A. contain are also earlier than their other chapters. A few, however, are in the strain of Brāhmaṇas and are, therefore, very old. We think that the age of the Āraṇyaka chapters may be taken to be from 2500 to 1500 B. C. and it may even be believed that the several Araṇas or Brāhmaṇas, as they must have been called, were put together even later than Pāṇini, who does not know of any Vedic treatise called Āraṇyaka. We will indicate the probable dates of individual chapters or Araṇas in the following note in which we also give their contents in more detail.

Note 1 :- The Name Āraṇyaka

This word arose, as stated already, after Pāṇinī and before Vararuchi. The sevaral chapters of the Taittirīya and Aitareya Āraṇyakas are always looked upon as separate, their beginnings being recited separately on the S'rāvaṇī day. They thus seem to have been originally treated as separate appendices. They are called Araṇas by the Vaidikas of both the Vedas. This word is explained by Vasudeva S'āstri Abhyankar of Poona as a short form of Āraṇyaka which, however, seems to be doubtful. Araṇa may mean a philosophical treatise from Ṛi to go and thence to know. 'Although this word Araṇa is not used in Vedic literature like Brāhmaṇa, we have the line ब्रह्मणः उदरणमसि in T. A. I 12, which indicates that Araṇa may mean a philosophical work. Āraṇyaka thus might be explained as a collection of Araṇas, though not by any sūtra of Pāṇinī, the word plainly coming into use after him. The ostensible derivation given by Vararuchi and Sāyaṇa is not wholly borne out by the contents of the Āraṇyakas. In T. A. I 32, no doubt, we have the dictum अरण्येऽधीयीत. But this is a special provision for this chapter, not for all. In II 12, the provision is made that S'aucha Āheya prescribes that Svādhyāya should be recited in the village and not outside (ग्रामे मनसा स्वाध्यायमधीयीत दिवा नक्तं वा इति ह स्माह शौच आन्हेयः). In the third chapter Chitti, we have the Purusha-sūkta and there is no provision and there can be no provision that the sūkta should be learnt or recited in a forest. But the idea that the Āraṇyakas should be learnt or recited in a forest, though recent, is now strongly rooted and it may be stated that Vaidika Brahmins at present learn the Āraṇyakas in a temple and rarely recite it in Vedic recitations.

Note 2 :- Further particulars about the Āraṇyakas

(1) Taittirīya Āraṇyaka

1. The first chapter or Araṇa called Bhadra contains the following śloka in Anuvāka 2 "स्मृतिः प्रत्यक्षमैतिह्यम् अनुमानश्चतुष्टयम् । एतैरादित्यमण्डलम् सर्वैरेव विधास्यते । Smṛiti, Aitihya and Anumāna are words which indicate a late date for this book. There is here a highly philosophical description of Kāla in which the following line अष्टिर्वाज्रिशतघ्नि च (15) is strange and almost inexplicable. S'ataghnīs could not have been known presumably before the Greek invasion under Alexander. The eight names of the sun given in I 7 are new, viz. आरोग, भ्राज, पटर, पतंग, स्वर्णर, ज्योतिषीमत्, विभास with the eighth काश्यप (this sun alone resides on Mahā-Meru). 'The Āchāryas believe the seven Sūryas to be the seven Prāṇas in the head. पंचकर्ण वात्स्यायन and सप्तकर्ण प्लाक्षि have seen the seven Suns but not the eighth, being unable to go to Mahāmeru.' सप्तर्त्विजः सूर्या इत्याचार्याः is another explanation. It does not appear whence the Ṛiks quoted here are taken ; but चित्रं देवानामुदगादनीकम् is clearly from the Ṛigveda. Vaiśampāyana holds (नानालिङ्गत्वादृतूनां नानासूर्यत्वम्) that there were thousands of Sūryas ; 'but Ṛishis believe they are eight above the one we see'.

Philosophical questions are asked, one of which is "By whom are the worlds held". The answer is "Vishṇu holds them according to Vatsa Ṛishi" (विष्णुना विधृते भूमी इति वत्सस्य वेदना). "By what power and how ?". The answer is वाताद्विष्णोर्बलमाहुः. In I 9 eight names of Agni are given (अग्निश्च जातवेदाश्च &c) and these are said to be the eight Vasus on earth. Eleven forms of lightning are then mentioned and he who knows them does not die by the same. But Pārāśarya Vyāsa desired death by lightning (विद्युद्वधमेवाहं मृत्युमैच्छम् I 9). Then eleven Gandharva names are given which are also in reality names of Agni. And there are Devas, Mahādevas, Raśmis and Garagiras (?). The Āraṇyaka Ācharyas are now full of the Brahman theory and reduce all deities to it.

असतः सद्ये ततक्षुः । ऋषयः सप्तात्रिश्च यत् (I 4) reminds one of the Upanishad असद्वा इदमग्र आसीत् ततो वै सदजायत and of the Bhagavadgīta line महर्षयः सप्त पूर्वे येषां लोक इमाः प्रजाः। The well-known Gāyatrī तत्सवितुर्वरेण्यं etc. is found here and is imitated in the next verse तत्सवितुर्वृणीमहे वयं देवस्य भोजनम् । तुरं भगस्य धीमहि. Similarly नाम नामैव नाम मे, नपुंसकं पुमाँस्स्त्र्यस्मि reminds one of the Chhāndogya sentence नामैव तत् or त्वं स्त्री त्वं पुमान् त्वं कुमार उत वा कुमारी. Also अन्धो मणिराविन्दत् तमनङ्गुलिरावयत्, of अपाणिपादो जवनो ग्रहीता &c. ऊर्ध्वमूलमवाक्शाखं वृक्षं यो वेद संप्रति is the precursor of the Bhagvadgīta verse ऊर्ध्वमूलम् &c

मेधातिथेर्मेष, वृषणश्वस्य मेने, गौरवस्कन्दिन्, अहल्यायै जार, कौशिक ब्राह्मण गौतम ब्रुवाण इन्द्र (I 12) reminds one of the Purānic stories concerned. अष्टयोनिमष्टपुत्राम्। अष्टपत्नीमिमां महीम्। (I 13) is probably the origin of the later अष्टपुत्रा भव blessing instead of the Ṛigvedic दशपुत्रा. अष्ट पुत्रासो अदितेः। मित्रश्च वरुणश्च धाता चार्यमा च। अंशश्च भगश्च। इन्द्रश्च विवस्वाँश्चेत्येते।. Instead of twelve sons, Aditi has now eight.

Four Narakas or hells are spoken of as विसर्पी in south-east, अविसर्पी in south-west, विषादी in north–east and अविषादी in north–west. We do not hear of these in later times.

यो अपां पुष्पं वेद पुष्पवान् भवति &c (I 22) and आपो वा इदमासन्सलिलमेव स प्रजापतिरेकः पुष्करपर्णे समभवत् &c (I 23) remind one of Upanishads and Purāṇas. अन्तरतः कूर्मंभूतं सर्पन्तम् is the precursor of the legend of Kūrmāvatāra of the Purāṇas. या विप्रुषो परापतन्। ताभ्योऽसुरा रक्षांसि पिशाचाश्चोदतिष्ठन् (I 23) is not the story of the Brāhmanas which look upon Asuras and Devas as cousins, but of the Purāṇas. The Vratas or vows expounded in I 26 are those given in the Grihya Sūtras and Smṛitis; वर्षति न धावेत्। नाप्सु मूत्रपुरीषं

कुर्यात्। न निष्ठीवेत्। न विवसनः स्नायात्। न पुष्करपर्णानि हिरण्यं चाधितिष्ठेत्। न कूर्मस्याश्नीयात्। नोदकस्य।

उत्तिष्ठत मा स्वप्त। अग्निमिच्छध्वं भारताः। Bhārata is applied here to the Ṛitviks; but it means really, as explained already, all Aryan inhabitants of the Bhārata land. 'अष्टचक्रा' नवद्वारा देवानां पूरयोध्या is a highly poetic and metaphoric description of the human body, the epithet अयोध्या being particularly suggestive of the story of Rāma.

Late marriages seem to be general, as unmarried pregnant girls are looked upon as sinful; कुमारीषु कनीनीषु जारिणीषु च ये हिताः। proscribes even bastard girls, though married (I 27). See also यत्कुमारी मन्द्रयते (ditto).

In I 31 the city of Kubera is described as follows:—
सुदर्शने च क्रौंचे च मैनागे च महागिरौ। सतद्वाद्वारगमन्ता संहार्यं नगरं तव॥ which Sāyaṇa explains as a city on each of the great mountains Sudarśana, Krauncha and Maināga (Maināka in Purāṇas) with one hundred gates, castles and big streets.

इति मंत्राः कल्पोऽत ऊर्ध्वम् (I, 31) mentions कल्प as meaning a ritual provision and after this is actually given the ritual in which oblations are to be offered to Kubera.

The book ends with special Niyamas to be observed, such as bathing thrice, fasting two days, eating food obtained by begging and giving oblations specially to be offered. This is the precursor of the Prāyaschittas prescribed in Smṛitis.

2. In Araṇa II called 'Saha vai' we may note the very first sentence सह वै देवानां चासुराणां यज्ञौ प्रततावास्ताम्। Here, as in the Brāhmaṇas, Devas and Asuras are put together and the Asuras perform a sacrifice. They are thus distinct from Rākshasas who never sacrificed, and who, on the contrary, obstructed them. Subsequently Asuras and Rākshasas were closetted together.

The Rākshasas were also opposed to Sun-worship. II 2, 2 has रक्षांसि पुरोऽनुवाके तपोग्रमातिष्ठन्त...आदित्यो नो योद्धा... इति तस्मादुत्तिष्ठन्तमादित्यं रक्षांसि योधयन्ति यावदस्तमन्वगात् तानि ह वा गाय

न्याभिमंत्रितेनाम्भसा शाम्यन्ति ।. This is the same story as in the Purāṇas; nay we further have here that this water thrown up throws the Rākshasas into मन्देहारुणद्वीप.

II 2 also prescribes meditation of the sun at the morning and evening Sandhyā, because the sun is Brahman itself. उद्यन्तमस्तं यन्तमादित्यमभिध्यायन् कुर्वन्ब्राह्मणो विद्वान् सकलं भद्रमश्नुतेऽसावादित्यो ब्रह्मेति ॥

In II 3, mantras are prescribed for Kūshmāṇḍa Homa which are plainly Ṛigvedic, the first यद्देवा देवहेळनं using even ळ which is foreign to the Yajurveda. These mantras must be traced. In II 4 debts of gambling are treated as so imperative that their non-payment takes the defaulter bound to the Yamaloka. Two Apsaras, Ugrampaśyā and Rāshṭrabhṛit, are prayed for paying them off! अग्निर्ऋषिः पवमानः पांञ्चजन्यः पुरोहितः (II 5) makes the fire Ṛishi, Purohita and Pāñchajanya which is explained by Sāyaṇa as meaning born among five peoples (निषादपञ्चमा वर्णाः). In II 7, Kūshmāṇḍa Homa is prescribed for expiation of sins like Bhrūṇahatyā &c. and the story is related that Vātaraśana Ṛishis, described here as S'ramaṇa, which Sāyaṇa explains as meaning Tapasin, once entered Kūshmāṇḍas (gourds) and so on. In II 9 Brahmayajña or Svādhyāya is praised.

It is to be noted that for Svādhyāya all the four Vedas are prescribed, viz. Ṛik (like milk oblation), Yajuḥ (like ghee), Sāman (like Soma), Atharvāngirasaḥ (like honey) as also Brāhmaṇas, Itihāsa, Purāṇa, Kalpa, Nārāśaṁsa and Gāthā (like flesh oblations). Atharvaveda seems to have been already compiled and to have attained the highest position as its recitation is compared to honey oblations. Kalpas too seem to have been formulated, a word not occurring in Chhāndogya in this connection. It seems that this Araṇa is later than even Kalpas and may be placed in the beginning of the Sūtra period. II 10 mentions the five Yajñas (to gods, manes, Bhūtas, men, and the Vedas) in the form of Agnihotra, Shrāddha, Bali, feeding of Atithis and Svādhyāya recitation. The whole ceremony of Svādhyāya is described here and it is first stated that the reciter should go out of the village to a place whence the village huts are not seen, either east, north, or north-east. But in II 12 we have the opinion of S'aucha Āhneya that Svādhyāya may be recited in the village either during day or night, but in mind; nay it is further added that it may be recited loudly and while standing, lying, walking or sitting; at noon it should be recited loudly. In II 17, Svādhyāya recitation in a forest is prescribed as a penance for sacrificing for a prohibited person. त्रिषत्या हि देवाः (II 18) is interesting; a thing thrice done or said is believed in by the gods. Lastly नमो नमो गंगायमुनयोर्मुनिभ्यश्च नमः (II 20) shows that the centre of religion had shifted from the Sarasvatī region into Antarvedi. This is probably the region where this Araṇa was composed.

3. In the third Araṇa 'Chitti', are given the mantras for Chāturhotra sacrifice described in the Taittirīya Brāhmaṇa III 12. The whole sacrifice is symbolical, beginning with Chitti or the mind which is to be the Sruk or sacrificial ladle. The mantras are mostly new, though some may be traced to the Ṛigveda such as पतंगमक्तमसुरस्य मायया. "Dakshinā, Uttāna Angirasa may take thee" shows that Dakshinā had come to be ridiculed (उत्तानस्त्वांगिरसः प्रतिगृह्णातु III 10). However some strange Dakshinās for different gods at this sacrifice are prescribed, such as a slave for Prajāpatī and an elephant for the Himālayas. Naturally the philosophical Purusha-sūkta is given herein as III 12. One important change in it deserves to be noticed. Before the last verse यज्ञेन यज्ञं &c are added three more verses, viz. वेदाहमेतं पुरुषं महान्तमादित्यवर्णं तमसस्तु पारे (this line appears in the White Samhitā), सर्वाणि रूपाणि विचित्य धीरः नामानि कृत्वाऽभिवदन् यदास्ते ॥ and धाता पुरस्ताद्यमुदाजहार।

शक्रः प्रविद्वान् प्रदिशश्चतस्रः। तमेव विद्वानमृत इह भवति। नान्यः पन्था अयनाय विद्यते॥ The last line is plainly borrowed from Kena Upanishad and it shows that this verse is a new one and that this Araṇa may be later than Kena. The White Saṁhitā line instead of the last is तमेव विदित्वाति-मृत्युमेति नान्यः पन्था विद्यतेऽयनाय॥

4. Commenting on the fourth Araṇa (युंजते) Sāyaṇa observes "In the third Araṇa Brahmāgni and Brahmamedha are described; now in the fourth Pravargya mantras are given and their explanation is given in the fifth." The mantras are generally new ones and alliterations and derivatives from the same verb are very often used, e. g. प्रमा असि प्रतिमा असि समा असि विमा असि उन्मा असि. इडा, अदिति and सरस्वती are names of cows (IV 8). There are Abhichāra mantras in 10 (i. e. अमुष्य त्वा प्राणे सादयामि). Some vows are interesting such as संवत्सरं मांसं नाश्नीयात्। न रामामुपेयात्। न मृण्मयेन पिबेत्. In 19 the names of the five years of a cycle are given viz. सवत्सर, इदावत्सर, परिवत्सर, इद्वत्सर, and वत्सर. In 20 the dark fortnight is said to be पुरीष. In 24 and 25 are given the names of Maruts in the मरुद्गण which strike one to be as fanciful as the names of Muhūrtas given in T. B. III. Mantras against evil-doers and bad omens are given, as for discovering a thief (26), against wolves killing calves, against भयेडक, दुहेणु (a she-crow,) against evil spirits who have seized a person (35) or against worms (36). Magic sacrifice with the enemies' blood is also given as also curses against them as ब्रह्मणा त्वा शपामि (37) or शिमिजावहि (?) to be used in their cowpens to kill their cows. It is strange that such Abhichāra mantras are found in this Araṇa, philosophical as it is.

(II) Aitareya Āraṇyaka

The first Āraṇyaka speaks of Ātman as Ekavīmśa (twenty-first) an idea of the Āchāryas leading up to that of the Sānkyas who called it the twenty-fifth. Brahma is said to be Vāsukra (?) (2) Bharadvāja is said to be the most learned Vedic scholar and very long lived. भरद्वाजो ऋषीणांमनूचानतमः दीर्घजीवी &c. (3) वयांसि वंगा वगधाश्चेरपादाः (II) is not well understood. But वगधाः probably stands for मगधाः and चेरपादाः refers to Cheras of the south. We know that the Aitareya Brāhmaṇa itself speaks of Āndhras and indicates Aryan advance into that country. The Aitareya Āraṇyaka, no wonder, speaks of the Cheras of further south; but this mention indicates a still later date. (4) In III 2 we have an explanation of the names शतार्चिनः, मध्यमाः &c. as applied to the Ṛishis of the Ṛigveda. तस्माद्यच्छतं वर्षमभ्यर्चन्तस्माच्छतर्चिनः । Madhyama is also similarly explained as also Pragātha (प्रायात् = प्रगाथ). We know that the classificatian of Ṛigvedic Ṛishis as शतार्चिन; मध्यमा ; प्रगाथाः, क्षुद्रसूक्ताः and महासूक्ताः is given by Āśvalāyana Grihyasūtra. The division is older than this Sūtra, as the names have already begun to be fancifully explained in this Āraṇyaka (III). (5) In III 4 we have प्राण उक्थः which is plainly copied from Upanishads. (6) बृहती सहस्र is explained as 36000, Brihati consisting of 36 letters. (7) The classification of sacrifices is already made. स एष यज्ञः पञ्चविधः अग्निहोत्रं दशपूर्णमासौ चातुर्मास्यानि पशुः सोमः ॥ These are detailed in the Sūtras. The first three appear to be food sacrifices. Where verses are quoted by the phrase तदेते श्लोकाः, they are not Vedic verses but are new ones though older than the Āraṇyaka.

X UPANISHADS

We now come to the noblest portion of Vedic literature, indeed of the whole range of Sanskrit literature, viz., the Upanishads, sublimest from the philosophical as well as literary points of view. The Āchāryas who developed the Brāhmaṇa literature probably got tired of Vedic sacrifices which involved tedious ritual as also the cruel slaughter of larger animals like cows, bulls and horses. And they seriously fell to consider whether the highest destiny of man could not be realised without these horrid sacrifices. The seeds of such thoughts had already been sown in the days of Ṛigveda hymns some of which strike us, even now, as embodying the highest philosophical speculations to which man can rise and evidencing the most serious attempts of man to solve the never-to be-solved mystery of man, nature and God. And the wonder is that these abstruse speculations of the older Upanishads are put forth in such convincing form and language, that it may be said, without the fear of contradiction that they are the most precious possession of posterity, surpassing, as they do, even the dialogues of Plato in eloquence and subtility of thought. Their language is both simple and eloquent and their style though still that of the Brāhmaṇas is yet without their *tedious* repetitions or *puerile* quibbles. Indeed it shows how at that ancient date the Sanskrit language could be used in prose with all the artifices of oratory used by Demosthenes or Macaulay. Some passages of the Chhāndogya and the Bṛihadāraṇya are master-pieces of eloquent Sanskrit prose and deserve to be learnt by heart by Sanskrit students. Interesting stories and dialogues, real or conceived, are given in illustration of high principles which are as charming and convincing as the parables in the Bible.

The *philosophy* of these older Upanishads is also the highest to which philosophers of the world, ancient or modern, have yet reached. These Upanishadic thinkers rose from the worship of nature and of numerous gods presiding over its manifestations, to the idea of one God different from man and nature and then to God no other than man and nature. They rose from personal God to Impersonal God, who is both the maker and the made, the mason and the material, an idea to which man is slowly coming round in these days of phenomenal advance in physical sciences. These thinkers gave the name of Brahman to this highest entity because it overspreads the whole creation, pervading and also controlling it. They also called it Ātman or Soul Supreme, because it is conscious and the human soul is itself the Soul Supreme, as also the fine essense which constitutes this world (य एषोऽ

णिमैहतदात्म्यमिद॑ सर्वं तत्त्वमसि-छां.). Along with this idea, they also rose beyond the idea of heaven, first conceived by them along with all peoples as containing all the blessings of this world made everlasting, to a still higher conception of final beatitude in which the individual soul merges into the Universal and enjoys Ānanda or joy, different from the joys of this mundane world (which are merely an iota of it (आनंदस्य मात्रामुपजीवान्ति &c). The older Upanishads, therefore, form, as said before, unquestionably the noblest portion of Sanskrit literature, both as literary and as philosophical productions and have been praised as such by all Sanskrit scholars, eastern as well as western. No praise can be higher than that bestowed on them by the German philosopher Schopenhauer who said "Oh Upanishads, you will be the solace of my life and the solace of my death."

We are not concerned here with the elucidation of this philosophy of the Upanishads, the theory of Brahman, that subtle principle by which the Vedic Ṛishis and Āchāryas sought to explain the phenomenon of this Universe, conceived as one and not manifold, as conscious and not unconscious. This philosophy has been studied by thinkers of India from the most ancient times down to the modern, from Bādarāyaṇa of 1st century B. C., the author of the Brahmasūtras, down to Śankara, Rāmanuja, Madhva and Vallabha of the 15th century A. D. as also by western scholars of modern days. But these Upanishads have historically been studied only in modern times, in the West by scholars like Deussen and others and quite recently in India by Belvalkar and Ranade. And they have propounded their views on the history of this philosophy and of this literature in their valuable works – views from which we widely differ, especially in respect of chronology, inasmuch as these scholars assign a much later date to the Ṛigveda itself than we assign. In the following pages, we will put forth our views, noticing where necessary the conflicting views of scholars, western and eastern.

The total number of Upanishads, according to the orthodox view, is 108, as mentioned in an Upanishad itself, viz. the Muktikopanishad. And these are assigned to different Vedas, as Upanishads are usually conceived to form part of some Vedic Āraṇyaka. This enumeration of Upanishads made by the Muktikopanishad (which we give in a note) may be taken to be later than Śaṅkara and earlier than Akbar for whom a special Upanishad called Allopanishad was composed. The Muktikopanishad, however, says:– "The Māṅḍūkya Upanishad is the highest among the 108 and would alone suffice for salvation. If not, ten Upanishads would suffice". This pre-eminence of the Māṅḍūkya may be ascribed to the fact that Gauḍapāda, the teacher of Śaṅkara, has commented upon it in his Kārikās. It may, however, be taken that from ancient times ten Upanishads have been looked upon as old and leading, as these ten only have been commented upon by Śaṅkara and others. These ten are usually given in the following order, 1 Īśa, 2 Kena, 3 Kaṭha, 4 Praśna, 5 Muṇḍaka, 6 Māṇḍūkya, 7 Taittirīya, 8 Aitareya, 9 Chhāndogya and 10 Bṛihadāraṇyaka (माण्डूक्यमेकमेवालं मुमुक्षूणां विमुक्तये । तथाप्यसिद्धं चेद्ज्ञानं दशोपनिषदं पठ ॥२६॥ ईशकेनकठप्रश्नमुण्डमाण्डूक्यतित्तिरि । ऐतरेयं च छान्दोग्यं बृहदारण्यकं तथा । ३०). The Muktikopanishad goes on to say "If ten do not suffice, study thirty-two, if not even these, then study 108"; and then it enumerates these 108. Most of the latter are, however, not real Upanishads, devoted to the teaching of the philosophy of Brahman, but are sectarian and even Tāntric, like the Dattātreyopanishad or the Rudrākshopanishad. On reading these latter, one is forced to say that their authors have abused the high name of Upanishad and have wrongly used the sacred authority of that Vedic word to preach their worthless doctrines. Winternitz calls them non-Vedic properly; we would even call them Puranic or Tāntric. Three of these, however, are really old ones, viz. Kaushītakī, Śvetāśvatara and Maitrāyaṇīya. Belvalkar and Ranade have, in their history of Indian Philosophy Vol II, treated these thirteen Upanishads only as the older ones and have discussed how, from the philosophy of Brahman developed in these thirteen, they can be chronologically arranged. Deussen also, as well as other European scholars, look upon these thirteen only as the older Upanishads. In this view we entirely agree and we shall, in the following pages, speak only of these Upanishads. One or two others may be noted in passing, such as the Nārāyaṇa and Kaivalya; but as these thirteen only fall within the Śruti period, according to our view and even according to that of Belvalkar and Rānade, though their limits of this period are different, it is but proper that we should speak, in this section, of these thirteen Upanishads only.

These unique Upanishads in which "for the first time in the history of human, thought we find the Absolute grasped and proclaimed" (Macd. p. 220) and "which may very well bear comparison with Plato's dialogues" (Winternitz p. 247) are, as said before, ten according to orthodox opinion and thirteen according to most European and Indian scholars. Winternitz adds a fourteenth, viz. the Nārāyaṇa which is, however, later and not so grand either. The ten have been enumerated in the verse quoted above of the Muktikopanishad. The three other Upanishads which modern scholars place along with these are Śvetāśvatara, Kaushītākī and Maitrāyaṇīya. The first two are referred to, along with the ten by Śaṅkara in his Bhāṣhya on the Vedānta Sūtra; but he has not commented upon them. The Vedānta sūtras themselves, according to the Bhāshyakāras, refer to eight distinctly. "The texts referred to by the several groups of commentators down to 1300 A. D. are the Chhāndogya and other 8, with Śvataśvatara, Kaushītakī, Maitrī and Māṇḍūkya as a second set and the recently discovered Bāshkala, Chhāgaleya, Ārsheya and Śaunaka, as *perhaps* forming a third set" (Belvalkar p 80.) We shall not speak about these last in this chapter, but shall confine our remarks to the thirteen generally accepted to be the older Upanishads, already enumerated.

These thirteen Upanishads form part of the Āraṇyakas or Saṁhitās of the different Vedas and they are actually found in them. Thus Īśa is the last chapter of the White Yajurveda Saṁhitā; Kena is a part of the Talavakāra Brāhmaṇa of the Sāmaveda; Kaṭha belongs to the Kāthaka Śākhā of the Black Yajurveda and is part of its Saṁhitā. Praśṇa, Muṇḍa and Māṇḍūkya are ascribed to the Atharvaveda which has, however, no Āraṇyaka; and as these Upanishads do not form part of its Śaṁhitā and of Gopatha, they may be supposed to belong to some lost Brāhmaṇa of that Veda. The Taittirīya Upanishad belongs to the Tittiri Śākhā of the Black Yajurveda and is actually found in its Āraṇyaka. The Āitareya belongs to the Ṛigveda and is contained in the Aitareya Āraṇyaka. The Chhāndogya belongs to the Sāmaveda and is said to be given in the Chhāndogya Brāhmaṇa not now extant. Lastly, the Bṛihadāraṇyaka Upanishad belongs to the White Yajurveda and is contained in its Śatapatha Brāhmaṇa. That Veda having no separate Āraṇyaka, this Upanishad itself is called an Āraṇyaka. Of the remaining three, Śvetāśvatara and Maitrī belong to the Black Yajurveda and are given in these Śākhā Brāhmaṇas, while the Kaushītakī belongs to the Ṛigveda and is contained in the Sāṅkhāyana Āraṇyaka.

How to arrange these Upanishads chronologically is a difficult problem indeed. European and Indian scholars have carefully studied them historically and even by parts with this object and have formulated their views as to the priority or posteriority of these parts relatively. Deussen has arranged them into four groups as follows:– I Ancient prose Upanishads :– 1 Bṛihadāraṇyaka, 2 Chhāndogya, 3 Taittirīya, 4 Aitareya, 5 Kaushītakī, 6 Kena or Talavakāra. II Early Metrical Upanishads:– 7 Kāṭhaka or Kaṭha, 8 Īśa or Īśāvāsya, 9 Śvetaśvatara, 10 Mahānārāyaṇa. III Later prose Upanishads. 11 Praśna, 12 Maitrāyaṇīya, 13 Māṇḍūkya. IV Ātharvaṇa Upanishads and minor Upanishads like Saṁnyāsa, Yoga, Śaiva, Vaishṇava, Śākalya and others. This classification as quoted by Belvalkar and Ranade (p 89, Vol II) seems to be somewhat inaccurate, as it omits to mention Muṇḍaka and incorrectly (in its place probably) mentions Mahānārāyaṇa which is obviously a later Upanishad. Winternitz takes the six Upanishads, Aitareya, Bṛihadāraṇyaka, Chhāndogya, Taittirīya, Kaushītakī and Kena as "representing the earliest stage of development" in Upanishadic thought (p 236). In the next stage he puts the four metrical Upanishads, viz. Kaṭha, Svetāśvatara, Mahānārāyaṇa and Īśa and the two, half in prose and half in verse, Praśṇa and Muṇḍaka, "in which we find interwoven Sāṅkhya and Yoga doctrines". And in the third and last stage he puts Māṇḍūkya and Maitrāyaṇīya. This classification is also not correct. The prose Māṇḍūkya can not be put in the last stage, included as it is by orthodox opinion in the oldest ten. Nor can Mahānārāyaṇa be placed in the second set as we shall show in detail later on. Winternitz, however, finally observes that "we must leave it to future scholars to decide to what degree the various philosophical doctrines mingled and how far such mingling was consequent upon retouched versions of the texts" (p 238). It must be admitted that the question of the priority or posteriority of these Upanishads has become a complicated one, owing to the certainty that these texts have more than once been retouched.

Macdonell also divides the Upanishads chronologically into four groups. The oldest group consists of Bṛihadāraṇyaka, Chhāndogya, Taittirīya, Aitareya, Kaushītakī "in prose still of the

Brāhmaṇa style". Kena comes next as a link partly in prose and partly in verse, while decidedly later are Kāṭhaka, Īśa, Śvetāśvatara, Muṇḍaka and Mahānārāyaṇa. "These are more attractive from the literary point of view." This grouping is generally correct; but the last view is certainly not; for the case is exactly the reverse. these five Upanishads, viz. Kaṭha, Īśa, Śvetāśvatara, Muṇḍaka and Mahānārāyaṇa cannot stand comparison, in literary excellence even, with the Bṛihadāraṇyaka and the Chhāndogya, as Macdonell himself admits further on where he says that "their language often rises to the level of eloquence" and that 'there is a pecu''ar charm in their liveliness, enthusiasm and freedom from pedantry" (p 226). This mistaken view apart, one may agree with Macdonell in looking upon Bṛihadāraṇyaka, Chhāndogya, Taittirīya, and Aitareya (Īśa, however, being taken to be also one of them) as the oldest Upanishads, Kena and others as following them, Śvetāśvatara, Kaushītakī and Maitrāyaṇīya as coming last.

In grouping the Upanishads or their parts Belvalkar and Ranade first give the criteria for deciding the priority or posteriority of Upanishads or their parts (Vol. II p. 88) as follows:- 1. The name, the newer ones being named after the initial word; 2. The style, language and form; 3. The similes, symbols and illustrations used, the older texts being tinged with ritualism and giving fancy etymologies; 4. Priority of sacrificial gods like Indra; 5. Prose according to Deussen; 6. According to Oldenberg the influence of Brāhmaṇic ideas of sacrifice, magic, or vratas and a phalaśruti with the words एवं वेद; 7. Specific mention of rivers, mountains, countries, peoples etc.; 8. Interquotation or analogies of words; and 9. Ideological development. But these in our view are mere indications which individually will be of no avail. For a subsequent author may write in prose – prose imitating the Brāhmaṇa style and giving fancy etymologies and even phalaśrutis. He again may simply take up an old idea and dilate upon that only. Interquotations again may be from a common source, as several teachers developed this philosoply such as Śāṇḍilya &c. who have left no works of their own. It must be noted here that no Upanishad quotes from another by name. And there is not one teacher and one sacred work as in Christianity or Mahomedanism. It is, moreover, a question whether prose comes first or verse. It is, therefore, difficult to rely upon any of these indications for determining priority and a general view must be taken upon all these indications, other arguments being also given their due weight. We will take the instance of Īśāvāsya which by its metrical form is looked upon as belonging to the second set. Now this Upanishad forms a part of the

White Yajurveda Saṁhitā which itself is wholly in verse, which indeed was formulated by Yājñavalkya with the avowed object of separating the metrical Mantras from the prose Brāhmaṇas. This Upanishad which forms the last chapter of this Saṁhitā is no doubt called Khila and cannot, therefore, be looked upon as forming part of the original Saṁhitā formulated by Yājñavalkya. But it must be treated as contemporary with the Bṛihadāraṇyaka, which also is the last chapter of the Śatapatha Brāhmaṇa and is also its Khila. Nay, it may be treated as even earlier, as it still sticks to sacrifice (कुर्वन्नेवेह कर्माणि जिजीविषेत् शतं समाः) and does not preach abandonment of the world preached by the Bṛihadāraṇyaka (पुत्रैषणायाश्च लोकैषणायाश्च व्युत्थायाथ भिक्षाचर्यं चरन्ति). These arguments themselves, it may be admitted, are not conclusive as a subsequent author may revert to verse and to the older doctrine of 'Karman without the desire of obtaining heaven.' It, however, seems probable that Īśāvāsya is one of the oldest Upanishads as it forms part of the White Saṁhitā. Belvalkar and Ranade also look upon it as one of the oldest Upanishads "as its metrical form was inevitable being a part of the White Saṁhitā and as its theme is a compromise between the old path of sacrifice and the new path of renunciation and as it heads the Muktikā canon (p. 91, Vol II). The Maitrayāṇīya may similarly be placed in the third group and not in the second, as it actually quotes from other Upanishads by using the words एवं ब्राह. It does not mention any Upanishad by name by stating who says it; but other and many indications show its lateness as we will point out when describing each Upanishad separately.

The task of arranging the Upanishads in chronological groups is thus very difficult. It is, however, attempted by Belvalkar and Ranade who, as recommended by Winternitz, have studied them philosophically and by parts and have compared them carefully with one another. It is well marked by most scholars that the several parts of these Upanishads mostly belong to different authors and were composed at different times; and these two scholars have carefully gone through these several parts and the development of their thought. And the result of this study has been exhibited in a table given at page 135, Vol. II, which shows four chronological groups with minor columns distinguishing the early from the late ones. This table, however, we are forced to say, is bewildering and does not give a clear idea on the subject.

In our view, two definite grounds may fairly enable us to group the Upanishads, as they are today, chronologically. The first is the mention of Vishṇu or Śiva as the highest god, nay, as Brahman itself. We know that the oldest Upanishadic philosophers rose above the idea of individual gods and left behind the Vedic deities, Indra, Vishṇu, Śiva and Āditya. They taught the impersonal Brahman, pervading, constituting and moving or restraining the whole universe. Later thinkers, however, reverted to one highest god, some first to Vishṇu and others to Śiva. We have already noticed in this behalf the very first sentence in the Aitareya Brāhmaṇa अग्निर्वै देवानामवमो विष्णुः परमः. But Vishṇu was not still taken up by the old Upanishadic thinkers as Brahman itself. The two Upanishads which are thus entirely free from sectarian bias and are solely devoted to the exposition of Ātman or Brahman are Chhāndogya and Bṛihadāraṇyaka; next to them come Īśa, Taittirīya, Aitareya and then Praśna, Muṇḍaka and Māṇḍūkya. Then comes Kaṭha which mentions तद्विष्णोः परमं पदम् । for the first time. The Black Yajurveda followers were, however, not satisfied with Vishṇu, as their favourite deity was Rudra and the Rudrādhyāya was the most popular section of their Saṁhitās. They raised Maheśvara, therefore, to the highest position in the Śvetāśvatara. Subsequently came the dea of three highest gods, the triad of the Purāṇas, Brahmā, Vishṇu, and Maheśa and the Maitrāyaniya Upanishad, the latest of the thirteen, takes up this idea.

The other indication is the mention of the Sāṅkhya doctrine of Purusha and Prakṛiti, and nore still, of the three guṇas, Sattva, Rajas and

Tamas. We do not take, along with this, the Yoga philosophy; for this philosophy as such is very modern. But the chief plank of it, concentration of the mind, is very ancient, indeed is to be found in the oldest Upanishads (आत्मा वा अरे श्रोतव्यो मन्तव्यो निदिध्यासितव्यः). If we apply this test, we come to the same arrangment, viz. Chhāndogya, Bṛihadāraṇyaka, Īśa, Taittirīya, Aitareya, Praśna, Muṇḍaka and Māṇḍukya. Kaṭha first mentions guṇas and thus follows, along with Kena. The Maitrāyaṇīya is the latest as it mentions the Prakṛiti doctrine and the guṇa doctrine in detail. Śvetāśvatara comes a little before it; for it mentions Pradhāna (क्षर प्रधान), Jñeya and Jña (ज्ञेय, ज्ञ) of the Bhagavadgītā as also Kapila (ऋषिं प्रसूतं कपिलं पुराणम्) and Sāṅkhya (तत्कारणं सांख्ययोगाधिगम्यम्) themselves. And it may also be noted that this Upanishad in the end recommends gurubhakti (यस्य देवे परा भक्तिः यथा देवे तथा गुरौ) and we are sure that it is one of the three latest Upanishads. Kaushītakī also cannot be placed in the early set of ten as it copies verbatim many sections from the older Upanishads with additions such as भूतमात्रा of the Sāṅkhya. We shall describe this Upanishad in fuller detail in our note, along with others.

Having thus far given our idea of the relative priority of the thirteen Upanishads, we proceed to discuss their age; and on this point we differ most emphatically from the views of European scholars and of Belvalkar and Ranade, who, perhaps without questioning, follow them. All are agreed that these older Upaṇishads are pre-Buddhistic as they show no trace of Buddhistic doctrines and hence their lowest limit is 600 B. C. As they must be placed after the compilation of the Ṛigveda, the earliest date of which according to European scholars is 1200 B. C., Belvalkar and Ranade accept it and take the Upanishadic period to lie between 1200 and 600 B. C." (Vol I, p. 13). It is strange that these scholars, with all their careful scrutiny of the Upanishads, fail to notice the astronomical statement in the Maitrāyaṇīya Upanishad, pointed out by B. G. Tilak, which indubitably establishes for it a date as early as 1900 B. C. This Upanishad, as we shall point out in our note, consists of three parts, first old, second later and third latest; and this statement occurs in the second part, making it certain that the first part is as old as 2000 B. C. The statement mentions that Uttarāyaṇa takes place in the middle of Śravishṭhā, which, compared with the modern position of Uttarāyaṇa in Pūrvāshādhā, can be made the basis of calculation, as shown in our note. If then the latest Upanishad, viz. Maitrāyaṇiya, is as old as 2000 B.C., the Upanishadic age must be placed between 2500 and 2000 B.,C., a conclusion fortified by the date which we have assigned to the compilation of the Ṛigveda, viz. 3100. B. C. There are indications in the

Chhāndogya and Bṛihadāraṇyaka Upanishads themselves which take these oldest Upanishads to about 2500 B. C. The first mentions Kṛishṇa Devakīputra as a pupil of Ghora who taught him a special Upanishadic tenet. Clearer than this is the proof afforded by the Bṛihadāraṇyaka which in a disputation of philosophers with Yājñavalkya refers to Pārīkshitas, viz. Janamejaya and his three brothers. "Where have the Pārīkshitas gone?" asks a philosopher and Yājñavalkya replies "To the place where Aśvamedha sacrificers go" and then goes on to describe that place. This question is very interesting and even European scholars admit that it 'suggests the inference that the sons of Parīkshit had recently come to a bad end.' We shall have to discuss the bearing of this question in another volume when dealing with the Mahābhārata. But we may state that the Śatapatha itself gives the story of the four sons of Parīkshit having celebrated four Aśvamedhas in expiation of sin. This question, therefore, shows that the story of their performing four Aśvamedhas was fresh in people's memory and if the date of the Mahābhārata fight be taken to be about 3100 B C., the Bṛhadāraṇyaka section mentioning Pārikshitas may fairly be placed about 2500 B. C. Vyāsa who compiled the Ṛigveda includes in the 10th Maṇḍala, the latest portion of the Ṛigveda, a sūkta of an uncle of Bhīshma; and the Śatapatha, which in Kāṇḍa I, its older part, makes the astronomical statement about the rising of the Kṛittikās, fixing its date at about 3000 B. C., refers to the compiled Ṛīgveda. We are thus also sure that Bhīshma and the Pāṇḍavas lived about 3100 B. C. and that Janamejaya and his brothers must have flourished about 3000 B. C. It is, we think, impossible to controvert the position which we have taken with regard to the age of the older Upanishads from astronomical statements; and it is to be regretted that the Indian scholars, Belvalkar and Ranade, have taken no note of Tilak's views, much less tried to refute them. According to our view and Tilak's, the older Upanishads were compiled between 2500 and 2000 B.C.

That the philosoply of these Upanishads is the highest and that the treatment of it in these "philosophic poems" is most charming is conceded by all European scholars. Schopenhauer looked upon it as "the fruit of human knowledge and wisdom and as containing almost superhuman conceptions whose originators could hardly be conceived as mere men". Deussen thought that the Upanishads gave "if not the most scientific yet the most intimate and immediate light upon the last sceret of existence." It is no wonder therefore, that we, Indians, have from most ancient times looked upon the Upanishads as revelation, as forming part of the revealed Vedas. The reverence with which they are treated during these four thousand years is thus justifiable. Even the doubting Winternitz is forced to concede on this opinion of Deussen "that these philosophical conceptions are unequalled anywhere in the world. Though the Upanishads do not contain superhuman conceptions, they wrestle so earnestly with truth ; and the eternally unsatisfied human yearning for knowledge has been expressed in them so fervently" (p.266).

There were, however, stronger doubters even in India and even in those early days ; doubters who denied the entire truth of the philosophy of the Upanishads and their character as revelation. For it may be noted that in opposition to the Upanishads arose the Sāṅkhya philosophy, first preached by Kapila, with its doctrine of Prakṛiti (unconscious but active principle) and Purusha (conscious but inert principle) and the three guṇas or properties of the former, Sattva (spiritual), Rajas (worldly) and Tamas (debasing). The theory of the guṇas became very popular and was adopted by all philosophers including Upanishadic ; and some later and most latest Upanishads even based their teaching upon it. There are also references in the Śvetaśvatara to atheists who denied Brahman altogether. (कालः स्वभावो नियतिर्यदृच्छा and स्वभावमेके कवयो वदन्ति कालं तथान्ये परिमुह्यमानाः ।)

It would be interesting finally to take a survey of the social and political condition of the country in the Upanishadic age, i. e.

between 2500 and 2000 B. C.

The Aryan land stretched from Gāndhāra on the west of the Indus to Videha beyond the Sadānīrā, from Peshawar to Patna in modern language. It contained many kingdoms or peoples such as Madra and Kekaya, Kuru and Pāñchāla, Kosala and Videha, Kauśāmbī and Kāśī. Gāndhāra was probably the last Aryan land and beyond were tribes given to abduction and dacoity even as they are now; and one is moved with wonder when one reads even in the Chhāndogya the illustration, given to show how one reaches the highest Brahman from conception to conception, of a man blind-folded and abducted and then liberated in a deserted place who making enquiries and going from village to village finally reaches Gāndhāra at last. These troublesome mountain tribes apart, the Aryan kingdoms in India were well-governed. We are proud of the boast of Aśvapati of Kekaya that there was no thief in his kingdom (न मे स्तेनो जनपदे – छां०) and no adulterer. Thieves and adulterers were most carefully watched by Aryan kings whose sole duty in those days was really that much and these crimes were most ruthlessly punished, the hands of thieves, caught red-handed, being cut off or they being put to death (अथ हन्यते – छां० ६, १६). It also appears that in case of doubt, Divya or ordeal was resorted to; but ordinarily eye-witnesses were relied upon and he who *saw* was more believed than he who deposed that he *heard* (अहमद्राक्षं तस्मै श्रद्धाति). The kings took taxes and carried on the administration which then related chiefly to the tracing out of thieves and the dispensation of justice. The country people were prosperous and the kings moved through their dominions with pomp, being received everywhere with delight by the villagers the leaders of whom (ग्रामणी) called Sūtas went forward to receive their kings and set up huts of straw and kept food and water ready as described by Bāṇa so graphically in Harshacharita. The simile taken in the Bṛihādaraṇyaka by Yājñavalkya from this reception in connection with the coming of Prāṇa into the body is equally graphic, if not more.

The kings were mostly Kshatriyas; they were well-versed in the Vedas and the Upanishadic philosophy. And they took very great interest in philosophical discussions. In the long-stretching Aryan land, Brahmins versed in the philosophy of Brahman moved about, from Kuru-Pañchala to Kāśī–Videha and from the latter to Aśvapati of Madra, teaching their doctrines and holding discussions in the presence of kings and under their patronage. These travelling teachers and professors made the new phlosophy popular and enabled its doctrines to be definitely determined. Their names are preserved to us in the several Upanishadic episodes, though the names given in the Vaṁśas are perhaps imaginary.

Yājñavalkya Vājasaneya and Uddālaka Āruṇi, Ayāsya Āṅgirasa and Satyakāma Jābāla are most probably real persons, though Nārada and Sanatkumāra, Bhṛigu and Varuṇa, Nachiketas and Mṛityu are imaginary beings.

As in the days of the Ṛigveda and the Brāhmaṇas, the Aryan people were divided into four castes only and not more. The Brahmins taught the Vedas and performed the duties of priests at sacrifices. The Kshatriyas ruled, but studied the Vedas and performed higher sacrifices. They occupied socially a higher position than the Brahmins (तस्माद्ब्राह्मणः क्षत्रियमधस्तादुपास्ते). But the Brahmins were higher religiously, as they were teachers. It is interesting to read in the Chhāndogya that Śvetaketu Āruṇeya went to Aśvapati to learn a philosophical doctrine and that Gārgya Bālāki went to Ajātaśatru of Kāśi and they at first declined to teach, observing that it was against rules that a Brahmin should learn from a Kshatriya. The teachers, however, demanded teaching fees but the only present that a student was expected to make when learning was that of a few samidhs (sacrificial fire-sticks). It is not mentioned if Vaiśyas learnt these doctrines. But they must have done so unquestionably, as even Śūdras are shown as learning them. The story of Jānaśruti, a Śūdra king, who, being first refused, was eventually accepted as a pupil by a great Vedānta teacher, given in

Chhāndogya (IV 1), shows that even Śūdras were taught these doctrines. The Brahmasūtras of Bādarāyaṇa, two thousand years thereafter, fruitlessly attempt to explain away this story by splitting up the word Śūdra and making it mean something else ! ! !

The Brahmins and the Kshatriyas were, however, the foremost castes both in society and in the development of philosophy. It is thought by some scholars that the Vedānta philosophy originated with Kshatriyas alone. It is true that some doctrines originated with them and remained with them for some time (यथैषा विद्या नास्मात्कुलाद्गता. छां.). But there are other and greater doctrines which were taught by Brahmins, notably by Yājña-valkya and Uddālaka Āruṇi, his teacher; and Janaka learnt them from the former. Ajātaśatru of Kāśi taught a lesson to a Brahmin student, explaining how Ātman comes into the body of man, by showing how a man goes into sound sleep and how he awakens from it,—a phenomenon not yet well explained by modern science. It must, therefore, be said that Brahmin and Kshatriya thinkers equally took part in the evolution of the Brahman theory and equally share the credit for it.

Along with the four Varṇas (Sūta and Kshattṛi being indicative still of professions aud not mixed castes), the theory of four Āśramas seems to have been established at the end of this Upanishadic age. The Āśramas were probably three in the beginning, the student's life, the married life and that of the recluse or the man who has retired to a forest to lead an austere life. The Brāhmachārins (students) resided and boarded at the house of their guru and in return rendered many personal services such as tending his cows. In the story of Satyakāma Jābāla he was asked to stay with the cows of the guru and return only when they had increased to a thousand. The importance of the guru was recognised even for Brahmavidyā and the Āchārya was the final resort in it (आचार्यस्तु ते गतिं वक्ता, आचार्याद्ध्येव विद्या विदिता साधिष्ठं प्रापयति &c. - छां॰). The subjects taught to students are enumerated in the Chhāndogya (VII, 1) as follows: 1 Ṛigveda 2 Yajurveda 3 Sāmaveda 4 Atharvaveda 5 Itihāsapurāṇa 6 Veda of Vedas (grammar ?) 7 Pitrya 8 Rāśi (Arithmetic) 9 Daiva 10 Vākovākya (logic ?) 11 Ekāyana 12 Devavidyā 13 Brahmavidyā 14 Bhūtavidyā 15 Kshatravidyā (art of war) 16 Nakshatravidyā (astronomy) 17 Sarpadevajaṇavidyā (that relating to serpents, Yakshas and Rākshasas). The list is interesting and it has already been many times referred to. Some of these vidyās are unintelligible; but that they are not imaginary cannot, in our view, be doubted. The students learnt the Vedas and having learnt them constantly recited them as a religious act called Vedānuvachana (वेदानुवचन) and he who recited all the Vedas correctly was called Anūchāna (अनूचान). Students sometimes prided themselves on such proficiency (अनूचानमानी). The Upanishadic philosophy led, in our view, to the addition of a fourth Āśrama, viz. Saṁnyāsa, a word not found in the Ṛigveda nor also in the Brāhmaṇas. The idea of giving up the world and living by begging is first given expression to in the Bṛihadārṇyaka (भिक्षाचर्यं चरन्ति). These begging philosophers were, however, few and were probably Brahmins only. It is creditable to those times that women were allowed to take up the philosopher's life and there were many noted Brahmavādinīs like Sulabhā and Gārgī, the latter of whom assailed Yājñyavalkya with a question in the famous Bṛihadāraṇyaka disputation before King Janaka. The cult of Saṁnyāsa was, however, restricted to the really retired men and women. It came into abuse later when it was taken up by Buddhism and made cheap. The Buddhistic monks and nuns were a cheap and broad-cast edition of the Vedantic Saṁnyāsins. Men and women of all sorts and ages became Buddhist Bhikshus and Bhikshuṇīs. These abused the institution so grossly and incurred so much contempt that eventually Hindu society, on the fall of Buddhism, suppressed Saṁnyāsa altogether as forbidden in the Kali age.

The Vedānta philosophy was, however, taught to the pupils in Brahmacharya as also to men in the Grihasthāśrama, though its actual practice lay with Śaṁnyāsins. Śvetaketu was taught it when he had just finished his student life and Yājnavalkya was famous as a philosopher when he led still a married life. Indeed, the nearest approach to Brahmānanda mentioned in the Upanishads was the bliss that the married man enjoyed (यथा प्रियया स्त्रिया संपरिष्वक्तो न बाह्यं किंचन वेद–बृ०). But apparently the married man had eventually to retire to a forest, as Yajñavalkya did, for attaining the final bliss. It could, however, be attained, immediately a man had true knowledge; for ignorance caused bondage and naturally true knowledge, when attained, led immediately to Moksha or deliverance and the man became Brahman itself. The first fruit he acquired was fearlessness (अभयं वै जनक प्राप्तोऽसि, ब्रह्माभयं भवति–बृ०).

Along with the four Varṇas and the three Āśramas, supreme importance was attached to great social purity. The Chhāndogya enumerates the five great sins or Mahāpātakas and Surāpāna is among them and was so for all men. It is only in America that this abstinence has now become an accepted principle, while it had been accepted by the Indo-Aryan society four thousand years ago. India has maintained this principle for Brahmins, to this day. Even some Kshatriyas like the Śisodias observe the vow rigorously even now.

The evil of marrying more wives than one continued from the Ṛigvedic days and even

Yājñavalkya had two wives; but they were respected and Yājñavalkya even taught Brahmavidyā to his wife Maitreyī who spurned wealth in favour of it. The Indo-Aryans generally burnt their dead bodies; but sometimes the bodies were left uncared for in jungles and no funeral ceremonies were performed for them, especially of those that had entered into forests and pursued Brahmavidyā. These also went to Brahmaloka from whence there is no return, by the Devayāna path (तस्माद्यद्यप्यस्मिञ्छव्यं कुर्वन्ति यदि च नार्चिषमेवाभिसंभवन्ति &c – छां०) The mentiou of an Āṭikī wife (आटिक्या सह जायया) in the Chhāndogya is to be noted. The word is explained as a wife married when she was very young. Early marriages seem thus to have been then derided.

Among the vices of the Indo-Aryans, that of gambling seems to have still continued from Ṛigvedic times. Thus Chhāndogya gives an illustration from gambling: "As to the winning Kṛita the other lower figures bow". Kṛita meant four and the dice had their faces marked with one, two, three and four dots, and when the dice thrown showed four dots, the thrower won. This method of gambling is still current in India. In contrast with this vice, the Indo-Aryans were remarkable for their truthfulness. The story of Satyakāma Jābāla in the same Chhāndogya proves this great virtue of the Indian people, a virtue which distinguished them still till the most recent times, as this virtue is noted by the historians of Alexander of 330, B. C. by Arab travellers of about 900 A. D. and by Marco Polo of about 1400 A. D.

The advance in civilisation is testified to by the progress in scientific knowledge. Many metals were now known and used. The sentence यथा लवणेन सुवर्णं संदध्यात् &c. has already bee noticed. The physical phenomenon was marked that eastern winds brought rain-clouds (पुरोवातो हिंकारः &c.) This also shows that the Aryan land then was the same as mentioned above consisting of the modern Panjab, U. P. and Behar where eastern winds from the Bay current usher in the rainy season. These rains brought fertility and gladness (अन्नं बहु भविष्यति). The different kinds of grain grown are enumerated in one place as व्रीहि (rice), यव (yava), तिल (sesamum). माष (Māsha), गोधूम (wheat), प्रियङ्गु (jungle rice) &c. Rice maintains its first place and this shows that the Indo-Aryans still inhabited the lands at the base of the Himalayas.

With regard to religion, it may be said that the cult of sacrifice was still supreme and every householder kept Agnihotra (नानाहिताग्निः-छां॰). But this as well as recitation of the sacred Vedas now became directed to the attainment of Brahman and not of heaven. Vedic recitation, sacrifices, gifts, austerities and fasts were now prescribed for the knowledge of Brahman (वेदानुवचनेन ब्राह्मणा विविदिषन्ति यज्ञेन दानेन तपसानाशकेन-बृ॰). But if practised for attaining heaven, the fruit was not everlasting but temporary. This new theory was set up to dethrone the cult of sacrifice or to place it on a lower plane. Vidyā was thus of two kinds, higher and lower, परा and अपरा; the first was Brahmavidyā, while the latter, viz. learning Ṛigveda &c. and performing sacrifices, led to heaven or Svarga from which after enjoying the fruit of one's merit, one returned to this mundane world. It gradually became established that for the former Vidyā only Saṁnyāsins were eligible (शिरोव्रतं यैस्तु चीर्णम्-नैतदचीर्णव्रतोऽधीते – मुण्डक). Tapas and Brahmacharya were also necessry. The idea of तपस् or mortification of the body of various kinds gained great strength at this time and for this reason. Fast or अनशन was supposed to be most efficacious. This idea was taken up later by Jainism which prescribes a forty days' fast as of the highest merit. The idea of refraining from flesh also arose (संवत्सरं मज्जो नाश्नियात् – छां०) at this time.

The ancient Aryan states or rather peoples were prosperous and well-governed. Pessimism did not exist among the people as is supposed by some to explain the rise of Vedānta philosophy. There was no misery inflicted by man on man which could lead to dissatisfaction with this world. The Vairāgya of even Buddha was due not to such misery but to misery inflicted by God on man as seen in this mortal world, viz. the misery of birth, death, old age, sickness and mental pain (जन्ममृत्युजराव्याधिदुःखदोषानुदर्शनम्

-भग०). But the Vedantic philosophers did not harp upon even this as the Buddhists did. For they were full of the joys of this world and rose from this joy to the idea of Brahmānanda, joy objectless and everlasting. To realise this state, they spurned the joys of this world as Nachiketas or Christ did to obtain the joy of true knowledge. And such philosophers like Sayugvā Raikva often lived the life of a Diogenes, sitting aimless under a chariot (यत्र वै ब्राह्मणस्यान्वेषणा – छां० 3. 1.)

Lastly, it may be noted that these philosophers enunciated and developed the doctrine of the transmigration of the soul and also the theory of Karman under which every person goes to good or bad births according to his Karman (पुण्येन पुण्यो भवति पापः पापेन). This doctrine is explained at length in the oldest Upanishads, viz. the Chhāndogya and the Bṛihadāraṇyaka and is noticed in brief or at length in almost every other Upanishad. To escape from the chain of rebirth is, therefore, the final goal of the human soul. The theory of the two paths also was propounded, viz. of the Devayāna and the Pitṛiyāṇa, by the first of which the soul goes to the Brahmaloka from which there is no return and by the second of which the soul, having gone as far as the moon, returns to this world. It is remarkable that at the final stage of the Devayāna, the man of lightning is believed to lead the soul to its final delivery (वैद्युतः पुरुषः स एतान्ब्रह्म गमयति–छां०)

Note :- Further Particulars about the Upanishads

We give in this note detailed information about each of the thirteen old Upanishads and about some of the later ones, in the probable order of their chronological position.

I. Chhāndogya

This Upanishad is, according to our view, the oldest of all (perhaps with the exception of the Īśa), as it belongs to the Sāmaveda and as the singers of that Veda seem to have been the first to turn to philosophical speculation. It is well known that singing leads to ecstacy and it is conceivable that the singers of Sāmans first fell to philosophic contemplation. We have already shown (Section I, p. 114) that Om, the symbolical note of these singers, for this very reason, became identified with Brahman, the highest impersonal entity propounded by Upanishadic philosophy.

The Chhāndogya contains eight chapters called Prapāṭhakas or lessons, divided into 154 Khaṇḍas (13+24+19+17+24+16+26+15); and these Khaṇḍas contain from one to more than ten prose sentences or Mantras. These Khaṇḍas may have been composed at different times and by different authors, as they relate to different topics (see for instance शाण्डिल्यविद्या, सर्वं खल्विदं ब्रह्म, &c. III 14). But the whole Upanishad must have been put together before the sacrificial cult descended to a lower position. For the last Khaṇḍa declares that a man goes to Brahmaloka, who leads a married life and does all the religious acts required of him, with his senses restrained. Such a man does not return to this mortal world (अभिसमावृत्य कुटुम्बे...धार्मिकान् विदधत्...सर्वेन्द्रियाण्यात्मनि संप्रतिष्ठाप्य

स खल्वेवं वर्तयन्यावदायुषं ब्रह्मलोकमभिसम्पद्यते न च पुनरावर्तते). The same doctrine is found only in the Īśavāsya, viz. that a man should do his due religious acts till the end of his life, but in a resigned spirit without greed (कुर्वन्नेवेह कर्माणि जिजीविषेच्छतं समाः । एवं त्वयि नान्यथेतोऽस्ति न कर्म लिप्यते नरे ॥). Secondly, the Chhāndogya speaks of three Āśramas only, the student life, the married life and the retired life in a forest (त्रयो धर्मस्कन्धाः &c. II 23). Thirdly अहिंसन् सर्वाणि भूतान्यन्यत्र तीर्थेभ्यः does not prohibit animal sacrifices. Lastly, the Āchārya-Paramparā given at the end is characteristically short, viz. Prajāpati, Manu and his prajās or descendants. One thus feels almost sure that this Upanishad is the oldest of all. Even the Bṛihadāraṇyaka teaches the life of the Saṁnyāsin beggar (भिक्षाचर्यं चरन्ति), hereafter adopted as the fourth Āśrama necessary for Moksha or absolution.

The Chhāndogya Upanishad naturally opens in I with the glorification of Sāman and of Udgītha, with the Sāman chant at sacrifices; and stories are related of Baka Dālbhya, Ushasti Chākrāyaṇa and others who were Sāman singers and Sāman philosophers. In II Sāman is identified with the whole world, the earth being Hiṁkāra and so on to the Sāman of five parts as well as that of seven parts; and in the end are given some actual notes of singing. In III, the sun is first identified with Ātman, the sun with its rays in the four directions; then Gāyatrī, the chief prayer of the Vedic Aryans to the sun. The human soul resides in the heart, the warmth of the living body and the sound heard in the closed ear indicating the burning within. The soul is next identified in the शाण्डिल्यविद्या with the whole world. Prāṇa is also identified similarly with the world and also mind and speech, sight, hearing and breathing. Lastly, the whole world outside is Ātman, the sun born out of the bursting of the egg of the universe; the atmosphere with the clouds and the ocean. Hereafter in IV we have very interesting parables related, viz., that of the S'ūdra king Jānaśruti Pautrāyaṇa, of Satyakāma Jābāla and of his pupil Upakosala Kāmalāyana, ending with a description of how the soul reaches the Brahmaloka by the Devayāna (divine path) through light, day, fortnight, month, year, the, sun, the moon and finally Vidyut. Chapter V opens with the parable of a dispute among the senses as to which is the highest among them (a parable copied in more than one Upanishad) and then gives a dialogue between S'vataketu Āruṇeya and the Pāñchāla king Pravāhana Jaivali, illustrating how the human soul migrates and describing the Pitṛiyāṇa (the path of Pitṛiloka) in complete detail. Next comes the charming dialogue between the five seekers after truth, Prāchīnaśāla and others, including the great Uddālaka Āruṇi on one side and the Kshatriya philosopher king Aśvapati Kekaya. In VI we have the still more charming dialogue between S'vetaketu and his father Uddālaka Āruṇi in which the docrine of तत्त्वमसि (That thou art) is explained with various illustrations. In VII is given the eloquent discourse on Ātman, preached by Sanatkumāra to Nārada, elucidating the docrine of Prāṇa and the really highest state of happiness wherein man is conscious of no want or desire. The eighth chapter comes last, forming the pinnacle so to speak of this glorious Upanishad, and gives the parable of Prajāpati and his two pupils, Indra, chief of the gods, and Vairochana, chief of Asuras with their material views, differentiating the West from the East from the most ancient times, as the word अश्रद्दधान used in VIII 8 clearly proves.

Having so far described in short the contents of this most important Upanishad and having indicated the probable basis of the arrangement of its eight chapters, we proceed to notice the many interesting historical facts which can be elicited from it. 1. I 38 proves that the Ṛigveda and the Sāmaveda were not only already compiled but fully studied. The tune, the ṛishi and the deity of each Sāman was fixed (तत्साम त-मृषिं तां देवतामुपधावेत्). 2. The singing was to the accompaniment of a Viṇā or guitar (वीणायां गायन्त्येतं ते धनसनय: I 7, 6). 3. मटचीहतेषु कुरुषु is explained as famine-stricken Kuru country (I 11). 4. The singing cries ओं, हाऊ, होई came to indicate different deities (I 12. 7, 13). 5. पुरोवातो हिंकारः मेघः प्रस्तावः (II 8) shows that the Aryan land then extended over the Panjab and U. P., the eastern wind bringing rain therein; and east-flowing rivers are mentioned, not rivers flowing north or south. 5. The parts of the Sāman song are seven now, with आदि and उपद्रव added (II 8). 6. Different Lokas are conceived in which Āditya or Sun is the 21st (एकविंशो वा इतोऽसावादित्य:) and in the 22nd beyond Āditya you have heaven or Nāka which is described as विशोक 'without sorrow' (II 10). 7. संवत्सरं मज्जो नाश्नीयात् shows that the cult of abstinence from flesh had begun (II 19) so also ब्राह्मणान् न निन्देत् is interesting (II 20). 8. The study of grammar had progressed and the letters of the alphabet grouped as Svaras, Ūshmans and Sparśas and the method of pronouncng them prescribed (सर्वे स्वरा घोषवन्तो बलवन्तो वक्तव्याः &c. II 22). 8. Atharvaveda was probably not put together at the date of this chapter, for अथर्वांगिरसः do not lead to अथर्ववेद as in the case of ऋग्वेद, यजुर्वेद and सामवेद, but to इतिहासपुराण which is treated as its Pushpa. Guhya Ādeśas or Upanishads are treated as separate from Brāhmaṇas and were not yet included in them, they leading to Brahman as flower. 10. It is difficult to understand how the sun could rise in the west and set in the east (III 8). It is, however, refreshing to find astronomy and geography so far advanced. 11. How is Gāyatrī चतुष्पदा and षड्विधा ? and how does the quotation तावानस्य महिमा apply to it referring as it does to Purusha and not to Gāyatrī ? 12. There is a reference to Mahidāsa Aitareya living upto the age of 116 (III 16) and one to S'rīkṛishṇa, son of Devakī, as being taught a doctrine by Ghora Āngirasa (III 17). The story of Jānaśruti is interesting in many ways; firstly, a Sūdra is here mentioned as learning Vedānta doctrine. Secondly Kshattā is mentioned as a chariot-driver. The S'ūdra offers his daughter to a Brahmin. Nishka means a fixed quantity of gold and not a coin (अयं निष्कः). And villages are given as Inams to Brahmins. 14. Upanayana was no more than going to school and being admitted as a pupil उप त्वा अयानि (IV 4). But the importance of a guru seems to have been established, आचार्याद्धैव विद्या विदिता साधिष्ठं प्रापयति (IV 9). 14. The students lived at the house of the teacher whose wife took a maternal interest in their welfare. 15. Advanced knowledge of metals is evidenced by सुवर्णेन रजतं &c. (IV 17). 15. The fourth priest still knows only the three Vedas and not the fourth (त्रय्या विद्यया वीर्येण यज्ञस्य विरिष्टं संदधाति यत्रैवंविद् ब्रह्मा भवति ibid.). 16. Horses were tied to four pegs driven into the ground and it was the test of a powerful horse that when it sprang, it pulled out the pegs (V 1 17. The words of Pravāhaṇa (यथेयं न प्राक् त्वत्तः पुरा विद्या ब्राह्मणान् गच्छति) do not mean that the *whole* Vedānta philosophy was developed by the Kshatriyas (V 3) 18. The theory of transmigration by the two paths with the law of Karman is detailed here. इष्टापूर्ते दत्तं is no doubt lower in status; but not अग्निहोत्र or daily sacrifice. A third path is, however, mentioned for those creatures that live an ephemeral life. 19. The five great sins (महापातक) are here first detailed, viz. theft of gold, liquor-drinking, adultery with the guru's wife, killing a Brahmin, and association with such sinners as the fifth (V 10). 20. Names are double, viz. that of the individual with that of the father, even as at present, such as उद्दालक आरुणि, बुडिल आश्वतराश्वि &c.; but there is also a third distinguishing appellation based on gotra-descent equivalent to our modern surname; thus उद्दालक is गौतम and बुडिल is वैय्याघ्रपद्य. The gotra system was firmly established at least among Brahmins at this ancient date (V 15). 21. The sixth chapter first mentions the usual period of Brahmacharya orschool-life, viz. from the 12th to the 24th year and famous schools sent out महाशाल or learned men. 22. We have a distinct mention of कार्ष्णायस or steel as distinguished from लोह or iron and of such sharp instuments as नख-निकृन्तन (nail-cutter). 23. Elements first appear to be three only: earth, water and fire. Five elements came later, especially Ākāśa, as conceived by Vedānta philosophy, later still. 24. We have already noticed the mention of Gāndhāra and of fire-ordeal at the end of this chapter. 25. The various subjects of study at school enumerated in VII have already been noticed. 26. The chapter also enumerates the various methods of worship in vogue viz. यज्ञ, इष्ट, सत्रायण, अनाशकायन and अरण्यायन which are all equated with Brahmacharya or worship of Brahman.

2 Bṛihadāraṇyaka

The next great Upanishad is the Bṛihadāraṇyaka which is in some parts even more eloquent than the Chhāndogya. It may, however, be placed after it in date. The several parts of it, like those of the Chhāndogya, are by different authors and composed at different times which can not be definitely determined. But the putting together of the whole may be taken to be late. The name at least is very late, for, as explained already, the very name Āraṇyaka is post-Pāṇinian. The several parts which are styled Brāhmaṇas were treated as forming a Khila or supplement of the S'atapatha Brāhmaṇa and not as Āraṇyaka. But the first Adhyāya is not a Khila as it forms part of the eleventh Kāṇḍa of the S'atapatha, the others forming the fourteenth.

These several Brāhmaṇas are put together into six chapters called Adhyāyas and not Prapāṭhakas. They are 57 in number as follows: 6+6+9+16+15+5. The S'āntimantra of this Upanishad is पूर्णमिदं पूर्णमदः &c. and is found at the beginning of the fifth chapter. Another important thing is that there are three different Vaṁśas given at the end of the second, fourth and sixth chapters and they are a study by themselves as will be noticed separately. They perhaps indicate that the Upanishad originally was in three parts of two chapters each, which were subsequently joined. The Brāhmaṇas consist mostly of prose sentences or Mantras of various length which run up to as many as twenty-three and more. There are S'lokas quoted in the midst of Brāhmaṇas as a sort of authority.

As this Upanishad belongs to the Yajurveda or the Veda of sacrifice, and as Aśvamedha is the highest Vedic sacrifice, it naturally opens with an idealization of that sacrifice into the phenomenon of sunrise, which itself is looked upon as an Aśvamedha. Then we have the creation of the world philosophically described as also of the five senses in man, the working of which has always arrested the attention of Indian philosophers. The second chapter opens with a dialogue between Dṛipta Bālāki Gārgya, a Brahmin, and Ajātaśatru of Kāśī, a Kshatriya, ending with the explanation of the phenomena of sleeping and awakening. The chapter then gives the well-known dialogue between Yājñavalkya and his philosophic wife Maitreyī, in which the greatest sage of Vedānta philosophy explains what Ātman or Brahman is and the state of Brahmībhāva wherein all cognition of duality is lost and the whole world is realised to be nothing else than Brahman. After describing the Madhuvidyā of Dadhyaṅ Ātharvaṇa, this chapter ends with a Vaṁśa. Chapter III contains the still more interesting story of the disputations at the court of Janaka wherein Yājnavalkya is assailed with searching questions by many philosophers including the redoubtable lady savant Gārgī Vāchaknavī. The fourth chapter is the most eloquent disquisition in the whole range of Upanishadic literature, containing an elucidation of the philosophy of Ātman alias Brahman by Yājñavalkya to Janaka. Curiously enough, the story of Yājñavalkya and his wife Maitreyī is again given at the end of this chapter and then comes the second Vaṁśa.

The fifth chapter begins with the S'anti Mantra पूर्ण-मिदं &c. and then gives a few short but pithy Brāhmaṇas while the sixth quotes two popular parables from the Chhāndogya, one about the dispute among the senses for supremacy (यो ह वै ज्येष्ठं च श्रेष्ठं च वेद &c.) and another called पंचाग्निविद्या relating to the migration of the soul by Devayāna and Pitṛiyāṇa paths, embodied in a dialogue between S'vetaketu Āruṇeya and the King of Kurus, Pravāhaṇa Jaivali. Then come two Brāhmaṇas which are really out of place here as they do not teach any Vedānta doctrine and are entirely sacrificial. Finally comes the third Vaṁśa which is the longest of the three.

The following interesting statements in this Upanishad may be noted. 1. Yājñavalkya is not the author of this Upanishad though he is the chief authority quoted in it (इति ह स्माह याज्ञवल्क्यः). 2. Man and woman originally were one and were then divided into two halves (स इममेवात्मानं द्वेधा पातयत् पतिश्च पत्नी चाभवतां तस्मादिदमर्धबृगलमिव &c. I 4, 3). 3. Caste distinctions were recognized even among gods, इन्द्र, वरुण, सोम, रुद्र, पर्जन्य, यम, मृत्यु and ईशान being Kshatriyas. But the Kshatriya is treated as the highest, as a Brahmin serves the Kshatriya in Rājasūya from a lower position. The higher *spiritual* position of the Brahmins is, however, equally clear, as killing a Brahmin is a great sin (ब्राह्मणः क्षत्रियमधस्तादुपास्ते राजसूये, सैषा क्षत्रस्य योनिर्यद् ब्रह्म य उ एनं हिनस्ति स पापीयान् भवति स्वां स योनिं हिंसति I, 4). The Vaiśyas are those gods who form groups like वसवः, रुद्राः, आदित्याः, विश्वे देवाः and मरुतः and whose names are in the plural while the only S'ūdra god is Pūshan because he supports all (*ibid*) The Aryans in the eastern countries left agriculture to the S'ūdras who were already tillers of the soil. But it speaks highly of the sublime sentiment of these philosophers when they place Dharma above all castes (क्षत्रस्य क्षत्रं यद्धर्मः) and Satya as the highest Dharma. Agni is a Brahmin and through him, men go to the highest Brahman. 4. Whence are the श्लोकाः (not Ṛiks) यत्सप्तान्नानि मेधया &c. that they should be explained in this Brāhmaṇa (I 5) ? 5. तस्मादेतां रात्रिं (अमावास्यां) प्राणभृतः प्राणं न विच्छिन्द्यादपि वा कृकलासस्य is the precursor of the Ahiṁsā doctrine subsequently preached by Buddhism, Jainism and even Christianity in 'Thou shalt not kill' (I 5). 6. The works born from Brahman's breath are Ṛigveda, Yajurveda, Sāmaveda, Atharvāngirasa, Itihāsa, Purāṇa, Vidyā, Upanishads, S'lokas, Sūtras, Anuvyākyānas and Vyākhyānas (II, 4). The occurrence of the word Upanishad here is very significant. It may be equated with गुह्या आदेशाः of the Chhāndogya. They were not parts of any Veda or Brāhmaṇa yet; they were separate, small, esoteric treatises taught to advanced students. Many of these old Upanishads have been incorporated into the existing thirteen Upanishads but many may have been lost. Then there were many S'lokas besides the sacred Ṛiks which were composed for embodying Vedānta doctrines in short form to help the memory, (यत्सप्ताननि &c. annotated in this very Upanishad, as mentioned above, probably being one of such S'lokas). And Sūtras in prose for the same object were also enunciated by this time; but these as preceding this Upanishad must be taken to have all been lost. Or the word refers to such short sentences as सर्वं खल्विदं ब्रह्म (as explained by S'ankara in his commentary on ब्रह्मसूत्रपदैश्चैव of गीता) followed by their Vyākhyānas and Anuvyākhānas, works which no longer now exist, nor even these their names. This list when compared with that in the Chhāndogya (VII 2) indicates that the Bṛihadāraṇyaka is a later Upanishad than the latter. 7. The reference to Pārikshitas in III 8 is very important. The memory of the four sons of Parikshit seems to have been fresh. Janamejaya and his brothers were the emperors of the Indo-Aryan world and performed four As'vamedhas. From this question here asked, क्व पारिक्षिता अभवन्, it is inferred by some scholars that the fall of the Pārikshitas was in some strange manner. But no such inference can be supported from the answer of Yājñavalkya who says "They have gone to the place where As'vamedha-sacrificers go, viz. there where Vāyu is and so on". The answer gives the then prevailing idea as to where the Brahmaloka is, beyond this visible world. 8. मद्रेषु चरकाः पर्यव्रजाम shows that the question was asked in the Madra country in the Panjab by a Gandharva or a spirit which had seized the daughter of Pāñchala Kāpya. Inquisitive spirits which seized human beings were believed in those days even as in the days of the Bible. 9. In III 5 we have कहोळ described as कौषीतकेय (son of कौषीतकि and not कौषीतक). 10. The Upanishads discuss Brahman only as is clear from the sentence तं त्वौपनिषदं पुरुषं पृच्छामि (III 9). The S'lokas at the end of this Brāhmaṇa are not from any Saṁhitā but from such floating works on these subjects as are noted already. They are often enigmatic ones, such as Vedantic philosophers delighted in composing, e.g. विज्ञानमानन्दं ब्रह्म रातिर्दातुः परायणम्. 11. In the fourth chapter we first find Janaka addressed as Samrāṭ, the title of Eastern monarchs, according to the Aitareya Brāhmaṇa. Then we have the same list of works of study with उपनिषद्, सूत्र, व्याख्यान and अनुव्याख्यान again. नाननुशिष्य हरेत may be marked as showing that Dakshiṇā was taken only for adequate service. Upanishads are again mentioned as Vedantic teaching and not secret (एताभिरुपनिषद्भिः समाहितात्मा IV 2). S'lokas are quoted here which are not Vedic, but Upanishadic (IV 3). The simile taken from the royal march has already been noticed (राजानमायान्तं सूतग्रामण्यः &c.). IV 4 again quotes the ancient S'lokas तदेते श्लोकाः, two of which अन्धं तमः प्रविशंति &c. and अनन्दा नाम ते लोकाः are clearly from the Iśāvāsyopanishad, or both borrow from the same source; but the quotation at the end एष नित्यो महिमा &c. is introduced by the words तदेतदृचाभ्युक्तम्. 12. Chapter V begins with an enigmatic Mantra composed by Kauravyāyaṇīputra ओं खं ब्रह्म खं पुराणं वायुरं खम्. 13. We have the three peoples देवाः मनुष्याः and असुराः who are preached the same letter द by the creator. The Devas understood it as दम or restraint, men as दान or gift and Asuras as दया. Are these three characteristics true of any historical peoples? In a previous Bārhmaṇa we are told that Devas and Asuras were both descendants of Prajāpati, the Devas belonging to the younger branch and the Asuras to the elder. Can this be explained as showing that Indo-Aryans were the last offshoots of the Aryan race who came to India from Persia? 14. V 5 states that a dying man sees the sun shorn of its rays. Is this so?

So also he does not hear the noise in the ear usually heard when closed (V 9.). 15. The three holes of रथचक्र, लम्बर and दुंदुभि are wider in gradation so is the path of the human soul when it goes to Vāyu, to Āditya, and to Chandramas. 16. The moon is placed higher than the sun by ancient Indian astronomical theory. 17. In V 14 the sacred Gāyatrī mantra is esoterically explained, the fourth unseen foot of it being the sun itself. 18. V 15 gives verses from the Īśāvāsyopanishad word for word. 19. Lastly in VI 3. we have a more reliable आचार्यपरम्परा, viz. उद्दालक आरुणि, his pupil वाजसनेय याज्ञवल्क्य, his pupil मधुक पैङ्ग्य, his pupil चूल भागवित्ति, his pupil जानकि आयस्थूण, his pupil सत्यकाम जाबाल. And 20. in VI 5 we have a detailed special sacrificial rite given, for begetting a learned son versed in all Vedas, which strikes us as somewhat obscene but was not so in reality then, as sexualintercourse was then looked upon as a sacred and solemn act.

3. Īs'āvāsya.

The Īśāvāsya or shortly Īśa Upanishad is really the last or fortieth chapter of the White Yajurveda Saṁhitā and as such must be very old though it is treated as a khila of that Saṁhitā. In a condensed form it gives the important doctrines of the Vedānta philosophy. But it does not preach Saṁnyāsa and teaches that karman should be performed till the end of one's life, for "thus only can salvation come". There is one interesting reference in it to Avidyā, not nescience nor the Avidyā of S'ankara; Vidyā is Upanishadic knowledge and Avidyā is plainly other knowledge. The word is, however, differently construed by different philosophers.

4. Kaṭha.

We next take up the Kaṭha which belongs to the Kaṭha S'ākhā of the Black Yajurveda while Is'a and Bṛihad. belong to the White. The Kaṭha is also the next important Upanishad after the preceding three. The S'ānti-mantra of this Upanishad is सह नाववतु and is given at its head, though not a part of it. It consists of two Adhyāyas each subdivided into three sections called Vallīs, a new and strange name. It is introduced by the story of Nachiketas who was cursed by his father Us'anas surnamed Gotama (of the Gotama gotra) to go to the world of Yama and who is taught the Vedānta philosophy by Yama himself, the very first question being "Does man live after death ?" The six vallīs contain verses oft quoted by later works, chiefly the Gītā, and these probably are taken from the various Saṁhitās, The original story of Nachiketas in the Kaṭha Saṁhitā is shorter and was concerned only with the sacrificial cult of the Nāchiketa fires. The language strikes us as later than that of the original story in the Saṁhitā.

The following interesting statements may be noticed. 1. Nachiketas not being tempted by riches or women or empire is like Jesus not being seduced by Satan in the Bible. This idea may, however, arise in different countries and peoples. 2. अयं लोको नास्ति पर इति मानी shows that atheists who did not believe in any hereafter had already arisen. 3. आश्चर्यो वक्ता is copied in the Gītā as also अणोरणीयान् and अजो नित्यः शाश्वतोऽयं पुराणो न हन्यते हन्यमाने शरीरे &c. 4. नैषा तर्केण मतिरापनेया indicates the rise of Tarka science. 5. नायमात्मा प्रवचनेन लभ्यः shows that Pravachana is college teaching (see Taittirīya) and is distinct from अनुवचन, the reciting of the Vedas (see also अनूचान). 6. ऋतं प्रविष्टौ सुकृतस्य लोके &c. is probably an old Ṛik. 7. आत्मानं रथिनं विद्धि &c. is a striking metaphor copied in many later works. 8. तद्विष्णोः परमं पदम् (I 3, 9) shows that Vishṇu is taken up by this Upanishad as Para Brahman. Though the Black Yajurveda in general praises S'iva as the highest god, the Kaṭha S'ākhā probably glorifies Vishṇu. 9. इन्द्रियेभ्यः परं मनः &c. is copied by the Gītā. 10. बुद्धेरात्मा महान् परः । महतः परमव्यक्तमव्यक्तात्पुरुषः परः । पुरुषान्न परं किंचित् ॥ is copied by the Sānkhya and not from the Sānkhya. The words महत्, अव्यक्त and पुरुष are also taken by the Sānkhya from here. 11. The Phalaśruti at the end of the first chapter and the line नाचिकेतमुपाख्यानं मृत्युप्रोक्तं indicates that the Upanishad consisted originally of one chapter only, the second chapter being a later addition. 12. That chapter is, however, older than the Gītā and even the Sānkhya philosophy as सर्वभूतान्तरात्मा, न तत्र सूर्यो भाति &c. ऊर्ध्वमूलमवाक्शाखम् are ideas copied from here by the Gītā. 13. भयादग्निस्तपति &c. is a grand idea copied by many later works. 14. इन्द्रियेभ्यः परं मनः । मनसः सत्त्वमुत्तमम् ॥ does not mention the सत्त्वगुण of the Sānkhyas; it is the same word as in सत्त्वानुरूपा सर्वस्य श्रद्धा भवति भारत of the Gītā 15. So also तां योगमिति मन्यन्ते स्थिरामिन्द्रियधारणाम् is different from Pātañjala Yoga philosophy and is its precursor; for Yoga is described as प्रभवाप्ययौ. 16. शतं चैका हृदयस्य नाड्यः and अंगुष्ठमात्रः पुरुषः embody an older idea taken up here. 17. मुञ्जादिवेषीकां धैर्येण is also a grand simile. 18. The chapter ends with a small phalaśruti. The योगविधि कृत्स्न mentioned is that of Vedāntic concentration described in the Bhagavadgītā in detail.

5. Taittirīya

We next take up the Taittirīya Upanishad which belongs to the Tittiri branch of the Black Yajurveda. Its relative chronological position can not well be defined and it may have preceded the Kaṭha. Its S'ānti-mantra is शं नो मित्रः शं वरुणः &c. (different from सह नाववतु) and this forms the first Anuvāka in it. For this Upanishad, like the Brāhmaṇa and Saṁhitā of the Tittiris is divided into Anuvākas, though the word Vallī is borrowed from the Kaṭha S'ākhā. The Upanishad has three Vallīs, the first being called S'īkshādhyāya, the second Brahmānanda and the third Bhṛigu. These names are given to them from thir opening words. These Vallīs are subdivided into thirty-one (12+9+10) Anuvākas. The Anuvākas consist of prose sentences which are always short, as elsewhere in this S'ākhā; and at the end of each chapter or Vallī there is an enumeration of sentences by tens as in the Taittirīya Āraṇyaka of which the Upanishad forms a part. These Vallīs may, however, have been composed at different times and finally included in the Āraṇyaka. For the S'īkshādhyāya mentions the sentences by tens and over in each Anuvāka, which is the older method of the Saṁhitā. This S'īkshā chapter gives many practical instructions which are of very high value such as those to the student who leaves his college: 'सत्यं वद' and so on. At the end of the third Vallī, a Sāman is given as sung by the man who has reached the Ānanda of Brahman. In a Yajurveda Upanishad this is remarkable.

The following noteworthy facts may be culled from this Upanishad. 1. अथातः संहिताया उपनिषद् has a different meaning for Upanishad. 2. Teachers mentioned by name are Prāchīnayogya, Rāthitara, Pauruśishṭi and Nāka Maudgalya. 3. The five elements are now well established; but they are produced one from the other and Ākāśa is produced from Ātman, a tenet developed later by the Sāṅkhyas. 4. The five kośas are a new tenet; but Ānanda is a remarkable advance over mere absorption. 5. आदेश आत्मा refers to Upanishad as distinct from Ṛik, Yajus, Sāman and Atharvāṅgiras. 6. The gods are classified as आजानज, कर्मज and others who are simply Devas. Indra is above them, above him is Brihaspati, above him Prajāpati, and above him Brahman. 7. The Bhṛiguvallī develops the same theory of five Kośas and praises Anna in various ways. But what is ब्रह्मणः परिमरः which kills the enemies, the haters and the cousins (भ्रातृव्य)?

6. Aitareya.

The Aitareya follows next. It belongs to the Ṛigveda and is the only old Upanishad of that Veda. Its S'ānti Mantra is वाङ् मे मनसि प्रतिष्ठिता &c., a Ṛigveda Mantra. It is a very short Upanishad consisting, as it does, of three short chapters (अध्याय), the first only being subdivided into four Khaṇḍas. These three chapters form the fourth, fifth and sixth chapters of the second Araṇa of Aitareya Āraṇyaka. The first chapter seems to be the earliest of the three speaking of अशनाया and पिपासा. It first gives the explanation of the word Indra on the esoteric basis इदंद्रं सन्तमिन्द्रमित्याचक्षते परोक्षेण and lays down the oft-repeated dictum परोक्षप्रिया इव हि देवाः. The second chapter speaks still of svarga as the highest goal: स्वर्गे लोके सर्वान् कामानाप्त्वामृतः समभवत्. The third chapter does the same. Here we have the functions of mind minutely distinguished and also the five elements mentioned clearly.

7. Pras'na.

We now come to the three Atharvaveda Upanishads: Praśna, Muṇḍaka and Māṇḍūkya, their S'ānti-mantra being भद्रं कर्णेभिः शृणुयाम देवाः. These are probably the latest of the old Upanishads as they contain all the latest developments of the Vedānta philosophy. The

Praśna is a dialogue between Pippalāda, the Ṛishi of the Atharvaveda and five seekers after Brahman; and in its five sections answers are given to the five questions asked by each of these sages. It is chiefly in prose but verses are usually quoted and are preceded by तदेते श्लोकाः, which are not Vedic but Upanishadic. The first Praśna details देवयान and पितृयाण and therein assigns a lower position to Karman. It also divides Brahman into Para and Apara. It also mentions the five elements. The word vrātya is used in its Atharvaveda sense, viz., the highest deity. The following two similes are striking, viz. यथा मधुकरराजान मक्षिकाः &c. and यथा सम्राडधिकृतान्नियुंक्ते एतान्ग्रामानाधितिष्ठ &c. The latter relates to the eastern countries, विदेह and others, and probably this Upanishad belongs to that part.

8. Muṇḍaka.

This Upanishad contains, as said above, all the latest developments of the Vedānta philosophy. The line of teachers given in the beginning is ब्रह्मा, अथर्वन्, अंगिरस्, भरद्वाज, सत्यवाह, अंगिरस् and शौनक who is no doubt a late Āchārya. The work is wholly metrical. It is a short one and has three chapters called Muṇḍakas, each divided into two Khaṇḍas, and each Khaṇḍa contains from nine to thirteen verses or mantras. Vidyās are of two kinds like Brahman, viz. Parā and Aparā. While Parā is the highest by which the Akshara is known, Aparā is Ṛigveda, Yajurveda, Sāmaveda, Atharvaveda and the six Vedāngas, Sikshā, Kalpa, Vyākaraṇa, Nirukta, Chhandas and Jyotisha. Itihāsa and Purāṇa are here omitted as also the other Vidyās of the Chhāndogya and Bṛihadāraṇyaka. The names and number of the Vedāngas are the modern ones. The ordinary sacrifices of Agnihotra, Darśapūrṇamāsa &c. are also given; but these sacrifices are frail boats (प्लवा ह्येते अदृढा यज्ञरूपाः। अष्टादशोक्तमवरं येषु कर्म।) Their fruit is not lasting. Their performers return to life and death. But the Saṁnyāsin who gives up the world and lives by begging goes to the eternal Ātman through the gate of the Sun. For this a Guru is necessary (गुरुमेवाभिगच्छेत्समित्पाणिः श्रोत्रियं ब्रह्मनिष्ठ). The Brahman theory is well presented and the simile taken from archery is grand, wherein however the bow is Praṇava or Om which has now become the highest goal as well as means (प्रणवो धनुः शरो ह्यात्मा ब्रह्म तल्लक्ष्यमुच्यते। अप्रमत्तेन वेद्धव्यं शरवत्तन्मयो भवेत्॥). The bow is previously called औपनिषद. Some verses are taken from the Ṛigveda. The word Vedānta is here found for the first time probably and Yatis alone realise Brahman. तदेतदृचाभ्युक्तं introduces क्रियावन्तः श्रोत्रियाः &c. which cannot be a Ṛigvedic verse, especially as it inculcates शिरोव्रत already noticed.

9. Māndūkya.

The third Atharvaveda Upanishad is the shortest of all Upanishads, consisting as it does of twelve prose sentences only. It describes how Om is the whole world, past, present and future. It is Ātman in its four stages: the waking, the dreaming, the soundly sleeping and the one beyond these three. Om has also four parts अ, उ, म् and the fourth अमात्र beyond. The philosophy of this Upanishad based on 'Om' has been elucidated by the Kārikās of Gauḍapāda and later Vedānta philosophers. The words प्रपञ्च and अद्वैत and the ideas conveyed by them are first found in this work. Its meaningful conciseness is an indication of its lateness.

10. Kena

We lastly come to Kena which is the second Upanishad of the Sāmaveda, called so from its first word Kena and also called Talavakāra as it belongs to that S'ākhā. This last but not least of the ten old Upanishads is also a short one, having four Khaṇḍas only, two in verse and two in prose, containing 34 Mantras (13 veres and 21 prose sentences). It opens with the unanswerable question, who sets the mind in motion or gives the first impulse to breath (the pendulum of the clock of life), and then describes the Brahman in pithy verses. In the prose part is given the parable of Indra, Vāyu and Agni trying to find out Brahman. Agni could not burn a straw nor could Vayu move it when asked to do so by Brahmaṇ. When Indra approached, Brahman disappeared and hence he is considered to be the greatest of the gods. Indra thus is still the highest deity; but he is not Brahman itself as Vishṇu is in Kaṭha. It may, therefore, be earlier than Kaṭha; but the mention of Umā, daughter of the Himālayas (उमा हैमवती) makes it nearly certain that it is a later one. How this Purāṇic deity comes in here and explains Brahman is a riddle.

11 S'vetās'vatara

Of the three next Upanishads, the S'vetāśvatara is probably the earliest, Kaushītaki and Maitrāyaṇīya being the next in order. All other Upanishads hereafter are sectarian and not devoted to the pure elucidation of the theory of Brahman. The S'vetāśvatara is attached to the Black Yajurveda and belongs to the S'ākhā of that name. Its S'ānti–mantra is, therefore, naturally सह नाववतु &c. It is divided into six chapters which are not, however, further subdivided. They contain metrical Mantras only, in all 113 (16+17+21+22+14+23). Many of them are old, being borrowed from the various Saṁhitās as also other Upanishads. The Upanishad is very thoughtful and eloquent and has not the verbosity of the Black Yajurveda Brāhmaṇa.

The first chapter treats of जीव, ब्रह्म, ज्ञ, and अज्ञ. Brahman pervades the world like सर्पि: in क्षीर. The second chapter treats of Yoga, giving the whole method of concentration (त्रिरुन्नतं स्थाप्य समं शरीरं &c.) and enumerates the Yogic experiences (नीहारधूमार्कानलानिलानां &c.). This progress of Yoga establishes its lateness and yet the philosophy is not that of Patañjali but its first stage giving the principles, not yet fixed in a system. The third chapter quotes from the Rudrādhāya (या ते रुद्र शिवा तनू: &c.) and from the Purushasūkta and from various other sources. The fourth identifies Brahman with Mahes'vara and distinctly mentions Māyā (मायां तु प्रकृतिं विद्यान्मायिनं तु महेश्वरम्). The fifth chapter mentions Kapila called Ṛishi (ऋषिं प्रसूतं कपिलं) and his Triguṇa theory. It may, therefore, be a later addition. The sixth mentions the Karman theory and the words Sāṁkhya and Yoga in their particular senses (तत्कारणं सांख्ययोगाधिगम्यं). It also details Sānkhya tenets in a line (प्रधानक्षेत्रज्ञपतिर्गुणेशः। संसारमोक्षस्थितिबन्धहेतुः ॥१). In the end the teacher S'vetās'vatara is praised and he taught his doctrines to अत्याश्रमिs (saṁnyāsis or those beyond the three Ās'ramas). It says that the philosophy should not be taught to अशान्त nor to a bad son or pupil. It first preaches गुरुभक्ति as necessary for the highest knowledge (यस्य देवे परा भक्तिर्यथा देवे तथा गुरौ। तस्यैते कथिता ह्यर्थाः प्रकाशन्ते महात्मनः ॥). These facts establish beyond doubt, the lateness of this Upanishad and it has been properly excluded from the list of the ten older Upanishads.

12 Kaushītaki

This Upanishad belongs to the Ṛigveda and forms part of the Kaushītaki Brāhmaṇa which, as we have shown already, follows the Aitareya. Its S'ānti-mantra is, threfore, वाङ्मे मनसि प्रतिष्ठिता &c. It is entirely in prose. It consists of four long chapters called अध्यायs and is not sub-divided into any sections. Each chapter contains long prose sentences or Mantras, in all 51 (7+15+9+20). There is no line of teachers given anywhere; but Kaushītaki is mentioned as a teacher (प्राणो ब्रह्मेति स्माह कौषीतकिः II) and the Upanishad mostly copies from other older Upanishads with amplifications of its own. Thus the first chapter speaks of the two (or three) paths and expands the Devayāna with so many details of its own (तं पञ्च शतान्यप्सरसां प्रतिधावन्ति शतं मालाहस्ताः &c. I 4). In chapter two, we have a mention of Paingya, who is usually opposed to Kaushītaki in this school, though both sanction the Saṁnyasin's rule of life, viz. begging in the village (ग्रामे भिक्षित्वा). What is Ekadhana or Daivasmara (II 3 & 4)? We have here a mention of यज्ञोपवीतं कृत्वा (II 7) as a preliminary to sacrifice and also the Vrata of observing the moon on the day following the Amāvāsyā as very meritorious (II 8). The seeing of the full moon and the performance of certain ceremonies are also prescribed and these latter include some which are out of place in an Upanishad. These are सर्वजितः कौषीतकेस्त्रीण्युपासनानि. The mention in II 13 of यमौ पर्वतौ दक्षिणश्चोत्तरश्च makes it certain that the author knows Vindhya and hence is a late one. The third chapter gives a dialogue between Indra and Pratardana Daivodāsi who has gone to heaven. The Upanishad here copies copiously from Chhāndogya and Bṛihadāraṇyaka, quoting even the very words, with many additions of its own such as प्रज्ञा and भूतमात्राs. The dialogue between Gārgya Bālāki and Kāsya Ajātaśatru in the fourth chapter is similarly borrowed from the Chhāndogya, almost wholly, with extensions of its own such as the प्राज्ञ आत्मा at the end, which is treated by the several senses like a S'reshṭhin, an interesting simile from life, wherein a rich merchant is followed and feasted by his compeers.

13. Maitrāyaṇīya Upanishad

Last comes the Maitrāyaṇīya or Maitri which furnishes us with the astronomical statement fixing the lower limit of the Upanishadic period at about 1900 B.C., as already explained. The Upanishad belongs to the Maitri S'ākhā of the Black Yajurveda. It has been published in the Bibliotheca Indica series with the commentary of Rāmakṛishṇa by Cowell. It is called Maitryupanishad also, as its teaching is that of Maitri, which word is derived by the commentator from Mitrā (मित्रायाः पुत्रः मैत्रिः). Indeed the Upanishad itself mentions in the beginning that the Vidyā was first taught by Maitri (इयं ब्रह्मविद्या राजन्नस्माकं भगवता मैत्रिणाख्याता). Maitrāyaṇīya seems to be a descendant of his and this Upanishad belongs to the Black Yajurveda.

The work is divided into seven Prapāṭhakas or lessons and the last two are known as Khila or appendices. The original portion, however, consists of the first four lessons. It begins with a discourse between king Bṛihardratha and the sage S'ākāyana who teaches the Brahman philosophy as it was taught by Maitri. He then recites a dialogue of old days between the Ṛishis called Vālakhilyas and the Prajāpati called Kratu. This dialogue ended originally with the fourth lesson; but in the present recension it is extended upto the 29th section of the sixth lesson, where S'ākāyana's discourse is shown to have ended with the usual caution "This knowledge should not be imparted to a sceptic" and so on (एतद्गुह्यतमं नापुत्राय नाशिष्याय कीर्तयेदनन्यभक्ताय सर्वगुणसम्पन्नाय दद्यात्). But the Upanishad again continues to the 38th section of this sixth chapter and a seventh chapter is added. Thus obviously there are three portions of this Upanishad ; the first consists of the old portion upto the fourth lesson, then an addition runs upto the 29th section of the sixth and thirdly there is a further addition to the end of the seventh. The astronomical statement appears in the second portion ; and the date furnished by it is about 1900 B. C. as we will again in detail show. As this Upanishad contains express words such as अथाह or 'so says' (a ṛishi) or अन्यत्राह or 'says a ṛishi else-where', quoting sentiments and even exact words* from other Upanishads like the Bṛihadaraṇyaka, Chhāndogya, Kena and others, we are sure that these oldest Upanishads must have been composed before 2000 B. C. The oldest portion of this Upanishad itself may be taken to be about 2000 B. C., the middle portion about 1900 B.C., and the latest addition may come to about 600 B.C. or a period preceding Buddha, to whom there is no reference in the Upanishad.

The following statements in the Upanishad are interesting :–

1. Ancient kings are mentioned in apparently two sets, viz. the solar and the lunar lines as given in the Purāṇas (सुद्युम्नभूरिद्युम्नेन्द्रद्युम्न-कुवलयाश्व-यौवनाश्व-वध्र्यश्वाश्वपति-शश-

*Such as य एष सम्प्रसादो (छां.), प्रतिपुरुषः क्षेत्रज्ञः य एष घोषं शृणोति (बृ.), मनोमयः प्राणशरीरो &c. (छां.), इंद्रियाणि हयाः रथः शरीरं (काठ.), अस्तीति ब्रुवता (कठ), खल्वयं सर्वं (छां.), अथ खलु स उद्गीथ &c., ऊर्ध्वमूलमवाक्शाखं &c. (कठ), प्राणः प्रजानामुदयत्येष सूर्यः (प्रश्न). It must be seen if there are extracts fom later Upanishads like श्वेताश्वतर.

बिन्दु-हरिश्चन्द्राम्बरीष-ननक्तुसर्यातिययात्यनरण्योक्षसेनादयः चक्रवर्तिनः, अथ मरुत्तभरतप्रभृतयो राजानः). 2. ध्रुवस्य चलनं दृष्टं shows advance of astronomical observation 3. The references to the Sānkhya theory af three guṇas are numerous: गुणमयेन पटेनात्मानमन्तर्धाय. This occurs in the second chapter and indicates even lateness for some ideas in the first portion. It can not be denied that the Sānkhya theory of guṇas is later than the chief old Upanishads as has already been shown. 4. नट इव क्षणवेषः and चित्रभित्ति show that acting and painting were known in those early days as also the ideas of the four Āśramas first noted in the Chhāndogya. 5. In the middle portion in 6-19 we have a reference to षडंगयोग, viz. प्राणायाम, प्रत्याहार, ध्यान, धारणा, तर्क and समाधि. This is different from the Yoga science expounded by Patañjali. There is no doubt that the study of the science of Yoga is as old as the ten Upanishads. There is even a reference to the pressing of the tongue against the roof of the mouth. तालुरसनाग्रनिपीडनात् (8-20). 5. यथार्द्रेन्धनाग्नेरभ्याहितस्य &c. महतो भूतस्य... ऋग्वेदो यजुर्वेद &c. is taken from the Chhāndogya (6-32) and mentions अथर्वाङ्गिरसः instead of अथर्ववेद but this is not strange. इतिहास and पुराण are mentioned here as usual. 6. शनिराहुकेतु mentioned in 6, 7 bring this last portion down to a very late period. 7. The idea of the triad ब्रह्मा, विष्णु and रुद्र seems to be already complete as their different functions are noted more than once. (रुद्रस्तामसोंऽशः ब्रह्मा राजसः विष्णुः सात्विकः V 2).

The following quotation, long though it is, shows that this last addition was made when there was an attack on the Vedic religion, probably Buddhist, though not necessarily, as Buddha is not directly mentioned, and as such attacks preceded even Buddha. ये चान्ये च पुरयाजका अयाज्ययाजका शूद्रशिष्या शूद्राश्च शास्त्रविद्वांसः अथ ये चान्ये चाटजटनटभटप्रव्रजितरङ्गावतारिणो राजकर्मणि पतितादयः अथ ये चान्येह यक्षराक्षसभूतगणपिशाचोरगग्रहादीनामर्थं पुरस्कृत्य शमयाम इत्येवं ब्रुवाणा अथ

ये चान्ये वृथाकषायाः कुण्डलिनः कापालिनः अथ ये चान्ये ह वृथातर्कदृष्टान्तकुहकेन्द्रजालैर्वैदिकेषु परिस्थातुमिच्छन्ति तैः सह न संवसेत् प्राकाश्यभृता वै ते तस्कराः अस्वर्ग्या इत्येवं ह्याह, नैरात्म्यवादकुहकैर्मिथ्यादृष्टान्तहेतुभिः। भ्राम्यन् लोको न जानाति वेदविद्यान्तरं तु यत् (7–8). So also बृहस्पतिः शुक्रो भूत्वाऽसुरेभ्यः क्षयायेमामविद्यामसृजत् and तस्माद्ब्राह्मणो नावैदिकमधीयीत. In this connection various S'lokas are quoted which do not belong to any Upanishads. They may be found in the Mahābhārata (e. g. मन एव मनुष्याणां कारणं बंधमोक्षयोः VI 34) though one is not sure. It can not, however, be decided which is the original source. The atmosphere of this Upanishad with its amplification of Sāṁkhya ideas and Yoga practises is the same as that of the Bhagavadgītā, which is, however, later and more methodical (e.g. प्रकृति, प्रधान, राजस, तामस, सात्विक, भूत, परमात्मा).

Lastly, the astronomical statement in the middle portion is as follows. Describing Kāla in detail, the Upanishad divides the year into two halves "एतस्याग्नेयमर्धमर्धं वारुणं मघाद्यं श्रविष्ठार्धमाग्नेयं क्रमेणोत्क्रमेण सार्पाद्यं श्रविष्ठार्धान्तं सौम्यं तत्रैकमात्मनो नवांशकाः &c. This plainly indicates that at this time the Zodiac had been divided into 27 equal parts allotted to the 27 Nakshatras. These equal parts, in modern language, would consist of $13\frac{1}{3}$ and the statement shows that the sun moved northwards at the middle point of S'ravishṭhā and ended his northern course at the beginning of Maghā. The Vedānga Jyotisha mentions that the sun moves northwards at the beginning of Dhanishṭhā and ends his northern course at the middle of Āśleshā. At the present day the reader will find from any Hindu calender that the sun turns northwards, in other words, Dec. 21 falls, when the sun is in the middle of Mūla. The present position of the winter solstice is thus nearly 4 Nakshatras or nearly 53° behind the Maitryupanishad position. Taking 72 years for each degree of precession, we have 53×72 or

3816 years between now and the Upanishad, which thus goes back to about 1900 B.C.

14. Later Upanishads.

Of these the Narāyaṇīya is the most important. It forms the tenth Araṇa ef the Taittirīya Āraṇyaka and is known to be a Khila or appendix. Its S'ānti-mantra is of course सह नाववतु &c. It is a very long Upanishad and is not divided into sub-sections though the Mantras are numbered 15 &c. It consists of verses except where sacrificial formulæ come in. These verses are taken mostly from the Saṁhitās. The familiar Sandhyā (संध्या) mantra स्तुतो मया &c. is found here. Herein are also found the popular त्रिसुपर्ण and मधुमती mantras. The Purāṇic deities are referred to and separate mantras for each imitating the Gayātri mantra are given (These deities are रुद्रो रुद्रश्च दन्तिश्च नन्दिः षण्मुख एव च । आदित्योऽग्निश्च दुर्गिश्च क्रमेण द्वादशाम्भसि ॥ गरुडो ब्रह्मा विष्णुश्च नारसिंहस्तथैव च ॥). The gotra of Gāyatrī is given as Sānkhāyana. तपो नानशनात्परम् and संवत्सराः परिवत्सराश्च ते अहर्गणाः is notable. Those who die in the Uttarāyaṇa go to the sun and those dying in the Dakshiṇāyana to the moon (84).

Next may be noted the Kaivalya which is a short Upanishad and is attached to the Black Yajurveda, its S'ānti being सह नाववतु. It is in the form of a dialogue between Āśvalāyana and Prajāpati. It is entirely in verse, there being only two Kāṇḍas of 24 (19+5) mantras in it. For Moksha it prescribes the Saṁnyāsa Āśrama and a Guru is prescribed 'in the S'rutis' (अन्त्याश्रमस्थः स्वगुरुं प्रणम्य). It is naturally devoted to S'iva worship (उमासहायं त्रिलोचनं नीलकण्ठं or शिवं ध्यात्वा). सर्वभूतस्थमात्मानं सर्वभूतानि चात्मनि is taken from the Gītā; as also वेदैश्च सर्वैरहमेव वेद्यः वेदान्तकृद्वेदविदेव चाहम् ॥ स्वमायया कल्पितजीवलोकम् and भोक्ता-भोग्य-भोग forming *trīpuṭī* are clearly modern.

The short Jābāla Upanishad is attached to the White Yajurveda. It is in prose and Yājnavalkya is naturally the teacher. It is also devoted to S'iva worship and teaches the Japa of the S'atarudriya. It prescribes Saṁnyāsa and living in deserted places (शून्यागारदेवगृहतृणकूटवल्मीक &c.; संन्यासेन देहत्यागं करोति स परमहंसः).

The Bṛihajjābāla is, however, a long Upanishad attached to the Atharvaveda, the S'ānti-mantra being भद्रं कर्णेभिः &c. It consists of eight parts called Brāhmaṇas and it is partly in verses and partly in prose. It is in the form of a conversation between भुसुण्ड and कालाग्निरुद्र and others on the merit of भस्मधारणा. The smearing of the body with ashes is a rite peculiar to the S'iva cult. The names of Bhasman are given as विभूतिर्भसितं भस्म क्षारं रक्षेति पंच नामानि भस्मनः। The Paramahaṁsas enumerated are संवर्तकारुणिश्वेतकेतुदुर्वासऋभुनिदाघजडभरतदत्तात्रेयरैवतकभुसुण्डप्रभृतयः. Those from Durvāsas onwards are Purāṇic names purely. The work treats only of the putting on of Bhasman and Rudrāksha.

The Jābālī Upanishad is attached to the Sāmaveda and its S'ānti-mantra is आप्यायन्तु ममाङ्गानि. It is in the form of a conversation between Jābāli and Paippalādi. It styles Jīva as Paśu and Īśa is properly Paśupati. It also treats of Bhasmadhāraṇā. In the Kalisantaraṇa is found the modern Mantra हरे राम हरे राम &c. Nārada is told by Brahman that sixteen names are saviours in the Kali age and their Japa to the number of three crores is prescribed. The Mahāvākyopanishad prescribes the Mantra असावादित्यो ब्रह्म. There are other Upanishads devoted to the worship of the Purāṇic gods such as Bahvṛichopanishad treating of Devī worship. The names of Devī are त्रिपुरसुंदरी, बालाम्बिका, बगला, मातङ्गी, तिरस्कारिणी, राजमातङ्गी, भुवनेश्वरी, वाराही, चामुण्डा, चण्डा &c. The Krishṇopanishad mentions Veṇu as Rudra and S'ankha as Vishnu; while Kṛishṇa is Brahman.

itself. उलूखल, रशना, अदिति, सुदामा, नारद and वृन्दा are also mentioned. We have a दत्तात्रेयोपनिषत्, a हयग्रीवोपनिषत् and others which need not be noticed here in detail.

The 108 Upanishads enumerated in the Muktikopanishad are as follows:– ऐतरेयकौषीतकिनादबिन्द्वात्मप्रबोधनिर्वाणमुद्गलाक्षमालिकात्रिपुरासौभाग्यबह्वृचानामृग्वेदगतानां दशसंख्याकानां वाङ्मे मनसीति शान्तिः ॥१ ईशावास्यबृहदारण्यजाबालहंसपरमहंससुबालमांत्रिकानिरालम्बत्रिशिखीब्राह्मणमण्डलब्राह्मणाद्वयतारकपैङ्गलभिक्षुतुरीयातीताध्यात्म्यतारसारयाज्ञवल्क्यशाट्यायनीमुक्तिकानां शुक्लयजुर्वेदगतानामेकोनविंशतिसंख्याकानां पूर्णमद इति शान्तिः ॥ २ कठवल्लीतैत्तिरीयकब्रह्मकैवल्यश्वेताश्वतरगर्भनारायणामृतबिन्द्वमृतनादकालाग्निरुद्रक्षुरिकासर्वसारशुकरहस्यतेजोबिन्दुध्यानबिन्दुब्रह्मविद्यायोगतत्त्वदक्षिणामूर्तिस्कन्दशारीरकयोगशिखैकाक्षराक्ष्यवधूतकठरुद्रहृदययोगकुण्डलिनीपञ्चब्रह्मप्राणाग्निहोत्रवराहकलिसन्तरणसरस्वतीरहस्यानां कृष्णयजुर्वेदगतानां द्वात्रिंशत्संख्याकानां सह नाववत्विति शान्तिः ॥ ३ केनछांदोग्यारुणिमैत्रायणिमैत्रेयीवज्रसूचिकायोगचूडामणिवासुदेवमहत्संन्यासवज्रकुण्डिकासावित्रीरुद्राक्षजाबालदर्शनजाबालीनां सामवेदगतानां षोडशसंख्याकानां आप्यायन्त्विति शान्तिः ॥ ४ प्रश्नमाण्डूक्यमुण्डकाथर्वशिरोथर्वशिखाबृहज्जाबालनृसिंहतापिनीनारदपरिव्राजकसीताशरभमहानारायणरामरहस्यरामतापनीशाण्डिल्यपरमहंसपरिव्राजकान्नपूर्णासूर्यात्मपाशुपतपरब्रह्मत्रिपुरतापनदेवीभावनाब्रह्मजाबालगणपतिमहावाक्यगोपालतापनकृष्णहयग्रीवदत्तात्रेयगारुडानामथर्ववेदगतानामेकत्रिंशत्सख्याकानां भद्रं कर्णेभिरिति शान्तिः ॥ ५

APPENDIX

1 Keith on the Rising of the Kṛittikās due east.

In his history of the religion and philosophy of the Vedas, Keith refers to the statement in the S'atapatha regarding the rising of the Kṛittikas due east and tries to brush it off in a cavalier fashion by observing "It is impossible to attach serious value to this assertion made in a passage which assigns *foolish* reasons for preferring one or other Nakshatra. We are in the same region of popular belief as when in the Sūtra literature the existence of Dhruva, a fixed Pole-star, is alleged" (p. 22). One may call it foolish for the Vedic sacrificers to say that fire should be consecrated when the moon is in the Kṛittikā Nakshatra, *because* that Nakshatra rises due east.* But how does this detract from the truth of the observation recorded in this reason ? It is illogical to argue that the observation is unreliable because it was foolish to give it as a reason.

There is some logicality in saying that the observation cannot be treated as absolutely correct because the Sūtra literature contains a similarly incorrect observation about the Pole-star treated as Dhruva or immovable. It must, however, be remembered that the star looked upon as Dhruva is fixed for all practical purposes, as it appears in the same place and region every night and does not move, as all other stars do, during the night

* But is it not equally foolish of the Romans that they should fix their Easter after a certain fullmoon and more foolish still of the Christians that they should even now keep Easter as a movable sacred day depending upon a full-moon instead of fixing it immovably in the Julian Calendar.

from east to west. The Dhruva observation, therefore, is correct practically though not absolutely. Similarly the observation of the Kṛittikās rising east cannot but be taken to be practically correct and even in this view it leads to a date much earlier than the date assigned to the S'atapatha by Keith and other European scholars. But there is a great difference between the Pole-star observation and the Kṛittikā observation. The east point can be very easily fixed with absolute correctness and was, we know, so fixed by the ancient peoples, Egyptians, Chaldeans and Vedic Aryans. The north point, on the other hand, in each lattiude, is difficult to fix in the sky with absolute correctness and hence the two observations cannot be treated on the same level. We have already shown how the Kṛittikā observation must be treated as absolutely correct, since the east point is easy to fix, and how it leads to a very ancient date for the S'atapatha.

It is not here suggested by Keith, as it has been by some scholars, that the Nakshatras themselves are not Vedic but borrowed from elsewhere. This argument has been advanced further on. At page 25, Keith remarks that the Nakshatras are foreign "because they are not mentioned in the Ṛigveda except in X 85 and that they are found only in the Taittirīya Saṁhitā and the Atharva Saṁhitā." But, as stated over again, the argument derived from non-mention is valueless. There may have been no occasion to mention the Nakshatras elsewhere in the Ṛigveda. But this mention in X 85 of the Ṛigveda is sufficient for our purposes as it shows conclusively that the Nakshatras were known before the Ṛigveda was compiled and that therefore their mention in the S'atapatha is not suspicious. But, further than this, we have shown that the Nakshatras cannot be foreign. They are found in China and

Arabia no doubt, but at a time when they may be taken to have been borrowed from India. Keith thinks that they must have been borrowed from Babylon; but he admits that there is no proof of their existence there. Moreover, if the Nakshatras came from Chaldaea, why did not the Rāśis also come from there, the Rāśis which are peculiarly Chaldean and which are not found in India till about 200 B.C. after the invasion of Alexander? Lastly, the Nakshatras have been mentioned in the Vedic literature at a time when they could not have come from outside. The rising of the Kṛittikās due east could not have been marked later than 2800 B.C. and as the precession of the equinoxes was not known in India till 600 A.D., no one could have made such a statement from inference. The statement in the S'atapatha is that of an actual observation and stands as a stumbling-block in the way of those who would assign a very late date to the Ṛigveda and the S'atapatha. The above-noted remark of Keith, therefore, strikes one as as hopeless and strange as the remark of Max Müller noted already in getting over the difficulty presented by the astronomical statement in the Vedānga Jyotisha, which also takes the Ṛigveda far behind the date Max Müller and Keith are inclined to assign.

II Keith's Dates for the Various Saṁhitās and Brāhmaṇas

Having thus summarily brushed aside the statement in S'atapatha, first brought to notice by S. B. Dixit, and withont having even mentioned the theory of B. G. Tilak based on the reference in the Ṛigveda to the vernal equinox being in Mṛigaśīrsha, propounded in his 'Orion', Keith tries to refute the argument advanced by Jacobi for placing the Ṛigveda in the third millenium

B. C., based on the mention of the vernal equinox in Phalgunī (R. X. 35, V, 13 &c.), as "of no value" in proving a date so early for the Ṛigveda. Keith holds that the Ṛigveda cannot be earlier than 1200 B. C., as the gāthās of Zoroaster and the hymns of the Ṛigveda are almost exactly the same and as the date of Zoroaster cannot be taken further back than this. The lowest date for other Vedic works are also assigned by him as follows. "The Upanishads undoubtedly precede Buddha, i.e. 480 B.C. The Brāhmaṇas precede the Upanishads and their lowest date is thus 600 B.C." Keith looks upon the Aitareya as the oldest Brāhmaṇa and the S'atapatha as the latest. "The Atharva-veda Saṁhitā and Yajurveda Saṁhitās precede the Brāhmaṇas and their lowest date may be taken as 800 B. C." The latest date for the Ṛigveda is, therefore, about 1000 B.C. The argument derived from the kingly dynasties given in the Purāṇas for placing the Ṛigveda in about 1200 B. C. is also noticed and dismissed as based on unreliable dynasties given in works unquestionably dated about 500 A.D.

These lowest limits for these works are undeniable, but they lead to nothing as to their actual probable dates; and further it is not possible to accept a century or two as the probable period intervening between the several works and chiefly between the Upanishads and Buddha. And the higher limit assumed, viz. 1200 B.C. for the Ṛigveda based on Zoroaster's date is open to grave objections. Many gāthās are no doubt exact counterparts of Vedic hymns and they were most probably composed at about the same time when Vedic Aryans and Iranians were together. But they may have preceded Zoroaster by thousands of years, being preserved intact by Parsi priests as Ṛigveda hymns have been preserved intact by Brahmins these five thousand years. Their date cannot, therefore, be the date of Zoroaster. Secondly, even Zoroaster can not be placed so late as 600 B.C. nor as 1000 B.C. It is really inexplicable how European scholars like Hertel and even Keith (who properly refutes Hertel's arguments by which he places Zoroaster a little before Darius) entirely ignore the statements of ancient Greek authors who are almost contemporaries (426 B.C.) and placed Zoroaster 6000 years before the invasion of Xerxes and Aristotle also placed him about the same period before Plato (Keith, ibid., p. 615). In the face of such ancient evidence it is impossible to place Zoroaster so late as 665 B.C. or even 1000 B.C. as held by Carpenter and R. C. Temple (J. R. A. S. 1926). As pointed out by Keith himself, no conclusion can be drawn from the non-mention in the gāthās of nature-gods worshipped by the Persians as described by Herodotus or of animal sacrifices or of the exposing of dead bodies to birds or beasts. It is admitted that the Medes who practised these rites were different from the Persians. The dissenting sect of Zoroastrian Persians may have long lingered before it was taken up by Darius and given royal support. Zoroastrians may have given up animal sacrifices long before Darius as the Upanishadic philosophers did so early as 2000 B.C. It can not, therefore, be argued that Zoroaster lived only a little before Darius nor about five or six centuries before him, as by ancient Greek tradition he is placed several thousand years before Darius. The date for the higher limit for the Ṛigveda, therefore, can not be taken to be only 1200 B.C.

Keith thinks that the separation of Iranians and Vedic Aryans can not be placed before 2000 B.C.; but no definite arguments are given for holding this view. Some of the Ṛigvedic hymns were composed beyond the Hindu-Kush when the two peoples were together; but many hymns were clearly composed in the Panjab and as the compilation of the Ṛigveda must be placed about 3100 B.C., the separation of the two branches must be placed earlier than 3100 B.C. The words Brahmadvish and Devanid in some hymns of the Ṛigveda may refer to the Zoroastrians or their predecessors who separated from the Vedic Aryans. The changed meaning of Deva among the two peoples and the changed meaning of Asura itself in the Ṛigveda also shows this. Many later hymns describing the Asuras as the enemies of Devas and as conquered by Devas and by Indra (pointed out by Keith himself) would point to the same conclusion. The Devanids can not, we think, be the Dravidians or the aboriginal Dāsas, as in one Ṛigvedic verse the three peoples have been distinctly and separately mentioned. यो नो दास आर्यो वा पुरुष्टुतादेव इन्द्र युधये चिकेतति mentions the Adevas as distinct from the Dāsas and the Aryans (Vedic people). The schism between Vedic Aryans and Iranians or Asuras *alias* Adevas must be placed before 3100 B.C. and it may be that Zoroaster may be the leader of the Iranians in this schism. But his name does not occur in any Ṛigvedic hymn; and it is likely that he was only a late teacher of that schism, especially as Asuras are spoken of in the Brāhmaṇas† as sacrificers. Some even consider

† The Chhāndogya speaks of the Asuras as decorating the bodies of their dead. The Zoroastrians have not this custom. It may, therefore, be suggested that Zoroaster's schism came later than the Chhāndogya or 2500 B. C. The Medes also are said to have exposed the bodies of their dead. But Herodotus, as stated above, does not speak of Persians as exposing the bodies of their dead to birds of prey and hence some Asuras must be taken to have the custom of decorating dead bodies like the Egyptians and the Assyrians and even the western Aryans.

Zoroaster and Vyāsa as contemporaries. We are not, however, concerned here with fixing the date of Zoroaster; our contention is that the gāthās may be more ancient than Zoroaster and that, therefore, the date of the Ṛigvedic compilation does not depend upon that of Zoroaster and that even the date of Zoroaster itself cannot be so late as 1000 B.C.

III. The Three Vaṁsas in the Bṛihadāraṇyaka.

These vaṁsas when studied carefully are inexplicable in many points. It is true that the name in the nominative is that of the pupil and that in the ablative is the name of the teacher. But names are sometimes repeated, the teacher's and the pupil's name being the same. Thus पौतिमाष्यो गौपवनाद्गौपवनः पौतिमाष्यात् (II 6). is strange. It may be suggested that the second पौतिमाष्य is another Ācharya oı the same name. In kingly dynasties, we have names repeated often and we distinguish them as George I and George II. This second Pautimāshya may be Pautimāshya I and his graud-pupil Pautimāshya II with whom the Vaṁśa starts. 2. शाण्डिल्यः कौशिकाच्च गौतमाच्च gives two names as teachers as च is used (and even twice as required). It must be understood that S'āṇḍilya learnt Vedānta doctrines from two teachers. But the Vaṁśa goes higher with Gautama only. 3. आनभिम्लातः आनभिम्लातात्. This is explicable only on the the supposition that the second is the father and bears the same name as it is a gotra name. 4. सैतवप्राचीनयोग्यौ again are two teachers or they are two brothers of the same name. 4. भारद्वाज and पाराशर्य ars next repeated. They must be different persons of the same gotra name. 5. Āsurāyaṇa and Yāska are two persons as noted above, but कैशोर्य काण्व is one person as च is not used here. So also are अयास्य आङ्गिरस, आभूति त्वाष्ट्र etc. The names now seem to be imaginary ending with परमेष्ठी, pupil of Brahman, which is swayambhu or uncreated, the first teacher.

The Vaṁśa at the end of the fourth chapter is the same as above with the exception that in section two new pupils are introduced from Āgniveśya, who is shown as a pupil of गार्ग्य, whose name is repeated. From कौशिकायनि the Vaṁśa is the same again upto the last, viz. Brahman.

The third Vaṁśa at the end of chapter VI presents an entirely different aspect. Instead of पौतिमाष्य and so on we have till the end of the section 2 पौतिमाषीपुत्र etc. Probably these are different persons altogether, पौतिमाषीपुत्र being sister's son of पौतिमाष्य. But why should these Vedānta philosophers be styled as their mother's sons? 2 The line of teachers from आसुरि is interesting as he is a pupil of याज्ञवल्क्य, he of उद्दालक, he of अरुण and so on. But here the line of teachers ends with Āditya, the sun, and not with Brahman (VI 3.) A second line of teachers is therefrom given in the next section commencing with the words समानमासाञ्जीवीपुत्रात् in which याज्ञवल्क्य is omitted and the line is taken to Brahman as in the other two Vaṁśas. The ṛishi तुरः कावषेयः is here mentioned as taught immedeiately by Prajāpati, taught by Brahman. Prajāpati here is the same as Parameshṭhin of the others.

Many of these names of teachers appear in the other Upanishads and they mostly seem to be real persons excepting some of the last names. Why these Vaṁśas should be given in the Brihadāraṇyaka alone is a riddle; it may be explained as showing the rigid traditions of the school of Yājnavalkya, the propounder of the White Yajurveda.

HISTORY
OF
SANSKRIT LITERATURE

Vol.3

VEDĀṄGAS &
BHAGAVADGĪTĀ

By

C.V.VAIDYA M.A., LL.B.
Author of Mahābhārata: a Criticism, Riddle of
the Rāmāyaṇa and Epic India; and
History of Mediaeval Hindu
India, in three Vols. etc. etc.

PARIMAL PUBLICATIONS
DELHI

Published by

Parimal Publications

Office : 27/28, Shakti Nagar, Delhi-110007 (India)
Retail Outlet : 22/3, Shakti Nagar, Delhi-110007 (India)
Ph. : +91-11-23845456, 47015168
e-mail : order@parimalpublication.com
url : http://www.parimalpublication.com

Edition : Year 2011

ISBN : 978-81-7110-047-7 (Set)
978-81-7110-050-7 (Vol. 3)

Price : ₹ 700.00 (Set of 3 Vols.)

Printed by

Vishal Kaushik Printers

Near G.T.B. Hospital, Jagat Puri Vistar,
Shahdara, Delhi-110093

SECTION III–VEDĀṄGAS

History of Sanskrit Literature

ŚRUTI PERIOD

Section III – VEDĀṄGAS

CONTENTS

HISTORY OF

SANSKRIT LITERATURE

S'RUTI PERIOD

SECTION III—VEDĀṄGAS

I INTRODUCTION

As in every other language, literature is originally religious, so also in Sanskrit the Vedas were the earliest literary works embodying the prayers, the sacrificial formulas and the psalms of the Indo-Aryan Vedic people They naturally soon became sacred utterances, so much so that every word and every ritual action acquired importance as securing merit not from their meaning but from their form. To utter a mantra exactly as the Ṛishis uttered it or to perform a sacrifice as the Ṛishis performed it or to sing a psalm in the very notes and modulations of the Ṛishis became the sine qua non for securing the favour of the gods and any mistake or change in them was productive of evil. The Āchāryas of the Brāhmaṇas, therefore, laid down many rules for the proper pronunciation of mantras and the proper performance of sacrifices. These rules became vastly more important when the progress of time changed the language of the Indo-Aryans, both in pronunciation and in grammar and sacrificial ritual developed by the addition of longer and higher sacrifices and of more complicated rites. These matters, therefore, had to be reduced to scientific precision in special works devoted to these subjects. It was thus natural that works were written on the proper pronunciation of Vedic mantras, on the proper performance of Vedic sacrifices and on the grammar of the Vedic language which had visibly changed in the course of a thousand years and owing to the extension of Aryan settlements into eastern and southern lands where new non-Aryan tribes were incorporated as Śudras. This explains how Śikshā, Kalpa and Vyākaraṇa became the subjects of new works on the topics of pronunciation, ritual and grammar.

The next necessary subject to be studied was vocabulary. Ancient Vedic words were going out of use or changing their meanings. The Vedic mantras were efficacious, no doubt, according to the reverent feelings of the Aryans, by their words and form and not by their meaning. But there were still generations which understood their meanings and they tried to indicate these meanings by the Pada-pāṭha, i. e. separat ing each word in the mantra and by fixing the meaning of obsolete words therein. Nighaṇṭu or what may be called in modern language Vedic vocabulary was thus needed. So also was needed a method of interpreting the Vedic sentences by explaining the nature of Vedic gods and the ideas involved in the Vedic hymns. How the names of gods were to be explained and how the names of objects or words arose was also naturally studied. The result was the development of a fourth Vedāṅga or subsidiary subject of study in connection with the Vedas, viz. Nirukta which tried to explain the meaning of Vedic words and mantras.

Along with this came the study of metres naturally enough. The Vedic hymns were in different metres. In the progress of time, Vedic metres which were somewhat rough and untūtored changed into more polished and regulated ones. The study of old Vedic metres was, therefore, necessary, as the mantras could not be changed and must be recited as the Ṛishis had composed them. Different metres again were supposed to be pleasing to different gods as the Āchāryas had said that Gāyatrī was pleasing to Agni, Trishṭubh to Indra, Jagatī to Varuna and the Viśvedevas and so on. The Vedic metres were, therefore, carefully studied; their supposed irregularities were explained and accounted for, and modern metres were compared with them.

Thus arose the fifth Vedāṅga, viz. Chhandas or prosody.

Lastly came the most important and scientific of all the Vedāṅgas namely Jyotisha or astronomy. Vedic sacrifices were to be performed not only daily, morning and evening, but the more important ones were to be performed on the full moon and new moon days. Some ritual was prescribed on certain Nakshatras; for with the Vedic Aryans not only the sun and the moon but the constellations also were very important. In their ancient home about the polar regions, the sun was invisible for months together; and time could be watched and measured by the progress of the moon among the constellations which were visible throughout the time (night and day being one long night lasting for two or three months) and the moon must have been, therefore, carefully watched. It is thus why with the Vedic Aryans, the Nakshatras, i. e. the positions of the moon among the constellations, naturally taken to be 27 by the moon's making a round of them in 27 days, were so important. Certain ceremonies were, therefore, fixed for certain Nakshatras such as Punarvasu, Hasta, Chitrā and so on. Again certain sacrifices were to be performed on the Vishuvan day, the day on which the sun is in the middle of its southern and northern travel Astronomy, therefore, was naturally studied and astronomical phenomena being regular and unchanging, the intelligent Vedic Aryans found out the laws regulating them and evolved rules for calculating the positions of the sun and the moon at any future time, so that full moons and new moons, Tithis and Nakshtras, Vishuvans and seasons which depended upon the sun's course northward and southward, could be predicted. The great advance in astronomical knowledge disclosed by the Vedāṅga Jyotīsha need not, therefore, be wondered at, as it was the result of a necessary study of the stars and the sun and the moon made for nearly two or even three thousand years. This Vedāṅga must necessarily have been preceded by a good knowledge of Arithmetic and the rule of three, called together राशिविद्या, mentioned in the Chhāndogya Upanishad.

These six Vedāṅgas or subjects of study ancillary to the Vedas are enumerated already in an Upanishad noted before as शिक्षा, कल्प, व्याकरण, छन्दः, निरुक्त and ज्योतिष. The word aṅga may even be taken to mean limb, as Chhandas is looked upon as the feet of Veda, Kalpa as its hands, Jyotisha as its eyes, Nirukta as its ears, Śikshā as its nose and Vyākaraṇa as its mouth : छन्दः पादौ तु वेदस्य हस्तौ कल्पोऽथ पठ्यते । ज्योतिषामयनं चक्षुर्निरुक्तं श्रोत्रमुच्यते । शिक्षा घ्राणं तु वेदस्य मुखं व्याकरणं स्मृतम् ॥ (पाणिनीय शिक्षा). These subjects must have been long studied before the works now recognised as Vedāṅgas were composed. For many teachers are mentioned not only in these works, but in the several Brāhmaṇas and Āraṇyakas. Whether these teachers had composed any works or not, we do not definitely know; but as the Mahābhārata mentions a Sūtrakāra Śākalya whose work on grammar we do not now possess, such works must have existed once though they have now disappeared. We must assign to these works dates ranging between 1900 and 800 B. C., the latter being the date of Pāṇini whose अष्टाध्यायी is the recognised Vedāṅga on grammar, disclosing as it does the highest development of that subject. We have already shown how our date for Pāṇini is vastly different from the date assigned to him by European scholars and how consequently the whole range of Vedic literature is dated by them much later than we date it. The date of Pāṇini is the sheet anchor, so to speak, in the history of Vedic literature and it will be discussed at length in a special note. If the date of Pāṇini is taken to be 800 B.C. as we do, the other Vedāṅga literature which unquestionably preceded Pāṇini may be placed between about 1900 B.C., the date of Maitryupanishad, and 800 B.C.

This literature, with the exception perhaps of the Kalpasūtras detailing many Vedic sacrifices in which the modern world including India has lost all interest, is of very great value. Language was so thoroughly studied by these ancient Āchāryas that the rules which govern the natural formation of words and grammatical forms discovered by them still serve as a guide to the study of modern languages. Grammar and etymology especially were scrutinized in a manner in which no nation of the world, ancient or modern, has yet done. The unassailable edifice of grammar which Pāṇini has built and into and from which not a word or letter can be put or taken out is indeed a worderful work in the literatute of the world. Even the Kalpasūtras disclose the logical intellect of the Indo-Aryans who have laid down maxims for the interpretation of revealed works, maxims which laid the foundation, later, of the Pūrva Mimāṁsā Śāstra, maxims which can guide lawyers even in modern times in the interpretation of codified law.

II S'IKSHA

This Vedāṅga relates to the proper pronunciation of Vedic mantras. The work now recognised as the Vedāṅga by the reciters of Ṛigveda, Yajurveda and Sāmaveda is a short book of about 60 verses divided into 11 sections. It is certainly a late work, later than Pāṇini whose teaching, it declares in the very beginning, it follows. It applies to both Sanskrit and Prakrit which also proves that it is later than Pāṇini. Pāṇini is said herein to be Dākshīputra. It treats of letters and accents and the method of pronouncing them. The arrangement of letters according to their Sthāna is perfect and shows the highest advancement of the science of phonetics. The science is supposed to have been taught by god Śiva to Pāṇini.

There are several references to Śikshā in Vedic works; but a complete work on this subject was not composed by any one and hence this work by an unnamed author became the recognised Vedāṅga on Śikshā. It may be dated about 300 B. C. and does not really belong to the Vedic period. Other Śikshās are known and there are several Prātiśākhyas but they are all probably later than Pāṇini and need not be treated of here.

III CHHANDAS

The same thing may be said about the work on Chhandas recognised as Vedāṅga by all the Vaidikas. It is attributed to Piṅgala who may have lived about 300 B. C. It treats of both Vedic and classical metres. It opens with the *abcd* of this science, viz. म, य, र, स, त, ज, भ, न, ल, ग, the names of the gaṇas adopted to secure the utmost brevity in giving the definitions of classical (लौकिक) metres. But these gaṇas have no application to Vedic metres; and it is somewhat absurd to begin the treatise with this string of letters. Vedic metres, like Śikshā, have been defined in several places in Vedic works and, as stated already, the names of the seven chief metres are found mentioned even in Ṛigvedic hymns. This is, however, perhaps the first work solely devoted to the subject of Vedic and classical prosody and has consequently been adopted as the Vedāṅga on the subject. The author probably is a follower of Piṅgala, called पिंगलनाग in the very first verse, whose intellect was chastened by the favour of Śiva like that of Pāṇini.

IV KALPASŪTRAS

The extant Kalpasūtras must have been preceded by others, now not existing. Sūtras are mentioned as early as the Bṛihadāraṇyaka Upanishad as subjects of study. And for the performance of elaborate sacrifices manuals, short and decisive, must have been found necessary at a very early age, as the procedure described in the Brāhmaṇas is desultory and as discussions are often given therein without decisions. Moreover, different schools soon sprang up, adopting different ritual and the four Vedas also soon led to four main schools. Though in the performance of the principal sacrifices, all the Vedas were required to be used, the Hotṛi using the Ṛigveda, the Udgātṛi the Sāmaveda, the Adhvaryu the Yajurveda and the Brahman or presiding priest all the three and latterly Atharvaveda particularly, still each Veda later on provided for all requirements by including the necessary mantras in its Brāhmaṇas and especially its Āraṇyakas. Hence the Sūtras also, like these works, attached themselves to the several Vedas and laid down their distinctive procedure. They were thus considered as an Aṅga or limb of that Veda along with other Aṅgas. The older Sūtras mentioned in the Bṛihadāraṇyaka disappeared, both because better Sūtras subsequently arose and because ritual also developed further. The extant Kalpasūtras which are recognised as Aṅgas of the four Vedas are as follows :-1 Āśvalāyana and 2 Sāṅkhāyana of the Ṛigveda; 3 Maśaka, 4 Lāṭyāyana and 5 Drāhyāyaṇa of the Sāmaveda, 6 Mānava, 7 Baudhāyana, 8 Bhāradvāja, 9 Āpastamba and 10 Hiraṇyakeśin also called Satyāshāḍha of the Black Yajurveda, 11 Kātyāyana of the White Yajurveda and 12 Kauśika and 13 Vaitāna of the Atharvaveda.

These Śrauta Sūtras relate to the Śrauta sacrifices performed on the higher fires with the help of one or more priests. But there were many sacrifices and ceremonies of a domestic nature which were to be performed by the householder himself without the aid of any priests and on the Gṛihya fire. For these, manuals subsequently arose called Gṛihya Sūtras. These Sūtras usually bear the same name as the above but their authors were without doubt not the same. They have the same names because they belong to the same school; or perhaps because their authors were born in the same gotra. Thus the author of Āśvalāyana Gṛihya Sūtra can not be the same as the author of the Āśvalāyana Śrauta Sūtra, though he poses as such in the very first sūtra of his Gṛihya work. Indeed that Gṛihya Sūtra was composed centuries after the latter as will presently appear. The Gṛihya Sūtras, according to our view, do not fall in the

Śruti period as defined by us. Their language is distinctly later. 'The literary development of the Śrauta Sūtras is earlier than that of the Gṛihya Sūtras' (Keith p. 26).* 'The language of the former is not yet classical Sanskrit and is distinctly pre-Pāṇinian' (ibid). Even according to Keith thus they are to be placed before Pāṇini. Keith places them about 400 B. C., Pāṇini according to him dating about 300 B.C. But, as will be shown later on, Pāṇini can not be placed later than 800 B. C., and these Kalpasūtras can not be later than 1000 B. C. It is difficult to determine their earlier limit. They are unquestionably later than the Upanishads and hence can not be earlier than 1900 B.C. We may, therefore, take the Śrauta Sūtras as falling between 1900 and 1000 B. C., i. e. in the third part of the Śruti period. There are one or two other indications of this early age of these Sūtras. They nowhere mention idols of Vedic gods or idol worship. Idol worship is mentioned in Pāṇini. Secondly they still stick to animal sacrifices which subse-

* Garbe observes that the style of Apastamba in the Gṛihya is much more concise than in the Śrauta (p. XVII, Vol. III). The same thing may be said of Aśvalāyana. The authors of these two Gṛihyas, therefore, must be different from Apastamba and Aśvalāyana, the authors of Śrauta Sūtras. It may also be noted that for Sāmaveda the authors of Gṛihya Sūtras are different from those of the Śrauta, viz. Jaimini, Gobhila and Khadira; and for the White Yajurveda, the author of the Gṛihya Sūtra is Pāraskara and not Kātyāyana.

quently became unpopular. The first indication, however, is not decisive, as non-mention is no evidence and as mention of idols is not necessary in treatises which treat of Śrauta sacrifices solely.

The word Kalpa means procedure or formula (प्रयोग) and in this sense frequently occurs in the Kalpasūtras themselves (Āpastamba VI 18, 11 e.g.). It is used in medicine also in the same sense, viz. formula of a medical preparation. As meaning a work on sacrificial procedure, the word is used in the Muṇḍaka Upanishad and also, as we know, in Pāṇini. His sūtra पुराणप्रोक्तेषु ब्राह्मणकल्पेषु shows that he knew of old and new Kalpas. The old Kalpas are probably all lost. They were probably not called Sūtras. This word is also old; but it originally meant a work with a continuous thread. The idea of brevity was subsequently developed. The earlier Kalpas must not have been as concise and short as the later ones are. This index may be used for fixing the relative priority of the extant Kalpasūtras, though it is not a decisive one. It can not be believed that these Sūtras were composed in opposition to Buddhism in support of animal sacrifices as Dr. Macdonell thinks (p. 145). It is more proper to suppose that the codification of the ritual of animal sacrifices took place long before Buddha arose and thus gave occasion for the rise of his philoosophy. The philosophy of sacrifice arose after Buddha and was embodied by Jaimini in his Pūrva

Mīmāṁsā Sūtras based on all the Kalpasūtras. Even the Dharmasūtras which are later than the Śrauta Sūtras preceded Buddha and even Pāṇini and also Yāska who, as mentioned by Macdonell himself, quotes maxims from some Dharmasūtras. These like the Gṛihya Sūtras now form part of Kalpasūtras no doubt, but are later additions. Thus Āpastamba Dharmasūtra, treated as the oldest by Macdonell, forms the 28th and 29th chapters of the Āpastamba Kalpasūtra, the 26th and 27th chapters forming the Gṛihyasūtra. The Śrauta Sūtras, however, form admittedly the earliest portions and we shall treat only of these in this section.

Note :–Detailed description of the extant Kalpasūtras

I Āpastamba

This Kalpasūtra seems to be the oldest of those we possess. It belongs to the Taittirīya S'ākhā of the Black Yajurveda which is also the oldest S'ākhā of that Veda. As Yajurveda is chiefly concerned with sacrifice, it is but natural that the Taittirīyins should first set about to lay down a Kalpasūtra for their S'ākhā. This S'ākhā is now chiefly found in Andhra.

The language of Āpastamba's Sūtra is simple and the sūtras are not enigmatic and difficult of understanding as Pāṇinīya and other sūtras, conspicuous for their brevity, are. According to most scholars, the Gṛihyasūtra which forms the 26th and 27th chapters of this Kalpa is less simple and belongs in our view to a different author. The S'rauta portion of which we speak here consists of 25 chapters, called Praśnas, a new name for chapter and each Praśna consists of several sub-sections called Kaṇḍikās, each Kaṇḍikā containing, on an average, about 13 sūtras, there being about 7590 sūtras in the 588 Kaṇḍikās of the 25 Praśnas.

This work has been edited in the Bibliotheca Indica series by Garbe in three parts. It speaks indeed volumes of the great labour the editor has taken, that he has traced all the quotations in it to their respective origins in the Saṁhitās and Brāhmaṇas and has given lists of these references. There are many quotations from the Ṛigveda taken bodily and also from its Kaushītaki Brāhmaṇa. There are very few quotations from the Sāmaveda; but "quotations from its Pañchaviṁśa Brāhmaṇa are copious especially in the Ahīna and Sattra sections". Twenty-five quotations are taken from the Atharvaveda; but as they are a little different from those in the S'aunaka recension, they probably belong to the Pippalāda one. Many Brāhmaṇas, not extant now, are quoted by name viz. Kankati, Kālabavi, S'āṭyāyani, S'aitali and Bhāllavika. Kalingāyanika is a name not found elsewhere. It is remarkable that Aitareya is not mentioned nor Kaushitaki of the Ṛigveda; but the word Bahvṛicha is often used for them. The Vājasaneyakam is also frequently mentioned and we think that the reference is to the S'atapatha; and one is justified in inferring that the Kātyāyanasūtra of the White Yajurveda had not yet been written, as Vājasaneya procedure is noticed here. The name S'atapatha also appears to be later than the Āpastamba Sūtra. We have already seen that the name Shashṭipatha was once current. When a Brāhmaṇa is quoted without name, the words इति विज्ञायते are used as also यथा ब्राह्मणम्, यथा समाम्नातं or यथा वदति. Very probably the Taittirīya Brāhmaṇa or Āraṇyaka is there meant, not a S'rautasūtra according to our view; but Garbe thinks that the Pravarādhyāya is taken from Āśvalāyana S'rautasūtra. We will discuss the question whether they both give independently what was common matter or whether one copies from the other, when we shall speak of Āśvalāyana. Several teachers are mentioned by name, e.g. Āśmarathya and Ālekhana; but they are probably not authors of Sūtras, but are two savants of opposite views. There is a commentary on this work by Rudradatta which extends only to fifteen Praśnas as published by Garbe.

The work treats of all S'rauta sacrifices, from the lowest Darśapūrṇamāsa to the highest Aśvamedha and Purushamedha, in all their details. The procedure is laid down in detail and every action is described in words which, as Brahmin sacrificers even now do, have to be repeated while doing the acts indicated. This method has enabled the several actions in al. rituals to be fixed without any change or omission. Mantras accompany every action which are either taken from Saṁhitās or Brāhmaṇas or are newly prescribed by this Sūtra, as suitable mantras were not found in the former. Elaborate preparations are necessary for every S'rauta sacrifice. A separate sacrificial shed (यज्ञशाला) has to be put up; every action connected with it such as the bringing of wood and of earth &c., the laying of the altars as well as the finding out of the required gold is described and has to be performed with certain mantras. One thus understands the propriety of the descriptions in the Rāmāyaṇa and the Mahābhārata of the preparations for As'vamedha, including the excursion into the Himalayas for obtaining gold and the performance of ceremonies there before searching for it (V. 2, 1). It seems that gold was then obtainable in the rivers issuing from the Himalayas and anybody could gather it. There could be no higher sacrifice without a sufficient quantity of gold, as in the Dakshiṇās, gold or हिरण्य alias सुवर्ण is always prescribed by शतमान or hundred measures or at least thirty (त्रिंशन्मानं V 21, 10). It is also prescribed that Māna meant the usual weight of gold (येन हिरण्यं मिमीते). This shows that there were no gold coins in use then but packets of gold-dust weighing a fixed amount: and these were called Nishkas.

The different officiating priests were to get different Dakshiṇās, but generally all were to get clothes, one pair of bovine animals and a new chariot. (वासो मिथुनं गावौ नवं च रथं ददाति साधारणानि सर्वेषाम् ५।२०।११). More may be given, even six-fold and twelve-fold. But the condition of a poor sacrificer is also provided for and one cow only is prescribed for him. The mention of a new chariot is remarkable: whether with or without animals, horses, bullocks or mules is not mentioned. The craft of making chariots seems to have flourished as we shall presently see.

These S'rauta sacrifices could be performed by all the three Aryan castes or Varṇas viz. Brahmins, Kshatriyas and Vaiśyas and a fourth class of Rathakāras is usually mentioned. But it seems from V 3, 19 that they belonged to any of the three Varṇas and the commentator adds the explanation that an Aryan took up this profession for poverty. And as no other mixed-caste man is mentioned, it is almost certain that at the date of this Sūtra, mixed castes had not arisen and the progeny of mixed marriages among the Varnas belonged to the Varṇa of the father according to the old rule mentioned in Manu. This indicates a very early date for this Sūtra.

S'ūdras were not only not allowed to perform these sacrificec, but also were prohibited from even milking the cows for sacrifice. Further on, in particular cases, permission is given to employ a S'udra in milking (VI 3, 12); a S'ūdra, however, was permitted to grind the corn (पत्न्यवहन्ति शूद्रा पिनष्टि I 21, 9). It is further to be remarked that different mantras were prescribed in case of particular sacrifices for Brahmins, Kshatriyas and Vaiśyas, thus emphasizing caste distinctions. For Agnihotra, however, they were all eligible and no difference of mantras is to be seen. In a ceremony in V 11, 7 Rājan is distinguished from Rājanya showing that ruling kings were distinguished from ordinary Kshatriyas, and were called Rājaputras, a word appearing in the S'atapatha even. The word Asura in V 12 can not mean a Persian but must mean an imaginary terribly strong being (असुर इव पुरुषः स्यात्). A Gāyatrī-metred mantra is for Brahmins, a Traishtubha for Kshatriyas and a Jāgata for Vaiśyas.

The usual prayer of the sacrificer was for cattle (पशु) progeny (प्रजा) and food and wealth (अन्न and र)–रायस्पोषाय

सुप्रजास्त्वाय सुवीर्यायेति तेष्वग्निहोत्रम्. The wife's presence at sacrifice was always necessary and this shows the importance attached to the wife. The householder in beginning the ceremony of Ādhāna had first to shave and bathe and put on a silken cloth. The wife had to get her nails cut and to bathe and put on also a silken Sārī (क्षौमे वसानौ). During the period of the sacrifice, they had to remain celebate and eat no flesh. Departure was allowed, however, at certain times and under particular conditions. Among desires, ग्रामकाम is mentioned, which probably meant the gift of a village in inam or headship of a village. For glory or यशस्, flesh oblations are prescribed and for spiritual power, Soma oblations (मांसेन यशःकामस्य, सोमेन ब्रह्मवर्चसकामस्य IV 15, i).

In higher sacrifices there were elected 16 priests, four in each branch and named as follows. In the Adhvaryu (oblation) branch, 1 Adhvaryu, 2 Pratipṛasthātṛi, 3 Neshṭṛi and 4 Unnetṛi. In the Brahman (supervisor) branch, 1 Brahman, 2 Brāhmaṇāchchhaṁsin, 3 Agnīdhra and 4 Potṛi. In the Hotṛi (reciter of hymns) branch, 1 Hotṛi, 2 Maitrāvaruṇa, 3 Achchhāvāka and 4 Grāvastuta. And in the Udgātṛi (singing) branch, 1 Udgātṛi 2 Prastotṛi, 3 Pratihartṛi and 4 Subrahmaṇya (X 1-9). The Kaushītakins, it is stated, added a seventeenth priest called Sadasya; but no Upadeshṭṛi was needed. Where only four priests were to be chosen, they were of course the first four in each branch, viz., Adhvaryu, Hotṛi, Udgātṛi and Brahman. The priests were chosen with great formality and special mantras are prescribed for their election (X, 1, 14).

The contents of this Sūtra, are as follows :- (Garbe's preface to Vols. II and III).

Praśna

1-4 Darśapurṇamāsa with Yājamāna in K 4

5 Agnyādheya with Punarādheya in K 26-29

6 Agnihotra with Agnyupasthāna in K 16-23
7 Nirūḍhapaśubandha
8 Chāturmāsya with वैश्वदेव (1-4), वरुणप्रघास (5-8), साकमेध (9-19), शुनासीरीय (20-22)
9 Prāyaśchitta
10-13 Agnishṭoma (प्रातःसवन 10-12, माध्यंदिनसवन 13, 1-8 and तृतीयसवन 13-9-25)
14 उक्थ्य, षोडशिन्, अतिरात्र, अप्तोर्याम, ऐकादशीन (1-12) and चातुर्होत्र, पंचहोत्र, षड्ढोत्र, सप्तहोत्र &c. (13-15) and प्रायश्चित्त
15 Pravargya
16-17 अग्निचयन
18 वाजपेय (1-7), राजसूय 8-22
19 Sautrāmaṇī with कंकति and वैश्वसृज, काम्य पशु, काम्य इष्टि
20 Aśvamedha in 1-23 and Purushamedha in 24-25
21 Gavāmayana, Utsargiṇāmayana, Dvādaśāha
22 एकाहाः, अहीनाः, सत्राः
23 सत्राणि
24 Paribhāshāḥ, Pravarāḥ and Hautrakāḥ.

After these general observations, we will notice important statements in the several chapters in their order. In the first Praśṇa, Darśa-Pūrṇamāsa sacrifice begins with releasing of sacrificial cows in the morning with suitable mantras and these are new Anushṭup verses given here. There was always a fear of Asuras and Rākshasas interfering with sacrifices at every step and mantras were recited for killing them, accompanied by suitable actions (अपहता असुरा रक्षांसि वेदिषद; these are supposed to sit about the Vedi). Then there is performed first a sacrifice to the manes called पिण्ड-पितृ-यज्ञ which is like an ordinary S'rāddha with अञ्जन and अभ्यञ्जन of the Piṇḍas. The Bhṛigus and Āngirasas were the oldest Vedic sacrificers and they are praised on this occasion. Vrīhi and Taṇḍula are words which occur, it appears, for the first time in these Sūtras, meaning grain separated from the husk and thus applying usually to rice. What is आतश्चन does not seem clear. त्रयो वै गतश्रियः शुश्रुवान्, ग्रामणीः, राजन्यः is remarkable, गतश्री meaning प्राप्तश्रीः. The process of sowing grain, of milking cows, of unhusking corn in उलूखल &c, is strangely enough done religiously, being performed with suitable mantras for each act. Whatever falls on the ground is for रक्षः and these and enemies (अमित्राः) are constantly driven away. Probably, in early Aryan settlements enemies and cannibals actually interfered with the Aryan sacrifices; but in the times of the Kalpasūtras, these had become imaginary beings. The Abhichāra or magic action is always levelled against them and against Sapatnas and Bhrātṛivyas, the phrase योऽस्मान् द्वेष्टि यं च वयं द्विष्मः constantly occurring, showing that these Taittirīyins were very strong in their feelings of hatred.

Having described दर्शपूर्णमास in I, II, III and Yājamana in IV, in V we have Agnyādhāna and Punarādhāna, the Nakshatras for the first being कृ. रो. मृ. पुन. पु. and उ. ह. चि. (only for Kshatriyas) वि; and for the latter पुनर्वसू. Phalguni Pūrṇamāsī is declared to usher in the new year. For seasons वसन्तो ब्राह्मणस्य, ग्रीष्मो राजन्यस्य, हेमन्तो शरद्वा वैश्यस्य, वर्षा रथकारस्य. (The commentator shows here that the new rule मीनमेषयोर्वसन्तः is not to be taken here but फाल्गुनचैत्रयोः, and the months may be चान्द्र or सौर. In the Vājasaneyaka, अश्वमेध is begun in वसन्त only, while सत्याषाढ and आश्वलायन give different times). They had to go out and build a shed according to S'ālīna, but not according to Yāyāvara. The erection of sheds is described in detail, with a shed for guests to the east. The trees for sacrifice or for building a sacrificial shed are mentioned as अश्वत्थ, उदुम्बर, पर्ण, शमी, विकंकत, अशनिहत and पुष्करपर्ण.

In VI one is surprised (in 18, 3) to find Agni as lord of the east, Indra of the south, Soma of the west,

Mitrāvaruṇan of the north and Bṛihaspati of the direction above (ऊर्ध्वन्). Rik-Mantras are named by their authors as वात्सप्र, गोषूक्त, आश्वसूक्त. &c. The householder is to sacrifice with श्यामाक in वर्षाः, with व्रीहि in शरत्, with यव in वसन्त, (यथर्तु वेति VI 3, 14). This indicates the seasons and their corns in the middle land (मध्यदेश) of India. The आग्रयणेष्टि is described at the end.

Praśna VII relates to पशुबन्ध or animal sacrifice which secures all heavens to the sacrificer!!! (सर्वान् लोकान् पशुबन्धयाज्यभिजयति (1, 1). The Sambhāras include गुल्गुलु, सुगन्धितेजन, श्वेता ऊर्णास्तुका and among vessels and instruments हृदयशूल, असि, कुम्भी &c. (स्फ्यमग्निहोत्रहवणीं वसाहोमहवनीं द्वितीयां जुहू पृषदाज्यधानीं द्वितीयामुपभृतं द्वे आज्यस्थाल्यौ हृदयशूलमसिं कुम्भीं प्लक्षशाखां शाकपवित्रं काश्मर्यमय्यौ वपाश्रपण्यौ द्विशूलां एकशूलां औदुम्बरं मैत्रावरुणदण्डं आस्यदघ्नं चुबुकदघ्नं वा रशने च VII 8, 3). The animal selected should not be काण, खण्ड, वण्ड, श्लोण, छिन्नपुच्छ, पङ्गु &c. An अवट (pit) is to be dug for receiving refuse and ऊवध्यगोह is mentioned for covering ऊवध्य (उदरगत अशुद्ध). तस्मिन्संज्ञपयन्ति प्रत्यक्शिरसमुदीचीनपादम्. (Com. explains संज्ञपन as अक्षतस्य मारणम्). यत्र यंति सुकृतो नापि दुष्कृतस्तत्र त्वा देवः सविता दधातु etc. इत्युक्त्वा पराङावर्तते यजमानः (VII 16, 7). निर्दग्धं रक्षो निर्दग्धा अरातयः is also pronounced. The division of the animal's body among oblations to gods and gifts to priests is clearly laid down. The शमितृ or cutter is a Brahmin; but if he is not, he gives his portion (VII 27, 13) to a Brahmin.

Praśna VIII describes the Avabhṛitha. It is to be taken in any direction; but not in the north in the view of some teachers (VIII 7, 18), why it is not clear. The Chāturmāsya sacrifices of which we have already spoken viz. वैश्वदेव, वरुणप्रघास and साकमेध in the three seasons follow.

The same chapter gives particulars about mantras and Sāmans to be recited at the morning, noon and evening Savanas. Many names are new to us, like विहार, महाबालभित्. The प्रतिगर, ओथामो दैवोम् is lengthened in different ways. Sampāta, Kadvanta and Kuntāpa Sūktas are to be recited in पृष्ठ, षळह &c. गौराषु is a new term. The Sāmans with their Yonis are detailed for each day and many details are given which it is difficult to grasp for a layman.

Praśna IX gives the Prāyaśchittas and begins with the well-known dictum विध्यपराधे प्रायश्चित्तं (श्रुतिलक्षणं विधीयते). They are जपो होम इज्या च (3); निहते दोषे पुनः कृत्स्नं कर्म. The faults include cows not giving milk for sacrifice or the wife's being in courses &c. or when insects fall into oblations or fire goes out or is not created in churning (then sacrifice is allowed on the palm of a Brahmin's hand or in Darbhas or in water), if the Sun or Moon rises before आहुति or the oblation milk fall out of hand, if Agnihotra is broken or one of the fires (स्तोत्रे शस्त्रे वा मृढे)

The tenth Praśna is very interesting and gives details of the Soma sacrifice, the basis of Agnishṭoma (सोमेन यक्ष्यमाणो ब्राह्मणानार्षेयान्वृणीते यूनान् स्थविरान्वानूचानानूर्ध्ववाचोनङ्गहीनान्) in which only young learned Brahmins of the same Pravara are to be elected as provided for in the Chhāndogya Brāhmaṇa. This is mentioned for the first time here, because the Soma sacrifice is chiefly accompanied by Sāma-singing. The sacrifice is identified with the universe, the Agni being looked upon as the Hotṛi, the Sun as Adhvaryu, the Moon as Brahman, Rain as Udgātṛi, the Ākāśa as Sadasya and sun's rays as चमसाध्वर्यव. Soma is also performed in Jyotishṭoma, Atirātra and other higher sacrifices. A Devayajana (देवयजन) or sacrificial ground is to be obtained from the king outside the town and a sacrificial shed is to be erected thereon. Every detail is prescribed with the special mantras for it, the erecting of प्राग्वंश, the keeping of doors on four sides, even the corners. The sacrificer is then ordained with several ceremonies as also his wife. They bathe and put on new silken garments; the wife has कुंबकरीर on the head and the sacrificer puts on a turban. After taking food they go to the यज्ञशाला reciting the Vedas (ऋक्, साम, यजूंषि is the order here given and Atharvaveda is not mentioned–ऋचस्त्वा दीक्षमाणमनुदीक्षन्ताम् । साम... । यजूंषि... X 11, 1). The Dīkshā is born of Brahman or Veda and hence when the sacrificer is ordained for Soma, even the Rājanya or Vaiśya is to be treated as a Brahmin (तस्माद्राजन्यवैश्यावेव ब्राह्मण इत्यावेदयेत X 11, 6). He enters upon a strict course of life. He should not speak with any woman or S'ūdra; should not spit or sneeze or vomit; and if he does by chance, special mantras are to be recited. (सूद्दान=नासास्रुतश्लेष्मादि is also to be avoided or atoned for). He is to eat only हविःशेष (दुग्ध for a Brahmin, यवागू for a Rājanya, and आमिक्षा for a Vaiśya). 'The fat sacrificer thus gets lean and thus becomes fit for Soma' (पीवो दीक्षते कृशो यजते).

Soma is called king (राजन्). He has to be purchased especially of a कुत्स-गोत्र Brahmin or else a S'ūdra. The seller is first asked to clean Soma (सोमं शोधय) by removing all other things mixed in it. (It is difficult to imagine what Soma was like). This cleaning was not to be done by the यजमान or any of the priests. Then the प्रायणीय ceremony was performed and the Soma was purchased for a particular kind of cow. It is taken in a chariot to a hill, taken to its top on the head and then brought back from it. (This is perhaps a reminiscence of the fact that Soma was to be brought from the Himālayas). The purchasing again takes place with a strange ceremony ending in payment of gold (which was a hundred in वाजपेय, two hundred in राजसूय and a thousand in अश्वमेध X 26, 9). It appears that the gold was taken back and a cow given. If the seller disputed, he was to be struck with sticks according to some savants (लकुटैर्घ्नन्तीत्येके X 27, 7). Then it is taken in a chariot to the sacrificial shed with mantras where, on arrival, it is given a regal reception and is placed on a throne (आसन्दी), with the present of an ox which is released after presentation

In XI further particulars are given about the same sacrifice with particular injunctions as to the sacrificial shed. विराडसि सपत्नहा सम्राडसि भ्रातृव्यहा स्वराडस्यभिमातिहा विश्वाराडसि विश्वासां ना(रा ?)ष्ट्राणां इंतेति बाहू उपावहरतोऽध्वर्युर्यजमानश्च (XI 12, 2) is inexplicable. प्रवर्ग्य, उपसद् and अग्नीषोमीय are described. The Soma is partaken of by the sacrificer after his wife and Amātyas are honoured. The word संतिष्ठते is everywhere used in this Sūtra to show that the ceremony is rightly finished. The sacrificer guards the Soma during the night.

In the next chapter (XII) is described the process of extracting the Soma, it being crushed with stones while रक्षोघ्न mantras are recited (what is वलगघ्न mentioned along with रक्षोघ्न XII 2, 15 ?). The rite differs in the morning, noon and evening Savanas. Yava and लाजा (of व्रीहि) are used (तण्डुलानोप्य धानाः करोति व्रीहीनोप्य लाजान्करोति XII 4, 10). Saktus mixed with water or ghee are called करम्भ. The मूजवत् mountain where Soma was originally found is remembered (सोमस्य त्वा मूजवतो रसं गृह्णामि (XII 5,11). यं कामयेत पण्डकः (क्लीबः) स्यात्तं प्रचरण्योपस्पृशेत् XII 7, 1 is strange. Juice came out in drops (अंशु) which were offered to fire and then taken. For अभिचार the words हतोऽसौ फट् are to be uttered (XII 11, 10). The juice is strained over a cloth into which होतृचमसेन धारां यजमानः स्रावयति. The mantra is पवित्रं ते विततं ब्रह्मणस्पते &c. while different Sāmans (रथंतर, बृहत्साम &c.) are sung. The ceremony is called महाभिषव. (घास=भक्ष XII 12, 11). To enable a man to return to the ग्राम or to turn out one, a rite is prescribed (XII 15, 2). The सोम flows (पवते) for the good of all, Brahmins, Kshatriyas and Vaiśyas &c. A Rājaputra protects the Soma extract till it is used (XII 16, 4). It is kept in द्रोणकलश (अर्धपूर्ण according to Kātyāyana, com.). यत्र धारा विरमति प्रपीड्य पवित्रं निदधाति (XII 16, 10). The Soma is poured with mantras and Sāmans by all. Different animal sacrifices follow in different higher sacrifices. New mantras are prescribed for offering Soma to Agni. For injuring enemies शण्डामर्क are mentioned. Each priest takes his चमस (wooden cup) full of सोम from the द्रोणकलश and offers it to the fire. If a Rājanya or Vaiśya wishes to eat Soma, a rite is performed and then it is given to him to eat. Then the priests eat with one another's permission (like tea) नानुपहूतेन सोमः पातवै सोमपीथेन ह व्यर्धुको भवति (XII 24, 14). The drinking is to the health of gods (dual इन्द्राग्नी &c.). Every action is minutely provided for, such as सर्वेषां सोमपात्राणां भक्षितानां मार्जालीये प्रक्षालनम् (XII 27, 10. (Even washing of tea-pots is thus not forgotten). The होता then cries शोसांवोम् or ओथामोद and अध्वर्यु replies ओथामोद एवं होतः &c. which is called व्याह्राव. Nārāśaṁsa follows and also S'astras. संतिष्ठते प्रातःसवनम् (Thus is completed प्रातःसवनम्).

In Praśna XIII we have the noon Savana described, particular injunctions being given also in XII. Special दक्षिणाs are provided for सदस्यs but not to him who asks and not to कण्व and कश्यप (Com. adds हेतुश्चिन्त्यः), nor to a non-Brahmin nor to an unlearned (XII 7, 7). Probably the same Soma is used, as no new one is bought. In Kārikās 8-24 the evening Savana is described.

Praśna XIV gives the Vikṛitis of Agnishṭoma viz. उक्थ्य, षोडाशन्, अतिरात्र and अप्तोर्याम and then describes them in detail. In one place we find a rite prescribed, if it is wished that the क्षत्र (in a Rāshṭra) should be superior to the विश्. The rite reversed would make विश् superior to the क्षत्र (XIV 6, 9). असौ ते पशुरिति द्वेष्यं मनसा ध्यायेत्। यदि न द्विष्यादाखुस्ते पशुरिति ब्रूयात्॥ (XIV 7, 5) shows that rats were then hated. वासिष्ठो ब्रह्मा ज्योतिष्टोमे

shows that in Soma sacrifices the Brahman was to be of the Vasishṭha gotra (XIV 8, 1). स्तोमभागानां दधाति द्वादशाग्निष्टोमे पञ्चदशोक्थ्ये । षोडश षोडशिनि । सप्तदश वाजपेये एकोनत्रिंशतमतिरात्रे त्रयस्त्रिंशतमप्तोर्यामे । XIV 10 4 should be marked. In all Somas they went towards the south for Avabhṛitha. सोमाय वासः । रुद्राय गाम् । वरुणायाश्वम् । प्रजापतये पुरुषम् । मनवे तल्पम् । त्वष्ट्रेऽजाम् । अग्नये वा निर्ऋत्या अश्वतरगर्दभौ । हिमवतो हस्तिनम् । विश्वेभ्यो देवेभ्यो धान्यम् । ब्रह्मण ओदनम् । समुद्रायापः । वैश्वानराय रथम् ।

Chāturhotra is hereafter described. A Brahmin who does not earn fame should perform it or a king who is fighting a battle (XIV 14, 5). Higher Hotras are also prescribed for other desires. Many mantras are taken from the Ṛigveda here such as those of the Ṛishi Gaurivita and कयाशुभीय of Agastya (पंचसवनो यज्ञः, त्रीणि सवनान्यवभृथोऽनूबध्येति). The contingeny of the sacrificer dying before अवभृथ is provided for (XIV 21, 8). When the sun does not come out after morning prayer, दाशतयी Ṛiks should be recited. Dāśatayī refers to the Ṛigveda (probably the अष्टक division had not yet been made or recognised). If Soma is obtained without purchase, it should be taken out and purchased. If Soma is unobtainable, other herbs are substituted such as पूतिका, श्वेततूलानि फाल्गुनानि or milky herbs, अरुणदूर्वा or हरितकुश as Vājasaneyins prescribe and if none of these, finally व्रीहियवs to be mixed with whole milk (प्रतिधुक्) in the morning, skimmed milk (शृत) in the noon and curds in the evening (XIV 24, 14). If the pounding stone is broken or the Kalaśa broken, certain mantras should be recited in प्रायश्चित्त (XIV 24). Hiraṇya appears to be of two kinds, सुवर्ण and रजत. Many other Prāyaśchittas are prescribed for untoward incidents, such as loss of Brahmacharya of the sacrificer, or black birds (crows) entering the shed and touching the Havis, or some danger coming (XIV 32, 5). Finally a सर्वप्रायश्चित्त is recommended with the mantra नमो ब्रह्मणे &c. if nothing could be done as previously prescribed.

Praśna XV relates to the Pravargya ceremony preparatory in higher sacrifices such as Jyotishṭoma. A Mahāvīra is to be made of earth dug out with ceremony. It is placed on Āsandī (throne) and certain ceremonies are performed. After Pravargya, many vows are to be observed for a whole year (संवत्सरं न मांसमश्नीयात् न रामामुपेयात् न मृण्मयेन पिबेत् नास्य रामा उच्छिष्टं पिबेत् । XV 12, 13). A human form is allegorically conceived (XV 15, 1). Then it is thrown in different ways for different desires including the killing of a hated person who is named: ताजगार्तिमार्छति (ताजक् = सद्यः com.). After this, Prāyaśchittas are prescribed for various mishaps and mistakes. The chapter ends with other minor Dīkshās for magic (अभिचार) and ill omens described in T. B. (दुहॄणु &c.).

The Praśnas from XVI onward relate to higher sacrifices and probably as these were never performed in the time of the commentator, he has not commented on them. The sūtras on these, read by themselves, show very elaborate preparations for these higher sacrifices, commencing with going out of the town and digging earth and bringing it on the backs of horses and even asses, with appropriate mantras for each action. A preliminary sacrifice of a तूपर अज (hornless sheep) is performed (XVI 8, 3). If rain is wanted, a rite is prescribed and another to prevent rain. Bricks are to be prepared and then altars built, the pit being deep as the knee (जानुदघ्न) for the man sacrificing for the first time and deep up to the navel (नाभिदघ्न) for others. Bricks are तुषपक्व i-e. burnt in husk fire. Ploughing of ground is also mentioned with six, eight or twelve bullocks drawing the plough (लाङ्गल) and grain is sown. The grains mentioned are तिलमाषाः, व्रीहियवाः, प्रियङ्गुवेणवः, गोधूमाः, वेणुश्यामाकनीवाराः and जर्टिलाश्च गवीधुकाश्च some of which can not be recognised. गार्मकससमाः or कुलत्थससमाः is added. Dūrvās are to be secured with the mantra now usually used (काण्डात्काण्डात्प्ररोहन्ति, probably first prescribed here–XVI 2, 1). It appears that human heads and animal heads were put in in the building of altars called चयन.

The elaborate detailed rites of the higher sacrifices show how the Aryans had developed a craze for sacrifice and a superstitious belief in its efficacy for securing each and every human desire. The mantras also had attained miraculous powers, irrespective of their meaning and so also the acts in the ritual which secured the desired fruit only if performed in the prescribed manner but which became harmful to the sacrificer, if wrongly performed. Ritual had thus attained an esoteric meaning and importance and was as unchangeable as the Vedic mantras recited in it; hence the importance of these Kalpasūtras which were enunciated by different schools of Vedic teachers. Some of these sacrifices were to be performed by kings only and the power of the Kshatriya rulers was enhanced by the performance of these sacrifices. It is wrong to suppose that Brahmins imposed their beliefs upon the Kshatriyas. As in philosophical speculation, so in sacrificial elaboration, both Kshatriyas and Brahmins were equally concerned; the former wished to impress the imagination of the people (the Aryan Viś and Non-Aryan S'ūdra subjects) by these gorgeous sacrifices; the latter wished to exhibit their skill and learning by multiplying ritual by permutations and combinations of different sacrificial rites. In the following descriptions of the different higher sacrifices, these observations will assist the reader and prevent wrong inferences.

The eighteenth Praśna describes Vājapeya, open to Brahmins and Kshatriyas (शरदि यजेत ब्राह्मणो राजन्यो वृद्धिकामः) for prosperity. In this sacrifice गोधूम and सुरा are used. Everything is to be seventeen. The Dakshiṇās also are to be 17 elephants or 17 horses, 17 nishkas, 17 dāsī and 1700 cows and 17 chariots. A Rājaputra throws 1' arrows. After the homa of Vāja, the sacrificer shoulc perform Sautrāmaṇī or Brihaspatisava.

Rājasūya is then described which only a king ca perform for obtaining Svarga (राजा स्वर्गकामो राजसूयेन यजेत) showing how Yudhishṭhira was asked to perform thi sacrifice by Pāṇḍu who was in heaven. It was the same as Agnishṭoma with Dakshiṇā a thousand-folc or a lakh-fold (शतसहस्रदक्षिणा). The sūtra XVIII 12, 7 i remarkable; एष वो भरता राजेति। एष वः कुरवो राजेति कौरव्यम् एष वः पंचाला राजेति पञ्चालान्। एष वः कुरुपञ्चाला राजेति कुरुपांचालान् एष वो जना राजेत्यन्यान् राज्ञः shows that there were generally three families of kings: Bharatas, Kurus and Pāñchālas. The Kuru-Pāñchālas must be different from the above The Brahmins were outside the power of kings; for they recited the mantra सोमोऽस्माकं ब्राह्मणानां राजेति ब्रह्मा जपति The king's Abhisheka was performed with waters of the sea and of the Indus or any other river which has a masculine name. This shows that by that time certain big rivers had names masculine in gender (पुंनदी e. g. सिंधुनद, शोणनद). The king then played dice which was thus a necessary function in Rājasūya. The S'aunaḥśepa Ākhyāna is recited or other Ṛiks with Gāthās (story verses). The king has to inform other kings that he wishes to perform a Rājasūya. This is like the modern custom of informing other powers of the assumption of royalty. The Rājasūya is practically a ceremony declaratory of the assumption of king's dignity.

Praśna XIX describes the Sautrāmaṇī wherein Surā (liquor) is offered as libation and drunk. The Surā and the Soma are brought together and offered to Indra (सुरा त्वमसि शुष्मिणी सोम एष मा मा हिंसीः XIX 3,). The hair of a lion, a tiger and a wolf are required. What is हरित रजत (XIX 2, 6) can not be explained. A special form of this sacrifice is also described viz. कौकिली सौत्रामणी.

We have next the Sāvitrachayana, described in T. B. with names of 15 days (संज्ञानं विज्ञानं etc.), 15 nights, 15 muhūrtas (चित्रः केतुः &c.), 13 month-names अरुणाः अरुणरजाः &c. (XIX 12). Then Nāchiketa and then Vaiśvasṛja come as described in T. B. Then we have various काम्य पशु and काम्य इष्टि "mentioned in Brāhmaṇa" in detail described (XIX 18, 2). आदित्यचरुं निर्वपेत्संग्राममुपयास्यन् (XIX 19, 1) प्राजापत्यां शतकृष्णलां निर्वपेदायुष्कामः &c. Other similar ceremonies are finally described.

The 20th Praśna describes the Aśvamedha which only an emperor can celebrate; but later even an ordinary king is permitted (राजा सार्वभौमो अश्वमेधेन यजेत। असार्वभौमो वा। XX 5, 2). It must begin on Vaiśākha Pūrṇimā with the sacrifice of a प्राजापत्य ऋषभ or तूपर on the following अमावास्या. Probably the word तस्याः here shows that the months ended with Amāvāsyā with the Taittirīyins. The four Brahmin chief priests were to be given as Dakshiṇā सहस्रान् सौवर्णान् निष्कान् and अश्वतरीरथान् (chariots drawn by mules). The details of the colour &c. of the horse selected for sacrifice are given and a dog is to be killed near its ears. It was then surrounded by a hundred Rājputs with the Adhvaryu, a hundred Ugras who are not kings (अराजभिरुग्रैः) with the Brahman, a hundred Sūta-Grāmaṇīs with the Hotṛi and a hundred Kshattṛi-sangṛihītṛis with the Udgātṛi on the four sides, as already described in Section II when speaking of the Brāhmaṇas. When sent on its wanderings, the horse with its party was to put up in the house of a Rathakāra (XX 5, 16). Even a Brahmin's house was to be looted for food if he did not know the Aśvamedha ritual. The party returned at the end of a year during which various ceremonies were performed in the sacrificial shed, accompanied by singing on the Vīṇā (वीणागायं गायति) and the Pāriplava was recited by the Hotṛi. If any mishap overtook the horse, another was to be substituted; but if an enemy seized and removed it, the Aśvamedha was destroyed (अमित्रा अश्वं विन्देरन् इन्येतास्य यज्ञः XX 8, 1). After its return, on the last Amāvāsyā of the year, the उखा ceremony took place with many animal sacrifices, and the Dakshiṇās given were the most astounding, viz. the property of all people except Brahmins in the four directions to the four priests (दक्षिणाकाले यदब्राह्मणानां दिक्षु वित्तं ... ददाति XX 9, 14). After many ceremonies and animal sacrifices, the principal sacrifice commenced with the decoration of the horse by the queens of the sacrificing king. The three queens mentioned are महिषी, वावाता and परिवृक्ती. These were to be attended by one hundred Rājaputrīs, one hundred wives of Ugras (not kings) and of Sūta-Grāmaṇīs respectively. The Mahishī put on the horse golden ornaments, the Vāvātā, silver ones and the Parivṛiktī, marine ones (shells, coral &c.). The horse was then led in procession by the king taking his bow and arrow to a pond to drink water and the horse drank water while a prescribed mantra was recited. After being brought back, it was killed along with a तूपर and गोमृग, how is stated as follows: वेतसशाखायां तार्प्यं कृत्यधीवासं हिरण्यकशिपु चास्तीर्य सौवर्णं रुक्ममुपरिष्टात्कृत्वा तस्मिन्नश्वतूपरगोमृगान्निघ्नन्ति ॥ प्लक्षशाखायास्त्वितरान्पशून्। (XX 17, 8) श्यामलेन क्षौमेण वाश्वं संज्ञपयन्ति। स्पन्द्याभिरितरान् पशून्। (9). We are reminded here of the description in Vālmīki Rāmāyaṇa wherein the horse is stated to be killed by Kausalyā with three sword strokes. The description is detailed and shows that the writer had accurate knowledge of the Aśvamedha ritual. But the word विशशास is strange: कौसल्या तं हयं तत्र परिचर्य समन्ततः। कृपाणैर्विशशासैनं त्रिभिः परमया मुदा (I 14, 33). The commentators refer here to the Sūtras but they speak of cutting the dead horse much as the lady of the house carves the meat on the dining table among western peoples. The subsequent ceremony of making the chief queen lie with from the other, as Dr. Lorinser and others do. Similar thoughts and expressions occur to great poets and spiritual teachers in different countries and at different times independently. When, therefore, the Bible has 'Many prophets and kings have desired to see these things which ye see and have not seen them' (St. Luke X 24) or the Gītā has त्वदन्येन अदृष्टपूर्वम् and देवा अप्यस्य रूपस्य नित्यं दर्शनकांक्षिण: (XI 52), we need not suppose copying. And if copying is to be inferred, it would be that the Bible embodies sayings which had gone westwards through Buddhist teachers. For the Gītā, as we proceed to show in the following note, was preached long before Buddha and necessarily, therefore, before Christ. It is, however, true that the sentiments and sayings of the Gītā have been copied in the several pseudo-Gītās which have been composed after the true Gītā and put into various Purāṇas and other religious works. These have been noticed by Tilak in his Gītārahasya and they have not even approached the excellence and grandeur of the original.

NOTE I–THE DATE OF THE BHAGAVADGITA

European scholars generally place the Gītā at the beginning of the Christian era or a little earlier. They place the Mahābhārata itself about 400 A. D. and naturally Gītā, as an old part of it, is placed some centuries before this date. Winternitz thus gives 200 B. C. as the date of the old Gītā (p. 438). Before discussing the propriety of this European view, we will first notice and discuss the views of Tilak who discusses this subject at length in his Gītārahasya and who strangely enough puts the Gītā about the fourth century B. C. only (p. 564). More strangely still, among the arguments detailed for this view, we find that the well-known Vedāntā Sūtras and the Bhagavadgītā are treated by him as two works by the same author viz. Bādarāyaṇa who is, most strangely, looked upon as the person who has also put the Mahābhārata into its present form. It is inexplicable how so great an author as Tilak whose deep research and piercing acumen enabled him to fix, almost beyond doubt, the date of the compilation of the Ṛigveda, should have entertained such palpably absurd opinions. We have, therefore, to controvert these views at the outset, reluctantly no doubt, as we have generally accepted Tilak's views on many Vedic subjects.

Tilak properly holds that the Gītā formed part of the Bhārata which was expanded by some one into the present Mahābhārata. But he looks upon the present Gītā as expanded by this author from its original form which was much smaller than the present. The most striking verse according to him, added by this author, is ऋषिभिर्बहुधा गीतं छन्दोभिर्विविधैः पृथक्। ब्रह्मसूत्रपदैश्चैव हेतुमद्भिर्विनिश्चितैः ॥ XIII 4. The ब्रह्मसूत्र mentioned here is the Vedāntasūtra of Bādarāyaṇa who is also treated as the author of the present Gītā and of the present Mahābhārata. For the Vedāntasūtra refers to the Gītā, though not directly yet questionably, in many sūtras (e. g. I 2,3, I 3,23, II 1,36, II 3, 45, III 3,31, IV 1,15 and IV 2,21). The words स्मृतेश्च, स्मर्यते, स्मरति and अनुमान in the Vedāntasūtra refer to the Gītā alone, as appropriate statements from any other authorities are not quoted by any Bhāshyakāra or commentator or can be quoted by any person even now. This makes the Gītā precede the Sūtra of Bādarāyaṇa. But the Gītā referring to Brahmasūtra makes the latter precede Gītā. This difficulty is solved by Tilak by holding that Bādarāyaṇa is the author of both the extended Gītā and the Vedānta Sūtra.

It is no doubt certain that the Sūtra of Bādarāyaṇa refers to the Gītā in the several sūtras noted above, for the Gītā was already a semi-divine (स्मृति) authority on Vedānta, next to the divine (श्रुति) authority of the Upanishads. But it seems equally certain that the Gītā by the word ब्रह्मसूत्र does not refer to the Sūtra of Bādarāyaṇa. In the first place, it would not be acceptable that Bādarāyaṇa, taking advantage of the established reputation of the Gītā as Smriti, would, in expanding it, introduce a verse mentioning his own Sūtra as authority. No respectable author would do it, much less a spiritually minded orthodox author. Secondly, Bādarāyaṇa is not mentioned anywhere in MBh. as having extended the Bhārata. It is Sauti who expressly says that he has extended the Bhārata to a hundred thousand verses (एकं शतसहस्रं तु मयोक्तं वै निबोधत). It is a commmon wrong notion that Krishṇa Dvaipāyana and Bādarāyaṇa are one and the same persons. Bādarāyaṇa has nothing to do with MBh. or the Gītā. The two names are confounded by the Marathi translator of the MBh. also. We even think that Bādarāyaṇa is wrongly called Vyāsa. Krishṇadvaipāyana is alone Vyāsa (वेदान् विव्यास यस्मात्स &c. MBh.). The gotra also is different as shown already, the former being पाराशर्य i. e. वासिष्ठ and the latter, आंगिरस (Section III p. 18). Thirdly ब्रह्मसूत्र in the verse quoted can not refer to the Vedānta

Sūtra of Bādarayaṇa, notwithstanding the opinion of Rāmānuja, Madhva, Ānandagiri and other great authorities. For the description of 'Kshetra,' given hereafter in the Gītā, differs entirely from that given in Vedāntasūtra (महाभूतान्यहंकारो बुद्धिरव्यक्तमेव च and इच्छा द्वेषः सुखं दुःखं संघातश्चेतना धृतिः are not acceptable to the latter). To what does the word then refer? The answer is, to some Sūtra which was current before Pāṇini who mentions a भिक्षुसूत्र by Pārāśarya and better still to the Upanishad sentences like सर्वं खल्विदं ब्रह्म तज्जलानिति as held by Śankara. If we scan the śloka carefully, we find that it refers to two authorities viz. the many scattered Ṛik mantras (छन्दोभिर्विविधैः पृथक्) by Ṛishis and to हेतुमद्भिर्विनिश्चितैः पदैः : or logical definite expressions (prose) *by Ṛishis.* Tilak and Prof. Amalnerkar who thought like him fail to notice that in the second line पदैः is करणे तृतीया like छन्दोभिः in the first line and that ऋषिभि : (कर्तरि तृतीया) has to be repeated in the second line. The ब्रह्मसूत्रपदानि are by Ṛishis and hence refer to the Upanishads. Brahmasūtra can not refer to the Sūtra of Bādarāyaṇa who is an Āchārya and not a Ṛishi. There are many statements in the Upanishads which assign reasons and are definite like the one quoted above. We are, therefore, certain that there is no reference here to the Vedāntasūtra of Bādarāyaṇa and that the Gītā precedes it by several centuries. Tilak also seems to have wrongly placed the Vedānta Sūtra about the 4th century B. C. For, as stated already, it contains a refutation of Buddhist doctrines and may properly be assigned to the revival of Hindu supremacy in the days of Pushpamitra after the downfall of the Maurya dynasty. It is also hence wrong to suppose that Bādarāyaṇa recast the MBh. which does not contain any refutation of Buddhism and also wrote the Vedānta Sūtra which refutes it.

The Gītā can not be a work of Bādarāyaṇa for many other reasons. The Gītā, even as we have it, does not condemn from Praśna 10 relate to Ukhā, Vājapeya, Rājasūya, Ishṭis, Soma, Aśvamedha, Dvādaśāhas, Atirātra, Brihaspatisava and Sāvitrachayana. The contents of Vol. III appear distinctly to be later additions. Praśnas 20 to 23 form what is called Dvaidhasūtra; 24 and 25 form the Karmāntasūtra; 26 to 29 form Prāyaśchittasūtra and 30 forms S'ulvasūtra. The latest addition is clearly that of the Pravarādhyāya, as shown in our note on Pravaras. The S'ūlvasūtra commences with defining the measures अंगुल, पद, प्रक्रम &c. and then describes how the Āyatanas (houses) are to be built of 8 प्रक्रम for Brahmins, 11 for Kshatriyas and 12 for Vaiśyas; how Prāgvaṁśa is to be set up, how bricks (इष्टका) are to be prepared and laid and how altars of different forms like श्येनचित् (vulture form, वक्रपक्षो व्यस्तपुच्छः and others) are to be built. This may be an earlier form of the separate S'ulvasūtra we have, but is itself a late addition.

The procedure of the highest sacrifices described in Praśnas 10 to 19 in the second volume shows, however, that this part is really older than Āpastambasūtra as the ritual differs in important particulars and embodies an earlier stage of the development of S'rauta sacrifices. We may first take for instance the Aśvamedha ritual laid down in Praśna 15. This sacrifice is for राजा विजिती सार्वभौमः and not for any king optionally as in Āpastamba. The guards of the horse are the same; but Rājaputras are described as Talpya (?) and their description is as simple as in T.B. There is no provision to the effect that the guards in their ramblings are to stay with a Rathakāra and live upon the loot of Brahmins who did not know the Aśvamedha ritual. The description of the preparations for the sacrifice in the meantime is very detailed and interesting. It shows how many callings there were and what things the artizans manufactured. (We give this description in the original in the Appendix). The sacrificing king is employed in various sacrifices in the interval such as वरुणप्रघास &c not mentioned elsewhere. When the horse returns, there is jubilation and the queens decorate it for sacrifice. Three queens only are mentioned, viz. महिषी, वावाता and परिवृक्ती, and not the fourth, पालागली. Ugras are not mentioned, but are described simply as Arājāḥ. While the horse is being killed, the priests ask one another philosophical riddle questions already noticed in T. B. There is a new query here: किंस्विदासीत्पूर्वचित्तिः किंस्विदासीद् बृहद्वयः । किंस्विदासीत्पिशङ्गिला किंस्विदासीत्पिलिप्पिला. And the reply is द्यौरासीत्पूर्वचित्तिरश्व आसीद्बृहद्वयाः । रात्रिरासीत्पिशङ्गिला त्रिरासीत्पिलिप्पिला ॥ (?) which is queer and not mentioned in Āpastamba. The three queens only are again mentioned as showing with gold, silver and lead Sūchis how the dead horse is to be cut with swords. The sacrifice over, subsidiary sacrifices like सौत्रामणि are performed for two years more and thus the Aśvamedha really lasts for three years (संतिष्ठतेऽश्वमेधस्त्रिभिः संवत्सरः). Finally there is no mention of stupendous or even any Dakshiṇā at the end as in the other Sūtras; once or twice only शतपलमान gold is prescribed as Dakshiṇā.

We will give the interesting portions of the contents of the other praśnas commencing with the 11th. The 11th Praśna describes Vājapeya without saying who can perform it and a minute list of its requirements is given at the very beginning which we quote in the appendix and which includes 17 of many things such as 17 elephants and 17 slave-girls. The usual (प्रसिद्ध) दीक्षा ceremony is gone through first on a day described as ग्रीष्मस्य जघन्याहस्सु पुरस्तादाषाढ्यै पौर्णमास्यै. This is the same nearly as in Āpastamba and shows that the rains commenced about Āshāḍhī Paurṇimā, leading to the same date as the earliest possible one for this Sūtra also.

Besides Soma, Surā is also prescribed, which is more than what Āpastamba does. But there is the same martial race of chariots as if for fight and the same beating of drums. When the sacrificer returns, the chariots are unhorsed with mantras and after offering Soma to the gods, especially Indra the god of fight, they all drink (or eat) the Soma, which perhaps gives the name to this sacrifice for fighters, viz. वाजपेय (the drink of strength). At the end we have संतिष्ठते वाजपेयः, as in Āpastamba.

Praśna 12 describes the Rājasūya in a greatly different manner from Āpastamba. It is not stated in the beginning that only a king can perform it; but this goes without saying. Various sacrifices are performed for a year. The king then goes to the house of (1) a Brahmin, (2) a Kshatriya, (3) a Vaiśya, (4) the Mahishī (chief queen,) (5) the Vāvātā queen, (6) the Parivṛiktī queen, (7) the Commander-in-chief, (8) the Sūta (chariot-driver), (9) the Grāmaṇī, (10) a Kshattṛi, (11) a Bhāgadugha and (12) an Akshāvāpa (dice-player). Here we again miss the Pālāgalī queen. These are important associates of the king and are in the beginning called Ratnas or jewels. When, the Abhisheka or chief ceremony of crowning begins, the Soma sacrifice in its three Savanas is first gone through with its attendant animal sacrifices. After Abhisheka, the declaration is made एष वो भरता राजा and Kuru-Pañchalas are not mentioned here as in other Sūtras. The word Bharata is the oldest word for Indo-Aryans. The king is then given a bow and arrows and putting on shoes made of boar-leather, he rides a chariot. Many ceremonies, not mentioned in other Sūtras, follow including a game at dice. Finally, the Hotṛi relates the story of S'unaḥśepa as prescribed in all Brāhmaṇas in this connection. Many subsidiary sacrifices, not mentioned in other Sūtras, have to be performed and the Rājasūya ends after seventeen months and a half. Other kings are informed by sending them some sacrificial offerings and those who refuse them are counted enemies. A दिग्विजय is not mentioned as preceding the Rājasūya. But this explains why a दिग्विजय was necessary for Yudhishṭhira before his Rājasūya.

Praśna 13 describes Kāmyeshṭis, i. e. sacrifices with particular desires such as प्रजा, अन्न, पशु, ब्रह्मवर्चस, ग्राम, भूति, वीर्य, आयुः &c., with special mantras in each case addressed to Agni, Indra or others. There are a few magical rites (अभिचार इष्टि) one of them being for killing the men and cows of an enemy (4), another for curing consumption (28). Abhichāra rites, however, are much fewer in this Sūtra than in Āpastamba. But there is one for inflicting leprosy (दुश्चर्म) or escaping from it (18). In these Ishṭis different kinds of milk or grain oblations are prescribed but not any flesh offerings. Thus in the Kārīrī Ishṭi (38), prescribed for bringing rain, the oblations are of करीरसक्तु and everything is black such as the sacrificer's clothes, the horse in attendance &c.

Praśna 14, which begins with the statement that Prajāpati first created serpents and then birds, is entirely of the nature of a Brāhmaṇa, discussing the philosophy of ceremonies. (Where the words इति ब्राह्मणं occur they do not refer to any previous Brāhmaṇa statement but simply mean, we think, "this is the explanation".)

The caste or order सौधन्वन is mentioned in 5. A story is told that Manu dividing his property among his sons gave nothing to Nābhānedishṭa, who complained and was given a share in the sacrificial oblations of Āngirasas. What is किक्किटा (18)? इति बौधायनः...इत्याञ्जीगविः, quoted as conflicting authorities (15), show that the Sūtra belongs to the Baudhāyana school only.. In 17 and 18 sacrifices are prescribed for the purposes of a Rāshṭra by the Rāshtrabhṛits and also against its enemies in war. In

20 a story is told how Vasiṣṭha, alone of all Ṛishis, actually saw Indra, who being pleased gave him Stomabhāgas and it is hence that a Vāsiṣṭha should be elected Brahman. In the latter part are given certain rites for प्रायश्चित्त against mishaps in Agnihotra or other higher sacrifices indicating that the Prāyaśchitta Sūtra, Praśna 29, is a later addition. In this we come across the remedy for the mishap in which Soma, bought or unbought, is stolen. It is that a certain फाल्गुन grass called आदार and described as Haimavata (growing in Himālayas) should be used; if that was not available, Parṇatsaru (पर्णत्सरु) leaves' sap (अभिषव) should be used. These substitutes are older ones not known to the other Sūtras.

In Praśna 16 is detailed Dvādaśāha which is the basis of year-long sacrifices. We find here a mention of न्यूङ्ख of the Ṛigvedins. The discussions (Mīmāṁsās) given, e.g. whether पशु should be ऐंद्राग्न or वायव्यीय or solely आग्नेय or ऐन्द्र, are of the nature of Brāhmaṇas and are out of place in a Sūtra which has to give definite rules without discussions. Year-long sacrifices like गवामयन are indicated. These are to begin four days before माघी पूर्णिमा or फाल्गुनी or चैत्री (13) and the reasons are given for these beginnings which are astronomically important. We merely notice that if माघी पूर्णिमा is the beginning of the year, this Uttarāyaṇa would be about a thousand years before that of the Vedāṅga Jyotisha. In explaining गर्गत्रिरात्र a story is told of रौहिणेयः क्रौंशुनिः कौलाश्वो यास्कः sacrificing and मशको गार्ग्य आरुणेरन्तेवासी explaining to him a rite. Here यास्क is only a gotra name and not the author of the Nirukta. The Sārasvata sacrifice is mentioned briefly with some difference and ending with the usual उत्थान at प्लाक्ष प्रस्रवण. Various sacrifices beginning with Pañcharātra and going up to Saptadaśarātra and Ashṭādaśarātra and so on to 36 nights are described with permutations and combination of rites. It is interesting to note that the sacrifice named Pauṇḍarīka is described here. In the MBh., it is mentioned that Duryodhana performed this sacrifice after the exile of the Pāṇḍavas, as he could not perform the Rājasūya performed by them. It is described as एकादशरात्रोऽयुतदक्षिणोऽश्वसहस्रदक्षिणः. This is one of the few places in this Sūtra where exhorbitant Dakshiṇā is prescribed, naturally as the sacrifice is performed by great kings.

Praśna 17 describes अतिरात्र in the first ten Kaṇḍikās and one may form an idea as to how sacrificial procedure is varied in different forms. Atirātra is a form of षोडशिन् in which there is an अरुणपिशङ्ग horse, औदुंबर षोडशिपात्र, चतुःस्रक्ति &c. and Soma is to be bought with a Rohiṇī पिङ्गला एकहायनी cow and so on; these differences continue in the actual performance. There is a sacrifice for killing an enemy (13) and by it he dies immediately: (ताजक् प्रमीयते). We may note मनसैव यं द्वेष्टि तमुपाकरोति यद्यु वै न द्वेष्टि आखुस्ते पशुरित्यनुदिशति (14) as in Āp. Sarpasatra is mentioned (18) as performed by serpent kings and a king's sons named जर्वर &c. (the names finally include अरिमेजय and जनमेजय) in Khāṇḍavaprastha for obtaining poison (विष) which they obtained. "Those who perform this Sattra do not kill serpents." We have already said that the Mahābhārata story of Janamejaya's Sarpasatra is a distortion of this imaginary Sattra. The last sentence and the name खांडवप्रस्थ is in addition to what we read in Āp. After this is explained कुण्डपायिनां सत्र (with mention of कुण्डाः—21), then उत्सर्गिणामयनम् (22), then तपश्चितामयनम् (23), then छन्दश्चित, श्येनचित, कङ्कचित &c. (24-30),—all imaginary sacrifices probably. Sautrāmaṇī is then described and a list of things required is given first. Both Surā and Soma are to be purchased and offered to Sutrāman (Indra) whose name is given to the sacrifice. The Surā is to be purified through the hair of a lion with suitable mantras, then of a tiger and then of a wolf (30-38). Then comes as usual संतिष्ठते सौत्रामणिः.

In 39-42 Samāvartana is described which is a Gṛihya rite and is out of place here. The new Anushṭup mantras prescribed show this to be a later addition as stated by Caland in his preface to Vol. II. Very probably it precedes the Gṛihyasūtra as it seems certain that at the time of this addition, there was no idea that a Gṛihyasūtra would be formulated. The rest of this chapter is also a later addition as we come across the line असिशूलैः प्रतुदन्ति यमस्य प्रतिषादने (44), an idea not to be found in Vedic literature. The name of Baudhāyana is as bad for interpolations as of the Purāṇas, especially Skanda Purāṇa. Several sacrifices by name यज्ञ are mentioned here as चतुश्चक्रयज्ञ, this use of the word being unusual. Then finally are described (55-62) चातुर्मास्य सोमाः such as वरुणप्रघास सोम, शुनासीरीय सोम, साकमेध सोम &c. with their different animal sacrifices.

Praśna 18 begins with Bṛihaspatisava. Among the many requirements for it, the Hotṛi should be परिस्रजी which means खल्ति (bald) as the Sūtra itself explains. He should also be मिर्मिर, which is explained as शुक्लो विक्लिधस्तिलकवान् पिङ्गाक्षः and also त्रिशुक्र or त्रिवेद. This is a strange provision not found elsewhere. The सव procedure includes a sacrifice to बृहस्पति. माध्यंदिन एव सवनेऽश्वं दद्यादिति मौद्गल्यः. This बृहस्पतिसव is both for Brahmins and Kshatriyas and is higher than राजसूय. We have next a स्थपतिसव for स्थपति or leader, a सूतसव for सूतग्रामणी, a सोमसव, a पृश्निसव and a गोसव which has, however, nothing to do with गो but the दक्षिणा is अयुत in it. There is next mentioned ओदनसव in which all the four Varṇas are invited and a Brahmin is given मधु in a golden pot, a Kshatriya सुरा in a silver pot, a Vaishya milk in a pot of bell-metal, and a S'ūdra water in an earthen pot. This is open to a ब्राह्मण, क्षत्रिय or वैश्य. Next is mentioned पञ्चशारदीय, a sacrifice for five years wherein eleven Vatsataris are sacrificed each year (11).

We have a story told of a sacrifice by ऋतुपर्ण भाङ्गाश्विन king of S'aphalas (13). This sacrifice is to be performed by one who incurs impurity by going into border lands viz. आरट्ट, गान्धार, सौवीर, करस्कर and कलिङ्ग. Thus at the time of this Sūtra, the Panjab, the lands beyond the Indus, Sauvīra (Ophyr, south of Sind), Eastern Bengal and Orissa were out of the list of Āryan countries. Aptoryāma is described (15) with its many Sāmans required by Chhandogas and the name is well explained also. A मृत्युसव is next described (16) a new name, whereby a king becomes unassailable in his kingdom. Like Rājasūya it is a national sacrifice and resembles it in most respects.

Sadyaskrī and Prāyaṇīya sacrifices being described (20, 21), we have next Vrātyastoma detailed (24-27). The particulars given here are very important and it is mentioned that among the Pāñchālas, गन्धर्वायण, वालेय and आग्निवेश्य were Vrātyas. After describing यज्ञक्रतु, the Sūtra gives (35) some particulars about Abhichāra (magic) rites.

We have hereafter stories related in the fashion of Brāhmaṇas and Purāṇas (38 to 51) one of which states that Purūravas had two sons by Urvaśī, Āyu and Amāvasū, and that Āyu went eastwards and founded Kuru-Pāñchāla and Kāshī-Videha nations, while Amāvasu went westwrds and founded गान्धारयः, स्पर्शवः and आरट्टाः (44). This is different from the account in Purāṇas. We have in 42 numbers mentioned up to the highest, viz. शत, सहस्र, अयुत, प्रयुत, अर्बुद, न्यर्बुद, समुद्र, मध्य, अन्त and परार्द्ध, names still used in modern times. In (43) we have two other words बद्व and पत्व. The author speaks familiarly of Kurukshetra and says "कुरुक्षेत्रे बिसवत्यो नाम पुष्करिण्यः" and "एते औशनसा नाम कुरुक्षेत्रे पर्वताः" (46, 47). The well-known mantra यन्तु नदयो वर्षन्तु पर्जन्या: is found in this Praśna.

The Sāvitrachayana described in Praśna 19 requires 8500 bricks of gold (पंचाशीतिशतं हिरण्येष्टका: 2). This is the total of the bricks to be laid for the 15 days of the first fortnight and 15 of the other, 15 nights of the same, 15 Muhūrtas of each day and night and 15 subdivisions of each Muhūrta, 12 first fortnights of the year and 12 second fortnights, 13 months and 4 Saṁvatsaras as prescribed in T. B. We could not arrive at the exact total 8500 from these; but the total does come up to about this number, when the different days, nights, Muhūrtas, fortnights &c. are added up.

Coming to the contents of Vol. III, Praśnas 20 to 23 are called द्वैधसूत्र as stated already, because they simply record differences of ritual according to Baudhāyana and other teachers like शालीकि (This is a new name in sacrificial literature). The Kaṇḍikās or paras state the procedure as laid down by Baudhāyana and that by others. This clearly shows that these praśṇas were added after the preceding work was ready. Indeed the subjects are taken up in the order of the previous praśnas, Agnyādhāna, Darśapūrṇamāsa &c.

Then follow Praśnas 24, 25 and 26 which are called Karmānta sūtras. These contain general discussions as to the propriety of the procedure laid down in the same previous 19 praśnas and in the same order. Differences of opinion among teachers are also noticed, especially between Baudhāyana and S'āliki.

Praśna 27 is called प्रायश्चित्तसूत्र and gives Prāyaśchittas for various mishaps, This is a very modern addition from its language and its quoting अनुष्टुप् verses, of others probably, the expression आचार्या ब्रुवते । तन्नोदाहरन्ति (11), followed by Anushṭup ślokas, is clearly an evidence of subsequent addition. The chapter gives Prāyaśchittas only in regard to Agnihotra mishaps (अनाज्ञात also).

It was probably added after other Sūtras were formulated, giving Prāyaśchittas separately. Several new mantras are prescribed for Āhutis suitable to the Prāyaśchittas.

Praśna 28 gives some higher Ishṭis as also Prāyaśchittas for the higher sacrifices. It first gives महापवित्रेष्टि by one who is struck with consumption or is cursed by a Brahmin, a cow or Pitṛis. Another purifies ज्ञातीन् जात्यन्तरे वर्तमानान्दुष्कृतैरुपरुद्धान् दशपूर्वान्दशापरानात्मनैकविंशम्, which shows the solidification of castes at this time. Then follows नक्षत्रेष्टि which begins with Kṛittikās and thus shows that this section precedes the first century B. C. when the Aśvinī enumeration came into force. Then follows Prāyaśchittas for mishaps in an animal sacrifice such as the selected animal dying before being sacrificed. It is important to note that in the case of गो or अश्व, a goat or sheep is allowed to be substituted.

In Praśna 29 we have further rites given of the nature of Prāyaśchittas for other kinds of mishaps which must have happened at all kinds of sacrifices. These include burning of the sacrificial shed, breaking of sacrificial pots and even राष्ट्रविभ्रम and व्याधि. These sections appear late as there are Anushṭup ślokas of modern type. And there is in the first section mention of Vādhūlaka whose Sūtra we possess. This Sūtra has not yet mentioned any known Sūtrakāra, though it mentions many teachers. In the end, other views are cited by इत्येके but सर्वानित्याचार्याः at the end refers to Baudhāyana and shows clearly that this section has been added by a follower of his.

Praśna 30 called S'ulvasūtra describes the construction of altars and also sacrificial sheds. It commences with the table of measurements as follows : — 14 Aṇus or sesamum (तिल) seeds make one Angula ; 10 Angulas form one क्षुद्रपद् and 12 form one प्रादेश (span) ; two padas form one प्रक्रम (step) and two spans one Aratni (hand or cubit). The building of altars in the form of श्येन (eagle), कंक (swan), रथचक्र with its navel and spokes, or कूर्म (tortoise) is the most difficult part of the subject and bricks had to be prescribed of a particular size. Their number was fixed in each case and sometimes the number was made up by half bricks (अर्धेष्टकाभिः संख्यां पूरयेत्). The subject involved a knowledge of mensuration. The chapter is evidently a late addition; but S'rauta altars only are treated of and this Sūtra seems to be the earliest of the S'ulvasūtras.

III Kātyāyana.

This Sūtra belongs to the White Yajurveda and is the only Sūtra we possess of that Veda. Its Gṛihya-sūtra is written by Pāraskara and not Kātyāyana, though in the Black Yajurveda and the Ṛigveda, the Gṛihya and S'rauta Sūtras go under the same name. This Sūtra has been published by Weber together with its commentaries. It was published in Berlin in 1859, which shows how German scholars since long have laboured in the field of Vedic literature. The well-known Bhāshya of Karkāchārya has not, we fear, yet been published; but in the commentary of Yājñikadeva, published by Weber, many extracts are taken from Karka's Bhāshya. Two other commentators, viz. Mahādeva and Mahīdhara, are also mentioned. Weber in the preface to his edition mentions two Bhāshyas, one by Upādhyāya Karka, fragments of which only exist in European libraries and another, very verbose, by Ananta who boasts of having performed many different sacrifices. Of commentaries, he first mentions the excellent Vyākhyā of Yājñikadeva of which many copies exist. There is a paddhati also of this author which gives the ritual in extenso as prescribed by the Sūtra for each sacrifice without referring to it. The next commentary mentioned is the Bhāshya of Mahādeva. The last and not the least is the Vedadīpa of Mahīḍhara who lived in Samvat 1654. The Sūtra of Kātyāyana is divided into 26 chapters called Adhyāyas which are subdivided into Kaṇḍikas containing about 10 to 15 sūtras. The sūtras are generally very brief. The idea that sūtras ought to be short seems to have been accepted at the time of Kātyāyana. The sūtras are again often in the form of the Indian syllogism typified in the sentence पर्वतो वन्हिमान् धूमवत्वात्. Indeed some sūtras contain one noun in the ablative only giving the hetu. This shows that logic had also advanced by this time. These two facts lead to the inference that this Sūtra is a very late one. Further, this Sūtra is solely devoted to sacrificial procedure as laid down by the S'atpatha Brāhmaṇa. The procedure in the ritual of other Vedas is never noticed as in Āpastamba Sūtra which frequently notices the Bahvṛicha and the Vājasaneyaka ritual. Indeed no other authority is mentioned except Jātūkarṇya and Vātsya in a few places. Optional procedure is provided for by इत्येके or एकेषाम्, these differing savants being most probably followers of the same White Yajurveda.

The contents of this Sūtra are similar to those of other S'rauta Sūtras and relate to the S'rauta secrifices beginning with Darśapūrnamāsa. The commentator everywhere shows, at the beginning of each Adhyāya, how the Sūtra follows the order of the S'atapatha. The commentary explains sūtras in the first twenty chapters and is full in the first twelve. The subsequent chapters relate to highest sacrifices like Aśvamedha rarely performed in post-Vedic days and had no interest whatever for modern writers.

The exact date of this Sūtra can not be determined.

It is treated as Pre-Pāṇinian by all scholars and if we take 800. B.C. as the date of Pāṇini, this Sūtra may be placed about 1000 B.C. It is pre-Buddhistic certainly as it shows the highest development of sacrifice which took place before Buddha in whose time the absurdity of the cult of animal sacrifices became nauseous to the people and made it necessary for a Buddha or a Mahāvīra to raise the standard of revolt. Hence also we feel assured that Kātyāyana must have long preceded Buddha. There are no specific indications, however, in this Sūtra as to its age, so far as we have scanned it.

The following interesting facts may be culled from the Sūtra. The first Adhyāya relates to general procedure and speaks of Ādhāna and Chāturmāsya. The difficulty of explaining how a Rathakāra is specially mentioned in the Brāhmaṇas is experienced here also. Whether the word indicates a special mixed caste or a special profession only, practised by any of the three Varṇas is answered here differently. Probably mixed castes, based on different avocations like the original three Varṇas, had arisen by this time, as further on Ṛibhus or Saudhanvas are referred to in IV 9, 5. The original provision in the Brāhmaṇas was in our opinion due to the fact that a Rathakāra who had to work for his profession in jungles during the dry season, cutting trees &c. was allowed to make Ādhāna in the rainy season when he was free. The further sūtra निषादस्थपतिर्गवेधुकेऽधिकृतः (I 1, 2), which entitles a Nishāda and a Sthapati for गविधुक ritual, indicates that Kātyāyana meant by Rathakāra, a S'ūdra or a mixed-caste person of that profession. (2) The distinction between यजति and जुहोति or यज्ञ and होम is clearly laid down in two sūtras तिष्ठद्धोमा वषट्कारप्रदाना याज्यानुवाक्यवन्तो यजतयः । उपविष्टहोमा स्वाहाकारप्रदाना जुहोतयः । (I 2, 6 & 7). Yajati is used when the oblation is to be made standing with the word

वषट् and with the Yājyā and Anuvākyā mantras; while Juhoti is used when the oblation is made sitting with the word Svāhā (3). The year began on the next day of Phālguna Pūrṇamāsī.

The second chapter relates to दर्शपूर्णमास and lays down the procedure in nearly the same manner as in other Sūtras. It may be noted that इवणी is the form used in this Sūtra also. Taṇḍula (तण्डुल) is clearly grain separated from the husk, the process of separating the grain being done by the sacrificer with special mantras. The word applies to व्रीहि or rice as also to other grains such as श्यामाक. The pounding of grain is mentioned and not grinding, we think, as perhaps grinding was not yet known or in sacrifice the oldest rudimentary process was still retained because considered sacred, as the creating of fire by churning one piece of wood in another. Match boxes are no doubt modern, but the method of percussion which is common even among Bhils is not used because of the same reverence for the oldest method. The पत्नी pounds and not a S'ūdrī. The election of Brahman follows that of Adhvaryu and every thing proceeds in a solemn manner, the motions to and by the Adhvaryu, the Brahman and the Yajamāna (sacrificer) being, as in a modern legislative Council, (e. g. ब्रह्मन्प: प्रणेष्यामि &c.), solemnly made.

Chapter III continues the same subjects. A special ritual or act is prescribed nearly everywhere to destroy the sacrificer's enemy. The sūtra अभावे द्विषन्तं भ्रातृव्यम् is however queer; if there is no enemy, the hating cousin should be destroyed. भ्रातृव्य in Vedic days, we have elsewhere shown, meant the Zends or the Asuras. But in Kātyāyana's days they were unknown in India. Probably the undivided family systeem always gave rise to these enmities between cousins.

At the beginning of IV, the commentator observes:

"Having described the पौर्णमास, the Sūtrakāra treating of दर्श first describes the पिण्डपितृयज्ञ' or sacrifice to the manes with balls of rice. The usual Srāddha ceremony is here described. The sūtra प्रकरणकाललिङ्गानुग्रहवचनेभ्यस्सन्निहितानि- श्रुतिभ्योऽनङ्गम् (IV 1, 29) shows the great advance the Pūrva Mimāṁsa method of interpreting the S'ruti procedure had made by the time of Kātyāyana. The Darśa procedure begins with the formal milking of the cow: वाग्यतो दोहयत्यशूद्रेण (IV 2, 22) shows that orthodoxy had increased and a S'ūdra is finally prohibited from milking a cow for sacrifice. अनुवादः पूर्वस्येति वात्स्यबादरी (IV 3, 18) mentions two authorities वात्स्य and बादरि; the latter can not be the बादरि of the Bādarāyaṇa Vedānta S'ūtra who lived nearly a thousand years hereafter. These are gotra-names only; and Bādari is the gotra progenitor probably of Bādarāyaṇas. वाजिन is the word for the liquid that remains after the substance is taken out of milk or curds. The Dakshiṇā prescribed here is पुनः संस्कृतो रथो (दक्षिणा); it is strange that a new chariot is prescribed elsewhere and here an old one repaired and repainted. The Nakshatras prescribed for अग्न्याधान are the same as in Āpastamba and the season for वैश्य and रथकार is वर्षा. The Nakshatra for पुनराधान is पुनर्वस्वोः only (IV 11, 5). Agnihotra is hereafter described in detail and different oblations are provided for different desires (पयसा स्वर्गकामः पशुकामो वा। यवाग्वा ग्रामकामः। तण्डुलैर्बलकामः। दध्नेन्द्रियकामः। घृतेन तेजस्कामः। (IV 15, 21 to 26).

Chapter VII takes up and describes higher sacrifices begining with अग्निष्टोम. For them sixteen priests are elected, their names being as in Āpastamba; if not possible, four leading ones only. They go out and select a spot for performing sacrifice called hence देवयजन on high ground and a S'ālā is erected with vacant space on all sides except the east where the entrance is. The sacrificer together with his wife enters on the दीक्षा with great ceremony, commencing with the cutting of his nails. For scratchig if necessary, a horn is tied to his cloth and is to be used and not his nails VII 3,36. (नापित is here mentioned in this Sūtra) They enter the S'ālā and live an ascetic life subsisting on milk only. शूद्रसंप्रवेशसंभाषाभ्युत्थान (VII 5, 5) are proscribed as in Āpastamba ; but a Sudra's not entering the S'ālā is an advance upon it. With regard to Soma, the same detailed provisions for its purchase from a Kutsa Brahmin or a S'ūdra (though before in a sūtra we have the Soma bought from somewhere else) are given. In the process of purchase higgling for price is also prescribed, the purchaser commencing with offering कला (1/16 of the price of a cow-com. VII 8, 6) and ending with gold. But subsequently the gold is taken back from him and a cow given ; if it is not taken, the seller is driven away with belabouring with sticks. Soma treated as king is placed on an Āsandī in the sacrificial pavilion and a reception ceremony is performed. After many more ceremonies including a sacrifice of eleven animals, the actual sutyā is performed the next morning.

Chapter IX describes this ceremony of extracting the Soma juice. The herb is to be ceremoniously pounded eight times or twelve times (IX 4, 17), a part is offered to the fire and four priests again press out the juice thrice (IX5, 1). The Soma juice taken in the द्रोणकलश is called śukra (19). There are three savanas, morning, noon and evening, for which different mantras are prescribed in certain ceremonies. Sāman songs in praise of Soma are recited as the juice is poured into the Kalaśas (IX 7,4). The last ceremony of offering oblations requires election of priests of good family with different mantras for Hotri, Adhvaryu, Brahman &c. and a Rājaputra is elected to protect the ceremony. The names शण्ड and मर्क in 10, 5, are old as they occur in V.S. (7, 12 and 17).

After oblations the priests eat the residue (हविःशेष).

In Chapter X are given special rites of the noon Savana. Probably the same material is again pounded and juice extracted. It is used with curds; the residue after oblation-offering is eaten by all. The priests अदीक्षित might have a smell of it which is called प्राणभक्ष as distinct from actual भक्ष. Dakshiṇā is hereafter given to priests. Afts अग्नीध्र is paid, a dakshiṇā is to be given to a Atrigotra Brahmin after calling out for him ; हालेय,वालेय, कौद्रेय, शौभ्रेय, वामरथ्य and गौपवन are to be excluded ; why it does not appear (2). Other Brahmins who have come in should also be given something except कण्व, कश्यप and याचमान. The two exceptions are also a riddle but the third shows Brahmin beggars rushing in for Dakshiṇā even at that time as now and the sūtra rightly orders that such Brahmins should never be given Dakshiṇās (X,2,35). Kaṇva is interpreted as Kāṇa (squint) and Kaśyapa as श्यावदन्त (black-toothed). पत्नी च ददाति makes it necessary that the wife should particitate in the act of giving, thus recognising her equal position. The third Savana for the evening is next described with the special procedure for it. Soma is mixed with curds when pressed again. After the ceremony is finished, they go out for Avabhṛitha to any pond; if such water is not available, to any unsteady water (stream) and then return to the यज्ञशाला. After giving दक्षिणा and सायमाहुति, this sacrifice ends and the sacrificer leaving the यज्ञशाला returns home. This अग्निष्टोम is the first necessary sacrifice for the higher ones उक्थ्य, षोडशिन्, वाजपेय, अतिरात्र, अप्तोर्याम &c. For Vaiśyas and Rājanyas some difference in procedure is here mentioned, though generally the ceremony is the same for all.

Chapter XI then details the duties of the Brahman (ब्रह्मत्व) in these sacrifices. It also describes the Dvādaśāha, a sacrifice which is the model for Sattra and Ahīna which are अदक्षिण (XII 1, 8) with दीक्षा and पत्नीसंयाज,

shaḍahas to be followed by उक्थ्य, छन्दोमा, सोमक्रय, शालाप्रवेश &c. as usual.

In Chapter XII we have all higher sacrifices mentioned and briefly described by the nature of गवामयन, the model of sacrifices lasting for one year. These are आदित्यानामयन with different sacrifices for each of the 12 months; 2 आंगिरसानामयन, 3 दतिवातावतोरयन, 4 कुण्डपायिनामयनं with many ordinary sacrifices during the 12 months, and 5 सर्पाणामयन. Then we have sacrifices described lasting for more than one year, probably imaginary, such as तापश्चित for 3 or 12 years with गवामयन for the first year and others for the next, प्राजापत्य for 12 years, शाक्त्य for 36 years (शाक्त्य means probably son of शक्ति son of Vasishṭha) and the 1000 years' sacrifice of Viśvasṛij (Creator). Finally, we have Sārasvata sacrifices described. On the left bank of the Sarasvatī, the first दीक्षा should be taken at उदकान्त (विनशन where the waters of the river disappear in sands). Then on the right bank following up the river every day by शम्याप्रास, Prāyaṇiyas were performed. There are three forms of the same further described viz. मित्रावरुणयोरयन, कुण्डपायिनामयन, and इन्द्राग्न्योरयन. In all these they finished at प्लाक्ष प्रस्रवण; and performed अवभृथ at कारपचव on the Yamunā. This explains the importance of the Sarasvatī as a sacrificial river. The vows of the sacrificer are all given in brief, such as abstaining from अनार्यभाषण, अनृत, क्रोध, वृक्षारोहण (नात्रे वा), अभिवादन and नृत्यगीतवादित्र. His food sould be chiefly milk. The animal sacrificed is divided among the priests and the sacrificer as minutely discribed. What the पत्नी gets she is to give to a Brahmin. The वैकर्त is distinguished from the शमितृ who if not a Brahmin should give his share to any Brahmin. The parts 36 in number "bear up the sacrifice". This description of the division would not seem strange to any European family, wherein the division of cooked whole animals constantly takes place; but in India of the present day animal sacrifice having almost disappeared, the description strikes one as revolting. In Kātyāyana's time some sentiment against obstinate division had set in. For in the next sūtra (XII 2) he says that if a wrong division is made, as the Selagas (mentioned in Aitareya Āraṇyaka as an aboriginal tribe) do, they would incur sin. This method of division was first known by Ṛishi Devabhāga; but he did not tell it to any body. It came to Bābhravya through a heavenly being much as an angel told Paul to have no scruples in eating animals.

This chapter finally gives the Pravaras necessary to be remembered in choosing priests for sacrifices. They are given last in Āpastamba and other Sūtras.

Chapter XIII treats of Gavāmayana in detail, the दीक्षा being on एकाष्टका (माघ कृष्णाष्टमी) or फाल्गुनी पूर्णिमा or चैत्री or four days before any पूर्णमासी, especially माघी. Here श्रुते: refers to Tāṇḍya Brāhmana (quoted by Weber). After several sacrifices mentioned, in the sixth month Agnishṭoma is performed and a singular ceremony follows in which the sacrificer is praised and censured alternately: अभिगरापगरौ आक्रोशत्येक: प्रशंसत्यपर: (XIII 5, 45); पुंश्चलीब्रह्मचारिणावन्योन्यमाक्रोशत: (6); शूद्रार्यौ परिमण्डले चर्मणी व्यायच्छेते (7). जयत्यार्य: (8) may be marked, as also गोधावीणाका; काण्डवीणा: पत्न्यो वादयन्त्युपगायन्ति. Cows are praised; न वै गावो मन्दारस्य गङ्गाया उदकं पपु: । पपु: सरस्वतीं नदीं ता: प्राच्य उज्जिगाहीर इदं मधु &c. is not commented on and is inexplicable. Perhaps the Panjab and Kurukshetra are praised here as having best cows and the latter as the most sacred land. Slave-girls (दासी) with pots on their heads walk round the fires thrice. If sacrifice ends before the year, procedure is detailed and then Avabhṛitha is gone through. Finally ten cows for each Brahmin are prescribed, and more if the sacrificer can afford it, as Dakshiṇā.

Chapter XIV describes the next higher sacrifice, viz. Vājapaya, which is for Brahmins and Kshatriyas (वाजपेयः शरद्यवैश्यस्य XIV 1, 1). There are seventeen Dīkshās and seventeen pieces of cloth are tied round the Yūpa. एकधनप्रवेशनकाले सुरां नेष्टा परेण प्रवेश्य खरं करोति (XIV 1, 26) and सोमग्रहाः and सुराग्रहाः अनुक्रमण (XIV 2, 6), अतिरात्रपशूनुपाकृत्य वशां पृश्निं मरुभ्य उज्जेषेभ्यः and सप्तदश श्यामतूपरान् बस्तान् show that वाजपेय includes offering of liquor and many animal sacrifices. सप्तदश सप्तदश शतानि ददाति गोवस्त्राजावीनाम् is as usual. सप्तदश वृषल्यो निष्ककण्ठयः is the first provision one comes across about slave-girls, these with golden ornaments (Nishkas being equal to 4 Suvarṇa coins) could not be merely for service; and seventeen chariots drawn by elephants are also given. After this, horses are yoked to chariots and they go out for a fight or race and on return the final Vājapeya ceremony takes place, the name of the Samrāṭ being loudly proclaimed.

Chapter XV speaks of Rājasūya, performed by a Rāja who has not performed Vājapeya (अनिष्टिनां वाजपेयेन XVI 2). माघीपक्षयजनीये दीक्षा (5) prescribes दीक्षा on फाल्गुन प्रतिपदा and shows that months were Amānta following Vedānga Jyotisha. The same king's followers are mentioned as elsewhere (सेनानी, पुरोहित, महिषी, सूत, ग्रामणी, क्षत्तृ, संग्रहीतृ, and भागदुघ (भोजयिता), अक्षावाप and गोविकर्तृ (XV, 3, 12). After various animal sacrifices on the फाल्गुनपक्ष यजनीय day (Chaitra 1) the Abhisheka takes place. The Hotṛi is to be a भार्गवगोत्रिन्. यस्याश्च जाते राजा भवति देशस्यानवस्थितत्वात् (XVI, 4, 17) shows that the old कुरुपांचालानां राजा formula is gone. The word जाति is also important and also देश. The king puts on a क्षौम cloth or त्रिषाणं घृतोक्षं; यज्ञरूपस्यूतं पापाण्डु (कम्बलं तार्प्यस्योपरि निवस्ते com.) and उष्णीष describe the apparel of kings in those days. The king takes up a bow; and seated on a tiger-skin is sprinkled with holy waters with suitable mantras. After certain other ceremonies including the king's son and brother

&c. is prescribed the throwing of dice in gambling. This explains how there was gambling after the Rājasūya of Yudhishṭhira. It was a usual game with Kshatriyas as with the ancient Germans. Different sacrifices of various kinds of animals are prescribed thereafter every month, ending with Sautrāmaṇi or some other higher sacrifice.

Chapter XVI describes Agni, Ukhā and Chayana and other minor matters. पंचारत्निः, पुरुषो, दशपदो, द्वादशागुंलं पदं, प्रक्रमस्त्रिपदः समविभक्तस्य (XVI, 8, 21) gives the current measures. The measure of sacrificial ropes is also given as also the number of bricks, यथाग्नि वेदीष्टकाप्रमाणम् (XV 6, 26) and जंघामात्रीं नाभिमात्रीं मुखमात्रीं सक्त्यां मिनोति gives the measures of the depth of the fire-pit.

Chapter XVII relates chiefly to Chiti and prescribes mantras with which bricks are to be laid.

Chapter XVIII first speaks of a शतरुद्रिय sacrifice which is a new one in S'rauta literature and shows that this Sūtra is probably the latest. (शतरुद्रियहोम उत्तरगक्षस्यापरस्यां सक्त्याम् । परिश्रित्स्वर्कक्काष्ठेन शातयस्सततं जर्तिलमिश्रान्गवेधुकान्सक्तून जाक्षीरमेके। तिष्ठन्नुदक् नमस्त इत्यध्यायेन I, II). वसोर्धारा is hereafter prescribed and then Vājapeya. In the last Kaṇḍikā, the Vratas given are: पक्ष्यमोजी, सवर्णापायी (com. explains that the Sūdrī wife should be avoided as also द्वितीये, the Kshatriya and Vaiśya wives); तृतीये न कांचन; in the third chayana thus perfect celibacy is ordained: यावज्जीवमविशेषात्संवत्सरं वा.

The next chapter XIX describes the सौत्रामणी which in this Sūtra is allowed to Brahmins only; but a king dispossessed might perform it (राज्ञोऽवरुद्धस्य 1, 3). After an ऐन्द्र animal sacrifice, सुरा and सोम are both to be purchased from a क्लीब. यवकर्कन्धूचूर्णानि बलमसीति आवपति (2, 20). कर्कन्धू com. explains as सूक्ष्ममतिमधुरमुत्तरापथे जायते. Milk is also to be mixed and hair of वृक, व्याघ्र and सिंह put in as in Āpastamba (2, 23). The sacrificer and the priests drink the हविःशेष; but an alternative is allowed, viz. प्राणभक्ष or smelling (3, 15). वसिष्ठशुनकानां नाराशंसः अन्नीणां चैके (6, 8). A sāman is sung at the end with a different Nidhana for Kshatriyas and Vaiśyas (5, 5). Various details are given finally of प्रयाज and अनुयाज.

Chapter XX describes the Aśvamedha, following the order in S'atapatha which the com. points out. It is to commence on Phālguna S'uddha 8 or 9, i. e. a shaḍaha before Pūrnamāsī. The queens put on different ornaments and take part. They are महिषी, वावाता, परिवृक्ता and पालागली. The com. describes the last as दूतपुत्री (St. Petersberg Dictionary gives पालागल as meaning दूत from S'. XIII 4, 1, 8 and 5, 2, 8) and the second as the favourite and the third as the detested consort. Āpastamba mentions the first three and not the fourth but that she is an ancient entity is proved from S'atapatha XIII 4, 11, 3. The queens are accompanied by one hundred daughters of kings, of Kshatriyas, of Sūtagrāmaṇīs and of Kshatra-Saṁgrahītṛis. The marks and colours of the horse to be selected are given in detail which are interesting to students of शालिहोत्र (horse-study). The rite in Āpastamba of killing a dog by an आयोगव or पुंश्चलु is mentioned here also. The horse starts on its ramble with guards mentioned already. They can take the wealth of Brahmins who do not know Aśvamedha ritual; but they are to stay with Rathakāras. The former provision is given even in S'atapatha VII 4, 2, 17. After the horse's return within a year, the chief sacrifice takes place on फाल्गुनी पौर्णिमा. There is दीक्षा and देवयजन and certain animal sacrifices. The three queens then decorate the horse, the fourth not being mentioned here (5-15). It is then taken out to drink water at a pond. When brought back, it is killed. हिरण्यवासोऽधिवासेष्वश्वसंज्ञपनम् shows that it was strangled or suffocated to death like other animals sacrificed. The usual obscene rite follows and it is accompanied here as elsewhere with obscene jests among priests; but it is remarkable that servants (अनुचरी) are allowed to be substituted for the queens in this Sūtra, evidencing its improved ritual, though later date. The three queens then show the way for cutting the dead body with a sword, by marking lines on it with needles of gold, silver and copper respectively. After the Vapā (entrails) of the horse sacrificed is thrown as oblation into the fire together with those of the other animals killed and after several subsidiary oblations, the Avabhṛitha takes place. When the sacrificer comes out, others take their bath in the water and they become purified of their sins without प्रायश्चित्त (अचरित्वा व्रतानि अश्वमेधपूतास्ते । 8, 18). उदवसानीयान्ते भार्या ददाति सानुचरीः । कुमारीं पालागलीं वाध्वर्यवे । is remarkable; but we find in stories that after Āśvamedha, girls were bestowed on the chief priests (e. g. S'āntā was bestowed on Rishyaśringa) and S'atapatha XIII 4, 5, 37 is referred to here by the com. (The following quotation from S'atapatha V, 3, 1, 11 using the word पालागल meaning दूत is interesting. It gives also the meanings of सूत &c., the eleven jewels of a king. सत्रो वै सूतः विशो वै मरुतः वैश्यो वै ग्रामणीः। सविता वै प्रसविता प्रसविता क्षत्ता । संग्रहीतृ-समोवी वा आश्विनौ सयोनौ सव्यृष्टि सारथी समानेष्ठिरथमधितिष्ठतः । पूषा वै देवानां भागधुक् एष वा एतस्य भागं दुहोति ॥ अक्षावाप and गोविकर्त are embers of fire. Finally in राजसूय we have प्रहेयो वै पालागलः अध्वानं वै प्राहित एति । एतानि एकादश रत्नानि.)

Chapter XXI describes Purushamedha, for प्रतिष्ठाकाम, lasting for five nights only, for both Brahmins and Kshatriyas. The vitims already described are not to be killed but released. The Dakshiṇā for Brahmins is सर्वस्व and for Kshatriyas the same as in Aśvamedha with the addition of men and wealth in the four regions !!!!!! Next is mentioned सर्वमेध for सर्वकाम, lasting ten nights, the ten higher sacrifices being performed on ten days and the Dakshiṇā being the same as for Purushamedha. Finally पितृमेध is described to be performed in ग्रीष्म, शरत्, and माघ.

Chapter XXII describes एकाह, विश्वजित् and other sacrifices, with previous ceremonies performed in different ways and with Dakshinā, usually a thousand. In the description of साद्यस्क are mentioned आजानेया अपरजने (2, 23) प्राश्वेषु हस्तिन: (2, 24) and अश्वतरीरथमुदीच्येषु (2, 25) showing the author's correct information about the important products of Āryan countries, viz. the good horses of the west, the elephants of the east and the mule chariots of the north. He does not apparently know the Deccan and the South. The श्येन (eagle) sacrifice for अभिचार (magic) is more detailed here than in Āpastamba. The sacrificial shed is to be erected on a barren ground facing the south (instead of east). The fire sticks (इध्म) are to be of बिभीतक and the fire-grass (बर्हि) of arrows. The priests are to be red-turbaned and red-clothed with निवीत (left shoulder being bare) and the Dakshiṇā is to be nine each of काण, खोर, कूट and बण्ड animals. These and many other distinguishing features show the evil nature of the sacrifice. Next is described व्रात्यस्तोम, the Dakshiṇā of it being given to मागधदेशीयब्रह्मबन्धुs who seem to be known as fallen Brahmins (4, 21). Agnishṭut is prescribed for various desires, for one who thinks himself to be impure (अपूत). Bṛihaspatisava is prescribed for a Sthapati who may be elected by kings or Brahmins (सराजानो ब्राह्मणा वा पुरस्कुर्युः). A सर्वस्तोम and four वाचस्तोमs are next described. A वैश्यस्तोम is prescribed for one who desires cattle (Vaiśyas being keepers of cattle) whether Brahmin or Kshatriya. उक्थ्यो गोसत्रोऽयुतदक्षिण: । सराजानो विशो यं पुरस्कुर्वीरन् । स एतेन यजेत (11, 8) describes the Gosava. Certain magical rites for political purposes are prescribed for kings as well as peoples (जनपद).

Chapter XXIII next describes the Ahīna sacrifices. द्वादशोपसत्काः मासापवर्गाः सहस्रदक्षिणाः । पौण्डरीकेऽयुतम् ; ज्योतिष्टोमविश्वजित्त्रिवृत्पञ्चदशसप्तदशैकविंशाः । यथासंख्यमृद्धिपशुब्रह्मवर्चसवीर्यान्नप्रतिष्ठाकामानाम् । shows the concise style of the Sūtra. आप्तोर्यामः प्रेव यस्मात्पशवो भ्रंशेरन् (19). There are other sacrifices described like अभिजित्, वैश्यस्तोम, ज्योतिर्गौ and सर्वस्तोम उत्तम. Of Daśarātras, ककुप् and कौसुरुविन्द are described, as also Chhandoma and Pauṇḍarīka for सर्वर्द्धिकाम.

Chapter XXIV describes Sattras beginning with द्वादशरात्र, एकोच्चयेन चत्वारिंशदन्तानि beginning with षडह and ending with अतिरात्र, with महाव्रत in the middle. The sacrifices गवामयनादि last a year or more such as आदित्यानामयन, आंगिरसानामयन, दतिवातेरयन &c. ; after six months मध्येव्रतम् । उत्तरतः प्रतिलोमम्. कुंडपायिनामयन commences on पूर्णिमा or चतुर्थ्यामपरपक्षस्य (com. फाल्गुनापरपक्षस्य चैत्र्यां वा. Months seem अमान्त). सर्पसत्र is hereafter described as also तापश्चित् of one or three years. Mahāsattras like प्रजापतिसत्र of twelve years and शाक्त्यानामयन of 36, शतसांवसर of साध्य्s and सहस्रसंवत्सर विश्वसृजाम् are described (अह्नां वा शल्यत्व तु may make a year a day). यात्सत्राणि सारस्वतानि are called so, because they are performed while travelling (यात्वा यात्वा &c). दीक्षा सरस्वतीविनशने । शम्याप्रध्वंसे शम्याप्रासे यक्ष्यन्तो यजमानाश्च दक्षिणेन तीरेण यन्ति (XXV, 6, 5). On the junction of सरस्वती and दृषद्वती a ceremony is performed. When प्लक्ष प्रस्रवण is reached, they return. Avabhṛitha takes place at कारपचव or the Jumna. A दार्षद्वत sacrifice is mentioned, to be performed at नैतन्धव which, the com. states, is an old village on the सरस्वती. The अवभृथ in this sacrifice takes place at त्रिप्लक्षावहरण on the Jumna. All these places were familiar to the Aryans in this period, the sacrificial cult having developed in the region of the सरस्वती and दृषद्वती, consequently called ब्रह्मसदन. A तुरायण sacrifice is next mentioned and सर्वाग्निष्टोम द्वादशमह ; and उत्सर्गिणामयन. A new sacrifice named नारायणपुरुष is finally mentioned as the best though not described, which indicates the late date of the Sūtra.

Chapter XXV gives Prāyaśchittas in all matters beginning with Agnihotra and Chapter XXVI describes the महावीर in Pravargya. It is a figure to be made of earth brought from a वल्मीक or a pond used by boars. महावीरं करोति प्रादेशमात्रमूर्ध्वमासेचनवन्तं मेखलावन्तं मध्यसंग्रहीतमूर्ध्वमेखलायास्त्र्यंगुलमश्वशकृतया धूपयति describes its figure and making. This is the first place where an idol is mentioned in sacrificial literature.

IV Ās'valāyana S'rauta Sūtra.

We now go on to Āśvalayana's S'rauta Sūtra which belongs to the Ṛigveda. Its style is concise and it avoids all repetitions, only using words which are absolutely necessary. Thus Chapter VII begins with the word सत्राणाम्, while other Sūtras would have begun with अथ सत्राणि व्याख्यास्यामः. As an instance of avoidance of repetitions may be quoted ग्रीष्मवर्षाशरत्सु क्षत्रियवैश्योपकुष्टाः।. Other examples will appear from the following. Āśvalayāna thus may be treated as the latest writer, though brevity of expression is a personal peculiarity and would not be a decisive factor. The contents, however, also show that his treatment of the subject is the latest.

The Sūtra is divided into two halves called पूर्वार्ध and उत्तरार्ध and each half contains six chapters called Adhyāyas. We will, however, for brevity number the Adhyāyas consecutively from I to XII. Each chapter consists of several sections called Khaṇḍas and the total number of these is 164 (96 + 68). Each Khaṇḍa is practically one continuous sentence and there are no separate sūtrās as such. The treatment of the subject is in the nature of a Paddhati giving the procedure without discussion as in Baudhāyana, or reasons as in Kātyāyana. Other opinions are noted now and then. The opinion of Āchāryas generally is frequently mentioned, but the name of S'aunaka, the Āchārya of Āśvalāyana, is not mentioned anywhere, except at the end where after Āchāryas, he is specially saluted (नम आचार्येभ्यो नमः शौनकाय). These Āchāryas are probably of Ṛigveda. Gāṇagāri and Kautsa are often mentioned and Taulvali only once or twice. The special views of Āitareyiṇaḥ are noted in VII 10, which shows that Āśvalāyana does not strictly follow Aitareya Brāhmaṇa, as Kātyāyana follows S'atapatha. The Ṛigveda Saṁhitā of course is constantly drawn upon as Ṛigmantras are constantly prescribed, the Sūtra being specially intended for the Hotṛi. These mantras are mentioned by their beginnings; and so many Ṛiks from such and such Sūkta is the usual method of reference.

The subjects are practically the same as those in other Sūtras but they are treated very briefly. The order is also nearly the same as in other Sūtras beginning with Darśapurṇamāsa, Agnyādhāna and so on, proceeding up to the higher sattras in the Uttarārdha. We will give the contents of the several chapters with the interesting facts found therein.

The Sūtra opens with the sentence अथैतस्य समाम्नायस्य (this only being recited at S'rāvaṇī to indicate this Sūtra). विताने योगापत्तिं व्याख्यास्यामोऽग्न्याधेयप्रभृतीन्याह वैतानिकानि follows. The com. explains this as शाकल्यस्य वेदस्य प्रयोगे, and वैतानिक is defined as rites on the वितान fire. Chapter I then takes up दर्शपूर्णमास. इत्येव जपित्वा कौत्सो हिंकरोति shows that Sāman procedure is also noted. एकश्रुति recitation is defined as उदात्तानुदात्तस्वरितानां परः सन्निकर्ष ऐकश्रुत्यम्. The reciting of Pravaras occurs in the very beginning; but यजमानस्यार्षेयान् प्रवृणीते यावन्तः स्युः requires the mention of as many as there may be and "not four nor more than four". But this rule is mentioned further on. पौरोहित्यान् राजविशाम् । राजर्षीन् वा राज्ञाम् । सर्वेषां मानवेति संशये । deserves to be noted and will be discussed in a note. इति शाट्यायनिकम् refers to a Sūtra and not the opinion of an आचार्य as in इति कौत्सः. S'āṭyāyana is the well-known author of a Brāhmaṇa or Kalpa not extant now. (See Pāṇini's पुराणप्रोक्तेषु ब्राह्मणकल्पेषु).

Chapter II describes अग्न्याधान and gives the नक्षत्रs for it; they are the same as in other Sūtras. The seasons are वसन्त for Brahmins and ग्रीष्मवर्षाशरदः for क्षत्रियवैश्योपकृष्टाः. Who is उपकृष्ट and why is रथकार not noticed here as in other Sūtras? (Probably the special importance of रथकार was gone and we find nowhere in this Sūtra mention of new or old Rathas as Dakshiṇā. Perhaps the mixed castes had arisen by this time and they are designated by उपकृष्ट. This would make this Sūtra the latest of all.) But for Soma sascrifice no particular Nakshatra or Ṛitu is necessary (this is also an indication of lateness as सोमेन यक्ष्यमाण ऋतुं न पृच्छेन्न नक्षत्रम् is added). प्रत्युष्टं रक्षः प्रत्युष्टा अरातयः occurs here only. The Rakshas and the enemy whom the Āpastambas constantly feared are no longer very troublesome. It may be noted that the kindled sacred fire was treated most respectfully by the Indo-Aryans, as his permission was sought when the house-holder went on a journey and he was prayed to for the safety of his kin and cattle during his absence and he was most respectfully approached on return and thanked with suitable mantras. Very often such mantras are newly prescribed by the Sūtrakāras. Then follows पिण्डपितृयज्ञ (offering of oblations to the manes), as in other Sutras, to be performed on Amāvāsyā. ये च त्वामत्रानु is explained by the remark तस्मै तस्मै ये एषां प्रेताः स्युरिति गाणगारिः When a Piṇḍa is offered to a dead father, along with his name the words ये च त्वामत्रानु ("and to those who are after you") are uttered even now. Gāṇagāri holds that the names of these should be separately recited. Perhaps this refers to the ancient practice that some followers burnt themselves along with their master and these were to be remembered along with the master. This explanation is likely as one finds the practice still obse_ved in Japan and as Bāṇa mentions it in Harshacharita. प्रत्यक्षमितरानर्चयेत् तदर्थत्वात्प्रेतेभ्यो निपृणीयादिति तौल्वलिः is also to be noted from which गौतम differs.

It is remarkable that पुनराधान is not described in detail as in other Sūtras, nor its Nakshattras given. Agrayaṇa is shortly noticed. The verses given in full and having accents are probably from other S'ākhās. The Kārīrī Ishṭi for वर्षकाम is also given here and mantras from the Ṛigveda with their Pratīka are given. Chāturmāsyas are briefly noticed but no Ṛituyājas are mentioned. The शुनासीरीय to be performed on Pañchamī after Pūrṇimā is also shortly noted.

Chapter III describes the पशु called इष्टि here and not बंध. अग्निप्रणयनमुक्तम् gives reference in short, to what has already been described. समिधमिति वसिष्ठानाम् notices a different method for Vāsishṭhagotrins (as in II, 12 वसिष्ठशुनकात्रिवध्र्यश्वराजन्येभ्योऽन्यत्र). Certain procedure differed in certain gotras. How the Paśu was to be killed is not even noted. Saūtrāmaṇi is also shortly described, but surā is not actualy to be taken as the direction is प्राणभक्षोऽस्त्र. This also indicates lateness as the permission to drink liquor in Sautrāmanī is taken away. In the 10th Kaṇḍikā we have prāyaschittas given, introduced by the well known dictum विध्यपराधे प्रायश्चित्तम्. These are very briefly given with the necessary mantras. Prāyaschittas for mishaps are also noted further on, such as the sacrificial cow not giving milk, the breaking of Kapālas and pots, spilling of oblations and so on. If the the fire goes out, the substitutes are given by the typically brief sentence पूर्वालाभे उत्तरोत्तरं ब्राह्मणपाण्यजकर्णदर्भस्तम्बाप्सु ।

काष्ठेषु पृथिव्यां हुत्वापि मन्थनम्. । But certain severe penitentia Vratas are prescribed, viz. ब्राह्मणपाणौ चेद्दासेऽनवरोधःकर्णे चेन्मां सवर्जनं स्तम्बे चेन्नाधिशयीत अप्सु चेदविवेक एतत्सांवत्सारिकं व्रतम् याव जीवं वा ।.

Chapter IV describes very briefly Soma sacrifice which is described with such interesting details in other Sūtras. The sixteen priests required for it are noted here also by name in four sets. There is no erection of a sacrificial shed. दीक्षा is briefly mentioned as also the purchase of सोम which here also is called Rājan and treated as such. Its reception is mentioned but not its pressing. Many mantras, however, are given. Mahāvīra is cursorily mentioned once. Pravargya is mentioned (इत्यंनुपूर्वः पटलम् can not be understood). A cow is then milked and fresh milk mixed with Soma. After many mantras in praise of Aśvins, Soma is offered to Agni and then it is drunk by the दीक्षिताः and गृहपतिः. A Paśu ends the sacrifice, followed by many mantras.

Chapter V describes the morning, midday and evening savanas (भूः स्वाहा for the morning, भुवः स्वाहा for the noon and भूर्भुवःस्वाहा for the evening). A verse is quoted which seems to be from some work of late date: ऋतुयाजान् द्विदेवत्यान् यश्च पत्नीवतो ग्रहः। अदित्यग्रहसावित्रौ तान् स्म मानुवषट्कृथाः ॥ How, when and in what order the Somá is to be taken is noted in detail with the mantras for each drink. Opinions differ here, as in formal tea-drinking (तेषां होताग्रे भक्षयेदिति गौतमः). Ṛituyāja is here noted in passing. Āhāva is described and the Sāman cries शोंसावोंम् &c., wherein Om is to be introduced in different places and on different occasions. Grāvāṇaḥ in the plural occurs, where many stones are used in pressing. The Abhishava is described. Dakshiṇā is here mentioned for the first time but the mantra for it seems to deprecate it (v 13). The Marutvatiya graha (taking of Soma) and other grahas are finally described. And everywhere the याज्या mantras are prescribed but nowhere the अनुवाक्या, the former being for Hotṛis and the latter for Adhvaryus. अथ तृतीयसवनमुत्तमेन स्वरेणादिश्यस्य prescribes the high pitch of voice for reciting mantras at the evening Savana.

Chapter VI speaks of उक्थ्य and other higher sacrifices called सप्तसंस्था in which Soma also forms a part. The mantras given in detail are mostly addressed to conquering Indra. Aśvins are also to be praised and the posture of the priest when praising is prescribed in an interesting way (यथा शकुनिरुत्पतिष्यन्नुपस्थकृतस्त्वेवाश्विनं शंसेत्। VI 15,). If the purchased Soma is lost or burnt and can not be purchased again, the substitutes recommended show that the Sūtra is the latest and belongs to a time when Soma was almost unobtainable (अनधिगमे पूतिकान्, फाल्गुनानन्या वा ओषधयः VI, 8). If a sacrificer dies before अवभृथ, the funeral ceremonies to be done including केशवपन, नखावकृंतन &c. are described in 10. Herein Ālekhana and Āśmarathya, the two differing authorities in Āpastamba, are mentioned. The सप्तसंस्थाः are enumerated in the beginning of 11 as अग्निष्टोम, अत्यग्निष्टोम, उक्थ्य, षोडशिन्, वाजपेय, अतिरात्र and अप्तोर्याम (इति संस्थाः) and these are noticed in brief. In each of these, formal invitations are to be given by the words श्वः सुत्या. In the pressing of Soma, द्रोणकलश is here mentioned; but घ्राणभक्ष is prescribed and not actual भक्ष. Devayajana or sacrificial shed is here mentioned with its four doors in four directions and which door is to be used by which person is prescribed carefully here as in other Sūtras.

The Uttarārdha relates to the Sattras, the general procedure of which is given in the first chapter (VII). The various sūktas of the Ṛigveda which are to be recited with the number of Ṛiks to be taken in them are given in detail and various Sāmans to be sung in the Stomas are mentioned. Tha number of verses is increased in the Stomas as follows: पंच सप्तदशे नवैकविंशे द्वादश चतुर्विंशे पंचदश त्रिणवे एकविंशति त्रयास्त्रिंशे द्वात्रिंशतं चतुश्चत्वारिंशे षटत्रिंशतमष्टाचत्वारिंशे एकाल्पसीर्वा (5). The Nyūnkha and Ninarda of the vowel ओ are a peculiarity of the Hotṛi recitation mentioned here; for they belong to the Ṛigveda reciters at such sacrifices only. They are probably borrowed from Sāman singers. The Sūtra gives examples actually how the Nyūnkha is to be made. Thus in the Ṛik आपो ३ रेवतीः क्षयथा हि वस्वः । क्रतुं च भद्रं विभृथामृतं च ।। the ओ of पो is to be lengthened in different ways. Ninarda seems to be a reduplication of the Nyūnkha.

Chapter VIII continues the same subject and mentions that certain Ṛiks are to be recited पच्छ: (by quarters) and अर्धर्चश: (by halves) and by permutations of the order of Ṛiks called Vyatimarśa. The Pratigaras given are curious, ending in जरितराथामोदैवोम्. Kuntāpa sūktas are here mentioned, viz. इदं जना उपश्रुता &c. (included in Atharvaveda). Various Sāmans are mentioned for use. The Chhandomā rite is described and along with Ṛigmantras are given many new Anushṭup mantras addressed to Agnāmarutau. In 13 Chāturhotra mantras are recited which remind one of T. B., where a symbolical sacrifice is described in which चित्तमग्निरासीत् । वाग्वेदिरासीद् । and so on. Lastly in 14 a sacrifice is mentioned for a Brahmachārin in which the word आचार्य is used. This is plainly a Gṛihya rite, for Āchārya is never mentioned in a S'rauta rite. This perhaps is like the समावर्तन rite in Baudhāyana and shows that a Gṛihya Sūtra was not yet in existence.

From Chapter IX we have higher sacrifices the प्रकृति of which is अहीन एकाह्. The details given here are not well understood. We have here the first mention of a large दक्षिणा in this Sūtra, viz. द्वादशशतदक्षिण: (1). We have उक्तानि चातुर्मास्यानि सोमान् व्याख्यास्यामः at the beginning of 2; but Soma has already been sacrificed. We have here the first mention of Varuṇapraghāsa and Sākamedha. In 3 Rājasūya is described very briefly. Abhisheka is merely hinted at; but the recital of the Saunaḥśepa Ākhyānā by the Hotṛi seated on a golden cushion to the annointed king seated with his son and ministers on a golden cushion, is mentioned. The Dakshiṇā to the Hotṛi is one thousand (gold or silver ?) and one hundred to the प्रतिगरितृ. Even when not sacrificing, a conquering king should hear this Ākhyāna. Other rites connected are mentioned, together with दशपेय (not mentioned in preceding sūtras). The Dakshiṇās mentioned in this Sūtra are very moderate and not excessive as in others: सौवर्णी स्रगुद्गातुरश्वः प्रस्तोतुर्धेनुः प्रतिहर्तुरजः सुब्रह्मण्याय द्वादश षष्ठौह्यो गर्भिणी ब्रह्मणे वशा मैत्रावरुणस्य रुक्मो होतुर्ऋषभो ब्राह्मणाच्छंसिनः कार्पासं वासः पोतुः (!!!) ·क्षौमीवरासी नेष्टुः त्रिवर्षः साण्डो ग्रावस्तुतः. (4). Many Stomas not mentioned elsewhere are mentioned such as उशनसः स्तोम, गोस्तोम, भूमिस्तोम &c. Next comes बृहस्पतिसव for which the दक्षिणा is एकादश or एकादशशत or एकादशसहस्र !!! (5). Other sacrifices for various desires अन्नकाम, ग्रामकाम &c. are noted including the अभिचार sacrifice where the priests have to wear red turbans (लोहितोष्णीषाः) as mentioned in other Sūtras. भूतिकामराज्यकामान्नाद्यकामेन्द्रियकामतेजस्कामानामेते कामा द्वयोर्द्वयोर्ऋषिस्तोमा वात्यस्तोमाश्च पृष्ठ्याहानि नाकसद ऋतुस्तोमा दिक्स्तोमाश्चाभिप्लवाहानि (8). Ṛitapeya, Atimūrti &c. show the further development of the sacrificial cult. Next is mentioned वाजपेय for आधिपत्यकाम (this is new) and every thing in सप्तदश in it (सप्तदश दीक्षाः &c.). After the Ṛik mantras for this are given, the दक्षिणा prescribed is any fabulous sum from शत to परार्ध्य including 17 gold-caparisoned elephants. (9). This is the only place where exhorbitant दक्षिणा is prescribed in this Sūtra. Finally अप्तोर्याम is described with its special procedure and mantras for obtaining cattle; the दक्षिणा is परःसहस्राः श्वेतश्चाश्वतरीरथो होतुः (11).

Chapter X gives further sacrifices for various desires;

अतिरात्र, पंचशारदीय and others with their special mantras such as पुरुरुबिन्दु &c. पौण्डरीक is next described. Finally Aśvamedha is described in detail for all desires or for conquering all. The guards of the horse are not, however, described in detail nor the queens. But the Pāriplava which is recited to the king during the whole year is given in detail and deserves to be compared with the details in S'atapatha in a special note. The philosophical conversation in which the Hotṛi and the Adhvaryu indulge is interesting and is not given in the other Sūtras. The questions are old ones as also new and we give these also in App. for the curious reader. After some further particulars, the दक्षिणा is given as भूमिपुरुषवर्जमब्राह्मणानां वित्तं in the four directions to the four chief priests. This is a little saner than in the other Sūtras.

Chapter XI in the first six Kaṇḍkās describes the Rātri-Sattras lasting from one night to 68 and एकोनशत nights with the various combinations in them of प्रायणीय, अभिजित्, विश्वजित, आप्तोर्याम and other rites as also the objects for which they are to be performed such as स्वर्ग, प्रतिष्ठा &c. In 7 it speaks of the गवामयन sacrifice extending over a year and details what sacrifices and rites are to be performed in the several months, the particulars of which, it appears, differ from those given in other Sūtras. And the last chapter XII gives the sacrifices higher than गवामयन which is their प्रकृति, such as आदित्यानामयनम्, अंगिरसामयनम्, दतिवातवतोरयनम्, कुण्डपायिनामयनम् in which सोम is bought and drunk, and the inexplicable सर्पाणामयनम्. A Gavāmayana lasting for three years compounded of three each year and four kinds of तार्पश्चित lasting for one, three, twelve and thirty-six years, Prajāpatisattra of 12 years, साध्यानां शतसंवत्सरं सत्रम् and finally विश्वसृजां सहस्रसंवत्सरसत्रम्, all of them imaginary Sattras, also mentioned in other Sūtras, are mentioned here perhaps for completeness without details. The Sārasvata sacrifices on the banks of the Sarasvatī going higher up each day ending with प्लक्षप्रस्रवण and with अवभृथ on the left bank of the Jumna, mentioned finally, may have been a sacrifice actually performed by some. In section 8, all the Vratas of a sacrificer (सत्रिन्) are given, thus avoiding repetition, And these include सर्वशश्च वर्जयेयुः ग्रामचर्यां सरणं त्रिवृतस्मयनं स्त्र्यभि-हासमनार्याभिभाषणमनृतं क्रोधं &c. He is further to live on milk of cows milked with certain restrictions, or fruit. Finally the division of the animal killed in sacrifice into 36 parts is describsd as seen by श्रौतऋषि देवभाग. "To divide it in any whimsical way as the Selagas do is sinful"; and this पशु alone is स्वर्ग्य, a statement made in other Sūtras also.

V THE AGE OF THE S'RAUTA SŪTRAS FROM ĀPASTAMBA

We have already fixed the age of the Śrauta-Sūtras as lying between 1900 and 800 B.C., the dates of Maitryupanishad and Pāṇini. An indication of this period is found in Āpastamba, though not as definite as that of the Vedāṅga Jyotisha. In Praśna VIII, the seasons are described by months named from Nakshatra Pūrṇamāsīs. These month-names came into vogue towards the close of the Brāhmaṇa period. Previously the month-names were मधु-माधव &c. and were connected with the seasons. In the Āryan habitat beyond the Himālayas, the seasons were five or six, viz. वसन्त, ग्रीष्म and so on. In the middle country of India, the seasons were practically three; and owing to the precession of the equinoxes, they had lost connection with the old names of months. The new month-names, however, did not lose connection with the Nakshatras on the full-moon day. These months by their new names are mentioned as concurrent with certain seasons. Then again, there was a disturbance between old seasons and old months. The two sacrifices Ṛituyāja and Chāturmāsya were, therefore, distinguished (VIII, 4, 12). The three season-sacrifices were at the commencement of वसंत, प्रावृट् and शरत् by the names of वैश्वदेव, वरुणप्रघास and साकमेध (13). By months the first was to commence on फाल्गुनी or चैत्री full-moon and the second वरुणप्रघास (for the deity of water) began on आषाढी or श्रावणी full-moon after four months (ततश्चतुर्षु मासेषु आषाढ्यां श्रावण्यां वोदवसाय वरुणप्रघासैर्यजते). This shows that while in ancient times of the Sanhitās the rainy season commenced with श्रावणी पूर्णिमा (a time still observed by Brāhmins for श्रवणाकर्म or stoppage of studies on account of the rains), in the days of the Sūtras the rainy season had shifted back and commenced usually about आषाढी Pūrṇimā. Whether we take the month-names as अमान्त or पूर्णिमान्त, both systems being then in vogue, the Pūrṇimā day is fixed and definite. Now in Kālidāsa's days, the rainy season usually commenced on the Pratipadā of Āshāḍha (आषाढस्य प्रथमदिवसे मेघमाश्लिष्टसानुम्); while in our days it commences usually on शुद्धप्रतिपदा of Jyeshṭha. (In our time also both अमान्त and पूर्णिमान्त months are used, the first, south of the Vindhya and the second, north of it.) Thus from the time of the Āpastamba Sūtra, whether we take its months to be अमान्त or पूर्णिमान्त, the rains have shifted back now by about a month and a half which means that the equinoxes have slided back by about 45 degrees. This procession would take about $45 \times 72 = 3340$ years and the date of Āpastamba Sūtra comes to about $3340 - 1920 = 1420$ B.C. The date of the Sāṁhitās would be the

श्रावणी पूर्णिमा rainy season or a month later i.e. 30 ×72 = 2160 years before Āpastamba, viz. about 3580 (1420 + 2160) B. C.

Though not connected with this Vedānga section, we may discuss the date of Kālidāsa for the curious reader as afforded by his 'आषाढस्य प्रथमदिवसे मेघमाश्लिष्टसानुम्'. If this आषाढ is अमान्त, his rainy season would commence about 15 days before that of Āpastamba and his date would be about 1080 (15 × 72) years after him, i. e. about 340 B. C. But if this month is पूर्णिमान्त, Kalidāsa's rainy season would commence 30 days earlier and his date would be 2160 years after that of Āpastamba or 720 A. D.

Of course these are calculations on a rough basis whether for Āpastamba or Kālidāsa. For the commencement of the rainy season is not a fixed phenomenon, as the coming together of the sun and the moon in Dhanishṭhā at the commencement of Uttarāyaṇa is, which gives us an unassailable date for the Vedāṅga Jyotisha or its falling in the middle of it which gives us the date of the Maitrāyaṇīya Upanishad. Moreover, Āpastamba might mention आषाढी पूर्णिमा in obedience to a long-continued practice, as श्रावणी is performed even now on श्रावणी पूर्णिमा in obedience to a practice of about 5000 years.

It is necessary to explain here certain adverse facts on which Garbe would assign Āpastamba Sūtra to the 6th century B. C. and to the

Andhra country, following Bühler who expresses this opinion in the preface to his translation of the Āpastamba Dharmasūtra (Preface, p. xvi Vol. III). The Aryans no doubt had gone into Āndhra in the days of A. B about 2000 B C. And as Āpastamba-Sūtra-Brahmins are mostly found even now in Āndhra, it is possible that this Sūtra was formulated there. But the date 600 B.C. can not be accepted and the various arguments advanced for this date have to be answered. (1) The occurrence of some Prakrit forms has led Bühler to observe with regard to the authors of the ritual in the Gṛihya Sūtras: "All these men were Yājnikas whose literary education, according to Pāraskara Gṛihya-sūtra 2, 6, 8, in ancient times was as deficient as in later times. All the Sūtras which have come down to us, belong to the time when the Prakrit dialects were in general use in daily intercourse and as the official language throughout the whole of India." This wrong notion has arisen from looking upon the autors of the Gṛihya Sūtras as those of the S'rauta Sūtras. Though the names are the same, the persons are different, as stated already, from language and method of treatment. The Śrauta Sūtras are pre-Pāṇinian as admitted by even European scholars. And in Paṇini's time the Prakrits had not even arisen, much less become the official language or even the language of the higher classes as in the days of the Mauryas.

to whose time (300 B. C.) European scholars wrongly assign Pāṇini. Pāṇini knows not the words Sanskrit and Prakrit and uses for the former the simple word भाषा. In his time Sanskrit was the spoken language of the Aryan people, the official language of the state and even the language of the generality. The Śudras and Dāsas spoke the same language in a debased form and thus arose Prakrits in later times which were adopted by the Aryans as their spoken language long after Pāṇini. The writers of the Śrauta Sūtras were again not illiterate Aryans; but even illiterate Aryans then spoke Sanskrit much as uneducated common people in England speak English a little different from the English of the cultured people. A few forms in this Sūtra, therefore, in which न is changed into ण and ऋ into इ are not to be wonderd at. (2) The word Ghoṭa for अश्व in XV 2, 13 is Sanskrit. The word Ghoṭa is looked unon as Hindustani; but Hindustani words are Sanskit unless shown to be Arabic or Persian or borrowed from a Dravidian language. The non-ocurrence of such words in classical Sanskrit does not make them Dravidian, as several common words of the original Vedic language dropped out of the classical liturature but were preserved in the language of the people and are used even now. A glaring instance of this is the word Achchha not foand in Sanskrit of the classical writers; but it is found even in Ṛigvedic verses.

Then again the names of many things of ordinary use which had no occasion to be mentioned in classical writings look like Dravidian words. Such things as different sorts of Vīṇās must have had different names in the common language of the people even then. The word तंबलवीणा found in XXI is one such word; it is not a Tamil word as supposed by some. A word used in common parlance may appear like a Dravidian word; but unless shown to be such, it leads to no inference. (3) Finally forms like इवणी found in this Sūtra occur because this Sūtra has been preserved in the Āndhra country. We have shown how ळ has crept into the Ṛigveda for ड because it has been preserved mainly in the Deccan by Deccani Brahmins. That sound was not originally used by the Ṛishis. Similarly the use of ण or ड in place of न or ऋ in a few places must have crept in in Āndhra, the people of which, formed of the admixture of Aryans and Dravidians, are addicted to utter ण instead of न and ळ instead of ड. इवणी alone being of common use, however, has this form and not many words and this form also occurs in Kātyāyana Sūtra which also has mostly been preserved in the Deccan.

VI GOTRA PRAVARA CHAPTERS IN THE S'RAUTA SŪTRAS

These chapters are found at the end of the Āpastamba, Āsvalayana and Baudhyāyana and in the middle of Kātyāyana Śrauta Sūtras. On comparing their contents, it can be inferred that Baudhyāyana is the latest. The chapter in Āpastamba is itself a late addition to it, but the contents are unmistakably earlier than those of the other three Sūtras. Pravaras appear to be a later development of gotras. Gotras were established even in Upanishadic days; since besides the name of a teacher and that of his father, we have a gotra name given, such as Gautama or Vaiyāghrapadya. The Pravaras grew out of sacrificial necessities. The priests at the sacrifices were to be selected from such gotras as were cognate. The election ceremony called प्रवरण gave rise to the word प्रवर. The rites in different Ṛishi families appear to have differed and in selecting priests, the Yajamāna had to see that they were of the same family of gotras. This practice gradually gave rise to Pravaras for which rules are found first given in Āpastamba. The rule मंत्रकृतो वृणीते shows that the Pravara Ṛishi must be the author of mantras to be found in the several Saṁhitās. If there were many such in one's family, only five were to be mentioned and not more, as also never four (न चतुरो वृणीते न पंचाति वृणीते-आप०). It had to be declared to what Gotra and Pravara the Yajamāna belonged as also the priests, so that the same ritual was assured. This practice of declaring one's Gotra and Pravara has enabled the Brahmins and Kshatriyas to remember their descent from particular ancient Vedic Ṛishis down to this day.

These Gotras and Pravaras, however, are not different for the different Vedas. Brahmins and Kshatriyas are now divided into Ṛigvedins, Yajurvedins &c., i.e. followers of particular Vedas. But this distinction does not appear to have arisen at the time of these S'rauta Sūtras. Sacrifices had to be performed with the help of all the three Vedas and hence learned Brahmins knew generally all the three; the Brahman especially had to be versed in all the three. Hence the Gotra and Pravara system is the same for all Brahmins and Kshatriyas. Āpastamba and Āśvalāyana belong to Yajurveda and Ṛigveda respectively; but they give the same Gotra-Pravara system. Āśvalāyana's list seems to be the later of the two; it takes the two rules मंत्रकृतो वृणीते and न चतुरो वृणीते न पंचातिवृणीते for granted (13, XII). But it attributes the necessity of enunciating Pravaras to Āvāpa at sacrifices which can not be well understood. Āśvalāyana's list is very brief; indeed brevity is the characteristic of his writing.

Many more gotras are givea by Āpaṣtamba than those in Aśvalāyana; thus एष एत्र अत्रिकृत: शठ-मर्षण-मद्रण-मद्रप-बादरायणानाम् as belonging to the Pravara आंगिरस पौरुकुत्सत्रासदस्यव: ; given by Āpastamba is not mentioned by Aśvalāyana. (It may be noted here that बादरायण is an Āngirasa and not a Vāsishṭha and hence is different from Dvaipāyana Vyāsa who is a Pārāśara or Vāsishṭha). But the Pravaras are the same in both of them; and they begin with Bhṛigu, who, though not one of the Saptarshis, seems to be the oldest or highest Ṛishi, as all Pravara enumerations begin with him. This explains महर्षीणां भृगुरहम् of the Gītā.

It must be noted that the Gotra Ṛishi is not always a Pravara Ṛishi or Maharshi and he is called Ṛishi, only by courtesy. For Ṛishi, according to the definition accepted by all, means the author of a Vedic mantra. The Gotra Ṛishi is always born of such (Pravara) Ṛishis and, being renowned, gives a new name to the family of his descendants. Thus the Vatsas ars descendants of Jamadagni who is a Bhārgava, and hence the name Vatsa does not come in, in the Pravara which is of five Ṛishis. viz. भृगु, च्यवन, अप्रवान, ऊर्व and जमदग्नि. All these five are authors of mantras in the Ṛigveda as will be found from the list of Ṛigveda Ṛishis given at the end of Section I. The importance of these lists, as already stated, is very great for Pravara chapters and also for determining the sequence of these chapters in time as we proceed to show.

The principle that the Pravara Ṛishi ought to be a composer of Vedic mantras seems to have been lost sight of by and by. (At the present day very few know it, even among learned Brahmins). The consequence was that in later lists Ṛishis other than the real ones got into Pravaras. If we scan the Pravarādhyāya at the end of Baudhāyana Śrauta Sūtra, such names will be found in some Pravaras. Thus Śaṇḍila-gotras (शंडिलाः) have their Pravara in Āśvalāyana as follows: शांडिलासितदेवलेति काश्यपासितदेवलेति वा. Now in Baudhāyana's list, not only the Śaṇḍilas are found and divided into many minor-gotras, but the Pravaras given for them all are काश्यपावत्सारशांडिल or काश्यपावत्सारदेवल or काश्यपावत्सारासित or शांडिलासितदेवलेति वा. Now Śaṇḍila is not to be found in any of the Ṛishi lists (see section I). The proper Pravara for Śaṇḍilas, therefore, is the second one given by Āśvalāyana, viz. काश्यपासितदेवल, all the three कश्यप, असित and देवल being Ṛigvedic Ṛishis. This pravara should not include अवत्सार who is a Vedic Ṛishi, but can not come in this line, Asita being called Kāsyapa and not Āvatsāra in the Ṛishi list. The name of Śaṇḍila began to come in Āśvalāyana's time but it not only came in but occupied a wrong place in Baudhāyana's list, and other alternatives also appeared. Lohita again is not the name of a Ṛishi and yet we find a new Pravara in Baudhāyana mentioning him, viz. विश्वामित्राष्टकलोहित, Ashṭaka being given as a Vaiśvāmitra. This Pravara is not given by Āśvalāyana at all. Another notable instance is that of the gotra वाद्भुतक whose Pravara is आत्रेयार्चनानसवाद्भुतक.—वद्भुतक being a name not found among Vedic Ṛishis.

A more explicit evidence of the lateness of the Sūtra of Baudhāyana is the Pravara which he gives for Kshatriyas. Brahmins and Kshatriyas were originally descendants of the same Ṛishi ancestors some of whom were Brahmins and some Kshatriyas like मान्धातृ, अम्बरीष, युवनाश्व and त्रसदस्यु, names which appear in some Pravaras of even Brahmins. These were two classes of different professions still and not hide-bound castes. The Sūtra of Āpastamba first lays down that kings should have priests of the Pravara of his Purohita. This dictum applies to kings *de facto* whether they be Brahmins or Kshatriyas. And the Sūtra further provides that those Kshatriyas *who do not know* their Pravara should give it as मानवैलपौरूरवस. As time went on, Kshatriyas lost memory of their Pravaras and Āśvalayana gives this Pravara as a rule for them, adding, however, यदि सार्ष्टं प्रवृणीरन् (this is not well understood). In Baudhāyana's Sūtra this is the rule without any condition. Āpastamba gives वत्सप्रि as the one Pravara Ṛishi for Vaiśyas. In Baudhāyana we have three Pravara Ṛishis, भलन्दन, वत्सप्रि and मंकिल. In the Ṛigveda there is a sūkta by वत्सप्रि भालन्दन, but

मंकिल is a name not found in the Ṛigveda Ṛishi list, nor in Sāmaveda list nor in White Yajurveda list. He has been added by Baudhāyana Sūtra, as by its time the principle of Pravara was lost sight of.

But this list of Pravaras (made according to the *views* of Baudhāyana and not *by* Baudhāyana himself; vide इति मतं बौधायनस्य) is the most detailed one and gives many interesting gotras. In the first place it propounds Pakshas (पक्षाः) or orders, a word used by the Agni-purāṇa also which contains a detailed chapter on Gotra and Pravara. The Pakshas are of eight Ṛishis, Agastya plus the well-known Saptarshis (Gotra being defined by Baudhāyana as अगस्त्याष्टमानां सप्तर्षीणां यदपत्यं तद्गोत्रमित्याचक्षते). Again, gotras are said to be innumerable while Pravaras are 49 only. This can be easily understood, as Pravaras contain composers of Vedic hymns only. Thirdly, Pārāśaras whose Pravara is composed of पराशर, शक्ति and वसिष्ठ (all Ṛigvedic Ṛishis) are said to be of various colours, viz. कृष्ण (black), गौर, नील, अरुण, श्वेत and श्याम (dark) and under each head five new gotras are given in Anushṭup verses. Fourthly, a family is mentinned which is Vāsishṭha by day and Kāśyapa by night (अहर्वसिष्ठाः नक्तं कश्यपाः) and their Pravara is given as काश्यपावत्सारवासिष्ठाः. This is absurd as Pravara always indicated descent and not discipleship. For the Hotṛi recited the names in the descending and the Adhvaryu in the ascending order with वत्

added to each original name. (काश्यपावत्सारासितेति होता, असितवदवत्सारवत्कश्यपवदित्यध्वर्युः). The theory of discipleship is sometimes put forward; but it is clearly negatived by the relationship known from the names given in the Ṛigveda and the Purāṇas. Thus वत्सप्रि भालन्दन means son of Bhalandana, शक्ति is known as a son of Vasishṭha and Parāśara as a son of शक्ति. It is, therefore, absurd to bring in वसिष्ठ in the काश्यप line. See also एक एव प्रवरो मनुरिति मानव्या हि प्रजाः and मानवैलपौरूरवस clearly indicates descent and not discipleship.

The Pravaras were originally intended to regulate the selection of priests; but they subsequently came to regulate marriages also which were always to be outside the Pravara, while the priestly selection was always to be inside it. Āśvalāyana gives Pravaras solely for sacrifice; so does Āpastamba. But the Baudhāyana list takes them as intended for marriage and prescribes certain rules for त्र्यार्षेय and पंचार्षेय. These are copied in the Āśvalāyana Śrauta at the end in a Pariśishṭa Khaṇḍa. Certain further provisions are given in Baudhāyana which are copied by the Smṛitis. But it is remarkable that Baudhāyana's list states, in a सप्रवर marrage, ब्राह्मणीं न त्यजेत्; apparently in other Varṇas the सप्रवर marriage was of no account. Further it is added that such Brahmin wife should be treated like a sister or a mother. But what is meant by गर्भो न प्रदुष्यति?

Lastly, certain interesting gotras may be noted. The Pāṇini gotra is given under Vatsas and Bhṛigu Pancha-Pravara. This makes this list later than Pāṇini or 800 B.C.; for Pāṇini is not a gotra under any other list. Vālmīki is also given under the same gotra heading. दीर्घतमाः is an Āṅgirasa Kākshīvata and उशनस् is an Āṅgirasa Gautama; शुक्र is a Bhāradvāja and कौत्स is an Āṅgirasa Yauvanāśva. Āśvalāyana has one pravara only, viz. Vāsishṭha (45) and Paippalādas are Kúṇḍina Vasishṭhas. Patañjala and Taṇḍin are found in the Kapi Pravara and are Āṅgirasas (Amahīyu and Urukshaya, author of R. X 118). Yāska gotra is also found among Bhṛigus (6) as also कौटिल्य (who is a Yāska Bhṛigu). There is a gotra by name कौशाम्बेय (6) which takes this list after the foundation of that city. आपस्तम्ब is probably different from आपस्तम्ब. The following नाराशंसाः are given at the end, viz. आत्रेय-वाध्र्यश्व-वाधूल-वसिष्ठ-कण्व-शुनक-संकृति-यस्क-राजन्यवैश्याः (?). These are probably authors of sūktas recited as नराशंस.

VII VEDĀṄGA JYOTISHA

This work is a short treatise treating of Vedic mathematical astronomy. In the Ṛigvedic recension. it contains only 36 verses divided into seven Khaṇḍas of five verses each, with one more verse at the end. The system shows the great advance then made by Vaidika observers of the sky as also by Vaidika mathematicians, as concise formulæ are given for calculating Tithis, Parvans (full-moons and no-moons) and Vishuvans (equinoxial days), the knowledge of which was necessary for performing Vedic sacrifices. Indeed the work opens with the statement " I give all the various positions of the sun and the moon for the proper performance of sacrifices, as approved of by Brahmins (ज्योतिषामयनं कृत्स्नं प्रवक्ष्याम्यनुपूर्वशः । विप्राणां संमतं लोके यज्ञकालार्थसिद्धये ॥) and ends with the praise of astronomy in these words " Vedas prescribe sacrifices and these are to be performed at particular times to be known by astronomy only " (वेदा हि यज्ञार्थमभिप्रवृत्ताः कालानुपूर्वा विहिताश्च यज्ञाः । &c). It is indeed to be wondered that the Indo-Aryans had, at so ancient a date as 1200 B.C. certain, already enunciated rules for calculating the future positions of the sun and the moon among the Nakshatras. They are of course not as accurate as those calculated under later

Siddhāntas (150 B.C. to 400 A.D.). But they are very approximate as mean positions, as shown by S. B. Dixit in his "History of Indian Astronomy" in Marathi.

The basis of calculation is a five-years' cycle called a Yuga. The solar year is taken to be of 366 days; and as in five years or 1830 days, there are 124 complete parvans (62 full-moons and 62 no-moons), the cycle of five years was properly taken as the basis of calculation. The Vedic sacrifices of Darśa–Pūrṇamāsa were the most important ones and hence the Vedic year was bound to be lunar. The five years' cycle contained 62 lunar months and thus two months had to be added to 5 lunar years to make the cycle a solar one. The cycle commenced with the coming together of the sun, the moon and the Nakshatra Dhanishṭhā on Māgha Pratipadā at the beginning of the sun's northern course i.e. at autumnal solstice; the Vedāṅga Jyotisha system with its five years (names संवत्सर, परिवत्सर, इदावत्सर, अनुवत्सर and इद्वत्सर already appearing in the Taittirīya Brāhmaṇa with their lords), therefore, started with the month of Māgha, white fortnight and Uttarāyaṇa (स्वराक्रमेते सोमार्कौ यदा साकं सवासवौ । तदादियुगं माघस्तपः शुक्लोऽयनं ह्युदक्–यजुःपाठ). This most important verse affords us the date of this work unmistakably, as shown already.

The five years' cycle of 60 lunar months and 2 intercalary months added at the end of every two years and a half, viz. one before Śrāvaṇa of the third year and another at the end before Māgha of the next cycle is made the basis of calculation of Tithis, Parvans and Vishuvans under rules hereafter given in verses which are not all intelligible. Great Indian scholars like Sudhākar Dvivėdi, Bārhaspatya (Lala Chhotalal), S. B. Dixit and B. G. Tilak and European scholars like Thibaut have attempted to explain these rules, by suggesting certain emendations of the verses in the Ṛigveda and Yajurveda recensions. But unfortunately, as Tilak observes, "the last word on this Vedānga has yet to be uttered" (p. 104 'Vedic Chronology and Vedānga Jyotisha). This difficulty arises from the fact, also noted by Tilak, that the calendar was abandoned in India when the astronomical Siddhāntas were formulated about the first century B.C.; and for the last two thousand years, we know nothing of the Vedānga Jyotisha calender, that work being only recited as a sacred work by Vaidikas without understanding a word of it as usual, and not used at all by astronomers. Further, the calculations of the Vedānga Jyotisha are made with the Vedic Zodiac of 27 Nakshatras and not of 12 Rāśis, the latter being introduced into India by the Greeks before the rise of the Siddhāntas which almost ignore Nakshatras and use Rāśis only. The Hindu ritual for the last two thousand years has taken up Rāśis and neglected practically the Vedic Nakshatras and thus Rāśis or Lagnas are now ingrained in the Hindu mind. Then again, the minute divisions of time and of the Zodiac of the Vedāṅga have also been forgotten. The Vedāṅga system of calculation divides each Nakshatra into 124 Aṁśas which is suitable to its method, as the number of Parvans in a cycle is also 124. The day is divided into 30 Muhūrtas, each of two Nāḍīs (modern ghaṭīs), each nāḍī being divided into $10\frac{1}{20}$ Kalās, the Siddhānta division of a day being into 60 ghaṭīs, each ghaṭī being of 60 palas. It is no wonder, therefore, that the Vedāṅga Jyotisha in the last two thousand years remained entirely neglected, till taken up by inquisitive European antiquarians and mathematicians.

The Vedāṅga Jyotisha is found in two recensions, viz. Ṛigvedic and Yajurvedic and there is a third, Atharvavedic, which is a very late one as we shall show. The verses in the Yajurvedic recension are 43 and are changed in order as shown by Dixit (p. 72). The work proposes to propound the knowledge as taught by Lagadha: कालज्ञानं प्रवक्ष्यामि लगधस्य महात्मनः. Who wrote this work and where cannot, therefore, be definitely determined, though it must have been written not long after Lagadha taught this system. The system of Lagadha itself must have been formulated about 1400 B. C. as shown by Dixit in detail in his work, from calculation made on the basis of the astronomical data found therein as also from other arguments (p. 90).

We have already quoted the verse wherein this datum is given, viz. the sun, the moon and the Nakshatra Dhanishṭhā being together at Uttarāyaṇa on Māgha Suddha 1. It is followed by another verse equally clear, viz. प्रपद्येते श्रविष्ठादौ सूर्याचन्द्रमसावुदक्. "In the begining of Śravishṭhā the sun and the moon turn towards the north." The tense is present and this conjunction was observed as occurring in the days of Lagadha. This datum can be made the basis for calculation of the date of this fact, as owing to the precession of equinoxes, the Uttarāyaṇa point has receded back upto our time, from the beginning of Dhanishṭhā to a point somewhere in Pūrvāshāḍhā. Naturally this position of the solstices recorded in these verses attracted the attention of early European sholars like Colebrooke and Sir William Jones, as stated already (Sec. I p. 36). The attention of Max Müller was drawn to it and it was pointed out to him that the date of the Vedāṅga Jyotisha evidenced by it was "about 1200 B. C." and was inconsistent with the date 1200 to 1000 B.C. assigned by him to the Ṛigveda itself. We have already shown how Max Müller vainly tried to get over this difficulty (*ibid*. p. 32). This date, whether we take 1400 B. C. as fixed by Dixit by taking the beginning of Dhanishṭhā as the star α Delphīni itself, or 1200 B.C. as fixed by Colebroke or 1192 B.C. as calculated by Archbishop Pratt for Max Müller, is the most important date in the history of Vedic literature, as the whole of that literature commencing with the Ṛigveda must be placed centuries before it. Most European scholars, however, seem to pay no attention to it, either ignoring it altogether or minimizing its value somehow. Thus Winternitz observes at page 289: "The very circumstance that it (Vedāṅga Jyotisha) is not written in prose refers this little work, which, moreover, has not yet been sufficiently explained, to a later period." Now even if we concede that the work as it is before us in verse is a late one, the astronomical observation recorded therein and the system of astronomical calculation based upon it remain and unquestionably go back to 1200 B. C. at the latest. The verses further in which these facts are recorded are clear and are not the subject of any controversy and do not require any explanation. Thus the cycle of five years, the month of Māgha commencing each cycle, Uttarāyaṇa commencing on Māgha Śukla 1, at the beginning of Dhanishṭhā are facts clear as day. On these facts this method of framing a calendar was eunnciated by Lagadha at a time when the whole Vedic literature had been written, viz. the Saṁhitās, the Brāhmaṇas and the 13 older Upanishads. For the Māitrāyaṇīya

Upanishad refers to an earlier position of the Uttarāyaṇa, viz. in the middle of the Dhanishṭhā division. Then again, the names of months Māgha &c. are not found in the Ṛigveda or the Yajurveda Saṁhitās; they were introduced about 2500 to 2000 B. C. And the first month was then taken to be Mārgaśirsha, as will be shown later on when we speak of the Bhagavadgītā. The new system of Lagadha made Māgha the first month and this mode of reckoning lasted till the first century B. C., when this month reckoning was again changed and Chaitra was taken as the first month. It does not in the least affect our argument based on the Vedāṅga Jyotisha system, if we concede that the *work* before us is a late one. The *system* of Lagadha is as old as 1400 B.C. or at the latest 1200 B.C as calculated by Archbishop Pratt and is itself posterior to the Brāhmaṇas and the older Upanishads, not to speak of the Saṁhitās.

But we need not concede that the work before us is a very late one. At most it may have been composed a few centuries after Lagadha. The objection that it is in verse is of no value. We have some of the older Upanishads themselves in verse, containing Anushṭup and Trishṭup ślokas. Ślokas again are mentioned in Brihadāraṇyaka and the Maitrī Upanishad quotes ślokas from the Vedic literature then current (1900 B.C.).

Further, as pointed out by Dixit, the work

uses old names of Nakshatras such as Śravishṭhā for Dhanishthā, Aśvayuk for Aśvinī and Śatabhishak for Śatatārakā (p. 90). As pointed out by Haug, the work uses the word चर्म for day which had disappeared even in the time of Yāska and Pāṇini (*ibid.*). Weber is clearly wrong when he says that the work uses the word Rāśi in the sense of the signs of the Zodiac; the word evidently means, from the context itself, a sum or a figure as in Chhāndogya where the word means arithmetic from this sense (as in त्रैराशिक). The Jyotisha is earlier than Garga and Parāśara who are mentioned in, and therefore, older than, Pāṇini (Kunte). It follows thus that we shall not be far wrong if we hold that the work, as it is before us, is itself as old as 1000 B.C.

The Ṛik recension is actually learnt by heart and recited by Ṛigveda Vaidikas; but the Yajuḥ one is, so far as is known, nowhere learnt by Yajurveda Vaidikas. It is, however, more correct than the former. From the statement about the longest and shortest day, viz. 24 and 36 nāḍīs, Dixit calculates that this applies to North Lat. 34°–46′ (p. 90) which falls about Kandahar and Kashmir and that is the place where Lagadha probably evolved his system.

It may be added that this work still gives the Yajurveda Nakshatra reckoning commencing with Kṛittikās. It appears that in consequence of this system, Dhanishṭhā began to be taken as the first Nakshatra. We have evidence in the Mahābhārata that subsequently owing to precession, Uttararāyaṇa began to take place in Sravaṇa and that Nakshatra was taken as the first (श्रवणादीनि नक्षत्राणि-अनुगीता). This must have been about 400 B C. as the precession over one Nakshatra or 13⅓° at 72 years per degree would take 960 or roughly 1000 years. There was a change again when the Siddhāntas were promulgated and Chaitra was taken as the first month and the year counted not from autumnal solstice but from vernal equinox, which then fell in the beginning of Āśvinī. This was, therefore, taken as the first Nakshatra, a reckoning which is still in vogue. The Vedāṅga Jyotisha which takes Krittikādi Nakshatras must, therefore, be very old, only a century or so later, if at all, than Laghdha, the author of the system.

Two or three interesting facts which appear from this work may be noted. 1 Names of Nakshatras are shortened by omitting all letters except the last. Thus Sravishṭhā is indicated by the letter ष्ठा; this shows that this work tries to secure the brevity of prose Sūtras. 2 The method of naming persons from their Nakshatra of birth, so prevalent in India, appears to be probably Vedic as it is referred to in this work नक्षत्रदेवता एता एताभिर्यज्ञकर्मणि । यजमानाय शास्त्रज्ञैर्नाम नक्षत्रजं स्मृतम् (१७). 3 Measures of weight are given in connection with the water-clock, which appears to have been used from those ancient days, as follows:—50 Palas make an Āḍhaka and 4 Āḍhakas make a Droṇa. One Droṇa less one Kuḍava (Kuḍava of Bhāskara-Dixit p.79) of water flows out in one Nādī of time. The weight Prastha is also mentioned which Dixit finds to be equal to 12½ Palas or 1/4 of an Āḍhaka. This pala subsequently, from being a measure of weight, became a measure of time, viz. 1/60 of a ghaṭī or Nāḍī.

The Atharva Jyotisha is described in detail by S. B. Dixit. As every work relating to this Veda is late, so is also this Jyotisha. It contains 162 verses distributed over 17 heads or प्रकरणs. It contains a description of Muhūrtas with the length of the shadow, cast in each, of a 12 aṅgula rod. It describes Tithis; and Karaṇas and Yogas are also mentioned further on. The latter two and the mention of Vāras or week-days makes it clear that this work was composed after the Vedic period as we have conceived it, viz. 1400–800 B.C. Nakshatras are also divided astrologically. But that this work is pre-Siddhānta is clear as it makes no mention of the 12 Rāśis of modern Indian Astronomy, borrowed from the Greeks. We might have omitted to notice this work in this Section; but as it claims to be a Vedāṅga, we have given Dixit's description of it (p. 98–100) to prevent misunderstanding.

VIII YĀSKA'S NIRUKTA WITH NIGHANṬU

This Vedāṅga treats of the derivation of Vedic words. The words selected for derivation are those which are collected in what is called Nighaṇṭu. Yāska is the reputed author of the Nirukta which is extant; but there must have been other works before his; at least there must have been other Āchāryas before him who had studied the subject and propounded their views. Some of these are mentioned in the Nirukta, Śākapūṇi and Aupamanyava being constantly mentioned among them. The Nighaṇṭu or collection of words prefixed to Yāska's Nirukta is not his work; and must have been in existence before him as a work which had already become sacred, since he calls it, in the very beginning of his work, a Samāmnāya (समाम्नायः समाम्नातः). Prof. Chandramaṇi of Kāṅgḍi Vidyāpītha thinks that in enunciating this Samāṃnāya, Yāska must have made some alterations in it; but if it was already treated as sacred, no orthodox author would have altered it. We will first describe in detail this Nīghaṇṭu on which Yāska has based his Nirukta.

(1) Nighaṇṭu.

Nighaṇṭu contains five Adhyāyas or chapters

the first three of which give synonyms and the last two homonyms. The contents of chapter I may be detailed here as follows:—

1	Gau and its synonyms	meaning earth	12	words.
2	Hema	... gold	14	„
3	Ambara	... sky	16	„
4	Svaḥ and other words	... sky and heaven	6	„
5	Svedayaḥ	... rays	15	„
6	Ātaḥ	directions	8	„
7	Śyāvī	... night	22	„
8	Vibhāvarī	उषा (dawn)	16	„
9	Vastoḥ	... day	12	„
10	Adri	... cloud	30	„
11	Śloka	...speech	57	„
12	Arṇaḥ	... water	101	„
13	Avanayaḥ	... rivers	37	„
14	Atya	... horse	26	„
15	Hari (name of Indra's two horses) &c. giving names of the special animals of ten deities		10	„
16	Bhrājate	to shine or burn	11	„
17	Jamat	burning	11	„

We give these details of the contents of the first chapter as a sample of the contents of these chapters. They show how the Vedic language was copious containing, as it did, a hundred and one words for water. Some words no doubt seem to have been interpreted in a different sense from the one in which they were used by the Ṛishis who composed the Vedic hymns. Thus both Asura and Vṛitra are interpreted as meaning a cloud also. The date of this collection of words seems to be several hundreds of years later than that of the Ṛigvedic hymns some of which had became unintelligible to the Āchāryas of the Vedāṅga period who tried to interpret them. Such words differently interpreted are not, however, many and the wonderful wealth of words in the Vedic language remains undiminished.

Chapter II gives 22 words for act (कर्मन्), 15 for progeny (अपत्य), 25 for men (मनुष्य) among which we find strangely enough तुर्वशाः, द्रुह्यवः, आयवः, यदवः, अनवः and पूरवः which are, historically speaking, names of Aryan clans of the lunar race; 12 for arm, 22 for finger, 18 for shining, 28 for food, 10 for eating, 28 for strength, 28 for wealth, 9 for cow, 10 for being angry and 11 for anger. A hundred and twenty-two words are catalogued meaning 'to go' and 46 words meaning fight or battle and 33 words meaning to kill.

Chapter III gives 12 words meaning many, 11 little or short, 25 great, 22 a house, 10 to worship, 20 happiness, 16 form or body, 10 good or praiseworthy, 11 intelligence, 6 true, 8 seeing, 44 praising, 24 a wise man, 13 praise and 15 sacrifice. Vishṇu, Indu, Prajāpati and Dharma are included among words meaning sacrifice or यज्ञ; the dictum विष्णुर्वै यज्ञः of the Yajurveda perhaps suggested this. Eight words meaning a priest include Bharatas and Kurus. These originally meant people of the two Indo-Aryan solar and lunar races. When this distinction was lost, to later interpreters of Ṛiks the words appeared to mean priests only. 17 words mean to pray and 10 to give. 14 words are given meaning a ditch or well, 14 a thief, 6 concealed, 5 distant, 6 ancient and 6 modern.

These three chapters are called together the Nighaṇṭu Kāṇḍa. The fourth chapter is called the Naigama Kāṇḍa. It does not give any synonyms, but simply collects together, according to our view, words in the Ṛigveda which had nearly become obsolete. They are given in three sets, on what principle can not be surmised. The first set gives 62, the second 84, and the third 133 without any specification of their meanings. The order also in which these words are given is almost inexplicable. Probably they are given haphazard and not in the order in which they occur in the Ṛigveda. The fifth chapter is called Devatākāṇḍa and brings together names which are used to indicate different deities. They are arranged in six sets, giving 3, 13, 36, 32, 36 and 31 words respectively. The order here in intelligible. Thus in Khaṇḍa 5, we have female deities, 21 in number, given together. Aṅgiras, Atharvan and Bhṛigu are ancestors of the Aryans and are included among names of deities naturally enough.

Having given the contents of these vocabularies, we may proceed to explain how the name Nighaṇṭu, given to them, arose. Aupamanyava, an ancient Nairukta Āchārya, says that the name originally was Nigantus or words *explaining* (निगमनात्) and was subsequently changed into Nighaṇṭus. We have already shown that the population of middle India is of mixed Aryo-Dravidian race. That the Dravidians have a tendency to aspirate letters is apparent, as even now Dravidians of the South, learned and unlearned, pronounce 'Tarpaṇa' as 'Tharpaṇa' and so on. The Śākala recension of the Ṛigveda, we have seen, changes ḍ into ḷ, also a Dravidian tendency. Yāska after giving this earlier derivation, however, suggests a second one, viz. that Nighaṇṭus means words 'separated', from the root 'han' (changed into ghan). This derivation is more probable, though how the t of 'ghnat' was changed into ṭ remains unexplained.

The author of these collections of words can not, as already stated, be Yāska though he may be the author of the last two chapters as explained later on. The question who their author is has been answered by Prof. Chandramaṇi by the help of a verse in the Mahābhārata (Śāntip. chap.342) in which Vṛishākapi is mentioned as the author of Nighaṇṭu and his guru's name is given as Prajāpati. It is, however, apparent that these authors are imaginary. Indeed in this chapter of MBh., Vedic works are generally ascribed to divine beings. Vṛishākapi is Vishṇu and Prajāpati is the father of all gods. Hiraṇyagarbha is similarly elsewhere looked upon as the promulgator of Yoga. Where authors were not known, sacred works were ascribed to gods themselves. Kapila alone seems to have been known as a human author, promulgating the Sāṅkhya philosophy. It seems that the author or authors of these collections of words were not known even in the days of the Mahābhārata (circa. 250 B.C.). In the next chapter (MBh. XII, 343, 71) Yāska is mentioned as praising Vishṇu in several sacrifices (नैकयज्ञेषु गीतवान्). He is undoubtedly the same as the author of our Nirukta; for he, interpreting various Ṛiks used by sacrificers, must himself have performed many sacrifices. Along with Yāska's name, that of his guru seems to have been mentioned, viz. Śipivishṭa. Prof. Chandramaṇi looks upon this name as the name of the real guru of Yāska and quotes for support Yāska's reference to his guru at the end of VII 6, 22. But the words used by Yāska here are simply इत्याचार्याः; no name is given here though this may be taken to be a reference to his guru by Yāska (the plural आचार्याः being used in reverence). Śipivishṭa is the name of

Vishṇu and we think does not indicate a human teacher. Having thus far discussed Nighaṇṭu, we proceed to describe in detail Yāska's Nirukta which is based on it.

(2) Nirukta.

The Nirukta of Yāska is divided into two halves called Pūrvashaṭka and Uttarashaṭka as each half contains six chapters. There are two more chapters added at the end which form the Pariśishṭa or appendix. (We will refer to these chapters by consecutive figures from I to XIV). The chapters are divided into Khaṇḍas or sections which consist of one sentence or mantra each. These Khaṇḍas are enumerated by their beginning words at the end of the chapter in what are called links, on the system of Yajurveda. On enquiring of Ṛigveda-Vaidikas, we were told that the system assisted correct recitation without Saṁchāra, as the Khaṇḍas ended usually with the same word भवति (तस्यैषा भवति). But curiously enough, the system is followed even in the Nighaṇṭu where there are no occasions for Saṁchāra. The words in the Nighaṇṭu have, naturally enough, accents, the same as those in the Ṛigvedic verses where they are found, sometimes with the accent on the last letter changed. The Nirukta, as now recited at least, has no accents. But in order to break monotony in recitation, the last letter in parts of sentences or after a number of letters is recited like Udātta and is marked in writing with an upward stroke. Of course where Ṛigvedic mantras are quoted, they are recited with their proper Vedic accents and are marked with their strokes in writing.

Yāska begins his work thus :—"The sacred collection (of Nighaṇṭu) has been collected; it is to be commented on" (समाम्नायः समाम्नातः सं व्याख्यातव्यः:). He first explains the word Nighaṇṭu as described before. Yāska then proceeds to divide Vedic words into four kinds, viz. 1 nouns (नाम), 2 verbs (आख्यात), 3 prefixes (उपसर्ग) and 4 particles (निपात). Extremely scientific definitions are given of these four terms, showing the great advance that grammar had made in the time of Yāska. These terms are adopted by Pāṇini who gives no definitions of these and who thus very probably came after Yāska. An interesting difference of opinion among savants is here noted by Yāska as to whether a prefix has or has not a meaning of its own, and several authorities on Nirukta are mentioned here. Thus Śākaṭāyana holds that prefixes (उपसर्गाः) have no meaning, but Gārgya holds that they have a meaning when joined to a noun or verb. These prefixes are not enumerated in the Nighaṇṭu and Yāska gives them all here in pairs of opposite meanings, such as आ and परा, अभि and प्रति &c. The expletives (निपात), also not given in the Nighaṇṭu, are given by him with their Vedic meanings, illustrated by quotation of Ṛigvedic mantras, as also their meanings in ordinary Sanskrit. Yāska like Paṇini uses the word भाषायाम् for the latter, which proves that Sanskrit was then a spoken language and that the word Sanskrit had not yet come into existence. Pāṇini uses the word छन्दसि to indicate Vedic language, but Yāska appears to use the word अन्वध्यायं or अधीते 'as recited' I. 4). The chief doctrine of the Nairuktas or etymologists is here enunciated, viz. that all words are derived from roots, a theory which has now been accepted by modern philologists. Three schools of thought existed in those ancient times in connection with the interpretation of Ṛigvedic verses, viz. Nairuktas, Vaiyākaraṇas and Aitihāsikas. Thus, with the Nairuktas, Vṛitra was a cloud while with the last, as stated before, he was an Asura and son of Tvashṭṛi. A fourth school, mentioned later on, was that of Yājñikas or sacrificers. This introduction by Yāska extending over chapter I is very interesting and deserves to be studied by students of Vedic Sanskrit.

The introduction is continued in chapter II and Yāska first details the method of Nirvachana or derivation, i.e. how words are formed from roots, how letters disappear or change, how Vibhaktis (cases) are altered and how Nirukta recognises changes other than those given by grammar. That Vedic words are often derived from roots used in ordinary language though they are not themselves in ordinary use or vice-versa is shown by illustrations such as उष्ण from the Vedic verb उष् to burn and घृत from घृ to flow. These words are used in माषा but the roots thereof are not used in the ordinary language. Nay, while some roots survive in the north, they have disappeared elsewhere, though their derivatives are still used there. As an instance of this, Yāska gives शवति (to go) as still used in the Kāmboja country and दाति (to cut) as used among Prāchyas, its derivative दात्र alone being used among Northerners. It is important to note here that Yāska like Pāṇini speaks of the differences in the spoken language of Easterners and Northerners. They both, however, do not refer to Southerners, which shows that the Aryan land then spread from Kāmboja in the north to Magadha in the east and that Aryans had not yet migrated southwards. This further shows that they both belonged to the central land (मध्यदेश), viz. the Panjab and Kurukshetra. Yāska here derives the word Kāmboja (following his practice of giving derivation of interesting words even as they crop up) from कम्बलभोजाः 'using shawls' (precious shawls being produced then as now in Kashmir and other adjoining parts). Thus simple words, as opposed to compounds or derivatives, are to be explained from their meanings and from

Vedic roots, current or not current in the spoken language of different parts of the country. In commenting on the latter, Yāska has occasion to mention the word Daṇḍa (दण्ड) and at once proceeds to give its derivation from the root दद् to hold. Here occurs the well-known sentence अक्रूरो ददते मणिम् (धारयते मणिम्) which was proverbial in his days (इत्यभिभाषते) and which refers to the story of Akrūra and Śrīkṛishṇa and the stolen jewel named Syamantaka. Aupamanyava, however, derives दण्ड from दमन.

Having explained further how compound words (समास) should be derived, Yāska in II 3 gives the caution that words unconnected (detached from the verses where they are used) should not be explained. Further, the निर्वचन should not be explained to one who does not know grammar or who is actuated by malice or असूया (One is reminded here of the line in Bhagavadgītā न चाशुश्रूषवे वाच्यं न च मां योऽभ्यसूयति) nor to one who does not know the rules of निर्वचन. It may, however, be given to an intelligent (though a बाल) or self-restrained person. Yāska, in II 4, quotes a Vedic mantra (from where has not been ascertained) in which Vidyā is said to come to a Brahmin for protection, promising that he would find her a treasure if imparted to a holy and intelligent student observing Brahmacharya.

After this long though instructive introduction, from II 5 Yāska takes up the words in the

Nighaṇṭu one by one and gives their derivations, quoting the Ṛigvedic verses where they are used. There are several derivations suggested for every word almost, some of which strike one as fanciful. Indeed one begins to think that a word may be derived from any root if one has enough ingenuity; especially as roots in Sankrit have almost innumerable meanings. Generally, however, words are well explained in the first derivation and Ṛigvedic verses are well interpreted. Where supporting Vedic verses are quoted, Yāska uses the expression इत्यपि निगमो भवति. Commentators and Prof. Chandramaṇi have generally given the references to these Vedic quotations which are mostly from the Ṛigveda. Yāska, when quoting from a Brāhmaṇa, uses the words इति ब्राह्मणम् and more often इति विज्ञायते. Historical references are given prefaced by the words अत्रेतिहासमाचक्षते. Here he either gives oral traditions of his days or those embodied in Itihāsa-Purāṇa, now lost, but preserved in later works like Bṛihaddevatā. We proceed to give such interesting historical legends as also such interesting derivations given by Yāska as deserve to be given, in the following note.

Interesting statements in Nirukta.

We have in II the story of Devāpi, a brother of S'antanu, hinted at even in a Ṛigvedic verse. We have next the story told of Viśvāmitra and King Sudāsa coming to the river Vipāṭ (Bias) and S'atadru (Sutlej). Paṇis are said to be Vaṇiks (merchants) from पण्यकर्म. This word is usually looked upon as equivalent to Phœnicians who were no doubt merchants and who went to distant lands like the British for trade. But Paṇis are mentioned in the Ṛigveda as stealers of cows !!! Perhaps they traded as well as stole cows.

Yāska, having finished the words in Adhyāya I of Nighaṇṭu in chapter II, takes up in chapter III words in the second Adhyāya. In deriving the word पुत्र, Yāska notices the law of Indo-Aryan inheritance by which sons alone and not daughters inherit and quotes Manu Svāyambhuva as authority. Manu, as an ancient lawgiver, is thus known to Yāska; but the verse quoted (अविशेषेण पुत्राणां दायो भवति धर्मतः) is not found in the modern Manusmṛiti. Yāska adds that females can be sold, gifted away or abandoned (स्त्रीणां दानविक्रयातिसर्गा विद्यन्ते न पुत्राणाम्) and quotes many Ṛigvedic verses here on the topic (III 3-6).

In III 8 असुर and पंचजन are explained. Yāska quotes a Vedic authority for deriving सुर from सु and असुर from असु (सोऽर्देवानसृजततासोरसुरान् इति विज्ञायते). But सुर is not a Vedic word at all; it was probably derived by dropping अ from असुर in Purāṇa times. Asura again has a higher sense even in the Ṛigveda and is properly derived from असु meaning प्राण. The word पंचजन frequently occurs in the Ṛigveda; but its meaning had become obscure in the days of Yāska. He gives the interpretations current at the time: गन्धर्वाः देवाः पितरः असुराः रक्षांसीत्येके । चत्वारो वर्णाः निषादः पञ्चमः इत्यौपमन्यवः. Yāska here derives निषाद (not mentioned in निघण्टु) in two ways; निषदनो भवति निषण्णमस्मिन्पातकमिति नैरुक्ताः It may be said that Aupamanyava is more reliable and निषाद meant really the people settled on the land, the Aryans being invaders.

In explaining खल meaning संग्राम (battle), Yāska gives the derivation of the words for numerals, which is very interesting though not quite convincing (एक इता संख्या द्वौ द्रुततरा त्रयस्तीर्णतमा चत्वारश्चलिततमा अष्टावश्नोतेर्नव न वननीया-नावाप्ता वा दश दस्ता दृष्टार्था वा विंशतिर्द्विर्दशतः शतं दशदशतः सहस्रं सहस्वदयुतं नियुतं प्रयुतं तत्तदभ्यस्तमम्बुदो मेघः स यथा महान् बहुर्भवति वर्षस्तदिवार्बुदम्. Here he gives the higher digits up to अर्बुद (III 10). We may next note that the verses quoted in III 30 include one नेमे देवाः &c traced to मैत्रायणी सं. (१।१।९ वाजपेये मैत्रायणीनाम्) by the commentator in which the word नेम means half, a word found in Persian also with the same meaning. This word is given in the Nighaṇṭu.

In beginning chapter IV, Yāska observes "We have given up to now many words having the same meaning. We will give now, in order, words having may meanings (एकार्थमनेकशब्दमित्येतदुक्तम् । अथ यान्यनेकार्था-न्येकशब्दानि तान्यनुक्रमिष्यामः) and Vedic expressions the grammatical explanations of which are not known (अनवगतसंस्कारांश्च निगमान्). This indicates the nature of the Naigama Kāṇḍa. He then takes up the words जहा &c. in the fourth chapter of Nighaṇṭu and quotes the Vedic verses where they occur. In explaining नाभि Yāska says अत एव ज्ञातीन् सनाभय इत्याचक्षते and derives ज्ञाति also from संज्ञान (21), those who are known as relatives. इति च ब्राह्मणम् specially mentions a Brāhmaṇa instead of the usual विज्ञायते.

In chapters V and VI are given further homonyms from Adhyāya III of the Nighaṇṭu. It is interesting to note that the Ṛik सप्तमर्यादाः कवयस्ततक्षुः is unsatisfactorily interpreted by Yāska as referring to the seven recognised sins, viz. १ स्तेयं २ तल्पारोहणं ३ ब्रह्महत्या ४ भ्रूणहत्या ५ सुरापानं ६ दुष्कृतस्य कर्मणः पुनः पुनः सेवा पातकेऽनृतोद्यम् (VI 29). Probably the five great sins enumerated in the Chhāndogya were later increased to seven. Bhrūṇahatyā was now looked upon as a great sin, because it had probably become more common; grown up unmarried girls becoming pregnant were given medicine to cause abortion as greater shame now attached to such lapses and the marriage of such girls became more difficult. In VI 28 S'ākalya, the author of the Ṛigveda Pada text, is mentioned and his padas criticised as improper. Parāśara, the name of Vasishṭha's son, is derived from पराशीर्णस्य (वसिष्ठस्य जज्ञे) in allusion to the story of Vasishṭha's 100 sons being killed by Viśvāmitra and then Vasishṭha's getting a son in old age (पराशरः शतयातुर्वसिष्ठः इत्यपि निगमो भवति). The next noticeable word is कीकटेषु which is described as an अनार्यदेशः and derived from किं कृतम्. मंगद is interpreted as कुसीदिन् and प्रमंगद as अत्यंतकुसीदिन्. This would show that money-lending flourished even in the days of the Ṛigvedic hymns.

We now come to the Uttarashaṭka or the second half consisting of six chapters, devoted to the derivation of names of deities given in the fifth Adhyāya of Nighaṇṭu and thence called Devatā Kāṇḍa. Yāska first, in a highly philosophical introduction, explains the nature of Vedic deities and also of the Ṛigvedic hymns in praise of them. The Upanishadic philosophy was fully developed by his time and Yāska seems to be a thorough Advaitī Vedantist who identifies the world with God or nature and Ātman, and therefore sees nothing wrong in the Ṛiks being divided into three classes-1 परोक्षकृत, 2 प्रत्यक्षकृत and 3 आध्यात्मिक. The परोक्षकृत verses are in the third person (called प्रथम पुरुष in Sanskrit) and in all Vibhaktis or cases of nouns (e.g. इन्द्रो दिवि &c.). The प्रत्यक्षकृत verses are in the second person (मध्यम पुरुष) and in Vibhaktis of the pronoun 'thou' (त्वमिन्द्र बलादधि &c.). The आध्यात्मिक verses are in the first person (उत्तम पुरुष) and in case forms of the pronoun 'I'. Such verses are of course few and they are both in praise as well as in prayer. Sometimes they are uttered in cursing or swearing. It may be noted here that many grammatical terms, viz. प्रथम पुरुष मध्यम पुरुष, उतम पुरुष, विभक्ति, नाम, सर्वनाम &c. had already come into use and become fixed and were used by Pāṇini without definitions as terms well-known.

Yāska then divides the deities also into three classes, viz. those of earth, sky and heaven. In fact there are three deities only according to the Nairuktas: Agni, Vāyu and Āditya. They have many different names assigned to them according to their many different functions, arising from their great glory, just as a priest becomes Hotṛi, Adhvaryu and Brahman according to his different functions. As to their forms three opinions are noted (1) that they have human forms (2) that they have no forms and (3) that they are of both descriptions. Where no deity is apparent in the hymn, it should be taken to be in praise of Prajāpati (प्राजापत्य) or of men (नाराशंस). Yāska speaks mostly of Ṛigveda mantras and mentions Ṛigveda by the name दाशतयी, which probably indicates that its division into Adhyāyas and Vargas is later than Yāska.

Yāska hereafter enumerates the seven metres and gives the derivation of their names, Gāyatri, Anushṭup &c. The Prayāja and Anuyāja mantras are next noted and these terms appear to be as old as the Ṛigveda hymns (VII 22). Indeed the cult and method of Vedic sacrifice must be very old.

From Khaṇḍa 14 (VII), Yāska takes up the words in the Devatākāṇḍa one by one, with the usual words अथातोऽनुक्रमिष्यामः. This Kāṇḍa may perhaps have been added by Yāska himself, as the words given therein are arranged on the plan given by him; and deities of the earth are first given, then of the sky and then of heaven. They first include even animals and inanimate objects also, praised in Ṛigvedic hymns. In explaining the various names, Yāska brings together most of the difficult verses in the Ṛigveda. It almost appears that the six chapters of the latter half of Nirukta are devoted rather to the interpretation of contested Vedic hymns than to the derivation of words, which is the proper subject of Nirukta. There are also noticed differences of opinion among various schools of interpreters, Yājñikas or sacrificers also having their own views. Yāska has thus rendered a great service to the study of the Ṛigveda; and interpreters of modern days or Bhāshyakāras of the Hindu period are greatly assisted as well as checked by it in their difficult work.

We now proceed to notice the interesting statements in the several chapters of the Uttarashaṭka. Vanaspati is interpreted as Yūpa by Kātthakya (a new name) and as fire itself by S'ākapūṇi (VIII 17). The eleven Āprīsūktas are mentioned and those by Vasishṭha, Atri, Vadhryaśva and Gṛitsamada are classed as Nārāśaṁsa,* those by Medhātithi and Dīrghatamas and the Praishas as उभयविध and the remaining by others are regarded as addressed to Tanūnapāt.

In beginning chapter IX Yāska says, "We will hereafter take up the objects on this earth which have received praise and Aśva is the foremost of these (अथ यानि पृथिव्यायतनानि सत्त्वानि स्तुतिं लभन्ते तान्यतोऽनुक्रमिष्यामस्तेषामश्वः प्रथमगामी भवति). Soma is described in a Ṛik as Maujavata; it is thus clearly an herb found in the higher Himālayas. Dundubhi is a word derived from the sound it produces, which is very probable. In IX 23 the story of Mudgala, son of Bhrimaśva, is given in explaining the word वृषभ. He is said to have conquered king Sūbharva and recovered his cows, clearly mentioned here to be one thousand and not a hundred thousand (सुभर्वं राजानं सहस्रं गवां मुद्गलः प्रधने जिगाय), referring to the verse न्यक्रन्दयन्नुपयन्तम् &c. (The words in the Ṛik are शतवत्सहस्रं गवाम् which may mean a thousand and one hundred or a thousand, as if they were one hundred.)

The next ineresting hymn interpreted is the well-known Nadī sūkta (IX 22) इमं मे गंगे यमुने &c. Yāska seems to look upon S'atadru and Parushṇī as independent rivers (परुष्णि स्तोममासेवध्वम्), Asiknī as, tributary of Marudvṛidhā, and Vitastā of Ārjīkīyā, the tributary rivers being apparently put in the instrumental case. Yāska gives the derivations of these names (शुतुद्रि

* A Nārās'aṁsa mantra is defined as येन नराः प्रशस्यन्ते.

from शुद्राविणी आशु तुन्नेव द्रवतीति वा &c.) and also mentions Irāvatī as a later name of Parushṇī. Asiknī means not white (अशुक्ला – असितमिति वर्णनाम). Marudvṛidhā is explained as मरुत एनां वर्धयन्ति and Vitastā as विदग्धा or विवृद्धा. He also mentions विपाट् (विपाश्-Bias) as another name of Ārjīkīyā even found in the Ṛigveda itself in another place. He here quotes a verse relating to the story of Vasishṭha wishing to commit suicide by drowning himself, bonds hand and foot, in the river; but the river broke his bounds and saved him whence the name विपाश्. (पाशा अस्या व्यपाश्यन्त वसिष्ठस्य मुमूर्षतः । तस्माद्विपाळित्युच्यते पूर्वमासीदुरुंजरा. It is clear that this Anushṭup verse is some Gāthā verse quoted by Yāska from current literature). Curiously enough Yāska gives Sushomā as another name of the Indus, a fact not much known, nor probable; the word being in the instrumental would indicate a tributary of the Vitastā. The word सुषोमा is derived as यदेना प्रसुवन्ति नद्यः. These particulars prove that Yāska was well acquainted with the Panjab and its rivers with their ancient and modern names. It is probable that Yāska like Pāṇini was an inhabitant of the Panjab, Takshaśilā being a famous place, even in the days of Yāska. The two rivers Vipāṭ and S'utudrī are together mentioned in another hymn, quoted here by Yāska, and are together mentioned as being the most important of the five, though they do not combine. Among words explained hereafter two may be noted: S'unāsīra is derived as शुना (वायुः, शु meaning अन्तरिक्ष) and सीर (आदित्यः सरणात्); and देवी ऊर्जाहुती (IX 42) is interpreted by Yāska as earth and heaven or day and night; but Kātthakya interprets it as सस्यं च समा च, which mean crop and years according to Prof. Chandramaṇi.

Chapter X next takes up the deities of the middle region, beginning with Vāyu. Yāska mentions a

Ṛishi Nābhāka who, as described in a Ṛigvedic verse, praised the raining waters called the seven sisters (possibly the seven rivers of the Panjab are referred to). In X 25 Viśvakarman is said to be Prajāpati, also called Dhātā and Vidhātā in the Ṛik quoted and it is interpreted in three ways as in Upanishads, viz. Adhibhūta, Adhidaivata and Adhyātma senses. And finally the legend is here related that Viśvakarman Bhauvana (a composer of Ṛigvedic hymns) first sacrificed all creatures and then himself (तत्रेतिहासमाचक्षते विश्वकर्मा भौवनः सर्वमेधे सर्वाणि भूतानि जुहवांचकार आत्मानमप्यन्ते । तदभिवादिन्येषर्क्-भवति स इमा विश्वा भुवनानि जुह्वत्). Asura is derived here from असु meaning प्रज्ञा and Tvaṣṭṛi is the name of this Asura (X 34).

Chapter XI takes up the words in the 5th section of Nighaṇṭu, Devatā-Kāṇḍa, beginning with S'yena. These deities belong to the middle region above Vāyu. S'yena (eagle) is interpreted as Moon and Chandramas is derived as चन्द्रो माता चान्द्रं मानमस्येति वा (XI 5). In explaining मृत्यु (XI 6), Yāska gives the derivation proposed by Maudgalya named S'atabalāksha, an author not yet mentioned. In the middle region along with सोम or चन्द्र are placed Maruts, Rudras, Ṛibhus and Pitṛis and Yāska begins section 13 with the words अथातो मध्यस्थाना देवगणास्तेषां मरुतः प्रथमगामिनो भवन्ति. Ṛibhus are explained in two ways, one of them a son of Sudhanvan and rays of the sun; in support of the first meaning Yāska says ऋभु[1] र्विभ्वा[2] वाज[3] इति सुधन्वन आङ्गिरसस्य त्रयः पुत्रा बभूवुस्तेषां प्रथमोत्तमाभ्यां बहुवन्निगमा भवन्ति न मध्यमेन, ऋभोश्च बहुवचनेन बहूनि दशतयीषु सूक्तानि भवन्ति. This is a historical remark worth noticing. Commencing section 22, Yāska says अथातो मध्यस्थानाः स्त्रियः and takes up Aditi and other female deities of the sky.

In chapter XII Yāska explains the names of the deities of heaven beginning with Aśvins, who are thus not deities of the sky. The question what these dual deities are even then puzzled the Nairuktas as they puzzle Vedic scholars to-day. "Who are the Aśvins" ? asks Yāska, "Some take them to be द्यावापृथिवी, some अहोरात्रे, some सूर्याचन्द्रमसौ and others two meritorious kings". Yāska derives the name from अश्नुवाते सर्वं रसेन; but Aurṇavābha derives the name form अश्वाः. Their time, however, was fixed, viz. before light begins to appear after midnight. Among the other deities, Sūryā is strangely enough considered to be Sun's wife (though the other meaning, viz. Sun's daughter, is also given) and Rodasī is declared to be Rudra's wife in XI 49 though the word usually means the two worlds heaven and earth. Rudra's wife is known as रुद्राणि in later Sanskrit.

The Pariśishṭa chapters XIII and XIV are clearly later additions as they take other words for explanation than those given in Nighaṇṭu. Chapter XIII is very short and explains some riddle Ṛiks such as the one containing the strange words जर्फरी तुर्फरीतू &c. and thus may be an earlier addition. Chapter XIV takes up subjects wholly foreign to Nirukta and propounds the philosophy of the Upanishads and the Bhagavadgītā, which it actually quotes (चतुर्युगसहस्राणि &c.). Sānkhya and Yoga are also referred to and the ideas of महानात्मा and भूतप्रकृति, words occurring in the Gītā also, are mentioned. Then a new list of words taken for derivation is given (XIV 11), introduced by the usual words अथात्मनो महतः प्रथमं भूतनामान्यनुक्रमिष्यामः at the end of 10. The new words thus probably denote Ātman of the Sānkhya philosophy. In 31 we have a reference to the custom of marrying the daughter of a maternal uncle in the verse मातुलस्येव योषा भागस्ते पैतृष्वसेयी वपामिव।. Whence this verse is taken can not be stated as no reference is given even by Prof. Chandramaṇi. In 35 the Ṛik त्र्यम्बकं यजामहे &c. is explained, त्र्यम्बक being interpreted as Rudra. This appears to be a riddle verse like चत्वारि शृङ्गा त्रयोऽस्य पादाः &c. describing Agni.

This added chapter ends with the significant line नमो ब्रह्मणे नमो महते भूताय नमः पारस्कराय नमो यास्काय ब्रह्मशुक्लमसीय. The mention of Pāraskara makes this addition to be the work of a pupil of his. If he is taken to be the author of the Gṛihyasūtra of the White Yajurveda, this addition falls entirely outside the Vedic period. Why a White Yajurvedic author makes an addition to this Ṛigvedic work is then inexplicable.

We may lastly state that there are two old commentators on Yāska's Nirukta, viz. Durgāchārya and Sāyaṇa. From Durgāchārya's commentory, it appears that there are a few interpolated sentences in Nirukta, according to Prof. Chandramaṇi, which is strange when we consider how rigidly Vaidika Brahmins have prrserved the texts of Vedic works. That Yāska himself in enunciating the Nighaṇṭu words may have altered a reading or added words and even added the Adhyāya V is possible from the fact that he does not consider the Padapāṭha of S'ākalya as unalterable and proposes a new pāṭha, viz. वायो instead of वा यो of S'ākalya (X 29). His view of the sacredness of the Nighaṇṭu may not have been as strong as that of the Vaidika Brahmins now.

IX GRAMMAR AND PĀNINI'S ASHṬĀDHYĀYĪ

The last Vedāṅga is grammar and the work recognised by Vaidikas on this subject is the Ashṭādhyāyī of Pāṇini. He comes also last in the Vedic period. Grammar had been studied before him for several centuries and many authors had also written on the subject. "The Padapāṭhas show that their authors had not only made investigations as to pronunciation and sandhi but already knew a good deal about the grammatical analysis of words, as they separate the parts of compounds and the prefixes of verbs as well as certain suffixes and terminations of nouns" (Macd. p. 267). Yāska had already distinguished the four parts of speech नामाख्यातोपसर्गनिपाताः, terms which Pāṇini uses, and there were many grammarians even before the days of Yāska such as Śākaṭāyana and Gārgya. "Even the Brāhmaṇas bear evidence of linguistic investigations, for they mention various grammatical terms such as अक्षर, वर्ण, वचन and विभक्ति (Macd. p. 268)", terms which Pāṇini uses without definition and "such terms are found more in Upanishads and Āraṇyakas." But all these investigations were taken to their highest development by Pāṇini who formulated his system with such ingenious devices and such all-embracing vision that his work supplanted all previous grammars and became the basis of most grammatical writings in later times. It was thus properly recognised as the last word on the subject and accepted as a Vedāṅga by all Vedic reciters. Pāṇini's work, however, does not treat of Vedic language only, but also and mainly of the spoken language of his time like Piṅgala's work which treats of the Vedic and later metres.

Most persons will agree with Prof. Belvalkar that the Aindra school of grammar is not pre-Pāṇinian. Indeed when the Brāhmaṇas speak of Indra separating padas, their authors, as usual, think of gods as doing anything and everything. Other schools no doubt existed from before Pāṇini like Apiśala, Kāśakṛitsna, Gārgya, Kāśyapa and Gālava and Pāṇini refers to them in his work. These authors had actually written works named above as also Śākaṭāyana, and Śākalya. Prof. Belvalkar even mentions extracts from their works in the writings of later grammarians. Most probably, all these works had disappeared by the time of सिद्धान्तकौमुदी.

Pāṇini lived about 900 B. C., as will be shown in a separate note and his work closes the Vedic period. Even Macdonell says, "It may be taken as the definite starting point of the Post-Vedic age" (p. 268) though our limits for the Vedic age differ from those of Macdonell and other European scholars. Pāṇini's birth-place, according to tradition, was Śalātura in Gāndhāra and he is, therefore, often called Śalāturīya. He was a Vātsa Bhārgava (see note on gotras). His mother's name was दाक्षी, a gotra-name; and he is called दाक्षीपुत्र in Piṅgala, as already noted. His father's name is not known. Pāṇini is not a gotra-name like Yāska, a word specially explained in IV 3,194. He must have studied at Takshaśilā or in the Sarasvatī region, the home of Vedic culture in his days. But he must have travelled far and wide as he notices the peculiarities of the spoken language of Easterners as well as of Northerners. Pāṇini is believed to have been killed, while passing through a forest, by a lion ignorant of the great grammatical genius and services of his victim, as a poet humorously remarks.

The grammar of Pāṇini is called Ashṭādhyāyī as it is divided into eight chapters. It is preceded by a list of letters in groups in which they are arranged differently from the arrangement according to their sthāna. This arrangement was revealed to him, so it is believed, by S'iva and hence these sūtras are called Māheśvara. It is an ingenious arrangement by which brevity is secured in the enuenciation of grammatical rules. Separate groups are made of letters which are subject to the same changes in the formation of words. The arrangement discloses a deep study of the natural evolution of sounds in words, besides evidencing great ingenuity in securing brevity; and it has been naturally looked upon as divinely inspired.

As stated above, Pāṇini gives mainly the grammar of the Sanskrit language as it was spoken in his time; but he does not use the word Sanskrit* for it, but simply भाषा. The Aryan settlements in India then extended from Kabul to Kaśī-Videha and naturally there were provincial differences. These were mainly three, the centres of Aryan culture being also three, viz. 1 Kāśī-Videha, 2 Kurukshetra and 3 Kekaya-Madra. Pāṇini naturally thus gives two main differences of language, viz. of Prāchām or Easterners and of Udīchām or Northerners, the middle Kuruskhetra being the home of the central language. Such differences exist in every living language. We have High German and Low German, English and Welsh, Eastern and Western Hindi and Marathi of Paithan, Poona and Phonda (eastern, central and southern). But such differences are very few and minor and hence there is one grammar for German, English, Hindi or Marathi. So does Pāṇini give one grammar for Bhāshā, noticing provincial peculiarities. He also notes the peculia-

* The word Sanskrit in IV, 4, 3 means cooked, दध्ना संस्कृतं दाधिकम्.

rities of the ancient Vedic language, using several words for it as explained in a note, viz. मंत्रे, छन्दसि, निगमे and once or twice आर्षे. Pāṇini seems to be conscious of the greatness of his work which he must have enunciated, after having taught grammar as professor for several years and hence in his sūtras he uses the word उपदेश (teaching) for his own work.

In the first chapter, Pāṇini gives the definitions of terms (संज्ञा) newly adopted by him as well as of some old ones. In the four quarters (पाद) of this chapter (each chapter being divided into quarters), there are altogether 351 sūtras (75,73, 93, 110). The second chapter treats of samāsas, the old names तत्पुरुष, बहुव्रीहि, द्वन्द्व and अव्ययीभाव being used by him. (कर्मधारय and द्विगु are also mentioned but as varieties of तत्पुरुष). The number of sūtras in this chapter is 261 (72+37+73+85). In the third quarter verbal terminations are given from sūtra 58 and this pāda rather queerly hereafter goes into the dropping (लुक्) of Pratyayas to be given hereafter. These sūtras, e.g. यस्कादिभ्यो गोत्रे, should have properly come after giving the Pratyayas themselves. In chapter III, forms and derivatives of verbs are treated. The names लट्, लिट् &c. are of tense-pratyayas and are newly invented by Pāṇini for brevity, the tenses before him being probably named वर्तमान, भूत and भविष्यत्, words often used by Pāṇini also as वर्तमाने लट् or भूतेऽपि दृश्यन्ते (III 3, 32). The chapter contains in all 631

(150 + 188 + 176 + 117) sūtras. The fourth and fifth chapters treat of formations of nouns, the stem of which is called प्रातिपदिक and of verbs, the stem being designated धातु. For forming the feminine, many sūtras are given in IV, and then gotra or family names are noted as also names of kings formed from peoples or countries. These sūtras supply interesting information about the geography of India in the days of Pāṇini which we will collect in a note. In 3 and 4 of IV various other derivatives from nouns are given including religious and literary terms. The number of sūtras in IV is 635 (178+145+168+144) and in V, 555 (136 + 140+119 + 160).

In chapter VI, the changes of vowels in सन्धि are given and also their accents उदात्त, अनुदात्त and स्वरित or middle, lower and higher; as also changes of letters in noun and verb forms. The rules relate to both Vedic and spoken languages and are very minute. Some changes are, however, too irregular and even Pāṇini contents himself by saying पृषोदरादि यथोपदिष्टम् (3, 09). These obey no rules. The number of sūtras is 736 (223+199+139+175).

In chapter VII, Pāṇini gives rules for changes to be made in his own pratyayas when applied to words. This device is adopted both for brevity as for other purposes. Thus फ, ढ, ख, छ and घ are to be changed into आयन्, एय, ईन्, ईय, इय (1,2). Next are given changes in nouns and verbs before pratyayas. The interesting इडागम in verbs is then detailed and next inflectional and conjugational forms are explained. The inflexions of pronouns, especially of युष्मत् and अस्मत्, being too strong for generalisation, take many sūtras and are always a difficult affair (note केचिद्भ्रमा युष्मदस्मत्क्रियायाम्). Many irregular forms in Vedic language are given like इष्ट्वीन and पीत्वीन and even a Ṛik verse is quoted (यजध्वैनमिति 1, 43). A new Āchārya, Bharadvāja, is quoted in 2,66. The number of sūtras in this chapter is 438 (103+118+120+97).

Chapter VIII begins with the changes in words when repeated and the प्लुत of vowels in invocation. In Sanskrit we have besides short and long, the प्लुत or treble, usually used in spoken languages in vocatives. हे हे प्रयोगे हैहयो: (2,85) brings home to us how Sanskrit was then a spoken language.* हे३ देवदत्त &c. as also विभाषा पृष्टप्रतिवचने हे: (2,13) instanced by अकार्षं हि३ ? or अकार्षं हि are very interesting. प्रत्यभिवादेऽशूद्रे (2,83) shows that even Śūdras spoke in Sanskrit and were answered in Sanskrit. 'अभिवादये तुषजकोऽहम्' says the Śūdra and the Arya answers 'आयुष्मानेधि तुषजक'. This brings out how Pāṇini properly uses the word भाषा. From quarter 2 to the end of the chapter, the sūtras are पूर्वत्र असिद्ध; i.e. they give changes which are not again subject to the operation of rules given previously.

* है हे प्राच्याम् shows that even in uttering है, हे the Easterners gave a different stress.

This is the most ingenious device used by Pāṇini for excluding forms from further changes. Here have been mentioned all Ādeśas such as ष् for स्, ण् for न्, श् for स्, च् for त् &c. In 3 we find in successive sūtras शाकटायन, शाकल्य and गार्ग्य mentioned as differing (16, 19 and 20); and in 4, 52 the mention of आचार्याणाम्, following शाकटायन in 50 and शाकल्य in 51 on the same subject, makes it clear that Pāṇini gives by आचार्याणाम् the view of his own guru.

This chapter contains 369 (74+108+119+68) sūtras. Thus the total of sūtras in Pāṇini's Ashṭādhyāyī is 3983 (351+268+631+635+555+736+438+269) according to Kāśikā.

Pāṇini gives roots in his sūtras in different forms; but they all indicate some special process upon them and these roots are given in the धातुपाठ by Pāṇini with the same forms (with इत् इ, उ, ऌ&c.) except the form ending in ति which is used in sūtras for the first time, indicating a special prakriyā. In the same way, all other *'it's* in his sūtras have a meaning, viz. some special grammatical process. This artifice seems to be older than Pāṇini inasumch as the old उणादिसूत्रs, which he includes in his work, were according to tradition among Indian grammarians, laid down by Śākaṭāyana*

* Prof. Belvalkar thinks that the उणादिसूत्रs are Pāṇini's but he admits that some of these sūtras are opposed to the Asṭādhyāyi. Secondly the terms ह्रस्व, दीर्घ &c are common because they are Pre-Pāṇinian. Pāṇini generally accepts them and hence he quotes them in his sūtra उणादयो बहुलम् which clearly indicates, to our mind, the priority of these Sūtras.

(शकटस्य तोकम् of Patanjali). As pointed out by M.M. Vasudeva Śāstri Abhyankar, they form an adjunct of the grammar of Pāṇini; but Pāṇini looks upon them as not always applicable, since he uses the word बहुलम् (III 3, 1 उणादयो बहुलम्).

Pāṇini callects words similar in any treatment in what are called gaṇas, indicating the gaṇa by the first word in it with आदि added as यस्कादिभ्यो गोत्रे (II 4, 63). These gaṇas must have been compiled by Pāṇini himself and the गणपाठ now recited is believed to be Pāṇini's work. But these gaṇas must have been extended from time to time; for under the above sūtra gaṇa, Kāśikā gives कर्णाटक which could not have been known to Pāṇini as stated already. Generally, however, these lists may be quoted as his. They are sometimes treated as incomplete by later authors and are called आकृतिगणाः. This is doubtful; for when Pāṇini wishes to indicate that there are many such words, he leaves the matter indefinite and uses words liks अन्येभ्योऽपि दृश्यते (III 2, 75). It may, however, be urged on the other side that Pāṇini himself looks upon these gaṇas as not exhaustive. Where the list was exhaustive, he gives it fully in his sūtras though they become long, e. g. III 2, 142; VIII 3, 87 or 4, 17 &c.

Though Pāṇini took the method of using इत्s from the उणादिसूत्रs, the Māheśvara sūtra arrangement of letters appears to be his, the most ingenious arrangement for securing brevity as stated already. The Pratyayas given for inflexions and conjugations are also his in the form they are given; though the terms आर्धधातुक and सार्वधातुक used for verbal Pratyayas are not his. They are too long to be his and Indian grammarians hold that they are older terms which Pāṇini could not but take up being too well-known. Indeed "brevity ought not to be looked for in Pratyaya names" is a maxim of Indian grammarians. The term भाषितपुंस्क is another such word (VII 1, 68).

The Sanskṛit language having ceased to be spoken since Pāṇini, there are several words used in ordinary parlance in Pāṇini's sūtras which can not now be understood. Even M. M. Vasudevas Śastri Abhyankar can not say what चिहण is in IV 2,125 (चिहणकन्थः).

Pāṇin's work is not without interpolations as even Indian grammarians admit. Some sūtras which were originally Vārtikas of Vararuchi, have crept in in the progress of time. Examples of this given by M. M. Abhyankar Śastri are (1) वृद्धस्य पूजायाम् (IV 1.166) on which Kāśikā remarks "वृद्धस्य ought to be in the nominative but विचित्रा सूत्रस्य कृतिः" This remark is undeserved if we remember that this was not Pāṇinis's sūtra originally and वृद्धस्य युवसंज्ञा would be inconceivable for Pāṇini. (2) Another example given is चरणाद्धर्माम्नाययोः. There are a few sūtras which have two readings as in आङोऽनुनासिकश्छन्दसि to which बहुलम् is added by some (Kāśikā VII, 126). That Pāṇini's sūtras had accents is undoubted; and we have elsewhere stated that the Sanskrit spoken in Pāṇini's time had accents as appears clear from several sūtras of his. These accents in Pāṇini have now been lost and Vaidikas recite his sūtras in एकश्रुति. Yāska's Nirukta also must have had accents; but they too are lost and Vaidikas recite it also in एकश्रुति with a few variations as previously noted The question whether Pāṇini's sūtras had accents or not is disputed among Indian grammarians and M. M. Vasudevaśastri Abhyankar mentions the controversy as त्रैस्वर्य controversy. But from the sūtra आदेच उपदेशे शिति taken in अनुदात्तस्य चर्दुपधस्यान्यतर-स्याम् (VI 1, 59) it is clear that Pāṇini in his उपदेश of धातुपाठ had given accents. If even in his धातुपाठ there were accents, his sūtras must have had them. Indeed if Sanskrit was a spoken language of the people generally at the time, accents must actually have been in use as in English. विभाषा भाषा-याम् explicitly mentions accents in the spoken language (VI 1,181.). The question why and when accents were lost is a difficult though interesting one and will be discussed in a note.

Another important change which may be noted is that Pāṇini's sūtras had here and there letters which were to be pronounced nasal (अनु-नासिक) and which are not now so pronounced by reciters or indicated by writers in written works. This change took place long before Bhaṭṭoji Dīkshita who clearly states that the original nasals have now to be inferred from the Kārya. Thus in VII 1,1 the यु, वु mentioned are अनुनासिक and when the Kāsikā cites the sūtra वासुदेवार्जुनाभ्यां वुन् for वु, it must be noted that वुन् was written and pronounced originally as वुँन्. Similarly (भुजिमृङ्भ्यां) युक्त्युकौ was युँक्त्युँकौ. This अनुनासिक was used by Pāṇini in Pratyayas with a purpose and also in धातुपाठ. Like accent, this nasal was later lost, being probably troublesome both in writing and reciting.

Note 1—Pāṇini's use of certain words.

Pāṇini always uses the word भाषायाम् when speaking of the spoken language, later called Sanskrit, e. g. VI 3, 20. When referring to the Vedic language, he uses three words मन्त्रे, छन्दसि and निगमे. When he uses मन्त्रे as in III 2, 71, VI 1, 151 or VI 4 53, he refers to the Saṁhitās or the metrical portion of the Vedas. When he uses छन्दसि, he refers to both Saṁhitā and Brāhmaṇa. The word छन्दस् means metre and it is difficult to see how it can apply to the prose portion of the Vedas, though in छन्दोब्राह्मणानि च तद्विषयाणि (IV 2, 66), it seems that Chhandas does not include Brāhmaṇas. In जुष्टार्पिते च च्छन्दसि followed by नित्यं मंत्रे, the word मंत्र is opposed to छन्दसि including both, a sense usually attached to it. Thus VI 1, 150 शीर्ष छन्दसि refers to शीर्ष्णो हि सोमं क्रीतं हरन्ति – a Brāhmaṇa quotation. So also वत्सरान्ताच्छन्दसि (V 1, 91) refers to इद्वत्सरीयः &c. appearing in Brāhmaṇas. The word छन्दस् is an old word appearing even in Zend and in Purushasūkta (छन्दांसि जज्ञिरे तस्मात्), where it means Ṛigvedic verses generally (see Sec. I, p. 175.) When the Brāhmaṇas were included in revelation (मंत्रब्राह्मणयोर्वेदनामधेयम् Ap.) the word was extended in its meaning. Mantra retained its meaning viz. the metrical portion of the Vedas. The third word निगम is a new word, used by Yāska for Veda generally, and is equivalent to छन्दसि, Pāṇini also uses it in the same sense (e. g. VI 3, 113 साढ्यै साढ्वा साढेति निगमे. Kāśikā quotes साढ्यै समन्तात् and साढ्वा शत्रून् which are probably from Saṁhitā). Pāṇini also sometimes names the particular Veda as Yajushi in यजुष्युरः (VI 1, 93).

When Pāṇini uses वा or अन्यतरस्याम् or बहुलम्, he gives optional forms generally used. But where he mentions the name of an Āchārya, he seems, we think, to indicate that the optional form is used by that Āchārya and his followers, but is not acceptable to him. Thus he mentions many Āchāryas by name such as आपिशलि, स्फोटायन शाकल्य, चाक्रवर्मण (VI 1, 130), काश्यप (1, 2, 25) &c. Modern grammarians, however, look upon the mention of an Āchārya as showing पूजा (sec. under V 3, 94). But historically speaking such पूजा was unnecessary; and if Pāṇini really honoured them and accepted their views, he would have given one form only or at best used वा. The sūtra वा सुप्यापिशलेः (VI 1, 92) gives वा along with the name of आपिशलि and this indicates that the optional form is taught by आपिशलि and not by Pāṇini. In one sūtra he uses the word एव (लङ् शाकटायनस्यैव III 4, 111). These other Āchāryas seem to have actually written works which were studied even later than Pāṇini, as in one place students and followers of अपिशलि are spoken of along with these of Pāṇini by the Kāśikā; आपिशलाः पाणिनीयाः or आपिशलपाणिनीये शास्त्रे (VI 2, 36). The word आचार्याः in VIII 3, 52, as stated before, however, stands for Pāṇini's guru and here the condition of the preceding vowel being long is acceptable to Pāṇini. We can not mean there by आचार्याः other teachers as others (अन्ये) would have sufficed, in that case one letter being less also. Who the Achārya of Pāṇini was is not mentioned anywhere.

Commentators similary interpret प्राचाम् and उदीचाम् as indicating merely optional forms. But historically speaking, one must restrict such forms to their province only. Pāṇini meant that the particular form would be correct when used by people in that province. Thus in III 1, 90 (कुषिरजोः प्राचां श्यन्परस्मैपदं च।) he means to say that कुष्यति would be correct when used in the eastern country, but in other provinces कुष्यते would be correct. Thus as the mention of the name of an Achārya would confine the form to his followers (a restriction by persons), the mention of प्राचां or उदीचाम् would confine the form to the province (a restriction by place). They are used in III 4, 18 and 19 in direct opposition. Generally acceptable optional forms are shown by वा or अन्यतरस्याम्. Of course these remarks apply to the time of Pāṇini only.

Note 2— Accents.

We were surprised to find on reading the Ashtādhyāyī carefully, that the Bhāshā spoken in the days of Pāṇini had accents, i. e., the svaras were pronounced उदात्त, अनुदात्त and स्वरित. Even noted S'āstris who study Vyākaraṇa did not, we found, seem to suspect this. Probably the स्वरप्रक्रिया in Pāṇini is usually neglected as applicable to Vedic Saṁhitās and not the language they use. That the spoken language of Pāṇini's days had accents is proved by many sūtras given in Chapter I, where these are defined and in Chapter VI, especially with regard to samāsas, as to how the svaras of the component words are changed. Nouns and verbs have svaras and even the pratyayas added to them in inflexion and conjugation and these are indicated by Pāṇini by certain letters (अनुबन्ध) added to the pratyayas. We have, therefore, to abandon our view expressed in Section I at page 55 that "Sanskrit lost accents in the days of the Brāhmaṇas".

Why did the Aitareya Brāhmaṇa then lose svaras is a riddle. The S'atapatha and the Taittirīya down to its Āraṇyaka and Upanishads, have svaras still. The riddle may be solved from the following sūtras of Pāṇini. Sūtra I 2, 34 lays down एकश्रुति recitation for even mantras in यज्ञकर्म, but not for जप, न्यूंख and सामन्. Sāmans had to be sung at sacrifices with their svaras, as also the न्यूंख (ओ lengthened in Rik verses). It appears that, in Brāhmaṇa and later times, the svaras of words changed, as changes slowly take place in every spoken language even in grammar. This difference in accents in Vedic hymns and the spoken language became troublesome. Gradually, tha Ṛigveda Saṁhitā and Brāhmaṇa began to be recited without svaras at sacrificse and Pāṇini had to sanction this proceeding optionally by his sūtra विभाषा छन्दसि (I 2, 36) but *not for the spoken language.* The Kāśikā comment on this sūtra is noticeable. छन्दसि विषये एकश्रुतिर्भवति पक्षान्तरे त्रैस्वर्यम् । व्यवस्थितविकल्पोऽयमिति केचित् । वेदे मन्त्रदले नित्यं त्रैस्वर्यम् । ब्राह्मणदले नित्यमैकश्रुत्यम्." This is thought by some to be an added sentence. Any how, historically this means that in Pāṇini's time, Ṛigvedic recitation was at option with or without svaras; but at the time of the Kāśikā or somewhat later (600 to 900 A. D.) it was a settled pratice with Ṛigvedins to recite the Saṁhitā with accents and the Brāhmaṇas without them, as the practice now is. The Yajurvedins seem to have stuck to their ancient practice of reciting both Saṁhitā and Brāhmaṇa with accents. We have to admit that the argument we gave in Section II that these Yajurveda Brāhmaṇas were older than Rigveda-Brāhmaṇas because they have accents and the latter not, therefore fails. Other arguments given in Section II, however, prove their priority.

Naturally even Pāṇini's sūtras had accents (see स्वरितेनाधिकारः I 3, 4) and his Dhātupāṭha also (I 3, 12); but they are now recited and written without sccents. The whole classical literature again is found written without accents. When Sanskrit lost accents is another riddle. M. M. Vāsudeva S'āstri Abhyankar thinks that accents existed in the days of Kātyāyana and even Patañjali. It seems, however, that these authors detail accents academically and not from spoken language. For Sanskrit was not a spoken language of the people in their time. A spoken language alone can have accents, not, a dead one, used only by Pandits in writing or in academic discussion. That Sanskrit had accents in Pāṇini's days is, as said before, ctrtain; the sutra एकश्रुतिदूरात्संबुद्धौ (I 2, 33) clealy shows this. 'When you call out a name from a distance, you have एकश्रुति, but not elsewhere or when called from near. Again from विभाषा छन्दसि Kāśikā draws the inference भाषायामपि एकश्रुतिर्विभाषा भवतीतिसिद्धम्; but this is not supportable. For विभाषा भाषायाम् (VI, 1, 181) which clearly proves the use of accents in भाषा allows option, only for भिः in षट्त्रिचतुर्भ्यः. We cannot, therefore, hold that accents were optional in the language spoken in the days of Pāṇini.

Lastly accents are important not only as showing correctly how the Aryan people pronounced the words, but as often marking difference of meaning. As in English con'duct and conduct' have diflerent meanings so in Panini's and Vedic language इंद्रशत्रु had a different meaning from इंद्रशत्रु, pronounced with a different accent, to take the example usually given, राजब्राह्मण (a Brahmin king) is differently accented from the same word meaning a king's Brahmin.

Note 3—Literature mentioned in Pāṇini

Several sūtras of Pāṇini, especially those commencing with तेन प्रोक्तम् (IV 3, 101), give us an idea of the literature current in the days of Pāṇini. That he knew all the four Veda Samhitās is certain from his mentioning Ṛiks, Sāmans, Vājasaneyin, Tittiri, and Ātharvaṇika. VII, 4, 38 mentions यजुषि काठके and VIII 3,104 यजुष्येकेषाम्. All this literature he includes in the word Chhandas, but he sometimes mentions Ṛiks, Yajuh and Sāmans also. He uses the word दृष्ट in connection with Sāmans and thus we feel certain that the theory of the divine origin of the Vedic hymns was already established. He even looks upon the Brāhmaṇas as revealed, since he appears to use the word प्रोक्त as higher than कृत used in कृते ग्रन्थे (IV 3,116). Tittiri, Varatantu, Khaṇḍika and Ukha (mentioned in IV 3 102) probably indicate their recensions of the Black Yajurveda Saṁhitā. The list can not be exhaustive but Varatantu is a name not found in चरणव्यूह. He seems to be a Saṁhitā proclaimer (प्रवक्ता), along with Tittiri. His name is not found in the list of Ṛishis given in Sec. I but he is mentioned even by Kālidāsa as a Vedic teacher (कौत्सः प्रेपेदे वरतन्तुशिष्यः). These are not Ṛishis in the strict sense i.e. मंत्रद्रष्टृ, as seems clear from the next sūtra (103) in which काश्यप and कौशिक are mentioned as Ṛishis, they being no doubt composers of individual sūktas and not proclaimers of Samhitās. Perhaps besides S'ākala and Bāshkala, there may have, been Kāsyapa and Kauśika Ṛigveda Saṁhitās. The

Kāśikā mentions a Kalpa of Kāśyapa, but a Rishi can not, we think, be the author of a Kalpa. The next sūtra mentions the pupils of Kalāpin and Vaiśampāyana as proclaimers or publishers of works. Their names are not given but the Kāśikā gives them as १ हरिद्रु, २ छगली, ३ तुम्बुरु and ४ उलप for Kalāpin and १ आलम्बि, २ पलङ्ग, ३ कमल, ४ ऋचाभ, ५ आरुणि, ६ ताण्डय, ७ श्यामायन ८ कठ and ९ कलापि for Vaiśampāyana. These publishers of Yajuḥ Saṁhitās are mostly unknown except हरिद्रु, छगली, कंठ and कलापिन् mentioned in चरणव्यूह. (Tāṇḍya here must be different from the Tāṇḍya of Sāmavedad; being a gotra-name this is quite possible). Then in the next sūtra (105), we have the mention of Brāhmaṇas and Kalpas and their proclaimers, both *old* and *new* (पुराणप्रोक्तेषु ब्राह्मणकल्पेषु IV 3,105). Thus Pāṇini looks upon even old Kalpas as प्रोक्त or proclaimed As old Brāhmaṇas, the Kāśikā instances भाल्लवि, शाट्यायनि and ऐतरेयि (the first two are now lost) and old Kalpas पैङ्गी and आरुणपराजी (both not extant now).

The next sūtra शौनकादिभ्यश्छन्दसि (IV 3,106) mentions other authors of Brāhmaṇas (छन्दसि) as also of other works by them which were not considered inspired. Thus शौनकि would mean a S'aunaka Brahmana but शौनकीय would be proper for a शिक्षा work (Kāśikā), or कठशाठि for a Brāhmana but कठशाठीय for other work (not known). The list of authors under शौनकादि contains 17 names of which वाजसनेय and तलवकार may be mentioned, as their Brāhmaṇas are extant; but those of others are lost. The next sūtra कठचरकाल्लुक् (IV 5,107) states that the Brāhmaṇas of कठ and चरक go by the same name while that by कलापिन् is कालाप (कलापिनोऽण् IV 3,108) but that by छगलिन् is छागलेय (छगलिनो ढिनुक् IV, 3,109). Kaṭha, Charaka, Kalāpin and Chhāgaleya are names mentioned in चरणव्यूह; but Katha-Kālāpa Saṁhitā alone survives. Brāhmaṇas are called त्रिशानि and

चत्वारिंशानि from their 30 or 40 chapters (V 1,62). This detailed survey would show how much Vedic literature known to Pāṇini has now been lost.

Similarly the Sūtra literature known to Pāṇini must also have been extensive. As already stated, Sūtras are mentioned even in Upanishads. In the next sūtra (IV 3,110), Pāṇini mentions a भिक्षुसूत्र by Pārāśarya and a नटसूत्र by S'ilāli. A code for Bhikshus or Saṁyāsins and a code for actors shows that the Bhikshus even then had separate disciplinary rules and that dramas were acted even then under systematic directions. There were opposing schools also, as in the next sūtra two other authors on the same two subjects are mentioned, viz. Karmanda and Kṛiśāśvin. The followers of the first would be पाराशरिणो भिक्षव: and शैलालिनो नटा:; but of the latter कर्मन्दिन: and कृशाश्विन: while their works would be called पाराशर and शैलाल and कार्मन्द and कार्शाश्व.

A third kind of works is treated by Pāṇini separaely as उपज्ञात (neither प्रोक्त nor कृत) which Kāśikā defines as विनोपदेशेन ज्ञातम् (IV 8,115); the example given is पाणिन्युपज्ञ व्याकरण which Pāṇini himself could not have given. Probably Pāṇini means by उपज्ञात works which though not revealed are extraordinary or original. The other instances given by the Kāśikā are आपिशल गुरुलाघव and काशकृत्स्न पुष्करण. What these works are can not be stated as they no longer exist. There were many authors on grammar as already stated, viz. शाकटायन, चाक्रायण, शाकल्य and others and their works are lost. Finally in the next sūtra, Pāṇini mentions ordinary works composed by other authors (कृते ग्रन्थे IV 3, 116). Their being called ग्रन्थ probably indicates that भूर्ज leaves written on were strung together as books. The instances given by the Kāśikā here can not have been before Pāṇini ; for वाररुचा: श्लोका: must be a later work, if Vararuchi is the same as the author of Vārtikas. We do not and cannot now know what other authors had written works and on what subjects before the time of Pāṇini, except Yāska; and his work probably was an उपज्ञात work and not कृत according to Pāṇini. Works named from the number of Adhyāyas are instanced by Kāśikā as त्रिकं काशकृत्स्नम् &c.

In IV 2, 64 we are told that those who study the प्रोक्त works are called by the same name, e. g. आपिशलाः, पाणिनीयाः &c. The next sūtra states the same with regard to Sūtras with names ending in *ka* (सूत्राच्च कोपधात् 65). Here we have names of Sūtras referred to, but not in the sūtra; the Kāśikā instances अष्टकाः पाणिनीयाः, दशका वैय्याघ्रपद्याः, त्रिकाः काशकृत्स्नाः. On what subject these works were can not now be known. In the next sūtra the same is stated of छन्दोब्राह्मणानि. Here Chhandas is differentiated from Brāhmaṇa and the examples gives in Kāśikā are, of the first कठाः, मौदाः, पैप्पलादाः, आर्चायिनः, वाजसनेयिनः and of the latter, ताण्डिनः, भाल्लविनः, शाट्यायनिनः, and ऐतरेयिणः.

Other kinds of works mentioned are आख्यान (VI 2, 103) and the instances given by the Kāśikā are पूर्वरामकम् and पूर्वयायातम्. Such Ākyānas were put in the Rāmāyaṇa and the Mahābhārata in their new editions later on. The Rāmāyaṇa was originally रामाख्यान by Vālmiki, as mentioned in the Vanaparva of the Mahābhārata.

Pāṇini must have had before him some astronomical works. Dixit (p. 103) points out that Pāṇini uses the words वर्ष (V 1, 88, VII 3, 16), हायन (IV 1, 27, V 1, 130) and नाडी (V 4, 159). He mentions the Nakshatra पुष्य alias सिध्य (III 1, 116), छन्दसि पुनर्वस्वोरेकवचनम् । विशाखयोश्च (I 2, 61-2) is objected to by Dixit; but Kāśikā cites without any reference पुनर्वसुर्नक्षत्रमादितिर्देवता and विशाखा नक्षत्रमादितिर्देवता R.V. (X 19, 1). T.S. and A.V. (XIX 7), use the dual. To what Vedic works does Pāṇini refer here?

The art of writing must have existed in Pāṇini's days, as collections of similarly behaving words could not have been made by mere memory. It is supposed by some that the sūtra style arose because writing was unknown. But such works were learnt by heart because it was considered meritorious to recite them, and the sūtra style probably arose to lessen the labour of learning by heart. Writing was no doubt troublesome in the absence of paper, and the word अक्षर for letters arose from notching them; but it proves the existence of ineffaceable writing, as ग्रन्थ proves that of books.

Note 4-Geography of India in Pāṇini.

We have already adverted to the fact that Pāṇini certainly knew two divisions of the Aryan land, viz. the Eastern and the Northern. Dr. Bhandarkar has inferred from the sūtra कम्बोजाल्लुक् (IV 1, 75), corrected by Kātyāyana into कम्बोजादिभ्यो लुक्, that Pāṇini did not know countries and peoples to the south of the Vindhya range where the peoples and kings Chola, Pāṇḍya, &c. lived and ruled. This is denied by M. M. Vāsudevaśastri Abhyankar who holds that Pāṇini includes the south in the word Prāchām and the west in the word Udīchām. In support of this opinion he points out the Kāśikā gloss on एङ् प्राचां देशे (I 1, 75) wherein is quoted an old verse प्राङुदञ्चौ विभजते हंसः क्षीरोदके यथा। विदुषां शब्दसिद्ध्यर्थं सा नः पातु शरावती ॥. This river S'arāsvati, it is argued, runs from northeast to southwest and divides India into Prāchām and Udīchām. Whence this verse is taken is not stated and we are almost sure that this is a Paurāṇa or grammarian śloka of later days. Probably this river is a Kurukshetra river and may be accepted as representing the two geographical divisions of India as contemplated by Pāṇini. We will take the examples given in the gloss on this sūtra by the Kāśikā, though we must caution our readers against taking them as really Pāṇinian. Unless a place is actually mentioned by Pāṇini in one of his sūtras, we can not be sure that it was known to him. The gloss gives एणीपचनीय, भोजकटीय, गौनर्दीय &c. as eastern places and दैवदत्तः, i. e. living in देवदत्त, a village in the Vāhīka country, as not eastern. Thus the Panjab and the Kurukshetra are, according to this description, northern lands and Bhojakaṭa and Gonarda, are in eastern lands. We would, however, divide India into three parts, historically speaking; (1) the middle land, viz. the Panjab and, or at least Kurukshetra and Rājpntana; (2) the land near the Indus and beyond the Himālayas as northern land and (3) the land beyond the Jumna as eastern land; and we hold that when Pāṇini speaks of the differences of the language of Northern peoples (उदीचाम्), he refers to the language of the people to the north of the Sutlej; and when he speaks of the peculiarities of the language of the Eastern peoples (प्राचाम्), he speaks of the lands to the east of the Jumna. Of course भोजकट (in Berar) could not be spoken of by Pāṇini; for he could not speak of the countries and the peoples to the south of the Vindhyas, though he knew Kathiawar (सौराष्ट्र); nor the countries to the west of the Panjab such as Baluchistan. These parts were not yet colonised by the Aryans, though not unknown to them and their people did not speak Sanskrit and these lands had, therefore, no peculiarities of language to present. This position is also consistent with historical facts. Pāṇini was a native of S'alātura which is said to be beyond the Indus (Hiuen-Tsiang's Travels); but he lived, learnt and gave lessons probably at Takshasilā or more probably in Kurukshetra.

The Vedic culture and civilization was, about the end of the Vedic period, centred in Kurukshetra. There were Aryan kingdoms in the east, i. e. eastwards of the Jumna as far as Behar and in the days of the Aitareya Brāhmaṇa, the Aryans had gone into Vanga and Kalinga even, though these tracts remained still outside the pale of Aryan civilization. This part, therefore, was the country of the Prāchām, viz. from the Jumna as far as Behar; and the Aryans there had developed certain peculiarities of speach which Pāṇini had to notice. It may be added that later commentators who had lost all memory of past geographical differences of language looked upon the words Prāchām and Udīchām as simply registering optional forms. But Pāṇini would then have simply used वा or अन्यतरस्याम् instead of these two words. The above śloka, however, gives us the view earlier than this, though it is itself not wholly correct.

This eastern, middle and northern division of the Aryan land in the days of Pāṇini is supported by the following sūtras in VI. 2; पुरे प्राचाम् ।, अरिष्टगौडपूर्वे च । and न हास्तिनफलकमार्देयाः । (99, 100, 101). The first sūtra lays down that names of towns in eastern lands are accented in a particular way. The second sūtra adds specially Arishṭa and Gauḍa which thus are clearly not in the eastern land. Gauḍapura is, therefore, not to be looked for in Bengal as one may be tempted to do. Upto Varāhamihira's time (500 A. D.), Gauḍa was not the name of Western Bengal but was the name of the country round Thanesar in Kurukshetra. The third sūtra states that even in the Eastern land, हास्तिन, फलक and मार्देय are not to be pronounced with that accent. This proves that according to Pāṇini, Hāstinapura was in the eastern part of the country. Being on the left bank of the Ganges beyond Kurukshetra, it is in the eastern country as per definition given above. So also are आहिच्छत्र and कान्यकुब्ज under I 1, 15.

The sūtra अमहन्नवं नगरेऽनुदीचाम् (VI 2, 89) is important as showing that besides प्राचाम्, there is a third division which is covered by अनुदीचाम्, viz. the middle country. For if there were two divisions only प्राचाम् and उदीचाम्, Pāṇini would have used here प्राचाम् which has one letter less. The examples given by Kāśikā for अनुदीचाम् are सुह्मनगर and पौंड्रनगर, clearly eastern towns; but विराटनगर is added by another commentary which is in the middle country. Northern towns given here by the Kāśikā are नान्दीनगर and कान्तीनगर which can not be indentified. VI 2, 87 treats of names of towns ending in प्रस्थ such as इन्द्रप्रस्थ &c. but names ending in पुत्र are not noted by Pāṇini. Pātaliputra given by Kāśikā under VII 3, 14 could not have been known to him as it was founded about 400 B. C.; Indraprastha must, however, have been known to him. पाटलिपुत्र is not mentioned in any sūtra, and hence this view can not be impeached.

With regard to the countries and peoples known to Pāṇini, Panjab peoples and those to the north of it mentioned by him are मद्र (VII 3, 13), कम्बोज (IV 1,175), कपिश IV 2, 99 (कपिश is Kabul from the instance given in Kāśikā कापिशायनी द्राक्षा, a well-known fruit of Kabul even now), वाहीक (IV 2, 47) उशीनर (IV 2, 118), गान्धार (IV 1, 169), साल्वावयव (branches of the Salva) * or शाल्व (IV 1, 173), युगन्धर (mentioned as a bad town of the Panjab in MBh.), त्रिगर्त (IV 1, 111), प्रत्यग्रथ, कालकूट, भर्ग and यौधेय (IV 1, 175), different form प्राच्य.

The भर्गादिगण people and the यौधेयादिगण people are from IV 9, 178 clearly northern people; and they are भर्ग, करूष, केकय, कश्मीर, उरश, साल्व, सुस्वात (Swāt) mentioned in the भर्गादिगण and यौधेय, शौभ्रेय, शौक्रेय, वार्तेय, धार्तेय, त्रिगर्त, भरत and उशीनर mentioned in यौधेयगण. The Bharatas mentioned as northern people are the original Bharatas.

Of the peoples to the east, actually mentioned in sūtras, are पाञ्चाल and निषध (IV 1, 192), काशी (IV 2, 116), मगध, कलिंग and सूरमस (IV 1, 170). Under प्राच्यभर्गादि-यौधेयादिभ्यः (IV 1, 178) the Kāśikā gives the following as Prāchya peoples, viz. पांचाल, वैदेह, अंग, नंग and मगध, Magadha and Kalinga are directly mentioned in IV 1. 170. The Aryans had advanced into Kalinga even in the days of the Aitareya Āraṇyaka. They were not then yet settled therein. Sauvīra (सौवीर) is mentioned in IV 1, 148; and in सौराष्ट्र the Aryans had long settled, as its milkwomen crying तक्रँ are mentioned in प्रातिशाख्यs. It is certain that Pāṇini knew not the Deccan and the South, no names from there occurring in his sūtras. The Aryans had, however, then settled as far as the Vindhyas as we have a direct mention of अवन्ति (Ujjain) and कुन्ति (कुतवाल in Gwalior) in IV 1, 176 and शूरसेन in Kāśikā under 177. The अन्धक and वृष्णि of Dwarka are directly mentioned in IV 1, 114 and the हैहय in the शिवादिगण (IV 1, 111).

The sūtra बहुच इञः प्राच्यभरतेषु (II 4, 66) shows, to our mind, that the Bharatas were a distinct people not of the east but of the middle land as also of the Panjab, which wae their original home, a fact wrongly denied by Kāśikā.

When it further gives under Bharatas here the example युधिष्ठिराः as indicating the descendants of Yudhishṭhira, it further forgets that from the Mahābhārata story, we are certain that Yudhishṭhira left no descendants. the only representative of Pāṇḍu's family after the massacre by Aśvatthāman in the dead of night being Parikshit in the womb of his mother. If we do take and must take Yudhishthira and Arjuna as Bharatas, we may hold that Bharatas were spread in both east and north and hence required a special mention. A similarly wrong remark is given by the Kāśikā under

न द्वचः प्राच्यभरतेषु (IV 2, 113).

The Kāśikā remarks here that the Bharatas were themselves an eastern people and, therefore, should not have been mentioned in addition to Prāchyas and thus finds out a ज्ञापक (hint). But we think that the Kāśikā, having no idea as to the geographical condition of Pāṇini's time, wrongly criticises him here.

The sūtra भौरिक्याद्यैषुकार्यादिभ्यो विधल्भक्तलौ (IV 2, 54) mentions many peoples and countries not now known or even suspected; भौरिकि and ऐषुकारि are unheared of even in Mahābhārata and their conntries with names ending in विध and भक्त such as भौरिकिविधः (देशः) and ऐषुकारिभक्तः. Under the former gaṇa we find सैकयत and वैकयत and under the latter सौवीर and दासमित्र.

Names of towns and villages are found mentioned in several sūtras such as कास्तीर and अजस्तुन्द mentioned already (VI 1, 155). Four sutrās explain how their names arise (IV 2, 70 &c.). (1) तदस्मिन्नस्ति, from something which is found there; (2) तेन निर्वृत्तम्, founded by some one, (3) तस्य निवासः inhabited by some one and (4) अदूरे, near something. Hundreds of names of towns and villages are given in illustation by the Kāśikā as also in the gaṇas indicated by the word आदि. वरणादिभ्यश्च (IV 2,82) includes मथुरा, उज्जयिनी, गया, तक्षशिला and उरशा in Kashmir. The sūtra उदक्च विपाशः (IV 2, 74) is very interesting. Firstly it mentions the Panjab river विपाशा or Bias. It further proves Pāṇini's minute knowledge of the villages of the Panjab. Wells dug north of the Bias are named in a particular way, while those to the south, in another. And thirdly, the names are accented in diflerent ways in different places. स्त्रीषु सौवीरसाल्वप्राक्षु (IV 2, 76) is important. For town names were often feminine like दात्तामित्री नगरी in सौवीर. Such towns in eastern lands are instanced by Kāśikā in काकन्दी and माकन्दी. (This sūtra further proves that according to

Pāṇini, सौवीर and साल्व were not in the east, the former being in the middle land and the latter in the north). River names are often formed in the manner of those found in the Mahābhārata list of rivers. उदीच्यग्रामाच्च बह्वचोऽन्तोदात्तात् (IV 2, 109) clearly shows that even in the names of towns there were accents in the spoken language in the days of Pāṇini. Where रङ्कु is, cannot now be determined (राङ्कवो गौः VI 2, 100). We have already mentioned towns ending in प्रस्थ ; but प्रस्थोत्तरपद-पलद्यादिकोपधादण् (IV 2, 110) includes many towns in the पलद्यादिगण of which यकृल्लोमन् and कालकूट are fit to be noted here as mentioned in the Mahābhārata and the Rāmāyana also. But तूदी, शलातुर, वर्मती and कूचवार mentioned in IV 3, 94 which are towns or countries probably in the north are not found in MBh. though तक्षशिला mentioned in the preceding sūtra is. In this gaṇa we may notice कश्मीर, उरस्, avd दरत्.

How Pāṇini's acquaintance with the Panjab was very close appears from वाहीकेषु ग्रामेभ्यश्च (IV 2,117) which states that names of villages in the Vāhika country only were treated in a certain way. Kāśikā instanses शाकलिका, शाकलिकी. Śākala was a well-known town in the Vāhika country (see MBh. शाकलं नाम नगरम्-कर्णप. where the Vāhikas are denounced as very irreligious.). Pāṇini in the next sūtra विभाषोशनीरेषु (IV, 1, 118) states that though Uśīnara was a part of the Vāhikā country, the names of villages in it were optionally subject to the same rule. Kāśikā mentions as instance आह्वजालिका–की aud आह्वजालीया, as also सौदर्शनिका–की and सौदर्शनीया, Pāñini's knowledge of the Panjab goes down even to optional forms of names of villages. Another sūtra gives कूल, सूद, स्थल and कर्ष as the usual endings of villiage names (VI 2, 127). Pāṇini seems to look upon Vāhīka as a general name for the Panjab in V, 3, 104. For he apparently classes क्षुद्रकाः and मालवाः as Vāhīka peoples.

But here they are not Kshatriyas as the Kāśikā seems to indicate !!! V, 3, 116 gives more fighting tribes, viz. दामन्यादि and त्रिगर्त with their five allied clans (त्रिगर्तषष्ठ.). The names given in these two gaṇas do not occur in MBh.-- The पर्श्वादि and the यौधेयादि fighting tribes mentioned separately in the next sūtra (V, 3, 117) taking certain Pratyayas contain some names of outsiders, viz. पर्शु, असुर, बाल्हीक (not वाहीक) and पिशाच (who gave their name to the पैशाची Prakrit). The latter gaṇa contains the well-known Indo-Aryans यौधेय, त्रिगर्त, भरत and उशीनर.

Note 5-Unusual words in Pāṇini

We have already noted that Sanskrit being the spoken language of the people in the days of Pāṇini, many words occur in his sūtras which are now out of use and hence not understandable, e.g. भाजी, कंस &c. There are also some unusual forms. मातरापितरावुदीचाम् (VI 3, 32) and सख्यशिश्वीति भाषायाम् (IV I, 62) may be noted. सखी and आशिश्वी used by the common people were सखा and अशिशु in Vedic language. स्थे च भाषायाम् (VI 3, 20) shows that विषमस्थ was विषमेस्थ in Vedic. गोत्रान्तेवासिमाणवब्राह्मणेषु क्षेपे (VI, 2, 69) shows how जंघावात्स्यः, कुमारीदाक्षः, भिक्षामाणवः, वृषलीब्राह्मणः were terms of contempt. दाण्डाजिनिक meant दाम्भिक (V 2, 76). रूप्य meant handsome: रूप्यः पुरुषः (V 2, 120) as also आहत in रूप्यः दीनारः (का.). The word रूपक (rupee) subsequently was perhaps taken from this use.

THE DATE OF PĀNINI

Next to the date of the Śatapatha Brāhmaṇa, the most important date in the history of Vedic literature is that of Pāṇini. It is also the subject of the greatest divergence of opinion between European and Indian scholars. While the former place Pāṇini generally "in the middle of the Sūtra period" (Macd. p.244) which is taken to range from 600 to 200 B.C., the latter including the late Dr. Bhandarkar place him before Buddha, i.e. before 500 B.C., at the latest, some placing him as early as even 1000 B. C. We place Pāṇini about 800 B. C.; and we detail our reasons for this view in this chapter. The late V. K. Rajawade, the well-known Maratha history researcher, also held the same view and detailed his arguments in a paper read before the Itihāsa Saṁśodhaka Mandala in 1911 A.D. in Marathi (see its Report for 1911). We will first give these arguments with such observations of our own as are necessary.

It must at once be pointed out that the story of the Kathāsaritsāgara that Pāṇini was a contemporary of Kātyāyana, both being pupils of Upavarsha who lived in the time of the 'Nine Nandas' is a pure fiction. The fact is that this 'ocean' of stories was composed in Sanskrit in about 1000 A. D., on the basis of a work of Guṇāḍhya in Paiśāchī. Realities had so far been forgotten that Paiśāchī from being a real Prākṛit spoken in the Panjab and the adjoining northern countries had become the language of goblins; and the work of Guṇāḍhya is represented in this ocean of absurd stories as written by goblins in blood. The story in this ocean about Pāṇini may, therefore, be safely rejected, bringing together, as it does, the three great authors on grammar, viz. Pāṇini, Vararuchi and Vyāḍi, much as modern tradition brings together the two best poets in classical Sanskrit, viz. Kalidāsa and Bhavabhūti.* We now know for certain that Kālidāsa preceded Bhavabhūti by at least two, if not seven, centuries. We must equally be sure that Pāṇini preceded Kātyāyana by two centuries at least. For when in his Vārtikas or 'Notes,' Kātyāyana suggests emendations or additions to the sūtras of Pāṇini, it is not because Pāṇini had committed mistakes and required correction, but mostly because language had changed since the time of Pāṇini up to the time of Kātyāyana. For such change, at least a period of two or three centuries must intervene between the two. We know for certain that Patanjali who wrote his unique Bhāshya on

* The further story that Pāṇini was originally a dunce is on a par with the similar story about Kālidāsa.

Pāṇini's grammar as emended by Kātyāyana's Vārtikas, lived about 150 B.C., as he refers to the invasion of India by the Greeks under Menander as a contemporaneous event. Kātyāyana may be taken to have lived about 200 years before Patanjali of 150 B. C., i. e. about 350 B. C., the age of the Nandas, and Pāṇini to have lived at least about 200 years before Kātyāyana, i. e. about 550 B. C. It may be noted that Macdonell in his last work gives 500 B. C. as the date of Pāṇini, though no reason is assigned for this change of opinion.

When Kātyāyana emends or adds to Pāṇini's sūtras, it may generally be taken, as stated above, that he does so because language had changed by his time. It is true that some of Kātyāyana's Vārtikas supply real omissions by Pāṇini, especially those wherein Chhāndasa or Vedic forms are noted in the Vārtikas; for we have to believe that Pāṇini must have had the Saṁhitās before him; and when any addition or emendation is made to Pāṇini's sūtras on their score, it supplies an omission by Pāṇini as in VI 2, 199* or VI 3,21, But ordinarily, looking to the genius of Pāṇini, and especially in matters of the spoken language, we must hold that Kātyāyana suggests alterations or additions simply because language had changed since the days of Pāṇini or new words had got into the language. This view,

* Even here no change of accent can explain Panini's silence.

underlies the arguments advanced by V. K. Rajwade as also by Dr. Bhandarkar.

(1) The sūtra of Pāṇini कम्बोजाल्लुक् (IV 1, 175) is emended by Kātyāyana by the Vartika कम्बोजादिभ्य इति वक्तव्यम्. Pāṇini mentions only कम्बोज as denoting both people and their king and Kātyāyana by कम्बोजादि adds four more words, viz. चोल, शक, यवन and केरल. Dr. Bhandarkar argued from this that while Pāṇini knew only the Kambojas (a people to the north of India), Kātyāyana knew the Cholas and the Keralas and that the Aryans must have advanced into Southern India after Pāṇini and before Kātyāyana, i.e. between 700 and 350 B.C., nay before 500 B.C., as in Buddha's days, towns in the south such as Śūrpāraka were known. Dr. Bhandarkar thus determined the date of the colonization of the Deccan and South India by Aryans with which question he was concerned. He naturally did not draw the inference derivable from the other two words शक and यवन. Rajawade takes up these words and discusses the natural inference from their non-mention by Pāṇini. These are northern peoples and Pāṇini who lived in Takshaśilā must have known them and the two words must have been current in the spoken language of his time. Indeed यवन is mentioned in one of his sūtras (IV 1, 49) and Śaka also in another sūtra. His omission of these two words in the sūtra कम्बोजाल्लुक्, therefore, shows that although he knew शक and यवन people, they had no

kings and, therefore, these words in his time did not denote any kings. We know that a Śaka kingdom was destroyed by Cyrus in 550 B.C. and that it had been founded by Deioces about 700 B.C. Rajawade, therefore, properly argues that Pāṇini who did not know of any Śaka kings must have lived before 700 B.C. Similarly Pāṇini did not know of any Yavana kings and, therefore, he must have lived not only before Alexander but before Darius in whose invasion of Greece, Indian soldiers formed part of the Persian army.

(2) Rajawade discusses next the sūtra इन्द्रवरुण... यवयवनमातुलाचार्याणामानुक् (IV 1, 49). It is clear from this sūtra that यवनानी in the language of Pāṇini meant a Yavana woman. But according to a Vārtika of Vararuchi, यवनानी meant यवनलिपि, the writing of the Greeks, a Yavana woman being called यवनी as in classical Sankrit. Yavana also meant to him both Greeks and Greek kings. It is thus clear that while Kātyāyana knew Yavana kings and Yavana writing, Pāṇini did not know either, though he knew the Yavana people and Yavanānīs, their women. This change of meaning of यवन and यवनानी indicates the dates of both. Kātyāyana must have lived after Alexander, at least after the invasion of Greece by Darius; but Pāṇini must have lived before both.

It may be objected that the sūtra इन्द्रवरुण...यवन &c. shows that Pāṇini knew the Greeks and consequently he must have known their kings and their writing, as there were kings in Greece and the Greeks were an advanced people. This objection, in our opinion, though plausible, is refutable. We know from the account of Arrian that the Greeks of Alexander found a colony of Greeks long settled in Afghanistan who were practically cut off from Greece and who were in a very backward condition. These Pāṇini knew; and as they had no kings, the word Yavana meaning a king had not yet come into use; and as they were illiterate, the word यवनानी could not have then meant यवनलिपि. Hence Pāṇini could not give यवन in कंबोजाल्लुक् nor could the latter word mean a special mode of writing.

(3) Rajawade next notes the sūtra अरण्यान्मनुष्ये (IV 2, 129) extended by Kātyāyana to पथ्यध्यायन्यायविहारमनुष्यहस्तिषु इति वाच्यम्. Thus आरण्यक to Pāṇini simply meant a forest man; to Kātyāyana it also meant a forest path, a book of study, a forest Vihāra &c. We have already noted (Sec. II p. 140) that the word आरण्यक as applied to certain Vedic works did not exist in the days of Pāṇini. But this fact does not supply us with a datum since we cannot determine when the word came into use. But the word विहार does so and indicates that Pāṇini lived before Buddha, as Vihāras came into existence after Buddha and the word आरण्यक as meaning a forest Vihāra came into use after him.

It may be objected that Pāṇini knew Śramaṇas from the sūtra कुमारः श्रमणादिभिः (II 1, 70) and must hence have lived after Buddha. But unlike the word विहार, the word श्रमण existed long before Buddha. It originally meant monks generally and is used in this sense in the Bṛihadāraṇyaka. It was appropriated later by Buddhism. Vihāra in the sense of monks' cell is post-Buddhistic and hence while Kātyāyana clearly followed Buddha Pāṇini must be taken to have preceded him.

(4) Winternitz in his 'History of Indian Literature' while placing Pāṇini about the 5th century B. C. (p. 44) does not place him before Buddha perhaps for the above sūtra. But there are other indications which make Pāṇini precede Buddha by several centuries. As stated above, Śramaṇa is an older word for monks generally and this sūtra is of no value in determinnig Pāṇini's date. But as Rajawade points out, we have the use of the word भाषा by Pāṇini to denote the language later called Sanskrit. We have already stated at length that the Prakrits arose after Pāṇini, and that by way of opposition, the ancient language which remained as the spoken language of pandits was called Sanskrit. Buddha preached in Pāli, the common language of the people at his time in Magadha, and hence must have been born at least two or three centuries after Pāṇini. It is conceded by Goldstücker also that Pāṇini preceded Buddha.

Professor Pāṭhak of Poona argues from the sūtra कुमार: श्रमणादिभि: that Pāṇini lived after Pārśvanātha and before Buddha. He thinks that the young female recluses mentioned by Pāṇini were Jains and that Pārśvanātha was the first Jain preacher who lived before Mahāvīra, the contemporary of Buddha, about 700 B.C. But Jainism does not believe that Pārśvanātha was the first Jain preacher, there being several before him like Ādinatha. And secondly, as stated already, the word Śramaṇa is a general word meaning monk and not necessarily a Jain monk.

The sūtra निर्वाणोऽवाते is taken by many as indicating that Pāṇini lived before Buddha. Both Goldstücker and Pāthak quote it in this connection. It is thought that Pāṇini did not know Nirvāṇa in the sense the Buddhists took viz. absolution. M. M. Vasudevaśastri Abhyankar thinks, however, that such an inference can not be drawn. The word निर्वाण in this sūtra is a verbal past participle, i. e. क्तप्रत्ययान्त adjective, e. g. निर्वाणोऽग्निः निर्वाणो मुनिः-का.; but the word निर्वाण in the sense of मोक्ष is a noun and ल्युट्प्रत्ययान्त formed under the sūtra ल्युट् च (III 3, 115); भावे धातोर्ल्युट् प्रत्ययो भवति e. g. शयनम्-आसनम्-काशिका. This opinion is well founded and makes it certain that the word निर्वाण like श्रमण existed from before Buddha in the sense of absolution or mere absorption in which sense it appears in the Bhagavadgītā also. The importance of this fact will appear further on, when we speak of the Gītā. It is only to be noted here that the sūtra निर्वाणोऽवाते has no bearing whatever on the question at issue and can not necessarily show that Pāṇini preceded Buddha.

(5) An argument is derived by Rajawade from the sūtra पर्श्वादियौधेयादिभ्योऽणञौ (V 3, 117) which shows that the पर्शुs or Persians were in the days of Pāṇini still an आयुधजीविसंघ (V 3, 114) or a community of soldiers living by their arms, fighting for any one who paid them; in short they had not yet founded the Persian empire. The Persians founded their empire under Cyrus about 550 B.C. Rājawade pointed out that in the brick records of the Assyrians, the word Persian is even spelt as Parśua and their mention goes back to 850 B.C. He quotes here Historians' History of the World Vol, I p. 388 and II p.560. We may, hold therefore, that Pāṇini must have lived between 850 and 550 B. C. It can not be argued, Rajwade urges, that the Persians again became an आयुधजीविसंघ after the destruction of their empire by Alexander and Pāṇini's sūtra refers to that time, as we are certain that Pāṇini lived be.ore Alexander himslf. It may be added that after the Persian empire was destroyed, the fame of their empire was too great and secondly history does not record that the Persians, after the destruction of their empire, again became renowned as a warlike people.

Rajawade sums up his arguments thus :— Pāṇini preceded Alexander and other Yavana kings and preceded Cyrus who destroyed the

Assyrian kingdom in 538 B. C. Pāṇini preceded Buddha and the rise of Prākrits. He lived at the time when the Persians were still an आयुधजीविसंघ, i. e. in the period between 850 and 550 B. C. Pāṇini preceded the establishment of the Śaka kingdom under Deioces about 700 B C. He adds that यवन or Ionions were known after the Trojan war (1200 B. C.) and that the Grecian alphabet was evolved about 900 B.C. Pāṇini's earlist date can not go beyond 1200 B. C. and his latest date can not be later than 700 B. C.

(6) The following sūtras, we think, futher support the date assigned to Pāṇini by Rajawade:- वासुदेवार्जुनाभ्यां वुन् (IV 3, 98) shows that Vāsudeva and Arjuna were worshipped as gods in the days of Pāṇini. We know that this position was lost by Arjuna in the days of the Mahābhārata. But the original work of Vyāsa, viz. Jaya, did look upon Arjuna as a god, as in the very beginning verse of salutation नारायणं नमस्कृत्य नरं चैव नरोत्तमम् &c., Arjuna is bowed to. This verse at least belongs to the same period as वासुदेवार्जुनाभ्यां वुन्. In the Bhagavadgītā we also find Arjuna treated as an Aṁśāvatāra in पाण्डवाणां धनंजयः. We will return to this subject when we speak of the Mahābhārata and the Bhagavadgītā in detail. Why Arjuna lost this position by the time of the Mahābhārata is an interesting question. It seems to us that the Gītā gave rise to the cult of Vāsudeva-worship, subsequently called Pāñchārātra, explained

at length in the Mahābhārata ; and in this cult, three near relatives of Vāsudeva, viz. Balarāma brother, Pradyumna son and Aniruddha grandson, were deified and the four looked upon as Vyūhas. Arjuna was thus left out and no longer was worshipped as a god. This sūtra leads to the inference that Pāṇini lived before the rise of the Pāñcharātra cult which is pre-Buddhistic.

(7) The most interesting sūtra which we adduce to prove the priority of Pāṇini to Buddha is VI, 2, 42, wherein to कुरुगार्हपत of Pāṇini, Kātyāyana adds वृजिगार्हपत, (कुरुवृज्योर्गार्हपतमिति वक्तव्यम्). One may safely infer from this that the Vṛijis were a people who were not admitted to the Vedic religion, being foreigners, in the days of Pāṅini but were so in Kātyāyana's days. The Vṛijis were known to Pāṇini from मंद्रवृज्योः कन् (IV2,131); but they were non-Aryans and had no गार्हपत. The Vṛijis, Lichchhavis and others figure in Buddhistic history and this proves that while Kātyāyana followed Buddha, Pāṇini preceded him by some centuries.

This emendation of Pāṇini's sūtra is important in another way, because it suggests a solution of the interesting question in Indian history, how did the Prakrits arise ? We are certain that they had no existence in the days of Pāṇini but had already come into being in the days of Buddha. What led to their rise is as yet a riddle. History establishes the principle that a general upheaval of society usually leads to the rise of new languages. We know that the incursions of Goths and other barbarian hordes not only destroyed the Roman empire but also the Roman language. We know that thereafter arose new languages based on Latin itself in Italy, France and Spain. Similarly in India, the modern Sanskrit-born vernaculars arose about the tenth century A. D. and the ancient Prakrits died because of the incursion of new ideas born of the philosophy of Śaṇkara and the downfall of Buddhism. The ancient Prakrits used by Buddhism fell into abeyance and Sanskrit coming into popular favour, modern vernaculars arose by the use of Sanskrit or Tatsama words. (See our history of Mediæval Hindu India Vol III p. 471 &c.). The political history of India before Buddha is almost a blank and we do not know yet definitely what happened in India which led to the death of Sankrit as a spoken language and the rise of Prakrits before the birth of Buddha, One fact we have already noted, viz. that Aryans went into and settled in Mahārāshṭra after Pāṇini and before Buddha. These Aryans married non-Aryan women to a far greater extent than they had hitherto done. We know from Harivaṁśa that the Yādavas who principally settled in the Deccan were Aryans born of Nāga women and the admixture of Dravidian blood is found to a larger extent in the Deccan than elsewhere.

Already in Pāṇini's days, they had settled in Dvārakā and other places and deteriorated. For the sūtra राजन्यबहुवचनद्वन्द्वेऽन्धकवृष्णिषु (VI 2, 34) discloses the fact that among the अन्धकवृष्णिs, there were tribes which were not Rājanyas. The Kāśikā names them as द्वैप्यand द्वैपायन (द्वीपे भवाः born in an island). Śrikṛishṇa, himself a Vṛishṇi (वृष्णीनां वासुदेवोऽस्मि), had married many non-Aryan wives. These mixed tribes must have begun to speak in softened and modified Sanskrit in the Deccan and in Gujarat and thus arose Māhārāshṭrī in the south. But what led to the rise of Pali in Oudh and the adjoining country? The Aryans were already long there and, having remained pure in race, spoke Sanskrit still with some provincialism of the प्राचाम्. This sūtra and its Vārtika bringing in the Vṛijis seems to indicate that after Pāṇini there was a great upheaval of society in Oudh by their incursion. These were admitted finally as Vrātya-Kshatriyas, vide Manu; peoples, such as Vṛijis, Lichchhavis, Daradas &c.of Tibetan origin adopted the religion and language of the more advanced local people but in adopting the language modified it into Pali. This incursion must have come via Nepal and not by the usual North-West route, as the population of the Panjab and Rājputāna still remains predominantly Aryan by race.

(8) if we scan further the history of the Parśus, ws can take Pāṇini two centuries before

Cyrus. From the obelisk of Shalmaneser we learn how the Assyrian king marched into the territory of Persia and received tribute. This was in 836 B.C. (H.H.W. Vol. II p. 589). The first king of Parśus and an ancestor of Cyrus was Teispes who flourished about 730 B.C., somewhat earlier than the foundation of the Median (शक) empire (p. 390 ibid). We may believe that the Parśus ceased to be freebooters about this time and hence Pāṇini who speaks of पर्शु as an आयुधजीविसंघ should be placed earlier than 730 B.C. Parśus later became Parsis, the Pārasīkas of Kālidāsa.

From all these arguments, we are justified in holding that Pāṇini preceded Buddha by three centuries and the formation of the Śaka and Parśu kingdoms in 700 and 730 B.C. by one century and he may thus be placed in the 9th century B. C. approximately.

It is inexplicable how Prof. Belvalkar puts Pāṇini about 650 B.C., accepting, as he does, all the arguments adduced by V. K. Rajawads, especially the one by which he places Pāṇini before 700 B.C., the date of Deioces (Systems of Sanskrit Grammar, p. 18). Instead of the 7th century B. C., Pāṇini should have been placed in the 8th and even the 9th. Probably Prof. Belvalkar thinks that "Pāṇini must have known some forms of Gṛihya and Dharma Sūtras" from IV 4, 71. But the Gṛihyas did not lay down rules *ab initio*;

they only embodied the current practice in rules; thus the अदेशकाल of अध्ययन must have been long established in practice. We have already shown how the Gṛihya Sūtras fall outside the Vedic period and how Pāṇini could not have known any Gṛihya sūtras.

It may be objected that such words as रोमक, बर्बर, अश्मक &c. occurring in the Gaṇapāṭhas go against our date for Pāṇini. But we have to remember that these lists have not come down to us as they were recited by Pāṇini. They were in fact intended to be आकृतिगणs or illustrative lists and additions must have been made to them from time to time. Then again Aśmaka may be a country or people in the north near Avanti (अवन्त्यश्मकम् a gaṇa given in VI 2, 37) from whence the name has been taken to the Deccan as several names clearly are. This argument, therefore, can not avail against the overwhelming data given above.

APPENDIX

I OTHER SRAUTA SUTRAS

I S'āṅkhāyana

This Sūtra which belongs to the Ṛigveda has been edited in the Bibliotheca Indica Series, by Dr. Hillebrandt in three volumes published at Calcutta (1888, 1891 and 1897). The first volume contains the original Sūtra and the next two volumes give the commentary of Varadattasuta Ānartīya. The S'āṅkhāyana S'ākhā is found in North Gujarat and naturally the commentator also belongs to Ānarta which means the same province. S'āṅkhāyana can not be the name of the author of this Sūtra as it is the name of an Āchārya in the Āchārya-tarpaṇa list of Ṛigvedins, who is therefore the author of a Brāhmaṇa. The author belongs to the S'ākhā only and gives the S'rauta riual of that S'ākhā. The Sūtra follows the Kaushītaki Brāhmāṇa which is also called S'āṅkhāyana, and this is clearly a gotra name from S'ankha--a Ṛishi.

The Sūtra is divided into 18 chapters subdivided into Kaṇḍikās or sections consisting of a number of short sūtras. The number of sūtras in this edition is different from the number given by the commentator; Dr. Hillebrandt thinks that the commentator has wrongly split up some sūtras into two or more. But the sections and the chapters are the same in both. The sūtra gives the ritual in all S'rauta sacrifices, chiefly in relation to the work of the Hotṛi whose duty it is to recite mantras from the Ṛigveda in praise of gods. The Sūtra as usual begins with the Darśapūrṇamāsa and ends with the highest sattras or sacrificial sessions like Aśvamedha.

The extreme care and erudition with which the Sūtra is edited will appear from the seven indices appended, the most important of which (V) gives references to the Ṛigveda of the S'ākala S'ākhā for all verses quoted in the Sūtra. Index VI gives the verses, only twelve in number, which could not be found. This shows that the Sūtra uses a slightly different version of the Ṛigveda. Lastly, an index of the Gāthās and S'lokas quoted in the Sūtrs is given. Whence these are taken cannot be found. We have already mentioned (See II p. 196) that the Bṛihadāraṇyaka Upanishad notices works known as गाथाs as also सूत्रs, व्याख्यानs and अनुव्याख्यानs which are now all lost.

The learned editor thinks that the Sūtra has been added to from time to time, especially in optional procedure. This is probable though to a limited extent. It is, therefore, difficult to determine the probable date of the Sūtra ; but it seems likely that it is anterior to the Āśvalāyana Sūtra as we find from its contents. The sūtras are short and simple and lay down detailed rules for reciting mantras at the various sacrificial and other acts.

The contents of the several chapters with the interesting statements in them may be noted shortly as follows : Chapter I gives provisions for recitations of mantras such as उपांशु or otherwise, with ओम् or without, and so on and ये यजामहे for याज्या. "The S'rauta sacrifices can be performed by the three varṇas". The mixed castes had apparently not arisen. The Darśapūrṇamāsa sacrifices are to be performed on Amāvāsyās and Pūrṇimās which are of two kinds, viz. when the moon is and is not seen, or when the moon is and is not full. This seems to show that astronomical calculation had not yet far advanced ; and the exact time of the full moon or no moon could not be calculated beforehand. The sacrificers had, therefore, to watch the sky. The word आवाप is defined as अन्तरेणाज्यभागं स्विष्टकृतं च यदिज्यते तमावाप इत्याचक्षते (16, 3). Differentiating याज्या from पुरोनुवाक्या, it is laid down that अद्धि, पिब, जुषस्व, मत्स्व आवृषायस्व, वीहि, प्रदेवतानामिति याज्यालक्षणानि। हुवे, हवामहे, श्रुध्यागह्येदं बर्हिर्निषीद प्रदेवतानामेति पुरोनुवाक्यानुलक्षणानि (17, 14, 15), This Sūtra uses ळ for ड् (e.g. अहेळता, पुरोळाश) and not ळ of the S'ākala recension.

In Chapter II the आधानकाल is given as in other Sūtras; but the रथकार is not here separately mentioned. This indicates a later date for it than Āpastamba and Kātyāyana. शुद्धे रक्षे वा पुण्ये नक्षत्रे is also later, especially the word शुद्ध. ऋतं त्वा सत्येन परिषिञ्चामि and सत्यं त्वर्तेन परिषिञ्चामि (प्रातः) are found here (6, 10). पयोयवागूर्दध्याज्यमित्यग्निहोत्रहवींषि shows that for daily अग्निहोत्र flesh was not prescribed.

Chapter III mentions various sacrifices connected with Agnihotra which are not mentioned elsewhere, one of which is बहुदेवता इष्टि (ज्ञातयोऽसंविदानाः i.e. families fighting among themselves should perform this for unity 6-1). In the end प्रायश्चित्तs are given for lapses in अग्निहोत्र; and Ṛigveda, Yajurveda and Sāmaveda lapses only are mentioned and not Atharvaveda.

Chapter IV begins with the remarkable provision that the sacrificer and his wife should eat before letting off the calf; but य इच्छन्मांसकृणमिथुनमावेश्यो येन च दण्डेन वक्ष्यमाणः स्यात्. Breakfast is thus allowed for an अग्निहोत्री. मध्यमपिण्डं पत्नी पुत्रकामा प्राश्नीयात् in पितृयज्ञ seems a late addition. The form (अग्निहोत्र) हवनी is found in this Sūtra also. कौषीतकिः is mentioned here as an authority. Some other rites are described including the burning of a dead अग्निहोत्रिन्. The शूलगव sacrifice is described in which a bull is sacrificed to propitiate S'iva who is पशुपति. The bull is killed by suffocating him (तं संज्ञपयन्ति प्राक्शिरसमुदक्पादमरवमाणम् (17-6). Finally मधुपर्क is described, to be offered to आचार्य, ऋत्विक्, श्वशुर, राजन्, स्नातक

and प्रिया. The bull offered is to be let loose optionally गोरुत्सृजते तृणान्यत्त्विति वा। (21, 22).

With Chapter V we have the higher sacrifices described begnining with सोम., with the usual details.

Chapter VI, saying that अग्निष्टोमीय is the प्रकृति or model of all पशुs, details the विकृतिs (changes) with the various mantras, especially so many verses in such and such सूत्र etc., So also Chapter VII gives detailed mantras for माध्यंदिन सवन with details of Sāmans sung and their metres.

Chapters VIII describes the तृतीय सवन. Everywhere the duties of the different priests नेतृ, पोतृ, अग्नीध्र &c. are given. The ceremonies प्रायणीया, उदयनीया, दीक्षणीय, अनुबन्ध्या are noticed and finally the अवभृथ. Sections 16-21 are in the nature of a Brāhmaṇa describing how different gods partook of the Soma. The sentences are short with alliterative words. We find here Yājuḥ mantras also..

Chapter IX begins with the sūtra व्याख्यातोऽग्निष्टोमः प्रकृतिर्द्वादशाहस्यैकाहानां च (१) The Paśus to be sacrificed are enumerated as follows—पुरुषोऽजोऽविर्गौरश्व इति पञ्च पशव :। अजो वा तूपरः (23-45). Human victims were released in the S'rauta Sūtra times; but an actual human sacrifice is described at the end. Chapter X describes the द्वादशाह with दशरात्र in the middle with increasing Stomas (9,15, 17, 21, 27, 33, 44, 48 and 54) and with different Sāmans. Chapter XI begins with व्याख्यातो द्वादशाहः प्रकृतिः सत्राहीनानाम् and describes अहीनs. पैङ्ग्य and कौषीतकि are quoted as opposing authorities. In XII we find Kuntāpa verses इदं जना &c., the same as in A. V. The Sūtra gives them because the Kaushītaki Brāhmaṇa does not give them as the Aitareya does. On comparing these with A. V. we find 4 is given at 6 and 7 – 10 about Parikshit are given later. The पारिक्षित्या four verses are last quoted, then the एतशप्रलाप and then other Purāṇic verses with न्यूंख at the end as अरितारो थामो दैवोम् &c (23).

Chapter XIII provides for minor matters such as the sacrificer's death (यदि दीक्षितेा प्रमीयेत दग्ध्वास्थीनुनपह्य पुत्रं भ्रातरं वा दीक्षयित्वा सह यजेरन् 41, 1). If Soma cannot be bought or obtained, पूतिकान् श्वेतपुष्पाण्यर्जुनानि कुशान् वाभिषुत्य is precribed (6–3). There is no higgling in the purchase of Soma as it is simply provided सामाहराय सोमविक्रायणे वा किंचिद्दद्यात् (6–21). Finally all the highest sacrifices are described together with the सारस्वत सत्र on the banks of the Sarasvatī and दार्शद्वत en the banhs of the दृशद्वती.

Chapter XIV curiously enough reverts to minor sacrifices like चातुर्मास्य, वरुणप्रघास &c. and in Brāhmaṇa fashion ascribes their origin to Prajāpati, Indra, Sāvitrī and others, these having first performed them. A special sacrifice to be performed by Brahmins and Kshatriyas is prescribed to make them united (29).

Chapter XV continues in the same Brāhmaṇa strain in short sūtras शरदि वाजपेयेन यजेत। पानं वै पेयः। अन्नं वाजः। and everything is seventeen as elsewhere. Aptoryāma is described and the name is explained in a sūtra. यमस्तोम and वाचस्तोम are new sacrifices. The several higher digits of number are given as अयुत, प्रयुत, नियुत, अर्बुद, निखर्व, समुद्र, सलिल, अन्त्य and अत्यन्त (II. 4); we do not come across कोटि yet. Rājasūya is seen by Varuṇa who wished to be king of kings. भार्गवो होता requires the Hotri in this sacrifice to be of भृगु गोत्र. दशपेय is for येषामुभयतः दशपूरुषाः श्रोत्रियाः (14, 9). Sautrāmaṇa is then described (the name being सौत्रामण) and a new mantra is prescribed for taking सुरा. Lastly, the शौनःशेप आख्यान is related here at length which is out of place in a Sūtra; but the Ākhyāna is not given in the Kaushītaki Brahmaṇa as in the Aitareya and hence its recital.

Chapter XVI concerns Aśvamedha which is said to have been seen and performed by प्रजापति to obtain *all* desires. It is said to be त्रिरात्र. The Hotri recites Pāriplava, derived as यत्पुनःपुनः परिप्लवते तत्पारिप्लवम् (2, 36). The ten Vedas recited on 10 days detailed here are nearly the same as elsewhere; but अथर्ववेद is mentioned as भेषज and आङ्गिरसवेद as घोर (घोरं निगदेत् 12). What is रक्षोविद्या to be recited to सेलगs who are plainly रक्षांसि or cannibals? पशवश्चैकविंशतिः is to be noted. Ṛig verses are recited at each action which are really in the Rigveda. Thus यदश्वाय वासः &c, recited when covering the horse with a cloth, is traced in the Index to I 162, 16 and A. B. This shows that the horse sacrifice ritual is very old. इन्द्रोतः शौनकः is mentioned here (7, 7) as performing अश्वमेध for जनमेजय पारीक्षित. His three brothers उग्रसेन, भीमसेन and श्रुतसेन are also mentioned. This is out of place in a Sūtra being in Brahmaṇa style. Sections 10 to 14 describe पुरुषमेध in a strange manner different from other Sūtras. It is seen by प्रजापति and performed by him for securing any and all things not secured by अश्वमेध. It follows the अश्वमेध ritual in all respects. A man, Brahmin or Kshatriya, is purchased and allowed to roam for two years ब्राह्मणं क्षत्रियं वा सहस्रेण शताश्वेनावक्रीय संवत्सरयोरुत्सृजन्ति (10, 9). Then a list of Rishis is given which requires to be scrutinized and their verses are recited, viz शुनःशेप, कक्षीवान् औशिज, श्यावाश्व आर्चनानस, भारद्वाज, वसिष्ट, मेधातिथि, कण्व, वत्स, प्रस्कण्व. पंचविंशतिर्यूपाः (Aśvamedha has twenty one). संज्ञप्तं वामेन सान्नोद्गातोपतिष्ठते (12,21) and संज्ञप्ताय महिषीमुपनिपातयन्ति (13, 7). The whole ceremony is different from the S'atapatha ceremony and is the latest absurdity developed in the Sūtra period by the craze of sacrificial cult. And it seems that this Sūtra or this portion is the latest of all.

The symbolical सर्वमेध is similarly described next. After some minor particulars about preceding sacrifices we have in the end एकोत्तरा अहीनाः from 2 to 11. त एते-पुरस्तादग्निष्टोमा उपरिष्टादतिरात्राः (30, 12).

The last two chapters describe महाव्रत ceremony in a strange way. The Hotṛi prepares a प्रेंखफलक of उदुम्बर

tree and some वीणाs (one शततंत्री) घाटकर्करीरवघटरिकाः काण्डवीणाः पिच्छोराः इति पत्न्य उपकल्पयन्ति (3, 12). उपमुखेन पिच्छोरां वादयेत वादनेन काण्डवीणाम् । तां घाटरीरित्याचक्षते (15) is inexplicable.

There are four दुन्दुभिs (big drums) and one भूमिदुन्दुभि made of a pit dug and covered with ox-hide. राजा वा राजमात्रो वा is invited. He goes round the srcrificial shed with bow and arrows. A S'ūdra and Ārya pair stand outside the gate and quarrel. This is the beginning of the ceremony which, however, consists of the reciting of various mantras from the Ṛigveda and Sāman-singing for the three Savanas.

This Sūtra quotes so many Ṛiks by Pratīkas and their number in the Sūkta that one is convinced that the Ṛigveda was then learnt by heart by almost every Brahmin; and just as quotations form the Bible by chapter and verse are easily understood in Christian countries, so the beginning of a verse or the name of the author of a Sūkta was sufficient to indicate the mantra. The metres and deities of mantras were also important and well-known.

This Sūtra by its simplicity and prolixity may, in its original forms, be older than Āśvalayana. No controversies almost exist and no savants are quoted except पैङ्गय and कौषीतकि. A pravarādhyāya is not given in it either added or original.

2 Lāṭyāyana

This Sūtra has also been published in the Bibliotheca Indica Series of Calcutta. It is edited by Ānandachandra Vedāntavāgiśa with the commentary of Agnisvāmin. It consists of 10 chapters called Prapāṭhakas subdivided into sections called Kaṇḍikās, 129 in all. It belongs to the Sāmaveda and is based on six works belonging to that Veda (प्रौढं ब्राह्मणमादिमम्[1] । षड्विंशाख्यं[2] द्वितीयं

स्यात् ततः [3]सामविधिः [4]संहितोपनिषद्दशा[५।६]). The contents are given in the Sanskrit preface as follows ; Chapter I Paribhāshās and the election of priests. II Stomayogas in all sacrifices, III The द्रव्यविधान in Shoḍaśin, IV Vājibhakshaṇa, V Chāturmāsyas, Varuṇapraghāsa and drinking of सोमचमसस, VI Sāmavidhāna and द्व्यक्षरप्रतिहार, VII चतुरक्षरप्रतिहार and नाद्वसीगान, VIII Ekāha and Ahīnasattra ending with Vājapeya, IX Rājasūya, X Sattras and their Paribhāshās.

The editor has prefixed two indices, one an alphabhetical list of sūtras with their beginnings and the other an alphabetical list of their subjects.

Lāṭyāyana is probably the author of this Sūtra and his school is that of the Kauthumas. There is another Sūtra of the Rāṇāyanīyas named Drāhyāyaṇa. The editor had that Sūtra also before him and has noted the difference of ritual wherever there is any. Such difference is, however, limited and it may be believed that Drāhyāyaṇa followed Lāṭyāyana as an author. The editor has not given the total number of sūtras in the work ; but it will appear from the following table :

chap.	sec.	sūtras.	chap.	sec.	sūtras.	Total.	
I	12	306	VI	12	219	sect.	sūtrs.
II	12	263	VII	13	235	129	2580
III	12	245	VIII	12	292		
IV	12	245	IX	12	269		
V	12	205	X	20	305		

Eight chapters have 12 sections each and VII has one and X has 8 more.

This is the chief Sūtra of Sāmaveda and gives many details about Sāman-singing. There are several interesting statements in it and we give the following for the curious reader.

एकश्रुतिविधानान्मंत्रान् कर्मापि चोद्गातैव कुर्यादनादेशे (1, 14) prescribes एकश्रुति recitation even of mantras generally at sacrifice. The ऋत्विक् should be आर्षेय (of the same प्रवर), अनूचान, साधुचरण, वाङ्मी, अन्यूनाङ्ग, अनतिरिक्तांग, द्वयसत्, अनातिकृष्ण and अनतिश्वेत, a long list of qualifications indeed (I, 1, 7). The sacrifical ground (देवयजन) is described as प्रागुदक्प्रवण, लोमश, अवृक्ष and सम (I, 1, 12). A पत्नीशाला is mentioned in I, 2, 22. The authorities quoted are शांडिल्य, शाट्यायनिक (I, 2, 24), गोतम (I, 3, 3) and धनंजय (I, 3, 4). General procedure for all sacrifices down to the सारस्वत and तापश्चित mentioned in other Sūtras are given for सुत्या. The Sūtra presupposes other Sūtras clearly.

In section 5 the first Sūtra lays down that the प्रस्तोता is to sing परिसामानि सर्वत्रानादेशे. Details are then given as to what Sāman. (रथन्तर, यज्ञायज्ञीय, वामदेव्य &c) is to be sung and from where. VI gives first how the parts are to be sung and how all are to join in the निधन. It then gives the other Sāmans to be sung (many names are given here), at the दीक्षणीय, प्रायणीय, उदयनीय, आतिथ्य and other rites of the higher sacrifices. Mahāvira is incidentally mentioned here. The succeeding sections describe him. The उद्गाता is to sing at औदुंबरी and other rituals. Section 9 describes how the उद्गाता with the प्रस्तोता on the left and प्रतिहर्ता on the right should sing at the प्रातःसवन. In 10 we find that a rite is pescribed while keeping the stone on the द्रोणकलश when it is desired that the राष्ट्र should be destroyed by the विश् (subjects). In 11 is given the order in which the priests should go out, viz. अध्वर्यु, प्रस्तोता, उद्गाता, प्रतिहर्ता and ब्रह्मन् and how they should come in and seat themselves facing a particular direction and then, looking at the junction of the sky with the earth, sing. Section 12 prescribes how these priests are to call upon one another and utter the Hinkāra.

Chapter II gives further general provisions about the priests and their postures, fire, savanas, the seats of Kuśa grass, praising &c. निष्क्रम्य पश्चिमेनाग्नीध्रीयं बहिर्वेदि मूत्रं कुर्यात

shows the minuteness of the details given). In 7 is described the ceremony of giving a horse-chariot as Dakshiṇā and in 8 that of ascending a chariot. Section 10 describes how different Sāmans are to be sung with their Stobhas, and how the Yajamāna and his wife (पत्नी) are to join the singing in the निधन. स्थविर गोतम is cited as an authority who is different from गोतम. We thus have the first mention of authors called subsequently वृद्ध. In 11, the eating of धाना with सोम is detailed, and in 12 the अवभृथ ceremony with its special Sāmans is described and then उपस्थान of the sun with the well-known mantras उद्वयं तमसस्परि &c.

Chapter III relates to the Somayāga and its दीक्षा, the Adhvaryu giving it in every sattra (सत्रेषु सर्वानध्वर्युर्दीक्षयेत 1, 5). The Sāmans to be recited at the time of churning are noted here and more mantras are here prescribed. Minute instructions are given as to the doors by which the priests and the sacrificer are to leave or enter the sacrificial shed. In describing the Mahāvrata a new Āchārya named भाण्डितायन is mentioned (9, 1).

Chapter IV gives details about वीणा which are interesting but which cannot be well understood. It has an औदुम्बर बाण (shaft) with आनडुह रोहित उत्तरलोम चर्मन् (I, 11) and तंत्रीs of मुंज or दर्भ in its ten holes and in touching it a strange mantra is given वदो वद वदा वदी वद मेरुः &c. (आ त्वा दुन्दुभीन् प्रवदन्तु वीणा इति ब्रूयात् I-11). An अलाबु वीणा is also mentioned in 2, 1 as also a महावीणा and शीलवीणा. That the Sāman-singing was always to the accompaniment of a Vīṇā, is clear from the Chhāndogya (ये वीणाया गायन्ति ते धनसनय: &c). The sacrificer's wife is to play on the काण्डवीणा and पिच्छोरा "called अपघण्टिका in the Brāhmaṇa" (?), but mildly (मृदु). A S'ūdra and a Vaiśya (in his absence even a Brāhmaṇa or Kshatriya) standing outside the shed are to strike a round चर्मन् (परिमण्डल). A पुंश्चली or a prostitute attends outside facing the south.

and is abused. Other strange things take place, (obscene rites are common to all ancient Āryan peoples at certain times of rejoicings), at this opening ceremony of the sacrificial shed.

Chapters V to VII give details about Sāmans to be sung, their metres, the Stomas and Stobhas, how the Pratihāras of Sāmans of particular Ṛishis are to be sung, the seventh chapter being wholly concerned with the technique of the singing of the various Sāmans and their parts.

Chapter VIII gives the essentials of all higher sacrifices. The time of beginning is generally उदगयन-पूर्वपक्ष-पुण्याह-सन्निपातः (अनादेशे). The Dīkshās are to be one, two, three or many (अपरिमित) as also Upasads (sittings) for all एकाह्s such as ज्योतिष्टोम, अभिजित्, विश्वजित् &c. The Dakshiṇā is usually to be सहस्र. In Sādyaskra and other rites, different Dakshiṇās are prescribed including a bed, a carriage, cooking pots and two pairs of slaves. Real Soma being unobtainable and substitutes being unsavoury, we have the provision अभक्षयन्तो ऋत्विजश्चमसानवजिघ्रयुः. After Avabhṛitha, the sacrificer is to stay for a night near a निषाद village, a new inexplicable provision.

For a श्येन sacrifice, which is a magic one, the priests are to be व्रातीनानां योधानां पुत्राः sons of fighting Brahmin clans,–a new provision. Section 6 describes व्रात्यस्तोम. "Vrātyas are those who put on turbans on the wrong side etc." The Dakshiṇā is to be given to a मगधदेशीय ब्रह्मबन्धु (6, 28). The Vrātyas then can become त्रैविद्यवृत्ति and are fit to dine with: तेषां भुञ्जीत कामं याजयेत (6, 30).

The ninth chapter begins with Rājasūya for kings, to commence on Phālguna S'uddha 1 (फाल्गुनीपक्षस्य प्रथमायां;–(the months are अमान्त apparently). The Dakshiṇā is द्वादशं शतं, a new figure, S'āṇḍilya prescribes Dīkshā on त्रयोदशी of अपरपक्ष and दक्षिणा द्वात्रिंशशतं and सहस्र for each priest. The sacrificer should call his subordinate kings with their wealth (अबलानस्य ज्ञातीन् सवित्तानावहेयुः--14). Their wealth should be divided into 3 parts, one to be given to the priests, one to Anusarpins, and the remaining third should be returned as presents. "These kings become chieftains and unfit for अभिषेक". This is a new provision; but it explains the importance of the Rājasūya and the action of the Pāṇḍavas in making a दिग्विजय and seeking large presents from conquered kings. The king should then go out of the sacrificial shed with shoes of deer-leather on and return with shoes of black-deer leather.

In section 2 दशपेय is described where ten drink besides the sacrificer. 26 is an important sūtra, showing that the rule of अनुलोम marriage, with the law of the caste of the father for the progeny, still obtained. In giving their ancestry the priests were to stop with the अब्राह्मणी mother. Ten generations are to be recited and this explains how usually 10 generation are also mentioned in Smṛitis (दशावरान्दश परान् &c). Many व्रतs are prescribed for a whole year to the sacrificer and strangely enough, all people in the राष्ट्र are not to shave – except Brahmins – for a year (नास्याब्राह्मणा राष्ट्रे वापयेरन् 25). In sections 3 and 4 minor sacrifices with new names are prescribed with their दक्षिणाs (among which are chariots with four horses each worth a hundred 4, 15). A गोसव is prescribed for a Vaiśya, अभिचार is levelled against kings and subjects also. In 5 Atirātras and Ahīnas are shortly noticed with their special Sāmans. A new आचार्य by name शौचिवृक्षि is mentioned in 5, 22. In 8, a new sacrifice called शबलीहोम is prescribed for one who wishes to have one thousand heads of cattle (सहस्रपोष) in which after the homa, you go out to a forest and cry शबली, शबली. "If a dog or an ass answers, you will not get any cattle.

In sections 9, 10 and 11 is described the Aśvamedha which is the most important of the higher sacrifices.

The description shows this Sūtra to be a late one. We have first राजाश्वमेधेन यजेत. In other Sūtras we have सार्वभौमोऽश्वमेधेन यजेत, then optionally any king. The details are few and relate chiefly to the उद्गाता. The definition of वावाता is new, महिषी being ignored. या पत्नीनां प्रियतमा यजमानस्य सा वावाता; राजपुत्री makes it necessary that the वावाता should be a Rajput lady; and one more queen is mentioned, viz. परिवृक्ती, who is described as अनपचिता (not honoured). The same mantras in reviling are used as elsewhere, in jocularity and the same riddle questions are asked. The same exhorbitant Dakshiṇās are prescribed; but they are optionally substituted by सहस्र on the first and on the last days. Finally, we find अश्वमेध made cheap, prescribed by a विकल्प, viz. पतन्तकोऽश्वमेधः (vi, 6), in which the horse is made to roam for half a month only, instead of a year. Jyotishṭoma is also made easier at the end.

In section 12 we have a जामदग्नय sacrifice prescribed which is not found elsewhere. Its दीक्षाs are to be विंशति and उपसदs द्वादश; and it is to be begun on the त्रयोदशी of the अमरपक्ष. The tithīs mentioned in this connection here and elsewhere are usually not अमावास्या or पूर्णिमा nor अष्टमी as in other Sūtras.

Chapter X describes Sattras, the Rātris of the sacrifices going up to 49 and then द्वादशाह, with their special Sāmans and their निधनs. A controversy among आचार्यs, (कौत्स is added here) is noticed regarding Sāmans and शक्वरी verses. Controversies are constantly noted in this Sūtra and the opposing Achāryās usually are the same (not much known elsewhere). Reference is often made to a Brāhmaṇa (उत्तमानुपूर्व्यं ब्राह्मणेन) which is, however, never named (4,13), a परब्राह्मण being mentioned in 4, 8. Gavāmayana and other sacrifices are cursorily mentioned. चतुःशतमैन्द्रा बार्हतप्रगाथा दशतयीषु (6,3) mentions there being 104 Bārhata Pragātha verses, addressed to

Indra, in the Rigveda, which is always called दशतयी referring to its division into ten Maṇḍalas. Ṛigveda was carefully studied by all and its verses counted and scanned. Other Pragāthas are also referred to by number and rules are prescribed as to which-metred Pragāthas are to be recited, in which month, at the Abhīvarta. सर्वे सहर्त्विजो महाव्रतेन स्तुवीरन् (9, 1) requires all priests to join at महाव्रत; but otherwise the उद्गाता is to sing all Sāmans. Another controversy is noted between ऊमकायन and क्षैरकलम्भि about the Sāmans to be sung in कौण्डपायिनामयन, इतिवातवतोरयन &c. Hereafter the procedure in several rituals is described in detail, which is rather unusual after these highest sacrifices. अमावास्येन पूर्वपक्षवितरं पौर्णमासेन (12,3) indicates पूर्णिमान्त months. Details about the पृष्ठ्य rites in तापश्चित for different deities are given in 13; 14 notes a difference of opinion as to whether अतिरात्र is सहस्रसाव्य (lasting for 1000 days). In sections 15, 16, 17, the सारस्वत sacrifice is detailed with its changing site each day as the sacrificer moves from place to place along the Sarasvatī and with its final rite at प्लक्ष प्रस्रवण. "There should not be अवभृथ on the Sarasvatī; if need arises, water should be taken out of the river and used for bathing" is a new provision in this old sacrifice. In 18, we have a sacrifice on the दृषद्वती, one function in which is the tending of the cows of a Brahmin on its bank for one year. It appears that about this river there were very good pasture lands. In 19, a place named परीण is mentioned in Kurukshetra and another named प्रभव्यमर्भ at the confluence of the Sarasvatī and the Dṛishadvatī, which shows the author's intimate acquaintance with Kurukshetra. The sacrificer after अवभृथ is not to return to any town but should retire from the world singing Sāmans. In 20, a new sacrifice named तौर is described and the work finishes with a reference to the mythical सहस्रसंवत्सर sacrifice of Prajāpati.

3 Drāhyāyaṇa.

This Srauta S'ūtra also belongs to the Sāmaveda and is said to appertain to its Rāṇāyaṇīya S'ākhā (Macd. p. 245) which is current in the Deccan. A portion of it has been published in England by J. N. Reuter, Ph. D. with a commentary by Dhanvin. In his introduction Dhanvin says that the Sūtra had been lost (लुप्तमासीत्) but that he obtained a copy of it from the banks of the Tāmraparṇī in the South (दक्षिणस्यां ताम्रपर्ण्यास्तीरे). This shows that the Sūtra, as we have it, is a late one. As already stated, it has been compared with the Lāṭyāyana S'rauta Sūtra by the editor of the latter and found to differ very little from it. A cursory view shows that the same differing ancient authorities are quoted in it, viz. धानंजप्य, गौतम, शाण्डिल्यायन &c. But the wording of the Sūtra and perhaps the arrangement is different. The Sāmavedins are numerous in the Tamil country and probably had their own Sūtra enunciated in this form. Some interesting statements from it may, however, be given here.

Chapter II relates to Somayāga with details about दीक्षा, यज्ञशाला &c. as in Lāṭyāyaṇa but a new Āchārya is mentioned in describing महाव्रत named Bhaṇḍitāyana (9,1). Chapter IV describes the Vīṇā with the body made of उदुम्बर wood (औदुम्बर) and strings (तन्त्री) of Muñja or Darbha &c. as in Lāṭyāyana. A prostitute (पुंश्चली) also attends outside facing the south, and she and a Brahmin abuse each other at the consecration of the sacrifical shed. In II Vājapeya is described in which everything is to be 17. यं ब्राह्मणा राजानश्च पुरस्कुर्वीरन् स वाजपेयेन यजेत. Where only 17 cows are given as Dakshiṇā instead of 17000 or 1700, the sacrifice is called क्षुद्रवाजपेय. Among the vratas of the sacrificer (वाजपेयी) is firstly क्षत्रवृत्तिं वर्तयेत् (12, 1) which means that he was to live thenceforth as a soldier. The sixth and the seventh chapters are concerned wholly with the technique of Sāmans, the metres of the stomas, how the Prātihara of Sāmans of particular Ṛishis is to be suing and how the Nidhana &c., which can not be understood by laymen.

4 Jaiminīya

This S'rauta Sūtra, not mentioned by Macdonell, is mentioned by Winternitz (p. 279 n.) as published by D. Gaāstra, in Leyden, in 1906 with a preface and translation in Dutch. This shows how European scholars in all countries take great interest in Vedic literature. We give here a short summary of its contents for the curious reader from the original as printed by D. Gaāstra.

The Sūtra is short and relates to the Agnishṭoma. It belongs to the Sāmaveda. It has only 26 Kaṇḍikās consisting of one long sentence each. At such sacrifices, S'āṭyāyani holds that Dakshaṇā should not be settled at the outset, as it would mean sale of one's qualifications; but Tāṇḍya holds that it should be, as it brings great fruit. कृष्णजन्मानं न याजयेन्नपापकर्माणम्. Nor with कृष्णजन्म and पापकृत् Ṛitviks is remarkable. The sacrifice begins with the purchase of Soma and its coming to the यज्ञशाला in a royal chariot drawn by oxen and then entering the S'ālā by the eastern gate. Subrahmaṇya invokes Indra by a well-known mantra. It is then declared in the town श्वःसुत्या and next day अद्य सुत्या. Details of Sāmans to be sung are then given such as वारवन्तीय, यज्ञायज्ञीय, वामदेव्य &c. The sacrificer ancestry and his name are then declared अमुष्य पुत्रः पौत्रः प्रपौत्रः नप्ता and even female ancestors' names are declared. With various mantras, the soma is then pounded and strained without a drop being allowed to fall on the ground.

Each of the 16 priests has his duty and his mantra and when Soma is offered to them, they eat it in order: चमसानुद्गृह्णन्ति हुतस्य भक्षयन्ति होतुर्भक्षमनुभक्षयन्ति, पुरोडाशान्भक्षयित्वा राजानं भक्षयन्ति राजानं भक्षयित्वा वा पुरोडाशान् । (१४).

संतिष्ठते प्रातःसवनम् as in other Sūtras finishes the morning ceremony. In describing the माध्यंदिनसवन and its दक्षिणा, it is prescribed आग्नेयाय प्रथमं गा दद्यात्. After many details as to the Sāmans sung, we have संतिष्ठते माध्यंदिनं सवनम् ।. In the ritual of the तृतीयसवन, offerings are made to Pitṛis (पितामह and प्रपितामह). Going out of the शाला the sacrificer looks at his shadow (छायां पर्यवेक्षेतात्मनोऽप्रणाशाय). After अनुयाज, हारियोजन (?) including eating of दधिघोम with चमस or with hands (पाणिभिर्वा २०), पत्नीसंयाज and अवभृथ, the sacrifice ends. Many new mantras are prescribed suited to the action.

अग्न्याधेये साम्नां गानकालमुपदेक्ष्यामः and names of Sāmans to be sung at different times are also given. कौत्सुद is a new name found here. The least दक्षिणा is one cow (इति पैङ्क्रम्).

Sāmans are given for प्रवर्ग्य (महावीर is mentioned here also), as also for दीक्षणीया and प्रायणीया and when सोम is being brought (राजन्यानीयमाने) and in सौत्रामणी and पशुबन्ध. पदाय पदाय अनुसंहरेदित्याचार्यसमयो यथार्थतान्येव गानानीति अनुब्राह्मणिनः refers to आचार्य and अनुब्राह्मण, which makes this Sūtra late. Its treatment is that of a Paddhati; but it probably belongs to the Vedānga period from its Brāhmaṇa-like treatment and prescribing of new Mantras.

5— Hiraṇyakes'in alias Satyāshāḍha.

This S'rauta Sūtra belongs to the Taittirīya Saṁhitā of the Black Yajurveda and the Hiraṇyakeśi S'ākhā. The author is named Satyāshāḍha. The Sūtra has just been completely published in the Ānandaśrama Series in several volumes. The Sūtra relates

12

to all S'rauta sacrifices from Darśapūrṇamāsa to the thousand years' sacrifice of Prajāpati. It is divided into twenty chapters called Praśnas, each Praśna being divided into eight Paṭalas or sections and each Paṭala consisting of many short sūtras. The last two chapters relate to उपाकरण and other Gṛihya rites. They in fact form the Gṛihya-sūtra of this S'ākhā. This Sūtra is thus probably of a later date than Āpastamba the chapters of which are also called Praśnas and the last two chapters of which also form its Gṛihya.

We give a few extracts from this Sūtra regarding the higher sacrifices for comparison. It begins with the dictum, यज्ञस्त्रिभिर्वेदैर्विधीयते । ऋग्यजुःसामभिर्ज्योतिष्टोमः । यजुर्वेदेनाग्निहोत्रम् । ऋग्यजुर्भ्यां दर्शपूर्णमासौ ॥. Atharvaveda is not brought in here. In the first ten Praśnas ordinary sacrifices being described, in 11 we have Chiti and in 12 Tāpaschit and Abhijit are described. In describing Vājapeya in 13 शरदि वाजपेयेन यजेत ब्राह्मणो राजन्यो वा । सप्तदश प्राजापत्यान् पशूनुपाकरोति । दक्षिणाकाले सप्तदश रथान् ददाति (३०). सप्तदश निष्कान् । सप्तदश हस्तिनः । सप्तदश गवां शतानि । सप्तदश महानसानि । सप्तदश शयनानि । सप्तदश वासांसि । सप्तदश दासान् । सप्तदश दासीः । (३२). As to Rājasūya we have राजा राजसूयेन यजेत स्वर्गकामः. In announcing him we have the old formula एष वः कुरवो राजेति ।. There is as usual a play with dice and the hearing of the शौनःशेप आख्यान. In Praśna 14 we have Aśvamedha detailed. राजाश्वमेधेन यजेत । चैत्र्यां पौर्णमास्यां सांग्रहण्येष्ट्या यजेत तस्या योत्तमामावास्या तस्यां संज्ञान्या । (अरातयो रातयः शत्रुमित्रे). १ शतेन राजपुत्रैः, २ अराजभिरुग्रैः, ३ सूतग्रामणीभिः, ४ क्षत्तृसंग्रहीतृभिः describes the guards. They may plunder a Brahmin who does not know अश्वमेध ritual for खानं पानम् । यज्जनपदेऽन्नं तदेषामन्नम् । रथकारकुले वसतिः पारिप्लवमाख्यानं भौमन्यत्रम् । परिसमाप्ते वीणागणगिनः पुराणैरिमं राजाभिः &c । त्रिंशिमासो संवत्सरो भवति (१९). ऊर्ध्वमेकादशान्मासादश्वस्थेऽवजेऽश्वं बध्नाति (२०). Three queens only are mentioned: महिषी, वावाता, परिवृक्ती. Among ornaments for the last काचा वा is mentioned. This reference to glass seems strange (3, 22). श्यामूलेनाश्वं संज्ञपयान्ति स्पन्द्याभिरितरान् पशून्. Com. explains श्यामूल as कम्बल. नाश्वस्य वपा विद्यते (?) (4, 21). येश्वस्य हुतस्य गन्धमाजिघ्रन्ति सर्वे ते पुण्यलोका भवन्ति ।. Purushamedha is next described. पञ्चाहः पुरुषमेधः। ब्राह्मणो राजा वा यः कामयेत सर्वेषां भूतानां ज्यैष्ठ्यं श्रैष्ठ्यं स्वाराज्यमाधिपत्यं गच्छेयमिति । मध्यमेऽहनि पौरुषमेधकान्पशूनुपाकरोति । पर्यग्निकृतान्पुरुषानुदीचो नीत्वोत्सृज्याज्येन तद्देवता । ६, ९, १४. Chapter 15 gives Prāyaśchittas and 16 and 17 द्वादशाह and एकाह अग्निष्टोम. Chapter 18 gives the highest sacrifices like दार्शद्वत and सहस्रसंवत्सर.

The Sūtra is voluminous and logical and seems to contain the latest development of S'rauta ritual. Mahīdhara, at the commencement of his commentary called वैजयन्ती, says that the S'ākhās of Tittiri are बौधायन, भारद्वाज, आपस्तम्ब, हिरण्यकेशि, वाधूल (of Kerala) and वैखानस. He looks upon Hīraṇyakeśin and Satyāshādha as names of ths same person. But this identification is doubtful, the former being always given as the name of the S'ākhā and the latter of the Sūtra.

III Description of preparations for As'vamedha in Baudhāyana S'rauta Sūtra (XV 14–16)

एनमेते कर्मकृत उपसंगच्छन्ते तक्षाणश्च रथकृतश्च मयस्कृतश्च कुलालाश्च द्वयाः कर्मारा नखकृतः सप्तमेऽथैतान्स्तक्ष्णः सꣳशास्ति ॥१३॥

एकशतं बैल्वानि दार्वाचितानि छिन्दत तानि प्रवकल्यानि कृत्वा चाथ चिनुतैकविꣳशतिं यूपान् छिन्दतैकविꣳशत्यरत्नीन् राज्जुदालमग्निष्ठं पौतुद्रवावुपस्थात्रानौ षड् बैल्वान् षट् खादिरान् षट् पालाशान् पालाशमुपशयं पालाशं पात्नीवतं पालाशं विशालयूपमेकतयानि दारुमयाणि पात्राणि कुरुत षट्त्रिꣳशतꣳ स्रुवान् दीर्घदण्डान् षट्त्रिꣳशतमनुवेषान् दीर्घदण्डांश्चत्वारि वाष्टौ वेन्द्राषासानि चतुश्चक्राणि बृहच्चक्राणि यथा समानि यूपाग्रैः स्युरपरिमितान्यारोहणमहानसानि कुरुतैकं वैतसं कटं कुरुताश्वस्योपस्तरणान्यथैतान् रथकृतः सꣳशास्ति स्वरथं कुरुतापरिमितान्रथान् कुरुतैतान् मयस्कृतान् सꣳशास्त्यपरिमितं चर्मण्यं कुरुतेत्यथैतान् कुलालान् संꣳशास्ति यथैकविंꣳशतिविधायाग्नय

एवमिष्टकाः कुरुत तिस्रो महतीः कुम्भीः कुरुत यथाश्वं तूपरं गोमृगमित्येतान् साङ्गान् श्रपयेयुरपरिमिताः स्थालीः कुरुतेति ॥ १४ ॥

अथैतान् कालायसकृतः स॰शास्ति सायकं कुरुत सित्तिमकल्पोदकं कृष्णं कृष्णत्सरु॰ सुवर्ण॰ सुवर्णत्सरुं चतुरः कालायसान् लोहायसत्सरू॰श्चतुरो लोहायसान् कालायसत्सरून् षट्त्रि॰शत॰ सुवर्णान् रजतत्सरू॰ षट्त्रि॰शत॰ रजतान् सुवर्णत्सरू॰श्चाणि च त्रयस्त्रि॰शतं च सौवर्णाना॰ सूचीनां त्रीणि च शतानि त्रयस्त्रि॰शतं च राजतानां त्रीणि च शतानि त्रयस्त्रिं॰शतं च सीसानामेकं कालायसस्य कमण्डलुं कुरुताश्वतेजन्यै श्रपणायेत्यथैतान् सुवर्णकृतः स॰शास्ति परः शत॰ शतपलान् निष्कान् कुरुत सुवर्णरजते महिम्नोः पात्रे कुरुतैकतयानि सौवर्णानि पात्राणि कुरुत यावत्यः पत्न्यस्तावतः सौवर्णानुपशयान् कुरुत रजतग्रन्थीन् राजतान् वा सुवर्णग्रन्थीन् यावत्यः पत्न्यस्तावन्ति सौवर्णानि कुम्बकरीराणि कुरुत रजतशंकूनि राजतानि वा सुवर्णशङ्कूनि यावत्यः पत्न्यस्तावतः सौवर्णान् कमण्डलून् कुरुत रजतरास्नान् राजतान्वा सुवर्णरास्नान् एक॰ सौवर्णं विधवनं कुरुत त्रीणि सौवर्णानि धवित्राणि कुरुत रजतदण्डानि राजतानि वा सुवर्णदण्डानि सहस्र॰ सौवर्णान् काचान् कुरुत सहस्र॰ राजतान् सहस्रा॰ सामुद्रान् हिरण्मयं कशिपु हिरण्मय॰ षड्वींश॰ हिरण्मय॰ संदानमिति ॥ १५ ॥

अथैतान्नखकृतः स॰शास्त्यपरिमितान्यष्टमानि कुरुतेत्यथास्यैतान्यन्यान्युपक्लृप्तानि भवन्ति शतं घृतचर्माणि शतं मधुचर्माणि शतं तण्डुलचर्माणि शतं पृथुकचर्माणि शतं लाजाचर्माणि शतं करम्भचर्माणि शतं धानाचर्माणि शतं सक्तुचर्माणि शतं मसूस्यचर्माणि शतं प्रियङ्गुतण्डुलचर्माणि । अथास्यैत एकवि॰शतिप्रतिप्रस्थातारः स॰शिष्टा भवन्त्यात्मना द्वावि॰शस्ते जनपदेभ्यः पशून् समचन्ति तथारूपान् यथारूपांस्ते विदुर्ग्रामेषु ग्राम्यान् रक्षन्त्यरण्येष्वारण्यान् गिरिषु गैरेयान् नदीषु नादेयान् पंजरेषु वया॰सि कुम्भीषु सरीसृपानिति ॥ १६ ॥

For Vājapeya.

वाजपेयेन यक्ष्यमाणो भवति स उपकल्पयते कृष्णाजिन॰ सुवर्णरजतौ रुक्मौ बस्ताजिन॰ शतमान॰ हिरण्य॰ सप्तदश सुवर्णानि कृष्णलानि हिरण्यपात्रं मधोः पूर्णमौदुम्बर॰ रथचक्र॰ सप्तदशार॰ सप्तदशफलकां च श्रितिं यूपं च तूपरं चतुरश्रि॰ सप्तदशारत्निं गोधूमकलापमिषुणीषं नैवार॰ सप्तदश शराव॰ सप्तदशोषपुटान् सप्तदश वायव्यानि सप्तदश पृथुबुध्नानुपयामान्सतं च बालं च सप्तदश निष्कान् सप्तदश वसनानि सप्तदश वासोभारान् सप्तदश रथान् सप्तदश दुन्दुभीन् सप्तदश हस्तिनः सप्तदश दास्यः सप्तदशाना॰सि युक्तानि सप्तदश गवा॰ शतानि वयसी वयसी वा सप्तदश सहस्रं वा तस्मिन् हि सर्वाणि वया॰सि भवन्ति चतुर्वि॰शतिं पशूनेकपञ्चाशतमश्वान् खादिरीं वितृण्णीं वध्रैर्व्यूतां प्रज्ञाता अग्निष्टोमिकाः सम्भाराः । (११-१)

.V The philosophical conversation among priests in As'vamedha. Ās'valā. S'. S. (X.9)

ब्रह्मोद्यं वदन्ति। कः स्विदेकाकी चरति क उ स्विज्जायते पुनः। किं स्विद्धिमस्य भेषजं किं स्विदावपनं महत् इति होताध्वर्युं पृच्छति। सूर्य एकाकी चरति चन्द्रमा जायते पुनः। अग्निर्हिमस्य भेषजं भूमिरावपनं महदिति प्रत्याह। किं स्वित्सूर्यसमं ज्योतिः किं समुद्रसमं सरः। किं स्वित्पृथिव्यै वर्षीयान् कस्य मात्रा न विद्यते। इत्यध्वर्युर्होतारं पृच्छति। सत्यं सूर्यसमं ज्योतिर्द्यौः समुद्रसमं सरः। इन्द्रः पृथिव्यै वर्षीयान् गोस्तु मात्रा न विद्यते इति प्रत्याह। पृच्छामि त्वा चितये देवसख यदि त्वमत्र मनसा जगंथ। केषु विष्णुस्त्रिषु पदेष्वस्थः केषु विश्वं भुवनमाविवेशेति ब्रह्मोद्गातारं पृच्छत्यपि तेषु त्रिषु पदेष्वस्मि येषु विश्वं भुवनमाविवेश। सद्यः पर्येमि पृथिवीमुत द्यामेकेनांगेन दिवो अस्य पृष्ठमिति प्रत्याह। केष्वन्तः पुरुष आविवेश कान्यन्तः पुरुष अर्पितानि। एतद्ब्रह्मन्नुपवल्हामसि त्वा किं स्विन्नः प्रतिवोचास्त्यत्रेत्युद्गाता ब्रह्माणं पृच्छति। पञ्चस्वन्तः पुरुष आविवेश तान्यन्तः पुरुष अर्पितानि। एतत्त्वात्र प्रतिमन्वानो अस्मि न मायया भवस्युत्तरोऽस्मिन्नित्याह। प्राञ्चमुपनिष्क्रम्यैकैकशो यजमानं पृच्छति। पृच्छामि त्वा परमन्तं पृथिव्या इतीयं वेदिः परो अन्तो पृथिव्या इति प्रत्याह (as in T. B.). This is a good way of whiling away leisure time during a long sacrifice like the Aśvamedha.

V The Pāriplava in As'vamedha as described in Ās'valāyana S'. S. (X 7) and its additions as compared with S'atapatha Br.

प्रथमेहनि मनुर्वैवस्वतस्तस्य मनुष्या विशस्त इम आसत इति **गृहमेधिन उपसमानीताः स्युः** (Householders are required to be brought and seated there, to represent men) तानुपदिशत्यृचो वेदः सोयमिति सूक्तं निगदेत् (a particular Sūkta from the Ṛigveda is to be recited). द्वितीयेहनि यमो वैवस्वतस्तस्य पितरो विशस्त इम आसत इति **स्थविराः उपसमानीताः स्युः** (old men represent ancestors) तानुपदिशति यजुर्वेदो वेदः सोयमित्यनुवाकं निगदेत् (an Anuvāka from Yajurveda is to be recited). तृतीयेहनि वरुण आदित्यस्तस्य गन्धर्वा विशस्त इमे आसत इति **युवानः शोभना उपसमानीताः स्युः** (Young handsome men represent Gandharvas) तानुपदिशत्यथर्वाणो वेदः सोयमिति यद्भेषजं निशान्तं (?) स्यात्तं निगदेत्. चतुर्थेहनि सोमो वैष्णवः (?) तस्याप्सरसो विशस्ता इमा आसत इति युवतयः शोभना उपसमानीताः स्युः (Beautiful young women brought represent Apsarasas) ता उपदिशत्यांगिरसो वेदः सोयमिति यद्घोरं निशांतं (?) स्यात् तं निगदेत्. पञ्चमेहन्यर्बुदः काद्रवेयस्तस्य सर्पा विशस्त इम आसत इति सर्पाः सर्पविद इत्युपसमानीताः स्युः (Serpents and serpent-knowers should be brought) तानुपदिशति विषविद्यावेदं (S'ata. mentions सर्पवेद) सोयमिति विषविद्यां निगदेत्. षष्ठेहनि कुबेरो वैश्रवणस्तस्य रक्षांसि विशस्तानीमान्यासत इति सेलगाः पापकृत इत्युपसमानीताः स्युः (These Selagas are mentioned in A. B. and were probably real cannibals, inhabiting some Orissa jungles) तानुपादिशति पिशाचविद्यावेदः सोऽयमिति यत्किंचित् पिशाचसंयुतं निशान्तं स्यात् तं निगदेत्. सप्तमेहन्यसितो धान्वस्तस्यासुरा विशस्त इम आसत इति कुसीदिन उपसमानीताः स्युः (Money-lenders represent now Asuras ! ! !) तानुपादिशत्यसुरविद्यावेदः सोयमिति मायां कांचित्कुर्यात् । अष्टमेहनि मत्स्यः सांमदस्तस्योदकेचरा विशस्त इम आसत इति मत्स्याः पुंजिष्ठा इत्युपसमानीता स्युः (Puñjiṣṭhas are a Nishāda caste which kills fish) तानुपादिशति पुराणविद्यावेदः सोयमिति पुराणमाचक्षीत (In the S'ata. इतिहास is mentioned). नवमेऽहनि तार्क्ष्यो वैपश्चितस्तस्य वयांसि विशस्तानीमान्यासत इति वयांसि ब्रह्मचारिण उपनीताः स्युः (Why pupils represent birds is a riddle) तानुपदिशतीतिहासो वेदः सोयमितीतिहासमाचक्षीत. दशमेहनि धर्म इन्द्रस्तस्य देवा विशस्त इम आसत इति युवानः श्रोत्रिया अप्रतिग्राहका इत्युपसमानीताः स्युः (Young men learned in the Vedas but taking no Dakshiṇā properly represent gods) तानुपदिशति सामवेदो वेदः सोयमिति साम गायात् । एवमेतत्पर्यायतः संवत्सरमाचक्षीत दशमीं दशमीं समापयन् संवत्सरान्ते दीक्षेत ॥

VI Alphabetical List of Sacrificial Words with their Meanings.

अभिप्लव sixth day's ceremony.

अभ्रि a wooden scrapper or shovel.

अवत्त proximity आवत् (अथर्व.), cutting of a divided sacrificial cake, अवद्यात cutting.

आमिक्षा mixture of boiled and coagulated milk.
आवाप mixing or arrangement of vessels.
इडा a name of Agni.
उदवसानीय concluding day of सोम.
उपसद् a particular fire; a sacrificial festival preceding सुत्या and forming part of ज्योतिष्टोम.
उपह्वय Invitation.
करणी (a surd number) a particular square.
कशिपु pillow, mat, cushion, (m.) food, (du.) food and clothing.
काश्मर्य The tree Gremlin Anora.
किक्किटा A particular exclamation.
कुंब enclosure round a place of sacrifice.
कुंबकरीर a kind of head-dress for women, a thick petticoat.
कृष्णल the black berry of a plant used as weight; a copper or gold coin of that weight.
खर a square ground for receiving sacrificial vessels.
गय (acquired) a house; its contents; propety.
गार्मुत a bean of a plant called गार्मुत्; a kind of hay.
चतुरस्र four-cornered, square.
चमस a vessel for drinking Soma, a flat dish of wood with a handle.
चषाल wooden ring on the top of a sacrificial post.
चात्वाल a hole in the ground for constructing उत्तरवेदि.
छन्दोमा The home of metres; the 8th, 9th and 10th days of the द्वादशाह; also name of Sāmans to be sung on those days.
तानूनप्त्र a ceremony in which तनूनपात् is praised.
तार्प्य a garment made of a vegetable substance or plant named तर्प्य.
तूष the border of a garment.
त्रिकद्रुक 3 Soma vessels. First 3 days of अभिप्लव.
द्रप्स a drop of Soma or semen.
धाय्या name of a Ṛik (Sāmidhenī)
निनर्द prolonging a note in chanting; slurring or trilling.
न्यूंख extension of ओ in recitation of Ṛiks.

पृश्नि Variegated, dappled, piebald, a dappled cow, name of a Ṛishi, Mother of Maruts.

प्रउग Forepart of a chariot, piled up. Name of 2nd S'astra.

प्रतिगर The responsive cry of Adhvaryu to the Hotṛi.

प्रायणीय Introductory libation, first day of सोम.

भाजी Rice gruel. भाजा a crooked stick.

मदन्ती Boiling water.

मनोता Name of a hymn in Ṛ (VI 1) having the word मनोता; and the deity praised in it.

मल्ह Having a dewlap (cow or goat).

महावीर An archer, a sacri. fire or vessel, white horse.

मार्जालिय Fond of ablution. 2 A name of S'iva. 3 Heap of earth on the right of Vedi on which secrificial vessels are cleansed.

मासर Mixture of yeast and grapes in which rice or millet has been boiled.

मेथिका The lowest seventh cubit of the sacrificial post.

मेंथी a pillar in the middle of a threshing floor to which oxen are bound.

लोकंपृणा Name of a brick used in building sacrifical altar, a Ṛik used at the building.

वपा Skin or membrane about viscera, secretion of bones, fat, marrow.

विहार Consecration for sacrifice.

वेहत् A barren cow desiring a bull. A pregnant cow.

व्याहाव A वौषट् for invocation of शस्त्र &c.

शम्या A stick, a staff, a peg ; a distance to which a stick or a peg can be thrown.

सौवीर Name of a country, a मूर्च्छना in singing, a fruit like sour बेर, a gruel which Bāhlikas drink.

स्यन्द्या A net, a plait or string.

स्फ्य A flat wooden instrument shaped like a sword for stirring.

SECTION IV–BHAGAVADGĪTĀ

History of Sanskrit Literature.

ŚRUTI PERIOD.

SECTION IV—BHAGAVADGĪTĀ.

CONTENTS.

HISTORY OF
SANSKRIT LITERATURE.

SRUTI PERIOD.

SECTION IV—BHAGAVADGĪTĀ.

I THE TWO ANCIENT EPICS OF INDIA.

It goes without saying that during the Vedānga period extending over about one thousand years, many other works were written, besides the Vedāngas already described, on various other subjects. We have thus already noted the Sūtras on monks and actors by Parāśara and Śilāli, Karmanda and Kṛiśāśvin, now not extant. Most important among these other works must have been Itihāsa and Purāṇa mentioned as early as the Chhāndogya Upanishad. The present Mahābhārata and Rāmāyaṇa developed out of Itihāsa; and the eighteen Purāṇas, by courtesy ascribed to Vyāsa, evolved out of the one Purāṇa which existed in the Vedānga period. The Śrauta Sūtras state that Itihāsa and Purāṇa were read on two separate days in the Pāriplava recited during the leisure hours of longer sacrifices, as two distinct Vedas, though the Chhāndogya speaks of Itihāsa and Purāṇa as one subject of study. The latest Śrauta Sūtra of Āśvalāyana states that to hear Purāṇa, Punjishṭhas (Nishadas who kill fish) were to be invited and to hear Itihāsa, students or Brahmachārins. Besides these we have mention of Ākhyānas in Upanishads; and in Pāṇini VI 2,103 we have Ākhyānas divided into eastern and western versions. The Kāśikā instances on this sūtra, पूर्वाधिरामकम् and अपराधिरामकम् and पूर्वयायातम् and अपरयायातम्. We may be sure from this that a रामाख्यान in two versions, eastern and western, already existed in the days of Pāṇini and also an Ākhyāna of Yayāti. All such stories or Ākhyānas have now disappeared, being absorbed into the Rāmāyaṇa and the Mahābhārata of the present day.

It may be conceded that the Rāmākhyāna spoken of by Pāṇini was by Valmīki–a Ṛishi name–and that it was subsequently developed into our present Rāmāyaṇa by an unknown unskilful recaster, gifted, however, with some poetic talent, about 100 B. C. The various arguments by which we are led to this conclusion have been stated by us at length in our ' Riddle of the Rāmāyaṇa". Rāma is a Vedic king of note, being mentioned in R. X. 93,14 and his exile into Daṇḍakāraṇya, the abduction of his wife Sītā by the cannibal king of Lankā or Ceylon and its conquest by Rāma assisted by monkey and bear nations are historical events, not copied from Homer; and this history is very similar to that of the conquest of Mexico with its cannibal population under Montezuma, by the Spaniards under Cortez, as detailed in our aforesaid work. We will not reiterate our arguments here, as the present Rāmāyaṇa falls outside the Vedānga period and the Rāmopākhyāna spoken of by Pāṇini no longer exists.

Going on to the Mahābhārata, we find that there is no mention of it in the Śrauta Sūtras or in Pāṇini. But Pāṇini knows a Bhārata, which word, meaning a work (ग्रंथ), may be derived by two sūtras of his, IV. 2,56 and IV. 3,87, the word first meaning a fight between Bhārata peoples and then a work describing this fight.* The word appears in VI. 2,38 but with a different meaning viz. a descendant of Bharata; and the word महाभारत which in this sūtra is stated to have a particular accent means most probably a great Bhārata warrior. The Kāśikā gives here the form महाभारतः and not महाभारतम्.

The Āśvalāyana Gṛīhya-Sūtra (c. 100 B. C.) mentions distinctly the two works, Bhārata and Mahābhārata separately, in सुमन्तुजैमिनिवैशम्पायनपैल-सूत्रभाष्यभारतमहाभारतधर्माचार्यास्तृप्यन्तु. This compound is often misunderstood; but there are in this sūtra, four authors and five works and hence each author must be taken to have written all the five works separately.† Anyhow Vaiśampāyana is clearly the author of a Bhārata which probably existed in the Vedānga period. This was

* संग्रामे प्रयोजनयोद्धृभ्यः and अधिकृत्य कृते ग्रंथे-भारतयुद्धमाधिकृत्य ग्रंथः भारतम्; so also यायातम्, सौभद्रम् &c.

† Indeed MBh. states that each of these four pupils of Vyāsa enunciated a separate Sanhitā of Bhārata (संहितास्तैः पृथक्त्वेन भारतस्य प्रकाशिताः—आदि ०)

enlarged by Sauti into the present Mahābhārata about 250 B. C. as shown in our "Mahābhārata : a criticism." We will give here the substance of our arguments, noticing the views of European scholars, as without determining the date of the present Mahābhārata, the date of Bhāṛata and of Bhagavadgītā which survives and which is to be described in this section cannot be taken back to about 1200 B. C. as we take it. We must also try to settle the date of the momentous Bhārata fight which is the theme of this epic as the date of the first Bhārata epic must be somewhere between this date and the date of the Mahābhārata we now possess.

Many European scholars, notably German, have studied the Mahābhārata carefully since long and have recorded their different views on this subject. But the latest view is that the historical background of this epic is an ancient conflict between two neighbouring tribes "which cannot be later than the tenth century B. C." (Macd. p. 285). Winternitz nowhere gives his view of the date of this fight, but merely leaves his readers to deduce it from the fact that the fight is not mentioned in the Vedas and that its first mention is found in the Śānkhāyana Śrauta Sūtra. He, however, refutes the date 3102 B. C. assigned by ancient Indian tradition, from the beginning of the Kaliyuga, to the Bhārata fight which took place a few months before it. This date, however, is the most probable one for the following reasons.

It is strange that European scholars are usually misled by the deceptive argument based on non-mention.

Non-mention argument can only be valid when mention is necessary. To argue because the Bhārata fight is not mentioned in the Brāhmaṇas, therefore it did not take place before the Brāhmaṇas were written is illogical. The Brāhmaṇas are religious works, written to elucidate sacrificial procedure; they are not works on history, so that the mention of the Bhārata fight was bound to appear therein. The Śatapatha mentions Janamejaya and his three brothers in its old part, in connection with the Aśvamedha sacrifice; and we may infer from this mention that the Bhārata battle must have been fought before the Śatapatha was composed about 3000 B. C. as deduced from an astronomical statement in it. That there is no reference to this fight or its actors in the Ṛigveda Sanhitā is not strange, as the compilation of that Sanhitā may be taken to have been made by Vyāsa before the fight. But there is a sūkta in the Ṛigveda by Devāpi who is uncle of Bhīshma and there is a reference to Somaka Sāhadeva, grandfather of Drupada, in another sūkta. And in the Kuntāpa sūktas, not included in the Ṛigveda, but taken in the Atharvaveda, plainly composed later than the compilation of the Ṛigveda, there is praise of king Parīkshit (राज्ञो विश्वजनीनस्य &c.). We may, thus, be sure that the fight took place soon after the compilation of the Ṛigveda and before the enunciation of the Śatapatha Brāhmaṇa and thus the date assigned by Indian astronomers viz. 3102 B. C. is beyond doubt the correct one.

This date is supported by a foreign piece of evidence viz. the statement of Megasthenes recorded about 300 B.C. and taken by Pliny and Strabo in their works. This evidence has not been noticed by European scholars. The Greeks under Alexander collected lists of dynasties in Egypt, Chaldaea and India and Pliny records that from Dyonysos to Sandracotos, the Indians count 154 kings and 6457 years and 3 months. Arrian in Strabo gives 153 kings and 6042 years with three republics, one of 300 years and another of 120 years, and states that "Dyonysos preceded Herakles by 15 generations". Now Herakles is plainly Hari or Śrikrishṇa, as it is recorded by Megasthenes that Herakles was worshipped in the town of Methora (Mathura); and if we take 153–15=138 kings between him and Chandragupta, we have, taking 20 years average for a generation of kings, 2760 years between them. Thus the date of Śrikrishṇa comes to about 2760+310=3070 B. C.; Śrīkrishṇa died 36 years after the Bhārata fight and hence the date of the fight comes to 3106 B. C. which is practically the accepted date. It clearly seems that this tradition is as old as Megasthenes at least.

It is true that the Purāṇas contradict this date; for they record that between the birth of Parīkshit and the coronation of the Nandas, the interval amounts to 1015 years (यावत्परीक्षितो जन्म यावन्नन्दाभिषेचनम् । एतद्वर्षसहस्रं तु ज्ञेयं पञ्चदशोत्तरम्—Vāyu and Bhāgavata). But the value of the Purāṇas as against that of the statement of Megasthenes, dated 300 B. C. is, in our view, nil. For the Purāṇas were reconstructed about 400 A. D. from traditions, mutilated and almost lost during the preceding Buddhist supremacy. Their value as regards

Buddhist and Hindu recent dynasties being fresh in memory may be great; but for dynasties before the nine Nandas, they cannot be relied upon. On the other hand, the information collected by Greek historians in Egypt and Chaldæa has been found to be correct. The lists of Menatho have been confirmed from bricks recently discovered. It is a pity that the list obtained in India by Megasthenes has been lost and we have only an aggregate statement of his, taken by Pliny and Strabo. Tilak who held, on the basis of the Purāṇas, that the Bhārata fight took place about 1015+400, Nanda's approximate date=1415 B. C., objected here that the average given by the figures of Megasthenes for one generation of kings is too large ($\frac{6457}{154}$=42 nearly). But in calculating Śrikrishṇa's date, we have taken the usually accepted average per reign. And secondly, in all genealogies, the first mythical kings are always allotted long reigns. Thus in the Jewish genealogy, for 11 generations from Adam to Noah are allotted 2262 years, giving an average of 200 years nearly per generation; for 11 kings from Shem to Abraham, 1310 years and for 12 kings from Moses to Solomon 408 years, giving an average of 130 and 34 years respectively. In Egypt also, the first kings were supposed to be gods, having long reigns and human kings begin with Menos. Similarly in India, from Dyonysos or Daksha to Śrikrishṇa, there were mythical kings and for these 15 kings (this is the number of generations actually given in MBh. Anuśa. p. 147,25–33), we have between them 6457 – 2760=3697 years, giving an average of 240 years per reign. This is acceptable for mythical reigns and the information given by Megasthenes is not absurd and as earlier, is more reliable than that of the Purāṇas. Then again, though the discrepancies among the Purāṇas may be disregarded, their assigning 1000 years to 32 kings of Brihadaśva's line in Magadha* is unreliable, firstly because this is a round number and secondly, no dynasty can last so long. The fact is that the Purāṇas knew not or had forgotten the dynasties which had intervened between Jarāsandha's line and the historical line of Śaiśunāgas in Buddha's days and they took the same Jarāsandha line to continue during the long interval.

It is really inexplicable how Tilak could take 1450 B. C. as the date of the Bhārata fight, when he himself assigned 1900 B. C. to the Maitryupanishad. For the Bṛihadāraṇyaka Upanishad, which must have preceded the latter by several centuries, mentions the Pārikshitas plainly and these four brothers named Janamejaya, Ugrasena &c. are mentioned in the Śatapatha in its earlier portion. We think that the date 3102 B. C. assigned by long tradition to Bhārata fight is unquestionably consistent with the date assigned to the whole range of Vedic literature.

Passing on to the present Mahābhārata, we find the same tendency in European scholars to ignore patent facts and assign as late a date as possible. Win-

*द्वात्रिंशच्च नृपाह्येते भवितारो बृहद्रथात् ।
पूर्णं वर्षसहस्रं च तेषां राज्यं भविष्यति ॥

ternitz puts "the transformation of the *epic* Mahābhārata into our present compilation *gradually* between the 4th century B. C. and the fourth century A. D." (p. 475). Macdonell similarly states that a land-grant dated 462 A. D. "proves incontrovertably that the epic about 400 A. D. was practically of exactly the same length as given in Ādiparvan" (p. 287). He is, however, candid enough to add that "further research in the writings of Northern Buddhists and their dated Chinese translations will enable us to put that date back by some centuries and we are justified in considering it likely that the great epic had become a didactic compendium by the beginning of our era." With such indefinite words as "some centuries, likely &c," European scholars at the utmost take the *principal* part of the present Mahābhārata to a little before A. D. It can, however, be positively proved that the epic with its present length of one lakh of verses was enunciated about 250 B. C. at the latest. In this view of ours, the late Lokamānya Tilak expressly agreed in his Gītārahasya.

It is firstly strange that European scholars, Hopkins included, take no account of the statement of the Greek traveller, Dion Chrysostom, who visited the Pāndya country about 50 A. D. that there was in India an Iliad of one lakh of verses. The reference is plainly to Mahābhārata and from his seeing the epic in Southern India, we may take it that the Iliad of one lakh of verses was enunciated by Sauti two or three centuries before in Naimishāraṇya in Northern India. This piece of evidence long pointed out by Weber remains unnoticed and European scholars still stick to 400 A. D. as the earlicst date when the epic acquired its present length But the lowest limit is really the beginning of the Christian era at the latest.

Other facts take this lower limit to 200 B. C. though not as definitely as Dion Chrysostom's statement. It seems almost certain that the present Mahābhārata is earlier than Patanjali and Bādarāyaṇa. The Vedānta Sūtra of Bādarāyaṇa contains a definite refutation of Buddhism and belongs to the time of the revival of Hinduism under Pushpamitra. The present Mahābhārata nowhere contains a refutation of Buddhism. Some tenets of Buddhism are noted but not condemned. Thus the Anugītā (Aśvamedha–p. 45) mentions that ' some believe that the soul does not exist after death ; others that this is not certain,' and also that 'everything is क्षणिक or momentary'. Again in Śāntip. chap. 316 we have Yoga minutely described and in chap. 236 we are given the twelve Upakaraṇas of Yoga ; in these things there are marked differences from the details given in the Yogasūtra of Patanjali. Patanjali's name is not given anywhere in MBh.; indeed Yoga is said to have been taught by Hiraṇyagarbha though Sānkhya is said to have been taught by Kapila (Śānti p. 348). Patanjali's name would certainly have been given when describing the teacher of Yoga, had he preceded the Mahābhārata. Patanjali's date, even if we take him to be the author of Mahābhāshya, is 150 B. C. nearly the same as that of Bādarāyaṇa and it seems certain that Mahābhārata with its extensive philosophical Śāntiparvan precedes 150 B. C.

The higher limit is afforded by the mention of Greeks, described as both valiant and learned. And as is generally conceded, Mahābhārata, as at present, is subsequent to Alexander's invasion. Its date, therefore, lies between 320 and 150 B. C. It further seems that Sauti enunciated his enormous version* before Aśoka established Buddhism as the predominant religion of the country. Indeed Sauti probably extended Bhārata into Mahābhārata to counteract the influence of advancing Buddhism, as explained at length in our महाभारतमीमांसा in Hindi; but we are not chiefly concerned with the question here. As Mahābhārata contains nowhere a condemnation of Buddhism, its date may be taken to be about 250 B. C. while that of the Rāmāyaṇa may be taken to be about 100 B. C. when Hinduism had triumphed under the Śungas and Buddha could be condemned as a thief (यथा हि चोरः स तथा हि बुद्धः—Rāmāyaṇa II).

As the Bhārata fight took place in 3102 B. C. and as the present Mahābhārata was enunciated about 250 B. C., we may safely place Bhārata, the intermediate stage of the epic, about 1400–1200 B. C., Vyāsa is said to have written a poem on the war soon after it, called Jaya or Victory; Vaiśampāyana recited the poem afresh at the Sarpasàtra of Janamejaya and Sauti recited it again in Naimshāraṇya to Śaunaka and other Ṛishis.

* एकं शतसहस्रं तु मयोक्तं वै निबोधत (MBh. I).

This story given in the Mahābhārata may be believed in effect. In the Mahābhārata itself, three beginnings are assigned to the poem and the length of the intermediate poem is given as 24000, that of the last edition being one lakh. It is wrongly supposed by Macdonell that the length of the original poem is given as 8800 verses. This figure is given respecting the Kūṭa-ślokas* put in by Sauti himself to exhibit his poetical powers. This trick can not belong to the Bhārata of Vaiśampāyana, much less to that of Vyāsa.

This date of the intervening Bhārata is practically admitted by all scholars; for it is conceded that Pāṇini knew of a Bhārata (Winternitz p. 317 n. on भारतः संग्रामः and वासुदेवार्जुनाभ्यां वुञ् &c.). It preceded the rise of Buddhism and Jainism as "many moral narratives and sayings in it are drawn upon from the 6th century B. C. by Buddhists and Jains" (Winternitz p. 474). It is wrong to say that "if an epic already existed in the 6th century, it was but little known in the native land of Buddhism" (ditto); for this contradicts the immediately preceding statement as also that "the Gāthās in the Tripīṭaka betray an acquaintance with the Krishṇa legend" and "in the Jātaka–books appear पाण्डव, धनञ्जय युधिष्ठिल, धतरट्ठ, विधुर and even the story of the marriage of द्रौपदी with five princes" (p. 472 ditto). This cannot be slight acquaintance and a Bhārata must surely have preceded Buddism and even Pāṇini. If the date of Pā-

* ग्रन्थग्रन्थिं तदा चक्रे and अष्टौ श्लोकसहस्राणि अष्टौ श्लोकशतानि च।
अहं वेद्मि शुको वेत्ति संजयो वेत्ति वा न वा॥

ṇini be taken to be ninth century B. C., it is probable that the Bhārata of Vaiśampāyana was composed in the 13th century B. C.; and the Bhagavadgītā which formed part of it can be assigned to about 1400–1200 B. C. as will be shown in the next chapter. Of course, if their author is Vaiśampāyana, he can not be a pupil of Vyāsa of the days of the Bhārata fight (3102 B. C.), but a descendant of his and the story of its recitation to Janamejaya, great-grand-son of Arjuna, is a fiction. Such fictions are often invented for magnifying the importance of a work and even Sauti's reciting MBh. to Śaunaka is a similar fiction.

II BHAGAVADGĪTĀ

The Bhagavadgītā is conceded by all to be the brightest jewel in the crown of Sanskrit literature, Vedic and classical. It has been studied and studied and studied and always admired by scholars, ancient and modern, Indian and foreign. It has been translated into almost all the modern civilised languages of the world and savants have written commentaries and Bhāshyas on it from their various points of view, during two thousand years at least. The commentary of Jnāneśvara, a Marathi poet-saint of 1390 A. D., is the most poetical and imaginative that has yet been written and deserves to be specially mentioned here. Being in the form of a dialogue, the Bhagavadgītā is most attractive in all its philosophical expositions and in this respect may be said to excel even the dialogues of Plato, though the latter's merit in putting opposite views in the most convincing form is unique in the literature of the world.

No praise of the poem can be higher than that bestowed on the Gātā by the German scholar Humboldt. It is as memorable as that bestowed on the Upanishads by Schōpenhaūr and deserves to be taken down in every work on Sanskrit literature. "This episode in the Mahābhārata is the most beautiful, nay the only truly philosophical *poem* we can find in *all* the literatures known to us" (Winternitz. p. 427). Even Macdonell praises the language of the poem. "The beauty and the power of the language in which the doctrine of doing one's duty is inculcated is unsurpassed in any other work in Indian literature." The Gītā is so catholic and at the same time so charming in its philosophical teaching that it is looked up to by thoughtful people of all nations and religions as a guide for their moral and religious beliefs. Christians, Mahomedans, Buddhists and Samajists, not to speak of Hindus, revere the book as teaching the best worship of God for all men, high and low, by performing one's duty, regardless of consequences and without love of fruit.

The Bhagavadgītā is highly praised in the Mahābhārata itself by Sauti. In introducing Anugītā which is an imitation of it, Sauti praises it skilfully, through the mouth of Śrīkrishṇa himself. Asked by Arjuna for the same teaching as had been given him at the beginning of the Bhārata fight, Śrīkrishṇa answers, "It is impossible for me to tell you again what I told you under the spiritual inspiration of that awful moment" (योगयुक्तेन चेतसा Āśva-p. 16). This is true of every great work, whether religious or philosophical. What is first written with the inspiration of the moment, on a subject firstly and fully grasped cannot be rewritten by the author himself. But this clearly shows also that the Bhagavadgītā is not Sauti's. Every dictum in the poem is constantly repeated throughout the MBh. and the stamp of the poem's philosophy is impressed on its whole philosophical thought. Even the विश्वरूप-दर्शन in the middle of the Gītā is not Sauti's. As supported by many, it is not an interpolation by him, either from language or the grandness of the conception. In fact Sauti has copied it in the Udyogap. ch. 131, where he makes Śrīkrishṇa give विश्वरूपदर्शन to Dhṛitarāshtra not only absurdly but ineffectually.

It would be profane, in a way, to subject this religio-philosophical gem to critical examination and to discuss its genuineness or value. In a work on the history of Sanskrit Literature, this has, however, to be done and we proceed to notice the various topics which arise in such examination. The name of the poem is Bhagavadgītā or "the Song of the Lord". It is probably a name bestowed on it by Sauti; for there are more than one such songs or गीताः in MBh., called so, because they are sung or recited by some great teacher. The author's name Bhagavat is not that of any individual as thought by some, but is a title bestowed on every spiritual teacher.* We find it in the Upanishads used for even a Kshatritya teacher (भगवो राजन्) by Brahmin pupils. We know Buddha was also called Bhagavat for this very reason. The word refers here to Vāsudeva and not to an imaginary teacher named भगवत् subsequently identified with Śrīkrishṇa, as supposed by an Indian critic.

The work is divided into 18 chapters and each chapter has a separate name in the colophon which is verv long; thus at the end of the first chapter we have इति श्रीमद्भगवद्गीतासु उपनिषत्सु ब्रह्मविद्यायां योगशास्त्रे अर्जुनविषादो

* See भूय एव भगवान् विज्ञापयतु &c. Chhāndogya.

नाम प्रथमोऽध्याय: This is usually prefaced by the words शतसाहस्र्यां संहितायाम् referring to the fact that the Gītā is a part of the Mahābhārata. It seems probable that these names of chapters and this colophon are also very old, as old as Sauti, in other words as 250 B. C. They are invariably the same in all copies of the Gītā whether made by Śānkara or Mādhva writers and are thus certainly as old as 800 A. D. at least. But they probably go back to Sauti himself who has put this poem in the middle of his MBh. with all the reverence due to it. He properly describes it as Upanishad or esoteric teaching, Brahmavidyā or the doctrine of Brahman and Yogaśāstra or the science of ascetic practices, these subjects being actually treated in the Gītā, not as they are seen in Sānkhya, Yoga and Vedānta Sūtras now existing, but in the original shapes these philosophies had before Pāṇini.

The Gītā is supposed by some to be purposely divided into 18 chapters by the author because the Bhārata fight lasted for 18 days and the MBh. has 18 parvans. But this is quite untenable, because the poem is conceded by all to be more ancient than Mahābhārata itself. The identity of number is, we think, accidental; nay if an inference is to be drawn, it is that Sauti divided his MBh. into 18 parvans and made the fight last for 18 days, because the Gītā was divided into 18 chapters and not vice-versa.

The number of verses in the Gītā is 700 and one unimportant and unnecessary śloka is generally considered as interpolated viz. प्रकृतिं पुरुषं चैव क्षेत्रं क्षेत्रज्ञमेव च। एत-

द्रेदितुमिच्छामि ज्ञानं ज्ञेयं च केशव ॥ at the beginning of the 13th chapter. This verse is probably added by some one to make the number of verses in the Gītā full 700, a number mentioned however by Śaṅkara in his Bhāshya. The Bombay version of MBh. gives two or three verses after the Gītā is finished, stating that there are in it 620 verses spoken by Keśava, 57 by Arjuna, 67 by Sañjaya and 1 by Dhritarāshṭra. But this brings up the total to 745 and further in the Gītā actually given in the MBh. of the Bombay version itself, the numbers are 573, 85, 44, and 1 respectively. These enumeration verses which are not found in the Gauda version are, therefore, inexplicable and may be Kūṭa-s'lokas by some unknown Deccani writer. Quite recently, a different version of the Gītā has been found in Southern India with a different total of verses and with 26 chapters. We can not take any account of this version, as it is opposed to the unanimous testimony of writers from ancient times in all parts of India.

The next question is whether the Gītā has grown to its present length, by several stages. It is supposed by many scholars that there are several contradictions in the Gītā and that some parts strike us as later additions. Rajaram Shastri Bhāgavat thought that the original Gītā ended in the middle of chapter II and the part from एषा तेऽभिहिता सांख्ये (II 39) is new. But this can not be accepted, though we admit that one feels a sort of hiatus at this śloka—a break in the context. This is so, we think, because we carry in our mind entirely different meanings of Sānkhya, Yoga and Vedavāda from their senses as understood by the writer of the Gītā. We know that the present Sānkhya philosophy is different from the philosophy as taught originally by Kapila himself. Indeed the philosophy has grown through several stages, the oldest, as it existed in the days of the Bhagavadgītā, being greatly different from the philosophy as taught in the MBh. itself in Śāntip. and this again vastly different from that taught in Sānkhyakārikā of Īśvara-Krishṇa, itself differing from that taught in the Sānkhya Sūtras which are as late as 1600 A. D. One proof of this would suffice; the line सांख्ये कृतान्ते प्रोक्तानि सिद्धये सर्वकर्मणाम् (XVIII, 13) gives a tenet of the Sānkhyas which is not found in their later works. Similarly Yoga means here Karmayoga and not Dhyānayoga. The Vedavāda similarly is not the Vedavāda of Jaimini or Kumārila but the embryo of it. Our modern ideas, therefore, make us think that there is a break in the context at this verse. Secondly, the reply of Śrikrishṇa upto verse II,32 merely teaches the immortality of the soul and the worldly considerations of honour. It contains no answer to Arjuna's question "Why should I fight instead of retiring from the world and attaining absolution". Thirdly, the Gītā would then contain nothing more than the doctrine of the immortality of the soul which was never denied by Arjuna or by any system of orthodox philosophy. The Gītā would then have had nothing new to tell and Śrikrishṇa's teaching would have been absolutely of no value. Lastly, after all the grand background painted by the first chapter, the principal picture would only be a tiny thing. As to the many contradictions pointed out by Rajaram Shastrī, they are in reality not such at all (e. g. तमेव चाद्यं पुरुषं प्रपद्ये which must be interpreted with इति added) and do not require to be noted at length. We are firmly of opinion that the Bhagavadgītā, as it is, is a consistent whole written by one gifted author, in language simple yet deep, having all the force, freedom, and fervour of a spoken language. The 18th chapter comes at the end properly and in a way summarises the whole teaching of the work in a grand peroration. Justice Telang and several European scholars are of the same opinion. (see Telang's preface to his English translation of the Bhagavadgītā) and we think that every one who reads the Gītā again and again and pores over its meaning will be convinced that the Gītā did not end at the eginning of एषा तेऽभिहिता सांख्ये and that there are no interpolations in it.

The question is often asked, could such a long discussion have taken place on the battlefield? It goes without saying that none can know what Śrikrishṇa actually said on the battle-field or indeed if any discussion did take place at all. It is an episode containing the teaching of Śrikrishṇa, given in the words of Vaiśampāyana or some other gifted author, represented as delivered on the battlefield, taking advantage of the momentous occasion and the natural feeling of dismay which would arise in a humane heart at the sight of thousands and hundreds of thousands of men of the same kith and kin ready to fly at one another's throat in a civil war. Let us take a parallel instance from the Bible. The unique Sermon on the Mount which contains the highest moral teaching that a divinely inspired person can give can not be supposed to contain the actual words of Jesus Christ, historically speaking, though they are indeed divinely straight, simple and spiritual. Nay it can not be said that this whole teaching was delivered at one time or that it was really delivered on the top of a hill. We are, however, certain that the words are those of St. Matthew (chapters V and VI) and that they give the whole moral teaching of Jesus Christ. In the same manner it may be taken that the Bhagvadgītā composed by a gifted author contains the philosophical teaching of Śrikrishṇa represented as delivered on the battle-field. The author discloses this when he says at the end अध्येष्यते च य इमं धर्म्यं संवादमावयोः, as Śrikrishṇa could not have uttered these words; for there was then no dialogue which could be *read*. Plainly the author is out here in recommending his work for reading by religiously minded persons.

Winternitz who has described and discussed the Bhagavadgītā in his "Indian Literature" at great length expresses the same views practically as Rajaram Shastri Bhāgavat. He thinks that the Gītā discloses three kinds of Krishṇa, the *hero* Krishṇa, the *sage* Krishṇa and the *god* Krishṇa and that the speech of *sage* Krishṇa from एषा तेऽभिहिता सांख्ये is 'in irreconcileable contradiction with the preceding speech of the *hero* Krishṇa (p. 429) ending with हतो वा प्राप्स्यसि स्वर्गं जित्वा वा

मोक्ष्यसे मद्दीम् &c. We have already explained the apparent contradiction, the change of front or the break in the context here. We may further add that this idea of three Krishṇas is like that of Dr. Bhandarkar who held that there were two Krishṇas, the Krishṇa of the Gopīs and the Krishṇa of the Gītā. But even Dr. Bhandarkar did not see three Krishṇas in the Gītā itself. The idea is due to the inability of modern thinkers to understand how certain human beings can be looked upon as divine. A German scholar has remarked "When Jesus Christ says that 'He was with God in the beginning' he is either a madman or an impostor." We will not discuss the question whether great religious teachers of the world were really divine beings or not; but we must point out that in ancient times and till recently, that perhaps even now, most people actually believed and believe that certain persons were Avatāras or incarnations of the Deity or born of God and that, therefore, works like the Bhagavadgītā or the Bible written under this belief represented Krishṇa or Christ as both divine and human. We need not suppose that these two aspects in these works arose at different times or that these are any contradictions as such.

Describing in detail the three paths preached in the Gītā for emancipation, "the path of dutiful desireless action, the path of knowledge and the path of the love of God," Winternitz again observes, "There are contradictions staring us in the face at every turn" (p. 433). "In one place Krishṇa is a personal god and in another he says he is in all beings and then quite abruptly he speaks of Brahman the highest principle of the monism of the Upanishads". 'Speaking of the Vedas in an almost scornful tone, in other passages he recommends sacrifices. The Sānkhya and the Yoga philosophies are also taught, though opposed to the doctrine of unity taught by the Vedānta'. 'How can all these contradictions be explained?' Various scholars have offered various explanations. Some say "the work is poetical and mystical rather than logical, and philosophical". "Others explain that the poem has not come down to us in its original form but that, like most parts of the Mahābhārata, it has received its present form as a result of interpolations and revisions." "Garbe thinking the poem to be originially pantheistic made a direct attempt to reconstruct the poem by printing in small type what he thought to be interpolations." Winternitz agrees with this view but thinks the poem to be originally theistic and that those portions which relate to Brahman and to ritual and sacrifices are interpolated, "I think too that the original Bhagavadgītā was much shorter and in the present form contains many interpolations and additions." In particular he points out the fact that the Bhagavadgītā has exactly eighteen chapters (p. 436), a fallacious view which we have already refuted.

We have given this long extract from Winternitz in order to place before the reader the arguments which lead him and other noted scholars of the West to hold the views they do. That this whole view is, on the face of it, unsound is clear from the fact that the Bhagavadgītā strikes one, throughout its length, with the beauty of its language and the charm of its poetry, a merit which no patched up work can possess. The supposed interpolations, necessarily made at different times, cannot have the same diction or dignity of expression, much less the same sonorous ring in its words or the same rhythm in its melody. The Gītā, it is clear, must be conceded to be the work of one gifted author as Justice Telang rightly maintained in the aforesaid preface to his translasion of the Gītā. But further, these apparent inconsistencies or contradictions of thought or teaching disappear, immediately we take into consideration the position of the Gītā by time in the history of the development of Indian philosophy and the vivid fact that the author of the Gītā strives to harmonise all the systems of thought that were current in its days. The Gītā plainly is not preached to teach the theistic doctrine alone. It clearly seeks to expound the different doctrines in vogue and to improve upon them in harmonizing all which is the special merit of its teaching. As Christ accepted the prophets, Moses and Elias, who had gone before him and their teaching, so also the Gītā accepts the teachings of the schools of thought which had already arisen; and like Christ it improves upon and harmonises them. Christ "came not to destroy but to fulfil" and go further. It would, therefore, be absurd to look upon the passages which speak of Brahman or those wherein the utility of sacrifice is preached, as interpolations.

Let us see what philosophies held the field wnen the Gitā was preached. We take the date of the Gītā, for reasons which will be presently given in detail, to lie between 2000 and 1000 B. C. i. e. after the date of the older 13 upanishads and before that of Pāṇini. The philosophy of Brahman preached by these Upanishads was already well established and held the first place in public estimation. Indeed this philosophy with its usual concommitant Sanyāsa (पुत्रैषणायाश्च लोकैषणायाश्च व्युत्थायाथ भिक्षाचर्यं चरन्ति) is shown to be on the brain of Arjuna, the protopype of the Indo-Aryan seeker after truth and the Bhagavadgītā begins with it and ends with it. In the first chapter Arjuna says it is better to be a sanyāsin and beg and after having heard all the preaching of Krishṇa Arjuna asks at the beginmng of the last chapter "what do you mean by Sanyāsa then". The pāth of Sanyāsa was thus at the head of all systems of religious thought and Srikrishṇa had to describe it and Brahman. How ne adds a touch of his own to this doctrine, it is not difficult to see (vide the descrintion of स्थितप्रज्ञ &c.). But that Brahman is the final goal is accepted, as indeed the Gītā must accept, if it is to be an orthodox preaching, the Upanishads being always treated as revelation. All paths finally lead to this goal; and how is shown in the sunming up of the 18th chap. beginning with the verse सिद्धिं प्राप्तो यथा ब्रह्म तथाप्नोति निबोध मे (XVIII, 50). The path of sacrifice was the next important one; it was even older than the path of Sanyāsa. It had, however, already been condemned partly but not wholly, and the Gītā in its inimitably charming expressions, condemns the

Vedavāda, namely the performance of sacrifice for the love of enjoyment and Svarga. The cult of sacrifice was at its highest as seen in the Śrauta Sūtras, hundreds of sacrifices being prescribed for hundreds of desires. The Gītā condemns this क्रियाविशेषबहुलां भोगैश्वर्यगतिं प्रति ॥ (II,43) cult of Śrauta sacrifice. But as the oldest path, it could not condemn it altogether and Śri Krishna preaches ब्रह्मार्पणं ब्रह्महविः etc; this is how tbe Gītā improves upon the old doctrine. Christ similarly accepts the law of Moses that a writ of divorce should be given but adds "do not divorce a wife except for adultery" The daily sacrifices must be performed to propitiate the gods who will requite by sending rain; but perform all sacrifices with the sense upon you that you are sacrificing to the highest Brahman in effect and that will secure salvation. The Gītā could neither omit the path of Sanyāsa nor the path of sacrifice, the two old orthodox paths; but taking them it improves upon them in detail.

The third philosophy which held the field was that of Sānkhya which had already come into exsitence in the days of the later Upanishads, Kaṭha and Kena (vide Sec. II p. 172). The theory of Purusha and Prakṛiti and twenty-our Tatvas, as well as of three Guṇas was well established, though not quite orthodox and the Gītā propounds this philosophy as it was then known, not the later Sāṅkhya of the MBh. or that of the Kārikās. It even expands the doctrine of the three Guṇas, by applying it to many things, vide chapters 17 and 18. But the Gītā improves upon and reconciles it with the orthodox systems by adding the entity of पुरुषोत्तम in the 15th chapter which is the finest conception in the Gītā.

Lastly there was the path of Bhakti or devotion to God who in this path can not but be a personal God. It is sometimes supposed that this philosophy came into being after and in consequence of the Gītā. But, we think, it was already in existence though the latest. Indra and other Vedic gods were no doubt personal; but they had lost that character in the days of the Upanishads and had become phases merely of the highest impersonal Brahman. The human mind ordinarily can not do without a personal god and impersonal Brahman could not be grasped by the multitude (XII,5). The worship of Vāsudeva had already come into being among the common people viz. स्त्रियो वैश्यास्तथा शूद्राः:; and the Gītā extols this theistic doctrine as राजविद्या or राजगुह्य and प्रत्यक्षावगम and सुसुख. This doctrine was, however, different from the later पांचरात्र system taught in the Nārāyaṇīya Ākhyāna of MBh. (Śantip.), Nārāyaṇa being the word adopted for the highest personal God. It is also not exactly the school of Bhāgavatas called after Bhagavadgītā probably. This Vāsudeva cult is mentioned in Pāṇini also. In its inimitable way, the Gītā describes the path of devotion or Bhakti with its ideal of a personal God; but at the same time identilfies this personal God with the impersonal Brahman. Under this view, there is no contradiction when Krishṇa says that he is immanent in all things but is not in them. This is another high merit of the Gītā that it reconciles and combines the theistic and pantheistic doctrines. It is this which makes the Gītā the accepted revelation of all schools of thought and sects in India.

Combining these four doctrines together in one exquisite structure, the Bhagavadgītā stands before us like the Taj Mahal, one among the seven wonders of the world, a wonderful literary monument, inlaid with letters of gold on its four walls of shining marble, declaring the doctrines of Saṇyāsa, Sacrifice, Ṣānkhya and Bhakti, having a gate in each side through which one can enter into the inner shrine of Brahman. In front of the chief gate, the gate of Vāsudeva, the terrace is gained by a slowly rising flight of steps on which may be seen multitudes of women, Śudras and Vaiśyas; and a few Brahmins and Kshatriyas are also there. They are singing the praises of their favourite gods, Vibhūtis only of Vāsudeva, and dancing with delight at the sight of the inner shrine. On the left side the terrace is gained only by three steps. Sānkhyas and scientists are standing on this side trying by their reason to find out the entrance which remains screened and which is the Purushottama gate. At the hind gate there are no steps to get on to the terrace; a few persons with the help of the ladder of Dhyāna have come upon the terrace and are sitting in various postures in meditation and with the help of Prāṇāyāma, Japa or other Yogic mental practice are trying to see through the difficult gate of Omkāra. On the fourth side are Brahmins and Kshatriyas trying to get on to the terrace by the help of the trees of sacrifice laden with luscious fruit, but falling down again and again in seizing it, the temptation being avoided by a few only whose gaze is fixed on the inner tabernacle through the ब्रह्मार्पण gate. There are domes on the four sides; but the central cupola rises above these domes inscribed in golden letters with कर्मण्येवाधिकारस्ते मा फलेषु कदाचन। मा कर्मफलहेतुर्भूः मा ते संगो ऽस्त्वकर्मणि ॥.

Which of these four gates is favoured by the Gītā is a question on which famous Bhāshyakāras from Śankara onwards have differed. There is no question of efficacy, though it is also raised by some; for in our view all the doors are open and there are doors on every side and not on one side only. The inner taberncale can be approached through any door, though there is only one access to the inside of the tabernacle viz. true knowledge of God (ततो मां तत्त्वतो ज्ञात्वा विशते तदनन्तरम् XVIII, 55). The only question is which is the easier way and the Gītā in plain terms describes भक्तियोग as the easiest (see राजविद्या &c.) But the Gītā always keeps Karmayoga in its front; its main object is to induce Arjuna to fight and hence the main purpose of the Gītā is to teach the path of Karmayoga namely the performance of one's duty, regardless of result dedicating one's actions to God.

There are hundreds who are not attracted towards any one of these gates, engrossed with their own false philosophy and immersed in the pleasures of this world. Their atheistic philosophy is also noticed by the Gītā only to condemn it. For it had already come into existence and was known as the Bārhaspatya doctrine. It is stated in one of the Brāhmanas that Brihaspati, the preceptor of Devas, taught this false doctrine to Asuras that they might be easily destroyed by the Devas. Asuras are Western Aryans and their materialism is noticed already in the Upanishads (see Sec. II p. 190). The tenets of this Āsura philosophy are glowingly described in XVI (असत्यमप्रतिष्ठं ते जगदाहुरनीश्वरम् &c.). They even perform sacrifices, only for pomp and show. This division of men into two camps, the Daiva and the Āsura, is older than the Sāṅkhya Triguṇa theory and is naturally noticed in the Gītā, coming as it does in time nearer the Upanishads. It has been eclipsed by the Sānkhya doctrine and is not found in subsequent works. This chapter also can not, therefore, be supposed to be an interpolation.

We have thus far shown how the Bhagavadgītā is one consistent whole, the exquisite workmanship of one architect who has properly put in the several parts of it, and not a small edifice to which incongruous additions have been made from time to time. Nobody has ever maintained that the Gītā was written before the Upanishads or the four Vedas. The argument, therefore, that the passages which speak of Brahman or sacrifice are interpolations is not understandable. It could not but speak of Brahman, since even Western scholars place the Gîtâ after the older Upanishads. And if it is taken much later, all the more reason there is why it should contain a description of the several doctrines then in vogue viz. the doctrine of Brahman, of sacrifice, of Bhakti, and of the Atheism of Bārhaspatyas. Inasmuch as the Gītā has condemned the last and harmonised the other and orthodox doctrines with its own doctrine of dutiful desireless action, it has naturally been accepted as revelation by all the orthodox teachers of Hinduism. The three now recognised works on Vedānta philosophy, are, therefore, the ten Upanishads, the Bhagavadgītā (called both उपनिषद् and ब्रह्मविद्या) and the Vetānta Sūtra of Bādarāyaṇa. All the great teachers of Hindu philosophy from Śankara onwards have written Bhāṣhyas on these three works and established their claim to be recognised as teachers of philosophy.

The Bhagavadgītā, like every other book of revelation, has its miracle. The विश्वरूपदर्शन chapter is often looked upon as an interpolation; but it is not so and is a necessary part of this sacred book. It is on a par with the story of the transfiguration of Christ in the Bible (St. Matthew ch. 17). Nay, it is far more in consonance with the high imagination and poetry of the author of the Gītā than such ordinary miracles as are believed in in every country or people, the raising of the dead or the curing of the blind. Indeed the विश्वरूपदर्शन is not a miracle, विश्वरूप being seen with दिव्यचक्षुः and not with human eyes as in the Bible. It is a prophetic vision, a cinema view of the whole uinverse, as the roll of time is unfolded before the mind's eye. Even Winternitz does not appear to look upon this whole chapter as interpolated. He takes objection to a few verses in it, " While I record my conviction that the author of the Gītā was a great poet, I hesitate to attribute to him such verses as XI 26 in which the heroes of the epic are visioned as hanging between the teeth of the god" (p. 437). We are afraid Winternitz has missed the Dhvani here viz. that there is praise here of the great valour of these heroes who are not easily swallowed even by the All-Devourer but who *stick* (not hang) in his teeth (विलग्ना दशनान्तरेषु).

It must be admitted that the Gītā being in verse and in the form of a dialogue, there is not that rigidity of treatment or precision of terms which is expected in a purely philosophical treatise. The word Yoga especially is used in different senses as also Brahman. But the difficulty arises because we are accustomed to use the two words in particular senses in modern times and are always obsessed with the Yogasūtras of Patanjali and the so-called Brahmasūtras of Bādarāyaṇa. If we could translate ourselves to the time when the Gītā was composed several hundreds of years before these Sūtras, nay even before the Sūtras of Pānini, when the Sanskrit languange was actually spoken, we shall be able to avoid this stumbling at the words योग, ब्रह्मन् or आत्मन्.

Finally it may be noticed that there are some sentences in the Gītā which strike us as riddles and are therefore susceptible of different meanings. Such sayings are, however, always pet with great teachers. Even in the Bible, we find sentences like 'He who loses his life shall save it and he who saves his life shall lose it.' या निशा सर्वभूतानां तस्यां जागर्ति संयमी or मयि सर्वाणि भूतानि and न च मत्स्थानि भूतानि contain a poetical Alankāra involving contrary statements. There are others which strike us as pithy sayings and which a great teacher usually utters. This is the chief reason why we see similar sayings in the Gītā and the Bible. We need not argue from this that either copied the dead horse, an old absurd custom, was then gone through. Eventually the वपा of the horse was offered as oblation into the fire. The ceremony ended with Avabhṛitha after many animals were sacrificed and Dakshiṇās were finally given again.

The Purushamedha, taken from the White Yajurveda by the Taittirīyins in their Brāhmaṇa, is hereafter described. It could be performed by any Brahmin or Kshatriya (ब्राह्मणो राजन्यो वा यजेत) for power and strength (ओजो वीर्यमाप्नोति). It lasted for five days. The victims as described in T. B. were to be tied to several sacrificial posts and after being offered formally, they were to be taken north and set at liberty, as expressly stated in sūtra XX 24, 10 (पर्यग्निकृतानुदीचो नीत्वोत्सृज्याज्येन तद्देवता आहुतीर्हुत्वा &c.). The Dakshiṇā was that in an Aśvamedha for a Kshatriya and in Sarvamedha for a Brahmin.

The Sarvamedha is finally described in this chapter which only a king could perform (सर्वमेधो दशरात्रः। राजा यजेत यः कामयेत सर्वमिदं भवेयमिति। XX 25, 4). It lasted for ten nights and every day a different sacrifice was performed viz. अग्निष्टोम, इन्द्रस्तुदुक्थ्य, सूर्यस्तुदुक्थ्य, वैश्वदेव उक्थ्य, अश्वमेध (तस्मिन्नश्वं मेध्यमालभते), पुरुषमेध, असोर्याम, त्रिणव, नवम, विश्वजित्सर्वपृष्ठोतिरात्रो दशममहः. Thus this was a combination of all higher sacrifices and the Dakshiṇā was accordingly the greatest; viz. यदब्राह्मणानां दिक्षु वित्तं तत्सभूमि सपुरुषं ददाति यथाश्वमेधे. This was probably symbolical and not real, as in the case of Paraśurāma's sacrifice in Purāṇas.

Praśna XXI describes first the द्वादशाह. In one sūtra, Prajāpati is said to be blamed by some for creating insects which bite (दंश) and mosquitos and thieves (XXI 12, 1). Then प्रायणीय and उदयनीय are described. Next गवामयन which secures progeny, prosperity and also Svarga, is described. It ends with Mahāvrata. Various differences are noted between शाट्यायनि, ताण्ड्य and

भाल्लविनः with whom Āpastamba agrees. A पुंश्चली and मागध are mentioned together in XXI 17, 19 where the former is a harlot and the latter is her singer. A curious festival of rejoicing marks the close of this year-long sacrifice and Āśmarathya and Ālekhana differ as to the manner of its celebration. अपाघाटलिकास्तंबलवीणाः निच्छोला इति पत्न्यो वादयन्ति (XXI 19, 3, 4). Tambala and other words are not Dravidian but are the names of instruments which are not now known and hence their absence from classical literature. Conches are blown and nādis. The harlot and her dancer fight. But more curious is the mention of a S'ūdra and an Ārya fighting a mock fight with skins: शूद्रार्यौ चर्मकौ व्यायच्छेते. The S'ūdra abuses and the Brahmin praises. Then Rājaputras throw arrows. Dāsa girls make three circuits dancing, about the मार्जालीय. (शंखान्नाळीस्तूणवानिति...ळ here is inexplicable; it belongs to Ṛigvedins). दुन्दुभीः समाघ्नन्ति । पुच्छकाण्डेन भूमिदुन्दुभिम्. The भूमिदुंदुभि mentioned here means a pit dug in the ground and then covered with a skin and it is to be struck by both S'ūdra and Ārya. This festival of rejoicing is called माहेन्द्र (held in praise of Indra the great.) Ālekhana prescribes a still more jubilant festival which is as follows:– हिल्लुकां द्वे गायेताम् हिम्बिनीं द्वे। हस्याबारां द्वे। सवत्सरगाथां द्वे। Cows are praised गावो घृतस्य मातरस्ता इह सन्तु भूयसीः। ननु गावो मंकीरस्य गंगाया उदकं पिबुः। पपुः सरस्वतीं नदीं प्राचीश्चोज्जगाहिरे॥ &c. यदा यखाल्यौ वदतः ग्राम्यमङ्गीरदाशकौ। क्षेमे व्यृद्धे ग्रामेणानङ्गस्तप्यते वहन्?। हैमहा इदं मधु हिल्लुं हिल्लिति सर्वासामृगन्तेषु समयः। This brings out the common language of the people of which many words are entirely lost.

The sacrifice, it is important to notice, began with the fourth day before Pūrṇamāsī of Māgha according to Āśmarathya and of Chaitrī according to Ālekhana. After 6 months came the विषुवत् or दिवाकीर्त्ये. If माघी full-moon be taken to be the winter solstice day of Āśmarathya's time, his date would be about 1900 B. C., the same as that of the Maitrāyaniya Upanishad given in Section II (p. 213).

In Praśna XXII Ekāha and Ahīna sacrifices are described which are of the nature of Agnishṭomas in which दक्षिणाs like सर्ववेदस are given. There are some curious practices as श्येनेनाभिचरन्यजेत्। अग्नये रुद्रवते लोहितः पशुः। बैभीतकः इध्मः। लोहितोष्णीषाः लोहितवसनाः निवीता ऋत्विजः प्रचरन्ति। (XXII 4, 22). Four stomas are described including व्रात्यस्तोम. Agnishṭoma with peculiar Sāmans are also described like बृहस्पतिसव. Various other sacrifices are prescribed for various desires (13), one of which is for a Kshatriya king who gets no kingdom for himself though he tries. A पुष्टिकाम Vaiśya may perform the बृहस्पतिसव in a particular way. Finally, a king's अभिषेक is detailed: राजाभिषेक्ष्यमाणो जनपदेषु समवेतेषु &c. (XXII 28).

In XXIII are described Sattras, अतिरात्र, गवामयन &c., their nature being that of द्वादशाह. The performer of पञ्चदशरात्र becomes a god (देवत्वं गच्छति). A S'atarātra is also mentioned. आदित्यानामयन, वृतिवातोरयन, शाक्त्यानामयन, (एतेन वै शाक्त्यो गौरिवीतिः &c. &c.) तपाश्चितामयन, प्रजापते द्वादशसंवत्सर, साध्यानां शतसंवत्सर, सारस्वत सत्र are described. The last was performed on the left right bank of the Sarasvatī and at different places. After a year a sacrifice in नैतन्धव is prescribed on the south bank of the दृषद्वती. त्रिप्लक्षं प्रति यमुनामवभृथमभ्यवैति. The sacrificer immediately disappears from men (तदैव मनुष्येभ्यस्तिरो भवति XIII 13, 15). A तुरायण is mentioned as also a सर्पसत्र by which old age is prevented (सर्पाणां सत्रेणाप जरां भते XXIII 24, 8). Finally comes the imaginary thousand years' Prajāpati's sacrifice by which he created the world. A śloka is here quoted, the same being not Vedic.

Praśna XXIV may be a later addition, as Garbe thinks, as it contains some later dicta, chief of which is the well-known मंत्रब्राह्मणयोर्वेदनामधेयम् and the sūtras here are in the later form of brief sentences.

It gives the general rules for all sacrifices Sacrifices were open to all the three Varṇas; but Brahmins alone could be Ṛitviks (priests). The Atharvavedin had not yet advanced to the highest position as Brahman; he still performed his duties with the help of the three Vedas, Hotṛi using Ṛigveda, Adhvaryu Yajurveda and Udgātṛi Sāmaveda. Full moons are of three kinds: पूर्णिमा, श्वःपूरिका and खर्विका. XXIV 12 gives some ritual for destroying one's enemies by using different forms of वषट् such as वाषट्, वौषट्, वौषाट्; वाक्षट्, वौक्षट्, वौक्षाट् which had different results (XXIV 12). The Pravara provisions are given here in Kaṇ. 4 to 10 and these appear to be older than those in Āśvalāyana, as will be separately shown.

II Baudhāyana

This Sūtra belongs to the Taittirīya S'ākhā of the Black Yajurveda and is looked upon as the oldest Sūtra of that S'ākhā. It has been published by Caland in the Bibliotheca Indica Series in three volumes, dated 1905, 1907, 1913. It consists of 30 Praśnas divided into Kaṇḍikās, which are again formed into arranged in Adhyāyas. The Kaṇḍikās consist of one long sentence in the Brāhmaṇa style (e.g. आयतनवान् भवति य एवं वेद 14, 5 &c.). The prose is simple and the description goes into the minutest details. The contents of Vol. II and III are printed from a complete and more reliable manuscript in the Mackenzie collection at the. India Office. The Sūtra, as given in this manuscript even, is more of the nature of a Paddhati than Sūtra. This perhaps shows that the Sūtra is older than Āpastamba which itself is in the not yet fully developed condensed style of Sūtras.

The contents of Vol. I relate, as usual in Kalpasūtras, to Ādhāna, Punarādhāna, Agnihotra, Darśapūrṇamāsa, Chāturmāsya and Paśubandha. The contents of Vol. II

Sānkhya and Yoga philosophies; but they are expressly and perfectly refuted by Bādarāyaṇa. Indeed, Sānkhya was the first and chief opponent to be refuted, the प्रधानमल्ल to be overthrown and Bādarāyaṇa does it clearly and cogently and overthrows Yoga also with the same stroke (एतेन योग: प्रत्युक्त :). The Sānkhya and Yoga thus overthrown are not the Sānkhya and Yoga of the Gītā; they are their later developments, as stated already, described in the MBh. admiringly and approvingly. Sānkhya and Yoga are orthodox and acceptable views in the present MBh. being nowhere controverted in it. Hence also Bādarāyaṇa can not be the last recaster of MBh. nor of course, of the Gītā. Bādarāyaṇa also refutes the Pāncharātra doctrine which is a late form of the Bhāgavata doctrine first propounded by the Gītā. Lastly, he even controverts the opinion of the Gītā in regard to the अर्चिरादिमार्ग and puts it on a lower level. This treatment of this subject in the Sūtra will convince any one that Bādarāyaṇa can not be the author of the Gītā and it is almost a riddle to us how Tilak did not or could not see all this.

Having wrongly looked upon Bādarāyaṇa as the author of the present Gītā and also of the present Mahābhārata from the verse discussed above, Tilak details other arguments in support of this view which to our mind lead exactly to the opposite conclusion. He rightly shows in his Gītārahasya (p. 507–520) that the Gītā is seven times referred to in the Mahābhārata itself, once even as हरिगीता (कथितो हरिगीतासु समासविधिकल्पित: Śantip. 346, 12. Mark the plu: हरिगीतासु). As noted already, it is praised at the beginning of Anugītā in Aśvam. p. 16, 9—13 through the mouth of Śrīkrishṇa himself. Complete sentences from the Gītā again recur at several places in MBh., 27 such instances being given by Tilak. Even thoughts are constantly repeated in the several philosophic disquisitions in the Mahābhārata. But these facts do not go to show that the authors of the Gītā and the Mahābhārata are the same, as Tilak argues; but they show on the contrary that the author of the present MBh had the whole Gītā before him as a work of established reputation. The same author would not praise one particular part of his own work in another part of it. Nay he would take care not to repeat his own sentences anywhere. Plainly the MBh. *quotes* and does not *repeat* sentences from the Gītā. It seems clear that the Gītā, as it is at present, existed and had attained reputation before the Mahābhārata was constructed in its present form. It must have formed part of the Bhārata of Vaiśampāyana of 24000 verses which was extended into the present MBh. of one lakh. The first or original work 'Jaya' of Vyāsa may have contained the germ of the Gītā. But Vaiśampāyana's Bhārata, we are sure, contained the Gītā as it is today, because the विश्वरूपदर्शन incident given in the middle of it which is often looked upon as an interpolation has been copied four times in MBh. as shown by Tilak, once ineffectually to Dhṛtarāshtra as noted already, next to Uttaṅka, again by Nārāyana to Nārada and by Rāma to Parasurāma (Aśvam. p. 55, Śantip. 339 and Vanap. 99). The original idea of the Gītā was grand and it was copied by Sauti thrice in his MBh.

On the basis of this wrong view, Tilak assigns the same date to the Gītā as to the present Māhabhārata which he fixes at about 300 B. C. (wrongly given as 500 before Śaka at p. 564 Gītārahasya) from arguments which we do not detail here, as they are already given in the preceding chapter. The original Gītā, Tilak places about 1400 B. C. as he takes this as the date of the Mahābhārata fight. We have already shown how this view also is wrong and the original Gītā of Vyāsa, if such existed. must be dated 3102 B. C. It was practically a negligible nucleus, and we have no idea of it. But the Bhagavadgītā which we possess and which must have been before the author of the present MBh. as a work of established fame may be placed about 1400 B. C. as we proceed to show.

That the Bhagavadgītā is later than the 13 old Upanishads is clear from the fact that it quotes sentences from Kaṭha, Kena &c ; and hence the higher limit for its date may be taken to be 1900 B. C., the date of Maitryupanishad fixed by Tilak himself. To fix the lower limit, we have certain statements in the विभूति chapter (X) which must be taken to be a part of the present Gītā being looked upon as a later addition. We are not, therefore, taking our stand on a portion of the Gītā which may be taken to be its oldest part. There is also further proof that it formed part of the Gītā as it was before the recastor of MBh., because he has copied it, though not cleverly, in the Anugītā. There are many interesting statements in this chapter which we will notice by and by ; but the most important one is मासानां मार्गशीर्षोऽहमृतूनां कुसुमाकरः. The mention of the name मार्गशीर्ष makes it certain that the Gītā is later than 2000 B. C. the names of months in the Samhitā and even the Brāhmaṇa period being मधु, माधव and so on, as shown by S. B. Dixit. But this placing of Mārgaśīrsha at the head of the list of months by their new names makes it probable that the Gītā precedes Vedānga Jyotisha. From this Vedānga onwards, months commenced with Māgha until the counting was again changed before the beginning of the Christian era and the month-list was made to commence with Chaitra, a method which still obtains. This argument is not, however, decisive ; for even now month-reckoning from Mārgaśīrsha obtains in the north-western parts of India. In the Mahābhārata itself, month-names are twice given in detailing Vishṇuvrata and they begin with Mārgaśīrsha (Anu. p. 106 and 109). Even Amarakosha details month names beginning with Mārgaśīrsha. It appears that when the new month-names based on the पौर्णमासी नक्षत्र were introduced at the end of the Brāhmaṇa period, the month list began with Mārgaśīrsha and hence मासानां मार्गशीर्षोऽहं, logically speaking, indicates a time that ranges from 2000 B. C. to 200 B. C. the date of the Siddhāntas roughly, which introduced the Chaitra reckoning. But the next sentence ऋतूनां कुसुमाकर: gives us reason to hold that this verse belongs to a period which is nearer the earlier limit. If मार्गशिर्ष is the first month, the first season should be हेमन्त. After the Vedānga Jyotisha, the months began with माघ and the seasons with शिशिर and we actually find in अनुगीता, श्रवणादीनि नक्षत्राणि ऋतव: शिशिरादय: (Asvam. p. 44,2) in consonance with the Vedānga Jyotisha. But the Gītā keeps up the old Vedic season reckoning in which वसन्त was the first season. This indicates that while the Gītā precedes, Anugītā follows Vedānga Jyotisha.

The sentence नक्षत्राणामहं शशी also suggests the same date. We know that the Vedic Aryans looked upon the moon as higher and more distant than the sun and indeed as one of the Nakshatras. Thus the Chhāndogya gives संवत्सरादादित्यमादित्याच्चन्द्रमसं चन्द्रमसो वैशुनं &c. It does not seem that the Vedānga Jyotisha looked upon the sun as lower or nearer than the moon. This would also make the Gītā come nearer the Upanishads.

The most interesting verse in this chapter is महर्षय: सप्त पूर्वे चत्वारो मनवस्तथा ॥. The Siddhānta idea is that in a Kalpa there are fourteen Manus and not four; and hence this line has become a tough riddle to scholars. Tilak takes here three categories instead of two, viz. the seven Maharshis, *the four preceding* and the Manus (seven including the present Vaivasvata). But this interpretation is unsatisfactory, to say the least; the word four stands in it without its noun. Tilak takes here, as understood, the four Vyūhas given in the Nārāyaṇīya Ākhyāna. But Vāsudeva can not include himself among the four and cannot describe Vāsudeva as born from Vāsudeva. We may note here one more wrong view of Tilak viz. that "the doctrine in the Nārāyaṇīya Ākhyāna is the same as that of the Gītā; indeed the Bhāgavata, Sātvata, Pāncharātra and Nārāyaṇīya Dharmas are one and are mentioned in and preceded the Gītā." This is clearly a mistaken view. When the Bhagavadgītā was recited, there was no doctrine of Chaturvyūha or any Vyūha current. The Bhakti doctrine then moved about Vāsudeva alone of the Vrishṇis and Arjuna of the Pāṇḍavas (XI 11). The doctrine subsequently developed into the Pāncharātra and the relatives of Krishṇa were brought in viz. his brother Śankarshaṇa, his son Pradyumna and his grandson Aniruddha. The Nārāyaṇiyākhyāna in MBh. refers to the Gītā respectfully and thus seems to have followed it after a long time. Nārāyaṇa is the highest deity in it and not Vāsudeva. The doctrine was first preached by Nārāyaṇa to Nārada. The Paramparā of the Gītā is given in itself as Vāsudeva and Vivasvat (इमं विवस्वते योगं &c). The Ākhyāna also refers to प्रवृत्ति and निवृत्ति or सन्यास as taught in the Gītā while in it is taught प्रवृत्ति as superior. Lastly the doctrine is entirely theistic and rigidly Vedic, the inexplicable Avatāra of Hayagrīva being conceived in it as reciting the four Vedas.

It seems, therefore, certain that the doctrine of the four Vyūhas did not exist at the time of the present Gītā nor the Nārāyaṇīya Ākhyāna and that, therefore, the words पूर्वे चत्वारः must be separated But no correct interpretation can be given of चत्वारो मनवः unless we remember the place of the Gītā in the history of the development of thought in ancient India. We see that the idea of 14 Manus is first found in Manu Smṛiti and the astronomical Śiddhāntas about 200 B. C.* It is not found

* The Kalpa of 1000 yugas was an old idea and also the idea of many Manus. The theory of संध्या between Manvantaras gives the number 14 only which can fit in with 1000 and hence the theory of 14 Manus was started by the mathematical Siddhāntas.

in the present MBh. nor in Vedānga Jyotisha. But that there are more Manus than one is accepted even in some hymns of the Ṛigveda. We find in the Vālakhilya sūktas 51 and 52 in Maṇḍala VIII two Manus यथा मनौ सांवरणौ and यथा मनौ विवस्वति. In a sūkta in X we have got a सावर्ण्य or सावर्णि Manu different from सांवरणि or son of Samvaraṇa. Taking this into account and Svāyambhuva Manu mentioned in Yāska's Nirukhta, we may believe that at this period only four Manus were known. The idea of there being more Manus than one is natural to man, as law usually changes and different lawgivers arise and are accepted. Thus we can split the line into two parts महर्षयः सप्त पूर्वे and चत्वारो मनवस्तथा. The word पूर्वे still offers a difficulty. We may at once reject the later idea that there were different Saptarshis for different Manus ; but पूर्वे requires that there were at least two sets of them, the earlier and the later. The Saptarshis are also Vedic and in interpreting the Vedic verse तस्यासत ऋषयः सप्त तीरे the Brihadāraṇyaka (II) names them as Gotama, Bharadvāja, Viśvamitra, Jamadagni, Vasishtha, Kāśyapa and Atri. They are all authors of Rigvedic hymns and they are identified with the seven stars in the Great Bear. But there are other Saptarshis both in ancient works and in the sky. Those mentioned in MBh. Śantip. 341* are, however, not those intended in this verse though MBh. here plainly copies the above verse in the Gītā; for Pulastya, Pulaha and Kratu are not known to the Vedas and Bhṛigu is not mentioned here. We know that Jamadagni is a descendant of Bhṛigu, while Gotama and Bharadvāja are descendants of Angiras. That Bhṛigu and Angiras are not mentioned in the Upanishad list of Saptarshis makes it certain that there was another list of earlier Saptarshis, the first in the list

* मरीचिराङ्गिराश्चात्रिः पुलस्त्यः पुलहः क्रतुः। वसिष्ठश्च महात्मा वै मनुः स्वायम्भुवस्तथा ॥ ज्ञेयाऽष्टौ ताः प्रकृतयो यासु लोकाः प्रतिष्ठिताः । अष्टाभ्यः प्रकृतिभ्यश्च जातं विश्वमिदं जगत् ॥

being Bhṛigu. Hence we can well understand महर्षीणां भृगुरहम् which follows in this very chapter. It is also worth noting, as stated elsewhere, that Pravara lists in all Śrauta Sūtras begin with Bhṛigu. We may further note that this verse महर्षयः सप्त पूर्वे &c is earlier than the Pravarādhyāyas in the Śrauta Sūtras. This verse seems to imply that the first seven Ṛishis were the progenitors of Brahmins and the four Manus, the progenitors of Kshatriyas and others. This naturally must have been the ancient view, as the professions of priesthood and princehood were from long hereditary. The Pravara chapters of Śrauta Sūtras, themselves later parts, give the same pravaras for Brahmins and Kshatriyas.

These two important statements viz. मासानां मार्गशीर्षोऽहमृतूनां कुसुमाकरः and महर्षयः सप्त पूर्वे चत्वारो मनवस्तथा । मद्भावा मानसा जाता येषां लोके इमाः प्रजाः ॥ lead thus to the inference that the present Gītā precedes Vedānga Jyotisha and the Pravara chapters of the Śrauta Sūtras. It thus belongs to the Vedānga period and is nearer to the Upanishads than to Pāṇini. There are other interesting statements also in this chapter which support the same inference. मरीचिर्मरुतामस्मि and पितृणामर्यमा चास्मि remain unexplained, so far as we know, by any legend in the Purāṇas or Śrauta Sūtras. अक्षराणामकारोऽस्मि is natural enough; but द्वन्द्वः सामासिकस्य च is earlier than Pāṇini; for Pāṇini in his Sūtra, when speaking of compounds, always begins with बहुव्रीहि. There are again several infractions of Pāṇini's rules in the Gītā. Thus, as pointed out by Telang, शक्यअहं, सेनानीनां, नमस्कृत्वा, are un-Pāṇinian. (युध्य may be added as also वर्तेयं, युध्यस्व and वर्ते being also found. For other infractions shown by Prof. Rajawade see note).

These facts and forms make Bhagavadgītā precede Pāṇini's grammar. The evidence of metre is also to the same effect. The longer-metred verses even in the eleventh chapter, supposed to be interpolated, do not follow the gaṇa restrictions of classical verse given by Piṅgala. They follow the Vedic rule of number of letters only. It would, therefore, seem that the Gītā is Pre-Pingala, in other words is nearer the Vedic times than classical times. It is possible to argue that even Kālidāsa in his Śākuntalā imitated the Vedic metre in a verse recited in praise of Agni. It goes without saying that a clever author might imitate Vedic metre even now. But it is more proper to hold that the author of the Gītā had no such idea before him viz, of making his verses appear like Vedic verses. He composed such verses simply because the classical restrictions had not yet arisen. He wrote in times in which the Vedic metre was still in vogue. All such verses have 11 letters without restriction of short and long, as shown by Tilak, of the Trishṭup metre of Vedic times.

Other statements also show that the author of the Gītā lived nearer the Vedic times. द्यूतं छलयतामस्मि exalts gambling in a manner which can only belong to the Aryan society as it was in Vedic or even Vedānga times, when the अक्षावाप was one of the eleven jewels of a king and when a game of dice was a necessary part of the Rājasūya celebration (Section III p. 30). Finally मुनीनामप्यहं व्यास : does not place Vyāsa among Ṛishis as post-Vedic literature does. From all these arguments, we think we shall be justified in placing the Bhagavadgītā in the Vedānga period about 1400-1200 B. C. nearer to the Upanishads than to Pāṇini who is the last writer of the Vedānga period of about the ninth century B. C.

We may finally notice the contrary view of European scholars and examine the arguments by which they arrive at the 2nd century B. C,, as the date of the Gītā. Winternitz observes (p. 437) "This didactic poem was originally, by its very nature, a text of the Bhāgavatas, wherein the doctrine of Bhakti, in conjunction with the Yoga doctrine of desireless action was taught on the foundation of Sānkhya. There is evidence from inscriptions that, as early as the beginning of the 2nd century B. C., the religion of the Bhāgavatas had found adherents even among the Greeks in Gāndhāra. It is perhaps not too bold to assume that the *old* Bhagavadgītā was written at about this time as an Upanishad of the Bhāgavatas. Its language, style and metre too prove the work to be one of the earlier parts of the Mahābhārata. There are references to the Gītā in the later parts of the epic and the Anugītā (XIV 16–57) is surely nothing but a late imitation of the Gītā than which it contains a still greater variety of doctrines." The extract is long but it shows how European scholars are aware of the various grounds which go, in our view, to prove a very ancient date for the Gītā. For if the Mahābhārata of one lakh of verses is itself about 250 B. C. including the Anugītā, the Bhagavadgītā which is a very old part of MBh. must be far older than 250 B. C. The language of the Gītā has all the force and freedom of a spoken language (verbal forms like व्यतितारिष्यति being usually used and not past participles as in classical Sanskrit); and thus the Gītā must belong to the times before Buddha. For in his days, the Prakrits had arisen and Sanskrit was a dead language. Hence also the Gītā must be earlier than 500 B. C. The evidence of unrestricted long and short in metre also shows the same thing as stated above. Speaking next of the argument based on the Besanagar inscription which records the erection of a Garuḍa-stambha by a Yavana Bhāgavata of the second century B. C. one is really surprised at the *boldness* of the guess that propably the *old* part of the Gītā was written at this time as an Upanishad of the Bhāgavatas. If a *Yavana* of Gāndhara was a Bhāgavata in 150 B. C. the Upanishad of the Bhāgavatas must be *fearlessly* taken several centuries before. But there are other and earlier historical records about the worship of Krishṇa Bhagavān. Megasthenes records that Krishṇa was worshipped in Mathura. Alexander's historians record that Porus was a worshipper of Krishṇa and had his image with him in battle. To suppose that the Gītā as an Upanishad, nay its old part only, was written in the second century B.C. is thas a too cautious or timid guess. The view taken in the first sentence about the nature of the didactic poem is lastly incorrect; for the Bhagavadgīta is, in its nature, not a text of the Bhāgavatas. Bhaktiyoga comes in as *one* of the paths to salvation like Karmayoga, Sanyāsayoga and Dhyānayoga. Indeed the Gītā reconciles all the paths then known for inciting Arjuna to action, *desireless dutiful action*, as Winternitz himself aptly puts it. And as was natural, each path takes the Gītā as its Upanishad; the Sanyāsa of Sānkhya and Vedānta, the Karmayoga of the Pāñcharātra, the Bhakti of Indian saints, the Dhyānayoga of Patanjali. But these are all subsequent developments and the Gītā was taught long before Pāṇini, when Vāsudeva and Arjuna were alone worshipped; and taking Pāṇini's date to be 900 B. C. its date may well be taken to be the second millennium B. C.

After having examined the arguments advanced by Winternitz thus far. it is not necessary to go into the arguments of other European scholars which practically are the same as his. If the Gītā is an old part of the Mahābhārata, if it is pre-Buddha and pre-Pāṇini, one must come to the date we have arrived at. The dates assigned by Western scholars to the present MBh. and to Pāṇini are different from those we have assigned them. But the date of Buddha is certain and uncontroverted and as the Gītā is clearly pre-Buddha, as it does not mention any of his views as it was bound since it takes notice of all the then existing systems of thought, the date of the Gītā mnst at least be taken to be some centuries before 500 B. C.

NOTE 2:—THE DIFFERENT INTERPRETATIONS PUT ON THE BHAGAVADGĪTĀ

There are no different versions of the Gītā, nor really different readings in it; yet the work is differently interpreted by great teachers and scholars along with the Upanishads and even the Vedāntasūtras of Bādarāyaṇa which profess to settle the real meanings of both these two sacred authorities. The fact is that each teacher or scholar has a preconceived theory which he wishes to propound and the power of the Sanskrit language is such that he can do so, though with some difficulty, with the help of the grammar of Pāṇini. The canons of Mīmānsā or the science of interpretation, developed to the highest in India (as is natural in a country believing in sacred word and relying upon it (शाब्दप्रमाण) as the only guide in religious matters) can also be appealed to with success by men of powerful intellect. Ordinary readers are thus puzzled by these different interpretations and have eventually to fall back upon their own view of the teaching of the Gītā. Although we are not directly concerned with these different interpretations in this historical treatise, these may still be briefly given for the curious reader in this note, with remarks of our own.

It may be stated at the outset that the historical method of interpretation is lo3t sight of by all these interpreters, though it is, we think, the only proper method. We must first assign the Bhagva1gītā its proper position by time in the development of philosophic and religious thought in India and then interpret it, with reference to that development and not its later aspect. The Gītā, as shown in the above note, belongs to the Vedāṅga period during which Srauta Śūtras were composed and probably Sūtras on other subjects also. The four paths of emancipation then were, as stated already, the path of sacrifice, of Sanyāsa taught by Vedānta and also by Sānkhya, of concentration or Dhyāna and Tapas, and of Bhakti. Even the Gītā itself says ध्यानेनात्मानि पश्यन्ति केचिदात्मानमात्मना । अन्ये सांख्येन योगेन कर्मयोगेण चापरे ॥ अन्ये त्वेवमजानन्त : श्रुत्वान्येभ्य उपासते ॥ तेऽपि चातितरन्त्येव मृत्युं श्रुतिपरायणा : ॥. The Gītā also describes minutely the different kinds of Yogins and Sanyāsins in XII. All paths lead to the final goal according to the catholic teaching of the Gītā which seeks to reconcile and even combine them. There must have been works of the nature of Sūtras on all these paths not yet developed to their present stage. There must thus have been a Sūtra on Vedānta indicated by the word Brahma-Sūtra in XV, a Sūtra on Sānkhya indicated by सांख्ये कृतान्ते प्रोक्तानि in XVII; a work on Dhyāna Yoga indicated by शुचौ देशे प्रतिष्ठाप्य स्थिरमासनमात्मनः (VI), and of Prāṇāyāma (अपाने जुव्हति प्राणं, प्राणान् प्राणेषु जुव्हाति &c). It is not probable that there was any work on Bhakti, as that path was not followed by intellectual Brahmins and Kshatriyas but was followed by women, Śūdras and also Pāpayonis and was, therefore, looked upon as inferior. It is the highest merit of the Gītā that it believes in the salvation of even these by the path of Bhakti; for the later Brahmanic view embodied in Bādarāyaṇa's Sūtra is opposed to this doctrine. (This also shows how the Gītā precedes that Sūtra and is not the work of Bādarāyaṇa). All such works have disappeared and historically speaking, the Gītā is the oldest work which we possess on Vedānta, on Sānkhya, on Yoga and on Bhakti and not having any contemporary or previous work on these subjects for guidance or comparison, we are often unable correctly to understand the various statements of the Gītā on these subjects. Thus no satisfactory interpretation is given by any commentator, as Telang points out, of the line नैते सृती पार्थ जानन् योगी मुह्यति कश्चन. So also, we think, स्वभावोऽध्यात्ममुच्यते and भूतभावोद्भवकरो विसर्गः कर्मसंज्ञितः must remain riddles; for they are sūtralike definitions of अध्यात्म and कर्म, probably taken from some Vedānta Sūtra of the time. The view of Bādarāyaṇa's Vedānta is entirely different and can not explain these sentences. There are again several apparently simple expressions in the Gītā which are difficult to understand. Under the placid and charmingly flowing surface of the language of this sublime poem are hidden rocks of difficult passages against which he who dives deep finds his head broken. As an example of this may be given the verse श्रेयो हि ज्ञानमभ्यासाद् ज्ञानाद्ध्यानं विशिष्यते। ध्यानात्कर्मफलत्यागस्त्यागाच्छान्तिरनन्तरम् ॥ or आरुरुक्षोर्मुनेर्योगं कर्म कारणमुच्यते । योगारूढस्य तस्यैव शमः कारणमुच्यते ॥. In our free rendering of the Gītā into Marathi, we have underlined all such apparently simple but really difficult expressions. These facts as also the use of some words like आत्मन्, ब्रह्मन्, योग &c in different senses at different places have enabled thinkers to interpret the poem in different ways, in consonance with their own theories. In spite of this difficulty, however, we still think that the historical method of interpretation yields the view already expressed viz. that the Gītā describes and reconciles the four paths of emancipation and looks upon them as independently leading to the final goal of absorption into Brahman. The Gītā in all such disquisitions, however, keeps before it the immediate object of its preaching viz. inducing Arjuna to fight without fear of incurring sin. This historical method, in the absence of contemporary or previous works on Vedānta, Sāṅkhya and Yoga, has not been followed by thinkers and they have freely put their own different interpretations on this philosophical poem.

The oldest interpretation we possess is that of Śankara, the great advocate of Monism and Māyā. The Gītā, he thinks, preaches Sanyāsa as all Karman is binding. Knowledge of Brahman can alone lead to absolution and the other paths described in the Gītā do not independently lead to

Mokshā but lead into the path of Sanyāsa which alone finally secures absolution. Śankara refers to and refutes the ज्ञानकर्मसमुच्चय theory which held the field in his time (this indicates how the Gītā was so interpreted before him). Śankara had thus to twist the meanings of many verses in the Gītā which plainly speak of Karmayoga as leading to absolution such as कर्मणैव हि संसिद्धिमास्थिता जनकादयः। or संन्यासः कर्मयोगश्च निःश्रेयसकरावुभौ. Nay more तयोस्तु कर्मसन्यासात्कर्मयोगो विशिष्यते plainly gives preference to Karmayoga. How could Śankara ignore the straight meaning of such passages? The answer is simple and there is no need of strongly animadverting Śankara's interpretation, as Tilak does. Śankara had to do it, owing to the exigencies of his time, as we proceed to show.

The human mind has, from the most ancient times, swung like a pendulum, between Sanyāsa and Karman, not only in India but in all countries. Thus among the ancient Greeks, while in the days of Homer they were full of the enjoyment of this world, in the days of Pythagoras, the doctrine of renunciation was in the forefront, so much so that not only flesh and wine but even marriage was forbidden to a philosopher and Diogenes passed his days in a tub. Epicurus raised a protest and Epicurianism went to the other extreme and was eventually sensualism. The Jews were sacrificers of animals; Christ forbade animal sacrifice and taught, like the Gītā, the golden mean between Sanyāsa (vide 'those who have made themselves eunuchs for the sake of God) and Karman (but this is not for all). Sanyāsa gained the upper hand soon and a monastic unmarried life was considered as leading to salvation. Monks and nuns established in monasteries, hereafter gained ascendency in Christianity so far that they eventually became supreme. Luther arose and protested and Protestantism denied Sanyāsa and abolished all monasteries. It is now swinging to the other extreme of the pendulum and Karman and enjoyment are becoming the highest aims of human existence.

The history of the swinging of the mind between Sanyāsa and Karman in India is exactly similar and may be noted at length. The Vedic Ṛishis were full of the joys of this world in their new settlements in India and they performed sacrifices and talked of Karman only in propitiating the Nature Deities they worshipped. This went on one side to the extremest point of the swing of the pendulum and the most fantastic sacrifices like पुरुषमेध for the attainment of all desires were proposed. Sanyāsa naturally came to the forefront and the Ṛishis, tired of such Karman, sought relief in renunciation in the Upanishads. Sanyāsa, however, also went to the other extreme and persons in every stage of life, began to resort to Sanyāsa and to begging alms for subsistence. But surely there must be some one to give alms. Karman was thus necessary and imperative. The Gītā was preached at this stage of the development of thought in India; and it properly lays stress on the golden mean; Sanyāsa was good, but Karman was also good, even better and both paths led to the highest goal.

We may note how the pendulum swung, after the Gītā, between the extremest points of Sanyāsa and Karman in India. Karman went to the opposite extreme point in later Śrauta Sūtras, Lāṭyāyana prescribing an actual Purushamedha after the model of the Aśvamedha (Sec. III p.). Naturally Sanyāsa again came to the front in the days of Buddha and soon went to the other extreme. Sanyāsa was allowed to men and women, young and old, Brahmin and Śūdra, so that in Aśoka's time, the land swarmed with monks and nuns leading a useless and even sinful life by begging and living in spacious comfortable Vihāras built by reverent kings and admiring laity.

There naturally was a rebound to the other side and Pushpamitra actually performed the condemned Aśvamedha to emphasise the sanctity of the path of Karman. Indeed the Sūtras of Jaimini arose at this time and established Karman on an intellectual basis. There was again a set-back and Buddhism triumphed in the days of Kanishka. The Guptas, however, reestablished sacrifice, the first Chandragupta performing the long unperformed Aśvamedha again. The Śabara Bhāshya probably belongs to this time; and Sanyāsa was so far condemned that it was treated as कलिवर्ज्य or prohibited in the Kali age. Harsha reestablished Sanyāsa so much so that from his imperial throne, having given away everything, he begged like a Buddhist monk his daily dole of food. When his empire was overthrown after him, Karman supremacy was reestablished by Kumārila who preached that Sanyāsa was not only Kalivarjya, but also not taught by the Vedas (त्रयो धर्मस्कंधाः only-Chhānd.). He not only reintroduced animal sacrifices but Śrāddhas with flesh offerings also. Śankara appeared at such a time and as Kumārila had gone to the extreme of Karman doctrine, he found it necessary to go to the other extreme and preach that there was no redemption through Karman but through Sanyāsa alone. He had perforce to twist the meaning of some verses in the Gītā which upheld Karman, along with Sanyāsa thus preaching the golden mean. The philosophy of Śankara going after him to the other extreme, there was a rebound again. Rāmānuja interpreted the Gītā differently in consonance with his doctrine of Bhakti joined to his विशिष्टाद्वैत doctrine. Madhva interpreted the Gītā in a third way consistent with his द्वैत doctrine. Vallabha went still further and preached wordly enjoyment as the Bhakti of Śrīkrishna. In Mahārāshtra, however, the Marathi poet-saints held fast to the teaching of Śankara and his interpretation of the Gītā, till the exigencies of the present time led Tilak to preach the doctrine of Karmayoga again and offer a new interpretation of the Gītā.

Tilak in his Gītārahasya or 'The Secret of the Gītā' maintains that the Gītā preaches Karmayoga as the highest Yoga leading independently to salvation. It teaches Karman, action-duteous action,-both before the attainment of the knowledge of God and after it, while Śankara maintained that Karman before such knowledge was only useful for चित्तशुद्धि and after it must be abandoned to secure absolution attainable only by Sanyāsa. Tilak has well explained the verses in favour of Karman of which Saṅkara had twisted the plain meaning; but it must be admitted that Tilak also has, in a few places, twisted the plain meaning of Yoga into Karmaryoga and has condemned the path of Sanyāsa rather too strongly. In spite of this defect, it cannot but be said that Tilak has explained the whole Gītā on the basis of Karmayoga, a task which Deussen thought very difficult and has thus rendered signal service to India and the world by focussing attention on the great philosophy of Karman, the doctrine of doing one's duty without desire of its fruit and dedicating one's actions to the Deity from whom all action springs. The theory of Gītārahasya has naturally become popular and the work has been translated into most languages of India.

But how to decide what is one's duty in particular difficult circumstances is a question which confronts one seeking for guidance. The simple answer of the Gītā is that Scripture will show you your duty (तस्माच्छास्त्रं प्रमाणं ते कार्याकार्यव्यवस्थितौ) Tilak ingeniously interprets शास्त्र as referring to the Gītā itself and not श्रुति and स्मृति. One of the greatest merits of Gītārahasya is that it treats the Gītā as a work giving the Indian ethical theory. There is no work in Sanskrit literature on ethics as such, the Indo-Aryan sages having from the beginning embodied rules of conduct in sacred works. Western thinkers, ancient and modern, have thought deeply on moral philosophy, independently of religion and enunciated their different doctrines. Modern moral philosophy propounds thus the doctrine of the greatest good of the greatest number as the basis of moral action. Tilak argues that the Gītā bases morality on the doctrine of Brahman pervading the world, आत्मौपम्य in other words or the precept "Do unto others as you would them do unto you."* Tilak's arguments (given at pp. 65–94 G. R.), we think, might well have been placed before the world in English, in a separate work on the ethics of the Gītā.

It may aptly be argued that the Gītā must be treated as a work on ethics as evidenced by the last line of the Gītā तत्र श्रीर्विजयो भूतिर्ध्रुवा नीतिर्मतिर्मम. Indeed the very question of Arjuna on which it is based is an ethical one. Arjuna asks "Is it proper, or in Indian phraseology, is it not sinful to kill thousands of our own kith and kin, though they are wrongfully attacking us (आततायि), for the sake of a paltry kingdom? Is it not better, more beneficial to the world, that we should live by begging rather than kill them? (श्रेयो भोक्तुं भैक्ष्यमपीह लोके does not necessarily involve any idea of Sanyāsa ; it merely means that the Pāndavas might as well live like poor men by begging). This question is purely one of ethics. It has been agitating the thinkers of the whole world. Plato answered it as Arjuna would. "It is better to suffer" he maintained, "than to inflict suffering." Christ similarly said "if any one strikes you on the right cheek offer your other cheek also." The answer of the Gītā is different. After explaining all the view-points of philosophy on the ways to secure absolution, Śrīkrishṇa says, "If without any pride (of power) in your heart and any prospect of profit clouding your mind, one kills the whole world, one does not incur the sin of killing." The Gītā nodoubt preaches Ahinsā already preached by the Upanishads. It

* यदन्यैर्विहितं नेच्छेदात्मनः कर्म पूरुषः न तत्परेषु कर्तव्यं जानता प्रियमात्मनः MBh.

prescribes it for a Sanyāsin or a Yogin trying to reach the final goal of existence. Nay it treats Ahinsā as the first quality of दैवी संपत् or the godly temperament. It even considers it as one of the steps to the highest knowledge (अमानित्वमदम्भित्वमहिंसा क्षान्तिरार्जवम् XIII 7). But it does not prescribe it in all circumstances and preaches the golden mean as in all other topics.

To return to the Gītārahasya, it riveted the attention of Indian thinkers on the philosophy taught in the Gītā and several scholars have formed new views and propounded new interpretations of the Gītā. Most notable is the view put forth by Mr. S. S. Budhiraj M. A. LL. B., Chief Judge of Kashmir, who holds that the Gītā preaches Buddhiyoga as the highest yoga and that the Gītā uses many words like कौशल in their Buddhitic senses, the Gītā being in his opinion post-Buddha. It is true that the word Buddhiyoga occurs in the Gītā three or four times as meaning a special condition of the reasoning mind leading to Moksha *e.g.* ददामि बुद्धियोगं तं येन मामुपयान्ति ते. But it is not mentioned as a निष्ठा or path and it is the last condition in every path. Secondly, the question is whether Buddhism borrows from the Gītā or the latter from the former. That the Gītā precedes Mahāyānism is accepted by all and Hīnayānism does not use Vedantic terms. It seems, therefore, certain that Mahāyāna Buddhism borrows words from the Gītā, its doctrines being infused with Vedantism. Lastly Nirvāṇa is a word which is always used with Brahman in the Gītā; it does not mean Moksha as in Buddhism, but merely extinction. Though we thus differ from Mr. Budhiraj, it must be acknowledged that his deep study of Buddhism has enabled him to find out many words having the same sense as in Buddhism and has drawn the attention of scholars to the word Buddhiyoga used in a peculiar sense in the Gītā.

Mr. V. G. Rele F. C. P. S. a medical practitioner of Bombay and author of the well-known philosophic book "The Mysterious Kundalinī," propounds quite a new interpretation of the Gītā, arriving at Karmayoga by applying its teaching to the physical body and not the universe outside. Dr. Rele expounds the psychic organism of the human body from the several chapters of the Gītā itself, with the help of modern science and psychology. Most striking is his interpretation of the Aśvattha tree, which he looks upon, not as an allegorical tree as is usually thought, but as the nervous system in the human body. Whether one agrees with his views or not, Dr. Rele has undoubtedly revealed, as only a medical man of philosophic turn of mind can do, another aspect of the greatness of the Gītā, composed as it was in a period of intimate knowledge of the anatomy of the human body, acquired in Śrauta animal sacrifices and has opened a new line of thought for students of this unique work.

NOTE 3—PROF. RAJAWADE ON THE GRAMMATICAL INACCURACIES IN THE GĪTĀ.

Mr. V. R. Rajawade, retired Professor of Sanskrit, Fergusson College, Poona in a contribution to the Bhandarkar Memorial Volume 1917 points out the many inaccuracies, in the Gītā, of grammar as well as of poetics, as taught by Pāṇini and Mammaṭa and finally observes: "The faults of grammar, style and reason in the Gītā are so many that when men assert that the Gītā has spoken the last word on ethics or that it is the best poem in the world, they lay themselves open to attack." "The tradition and faith, the ignorance and superstition, of the authors of such poems come into play and leave their impressions on their works" (p. 338). This singular opinion of Prof. Rajawade, opposed as it is to the almost unanimous opinion of scholars, eastern and western, is, we think, due to the fact that the Prof. forgets that the Gītā was written about five centuries before Pāṇini and twenty before Mammaṭa, both of whom base their rules on the language and poetry of their times and that, therefore, the Gītā cannot be criticised by the standard of Pāṇinian grammar or Mammaṭian poetics. The maxim is well-known that the test of the pudding lies in the tasting thereof. Even Prof. Rajawade observes (p. 337) that "the test of good poetry lies in the increase and renewal of pleasure at every fresh perusal." A Sanskrit poet has also said क्षणे क्षणे यन्नवतामुपैति तदेव रूपं रमणीयतायाः. Now the experience of hundreds is opposed to that of Prof. Rajawade on this point and, in spite of the inaccuracies which strike one who is full of the rules of Pāṇini or the canons of Mammaṭa, the Gītā strikes us as the most poetical philosophical work in the world both in thought and in language, as Humbolt and Macdonell, Tilak and Telang testify.

A recent (1922) European testimony may be fitly quoted here. Dr. St. Fr. Michalski Iwienski of Warsaw in the preface in French to his Bhagavadgīta says :—"The flight of its ideas and the grandeur of its conceptions, the gigantic amplitude of its images and the choice beauty of its language, the simplicity with which it solves the eternal enigmas and the profound clear wisdom of its teaching—all this makes one feel that we can scarcely find in the whole European literature, a book which we can put by the side of the Gītā."

Keeping aside this mistaken view of Prof. Rajawade, we may give here, for the curious reader, the several grammatical inaccuracies pointed out by him, per Pāṇini, "In Sanskrit युध्, यत्, रम्, पू, च्यु, स्था with अव, वृत् with नि and लभ् are Atmanepada; but in the Gītā they are almost always used in Parasmaipada. निवासिष्यासि ought to be निवत्स्यसि. मा शुचः means do not be pure; it ought to be मा शोचः or मा शोचीः. प्रसविष्यध्वम् is unaccountable; संयमतां ought to be संयच्छतां ; हे सखेति is a wrong sandhi (सखे इति). प्रियायार्हसि is wrong, it ought to be प्रियायाअर्हसि. (This is a mistake; it really is प्रियाय अर्हसि). शक्य अहं is wrong as also मय्येव अत ऊर्ध्वं where there is no sandhi made. सेदानीनाम् should be सेनान्याम्., सर्वेभ्यः पापकृत्तमः, तस्मात्प्रियकृत्तम and तेषां के योगवित्तमा: use wrong cases. तेषु and तरा: is proper. ते प्रतिजाने does not come under प्रत्याङ्भ्यांश्रुवः (Pāṇ). So also योगस्य जिज्ञासुः and धर्मस्य अश्रद्दधानाः should have योगं and धर्मं. मद्भक्तेषु अभिधास्यति should have भक्तान्, आदिकर्त्रे नमेरन् should have कर्तारम्, कथयिष्यामि दिव्याः विभूतयः ought to have विभूतीः. मे श्रुणु, मे निबोध appear Prakrit forms. एतत् संशय and इदं महिमानं may be misreadings. प्रकृतेः क्रियमाणानि कर्माणि ought to have कर्मणाम्–being followed by कर्ताहमिति मन्यते ॥" (pp. 326, 327).

These inaccuracies, even if they be judged so by Pāṇini's later rules, being scattered over 700 verses, are so few that they do not jar on the reader's ear and do not in any way diminish the beauty of the language. When forms differing from those sanctioned by Pāṇini are found in works earlier than Pāṇini, they must be treated as sanctioned by the usage then current. When they appear in works undoubtedly later, specially when Sanskrit was a dead language, they are incorrect and indicate a very late date as also ignorance of the author as in the Purāṇas.

It must further be pointed out that even according to Pāṇini, in the Vedic language verbs take both padas and that vibhaktis are also not fixed in their meanings. The genitive especially is used in many senses. धर्मस्य श्रद्दधानाः and योगस्य जिज्ञासुः are not, therefore, wrong nor युध्य or वर्तेयम्. Sandhi is optional except in Samāsa or Ekapada; and secondly, sandhi rules were not fixed in Vedic language yet; शक्य अहं नृलोके is thus not wrong, for we have in पुरुषसूक्त, पद्भ्यां शूद्रो अजायत. In short, the Gītā being far earlier than Pāṇini and nearer the Brāhmaṇas, these inaccuracies are really not such. Prof. Rajawade forgets the position of the Gītā in the development of the Sanskrit language and hence his wrong view.

It is unnecessary to give the poetical lapses of the Gītā pointed out by Prof. Rajawade as per Mammaṭa who is a far later writer than Pāṇini and whose canons are based on classical poetry written fifteen hundred years after the Gītā. Real poetry again is far less subject to fixed canons than language to grammar.

Lastly we may note Rajawade's view that "the Gītā unnecessarily uses expletives like च, एव, अपि, तु, ह, उत, and that another method of filling out lines is a host of unnecessary vocatives like हृषीकेश, गुडाकेश, परंतप, कौन्तेय, धनंजय, अरिसूदन." Does the

Professor think that the Gītā should only have used two vocatives अर्जुन and कृष्ण ? The Professor is really unpoetical when he observes that भूतभावन भूतेश देवदेव जगत्पते XI 5 is simply a string of expletives (useless vocatives ?); for these are used with full meaning in praising the divine nature of Krishṇa. And meaningless expletives are used in all spoken languages (*e. g.* भला in Hindi or वरी in Gujarati) and are found even in Rigvedic hymns (*e. g.* स इद्देवेषु गच्छति) They always add a peculiar force to the spoken sentence.

III GENERAL CONDITION OF THE PEOPLE

(1400—900 B. C.)

From the Śrauta Sūtras and from Pāṇini as well as even the Bhagavadgītā, many facts can be culled which throw a light on the general condition of the people in the Vedānga period; and we propose in this chapter to describe it at length by the help of such facts. We give references for the leading statements; but it is needless to cite page and chapter for every statement as the facts mentioned in the preceding chapters must be fresh in the mind of the reader.

The Aryan land extended from Kabul to Kalinga and from the Himalayas to the Vindhya, Kurukshetra being, however, the centre of Aryan religion and civilization. There were three main divisions of the land viz. the east, the middle land and the north. The eastern-most portions Anga, Vanga and Kalinga had a few Aryan settlements; but the Aryans there were looked down upon as degraded. Similarly on the west, Sind and Sauvīra were outside the pale of Aryan religion. The distant parts of the north were not staunch followers of the Aryan religion; especially the cult of Aryan sacrifice was not followed there and the people there were also looked down upon. In the mountainous country bordering on the south of this land, from the hills of Chhota Nagpur through the Vindhya and Śatpuda regions, as far west perhaps as Malwa, there were aboriginal peoples some of whom like the Selagas were even cannibals. Remnants of this race are now found in the Andamans only. The aboriginal population in the plain country was long incorporated into the political body as Śūdras, some of whom like the Nishādas lived in separate villages. The other Śūdras though allowed to live in towns and villages with the Aryans, were like the natives in South Africa, still kept apart in religious and political matters. The Śūdras were not allowed even to milk sacrificial cows; they were of course debarred from performing sacrifices. And they were not counted as Rāshtra or part of the nation, the Kshatriyas and Vaiśyas alone forming it and the Brahmins remaining above it. Thus, when the king was in sacrificial vrata, all the people in the country had to stop shaving *except Brahmins* (Lātyā. S. S. II 2, 5). Certain degraded people with uncleanly habits and food were to reside outside the village or town; but they were Śūdras still and not called Panchamas as now in South India. Pāṇini divides Śūdras into निरवसित (kept out) and अनिरवसित(not kept out,)and we have not actually come across the word अस्पृश्य. But even the Gītā calls these पापयोनि and the Chāṇḍālas certainly lived outside the villages. The others viz. the Nishādas and Śūdras were not to be talked to, much less touched, when the Aryan sacrificer had entered on the Dīkshā or ordainment for sacrifice.

All the kingdoms were small in extent except a few in the east where Samrāṭs ruled. The number of peoples mentioned in Pāṇini is very great and, as stated already, many of them disappeared after Pāṇini. The name of the country as also of the king was usually the same as that of the people. There was thus identity of interest between them, though probably the despotic form of government generally obtained. There were, however, kings who ruled with the help of councils and they were called परिषद्वल (V 2,112 Pāṇ.) The kings who became troublesome were often driven away by the people; and these performed a particular sacrifice to regain kingship. The Kshatriyas sometimes oppressed the people or विश् and the latter sometimes gained the upperhand, as appears from sacrifices prescribed for the oppressed राजन्य or विश् to gain supremacy. Brahmins, being outside, could perform these sacrifices for either of them.

The inhabitants were divided into the four well-known castes, Brahmins, Kshatriyas, Vaiśyas and Śūdras, with their typical occupations priesthood, arms, agriculture and service respectively. These castes and their professions were hereditary and generally unchangeable.* Cattle-keeping however, was practised by all the three higher castes. Cows especially were prized by all; they in fact served as medium of exchange. The jungles were plentiful and pastures many. The Dārshadvata sacrifice was simply tending the cows of a Brahmin in Kurukshetra for a year. Thousands of cows were given as Dakshinā by kings who had their own herds. A three year old pregnant cow

* (See ब्राह्मो जातौ Pāṇ. VI 4,171, ब्रह्मणोऽपत्यं ब्राह्मणः)

(षष्ठौही) was the best Dakshinā. Special sacrifices were laid down for a Vaiśya who had lost his cattle. पशुकाम was as general as प्रजाकाम, cattle and progeny being valuable in a newly settled agricultural country.*

The Kshatriyas formed the military caste; but some Brahmin tribes also followed the profession of arms, even as now, see आयुधजीविगोपालवा: under V 3,114 Pāṇini. This sūtra is very important. आयुधजीविसघाञ्ञ्य् वीहोकष्वब्राह्मण राजन्यात् shows that among the Vāhīkas (Punjab people) there were also fighting tribes other than Brahmins and Kshatriyas, such as कौण्डीवृस, क्षुद्रक, and मालव (Kāśikā); but the Malloi and the Oxidrae were Kshatriyas! The Kāśikā is apparently wrong here. Brahmins sometimes even became kings as appears from 2, Pāṇ VI 2,59. राजा च and आर्यो ब्राह्मणकुमारयोः (VI 2,58) make राजब्राह्मण, accented in a particular way, mean राजा चासौ ब्राह्मणश्च, (कर्मधारय) i. e. a king and Brahmin. But Kshatriyas appear never to have been priests.

The intermediate castes had not yet probably arisen. Some caste sections had no doubt become degraded or उपकृष्ट (आश्वलायन श्रौ. सू.) The Rathakāra separately mentioned in Sūtras belonged to any of the three Varṇas. The Sūtagrāmaṇis were सूताश्चग्रामण्यश्च (Kâṣ) and probably were also heads of villages but belonging to the Aryan race. The क्षत्रसंगृहीतृ are also a riddle; they were accountants and bankers and were probably Vaiśyas. The words सूत and क्षत्तृ after Pāṇini became names of two

* Lāṭyāyana prescribes a शबलीहोम for one who wishes to possess one thousand heads of cattle (II, 8).

mixed castes in Smritis as marriages with lower caste women were gradually banned or became lowered in public estimation.

The verse स्त्रियो वैश्यास्तथा शूद्रा: in the Gītā offers a riddle. If the Vaiśyas were Aryans, they could learn the Vedas and could perform all sacrifices, Gṛihya and Śrauta; why are they classed with Śūdras?* Commentators offer no explanation. It seems to us that most Vaiśyas had ceased to perform sacrifices, though, by the Sūtras, they were allowed to perform them. Their constant association with Śūdras and also greater mixture of race made them strangers to Vedic rites even in the Vedānga period. A strong proof of this may be found in the fact that they have only one gotra and pravara assigned them in the Pravarādhyāyas. They had forgotten their original gotras and pravaras so necessary to be recited in sacrifices. The Vaiśyas, however, later devised Nukhs, instead of gotras, to prevent further mixture of race and endogamy and have thus preserved the purity of their blood.

The word Pratyenas in Pāṇini VI 2, 60 offers another riddle. It has not been taken up in Smṛitis as indicative of any sub-caste. It means an armed soldier and it appears in the Bṛihadāraṇyaka in that sense. But his varṇa was either Kshatriya or other. The word राजप्रत्येना: according to Pāṇini meant either राज्ञ: प्रत्येना: or राजा चासौ प्रत्येनाश्च according to its different accent.

* In modern times, both Brahmins and Kshatriyas are ordinarily classed with Śūdras, स्त्रीशूद्रद्विजबन्धूनां त्रयी न श्रुतिगोचरा । भाग·

Marriages of Aryans with lower caste women, though in disfavour, were however allowed. For we find that there is a provision in Śrauta Sūtras to the effect that a sacrificer, when observing vrata, should cohabit with his savarnā wife only, at best a lower caste wife, but never with the Śūdrā wife. This shows clearly that the Sūdrā wife had already come into disfavour as also other असवर्ण wives. This led in later times to the stoppage of Anuloma marriage altogether. The Pratiloma marriage was already long banned; the Bhagavadgītā strongly denounces वर्णसंकर by which word we must understand mixture of race in the Pratiloma way. प्रदुष्यन्ति कुलस्त्रियः । स्त्रीषु दुष्टासु जायते वर्णसंकरः refers to Kulīna or noble ladies mating with lower class males.

Illegal connections were, of course, severely condemned. The institution of prostitutes was, however, countenanced, as a harlot (पुंश्चलु) was invited at the consecration of a sacrificial shed. Adultery existed, as it does at all times and in all climes. But the sacrificer had to see that his wife who had to take part in the religious ceremony was pure. He, therefore, at the commencement of the sacrifice, bluntly asked his wife पत्नि कति ते जाराः ? If the wife, in the presence of the sacred fire, was conscientious enough to name some persons, oblations with suitable mantras were thrown into the fire to destroy them. The confession probably purified the wife and the sacrifice proceeded.

The inference that intermediate castes arose after Pāṇini is supported by an interesting sūtra of his emended by a Vārtika of Kātyāyana (noticed by V. K. Rajawade also in his Marathi preface to the राधामाधवचम्पू). The sūtra VIII 2,83 (प्रत्यभिवादेऽशूद्रे) provides that when a Kshatriya or Vaiśya salutes a Brahmin, in returning the salute or in blessing him, the last vowel of the vocative should be changed to प्लुत, but not for a Śūdra as it did not require a tone of respect * Kātyāyana's Vārtikas to this give two provisvs (1) स्त्रियां प्रतिषेधो वक्तव्यः which states that for women the प्लुत tone of respect should not be used. This proves that women had descended in estimation as they often belonged to lower castes. (2) भो राजन्यविशां वेति वक्तव्यम्। This means that the tone of respect was optional in returning the salutation of a Kshatriya or Vaiśya.* These also had somewhat desecnded in estimation after Pāṇini and before Kātyāyana; for we have seen that there were incursions of foreign races and these had been admitted as Vrātya Kshatriyas or Vaiśyas. Many being born of Śūdra wives had probably been assigned an intermediate position. Thirdly, many had turned Buddhists and did not deserve respect from orthodox Aryans. This sūtra with its Vārtikas is historically very important, as evidencing social changes among the people of Northern India.

The artisans in villages and towns were probably of the Vaiśya caste, though the indication given by Pāṇini VI 2,60 is faint. The Kāśikā gives instances

* आयुष्मानेधि देवदत्त ३ for a Brahmin but आयुष्मानेधि तुषजक २ आयुष्मती भव गार्गि। १ आयुष्मानेधीन्द्रवर्मन् ३ or आयुष्मानेधीन्द्रवर्मन् and आयुष्मानेधीन्द्रपालित ३ or आयुष्मानेधीन्द्रपालित. Kāśikā.

on the sūtra ग्रामः शिल्पिनि, such as ग्रामकुलालः and ग्रामनापितः and on राजा च प्रशंसायाम् (VI 2,61) as राजनापितः both having particular accents.

Marriage customs seem to have remained the same as in Sanhitā and Brāhmaṇa times. We have elsewhere noted that Bhrūṇahatyā was now treated as one of the seven heinous sins and this proves that girls married late and often going astray before marriage, resorted to procuring abortion. And this appears to have led to early marriages. We find a faint indication in Pāṇini that there were early marriages already in his days. VI 4,84 (वर्षाभ्वश्च) of Pāṇini is added to by Kātyāyana by पुनर्भ्वश्चेति वक्तव्यम्. It cannot be argued that Pāṇini failed to notice that the word पुनर्भू also behaved like वर्षाभू. The proper inference is that the word पुनर्भू had no existence in the days of Pāṇini. In Vedic times along with late marriages, there was prohibition of widow-marriage as among the ancient Germans. The class of पुनर्भूs probably arose later as a result of early marriage coming into vogue and early married young girls becoming widows were naturally allowed to remarry (सा चेदक्षतयोनिः स्यात् पुनःसंस्कारमर्हति–Manu).

We have seen that the Aryans often married women from lower classes and that their progeny was treated as belonging to the varṇa of the father. This is shown even in the latest Lāṭyāyana Śrauta Sūtra which gives a rule that every priest must recite his pedigree to the 14th generation, but should stop at an ancestress who was not a Brāhmaṇī (IX 2, 6). This leaves Manu's dictum untouched that the varṇa of the progeny is that of the father in two lower wives only (द्वयोरात्मास्य जायते). The rule also shows how the pedigree of Brahmins upto the 14th generation was scrutinised and why the number 14 subsequently became important in Smritis in determining Sāpindya or cognateship.

Going on to the food and drink of the people, we find पान देशे a very interesting sūtra in Pānini (XII 4,9) as the favourite drinks of different peoples are given under it by the Kāśikā as क्षीरपाणा उशीनराः, सुरापाणाः प्राच्याः, सौवीरपाणा बाल्हीकाः and कषायपाणा गान्धाराः. The Uśīnaras in the Panjab drank milk; the easterners like Maithilas drank liquor; the Bālhīkas drank सौवीर (sour gruel) and the Gāndhāras drank कषाय, probably tea. Even now, the Panjabis drink milk and the Maithilas drink liquor. But drinking liquor was already looked upon as one of the five greatest sins and was avoided by all Aryans. At the Sautrāmaṇi sacrifice, liquor had to be offered to Indra who, like the German lord, was the patron of beef and beer. The sacrificer and priests had to take हविःशेष. A substitute was, however, provided soon in प्राणभक्ष or smelling instead of actual taking. As to food, flesh food was common to all. But among the vratas of sacrificers is mentioned abstaining from flesh and this subsequently became the lifelong vow of many Brahmins. Not to eat flesh during the month of Śrāvaṇa, the first month of the rainy season, is a custom among Kshatriyas even to this day. The grains used were chiefly rice and yava mixed with curds. Cow's milk alone was used as being sacrificial and cows were kept in every household. It seems that beef was never eaten except at certain higher sacrifices and only as हविःशेष, cows being considered sacred; and even there, प्राणभक्ष came into vogue.

The dress of the people was the same as in the Brāhmaṇa period, viz. two pieces of cloth for both men and women. The men had often a turban called उष्णीष and it was usually white as also the two pieces of cloth. A red turban was prescribed for priests who were engaged in performing magic rites and also red clothes (लोहितोष्णीषा लोहितवाससः–Śrauta S.). A red turban in modern times became, however, a sign of gentility and only Kshatriyas and Rajputs used it (See our History of Mediæval Hindu India Vol. I). The women, when ordained for sacrifice had for head dress कुम्बकरीर of which no idea can now be formed. Silk clothes were considered best and holy, being prescribed for both the sacrificer and his wife when ordained. But the Panjab did not produce silk and Bengal and China alone, as now, were producers of silken cloth. The क्षौम mentioned in Ś. S. must be imported silken cloth and it has become in modern India a sacred cloth with Hindus along with linen and woolen. The people generally kept a tuft of hair on the head called शिखा or चूडा; but some had heads clean shaven. The words यवनमुण्ड and कम्बोजमुण्ड which are given first in the gaṇa under II,1,72 Pāṇini, show that Greeks and Tibetans were even then shaven-headed.

A great many sūtras of Pāṇini give the surnames, as we may now call them, that were current among Brahmins and Kshatriyas. Brahmins used gotra-names as surnames and Pāṇini gives many rules for their formation. The Pravara stocks such as आंगिरस, भार्गव, वासिष्ठ &c. were also known but not used; but under these, the gotra-names some of which were often the same in different Pravaras were used with some differences. Thus कपिबोधादांगिरसे (IV 4, 107) provides that a Kappi-gotra man, if he was an Āngirasa, should be called काप्यः, if not कापेय; similarly बोध्य was an Āngirasa distinct from बौधेय a Vāsishtha. The Kshatriyas took names from the peoples (IV 1,168) or some ancestor. भर्गात्त्रैगर्ते (IV 1,191) shows that भार्गायण was a त्रैगर्त but भर्ग was other than त्रैगर्त. ऋष्यन्धकवृष्णिकुरुभ्यश्च (IV,1,114) brings together Brahmins and Kshatriyas, the अन्धकs the वृष्णिs and the कुरुs being Kshatriya tribes. There was a difference in the form of the surname from गोत्र (which is fitly defined by Pāṇini as पौत्रप्रभृत्यपत्यं गोत्रम् and thus meant *descendants* from grandson downward,) and of the name derived from the father only. We thus see how the modern practice of giving a man's name, his father's name and his family or gotra name is very old

Pāṇini II 4, 65 shows that certain ancient gotra names in the plural meant descendants. These gotras are अत्रि, भृगु, कुत्स, वसिष्ट, गोतम and अंगिरस्; thus अत्रयः (Atris) and भृगवः Bhṛigus would mean any descendants but आत्रेय and भार्गव would mean a son of Atri and Bhṛigu. Similarly among eastern peoples and Bharatas the plural meant descendants. The Kāśikā instances युधिष्ठिराः

and अर्जुनाः as meaning descendants of Yudhishthira and Arjuna; but Ārjuneya meant a son of Arjuna.

With regard to trade and imports, we have the sūtra उत्तरपथेनाहृतं च (V 1,77) of Pāṇini added to by Vararuchi in the Vārtika वारिजङ्गलस्थलकान्तारपूर्वपदादुपसंख्यानम्. This shows that in Pāṇini's days imports chiefly came from the north i.e. from Afghanistan, Persia, Chinese Turkestan and Tibet, while in Kātyāyana's days, under the rule of the Nine Nandas, imports by river and by jungle, land and forest routes were added. These river routes were the Ganges and the Mahānadī, the land routes were from Malwa and Kathiawar, the forest routes were through the Vindhyas and the jungle routes were from the treeless tract of Rajputana. A second Vārtika adds अजपथशंकुपथ ; the first indicates mountain routes fit to be used by sheep only. And a third मरिच-मधुकव्यारण् स्थलात् mentions two imports Mahua and Maricha brought by land. In वंशादिगण of Pāṇini, we have several products mentioned which were brought from forests even in his days viz. वंश, कुटज, बल्वज, मद्य, अक्ष, स्थूणा, अश्मन, इक्षु, खट्वा it is to be noted that मद्य (liquor) and इक्षु (sugarcane) were forest products.

Cultivated fields were not described by their superficial measurements such as Nivartana or Bīghā, but by the seed required for them; thus a field for which a प्रस्थ of seed was required was called प्रास्थिक, or a द्रोण, द्रौणिक (तस्य वापः V 1,46 Pāṇ.). This method of measuring fields for taxation was in vogue in hilly tracts even till the British rule. Among corns grown was one that ripened within sixty days and was called षाष्टिक (V 1,80 Pāṇ.). आढक, आचित, पात्र were other measures of weight or capacity besides द्रोण and प्रस्थ (V, 1,53).

People travelled generally on foot; but there were horses also and chariots drawn by bullocks, mules or horses for travel and draught. The importance of chariots prescribed as Dakshiṇā in Śrauta Sūtras can thus be understood. An अश्वतरीरथ was much prized as it travelled fast and carried much weight. And mules were to be had in plenty in the Panjab which was then the home of Aryan civilization and of Śrauta sacrifices, though it is not so now.

The people generally were agriculturists and this life is reflected in such common words as आयतियव, लूनयव, लूयमानयव, खलेयव "corn standing, corn cut, corn being cut, corn in the threshing place." The chief corn seems to be Yava (यवोसि धान्यराजोऽसि) a rough kind of wheat which indicates that the Panjab and the Sarasvati region were still the principal land of the Aryans at this period. These agriculturists were chiefly Vaiśyas who were called अर्य. Pāṇini gives अर्यः स्वामिवैश्ययोः (III 1,103); and in an agricultural country, the agriculturist is also the lord. The word is Vedic and is derived from the root ऋ 'to go' from which Ārya is also derived which denoted all the three higher classes.

It is important to note that among the desires with which sacrifices were performed, ग्रामकाम, प्रजाकाम and पशुकाम were the usual ones. As stated before, cattle and progeny were valuable in an agricultural country. But

ग्रामकाम indicates that whole villages were prized by the Aryans. This either refers to the obtainiug of new villages entirely for settlement by a prosperous family or to the settlement system then existing and continuing to this day by which headship of villages was a position of influence. It could be granted by kings or obtained by purchase. We have already noted that these Grāmaṇīs, mentioned even in Upanishads, were an important people and they were also called Sūtas which did not mean a separate intermediate caste as in Smritis. They probably were both Kshatriyas and Vaiśyas. Curiously enough, grants of villages (in inam) are not mentioned among the Dakshiṇās to be given to priests in any sacrifice in any Śrauta Sūtra, so far as we remember. It is, therefore, certain that Grāmanīs were not Brahmins. In the Panjab and the U. P., there are Kshatriya and Jāt owners of villages mostly, but there are also Brahmin owners. These were originally not priests but probably followers of the profession of arms.

Turning to commercial and money dealings, we may at once state that the profession of money lending was old and long established. The borrower was called अधमर्ण and the creditor उत्तमर्ण (Pān. & Smṛi.). We have noted that Yāska interprets मगंद in a Rigvedic verse as meaning कुसीदिन् or one who lives on interest. This profession was looked down upon as creditors were, as always, often oppresive (Sec III p. 110). The Vaiśyas and some Brahmins probably even then, followed this profession. The Vaiśyas were also traders and sellers of goods as the Gītā gives कृषि, गोरक्ष्य and वाणिज्य as the natural avocations of Vaiśyas and the agriculturist Vaiśyas, the cattle-rearing Vaiśyas (like Nanda of Vrindāvana in the Bhāgavata) and the trading Vaiśyas became probably distinct classes. Money was a *sine qua non* for trade and lending transactions and must have been in use. Pāṇini mentions many coins and the Śrauta Sūtras also refer to these coins. Nishka as coin is more than once mentioned in the Śrauta Sūtras for Dakshinā. It was most probably a stamped piece of gold. (See हिरण्यपरिमाणं धने P. VI 2,55 e. g. द्विसुवर्णं धनम्. Hiraṇya meant both gold and silver). Nishka is twice mentioned in Pāṇini and the lower coins given in निष्कादि्द (V. I. 20) are पण, पाद, माष (all mentioned directly in 34), वांर्ह, द्रोण and षष्टि. Other words which appear to be coins are गोपुच्छ (19), कंस (25), शूर्प (26 शूर्पेण क्रीतं शौर्पम्-काशिका),* कार्षापण (29) a copper coin, शाण (35) and खारी, (33). Vararuchi adds काकिणी to this Sūtra which thus appears to be shell-money used later on, कार्षापण, शत्त, विंशतिक, बिस्त are other words probably meaning coins given in 29,31,32. Coins were struck in Pāṇini's days (आहत V, 2, 120).

The religion of the Indo-Aryans was still Vedic, Gṛihya and Śrauta sacrifices being performed by the three higher castes. The sacred fire could be kept and worshipped by (Ś. S.) in every Aryan home. But the Vaiśyas had probably ceased to do so and had generally taken to the path of Bhakti and had thus

* Perhaps these coins were stamped with गोपुच्छ and शूर्प; but what is कंस and शाण ?

descended to the level of Sudras and women who could not perform Vedic sacrifices. Hence the propriety of the line in the Gīta स्त्रियो वैश्यास्तथा शूद्रा : &c. Nay many Brahmins and Kshatriyas also had ceased to keep firc and the Gītā also speaks of two classes of Brahmins and Kshatriyas, the pious Brahmins (ब्राह्मणाः पुण्याः) and the Vedic Kshatriyas (राजर्षयः) who still followed the sacrificial cult of the Vedas and others who were lax like the मागधदेशीय ब्राह्मण mentioned in Śrauta Sūtras. The former particularly exulted in performing the higher Śrauta sacrifices, the Soma sacrifice being most sumptuously celebrated. We can understand how the Gītā belongs to this period of the predominence of Soma sacrifice performed for the attainment of Svarga, when it specially refers to them in the verse त्रैविद्या मां सोमपाः पूतपापाः यज्ञैरिष्ट्वा स्वर्गतिं प्रार्थयन्ते ॥. The three Vedas are mentioned here not because the fourth Atharvaveda was not known (P. IV 3, 133) but because it was concerned chiefly with magic and mundane purposes.

The Upanishadic doctrine of Sanyāsa was also in the field and many Brahmins and Kshatriyas took to Sanyāsa and Tapas by retiring from worldly pursuits and living in forests. These also followed in one way the Vedic religion, as the Sanyāsāśrama and the Vānaprastha Āśrama were now recognised by it and a few Aryans of the three higher classes lived as recluses in forests.

The Śūdra, though admitted to the Aryan society, could not perform sacrifices nor take to Sanyāsa or Tapas. To this time belongs the story in the Rāmāyaṇa that Rāma punished with death a Śūdra who took to Tapas. Buddhism naturally came as a revolt after this and threw open Sanyāsa and Tapas to all. Brahmins who led a religious life were exempted from taxes and sometimes others than Brahmins pretended to be so to obtain this privilege. The sūtra of Pāṇini IV. 2. 69 is instanced by दासीब्राह्मण and भयब्राह्मण. It is inexplicable why मगधदेशीय Brahmins were stamped as degraded. In magic rites Dakṣhīnā was to be given to these Brahmins only (see Ś. S.). Probably they worshipped fiends like the Satanists of Europe.

The common people, the women, the Śūdras and many Vaiśyas followed generally the religion of devotion by worshipping Vāsudeva and other personal gods. Idolatry was probably well established among these people, as Pāṇimi speaks of the idols of Vāsudeva and Arjuna. We have already seen that even in the religion of sacrifice, an image of Mahāvīra made of mud brought from a Valmīka or a pond was worshipped. (This perhaps is the precursor of the later practice, even now subsisting, of worshipping idols of Gaṇapati made of clay every year in Ganesha Pūjā days). It can not be definitely stated if there were temples wherein idols were permanently installed and worshipped; for we have not come across any mention of such temples in Vedānga works. But non-mention leads to no inference where mention is not necessary. Temporary sacrificial sheds were erected for higher sacrifices which may be called fire temples. Their consecration was made with great ceremony and many public rejoicings. It is difficult to say whether the liṅga worship of the Non-Aryans referred to in the Vedas had been by this time accepted by the Aryans as the worship of the Vedic god Rudra, though a separate sacrifice to Rudra by the recitation of the Yajurvedic Rudrādhyaya called Śatarudrīya had come into vogue in the time of the late Kātyā. S. (Sec III p. 57). The identification of Vishṇu with the highest Brahman had already taken place in the Upanishads and according to the cult of sacrifice, Vishṇu was sacrifice itself. But it is also not quite certain if the identification of Shrīkrishṇa with Vishṇu had taken place by this time. The Gītā identifies Śrīkrishṇa with Brahman and with both Śankara and Vishṇu as Vibhūtis of God. The theory of Avatāras developed hereafter and the Pānchrātra and Nārāyaṇīya cults finally represented Vāsudeva as an Avatāra of Vishṇu. These two deities, Śiva and Vishṇu, became the two prominent gods of the Indian people hereafter; and thousands of templcs were built to them probably even before Buddha. We do not also find any mention of Devī-worship in the Vedānga works though, as stated before, non-mention leads to no inference. The Kena Upanishad mentions Umā Haimavatī not as a goddess and the Bhagavadgītā among female deities mentions only कीर्तिः श्रीर्वाक्च नारीणां स्मृतिर्मेधा धृतिः क्षमा. Yāska mentions many female Vedic deities, but not any Puranic ones.

The people generally were thus religiously divided into two sections the Aryans and the Śūdras (शूद्रार्यम् II 2,31 Kāśikā) and they often abused or reviled each other. It is interesting to note that the consecration of sacrificial sheds was accompanied specially by a mock quarrel between a Sūdra and an Ārya, the latter worshipping fire and the former not. The lowest grade of the Śūdras worshipped fiends and demons and they are referred to in the Gītā. The difference between the higher and lower classes is noted by the Gītā in the verse यजन्ते सात्त्विका देवान् यक्षरक्षांसि राजसाः। प्रेतान् भूतगणांश्चान्ये यजन्ते तामसा जनाः! Manes were also worshipped by many (पितृन्यान्ति पितृव्रताः).

Lastly several sūtras of Pāṇini give us hints about the food, apparel, avocations &c. of the people. Thus V. 2, 7–9 speak of सर्वपथीन रथ a chariot which can take all paths, सर्वपत्रीण सारथि a driver who can drive all animals, सर्वान्नीन भिक्षु a Sanyāsin who eats all kinds of food, आप्रपदीन पट a scarf which covers the body upto the ankle, अनुपदीन उपानत् a shoe that fits the foot. V. 2, 71 states that a country inhabited by Brahmins living by arms is called ब्राह्मणक. The Sūtra of Pāṇinī, though treating of grammar, is a mine of information on the general condition of the people in his time.

From the various facts above set forth, it will amply appear that the Indo-Aryans were, in the Vedānga period, a highly advanced people with ordered kingdoms and communities, living in walled towns (नगरमर्दिन्, प्राकारमर्दिन् Pan. VI 1, 26 गण), and with councils assisting kings, with intellectual pursuits resulting in such finished works as Pāṇini's grammar and in philosophical treatises like the Bhagavadgītā. They had advanced in mathematical astronomy and also in the knowledge of metals, using gold, silver and copper coins of various weights. Industry and agriculture flourished and trade by boats from the eastern and western seas was carried on with many distant lands. Fine arts had also progressed; music was studied, with stringed instruments like Vīṇas and dramas were acted, there being even works on actors. Rules for the building of altars had been laid down on the basis of geometry and arithmetic. Yet the question whether writing was known in the days of Pāṇini is a topic of controversy among scholars. Goldstücher held that "writing was known to Indo-Aryans from various sūtras of Pāṇini such as उदात्तस्वरितोदयम्. The roots लिप् and लिख् show that words were painted as also inscribed." If the Chaldeans knew inscribing on bricks, at least two thousand years before Christ, it is no wonder that the Indo-Aryans knew writing in the Vedāṅga period. The Vedas were no doubt taught from mouth to mouth, but other works were written down. Indeed we think that Pāṇini could not have prepared his gaṇas or lists unless he could note down words as they were found. He could not have kept them stored in his mind. The material on which writing was inscribed was Bhūrjapatra, as stated already and Bhūrja leaves could be had in plenty in the Himalayan regions. Patra consequently in Sanskrit means a letter, as paper in English has come to mean a disquisition written on paper. Such leaves strung together were called a grantha properly enough and grantha in the sense of a work is used even by Pāṇini (कृते ग्रन्थे).

GENERAL APPENDIX.

I NOTES OF Y. V. TALAVALKAR OF POONA on Sec. I with our remarks thereon.

(1) P. 3. "The ancient Indo-Aryans had a system of chronology. The Manvantara system counts time from Manu's being saved from the deluge. This system was known all the world over, Manu or Noah being treated as the saviour of the human race. Before this system, different forms of Yugas were in vogue, of four, five, ten &c years. The Manvantaras are described in the Purāṇas in detail."

The determination of Vedic dates from Puranic accounts of Manvantaras is an impossibility. These are differently interpreted by different scholars. The Puranic accounts of kingly genealogies are also unreliable, the orginal genealogies seen by Megasthenes being lost. The modern Purāṇas give imaginary ones, as their total differs from the total in the short summary given by Megasthenes. Thirdly, Manvantaras are a fabrication of astronomical Siddhāntas which are all later than 200 B. C.

(2) P. 47 and 55. "The पदपाठ must be taken to have preceded Vyāsa. It was recited by शकल or शाकल्य and it omits some of the verses in the Ṛigveda as now recited. Had Śākalya come after Vyāsa, he could not have omitted these verses. Again गालव, author of क्रमपाठ, according to the Purāṇas, lived in the reign of Brahmadatta, a contemporany of Pratīpa, father of Śantanu. He too, therefore, preceded Vyāsa. The above शाकल्य counted every Pada and hence we have शाकल्यदृष्टे पदलक्षमेकम्" We are of the opinion that no value attaches to the Purāṇa story historically. The पदपाठ no doubt omits certain sūktas or rather mantras. The important question why certain

mantras are omitted in पदपाठ is difficult to solve; for the present Sanhitā is known as of Śākala Śākhā. Probably when Śākalya enunciated his पदपाठ he thought these mantras to be spurious. Again the idea of reciting a पदपाठ can only arise after the mantras had become difficult to be understood owing to change in language. It is also possible that when Śākalya enunciated his पदपाठ, these mantras were not found in the compilation made by Vyāsa and were added subsequently by some one, like the Khailikas.

The following mantras only, included in the Ṛigveda Sanhitā always, have no पदपाठ. They are, however, commented on by Sāyana :—VII 59,12 (त्र्यम्बकं यजामहे from यजुर्वेद), X,20,1, X 120, 10 and X 190 (ऋतंच सत्यं सूक्त).

(3) P. 84. "The words Brāhmaṇa, Rājanya, Vaiśya and Śudra are not indicative of castes but are ताद्धित forms showing occupation. For these words do not occur elsewhere in the Ṛigveda. Brāhmaṇa thus is from ब्रह्मन् (mantra) "

This is an ingenious guess as राजन्य also seems, from राजन्, to be a collection of kings and Vaiśya, of विश् or settlers. But how is शूद्र a ताद्धित and what is its meaning?

(4) P. 110. "The Vāyu Purāna gives the following information about Sāmaveda. This Veda was taught by Vyāsa to his pupil जैमिनि, he taught it to his son सुत्वन्, he to his son सुकर्मन् who made 500 Samhitās and taught them to his pupil पौष्यिञ्ज who taught them to his disciples लोगाक्षि, कुथुमि, कुशीतिन्, and लांगली. These Sāmans are called औदीच्य, and are distinct from the प्राच्य or कार्त Sāmans of हिरण्यनाभ कृत."

The Purāna brings together known authors on Sāmaveda and the supposed 1000 Śākhās of it, in this imaginary story.

(5) P 137. Kālāpas are the same as मैत्रायणिs." Why?

(6) P. 140. "In Pāṇini's time, Āraṇyakas were not looked upon as separate from Brāhmaṇas."

II THE KHAILIKA ALIAS PARIŚISHṬA HYMNS OF THE ṚIGVEDA.

We have already noted in App. I that there are certain other hymns of the Ṛigveda on which there is no padapātha. They are called Khila or Khailika alias Pariśishta which may be rendered by 'remnant'. They are not given together at the end like an appendix in modern books but are given at different places throughout the Ṛigveda in some written books only. They are, however, not usually given in printed books; nor has Sāyaṇa commented on them. But they are almost always learnt by heart by Vaidikas. They have accents which Max Muller says are not proper, and they are omitted in many Mss. We give below a list of them supplied to us by Govindabhat Phatak, a noted Vaidika of Poona, both from a manuscript copy and from memory.

No.	*Ashtaka*	*Adhyaya*	*Varga*	*Pratika or beginning*	*No of verses*
1	II	5	16	मा बिभेर्न मरिष्यसि	8
2	,,	8	12	भद्रं वद दक्षिणतः	6
3	IV	2	25	जागर्षि त्वं भुवने जातवेदो	1
4	,,	3	3	स्रुक्कान्ते तृणान्यग्ना	1
5	,,	3	7	स्वस्त्ययनं तार्क्ष्यं	2
6	,,	4	29	वर्षन्तु ते विभावरि	1
7	,,	4	34	हिरण्यवर्णां हरिणीं (श्रीसूक्त)	16
8	,,	7	20	चक्षुश्च श्रोत्रंच	3
9	,,	8	4	स्रुक्कान्ते तृणान्यग्ना	1½
10	V	3	30	शंवती: पारयन्त्येते	6
11	,,	4	22	स्वप्नस्वप्नाधिकरणे	11
12	,,	7	4	उपप्लवद् मंडूकि	1
13	VII	21	9	पावमानीः स्वस्त्ययनीः	20
14	,,	5	28	यत्र तत्परमं पदं	5
15	VIII	3	6	सितासिते सरिते	1
16	,,	3	29	अविधवा भव वर्षाणि	6

No.	*Ashtaka*	*Adhyaya*	*Varga*	*Batika or beginning*	*No of verses*
17	VIII	5	23	असौ यां सेना मरुतः	2
18	,,	6	2	हविर्भिरेकेस्वरिन	1
19	,,	7	14	आरात्रि पार्थिवं रजः	25
20	,,	7	16	अर्वाञ्चमिन्द्रममुतो (यजुर्वेद)	1
21	,,	7	16	आयुष्यं वर्चस्य	11
22	,,	8	9	मेधा मह्ममाङ्गिरसो	9
23	,,	8	42	नेजमेष परापत	3
24	,,	8	45	अर्नीकवन्तमुतये	1
25	,,	8	49	संज्ञानमुशनावदत्	9 or 14

It may at once be said that these are additions most certainly made after Vyāsa the compiler of the Ṛigveda and Śākalya the enunciator of the Pada-Pātha. The Vālakhilyas are, however, earlier than Śākalya and later than Vyāsa as they have been separated into padas. Max Muller has shown in his edition of the Ṛigveda that these Pariśishṭas are older than Kātyāyana who does not include them in his सर्वानुक्रमणी as also Śaunaka who mentions them in his अनुवाकानुक्रमणी. They are, of course, not counted by him in the number of hymns and of padas. Some of these verses like तच्छंयोरावृणीमहे are found in the Atharvaveda and in Śrauta and Grihya Sūtras. We think that their being given in different places indicates that they were believed to be seen by those Ṛishis after or in whose hymns they are inserted. They are certainly allied to them in matter. Thus X 75 is a hymn to the rivers and the Khailika सितासिते सरिते यत्र संगथे &c. referring to the confluence of the white Ganges with the dark Jumna naturally comes after इमं मे गंगे यमुने &c. The first remnant hymn is inserted at the end of the first maṇḍala and the last (25) at the end of the Ṛigveda itself, the matter of it संज्ञानमुशनावदत् being allied to the matter of the last sūkta and its last verse समानीव आकूतिः &c.

Max Muller, in his edition, has given 32 Khailikas while Govindabhat's list gives 25 as also Ganapat Krishnaji's edition which also notes the place where each khailika is inserted. On comparison we find Nos 1,9,10,15,18,20 (ससृषीस्तद्पसो &c. is here given) and 29 of Max Muller's edition to be additional sūktas (29 ह्रिमस्य त्वा not given by G. K. edition is, however, accepted by Govindabhat, though it is not in his list). There are additional verses also, added still later in these remnant hymns, the most notable being 13 verses added at the end of the 8th of Max Muller called श्रीसूक्त. These clearly are later additions, for they come after the finishing verse यः शुचि : प्रयतो भूत्वा &c. श्रीकाम : सततं जपेत्.

The language of some hymns is post-Vedic and one hymn mentions even Kapila. The hymns Nos 8 and 9 given by Max Muller and omitted in our list are to Śiva and Krishṇa which are plainly spurious, the latter containing the line कृष्णाय गोपिनाथाय. The majority of the hymns and verses are, however, in Vedic language and style. यत्र सोमेश्वरो देवः यत्र प्राची सरस्वती यत्र गंगा च यमुना probably describes Prayāga. Is there Someśvara there? जनमेजयस्य सत्रांते आस्तीकवचनं स्मर and यो जरत्कारुणा जातः remind us of the Bhārata which probably takes these verses from here. यस्यां हिरण्यं प्रभूतं गावो दास्योऽश्वान् विन्देयं पुरुषानहम् embodies the Indo-Aryan conception of riches (7). कालिको नाम सर्पः यमुनाह्रदेह सो जातो यो नारायणवाहनः (11) is a prior version of the story of Krishṇa in Harivaṁśa.

III THE VEDĀNGA CYCLE OF 5 YEARS.

This cycle is certainly old, as the names of the five years are mentioned in the Taittirīya Brāhmaṇa III 4 and also the Vājasaneyi Sanhitā XXX 18 (Sec. II p. 48). These are, of course, their later portions; but the cycle must be older still as two extra months named Sansarpa or Malimlucha and Anhaspati are found in the Taittirīya Sanhitā which can only appertain to the cycle of five years. Mr. Y. V. Talavalkar thinks that there was previously a four years' cycle with three years of 360 days and the fourth of 381. He has not given the proof of this. But this is probable as the Taittirīya Brāhmaṇa (I 4,10) mentions the names of four years only and their lords. The extra month is certainly older as Adhimāsa is mentioned in R I 25, 8; and is likened to the hump of an ox in the Taittirīya Brāhmaṇa III 8. 3. The ancient Ṛishis must first have tried to equate the solar with the lunar year, in other words, the seasons with the full moon and new moon months, by adding 21 days or one month after 3 years and finding the inequality still remaining, by adding 2 months in five years.

IV Dr. V. G. Rele's new explanation of Vedic deities. (Sec I pp. 74-81)

Mr. V. G. Rele L.M.& S; F.C.P.S. whose new interpretation of the Bhagavadgītā we have already noticed, has suggested a new explanation of Vedic deities also on the physiological basis. Dr. Rele has studied the Ṛig-Veda deeply and with his wonderfully imaginative power and his intimate knowledge of anatomy has evolved the theory that the Vedic deities represent the several centres of activity in the nervous system of the human body. I have had the privilege of reading in manuscript his book expounding this theory and I am sure that when this book is out, it will take the learned world by surprise. He has not only accounted for the various attributes of each Vedic deity but has also shown how the various legends about each god given in this highly poetical work of the ancient Rishis can be explained.

Even in the time of Yāska, the Vedic deities had become a riddle. Some teachers thought that they were powers of nature looked upon as gods ; others that they were ancient kings. Thus Vritra was supposed by some to represent a cloud; by others to be a son of the Asura Virochaṇa. Modern Vedic scholars generally explain the Vedic deities and the legends connected with them on an astronomical basis. They explain these legends as poetical fancies of the ancient Rishis suggested by particular appearances in the starry regions. Some again believe that these deities represent but the Sun in its different aspects seen in the Arctic regions. Even Yāska thought that there were three deities only viz. Sun, Wind and Fire; and all other deities were only their different positions. But it is patent to all that these different theories cannot satisfactorily explain all the attributes of the Vedic deities described in the Ṛig-veda, nor all the legends in connection with them found therein. Thus, as pointed out by Dr. Rele, the name Rodasī in the dual, defies proper explanation. Even Yāska gave different meanings ; and many following him take it as heaven and earth (द्यावापृथिवी). But in many hymns of the Ṛig-Veda, Rodasī is mentioned along with earth and sky separately (III 54,4, VI 70,41, X 88,3) and there Rodasī must mean two heavens. Now in the outer world there is but one heaven. The idea of two heavens, however, seems to have been suggested by the two hemispherical brain vaults placed side by side, as well explained by Dr. Rele in his book. The Ṛishis in their sacrifices must have studied animal anatomy and even human dead bodies and they saw minutely both the inner world and the outer world and thought them to be alike. We may next mention the next most troublesome Vedic deity viz. the two Aśvins. Yāska, as usual, suggests many explanations. The astronomical explanation that they are two stars or two planets (Venus and Mercury) fails; for these do not constantly appear together. The Aśvins are always said to appear in the early morning before dawn. They are physicians. And they succour men when foundered at sea. It is almost impossible to suggest an explanation which can bring in these attributes. Dr. Rele's physiological explanation is, therefore, worth noting. Other troublesome deities such as Ṛibhus and Pūshan are also explained in this theory of Dr. Rele. Indeed his great merit is that he has collected together all the legends connected with each deity found in the Ṛigveda as also all attributes and has explained them on the theory that the Vedic deities represent the different centres of activity in the brain and the spinal cord of the human body. It is possible that the Vedic seers knew the human nervous system well and looking upon the outer world as a replica of the inner world, described both in the same fashion. This theory of Dr. Rele will certainly be carefully scrutinized by the learned world when it is placed before it. The German Pandits especially who are both good Vedic scholars and medical experts will study it deeply and pronounce their valuable opinion upon it. In the meanwhile, we think the theory to be so ingenious and thorough-going, that we feel it to be our duty briefly to notice it in this History of Sanskrit Literature, even before Dr. Rele's book is printed and published.

V DATE OF BHAGAVADGĪTĀ, Sec. IV pp. 34–46.

A further argument in support of the date we have assigned to the Bhagavadgītā may be found in वेदानां सामवेदोऽस्मि (X 20). Srikrishṇa was probably a Sāmavedin, as in the Chhāndogya he is described as a pupil of Ghora Āngirasa कृष्णाय देवकीपुत्राय प्राह (Sec. II p. 192). But the preeminence of Sāmaveda as the highest Veda also belongs to the Brāhmaṇa and Vedanga periods. It was a Veda recited by gods. T. B. says that all light was derived from the Sāmaveda (Sec. II p. 37). The Pāriplava, described in the Srauta Sūtras and Brāhmaṇas, provides that when the Sāmaveda was recited, gods were to be invited and learned Brahmins in the Vedas represented gods (Sec. I. p. 197 and III). But this position among the Vedas was lost subsequently by it. As noted by Telang in the preface to his translation of Anugītā, Gautama Dharmasūtra provides that Sāmaveda should not be heard in the house. Sāmavedins are now treated as almost fallen. The reason appears to be that Sāmaveda recitation was necessary at the time of burning the dead body of a king or a householder and became inauspicious as a funeral rite. Even the Mahābhārata depicts that the loud chanting of Sāmans distinguished the ceremonial burning of Bhishma's body. This lower position of the Sāmaveda was thus established by about 500 B. C. The Gītā must be taken to belong to the Śrauta Sutra period, in other words, to about 1000 B. C. at the latest.

VI MAP OF VEDIC-CHIEFLY PĀṆINIAN-INDIA

In preparing the Map of Vedic India hereto appended, we have had to contend with many difficulties. So many countries, towns and villages are mentioned in Pāṇini's sūtras and gaṇas and in Kāśikā by way of illustration and so few of these can be identified now, that we are at a loss to locate most of them on the map. Secondly, the situation of many has not been indicated, Pāṇini's work being on grammar and not on geography, though some of them are mentioned in the Mahābhārata. Thirdly, many peoples and towns have disappeared since Pāṇini's days. The map, therefore, does not fully represince Pāṇini's time. But we give here lists of countries, towns &c. mentioned in Vedić works from the Sanhitās down to Yāska and Pāṇini, so far as we could collect them, for the curious reader. The lists cannot of course claim to be exhaustive. It must be added that the gaṇas as recited in Kāśikā and the Sidhānta-Kaumudi differ ; the latter contains more names and also gives different readings. Kāśikā again in giving illustrations mentions names of towns which could not have been in existence in the days of Pāṇini such as Pātaliputra and hence one must take only those names which are actually mentioned in Pāṇini or Yaska as undoubtedly existing in the Vedānga period. Lastly, more than a hundred names of towns are mentioned in the 17 gaṇas mentioned in Pāṇ. IV 2,80 which we do not give here for fear of inordinate and unnecessary extension of lists.

RIVERS

We will first give the rivers of India mentioned in Vedic works. In R. X. 75,5 are given the rivers of India known in Ṛigveda Sanhitā times, from east to west in order (Sec I p. 89.) Their names with subsequent equivalents down to the time of the Greeks and modern days are as follows :—

U. P., DELHI AND PANJAB

1 Gangā (Ganges) 2 Yamunā (Jumna)
3 Sarasvatī (Sarsūti)
4 Śutudri (Sutlej), Gr. Hesidrus
5 Parushṇī (Ravi) also called Irāvatī, Gr. Hydraotes.
6 Asiknī (Chenab) modern Chandrabhāgā, Gr. Akesines
7 Marudvṛidhā (not identified)

8 Vitastā (Jhelum), Gr. Hydaspes
9 Arjikiyā (not identified). Yāska gives Vipāt as another name of it, but this is probably wrong. Yaska gives Urunjarā also as another name of Ārjīkiyā
10 Sushomā (not identified. Yāska looks upon it as Indus)
11 Sindhu (Indus) praised in R. X 75,
12 Rasā
13 Śvetyā (Swat)
14 Kubhā (Kabul) R.V 53,9
15 Kramu (Kurrum) „
16 Gomatī (Gomti)
(12–16: R.X 75,6)
17 Vipāśā R III 33,1 and P. IV 2,74. (Bias) Gr. Hyphasis. R. speaks of Vipāśā and Śatadru together and they combine first. This shows that Yāska is not right in looking upon Asikini as Vipaśā.
18 Śarayū in Oudh R.IV 30,18, V 53,9. X 64,9 mentions it along with Sarasvatī and Sindhu.
19 Śarāvatī given in Kāsikā as dividing east from north as conceived by Pāṇini (not identified).
20 Sadānirā in Behar (See II p. 15) mentioned in Ś. B.
21 Varṇu P. IV 2,77 ग. (not identified),
22 Suvastu P IV 3,93.
23 Dṛishadvatī (S. S.)
24 Rathasthā VI, 157 ग.

We go on to give a list of the countries known in Vedic times. There are very few countries mentioned in the Saṁhitās, though many *peoples* are mentioned like Bharata, Yadu, Anu, Dhruhyu, Pūru &c ; but these were not names of countries yet. In the Brāhmaṇas including Upanishads, we have Kuru, Pānchāla, Kāśi, Videha, Madra, Gāndhāra and Āndhra mentioned. Baudhāyana Ś. S. mentions आरट्ट, गांधार, सौराष्ट्र, कारस्कर and कालिंग as countries not to be visited by Aryans. Pānini's grammar, however, contains many names of countries and their situation whether east, middle or north can be tolerably known. There are more than a hundred names in the gaṇas recited by Pāṇini and Kāśikā adds many in illustration of Pāniniś sūtras. The latter not being always trustworthy, we add ग. and का. to indicate their source. The list is arranged alphabetically and names given in the map are marked.*

Abhisāra IV 2,124 का.
Aishukāri IV 2,54 ग.
Aindravakra IV 2,126 का.
Ajamīdha IV 2,125 का.
Ajaskanda P,
Andhaka IV 2, 114
*Āndhra (A.B.)
Anūpa IV 2,133 ग.
Anushanda ,,
Āraṭṭa (Baudh.S.) a general name for Panjab countries.
*Aśmaka IV 1,173, VI 2,37 ग.
Asura V 3,117 ग.
*Avanti IV 1,176, VI 2,37 ग.
Andarāyaṇa IV 2,54 ग.
*Bālhika V 3,117 ग. IV 1,154 ग.
Bharga IV 1,175
*Bharata IV 1,178 ग. &c. P.
Bhaurikāri IV 1,154 ग.
Bāhlīka
Chakrāvarta IV 2,126 का.
Chāndrāyaṇa IV 2,54 ग.
Chāpayata ,,
*Chedi IV 2,115
Chinti VI 2.37 ग.
Chitraratha II 2,31.
Dakshiṇāpatha IV 2,127 ग.
*Darada IV 3,93 ग.
Dārukachchha IV 2,126 का.
Dārva IV 2,125 का.
*Daśārṇa V 3,117 ग.
Dāsamitra P.
Dhārteya IV 1,178 ग.
Dhaurteya ,,
Drākshāyaṇa IV 2,54 ग.
Gandikā IV 3,93 ग.
*Gāndhāra IV 2,133 ग.
IV 1,169 Brih. B. S.
*Gauda P.
Haihaya IV 1,111 ग.
Jambu IV 2,125 का.
Jyābāṇeya IV 1,178 ग.
*Kachchha IV 2,133
*Kālakūta IV 1,173
*Kālañjara IV 2,125 का.
Kaṭūtara IV 2,133 ग.
*Kalinga IV 1,170
*Kamboja IV 1,175
Kāndāgnika IV 2,126 ग.
Kāṇeya IV 2,54 ग.

Kapiśa IV 2,99.
Karusha IV 1,178 ग.
Kāśī IV 2,115
*Kaśmīra IV 1,178 ग.
*Kekaya IV 1,178 ग.
Khāndāyana IV 2,54 ग.
Kīkata (Rigveda).
Kishkindhā IV 3,93 ग.
*Kshudraka IV 2, 45 ग.
*Kunti IV 1,176, IV 2,37
*KuruIV 2,81का.&c.IV 2,37
Madhumat IV 2,133 ग.
*Madra IV 2,131, IV 3,13.
*Magadha IV 1,170
*Mālava IV 2,45 ग.
*Nishadha IV 1,142 का.
*Pānchāla IV 2,81 &c.
Pāraskara VI 1,157
*Parśu V 3,117
*Paundra (A.B.)
*Piśācha V 3,117 ग.
Pratyagratha IV 1,175
Pulinda (A.B.)
Rauku IV 2,133 ग.
Rohita (Tāndya B.Sec.II p.72).
Saīkayata IV 2,54 ग.
Śailūsha IV 2,53 ग.
*Sālva IV 1,178 ग. IV 2,135, VI, 2,133 ग. &c
Sankāśa IV 2,80.
Sārasyāyana IV 2,54 ग.
Satvata V 3,117 ग
Śaukreya } IV2, V3
Śaubhreya } 178 ग. 117 ग
*Sauvīra P. &c.
*Sindhu IV 2,113 ग &c.
Śitikaksha VI 2,37 ग.
Sūramasa IV 1,170
*Śurasena IV 1,177 ग. IV 1,170.
*Surāshtra IV 2,37 ग.
Susthāla IV 1,178 ग.
Susvāta IV 1,178 ग.
*Trigarta IV 1,111, IV I, 178 ग.
Udasthāna IV 1,86 ग
Udumbara ,,
Uraśa IV 1,178 ग
*Uśīnara (A. B.) IV I, 178 ग.
*Vaideha IV 1,178 ग
Vaikayata IV 2,54 ग.
Vāṇijyaka ,,
*Vanga IV I, 178 ग.
Varṇa IV 2,133
Vāhīka IV 2,47 (general name for the Panjab).
*Vṛiji IV 2,131
Vṛishṇi IV 1,114
Yaudheya IV 1,175, V 3,107
Yugandhara IV 1,99 ग, IV 2,131

A similar alphabetical list of towns is given below. As stated already, many unimportant towns have been omitted, chiefly those given in gaṇas and Kāsikā.

Anakasthalī IV 2,127 ग.
* Ānarta ,,
Arishṭa IV 2,80 ग.
Aśman ,,
Aśmarε ,,
Aśoka ,,
Barbara ,,
Bhojakaṭa (east) I 1,75 का.
* Champā IV 2,82 ग.
Dāttāmitrī(Sauvīra)IV2,16का
Dārva IV 2,97 ग.
Devadatta I 1,75 का (north)
Dhūma IV 2,127
Drākshīprastha VI 2,87 ग.
Eṇīpachana (east) I 1,75 का.
Garta IV 2,127 ग.
Gaudapura
* Gayā IV 2,82 ग and Yāska
Gonarda (east) I 1,70 का.
* Hāstina VI 2,101
* Indraprastha IV 2,87 ग.
Jambu IV 2,82 ग.
Kairamedura IV 3,93 ग.
Kākandī (east) IV 2,76 का.
Kāṇḍavāraṇa IV 3,93 ग.
Kapila ,,
Karavīra IV 2,80 ग.
Karkīprastha VI 2,37 ग.
Karṇakoshṭha IV 3,93 ग.
Kāśapari IV 2,97 ग.
Kauśāmbi IV 2,97 ग.
Khādiri ,,
Kinnara IV 3,93 ग.
Kroshṭukarna ,,
Kūchavāra IV 3,94
Kuṇḍaprastha VI 2,87 ग.
Lankā IV 1,158 ग.
Madrákūla IV 2,127 ग
Mahī IV 2,97 ग
Mahakīprastha IV 2,87 ग
Māhishmatī IV 2,96 ग
Māhishasthali IV 2,127 ग
* Mūkandi (east) IV 2,76 का.
Majjāli IV 2,127 ग.
Mārdeya VI 2,101
* Mathurā IV 2,82 ग.
* Māyā IV 2, 97 ग.
Nāndīpura (East) का.
Pampā IV 2,82 ग.
Phalaka VI 2,101
Plaksha Prasravaṇa (S. S.)
Potā IV 2,97 ग.
Pushkara IV 2,82 ग.
* Rājagṛiha IV 2,127 ग.
Romaka IV 2,80 ग.
* Śākala IV 2,117 ग (?)
Sānkāśya IV 2,80 ग
* Śalātura IV 3,94
Śālmali IV 2,82 ग.
Śansphāya IV, 2,127 ग
Śasūdana ,,
Śātrājita ,,
Sinhakoshṭaka IV 3,93 ग
Śivadattapura (east) का.
Śrāvastī IV 2,97 ग
Śrigālapura IV 2,137 ग

Śinhanagara (east) का.
* Takshaśilā IV 2,82 3,93.
Tāmraparṇī IV 2,82 ग
Tūdī IV 3,93.
Udumbara IV 1,99 ग
* Ujjayini IV 2,82 ग
Uraśa „
Vaidhūmāgni (Sālva) IV 2, 76 का
Valabhi IV 2,82 ग
Valgu „
Varaṇa IV 2,82
* Vārāṇasī IV 2,97 ग
Varjya IV 2,127 ग
Varmatī IV 3,97
Vatsoddharaṇa IV 3,93 ग.
Videha IV 2,127 ग
Vinaśana (S. S.)
* Virāṭanagara (का.)
Vṛikagarta IV 2,137 ग.
Yakrilloman IV 2,110 ग
Yugandhara IV 1,99 ग.

VII JANAMEJAYA PĀRĪKSHITA ND DATE OF BHARATA FIGHT. See II p. 17 and IV p. 5.

There is no mention of the Pāndavas in Sanhitās or Brāhmaṇas and Weber as also Dutta thought that they were imaginary beings, "Arjuna being still the name of Indra" (Dutta). The mention of Janamejaya and his three brothers and of their performing four Aśvamedhas for expiation from guilt occurring in the Śatapatha led Dutta to think that "Janamejaya Pārīkshita was, according to contemporaneous testimony, himself stained with the guilt of war". Similarly, the Brihadāraṇyaka contains a question 'Where have the Pārīkshitas gone' and Weber thought that this question showed that something marvellous had happened to the Pārīkshitas and that "this unknown something was the basis of the legend of the Mahābhārata". That these surmises are wrong we have shown at length in our Mahābhārata: a criticism (p. 60) and our महाभारतमीमांसा (हिंदी Chap. III.) We would give here our arguments in short as detailed there. Non-mention, first, affords no basis for inference, unless mention is necessary. The Vedic Sanhitās and Brāhmaṇas being religious books need not contain a reference to any past historical event or person. That Janamejaya and his three brothers performed Aśvamedhas for expiation of sin as mentioned in Śatapatha proves that the Pāndavas whose great grandsons they were must have lived before Śatapatha. The sin mentioned is a Brahmahatyā and can not be confounded with the guilt of war. For Droṇa's being killed in fight does not involve Brahmahatyā, as killing a Brahmin warrior who comes to fight and kills thousands by his Brahmāstra is not a sin: श्रोत्रियं वा बहुश्रुतम् आततायिनमायान्तं हन्यादेवाविचारयन्. It is true that we are nowhere told in MBh. or in Ś. B. how Janamejaya committed the sin of Brahmahatyā. But it is unquestionable that the Bhārata fight involved no sin of Brahmahatyā. Thirdly, the question 'Where are the Pārīkhsitas' does not suggest the idea that their end was terrible. The answer of Yājnavalkya in the Brīhadār. makes this clear. He says "There they have gone where the Aśvamedha-sacrificers go, viz., where" &c. Thus the fact of their performing Aśvamedha was well-known and sacrificers of Aśvamedha, according to Yājnavalkya, went to the highest goal attained by Vedantins. There is in fact praise of Aśvamedha involved here.

Lastly, it may be noted that some have suggested that Janamejaya mentioned by S. B. is an ancestor of the Pāndavas, mentioned in MBh. Ādip. There is, no doubt, another Janamejaya who is an ancestor. But he is not Pārīkshita and he has not three brothers named Ugrasena, &c, as mentioned in Ś. B. in detail. Hence the Janamejaya of Ś. B. is unquestionably the great-grandson of Arjuna. Arjuna may be Indra in Ṛigveda hymns; but it is a name properly given to one of the Pāndavas supposed to be born of Indra and the hero of the Bhārata fight which took place after the compilation of the Ṛigveda Sanhitā and before Ś. B. was composed about 3000 B. C.

INDEX (of Names).

(The bigger figures indicate sections and the smaller, pages)

INDEX (of Subjects).

(The bigger figures indicate sections in smaller pages)